A Companion to John Adams and John Quincy Adams

WILEY-BLACKWELL COMPANIONS TO AMERICAN HISTORY

This series provides essential and authoritative overviews of the scholarship that has shaped our present understanding of the American past. Edited by eminent historians, each volume tackles one of the major periods or themes of American history, with individual topics authored by key scholars who have spent considerable time in research on the questions and controversies that have sparked debate in their field of interest. The volumes are accessible for the non-specialist, while also engaging scholars seeking a reference to the historiography or future concerns.

Published:

A Companion to the American Revolution
Edited by Jack P. Greene and J. R. Pole

A Companion to 19th-Century America
Edited by William L. Barney

A Companion to the American South
Edited by John B. Boles

A Companion to American Women's History
Edited by Nancy Hewitt

A Companion to American Indian History
Edited by Philip J. Deloria and Neal Salisbury

A Companion to Post-1945 America
Edited by Jean-Christophe Agnew and Roy Rosenzweig

A Companion to the Vietnam War
Edited by Marilyn Young and Robert Buzzanco

A Companion to Colonial America
Edited by Daniel Vickers

A Companion to American Foreign Relations
Edited by Robert Schulzinger

A Companion to 20th-Century America
Edited by Stephen J. Whitfield

A Companion to the American West
Edited by William Deverell

A Companion to the Civil War and Reconstruction
Edited by Lacy K. Ford

A Companion to American Technology
Edited by Carroll Pursell

A Companion to African-American History
Edited by Alton Hornsby

A Companion to American Immigration
Edited by Reed Ueda

A Companion to American Cultural History
Edited by Karen Halttunen

A Companion to California History
Edited by William Deverell and David Igler

A Companion to American Military History
Edited by James Bradford

A Companion to Los Angeles
Edited by William Deverell and Greg Hise

A Companion to American Environmental History
Edited by Douglas Cazaux Sackman

A Companion to Benjamin Franklin
Edited by David Waldstreicher

In preparation:

A Companion to American Urban History
Edited by David Quigley

A Companion to American Legal History
Edited by Sally Hadden and Alfred L. Brophy

A Companion to the History of American Science
Edited by Mark Largent

A Companion to Supreme Court History (2 volumes)
Edited by John Vile

A Companion to American Sports History
Edited by Steven Riess

A Companion to Custer and the Little Big Horn Campaign
Edited by Brad D. Lookingbill

A Companion to the U.S. Civil War
Edited by Aaron Sheehan-Dean

A Companion to the Meuse-Argonne Campaign, 1918
Edited by Edward G. Lengel

PRESIDENTIAL COMPANIONS

Published:

A Companion to Franklin D. Roosevelt
Edited by William Pederson

A Companion to Richard M. Nixon
Edited by Melvin Small

A Companion to Theodore Roosevelt
Edited by Serge Ricard

A Companion to Thomas Jefferson
Edited by Francis D. Cogliano

A Companion to Lyndon B. Johnson
Edited by Mitchell Lerner

A Companion to George Washington
Edited by Edward G. Lengel

A Companion to Andrew Jackson
Edited by Sean Patrick Adams

A Companion to Woodrow Wilson
Edited by Ross A. Kennedy

A Companion to John Adams and John Quincy Adams
Edited by David Waldstreicher

In preparation:

A Companion to James Madison and James Monroe
Edited by Stuart Leibiger

A Companion to Harry S. Truman
Edited by Daniel S. Margolies

A Companion to Abraham Lincoln
Edited by Michael Green

A Companion to Dwight D. Eisenhower
Edited by Chester J. Pach

A Companion to Ronald Reagan
Edited by Andrew L. Johns

A Companion to the Antebellum Presidents, 1837–61
Edited by Joel Silbey

A Companion to the Reconstruction Presidents, 1865–81
Edited by Edward Frantz

A Companion to Gerald R. Ford & Jimmy Carter
Edited by V. Scott Kaufman

A Companion to Warren G. Harding, Calvin Coolidge, and Herbert Hoover
Edited by Katherine A. S. Sibley

A Companion to John F. Kennedy
Edited by Marc Selverstone

A COMPANION TO JOHN ADAMS AND JOHN QUINCY ADAMS

Edited by

David Waldstreicher

WILEY-BLACKWELL

A John Wiley & Sons, Ltd., Publication

This edition first published 2013

Wiley-Blackwell is an imprint of John Wiley & Sons, formed by the merger of Wiley's global Scientific, Technical and Medical business with Blackwell Publishing.

Registered Office
John Wiley & Sons, Ltd, The Atrium, Southern Gate, Chichester, West Sussex, PO19 8SQ, UK

Editorial Offices
350 Main Street, Malden, MA 02148-5020, USA
9600 Garsington Road, Oxford, OX4 2DQ, UK
The Atrium, Southern Gate, Chichester, West Sussex, PO19 8SQ, UK

For details of our global editorial offices, for customer services, and for information about how to apply for permission to reuse the copyright material in this book please see our website at www.wiley.com/wiley-blackwell.

Library of Congress Cataloging-in-Publication Data

A companion to John Adams and John Quincy Adams / edited by David Waldstreicher.
pages cm. – (Wiley-Blackwell companions to American history)
Includes bibliographical references and index.
ISBN 978-0-470-65558-0 (cloth : alk. paper) – ISBN 978-1-118-52435-0 (adobepdf) – ISBN 978-1-118-52428-2 (bro) – ISBN 978-1-118-52439-8 (emobi) – ISBN 978-1-118-52429-9 (epub) – ISBN 978-1-118-52438-1 (vol) 1. Adams, John, 1735–1826. 2. Adams, John Quincy, 1767–1848. 3. Presidents–United States–Biography. I. Waldstreicher, David.
E176.1.C7744 2013
973.09′9–dc23
[B]

2012050382

A catalogue record for this book is available from the British Library.

Cover image: Left: Portrait of John Quincy Adams, 1824, by Thomas Sully (National Gallery of Art, Washington, Andrew W. Mellon Collection 1942.8.30). Right: Portrait of John Adams, c.1800, by Jane Stuart (Adams National Historical Park, Quincy MA)
Cover design by Richard Boxhall Design Associates

Set in 11/13pt Galliard by SPi Publisher Services, Pondicherry, India
Printed and bound in Malaysia by Vivar Printing Sdn Bhd

1 2013

In Memory of
Page Smith
and
Stephen Innes

Contents

List of Figures

About the Contributors

Sean Patrick Adams (no relation) is associate professor of history at the University of Florida and author of *Old Dominion, Industrial Commonwealth: Coal, Politics, and Economy in Antebellum America* (2004) and editor of *The Early American Republic: A Documentary Reader* (2008). He is currently writing a book on energy transitions and home heating in 19th century America.

Catherine Allgor is a professor of history at the University of California at Riverside and a University of California presidential chair. She is the author of *Parlor Politics: In Which the Ladies of Washington Help Build a City and a Government* (2000) and *A Perfect Union: Dolley Madison and the Creation of the American Nation* (2007). She is currently at work on a family history of the Grimké family.

Karen N. Barzilay is a former assistant editor of the Adams Papers at the Massachusetts Historical Society. She holds a doctorate in American Studies from the College of William and Mary, where she wrote a dissertation titled *Fifty Gentlemen Total Strangers: A Portrait of the First Continental Congress* (2009).

John M. Belohlavek is professor of history at the University of South Florida where he teaches nineteenth-century US political and diplomatic history. His publications include *George Mifflin Dallas: Jacksonian Patrician* (1977), *"Let the Eagle Soar:": The Foreign Policy of Andrew Jackson* (1985), and *Broken Glass: Caleb Cushing and the Shattering of the Union* (2005). He is presently completing a volume on women and the Mexican War.

R. B. Bernstein is distinguished adjunct professor of law at New York Law School, where he has taught since 1991. His books include *Thomas Jefferson* (2003); *The Founding Fathers Reconsidered* (2009); and *The Education of*

John Adams (forthcoming). He has written extensively on the era of the American Revolution and the making of the constitution.

Douglas Bradburn is associate professor of history at Binghamton University. He is the author of *The Citizenship Revolution* (2009) and coeditor (with John C. Coombs) of *Early Modern Virginia* (2011).

Andrew Burstein is the Charles P. Manship professor of history at Louisiana State University, and the author of numerous books about Early American political culture. These include *The Inner Jefferson* (1995), *The Passions of Andrew Jackson* (2003), and *Jefferson's Secrets: Death and Desire at Monticello* (2005). With Nancy Isenberg, he coauthored *Madison and Jefferson* (2010) and coedited *Mortal Remains: Death in Early America* (2003).

David P. Callahan is a doctoral student at Temple University. His scholarly interests include US early republic/antebellum political history with a focus on the presidency. He wrote a Masters thesis on the presidential succession of John Tyler and is presently researching a dissertation on the presidential election of 1824.

Elaine Forman Crane is professor of history at Fordham University. She is the author of *A Dependent People: Newport, Rhode Island in the Revolutionary Era* (1985), *Ebb Tide in New England: Women, Seaports and Social Change, 1630–1800* (1998), *Killed Strangely: The Death of Rebecca Cornell* (2002), and *Witches, Wife Beaters, and Whores: Common Law and Common Folk in Early America* (2011); and the editor of *The Diary of Elizabeth Drinker* (1991).

David F. Ericson is an associate professor in the department of public and international affairs at George Mason University. His most recent book, *Slavery in the American Republic: Developing the Federal Government, 1791–1861* (2011), examines the prominent role played by slavery, slaveholders, and slaves in the development of the American state.

John Fea is associate professor of history and chair of the history department at Messiah College, Grantham, PA. He is the author of *The Way of Improvement Leads Home: Philip Vickers Fithian and the Rural Enlightenment in Early America* (2008) and *Was America Founded as a Christian Nation: A Historical Introduction* (2011).

Edith B. Gelles is a senior scholar at the Michelle R. Clayman Institute for Gender Research at Stanford University. She is the author of *Portia: The World of Abigail Adams* (1992, winner of the American Historical Association's Herbert Feis Award); *Abigail Adams: A Writing Life* (2002); and *Abigail and John: Portrait of a Marriage* (2009, a finalist for the George Washington Prize). She edited *The Letters of Abigaill Levy Franks: 1733–1748* (2004).

Margery M. Heffron was formerly an associate vice president for university relations at the State University of New York, Binghamton. She ended her career as an independent scholar in Exeter, NH, at work on a biography of Louisa Catherine Adams, for which she received the Marc Friedlander Fellowship for 2008–2009 from the Massachusetts Historical Society. She died in December 2011.

Margaret A. Hogan is the managing editor of the Adams Papers project at the Massachusetts Historical Society and has served as the series editor for *Adams Family Correspondence*, vols. 7–10 (2005–2011). She is presently preparing vol. 11 (forthcoming) and is coeditor of the *Diary and Autobiographical Writings of Louisa Catherine Adams* (forthcoming).

David W. Houpt is a PhD candidate at the City University of New York's Graduate Center. His dissertation explores political mobilization in Pennsylvania during the early Republic. Selected publications include "Securing a legacy: the publication of James Madison's notes from the Constitutional Convention" (2010) and "Contested election laws: representation, elections, and party building in Pennsylvania, 1788–1794" (2012).

Nancy Isenberg is professor of history at Louisiana State University, and the author of two prize-winning books, *Sex and Citizenship in Antebellum America* (1998) and *Fallen Founder: The Life of Aaron Burr* (2007). With Andrew Burstein, she coauthored *Madison and Jefferson* (2010) and coedited *Mortal Remains: Death in Early America* (2003). She is currently at work on a book about the myth of the classless society.

Matthew Mason is associate professor of history at Brigham Young University. He is the author of *Slavery and Politics in the Early American Republic* (2006), and the coeditor (with John Craig Hammond) of *Contesting Slavery: The Politics of Bondage and Freedom in the New American Nation* (2011).

Colin Nicolson of the University of Stirling, Scotland, is the author of *The "Infamas Governor": Francis Bernard and the Origins of the American Revolution* (2001) and several articles on Massachusetts politics. He is editor of *The Papers of Francis Bernard, Governor of Colonial Massachusetts, 1760–1769* (6 vols., from 2007; the second volume covering the Stamp Act Crisis of 1764–1765, was published in 2012, and he is presently working on the third and fourth volumes). He is also coauthoring, with Owen Dudley Edwards, a book about John Adams's friendships and revolutionary writings.

Marlana Portolano is associate professor of rhetoric and directs a Masters program in humanities at Towson University. She is the author of *The Passionate Empiricist: The Rhetoric of John Quincy Adams in the Service of Science* (2009) and articles on Early American rhetoric and rhetorical theory in *Rhetoric Review*, *Isis*, *Kairos*, *World Englishes*, and *Utopian Studies.* She is currently working on a book of biographical essays about deaf priests and their experiences as orators.

Padraig Riley is an assistant professor of history at Dalhousie University. He has recently published "Slavery and the problem of democracy in Jeffersonian America" in *Contesting Slavery: The Politics of Bondage and Freedom in the New American Nation* (2011). He is presently working on a book about Northern democracy, Jeffersonian politics, and the power of slavery, from 1800 to 1828.

Bethel Saler is associate professor of history at Haverford College and the author of *A Settler's Empire: Colonialism and State Formation in America's Old Northwest, 1783–1854* (forthcoming).

Andrew Shankman is associate professor of history at Rutgers University, Camden. He is the author of *Crucible of American Democracy: The Struggle to Fuse Egalitarianism and Capitalism in Jeffersonian Pennsylvania* (2004), a History Book Club selection, the editor of *The World of the Revolutionary American Republic* (forthcoming), and author of the prize-winning article "A new thing on Earth: Alexander Hamilton, pro-manufacturing Republicans, and the democratization of American political economy" (2003). His current book project is titled "Ungovernable republic: nationalist Jeffersonians and the failure to make a nation."

David J. Siemers is professor and chair of the department of political science at the University of Wisconsin-Oshkosh. Siemers specializes in the American presidency and American political thought and is particularly interested in discerning the connections between political philosophy and practical politics. He is author of *The Antifederalists: Men of Great Faith and Forbearance* (2003), *Ratifying the Republic: Anti-Federalists and Federalists in Constitutional Time* (2004), and *Presidents and Political Thought* (2009).

Herbert E. Sloan is professor of history at Barnard College, Columbia University. The author of *Principle and Interest: Thomas Jefferson and the Problem of Debt* (1995), he specializes in the history of the early republic. He is at work on a study tentatively titled *Disappointed Founders.*

Darren Staloff is professor of history at City College of New York and the graduate center of City University of New York. He is the author of *The Making of an American Thinking Class: Intellectuals and Intelligentsia in Puritan Massachusetts* (1998) and *Hamilton, Adams, Jefferson: The Politics of Enlightenment and the American Founding* (2005). He is currently working on a study of the American Enlightenment.

David Waldstreicher is professor of history at Temple University and author of *In the Midst of Perpetual Fetes: The Making of American*

Nationalism (1997), *Runaway America: Benjamin Franklin, Slavery, and the American Revolution* (2004), and *Slavery's Constitution: From Revolution to Ratification (2009)*. He has also edited *A Companion to Benjamin Franklin* (2011), and is coeditor of the *Journal of the Early Republic.*

Wendy H. Wong is a PhD candidate in the department of history at Temple University. Her main research interests are US foreign relations, particularly during the early American republic, as well as diplomatic and political culture. She is currently finishing a dissertation entitled "Diplomatic subtleties and frank overtures: print, publicity and neutrality in the early American republic, 1793–1801."

Introduction: The Adams Paradox

David Waldstreicher

The Adamses are a great paradox, especially when viewed through the lens of the American presidency. One of only two father and son "dynasties," they each failed to win re-election, suggesting something less than dynastic reach. They scorned, even rejected partisanship – especially while president – but proved able to fight hard at other times. They were popular, and appreciated for their skills – except when they were not.

They loved America, practiced nationalism, but were also experienced diplomats and cosmopolitans who spent many years abroad. Both Adamses preached union but were sometimes seen as provincial New Englanders. They were admired, and scorned, for their intellectualism and oratory. They were conservative, except when they were radicals. They chose brilliant wives who helped make them who they were, and who pushed at "the bonds of womanhood" (Cott, 1977), which they themselves hardly questioned. They led intense inner lives, which they committed to paper, along with a record of their immensely social interactions with others, their harsh criticisms of those people, and of themselves.

The tendency in recent years has been to put the Adamses up on a pedestal. To say that it has not always been so risks understatement. To some extent we may be seeing the emergence of a cycle of American memory: when Thomas Jefferson and Andrew Jackson are down, the Adamses are up. Or perhaps it is the paradoxes at work: we will never be convinced, for long, that the Adamses had all the answers; but we will never forget for long that they all had heroic moments. Some of those moments shaped our national history. If they did not occur in presidential time, perhaps this suggests

A Companion to John Adams and John Quincy Adams, First Edition.
Edited by David Waldstreicher.

something of the need for a broader approach to presidents themselves, as Adams biographers have long appreciated.

The twenty-seven scholars in this volume do not always agree about what is important about John Adams, John Quincy Adams, Abigail Adams, and Louisa Catherine Johnson Adams. But they ask great questions and describe the range of answers historians have offered. They introduce us to what people have been writing and saying about the Adamses for more than two hundred years, not least the prolific, diary-keeping, history-writing Adamses themselves. They make it clear what the difference is between hero-worship or partisanship and careful interpretation based on examination of the original sources and consideration of the work of other scholars. Most of all, they demonstrate how the best history writing always builds on, rather than arrogantly ignoring, the work that has come before.

The chapters move chronologically and thematically through a first generation – John and Abigail – and then that of their son John Quincy. Parallel essays cover key segments of their political careers, including their diplomacy and presidencies; biographies and life-writing; ideas and political thought; key issues in their times, such as religion and slavery; and the striking importance of their spouses to them and to historians subsequently. A final section of three essays by leading scholars assesses experiences and images of both generations, in light of their friend and rival Thomas Jefferson; the profusion of films about them in recent decades; and, in Edith B. Gelles's virtuoso retrospective, the portraits others painted of them and the ones they, as writers, created for each other and us.

I am proud of having brought together this creative and erudite group of scholars and writers. They make pointed arguments, like the Adamses themselves, but also – like the Adamses – with more than a little sense of style.

This volume is dedicated to two historians who were interested in all kinds of history – political, social, cultural, intellectual – and who also saw history as an art form with public consequences. Page Smith, whom I did not know personally, inspired me as a teenager with his brilliant, and I think still unsurpassed, two-volume biography of John Adams. Later, his essays on history and education provided eye-opening accounts of the perils of academic excess, and suggested that historians can aspire to write for a large audience (P. Smith, 1961, 1984). Stephen Innes was a model teacher, intellect, and mentor. While his own work explored finer points of town life and political economy in early New England (Innes, 1983, 1995), he thought big and seemed just as enthusiastic and informed about *The Federalist*. Both Page Smith and Steve Innes made early America interesting; both suggested that there is no inherent conflict between paying attention to the ordinary people and the presidents in our past. I hope we can remember their teaching and their example.

Part I

The First Generation

Chapter One

John Adams: The Life and the Biographers

R. B. Bernstein

In the early twenty-first century, after generations of neglect, John Adams's historical reputation experienced a renaissance. Not only was he the subject of a prize-winning biography (McCullough, 2001), but that book also became the basis for an Emmy Award-winning 2008 HBO television mini-series. Even so, most Americans do not remember Adams for the reasons that he would have wished. Adams's place in historical memory is founded on perceptions of him as a character, an American version of Winston S. Churchill – by turns gruff, voluble, irritable, neurotic, and polysyllabic, yet blessed with courage, a self-mocking sense of humor, and a wondrous marriage. The things for which he hoped to be remembered – his contributions to the theory and practice of constitutionalism, his labors for independence, his role in negotiating the Treaty of Paris of 1783, and his averting of a war with France in 1800 – remain of concern principally to academia. Even though Adams may offer posterity unpalatable but necessary lessons, the clash between the Adams of historical scholarship and the Adams of historical memory persists.

That divide defines this chapter's organization. It first presents a concise life of John Adams, from his birth in 1735 as the oldest son of a colonial Massachusetts family to his death in 1826 as an American sage and patriarch of the Revolution. It then assesses portrayals of Adams in biographies and monographs. In sum, it first examines the history that John Adams made, and then studies what history has made of John Adams (see Peterson, 1998).

A Companion to John Adams and John Quincy Adams, First Edition.
Edited by David Waldstreicher.

1.1 The Life

John Adams was born on October 19, 1735, OS (Oct. 30, NS calendar), in Braintree, Massachusetts, the oldest of three sons of Deacon John Adams (1691–1761) and Susanna Boylston Adams (1709–1797). His father was a farmer, shoemaker, deacon of his church, and holder of various offices in local government and the militia. His mother, eighteen years younger than his father, was the daughter of an eminent minister who belonged to a prominent Massachusetts family.

Little is known of Adams's childhood beyond the reflections and anecdotes preserved in his unfinished *Autobiography* and his *Diary*. A healthy, sturdy child, he enjoyed exploring the land surrounding his father's farm. Educated by local tutors, at first he had little interest in schooling. The elderly Adams left two colorful but clashing versions of the battle between his father and himself over going to school. John insisted that he wanted only to be a farmer. Deacon Adams proposed that John do the hard work of a farmer. In one version, after a few days of toil, John capitulated and agreed to go to school; in the other version, John insisted that he liked the farmer's life well, to which Deacon Adams growled, "Ay, but I don't like it so well." Whichever version is correct, John took to his studies after his father transferred him to a school run by Joseph Marsh; it was then that he acquired his first book, a selection of Cicero's *Orationes* in which he scribbled, "John Adams His Book 1749/50."

Deacon Adams intended his eldest son to become a minister, a goal requiring John to earn a degree from Harvard College. In return for his father's paying his college tuition, John agreed that this payment would represent his share of his father's estate. Harvard ranked him fourteenth of the twenty-five matriculating students, based on "dignity of family." While at Harvard, John began a diary, which he kept, on and off, for the rest of his life, as a means of critical self-examination. Achieving distinction in his studies, he received his BA degree in 1755.

Accepting a post as a schoolmaster in Worcester, John pondered the choice among "Divinity, Law, or Physick." Having witnessed the ordeal of Rev. Lemuel Bryant, whose liberal theological views had so incensed his congregation that they put him on trial in Deacon Adams's parlor, John realized that his veering from the Calvinistic doctrines of his Congregationalist upbringing might subject him to Bryant's fate. He also felt an increasing attraction to law as a subject of study and as a means to develop his gifts of reasoning, writing, and oratory.

In 1756, Adams signed a contract with Worcester's only lawyer, James Putnam, under which Putnam would supervise his legal studies for two years. Teaching school by day while studying law at night, Adams pored over such standard treatises as the *Institutes* of the English jurist Sir Edward

Coke. Ranging beyond those texts, he also studied such legal and jurisprudential writers as Hugo Grotius and Samuel Pufendorf.

Adams found Putnam to be at best a passive mentor; after two years of largely self-guided study, he realized that he would have to forge a network of connections to support his bid to join the bar. He approached several established attorneys, the most important for his future being Jeremiah Gridley. Gridley questioned Adams about his studies and counseled him to pursue the study of the law rather than the gain of it; he then sponsored Adams's admission to the bar of Suffolk County (including Braintree and the city of Boston).

After a few false starts, including losing his first case because he had worded a writ incorrectly, Adams gained ground as a lawyer. By the mid-1760s, he was in demand throughout the colony. Admitted as lawyer and barrister to the province's highest court, the Superior Court of Judicature, he vigorously advocated professionalization of the Massachusetts bar. On Gridley's death in 1767, Adams absorbed much of the older man's practice.

Having established himself as a lawyer, Adams was ready for the next major step in his life. On October 25, 1764, after two years of courtship, he married Abigail Smith (1744–1818), daughter of a local minister and member of one of the area's leading families. Cementing this extraordinary marriage was their rich, eloquent correspondence, made necessary by Adams's frequent absences from home, caused first by the demands of riding circuit and then by his political career. Some biographers minimize the couple's stormy conflicts over John's absences from home and his frequent failures to write home. Nonetheless, these two intelligent, strong-willed people formed a remarkable partnership, owing as much to their political and philosophical harmony as to their love for each other. Throughout his life, Abigail was John's most trusted advisor; indeed, she often was a sterner, tougher-minded politician than he was.

As he recognized in his old age, the American Revolution transformed John Adams's life, creating new career paths for him and other Americans (Morgan, 1976). Adams was drawn early into the controversy. In 1761 (as he recalled in his autobiography), as a young lawyer observing court sessions, he was entranced by the brilliant lawyering of James Otis against the writs of assistance (M.H. Smith, 1978; Farrell, 2006). British officials saw writs of assistance – warrants granting customs officials unrestricted power to search anywhere they wished and to seize anything they deemed evidence or contraband – as valuable tools for customs enforcement, but Otis condemned them as violating the constitutional rights of Englishmen.

In 1765, Adams joined a legal reading and debating society organized by Jeremiah Gridley. Responding to that year's Stamp Act crisis, he presented an essay to this "sodality" that won praise from the other members. He published "A Dissertation on the Canon and Feudal Law," as a series of four newspaper articles; they were reprinted in London later that year and in 1768 appeared as a book (G.S.Wood, 2011a: 114–125, 130–136). Expounding the colonists' view of the unwritten British constitution and its protections of the rights of Englishmen in America as well as in the mother country, Adams warned that British policy was bringing tyranny to America, just as the ancient, dangerous alliance between canon law and feudal law had tyrannized England. Declaring, "Let us dare to read, think, speak and write," Adams issued an eloquent call to his countrymen to defend their liberties, invoking the synthesizing habits of thought of the transatlantic Enlightenment and Anglo-American constitutional argument. In the fall of 1765, the Braintree town meeting adopted his draft instructions to the town's representatives to the Massachusetts legislature spelling out opposition to the Stamp Act (G.S. Wood, 2011a: 125–128):

> We further recommend the most clear and explicit Assertion and Vindication of our Rights and Liberties, to be entered on the Public Records; that the World may know, in the present and all future Generations, that we have a clear Knowledge and a just Sense of them, and, with Submission to Divine Providence, that we never can be Slaves. (G.S. Wood, 2011a: 128)

Printed in the *Massachusetts Gazette*, these instructions circulated through the province and at least forty other towns adopted them.

The "Dissertation" and the "Braintree Instructions" won Adams a reputation as an advocate of resistance to unconstitutional British policies. His second cousin Samuel Adams practiced a different kind of leadership in the same cause (Irvin, 2003; Maier, 1972, 1980), but John was disturbed by Samuel's radical, bottom-up activism and wary of his ultimate goal; John believed that Samuel was aiming at independence, a step he then found unwarranted and dangerous. His preferred means of action was to set forth the colonists' constitutional case with his pen.

In early 1770, a violent clash between British forces occupying Boston and an unruly Boston crowd thrust John Adams into the spotlight. On March 5, 1770, a detachment of British soldiers shot five Bostonians dead in what became known as the Boston Massacre. Indicted for murder, the soldiers and their commanding officer retained John Adams as lead defense counsel, with the young attorney Josiah Quincy. Adams's defense helped to win the acquittal on all charges of Captain Thomas Preston and six of the eight soldiers; two were convicted of the lesser crime of manslaughter, saving them from the gallows (Zobel, 1970; Reid, 1974; Archer, 2010). Despite his fears, his role in that trial did not damage his reputation; indeed, Samuel Adams and other radicals were delighted that John had demonstrated Massachusetts's commitment to the rule of law. Nonetheless, in 1771, Adams fell ill, the first case of a lifelong pattern in which illness succeeded severe professional or personal stress; moving his family back to Braintree, he withdrew from public life for a year.

In 1773, Adams drafted the answers of the Massachusetts House of Representatives to Governor Thomas Hutchinson, who in his opening address to the legislature and a follow-up address defended parliamentary supremacy over the colonies (Reid, 1981; G.S. Wood, 2011a: 234–250, 268–283). This debate returned Adams to the intellectual leadership of Massachusetts resistance. Though the House elected him to the governor's council, Hutchinson vetoed his election.

At the end of 1773, opponents of British policy rallied against the Tea Act and the British government's efforts to assist the floundering East India Company by shipping cut-rate tea to the colonies. On the ministry's theory, the tea's price was so low as to camouflage the threepenny tax on tea. Instead, on December 16, 1773, Bostonians disguised as Native American warriors stormed the tea ships anchored in Boston Harbor, broke open their holds, and dumped the tea into the harbor. When in early 1774 Parliament learned of this Boston Tea Party (Labaree, 1964; Carp, 2010), it enacted a set of statutes, the Coercive Acts, to punish Boston and Massachusetts for destroying company property and resisting the tea tax.

Responding to these punitive measures, delegates from twelve of the thirteen colonies gathered in Philadelphia in September 1774 as the First Continental Congress. John Adams, Samuel Adams, Robert Treat Paine, and Thomas Cushing represented Massachusetts, winning praise for their tact and deference to other colonies. On his return home, John penned twelve learned newspaper essays answering a series of essays by "Massachusettensis" (the pen-name of Daniel Leonard, though Adams at first thought Jonathan Sewall to be the author) defending British policies. Adams's essays, signed "Novanglus;" set forth his most thorough statement of the American position on the constitutional dispute with Britain (G.S. Wood, 2011a: 327–349, 352–556, 559–614).

In May of 1775, after the battles of Lexington and Concord, Adams returned to Philadelphia to attend the Second Continental Congress, emerging as a vigorous advocate of independence. When in June Congress created the Continental Army, Adams nominated Virginia delegate George Washington to command it. While the Continental Army faced British forces near Boston, Congress adopted a last appeal to George III as an impartial "patriot king" duty-bound to mediate the claims of all his subjects. Though skeptical of this "Olive Branch Petition," Adams nonetheless signed it with his colleagues on July 5, 1775. On July 24, however, he wrote to his friend James Warren mocking the petition's draftsman, John Dickinson of Pennsylvania, as "a certain great Fortune and piddling Genius … [who] has given a silly cast to our whole Doings" (G.S. Wood, 2011b: 14). After the British captured Adams's letter and published it, Dickinson and his allies ostracized Adams. Nonetheless, Adams served on dozens of congressional committees as well as on the Massachusetts provincial council, demonstrating his commitment to the American cause.

The collapse of colonial governments in late 1775 and early 1776 left a void of legitimate government. For months, Adams answered requests for advice about restoring constitutional government from such colleagues as Richard Henry Lee, John Penn, and Jonathan Dickinson Sergeant. In April 1776 he distilled his advice into a pamphlet. *Thoughts on Government* was a terse, eloquent manual for devising state constitutions (G.S. Wood, 2011b: 49–56). Extolling "the divine science of politicks" and counseling that "good government, is an empire of Laws" (G.S. Wood, 2011b: 49, 50), Adams prescribed a constitution creating a bicameral legislature balanced by an independent governor armed with ample powers.

Thoughts on Government also answered Thomas Paine's *Common Sense*, published in January 1776. Though Adams admired and endorsed Paine's case that American independence was necessary, justified, and feasible, he scorned Paine's rejection of checks and balances and separation of powers as flying in the face of experience (G.S. Wood, 2011b: 44–46). Writing to Abigail on March 19, 1776, he observed, "This Writer has a better Hand at pulling down than building" (G.S. Wood, 2011b: 45).

In May, Adams built on *Thoughts on Government* by framing a resolution authorizing the colonies to form new constitutions; the Second Continental Congress adopted this resolution on May 10, adding on May 15 his justificatory preamble (G.S. Wood, 2011b: 68–69). Adams regarded this resolution as the substance of independence. In June of 1776, following the introduction by Richard Henry Lee of Virginia of three resolutions demanding independence, Adams was named to the committee assigned to frame a declaration of independence. Urging his friend Thomas Jefferson to prepare the draft, he became Congress's leading advocate for independence and supporter of Jefferson's Declaration (Maier, 1997). On July 2, 1776, Congress adopted Lee's resolutions; two days later the body adopted a revised version of Jefferson's draft Declaration (G.S. Wood, 2011b: 89–91, 91–93). On the night of July 2–3, exalted by his victory, Adams wrote to Abigail: "[T]hrough all the Gloom I can see the Rays of ravishing Light and Glory. I can see that the End is worth more than all the Means. And that Posterity will tryumph in the Days Transaction, even altho We shall rue it, which I trust to God We shall not" (G.S. Wood, 2011b: 93).

Up to this point, Adams's political ideas revolved around Anglo-American constitutionalism as informed by classical political thought going back to Aristotle. Though on occasion, as in *Thoughts on Government*, he seemed to endorse what later generations call American exceptionalism, Adams argued for an exceptionalism of opportunity rather than the view that Americans were inherently different from other peoples past or present. While extolling Americans and the chance they had to make their success a blessing to humanity, Adams still maintained that Americans were subject to the same internal and external forces that shaped and corrupted human nature, and that they still had to guard against falling prey to these dangers.

Adams became one of the Continental Congress's workhorses, serving on many committees and chairing dozens. In particular, he worked with Benjamin Franklin, John Dickinson, Robert Morris, and Benjamin Harrison V to frame a model treaty for the United States. This plan distilled the idealism that Adams hoped would guide American foreign relations, seeking the goal of free and reciprocal trade among the signing nations while avoiding American entanglement in European affairs (G.S. Wood, 2011b: 113–124). At other times, however, Congress filled him with frustration. On April 26, 1777, he vented this frustration by writing to Abigail, "Posterity! You will never know, how much it cost the present Generation, to preserve your Freedom! I hope you will make a good Use of it. If you do not, I shall repent in Heaven, that I ever took half the Pains to preserve it" (Butterfield et al., 1963: 2.223–224).

In late 1777, Congress assigned Adams his first diplomatic mission, based on his work on the model treaty and his mastery of the foreign policy issues facing the United States (Ferling, 1994a). Benjamin Franklin, Silas Deane, and Arthur Lee represented the United States in Paris, seeking a treaty of alliance with France. Responding to charges of incompetence and corruption that the prickly, distrustful Lee brought against Deane, Congress recalled Deane and named Adams to replace him. After a harrowing transatlantic voyage with his 10-year-old son John Quincy Adams, Adams arrived in April 1778 to find that Franklin already had negotiated the treaty. Adams worked hard to establish a role for himself in Paris; he systematized the mission's paperwork and finances, sent home news of European developments, and provided a needed third vote to avoid deadlock between Franklin and Lee, who detested each other.

Adams worked well with Franklin, as he had while they served in Congress (Ferling, 1994a), though he could not see the point of Franklin's subtle, indirect practice of diplomacy at dinner parties and soirees. As American fortunes suffered in 1778 and 1779, Adams increasingly worried about what he saw as Franklin's undue deference to the French and his slipshod administration of American affairs. Believing that a diplomat should be an attorney for his country, Adams brought the mindset of a seasoned litigator to the subtle, delicate sphere of diplomacy. Also, despite his cordial relations with Franklin, Adams took Lee's part in the festering controversy over Silas Deane. Further, as a Protestant New Englander, he shared his region's longstanding distrust of the French; he also became suspicious of the French foreign minister, the comte de Vergennes. In turn, Vergennes was suspicious of Adams, influenced by reports from Conrad Alexandre Gerard, the French minister to the United States, that Adams was secretly pro-British. In addition, Adams's blunt demands that France do more for the Americans exasperated Vergennes. Acting through Gerard, Vergennes induced Congress to rescind the three-man commission and name Franklin sole American minister to France. Having no role in Paris, Adams returned to America.

Soon after his arrival in Boston in August of 1779, Adams was elected as a delegate to the Massachusetts constitutional convention. That body, the first specially created to frame a constitution, named John Adams, Samuel Adams, and James Bowdoin as a drafting committee. After this committee assigned the drafting task to John Adams, he prepared the most eloquent and carefully devised state constitution yet adopted (Reid, 1980; R.J. Taylor, 1980; G.S. Wood, 2011b: 249–277;. Adams rejected the tendency of the first wave of Revolutionary constitution-making to exalt the legislature while cutting back the powers and independence of the executive and judiciary. Developing the plan of *Thoughts on Government*, Adams's draft established a bicameral legislature, a powerful governor elected by direct popular vote, and an independent judiciary. Following the example of Virginia's 1776 constitution, Adams prefaced his draft constitution with an elaborate declaration of rights – more accurately, a declaration of right principles including provisions recognizing individual rights and defining the citizen's duties or responsibilities. Adams had to return to Europe before the convention finished its labors, though he kept careful watch over the constitution's ratification and subsequent history. *Thoughts on Government* and the Massachusetts constitution of 1780 shaped all later American constitution-making, as to both a constitution's content and the manner of its framing and adoption, including the US constitution in 1787–1788.

By contrast to his achievements as a constitution-maker, Adams's work as a diplomat plunged him into difficulties personal and political. In February of 1780, he returned to France with a congressional commission to open peace talks with Britain, but his arrival, and his aggressive lobbying of Vergennes, agitated the Frenchman and strained Franklin's good humor. Adams and Vergennes clashed over whether and when to inform the British of his mission; Adams also sought from Vergennes a passport to the Netherlands for a mission seeking an alliance and financial aid – but Vergennes delayed issuing the passport till the summer, when he may have granted it as a means to get rid of Adams. Negotiating with the Dutch authorities while shuttling between Holland and Paris, Adams secured Dutch recognition of American independence and crucial Dutch loans to the United States (Schulte Nordholt, 1981, 1982). He also wrote two series of essays for European publications presenting the American case for independence (G.S. Wood, 2011b: 340–387, 392–442).

Returning to Paris in mid-1781, Adams discovered that Congress (again at the behest of the French) had rescinded his sole appointment as peace commissioner and named Franklin, John Jay, Henry Laurens, and Thomas Jefferson to join him in conducting talks with Britain, instructing them to coordinate their efforts with France. Adams accepted this new arrangement, though he resisted the congressional mandate. At the same time, letters from Abigail, from his friend and political ally Elbridge Gerry, and from

James Lovell, a Massachusetts delegate to Congress, told him that Congress had recast the commission in part because of French influence and Franklin's machinations; Franklin had sent Congress the testy 1780 correspondence between Adams and Vergennes with Franklin's cover letter criticizing Adams's conduct. Increasingly distraught, Adams filled his diary with criticisms of Franklin's ethics, laziness, inefficiency, and deference to France (Ferling, 1994a: 245–247).

Of the five commissioners, only Franklin, Adams, and Jay negotiated the treaty; Laurens had been captured by the British, and Jefferson was unable to serve. Over the next eighteen months, the Americans pursued negotiations, punctuated by pauses for British diplomats to consult with superiors in London and for Adams to make an emergency trip to the Netherlands to negotiate further American loans. Returning from Holland in October 1782 at Jay's behest, Adams discussed the negotiations with Jay. Making common cause, they told Franklin that they would disregard Congress's instructions to take no action "without the knowledge and concurrence" of France. Though questioning their decision, Franklin concurred with it.

The product of these exhausting negotiations was the Treaty of Paris, agreed in preliminary form on November 30, 1782 and signed in final form on September 3, 1783 (G.S. Wood, 2011b: 689–698). Under this treaty, Britain recognized American independence and American fishing rights along the Newfoundland coast and ceded all territory between the Allegheny Mountains and the Mississippi River, doubling the new nation's size. The treaty also offset Loyalist claims for confiscated property in America against Americans' claims for property destroyed by British and Loyalist forces. In sum, the treaty was an American victory (Morris, 1965; Ferling, 1994a).

Following completion of the negotiations, Adams brooded over his future. Though eager to return home, he hoped that Congress might name him the first American minister to Great Britain. He believed that he had earned the appointment; he also hoped that his diplomatic labors, on top of his efforts in Congress, would earn him enduring fame, the ultimate reward for devoted labors for the public good. Though Adams shared this way of thinking with every leading member of the Revolutionary generation, Adams was more candid about it than most (Adair, 1974).

Adams spent most of 1783 fretting that Congress would neither recognize his past services nor give him any new diplomatic assignment. Instead, he feared, those prizes would go to Franklin or to Franklin's nominee. Haunted by reports from home of schemes in Congress against him spurred by Vergennes's agents and by Franklin, and unable to contain himself, Adams denounced Franklin in letters and private conversations. Insisting that he and Jay and not Franklin deserved principal credit for the treaty, he made Franklin the target of his disappointment and wrath. The New Englanders to whom he unburdened himself shared his views and echoed them back to him, filling Adams with resentful vindication. Even so, Adams's explosions were extraordinarily indiscreet, illustrating his tendency to self-sabotage, confirming the doubts that many in Congress had of his judgment, and fueling the charge that he was vain and mentally unstable.

Adams's attempts to argue his case to Congress and to posterity backfired. It was almost impossible to practice national politics by letters sent across the Atlantic. Further, each letter Adams wrote defending himself seemed to most in Congress to reinforce the case against him. Finally, Franklin, a seasoned veteran of epistolary politics, knew how to get his revenge (Middlekauff, 1996). On July 22, 1783, his exasperation with Adams breaking through his genial veneer, Franklin complained to Robert R. Livingston, the Confederation's secretary for foreign affairs, about Adams's lack of discretion, adding, "I am persuaded however, that [Adams] means well for his Country, is always an honest Man and often a Wise One, but sometimes and in some things absolutely out of his Senses" (http://franklinpapers.org/franklin/framedVolumes.jsp). Franklin's letter soon became notorious, within Congress and among American politicians, pursuing Adams for the rest of his life (and thereafter) as the most devastating critique of him ever written.

Despite his desire to go home, and his December 1782 letter submitting his resignation to Congress, Adams stayed in Europe hoping against hope for news. Finally he learned that he had been named to act, with Franklin and Jefferson, to negotiate commercial treaties with such European powers as Prussia. In August 1784, after nearly five years apart, he and Abigail were finally reunited in London.

Several months later, Adams got the news he had long hoped for, and welcomed as validation and vindication: in early 1785, Congress notified him of his appointment as American minister to Great Britain. On June 1, he presented his credentials to George III and had a successful face-to-face audience with the king. Once that triumph was on record, however, Adams found his appointment a source of perennial frustration and disappointment. Try as he might, he could not induce the British to grant the United States "most favored nation" status, nor could he persuade the British to end their occupation of the western territories ceded to the United States under the Treaty of Paris. Finally, after two years of banging his head against a British wall, he wrote to Congress seeking permission to return home. In October of 1787, Congress granted his request, and he and Abigail sailed from Portsmouth in April of 1788.

While Adams struggled to carry out his diplomatic responsibilities, he also brooded over Europeans' condescension toward the Americans' experiments in government. He found particularly vexing a 1778 letter by the French economist and government official Anne Robert Jacques Turgot to the English dissenting clergyman and political activist Richard Price. Adams read this letter reprinted as an appendix to Price's 1784 pamphlet,

Observations on the American Revolution, and on the Means of Making It a Blessing to the World. Irritated by Turgot's insistence that checks and balances and separation of powers were not just unnecessary but pernicious mystifications, and that the people should concentrate all political authority in one center, Adams covered the pamphlet's margins with testy handwritten comments. Turgot's praise for the Pennsylvania constitution of 1776, which he extolled as the work of Franklin, exasperated Adams. Finally, news from America of the outbreak in Massachusetts in 1786 of Shays' Rebellion, a debtors' insurrection seemingly threatening the government whose constitution he had done so much to create, filled Adams with urgency (Szatmary, 1980; Gross, 1993).

In early 1787, the first volume of Adams's response to Turgot, *A Defence of the Constitutions of Government of the United States of America*, appeared in London and was reprinted in Philadelphia in time for the opening of the Federal Convention, the body that framed the constitution of the United States. Two more volumes followed within the year. This large, disorderly work ranged throughout Western political and constitutional history to support one theoretical point. Adams defended separation of powers and checks and balances as integral components of what he deemed to be the best constitutional government: a mixed republic with a two-house legislature and a powerful, independent chief executive, recreating the balance among the one, the few, and the many central to classical political thought. The history of every society, whether ancient, medieval, or modern, Adams insisted, taught the necessity of striking that balance among the three great orders. As he wrote at the close of Volume III:

> All nations, from the beginning, have been agitated by the same passions. The principles developed here will go a great way in explaining every phenomenon that occurs in the history of government. The vegetable and animal kingdoms, and those heavenly bodies whose existence and movements we are as yet only permitted faintly to perceive, do not appear to be governed by laws more uniform or certain than those which regulate the moral and political world. (C.F. Adams, 1850–1856: 6.218)

Adams wrote his book as part of his continuing effort to guide his countrymen's efforts to create sound constitutions, which he had begun in 1776 with *Thoughts on Government.* Adams also sought to strike a blow in America's war for intellectual independence, just as Thomas Jefferson's *Notes on the State of Virginia* defended America from the "natural degeneracy" thesis advocated by European *philosophes* led by the comte de Buffon. Like Jefferson, but in a different front of this intellectual war, Adams sought to set the *philosophes* straight.

Adams later bemoaned the *Defence*'s "want of method." Frantically compiling a sourcebook on comparative constitutional government, he left himself almost no time to give his book the literary finish and clear organization of *Thoughts on Government*. Moreover, as with his *Novanglus* essays, Adams was so intent on refuting his adversaries point by point that only someone equally immersed in the writers whom he disputed could follow his argument.[1] The *Defence* won Adams praise and criticism – praise for his learning, criticism for his apparent embrace of corrupt European habits of thought, in particular his lack of hostility to monarchic and aristocratic government. Yet Adams's contemporaries failed to grasp that he was not advocating aristocracy but rather arguing, first, that every society had or would develop an aristocracy; second, that that aristocracy would seek to control the government to protect itself and extend its power; and, third, that the best way to meet this challenge was to give aristocracy a place in government but hem it in with constitutional safeguards so that it could do as little harm as possible.

While his countrymen argued about the *Defence*, John and Abigail Adams sailed home. When on June 17, 1788 their ship docked in Boston, Adams returned to a country significantly different from the one he had left nine years before. The United States had ratified the constitution proposed by the Federal Convention in 1787 – a document that in his view approximated the prescription for sound government in his *Defence*. Later that year, Adams was elected to represent Massachusetts in the last session of the Convention Congress, but he never took office, for his countrymen had another role for him.

In April 1789, Adams learned of his election as the first vice president of the United States, and of George Washington's unanimous election as the first president. Adams had received only 34 of the 69 electoral votes cast – outdistancing all other candidates, but falling short of the acclamation accorded Washington. On receiving word of his election, he journeyed to New York City, the new nation's first capital under the constitution, and on April 23, 1789 he was sworn in before the Senate; a week later, he attended Washington's inauguration. That occasion's confused protocol led him to betray the first signs of a self-damaging preoccupation with ceremony. At one point, anxious about his status as president of the Senate when Washington was present, he asked, "When the president comes into the Senate, what shall I be? … I wish gentlemen to think what I shall be" (Bowling & Veit, 1989: 5–6).

Vice President Adams accelerated the erosion of his reputation with two missteps. First, he launched a doomed effort to bolster the new government's dignity by proposing that Congress adopt titles of office. In particular, Adams insisted, the president required a grand title beyond "His Excellency," usually accorded to state governors. A committee of Senators proposed to call the president "His Highness the President of the United States of America, and Protector of Their Liberties." Though the Senate approved the proposal, it met a crushing defeat in the House, and Adams became a laughing-stock. The only title emerging from this debacle was "His Rotundity," bestowed on Adams to ridicule his stout physique.

Second, though Adams sought to be a kind of senatorial prime minister, the senators made clear that he was merely their presiding officer, with power only to decide questions of procedure and break tie votes. Painfully, he learned to restrain his impulses to expound to the senators what he had learned about procedure in parliament or about comparative constitutional government.

News of the French Revolution prompted Adams to take up his pen once more. In 1790, he began a series of newspaper essays commenting on a history of the sixteenth-century French civil wars by the seventeenth-century Italian historian Enrico Caterino Davila. He hoped that his *Discourses on Davila* would echo Niccolo Machiavelli's *Discourses on the First Ten Books of Titus Livius.* Again, however, he bounced from subject to subject, launching a disquisition on emulation and the desire for fame inspired by a passage from Adam Smith's *Theory of Moral Sentiments.* His efforts to explain what he saw as the French Revolution's potentially disastrous consequences backfired. His foes cited the *Discourses* as further proof that he had forsaken republicanism for monarchism. Despite Adams's protests, even Jefferson concluded that Adams backed kingly government. When an American printer proposed to republish Thomas Paine's *Rights of Man*, Jefferson sent him the book with a friendly letter praising it as likely to refute "the political heresies which have sprung up among us." Jefferson was mortified when the printer used his private letter as a preface to Paine's polemic. Despite his apologetic explanations, the damage was done – the public saw Adams and Jefferson opposing each other, with Adams branded as an apologist for monarchy and aristocracy. Disgusted, in 1791 he discontinued his *Discourses on Davila.* It was his last sustained effort in political philosophy.

Adams's views of human nature had darkened since the early days of American independence. His growing pessimism had many sources: his stormy experience of representing his nation in indifferent or hostile European capitals; his exacerbated self-consciousness about his origins on the periphery of the Atlantic world; his bitter realization that Congress no longer followed the public-spirited standard of 1776; his sense of betrayal by Franklin and former colleagues in Congress; and his dismay at the turbulence of American politics as dramatized by Shays' Rebellion. If anything, the emergence of partisan divisions in the United States under the constitution intensified his pessimism.

Though Adams cast more tie-breaking votes in the Senate (29) than any other vice president, the partisan battles of the 1790s sidelined him. Abigail Adams's absence intensified John's sense of his own uselessness: citing her ill health, she returned to Braintree in 1792, not returning to Philadelphia for the rest of his term as vice president. As he wrote to her on December

19, 1793, "[M]y country has in its wisdom contrived for me the most insignificant office that ever the imagination of man contrived or his mind conceived" (Letter from John Adams to Abigail Adams, Dec. 19, 1793).[2]

Following Washington's announcement that he would not seek a third term, Adams became the presidential candidate of the Federalist partisan alliance in the 1796 elections, with the diplomat Thomas Pinckney of South Carolina for vice president. Facing him were Thomas Jefferson and Senator Aaron Burr of New York, the choices of the Republican partisan alliance. Adams defeated Jefferson by 3 electoral votes, 71 to 68; Jefferson, not Pinckney, became Adams's vice president.

On March 4, 1797, John Adams was sworn in before a joint session of Congress as the new nation's second president. His inaugural address reintroduced himself to the American people as a warm supporter of the Revolution, a firm advocate of republican government, an admirer of President Washington, and a man seeking to transcend partisan divisions (Richardson, 1897: 1.218–222). Though this address was well received, Adams then and afterward felt overshadowed by Washington. Wanting to avoid the appearance of criticizing Washington, Adams retained his Cabinet, though its members were more loyal to Washington (secretary of war James McHenry) or to Hamilton (secretary of state Timothy Pickering and secretary of the treasury Oliver Wolcott) than to himself. Adams compounded his problems by treating the presidency as a part-time office. Solicitous of Abigail's delicate health, he spent months at a time in Braintree. His Cabinet, left to fend for itself, sought guidance from Hamilton, then a lawyer in private practice in New York. Driven by impatience with Adams and by his conviction that he knew what to do, Hamilton provided that guidance. Adams had created a recipe for trouble; not until late in his term did he realize that he was not leading his own administration.

The division in Adams's administration indicated that, rather than being a coherent and unified movement, the Federalists had split into so-called High Federalists aligned with Hamilton and Adams Federalists loyal to the president. Any issue highlighting the differences between the two groups might rupture the fragile Federalist partisan alliance (Dauer, 1953); too many issues had that potential.

Troubles with France plagued Adams's presidency almost from the beginning. In 1797, after the French refused to receive Charles C. Pinckney as American minister, Adams sought a peaceful resolution of French–American differences. His mission to Paris (Pinckney, John Marshall, and Elbridge Gerry) failed at the outset when three French officials (whom the Americans identified as X, Y, and Z) demanded bribes before opening talks. Rejecting this demand, Pinckney and Gerry sent Marshall home with their report. For once showing a shrewd grasp of public opinion, Adams kept it confidential until Republicans demanded its disclosure. Then he released the report, embarrassing the Republicans and infuriating the public against

France. As American and French naval vessels clashed in a "quasi-war," Adams for once savored national popularity.

Another aspect of the Adams administration's response to the crisis was more controversial. In 1798, Congress enacted four statutes – a Naturalization Act, an Aliens Act, an Alien Enemies Act, and a Sedition Act – modeled on statutes enacted by Great Britain in the early 1790s. The first three measures tightened immigration law, empowering the president to deport any resident alien whom he deemed hostile to the United States or who was a citizen or subject of a nation at war with the United States. The Sedition Act made it a federal crime to bring into disrepute the general government, either house of Congress, or the president – but not the vice president. The Sedition Act empowered the government to use the full force of law against critics of Adams or his administration – though it allowed defendants to prove the alleged sedition's truth and left the jury free to determine issues of law and fact (Smith, 1956). Biographers are divided on Adams's responsibility for these measures; even such ardent Federalists as Alexander Hamilton and John Marshall doubted the statutes' wisdom. By contrast, Abigail Adams was firmly convinced of the need to punish sedition, as she maintained in a testy 1804 correspondence with Jefferson. Like others backing the Sedition Act, she insisted that, as the government under the Constitution was still fragile, the reputations of those holding office under it were key to its success, and any criticism of those officials would not only injure their individual reputations but damage the constitutional system as a whole (Freeman, 2003).

Republicans led by Jefferson and Madison sought to counter these Federalist measures. Later in 1798, the Kentucky and Virginia legislatures denounced the Alien and Sedition Acts as unconstitutional. The Kentucky Resolutions (secretly written by Jefferson) asserted a state's power to declare federal statutes null and void within its borders (*nullification*); the more moderate Virginia Resolutions (secretly written by Madison) declared that a state had the power to interpose its authority between a federal law and any of its citizens prosecuted under that law (*interposition*). Though the other states rejected these resolutions, Kentucky and Virginia put the measures' constitutionality in dispute, in the process highlighting a major issue that Republicans would use against Adams's bid for a second term.

The Adams administration's preparations for war included organizing an army. Adams named Washington as the army's commander-in-chief – but without first asking him. This appointment led to a cascading series of misunderstandings and clashes. First, Washington was irked that Adams had not consulted him. Second, he insisted on conditions, including his freedom to name his own staff. Washington wanted three men to serve under him: Alexander Hamilton, his most trusted advisor; Henry Knox, who had commanded artillery under Washington during the Revolution and had been secretary of war under the Confederation and the Constitution;

and Charles C. Pinckney. Though Adams bridled at including Hamilton, the real issue was the order of seniority of the officers' commissions. Adams preferred to put Knox or Pinckney first; Washington made it clear that Hamilton was his first choice; Pinckney graciously offered to serve without regard to seniority; and Knox was so hurt by the controversy that he withdrew his name. The imbroglio exasperated Adams. Already doubting the quasi-war's wisdom, he now began to seek a means to avert a full-blown war with France. Secretly, he asked William Vans Murray, American minister to the Netherlands, to sound out the French about reopening negotiations.

Meanwhile, a federal tax enacted to raise revenue for the war sparked outrage in Pennsylvania. John Fries, a veteran of the Continental Army, organized a tax-resistance movement. After clashes pitting the insurgents against local authorities, state militia, and US marshals, Fries and twenty-nine other men were arrested and tried for treason and other crimes in a federal court; Fries and two others were convicted of treason and sentenced to hang. Adams reviewed the sentences, determined that Fries and the other convicted defendants had not committed treason as defined by the constitution, and pardoned them; he then issued a blanket amnesty. These generous measures came too late, however – Adams's administration had alienated Pennsylvania's German population by its punitive enforcement of the tax, and Pennsylvania's voters swung away from Adams and the Federalists (P.D. Newman, 2004).

Washington's death on December 14, 1799 freed Adams to reassess his presidency. In 1800, he disclosed his efforts to seek peace with France, accepting the demands by congressional Federalists that he send Chief Justice Oliver Ellsworth and North Carolina's Governor William Richardson Davie to join William Vans Murray. He also discovered that for months his Cabinet had been following Hamilton's leadership rather than his own. Enraged, he forced secretary of war McHenry to resign and fired secretary of state Pickering, replacing them with men loyal to him and sharing his views. His explosive face-to-face confrontation with Hamilton left each man convinced that the other was insane. Infuriated, Hamilton wrote an inflammatory pamphlet denouncing Adams as unfit for office. Intending to circulate his *Letter from Alexander Hamilton Concerning the Character and Conduct of John Adams, Esq., President of the United States* only to leading Federalists, he hoped to persuade them to abandon Adams for his running-mate, Charles C. Pinckney – but the pamphlet leaked to the newspapers, splitting Federalist ranks and injuring both Adams's and Hamilton's reputations (Freeman, 2001a).

The split between Adams Federalists backing the president and High Federalists backing Hamilton and Pinckney, together with growing public unhappiness with prosecutions under the Sedition Act and desire for peace with France, played into the hands of the Republicans, who again backed Jefferson and Burr. In the 1800 election, Adams and Pinckney garnered 65 and 64 electoral votes respectively, behind Jefferson and Aaron Burr, who tied at 73 votes each.

Wounded by his defeat, Adams found bitter amusement in the election's results, noting that Hamilton's efforts had elevated above him the two men he least wanted to be president. Some Federalists tried to make a deal with Burr because they thought him less doctrinaire than Jefferson. Jeffersonians demanded that Burr defer to Jefferson, which he was prepared to do, and that he deny that he was fit to be president by comparison with Jefferson, which he was *not* prepared to do. Rejecting what he saw as a dishonorable slap at his fitness for leadership, Burr began to entertain Federalist offers of support. Appalled, Hamilton begged Federalists not to back Burr – even at the price of accepting Jefferson's election (Freeman, 2001a: ch. 5).

Adams rejected suggestions that he remain in office until the House broke the deadlock; once the House resolved the deadlock in Jefferson's favor, Adams worked to ensure an orderly transfer of power. His actions during this crisis rendered a service to the nation and its constitutional system as great as that rendered by Washington in refusing to seek a third term. As Washington set a two-term precedent honored until the 1940s, Adams helped to ensure that ensuing presidential elections would be marked by peaceful transfers of authority and power from losers to victors.

And yet the closing months of Adams's presidency gave rise to a myth of political retribution against Republicans that damaged his reputation though it had only partial basis in fact. Since the beginning of government under the Constitution, the federal judiciary's structure posed problems for the judges and for the nation (Preyer, 2009). The Judiciary Act of 1789 created a three-layer court system, with the Supreme Court at its apex and specialized federal district courts at its base. In the middle were the federal circuit courts, trial-court workhorses staffed by each state's federal district judge and by Supreme Court justices riding circuit. Congress imposed circuit-riding on the justices both to give them something to do while the Supreme Court awaited the development of a caseload and to occupy them so that they would not be idle and thus a danger to the system.

Circuit-riding was onerous, however, sometimes endangering the justices' health. For a decade, the justices sought relief from this burden, to no avail. After the 1800 election, the lame-duck Federalist Congress seized the chance to mix judicial reform with partisan advantage. The 1801 Judiciary Act abolished circuit-riding and redesigned and enlarged the federal circuit courts; in the last two weeks of his term Adams nominated, and the Senate confirmed, loyal Federalists to these new offices (Preyer, 2009).

Even before Congress redesigned the federal judiciary, Adams faced a decision about the Supreme Court. In 1800, Chief Justice Ellsworth resigned, citing ill-health. At first Adams named John Jay (without consulting him) to his former post, and the Senate confirmed him. Jay declined to serve, however, citing the post's onerousness and the prevailing lack of respect for the nation's courts. Learning of Jay's refusal, Adams named his secretary of state, John Marshall, to succeed Ellsworth. For once, an impulsive appointment by Adams succeeded far better than he had hoped.

Adams did not attend Jefferson's inauguration, leaving the capital very early on March 4, 1801. There is no evidence that he refused to attend out of spite; historians may confuse John Adams's failure to attend Jefferson's inauguration in 1801 with John Quincy Adams's refusal to attend Andrew Jackson's inauguration in 1829. Adams's cordial letters to Jefferson in early 1801 do not support the idea that he was boycotting Jefferson's swearing-in. Two family reasons may explain his departure. First, Abigail's frail health and her dislike for the capital had confined her to Braintree for weeks. Second, on November 30, 1800, their son Charles died at the age of 30 from alcoholism, leaving a wife and two small children.

Humiliated by his defeat, embittered by what he saw as Hamilton's dangerous ambition and Jefferson's deviousness, and heartbroken by his son Charles's death, Adams spent the first years of his retirement writing his *Autobiography*, though he never finished it. In 1805, aghast at his old friend Mercy Otis Warren's description of him in her *History of the Rise, Progress, and Termination of the American Revolution* (M.O. Warren, 1988), Adams wrote her a series of hurt, angry letters defending himself; Warren, a prolific author and one of the first historians of the Revolution, defended her book, but the correspondence did not heal the breach between them (C.F. Adams, 1878a). In 1809, Adams began a series of newspaper articles for the Boston *Patriot*, a defense of his public career against Hamilton's 1800 pamphlet that he continued for three years (Freeman, 2001a: ch. 3). Finally, Adams continued or restarted correspondence with such old friends from the Revolution as Benjamin Rush (Schutz and Adair, 1966). These letters and autobiographical writings focused Adams's attention on how posterity would remember him, prompting on occasion written explosions of hurt, resentment, and envy against patriotic icons such as Washington, Franklin, and Jefferson.

Noting signs in Adams's letters that he was mellowing toward Jefferson, Rush, who valued his friendship with both men, urged them to reconcile their differences. The thin-skinned Jefferson rejected the idea (Schutz and Adair, 1966: 200–202). Writing on Christmas Day 1811, Adams mocked Rush's suggestion, asking what reason either man would have to write to the other, but hinting, "Time or chance, however, or possibly design, may produce ere long a letter between us" (Schutz and Adair, 1966: 202). The "time" was one week. True to his word, on New Year's Day 1812, Adams sent Jefferson a gentle, friendly letter hinting at the delivery of a gift, two pieces of "homespun" from a person in whose education Jefferson had taken an interest (the gift was a two-volume set of lectures on rhetoric and oratory by John Quincy Adams, then Boylston Professor of Rhetoric at Harvard). Jefferson eagerly wrote back, launching one of the great correspondences in American history (Cappon, 1959; Peterson, 1976).

Adams wrote nearly four letters to Jefferson for every one that Jefferson wrote to him. Hungry for an intellectual sparring partner, he baited Jefferson on politics past and present, as when he wrote on July 13, 1813:

> The first time that you and I differed in opinion on any material Question was after your arrival from Europe, and that point was the French Revolution. You was well persuaded in your own mind that the Nation would succeed in establishing a free Republican Government: I was as well persuaded, in mine, that a project of such a Government, over five and twenty millions of people when four and twenty millions and five hundred thousands of them could neither write nor read, was as unnatural irrational and impracticable; as it would be over the Elephants Lions Tigers Panthers Wolves and Bears in the Royal Menagerie, at Versailles. (Cappon, 1959: 358)

At the same time, he happily shared with Jefferson his extensive reading on comparative religion and his musings on the classics, philosophy, the nature of aristocracy (the subject of another extensive correspondence with the Virginia agrarian writer John Taylor of Caroline), and such questions as whether they would be willing to live their lives over again. Both men often discussed the history of the Revolution, their own places in it, and the conflict between posterity's need to understand that history and the forces depriving posterity of reliable historical knowledge. Adams's letters display the intellectually venturesome, playful, and self-mocking facets of his personality that have endeared him to later generations. Jefferson's letters are graceful miniature essays, modeled on Cicero's letters to his friend Atticus, a body of Roman literature that both men treasured.

In 1818, Adams reported to Jefferson that Abigail had fallen gravely ill; on October 28, 1818, before Jefferson even received Adams's letter, Abigail Adams died, three days after their fifty-fourth wedding anniversary. Jefferson learned the news from the press and wrote an eloquent condolence letter that touched Adams's heart.

The letters that Adams wrote in retirement form a remarkable mix of wisdom, humor, learning, combativeness, and occasional sourness about his own historical reputation and his likely fate at posterity's hands. In some ways, Adams began to recover his youthful optimism about America, though he still disputed Jefferson's views on American exceptionalism, insisting that Americans were not exempt from the forces that had shaped human nature and experiments in government throughout history.

Two issues on which the two statesmen's ideas converged were religion and the relationship between church and state. Having left behind the Congregationalism of his ancestors as a young man, in his old age Adams embraced Unitarianism. By contrast with Jefferson's deist Unitarianism, Adams's was a Christian Unitarianism preserving belief in a personal deity, Jesus as the redeemer of humanity, and the miracles of the New Testament as true (Holmes, 2006: 73–78). Further, as a Quincy delegate to the Massachusetts constitutional convention of 1820, he tried but failed to rewrite the 1780 constitution to provide that "all men of all religions, demeaning themselves peaceably, and as good subjects of the Commonwealth, shall be equally under the protection of the law."[3] His service in that convention was the closing act of a political career that had begun more than half-a-century before. The convention delegates elected him president, an honor that he declined on account of his age (Journal, 1821: 9–10); when he entered the hall for the first time, the other delegates stood, their heads uncovered, as a mark of respect.[4]

Despite their increasing frailty, both men were determined to see the fiftieth anniversary of American independence, on July 4, 1826. Jefferson died first, early in the afternoon; Adams died several hours later, murmuring, "Thomas Jefferson survives." Americans regarded the news that these two great men had died on the same day, the fiftieth anniversary of the Declaration, as providential – a sign that the torch was passing from the Revolutionary generation to their successors.

1.2 The Biographers

Scholarship on John Adams falls into three categories – editions of his writings and papers; biographies and character studies (books focusing on key themes of the subject's psychology or personal qualities); and monographs studying his constitutional or political thought or key periods or themes in his life and thought. The balance of this essay groups these works accordingly.

Editions of Adams's Writings and Papers

Until modern times, all studies of John Adams have depended on *The Works of John Adams, Esq., Second President of the United States*, edited by Charles Francis Adams and published in ten volumes (1850–1856). In 1829, John Quincy Adams had started writing a life of John Adams after his defeated 1828 bid for a second term as president, but he set it aside after his election to the House of Representatives in 1830, with only seven chapters written. Charles Francis Adams had trained himself in documentary editing with selected volumes of John and Abigail Adams's Revolutionary era correspondence (C. F. Adams, 1840). When John Quincy Adams died in 1848, Charles Francis Adams revived the project. The first two volumes of the *Works* present the completed biography. The remaining eight volumes contain John Adams's *Diary* and unfinished *Autobiography*, his major political works, and a selection of his letters and speeches.

The *Works* both fostered and constricted understanding of John Adams. Although, as L. H. Butterfield noted, Charles Francis Adams was "a gifted and painstaking editor, well in advance of the standards of his day" (Butterfield et al., 1975: 11), he also was a nineteenth-century Boston Brahmin who, discomfited by his grandfather's earthiness and his idiosyncratic spelling and capitalization, regularized and sanitized Adams's prose, rendering Adams chilly, formal, and pompous. Compounding this problem, the Adams family closed the Adams papers to research for more than a century, pointing scholars to the *Works.* Most modern selections of Adams's writings (Koch and Peden, 1946; Peek, 1954; C.B. Thompson, 2000; Carey, 2000; Diggins, 2004) still use the *Works* as their source.

In 1956, the Adams Manuscript Trust transferred the Adams papers to the Massachusetts Historical Society, host of *The Adams Papers* project, founded in 1954. This landmark donation opened the Adams papers to scholarly research. The first major beneficiary was Lester J. Cappon's fine edition of the correspondence between John and Abigail Adams and Thomas Jefferson (Cappon, 1959). *The Adams–Jefferson Letters* is a landmark of American literature as well as historical scholarship and documentary editing; among its virtues, it reintroduced modern readers to the human side of John Adams.

The first letterpress installment of *The Adams Papers* appeared in 1961 – L. H. Butterfield's edition of John Adams's *Diary* and *Autobiography* (Butterfield 1961, 1966). This publication received extraordinary media attention, including serialization in *Life* magazine and many appreciative reviews, including a review for the *American Historical Review* by President John F. Kennedy (J.F. Kennedy, 1963). Next came L. Kinvin Wroth's and Hiller Zobel's edition of John Adams's legal papers (Wroth and Zobel, 1965), ten volumes of Adams family correspondence (Butterfield et al. 1963–); *The Book of Abigail and John*, which contains selections from the Adams family's correspondence between 1776 and 1784 for the American Revolution's bicentennial (Butterfield et al., 1975); sixteen volumes of John Adams's general correspondence and papers (R.J. Taylor, 1977–); a study of the portraits of John and Abigail Adams (Oliver, 1967); and *My Dearest Friend*, a selection from the correspondence of John and Abigail (Hogan and Taylor, 2007). The Adams Papers have four series – series I, "Diaries"; series II, "Family Correspondence"; series III, "General Correspondence and Other Papers of the Adams Statesmen"; and series IV, "Adams Family Portraits." In 2011, Gordon S. Wood presented the most thorough, scholarly selection of Adams's writings available, a two-volume *Revolutionary Writings* based on the volumes of the Adams Papers devoted to John Adams and covering the period between 1755 and 1783 (G.S. Wood, 2011a, 2011b).

The next major publication of Adams material appeared in 1966, when John Schutz and Douglass Adair published a selected edition of the correspondence between John Adams and Benjamin Rush – *The Spur of Fame: Dialogues of John Adams and Benjamin Rush, 1805–1812* (Schutz and Adair, 1966). Based on an 1892 limited edition of the Rush–Adams correspondence (Biddle, 1892), this carefully annotated selection by two distinguished historians cast new light on Adams's and Rush's ideas of fame and their preoccupation with posterity's understanding of the Revolution.

Biographies and Character Studies

In writing the life of John Adams, biographers face a great advantage and an equally great challenge. Adams was a prolific writer who often reflected on his own life and his emotional makeup. Further, in assessing his life, Adams was preoccupied by his desire for justice from posterity and his fear that posterity would deny him the enduring fame granted to Washington, Franklin, and Jefferson. These emotions drove him to exaggerate his contributions' merit and significance and the ways that contemporaries assessed him. At the same time, he often mocked himself, as when he noted to Benjamin Rush on July 23, 1806, that Washington, Franklin, and Jefferson had a great gift that he lacked – the gift of silence (Schutz and Adair, 1966: 59–61). Readers of biographies of Adams should keep these cautionary points in mind.

The first biography of John Adams was a reverent summary by the geographer and historian Rev. Jedidiah Morse (1761–1826), reprinted from Morse's *American Geography* as a preface to the third edition of Adams's *Defence of the Constitutions*, issued in 1797, after his inauguration as president (J. Adams, 1797).

The next contributions to biographical literature on Adams were the memorial orations delivered after Adams's and Jefferson's deaths in 1826, treating them together. Later orators discussed Adams in addressing the shift from the founding generation to the generation of those charged with preserving the founders' legacy. The most valuable oration of this group, delivered on January 4, 1859 in Boston, was the work of the Unitarian clergyman, author, and abolitionist Theodore Parker (1810–1860). Parker's illuminating miniature biography shows rare sensitivity to Adams's psychology. Unpublished during his lifetime, it first appeared in his 1870 book *Historic Americans* (Parker, 1870).

The appearance in the 1850s of *The Works of John Adams*, including the biography by Charles Francis Adams, established the conventions of Adams biography for decades thereafter. Oddly, the greatest scholar among Adams's descendants, the historian, essayist, and memoirist Henry Brooks Adams (1838–1918), never wrote about his famous ancestor, though he scandalized his students at Harvard by calling John Adams a demagogue. He even began his greatest historical work, *The History of the United States during the Administrations of Thomas Jefferson and James Madison* (1889–1896), with six chapters on "The United States in 1800" that fail to mention President John Adams even once (Henry Adams, 1984a, 1984b).

The other nineteenth-century biographers of John Adams were content to restate the conventional biographical wisdom as defined by his grandson. John Robert Irelan, a physician and author, published an eighteen-volume history of the American Republic, devoting each volume to a different president (Irelan, 1886). The prolific biographer John T. Morse (1840–1937) wrote his biography (J.T. Morse, 1898) as part of the *American Statesmen* series that he edited between 1898 and 1916. Finally, Mellen Chamberlain (1820–1900), librarian of the Boston public library, delivered an 1884 address, "John Adams, statesman of the American Revolution" (Chamberlain, 1898), tinged with his era's ethnocentric and racialist rhetoric and arguing for the central roles of Adams and New England in the creation of the United States.

The first scholar to write an intellectually distinguished life of John Adams was the French-born intellectual historian Gilbert Chinard (1881–1972). Chinard had won fame as a Jefferson scholar, especially for his widely read biography (1929). Turning from Jefferson to Adams, Chinard, deeply impressed with what he found, wrote a thoughtful, affectionate biography, *Honest John Adams* (1933), assessing him as statesman, political thinker, and revolutionary, and praising him as the most realistic American statesman of his generation. Chinard paid Adams the great compliment of taking his ideas and his personality seriously. For decades Chinard's biography stood as the best life of Adams, and it still maps the prevailing currents of Adams scholarship. Because he had no access to the Adams papers, however, he based his book on the *Works.* Thus, while remaining enlightening and valuable, *Honest John Adams* shows its age, given the outpouring of primary sources and scholarship since its publication. Standing in contrast to Chinard's work is *John Adams and the American Revolution*, by the popular biographer Catherine Drinker Bowen (1950). Her admiring book's chief flaw is her frequent resort to fictionalized passages; further, despite its title, it extends only to 1776.

The opening of the Adams papers was a catalyst for a wide range of biographical and historical scholarship. The massive two-volume biography published in 1961 by Page Smith of the University of California at Berkeley was the first based on the microfilm edition of the Adams papers (Page Smith, 1962). Smith's book won a Bancroft Prize and was widely praised as definitive, but other scholars faulted its scanty attention to Adams's ideas, its failure to hold Adams's public and private lives in coherent balance, and its diffuseness (see especially Garraty, 1963).

In 1976, Peter Shaw, a professor of English at the State University of New York at Stony Brook, published *The Character of John Adams.* Acknowledging Adams as a constitutional and political theorist, and tracing continuities between Adams's personality and psychology and his constitutional and political ideas, Shaw used the latter to illuminate the former. Though giving his readers valuable insight into Adams as a human being, Shaw inadvertently obscured Adams's intellectual labors. Well documented and beautifully written, Shaw's book is enlightening but limited in its assessment of Adams.

More than three decades after Page Smith's biography, John E. Ferling of West Georgia College, a specialist in the military history of the Revolution and a biographer of George Washington, published *John Adams: A Life* (Ferling, 1992), the first full-length biography since 1961. Ferling emphasized John Adams's inner life and psychology but sought with considerable success to strike a balance between Adams's public and private lives. Ferling followed up his valuable study with a bibliography of Adams (1994b).

Joseph J. Ellis of Mount Holyoke College published *Passionate Sage: The Character and Legacy of John Adams* (1993) a year after Ferling's biography. Perhaps Ellis's best book, *Passionate Sage* examines Adams's life along the lines of Peter Shaw's character study. Again, it is not a full biography, nor does it plumb the depths of Adams's political and constitutional thought, though it effectively illuminates Adams in his later years.

The acclaimed popular historian David McCullough (2001) made his first venture into the era of the American Revolution with his massive one-volume life of John Adams. Though his best-selling book won the Pulitzer Prize and inspired an acclaimed 2008 HBO mini-series, historians faulted it for its uncritical stance towards Adams and its failures to take him seriously as a political thinker and constitutional statesman or to engage with the growing body of Adams scholarship.

Four years after McCullough's biography, the financial journalist James Grant published *John Adams, Party of One* (2005). Ranking with the books by Chinard, Shaw, Ellis, and Ferling, this excellent book is grounded in the primary sources, in the burgeoning Adams scholarship, and in the profusion of recent scholarly work on the American Revolution and the early republic.

Monographs

The first monograph focusing on John Adams appeared in 1915, when the economist and political scientist Correa M. Walsh published *The Political Science of John Adams.* Analyzing the structure and coherence of Adams's political thought, Walsh also rejected it, arguing that separation of powers and checks and balances were irrelevant to modern problems. Walsh's book won praise for its rigor, but attracted criticism for its divorce of Adams's political thought from his life.

The next monographic study of John Adams, appearing nearly four decades after Walsh's study, remains one of the most innovative studies in

Adams scholarship and the history of ideas. Zoltan Haraszti, keeper of rare books at the Boston Public Library, explored the collection of Adams's books deposited in his library's rare book collection. In *John Adams and the Prophets of Progress* (1952), Haraszti used Adams's marginal notations, particularly those from the 1790s and early 1800s, to illuminate his evolving political thought. Appearing almost simultaneously with Haraszti's book was *John Adams, Scholar*, by Alfred Iacuzzi, a professor of Italian at Brooklyn College, which covered much of the same ground but from a different perspective, stressing Adams's gift for foreign languages and his wide and extensive reading (Iacuzzi, 1952).

On the heels of Haraszti's and Iacuzzi's monographs came a cornerstone work of political history informed by political science – Manning J. Dauer's *The Adams Federalists* (Dauer, 1953). Dauer illuminated historical understanding of politics in the 1790s by tracing the evolution of a factional split between so-called High Federalists, led by Hamilton, and more moderate "Adams Federalists," backers of John Adams. Dauer both reflected and cut against prevailing currents of analyzing the early republic's political history. Like many of his colleagues, Dauer sought to illuminate the origins of American political parties, yet at the same time he showed how the politics of the 1790s was more complicated than the conventional, stark dichotomy between Federalists and Republicans.

In the mid-1960s, two scholars re-examined Adams's political thought. Edward Handler of Babson College published *America and Europe in the Political Thought of John Adams* (Handler, 1964). Reflecting the influence of Louis Hartz's *The Liberal Tradition in America* (Hartz, 1955), Handler echoed Hartz's contention that America was the first liberal nation, not having known a feudal or quasi-feudal past, while also reacting against Hartz's thesis; the book is as much about Hartz as it is about Adams. Two years later, John R. Howe, Jr., a professor of history at the University of Minnesota, published *The Changing Political Thought of John Adams* (1966), long regarded as the most useful study of Adams's political thought. Howe traced a line of development from an early, radical Adams to an increasingly conservative Adams, though at times implying that he was examining Adams's political thought for insight into his psychology rather than for its independent significance.

Adams had to wait more than two decades for the next monograph analyzing his political thought. *John Adams and the Spirit of Liberty*, by the political scientist C. Bradley Thompson (1998), appeared in the University Press of Kansas series "American political thought". The first sustained examination of Adams's political thought since John Howe's monograph and the first to stress its coherence and consistency since Correa Walsh's study, Thompson's award-winning book analyzes Adams's political writings from his early newspaper essays through his *Discourses on Davila*. Its strength is that Thompson takes Adams seriously as a political thinker; its weakness is that Thompson champions Adams across the board, rather than trying to understand his strengths and his weaknesses. As a companion volume, Thompson edited *The Revolutionary Writings of John Adams* (2000).

After the ponderous tome of John Henry Irelan (1886), three scholars addressed Adams's presidency. In 1957, Stephen G. Kurtz published a lively, perceptive history situating Adams's presidency within the emerging partisan battles of the 1790s. Nearly twenty years later, Ralph Adams Brown published his study in the University Press of Kansas's *American Presidency* series, offering a ringing defense of Adams against critics past and present (Brown, 1975). In 2003, John Patrick Diggins, professor of history in the graduate school of the City University of New York, wrote on John Adams for a series on the American presidents edited by the late Arthur M. Schlesinger, Jr.. Ranging beyond the presidency, Diggins took Adams seriously as a political thinker and a politician. Though often insightful, his book is also flawed by chronological errors and eccentric interpretations undermining its reliability. Diggins also published a volume of selection from Adams's writings, *The Portable John Adams* (2004).

As a contribution to the commemoration of the American Revolution's bicentennial, the leading Jefferson biographer Merrill D. Peterson delivered an elegant set of lectures (1975) on John Adams's relationship with Thomas Jefferson. Peterson characterized their correspondence as "a Revolutionary dialogue," and traced their lifelong argument about the meaning of the Revolution in their time and for posterity (see also Allison, 1966; Koch, 1963).

Other focused monographs on John Adams include James H. Hutson's *John Adams and the Diplomacy of the American Revolution* (1980), which seeks to explain Adams's achievements and failings as a diplomat by reference to his psychology; Linda Dudik Guerrero's *John Adams' Vice Presidency, 1789–1797: The Neglected Man in the Forgotten Office* (1982). the only close-focus examination of Adams's ordeal as vice president though defending Adams rather than understanding him; and Walt Brown, Jr.'s study of the president's relationship with the American press (1995).

Many scholars and writers have published new accounts of the presidential election of 1800. The most useful are the symposium volume edited by James Horn, Jan Ellen Lewis, and Peter S. Onuf (2002); the histories by John E. Ferling (2004), Susan Dunn (2004), Edward J. Larson (2007), Bernard A. Weisberger (2000), John Zvesper (2003), Garry Wills (2003), and James Roger Sharp (2010); and a valuable article and book chapter by Joanne B. Freeman (1999, 2001a). These volumes join the older study by Daniel J. Sisson (1974) focusing on republican political ideology.

Two valuable collections of essays were spawned by conferences organized by the Massachusetts Historical Society: *John Adams and the Founding of the Republic*, edited by Richard Alan Ryerson (2001); and *The Libraries, Leadership, and Legacies of John Adams and Thomas Jefferson*, edited by Robert C. Baron and Conrad Edick Wright (2010).

Other historical studies include notable chapters on Adams. For example: Joseph Dorfman (1946) situated Adams within the evolving economic history of American civilization. Joseph Charles (1956) juxtaposed Adams and Jefferson in his *Origins of the American Party System: Three Essays.* H. Trevor Colbourn (1965) used Adams to illustrate the scope, depth, and uses of historical thought in Revolutionary America. Gordon S. Wood (1969, 2004) examined Adams's political thought in the 1770s and 1780s as a counterpoint to the development of American political thought in the same period. Richard B. Morris (1973) included Adams among his seven portraits of leading American founders as revolutionaries. Douglass Adair (1974) made Adams the focal point of his anatomization of the relationship between history and democratic theory in the American founding. In a sparkling series of lectures, Edmund S. Morgan (1976) assessed the meaning of independence for Adams, Washington, and Jefferson, an enterprise that John E. Ferling (2000) pursued in greater depth. Robert Middlekauff (1996: ch. 7) presented a fascinating analysis of the Franklin–Adams relationship in a study of Franklin's enemies. Joanne B. Freeman investigated the long series of self-justifying newspaper essays that Adams published between 1809 and 1811 in the Boston *Patriot* to illuminate "paper war" as a method of political combat in the early Republic (Freeman, 2001a: chs. 3 and 5), and examined the election of 1800 as "an honor dispute of epic proportions" (Freeman, 1999). Andrew S. Trees (2004) analyzed Adams's struggles with the challenges of creating a constitutional and political order that would sustain the virtue of the people and those whom they chose to lead them. Darren Staloff (2005) distinguished among Hamilton's, Adams's, and Jefferson's approaches to the Enlightenment in his examination of the politics of the Enlightenment and the American founding. And David L. Holmes (2006) wrote an illuminating, terse assessment of Adams's religious views. Readers also should consult a valuable series of articles by James M. Farrell (1989, 1991, 1992b, 1994, 2002, and 2006) tracing Adams's lifelong fascination with the Roman statesman Marcus Tullius Cicero.

Finally, though further discussion appears in this volume on Abigail Adams (Chapters 10 and 11), this historiographical overview notes a growing literature dealing with the marriage of John and Abigail Adams. This scholarship was made possible by the extraordinary correspondence between them, which in turn was made necessary by their frequent separations due to John Adams's public service at home and abroad and Abigail Adams's periods of illness in her later years. This genre began in 1876 with Charles Francis Adams's edition of their *Familiar Letters* (1876), issued for the centennial of American independence with modern annotations by the late Frank Shuffelton as a Penguin Classic (Shuffelton, 2004); a comparable volume published by *The Adams Papers* and based on accurate modern transcripts of the documents is *My Dearest Friend* (Hogan and Taylor,

2007). The leading study is the fine joint biography by Edith Gelles (2009), joining her previous pathbreaking studies of Abigail Adams (1992, 1998). More recently, Joseph J. Ellis published *First Family: Abigail and John Adams* (2010) and the historian G. J. Barker-Benfield published *Abigail and John Adams: The Americanization of Sensibility* (2010). Interested readers also should consult the Bancroft Prize-winning life of Abigail Adams by Woody Holton (2009).

1.3 Conclusion

This historiographical examination of John Adams reveals an irregular rhythm of publications keyed to the appearance of documentary editions and to the changing emphases of American historical scholarship. Until the twentieth century Adams has not been a favorite subject for historians or biographers; even after the increasing attention to Adams's life and work, the bifurcation between the Adams of scholarship and the Adams of popular culture remains firmly in place. Why should this be so?

The first reason, as noted, is the Adams family's closing of the Adams papers until the 1950s. Not until the 1960s did a scholarly edition of Adams's papers begin to supplant the only previous edition and to make previously unpublished papers available.

Second, Adams never fit the partisan dichotomy that captured the imagination of posterity and American political historiography. Ideological adherents of Jefferson and Hamilton have long traced an unbroken lineage of intellectual and political descent to their respective parent sources. By contrast, Adams never had a band of intellectual and political heirs claiming him as a forebear. So too, as noted, historians' emphasis on political parties' origin and development works to the disadvantage of Adams, who was wary of party and, as one biographer wrote, constituted a "party of one" (Grant, 2005).

Third, the issues and policies associated with Adams shape his treatment by scholars and popular writers alike. For example, when constitutional origins and their intellectual contexts become focal points for historical scholarship, work on Adams has flourished. By contrast, when the origins and development of political parties have taken the fore, scholars have relegated Adams to the sidelines, focusing instead on the Federalists led by Hamilton and the Republicans led by Jefferson and Madison. Finally, the Alien and Sedition Acts of 1798 are generally seen as the greatest blot on Adams's presidency. Given the growing attention to civil liberties in public discourse and historical scholarship, these measures increasingly appear as the first grave threat to American civil liberties, damaging the historical standing of the president who signed them into law (Smith, 1962). Not until recently have historians sought to understand the ideas and assumptions undergirding the 1798 Sedition Act (Freeman, 2003) or the public controversy that they engendered (Bradburn, 2008). By contrast, though Adams nominated John Marshall to the Supreme Court in early 1801, launching the career of the man deemed the greatest chief justice of the United States, the veneration accorded Marshall almost never touches the man who appointed him. Instead, Adams gets undeserved blame for the "midnight judges" (a catchphrase popularized by Jeffersonian Republicans at the time and by Jefferson scholars for generations thereafter), while Marshall almost appears to be a self-created titan of American law and constitutionalism.

Adams himself would have argued that his constitutional and political thought, and its effects on American constitutional government, warranted his claim to fame – and yet only scholars remember him for these achievements. An illuminating perspective on this vexed question appears in the most influential short discussion of John Adams and constitutionalism. Gordon S. Wood maintains, in "The Relevance and Irrelevance of John Adams," chapter 14 of his classic study *The Creation of the American Republic, 1776–1787* (1969), that in the 1780s Adams drifted away from the defining currents of American political thought. Adams continued to think and argue within the context of classical political thought, in which the people and the government are opposed, and society falls into the immemorial categories of the one, the few, and the many. By contrast, most Americans accepted the idea of popular sovereignty, under which the people rule themselves through a government devised and elected by and responsible to them. By winning independence, Americans believed, they had purged themselves of monarchy and aristocracy and were working to tame and constitutionalize democracy. Thus, in their eyes, Adams was increasingly irrelevant to the evolving nature of American constitutional democracy. And yet being outside the currents of American political thought, Wood added, conferred insight on Adams as well as seemingly consigning him to irrelevance. Wood concluded that, from his intellectual vantage point, Adams was better able to see and expound on aspects of American life that his countrymen did not see or chose not to acknowledge – specifically, the persistence of a functional equivalent of aristocracy in a seeming democracy. Thus, Wood praised Adams for his realistic grasp of truths that his countrymen were unprepared to learn. We are left with a brilliant Adams who is nevertheless out of step (whether rightly or wrongly) with both Americans and other contemporary leaders. To some extent, Adams scholarship has yet to recover from Wood's brilliant yet faint praise.

In a superbly insightful essay meditating on Adams's statecraft, Stephen G. Kurtz (1968) marked out a sensible, thoughtful approach. Kurtz points out that, although Adams's political and constitutional thought is less original than some have supposed, Adams never claimed originality; rather, he was committed to distilling and expounding what he deemed to be the lessons of history. In that enterprise, Adams was true to the synthesizing habits of thought associated with the Enlightenment, and (as Kurtz notes) to the rhetorical and argumentative tactics of the skilled and learned attorney. As an attorney overcomes his adversary with a mass of authorities, Adams sought to overcome his intellectual and constitutional adversaries by piling up examples, authorities, and the lessons of experience.

Building on the insights afforded us by Kurtz and Wood, we can see how these currents of thought, argument, and inquiry come together in John Adams's life and work. As an exemplar of the Enlightenment, Adams's insistence on the lessons of experience points to the centrality to his legal, political, and constitutional thought of an empirical exploration and sifting of history. Though Adams was fascinated by the study of human nature, he approached that subject always by considering how an understanding of human nature emerges from studying how it made itself felt in the record of history. Given that he always understood human nature historically, it was only natural that he should reject the idea (beloved by his adversary Thomas Paine and his sometimes-friend, sometimes-adversary Thomas Jefferson) that Americans were inherently exceptional by contrast with the rest of humanity. Whatever exceptionalism Adams recognized in the American story was one of opportunity only, and the uses to which Americans could put that opportunity were both defined and limited by their not being free of the strengths and weaknesses of human nature as revealed by history. Adams's historical empiricism and his applications of it, united with the forensic skills that he honed first in the courtroom, then in pamphleteering, and finally in his ponderous works of comparative constitutionalism and his sparkling letters, comprise the legacy that he hoped to leave posterity, and for which he wanted to be remembered.

Notes

1 For an analysis of the rhetorical design of the *Defence*, see Paynter (1996).

2 This is an electronic edition: *Adams Family Papers: An Electronic Archive*, Massachusetts Historical Society. At www.masshist.org/digitaladams/, accessed Nov. 10, 2012.

3 *Journal of Debates and Proceedings in the Convention of Delegates, Chosen to Revise the Constitution of Massachusetts, Begun and Holden at Boston, November 15, 1820, and Continued by Adjournment to January 9, 1821. Reported for the Boston Daily Advertiser*. Boston, MA: 209; see also p. 193.

4 *Journal of Debates...*: 11–12.

Further Reading

Adams, Willi Paul (2001). *The First American Constitutions: Republican Ideology and the Making of State Constitutions in the Revolutionary Era*. Expanded edn., trans. Rita and Robert Kimber. Lanham, MD.

Bernstein, R.B., with Rice, Kym S. (1987). *Are We to Be a Nation? The Making of the Constitution*. Cambridge, MA.

Bernstein, R.B. (2003). *Thomas Jefferson*. New York.
Bernstein, R.B. (2009). *The Founding Fathers Reconsidered*. New York.
Chinard, Gilbert (1929). *Thomas Jefferson: Apostle of Americanism*. Boston. (2nd rev. edn., 1939: paperback repr., 1965. Ann Arbor.).
Commager, Henry Steele (1975). *Jefferson, Nationalism, and the Enlightenment*. New York.
Commager, Henry Steele (1977). *Empire of Reason: How Europe Imagined and America Realized the Enlightenment*. Garden City, NY.
Hartz, Louis (1955). *The Liberal Tradition in America*. New York.
Hill, John E. (2000). *Revolutionary Values for a New Millennium: John Adams, Adam Smith, and Social Justice*. (2nd edn. titled *Democracy, Equality, and Justice: John Adams, Adam Smith, and Political Economy*, 2007.) Lanham, MD.
Lutz, Donald S. (1980). *Popular Consent and Popular Control: Whig Political Theory in the First State Constitutions*. Baton Rouge.
Lutz, Donald S. (1988). *The Origins of American Constitutionalism*. Baton Rouge.
Morris, Richard B. (1965). *The Peacemakers: The Great Powers and American Independence*. New York.
Palmer, R.R. (1959). *The Age of the Democratic Revolution: A Political History of Europe and America, 1760–1800*, vol. 1: *The Challenge*. Princeton.
Palmer, R.R. (1964). *The Age of the Democratic Revolution: A Political History of Europe and America, 1760-1800*, vol. 2: *The Struggle*. Princeton.
Pocock, J.G.A. (1976). *The Machiavellian Moment: Florentine Political Thought and the Atlantic Republican Tradition*. Princeton. (2nd edn. with new introduction, 2003).
Wood, Gordon S. (2009). *Empire of Liberty: The United States, 1789–1815*. New York.

Chapter Two

John Adams and Enlightenment

Darren Staloff

By most measures, John Adams was an exemplary representative of the American Enlightenment. From his early education at Harvard where he studied Newtonian science with John Winthrop, the Hollis professor of mathematics and natural philosophy and the most accomplished mathematical astronomer in British America, Adams became a fierce champion of the "new learning" of the Enlightenment. In a letter written in his mid-twenties, he sided unequivocally with the moderns against the ancients, a standard position within the Enlightened commonwealth of learning. The superiority of the Enlightenment over previous epochs could be found in any number of fields of inquiry, but it was particularly evident in "Mathematics, and what is founded on them, Astronomy and Phylosophy." These "Modern Discoveries" had not only brought distinction to the age of Enlightenment over its predecessors but had "done Honour to the Human Understanding" in its broadest dimensions, revealing "the true sphere of Modern Genius" (*Adams Papers*:1.42–43). More than five decades later his faith in and commitment to the Enlightenment remained intact. Of all previous ages, he told Thomas Jefferson, "the Eighteenth Century" had been "the most honourable to human Nature." It was not only that "knowledge and Virtues were increased and diffused," but entire fields of knowledge "useful to men" had been vastly "improved." This improvement had ameliorated the human condition, promoting social, political, and moral progress and reform to a greater extent "than in any former equal period" (Cappon, 1959: 456).

A Companion to John Adams and John Quincy Adams, First Edition.
Edited by David Waldstreicher.

The vast bulk of Adams's convictions, like his faith in science, progress, and reform, were utterly typical of the American republic of letters. As a young man Adams had adopted a distinctly liberal religious posture. Like most Enlightened Americans of his day, his liberalism was tempered with moderation, embracing rationalism and tolerance while accommodating popular pieties and established church orders. Similarly common was his commitment to the diffusion of knowledge and useful information. A founding member of the American Academy of Sciences, Adams was a lifelong champion of public education and higher learning. His constitutional principles, combining the checks and balances of the separation of powers with the structures of mixed government, were also broadly shared by most Enlightened statesmen in the new nation. Indeed, one of the leading scholars of the early republic has characterized his political writings, particularly his three volume *Defense of the Constitutions of the United States of America*, as "the finest fruit of the American Enlightenment" (G.S. Wood, 1998: 568). Even his purely philosophical convictions were typical. His combination of Lockean empiricism, Scottish moral sense doctrine, and physic-theology were well within the moderate mainstream of the American Enlightenment (H. May, 1976).

Although Adams continued to hold these conventional views throughout his life, his understanding of and relation to Enlightenment changed dramatically over the course of his life. From his college years Adams had embraced the moderate American Enlightenment with great alacrity. His political writings echoed its phrases and his public actions were informed by its principles. But if Adams's commitment to Enlightenment was sincere, his understanding of it was, by his own admission, superficial. With the coming of independence he now saw the need to deepen his understanding of Enlightened philosophy in general and political and constitutional science in particular. Adams's researches and his years in Europe as a diplomat beginning in the late 1770s exposed him to a new world of learning that profoundly altered his understanding of Enlightenment. Two strains of thought had a particularly important impact; the latter Scottish Enlightenment and the philosophical radicalism of the French "high" Enlightenment.

Perhaps the most profound result of his mature researches was his embrace of two strands of Scottish social science. By the mid-1780s, Adams became a disciple of the philosophical history of William Robertson, David Hume, and their English acolyte Edward Gibbon. At roughly the same time he came to adopt the moral psychology of Adam Smith. These two strains of the late Scottish Enlightenment deepened Adams's understanding of his previously embraced beliefs. They did not lead him to reject those beliefs, but rather to see their significance in a new light. The Scottish Enlightenment pushed Adams's thought in a more worldly direction. His arguments became increasingly consequentialist in form and his youthful idealistic calls for virtue gave way to a more realistic, occasionally world-weary, perspective.

During Adams's diplomatic tenure in Paris he was directly exposed to the flowering philosophical radicalism of the late French Enlightenment. As Jonathan Israel (2011) has recently argued, beginning in the 1760s what had previously been a marginal coterie of radicals began to displace the Voltairean and Montesquiean moderate mainstream from the center of the Parisian republic of letters. These radicals rejected the empiricism of John Locke in favor of a deterministic and monistic metaphysical materialism from which they rigorously deducted the rights of man, the rules of morality, and the principles of political organization and practice (Israel, 2011: 633–683). Adams was both fascinated and deeply disturbed by this new strain of radical Enlightened thought. Much of his subsequent published writing and correspondence was devoted to refuting it. Adams sought to expose the new radical philosophy as both politically dangerous and intellectually untenable. Indeed, he came to utterly deny that it was enlightened at all but rather a new fanatical enthusiasm. In reaction to debate with such radicals as Condorcet, Turgot, and Tracy, Adams clarified the limits of his understanding of Enlightenment, albeit by negative reference. If Adams's immersion in the new Scottish learning added depth to his Enlightenment, his rejection of radical French thought gave it focus and definition.

2.1 A Youthful Enlightenment

Like all acolytes of Enlightenment, the young John Adams reveled in the accomplishments of modern science. The ancients of classical Greece and Rome might lay claim to priority in poetry and oratory, but when it came to the mathematical sciences of physics and astronomy, modern learning seized the laurel. In a letter to his old college classmate Jonathan Sewell in 1760, Adams extolled those "Modern Discoveries" that had both "done Honour to the human Understanding" and opened "a noble Prospect of the Universe" teeming with "Millions of Worlds and systems of Worlds." Each of these worlds, he imagined, were filled with rational animals "engaged in some Active investigation" of the mysteries of the physical universe, and therefore "overflowing with Felicity" (*Adams Papers*: 1.42–43).

Adams's allusion to the "felicity" of scientific knowledge was hardly unique. The notion that scientific investigation (like all higher learning) was inherently pleasurable and that the diffusion of its findings a great source of happiness, was near-axiomatic among those who aspired to membership in the Enlightened commonwealth of learning. A life bereft of "the Acquisition of Knowledge" would be "a Punishment" (*Adams Papers*: 1.42). Adams also shared the modern equation of science and happiness first articulated by Francis Bacon in *The New Organon*. Bacon had optimistically predicted that a newly emerging scientific method of empirical observation, experiment, and induction would generate a host of new technologies. These technologies in turn would allow mankind to not only penetrate the secrets of nature, but literally master her and extract whatever was necessary to satisfy human needs. Winthrop's lectures seem to have had a decidedly Baconian cast; Adams recorded one demonstration where the professor calculated the manpower requirements for an ancient battering ram that could deliver a concussive force equal to a canon. A suitably impressed Adams noted that a mere six-man crew of his day "can do as much execution" as had once required a thousand men (Butterfield, 1966:1.61). For Adams, the lesson was obvious. It was modern science that had produced the advanced "state of all the Civilized nations of Europe" compared to the more underdeveloped regions of the world whose inhabitants were fully "of as quick natural parts as Europeans" (Butterfield, 1966:1.60). Confidence in the advance of science and happiness underwrote Adams's Enlightened faith in progress.

Adams's religious views were also typical of the American Enlightenment. Although his father had hoped his son's Harvard education would result in a ministerial career, the teenager's exposure to Enlightened thought raised doubts about the received Calvinist orthodoxy of New England's Congregational establishment. If anything, these doubts were deepened by his exposure to a circle of free-thinkers and deists in Worcester, MA, where he taught school after graduation (Thompson, 1998: 7–10). The doctrines of innate depravity and human reprobation struck him as frigid and absurd, and his hostility to predestinarian theology only deepened with the passage of time. "Howl, Snarl, bite, Ye Calvinistick," he wrote to his old friend Thomas Jefferson in retirement, "Ye will say I am no Christian: I say Ye are no Christians: and there the Account is ballanced" (Cappon, 1959: 373–374). Adams also came to doubt other tenets of orthodox Christianity and, by his early twenties, had become a Unitarian who rejected both the trinity and the divinity of Christ. Upon hearing an argument that only a divine being "could make Satisfaction to infinite Justice" for human depravity, and that the nature of this divinity was "very mysterious," a youthful Adams caustically remarked in his Diary that "thus mystery is made a convenient Cover for absurdity" (Butterfield, 1966: 1.6). The source of such "absurdity" for Adams was not the scriptures *per se*, but their distortion by self-aggrandizing clerics. "Where do we find a praecept in the Gospell," he demanded, "requiring Ecclesiastical Synods, Convocations, Councils" and all the "other trumpery, that we find Religion incumbered with in these Days?" The purpose of the Christian creed was to inculcate moral virtue and humanity, but the priestcraft of divines had perverted it into a scheme to "make men good Riddle Solvers or good mystery mongers" (Butterfield, 1966:1.8) As he matured, Adams's rejection of theological dogma stiffened. By the end of his life he had embraced Universalism as well as Unitarianism, rejecting the doctrine of the eternal damnation of the sinful. Was it possible that a God of "infinite Benevolence, Wisdom and Power" had created "innumerable millions" solely to "make them miserable, forever" for the sake of "exulting and triumphing in his Power and the Sweetness of his Vengeance?" Adams found such orthodox doctrines preposterous and did not hesitate to declare "I believe no such Things" (Cappon, 1959: 373–374).

Despite his Enlightened rejection of dogma, Adams was no deist, much less an atheist. Like Newton before him, Adams affirmed the argument from design that the evident orderly nature of the universe, its "surprising Diversity" amid "Uniformity," entailed belief in "the continual and vigilant Providence of God." "God exists by an absolute Necessity" he wrote in his diary, and "it implies a Contradiction to suppose him not to exist" (Butterfield, 1966:1.38–39). Like most members of the moderate mainstream of the Anglophone Enlightenment, Adams embraced a latitudinarian conception of Christianity, one that stressed its moral teachings over its theological creeds and ecclesiastical arrangements. These salutary and "general Principles of Christianity" he forthrightly held as "eternal and immutable" truth shared by all true Christians (J. Adams, 1823: 340). "I have often attended public worship in all countries and with all sects and believe the'm all better than no religion," he wrote in retirement, ruefully noting: "I have not thought myself obliged to believe all I heard" (Schutz and Adair, 1966: 116). Despite his misgivings, he always considered himself a Christian and believed that religious belief was essential to the moral order of society. "Without Religion this world would be Something not fit to be mentioned in polite Company," he informed Jefferson. "I mean Hell" (J. Adams, 1823: 509).

Just as Adams's views on religion and science were typical of the Enlightenment, so too was his understanding of the relationship of liberty and learning. Not surprisingly, the conviction that the inculcation of knowledge and Enlightenment was itself critical to the spread of modern liberty was nearly universal among the citizens of the republic of letters. Adams was no exception. In his first major political writing, *A Dissertation on the Canon and Feudal Law* (1765), Adams argued that the diffusion of knowledge and learning among the common people had been the principal cause of liberty throughout human history. The first civilizations of the ancient world had been under the sway of "absolute monarchy," but the spread of mass literacy and enlightenment in the classical age had produced the first glimmers of liberty and popular government in Greece and Rome. Similarly, it was the spread of literacy and learning among the general populace that had ended the despotism of the medieval "dark ages" and given rise to the progress of liberty and republicanism in the modern age. The lesson Adams drew was direct: "wherever a general knowledge and sensibility have prevailed among the people, arbitrary government, and every kind of oppression, have lessened and disappeared in proportion" (*Adams Papers*:1.111) Indeed, no small part of what disturbed him about the Stamp Act was that it represented a "design" to undermine the diffusion of Enlightenment in British America "by loading the Press, the College, and even an Alamanack and a News-Paper, with restraints and duties. Such an assault on "the means of knowledge" clearly portended a broader assault on popular liberty (*Adams Papers*:1.128).

Adams reiterated his belief in the central role of learning in preservation of liberty throughout the years leading to the break with Great Britain in 1776. In 1772 he told his fellow residents of Braintree that the "Preservation of Liberty depends upon the intellectual and moral Character of the People," and that as "long as knowledge and virtue are diffused generally among the Body of a Nation, it is impossible they should be enslaved." All of the European states had once enjoyed freedom but had lost it "by the Ignorance" and disunion of the people at large (Butterfield, 1966: 2.58–60) That was because, as he wrote in *A Proclamation by the General Court of Massachusetts* in early 1776, a truly popular and republican government "can be Supported only by universal Knowledge and Virtue, in the Body of the People" (*Adams Papers*: 3.385–386).

For Adams, not only was the spread of learning and Enlightenment critical for the survival of liberty, but the struggle for liberty was itself a source of Enlightenment. Throughout history the fight for popular freedom against tyranny had inspired the noblest minds to deepen their understanding of those arts and sciences that were essential to the birth and defense of popular government. In the first installation of *Novanglus* (1774) he insisted that it was ancient Rome's overthrow of monarchy and subsequent installation of republican government that had produced "the great Roman orators, poets, and historians, the greatest teachers of humanity and politeness" who became "the pride of human nature, and the delight and glory of mankind of seventeen hundred years" (C.F. Adams, 1850–1856: 4.17–18). Almost a decade earlier Adams had argued that the same process had occurred during the reign of Charles I in England. The Stuart monarch's "encroachments upon liberty" had inspired the learned to focus their minds on questions of government and public freedom. The result of these struggles against royal absolutism was not merely the recovery of English liberty but the critical works of such luminaries as Algernon Sydney, James Harrington, and John Locke, as well as the production of "the greatest number of consummate statesmen, which has ever been seen in any age or nation." Indeed, the struggle in his own time against metropolitan oppression offered learned American patriots an excellent opportunity to reflect on their current plight and further the advance of republican learning. As early as his *Dissertation*, Adams issued his call to his fellow patriot philosophes; "let every sluice of knowledge be open'd and set a flowing" (*Adams Papers*:1.127).

Given the centrality of Enlightened learning for republican liberty, Adams persistently urged its diffusion throughout the revolutionary struggle for American independence. In 1765 he championed the freedom of the

American press. "The art of printing should be encouraged," he insisted, so that "it should be easy and safe for any person to communicate his thoughts to the public" (*Adams Papers*: 1.121) Seven years later he urged his auditors in Braintree to "cherish the Means of Knowledge," particularly "our Schools and Colledges" (Butterfield, 1966: 2.59–60) If anything, the imperative to support education increased as independence approached. Breaking with the empire meant eschewing all monarchical elements in government in favor of a purely republican scheme, and "a Government so popular can be Supported only by universal Knowledge" among the common people (*Adams Papers*: 3.385–386). Thus in *Thoughts on Government* (1776), Adams proposal for republican state constitutions, he insisted that "Laws for the liberal education of youth, especially of the lower class of people, are so extremely useful, that, to a humane and generous mind, no expense for this purpose would be thought extravagant" (*Adams Papers*: 4.91). Predictably, when Adams drafted the constitution for Massachusetts in 1779, he inserted a paragraph enjoining the government of the Bay state "to cherish the interests of literature and the sciences, and all seminaries of them, especially the university of Cambridge, public schools, and grammar schools in the towns" as well as "private societies and public institutions" for the advancement of knowledge. Adams's reasoning was simple and direct. "Wisdom and knowledge" must be "diffused generally among the people" if they were to be able to preserve "their rights and liberties" (*Adams Papers*: 8.260).

The most important and central tenet of John Adams's Enlightenment, however, one that underlay and informed all his other beliefs and commitments, was the empiricism of John Locke. A youthful Adams likened Locke to a great explorer who had "steered his Course into the unenlightened Regions of the human Mind," a "new World" lacking the innate ideas of Descartes and filled solely by the evidence of our senses (*Adams Papers*:1.42–43). More particularly, Locke had essayed the limits of human understanding and the result was a powerful if modest skepticism (Osler, 1970). The only truly certain knowledge was that resulting from intuitively self-evident propositions or those which could be logically deduced from them. "Whatever comes short of one of these," Locke insisted, "is but Faith, or Opinion, but not knowledge" (Locke, 1975: 536–537). Our immediate phenomenal awareness of sense experiences "comes not only short of the reality of Things, but even of the extent of our *Ideas*" insofar as we have no way of knowing how these ideas are caused by external objects much less whether they adequately represent or resemble them. Even science itself afforded no more than probable judgment that might be sufficient for practical purposes but was nonetheless inherently fallible (Locke, 1975: 390, 539, 541–545, 653). If the truths of Newtonian physics were themselves merely probable, then the claim to metaphysical and other abstruse forms of knowledge was clearly chimerical. "I have a prejudice against what they call Metaphysics," Adams confessed, because it pretends to "fathom deeper than the human line extends" (Cappon, 1959: 561). The debates between the doctrines of materialism and idealism, determinism and freedom, and even the foundation of our knowledge of cause and effect struck Adams as questions that could never be answered by human intelligence. "The faculties of our understanding are not adequate to penetrate the Universe," he wrote to Jefferson in retirement. "Let us do our duty which is, to do as we would be done by, and that one would think, could not be difficult, if we honestly aim at it" (Cappon, 1959: 607).

The empiricism of Locke and his followers such as George Berkeley and David Hume profoundly influenced the thinking of John Adams in two distinct ways. Perhaps most pointedly, Locke's mitigated skepticism inculcated the value of moderation that characterized the mainstream of Anglo-American Enlightenment. In the absence of certainty in matters of theology and political theory, a judicious-reasoned man would practice prudence with regard to his own convictions and tolerance and forbearance towards those of others. Locke himself had insisted that our "mutual ignorance" of most contested issues left us with no excuse to "treat others ill" for not sharing our opinions "when 'tis more than probable, that we are not less obstinate in not embracing some of theirs" (Locke, 1975: 660). For empiricists like Locke and Adams, uncertainty entailed a moderation of belief and an attempt to balance one's convictions with the opinions of others.

This ethos of moderation and balance informed all of Adams's Enlightened commitments. Despite his admiration of science and his hope for future progress, the notion of human and social perfectibility struck him as romantic nonsense. In religion he rejected many of the theological creeds of orthodox Christianity, but he never doubted the existence of God or the salutary effect of religion on public morality. Even his enthusiasm for the diffusion of Enlightened learning was tempered by his acknowledgment that not all people could absorb it in equal fashion, that "bad men increase in knowledge as fast as good men," and that even "science, arts, taste, sense, and letters" could be used to spread "injustice and tyranny" as well as "law and liberty" (C.F. Adams, 1850–1856: 6.276). It was this moderation that characterized Adams as an Enlightened statesman, a revolutionary who rejected radicalism and a republican who insisted on restraining the will of the majority within a system of check and balances.

The other effect of Locke's empiricism on Adams was methodological. While Adams shared Locke's natural-right treatment of the principles of liberty, when it came to the actual science of constitutional design and government that he referred to as "the principles of political architecture," Adams insisted that only empirical observation and factual analysis could offer reliable insight (C.F. Adams, 1850–1856: 6.411–412; Thompson, 1998: 107–125). "The Science of Government," Adams insisted in 1772, "is best pursued by Observation and Experiment." Observations ought be focused on the experience of human history "in different Soils and Climates, in different Nations and Countries" as well as "under different Religions and Customs" (Butterfield, 1966: 2.56–57). Experiments were to be found in "the systems of legislators" (C.F. Adams, 1850–1856: 4.297). In the years leading up to 1776, Adams had, by his own admission, studied political science and theory "with very little Application to any particular Views." But with the break from Britain and the need to create a new American system of republican government, Adams immersed himself in "those Researches, which produced the Thoughts on Government, the Constitution of Massachusetts, and length the Defense of the Constitutions of the United States and the Discourses on Davila" (Butterfield, 1966: 3.358–359). These researches exposed him to the "philosophical history" of David Hume, William Robertson, and Edward Gibbon as well as to the moral sentimentalism of Adam Smith. These sources would profoundly influence Adams's mature writing and thinking, marking him as their chief exponent in North America. His researches and travel would also expose him to the emerging strain of Enlightened radicalism in Paris and beyond. His almost violent rejection of that strain would define his position within the Enlightenment every bit as much as his embrace of its moderate Scottish counterpart.

2.2 Adams and the Scottish Enlightenment

John Adams's study of the principles of political architecture in the years following the American Revolution led him to a host of writings ancient and modern. Two sources, both of largely Scottish provenance, however, had a particularly powerful influence on his understanding of Enlightenment and informed his subsequent writings. The so-called philosophical history of David Hume and William Robertson – as well as that of their English disciple Edward Gibbon – transformed Adams's understanding of the historical past and the processes and forces that had produced change and progress. The moral-sense doctrines of the Scottish Enlightenment, particularly the account he found in Adam Smith's *The Theory of Moral Sentiments* (1759) shaped his understanding of moral psychology and human nature. Neither of these sources fundamentally transformed the core elements of his political philosophy or his constitutional preferences. He continued to believe in a system of checks and balances between a bicameral legislature, an independent judiciary, and a separate executive armed with a legislative veto. But they did alter the way he understood these features and his justification for them. Adams's adoption of the lineaments of Scottish social science both broadened and deepened his Enlightened politics in ways that would lead him to sharply reject the radical thought he discovered in France.

That Adams would turn to the new philosophical history for insight and information was hardly surprising. Historical exegesis and examples had been a critical element in most of his previous writings and the multivolumed works of Hume, Gibbon, and Robertson were justly celebrated in their day as the greatest historical works of the age. Several features distinguished this philosophical history from the whiggish writings of contemporary popular historians like Rapin, Raynal, Rollin, and even Voltaire. Where the latter historiography was profoundly didactic and partisan, pitting the heroes of liberty and reason against the forces of tyranny and superstition, the philosophical historians sought to achieve a more moderate and balanced treatment by offering a more nuanced depiction of historical antagonists (Smitten, 1985). They also eschewed the heroic and elegiac forms of historical narrative in favor of an ironic tone of worldly detachment. But their most striking feature – one that strikes present-day readers as presciently revisionist – was their predilection for highlighting the disparity between the expressed intentions and goals of historical actors and the actual long-term consequences of their actions (Wexler, 1976–1977).

This privileging of consequences over intentions had been a central feature of Anglophone Enlightenment since the writings of Bernard Mandeville in the early eighteenth century, but it was Hume and Robertson (later followed by Gibbon) who first applied its logic to the study of history. The lessons drawn from such unintended consequences could completely invert traditional understandings. Thus the atheist Gibbon showed that the attempts of the Julian the Apostate, the traditional Roman hero of the Enlightenment, to revive philosophy and religious toleration as emperor had been both puerile and childish; the true preserver of the classical inheritance were superstitious monks who transcribed the great works in their scriptoria. Hume notoriously argued that in the great struggle in the mid-seventeenth century between Charles I and Parliament that culminated in civil war, all of the arguments based on legal precedents and historical constitutional principles lay on the side of the absolutist monarch and his royalist supporters. Fortunately, the royalists lost, but the subsequent rise of English liberty owed less to republican principle than to the fanaticism of Puritan Roundheads whose enthusiasm proved blessedly short-lived (Stockton, 1971: 278–279). It was from these ironic inversions of intention and consequence that philosophical history drew its lessons – whether the grand lesson that consequences trump purposes, or smaller ones such as the role of superstition in preserving learning or the importance of ignorance and enthusiasm in sparking the defense of liberty.

Adams drew widely on the themes and teachings of the philosophical historians, but the most central lessons he drew came from their treatment of feudalism. As the symbol of both the ancient regime and the social and political system from which early modern liberty had emerged, feudalism had loomed large in most of Adams's early writings. Beginning with his

Dissertation on the Canon and Feudal Law, Adams focused on feudalism as a system of monarchical tyranny and absolutism. Although originally a military system "for the necessary defense of a barbarous people against the inroad and invasion of her neighboring nations," feudalism was adapted by monarchs through the abuse of feudal land tenures to reduce the lieutenants and soldiers to the status of "servants and vassals" while binding "the chains faster on every order of mankind" (*Adams Papers*:1.112–114) The monarchical absolutism of feudalism, when combined with the canon law, had ushered in a veritable dark age that covered Europe in ignorance, superstition, and royal despotism. Only the revival of learning and, in England, the alliance of the populace and aristocracy against their royal overlord had ended this oppression and brought to light the first glimmerings of modern liberty (Butterfield, 1966: 2.59–60).

Adams's theory of feudal absolutism had been critical to his defense of the colonial assemblies against the claims of parliamentary sovereignty. In one of his replies to Governor Thomas Hutchinson on behalf of the Massachusetts House of Representatives, Adams claimed that because the colonists held their land "of the king" rather than allodially, these feudal tenures obviated any subjection to parliament: "We conceive that upon the Feudal Principles all Power is in the King." Indeed, the charter that Charles I issued to the settlers of Massachusetts, in keeping with his absolutist feudal pretensions, was "without any Reservation to the English Parliament, of authority to make future laws binding therein" (*Revolutionary*: 135–136). Adams made the same point in his *Novanglus* essays. Although according to the feudal laws "the king was absolute in America" at the time of settlement, such royal absolutism did not imply that the king-in-parliament held any legal authority in the colonies since the feudal relation of homage was personal and absolute, not institutional. Even if one argue that somehow the settlement of North America constituted a sort of royal conquest and annexation, "it will not follow that the lords and common have any authority over them" (*Revolutionary*: 241, 247–248).

Adams's understanding of feudalism was fundamentally transformed by his reading of philosophical history. Feudalism was not a defensive policy against barbaric incursion but instead the result of a successful conquest of a native population. Nor was it as system of royal absolutism. On the contrary, feudalism ushered in an aristocratic age of baronial lawlessness and anarchy. And it was not the revival of learning and a popular front by nobles and commons that finally brought feudalism to an end. Quite the reverse: modern liberty and enlightenment were the unintended consequences of the rise of commerce and popular support for absolute monarchy.

Contrary to Adams's whiggish account, feudalism was the result of barbarian conquest rather than the means of resisting it. After subduing a people, the successful warlord would distribute land to his principal followers in payment "for their personal service" (Robertson, 1827: 1.13). These followers (barons) would then distribute land among their knights who held the same feudal relationships of homage and clientage to their lord that the barons did to the king. David Hume traced the origins of this system to the Norman conquests of England and Italy in the eleventh century (Hume, 1778: 1.114–1.225, 1.203). William Robertson pushed it farther back, to the decline of the Merovingian dynasty in the seventh century (Robertson, 1827: 3.15) Edward Gibbon accepted Robertson's demarcation in "the silent decay of the Merovingian line" (Gibbon, 1994: 2.481) but argued that the core of the feudal principle could be found in any successful band of marauding pastoral nomads: "The rudiments of a feudal government may be discovered in the constitution of Scythian or Tartar nations"(Gibbon, 1994: 1.1032).

Far more important, the feudal system was in no way a form of absolute monarchy. As the benefice gave way to the fief, the land held "of the king" by the great barons increasingly took on the tincture of private property, and the construction of castles and armed fortifications on aristocratic estates signaled a profound decentralization of power and the near eclipse of the state (Gibbon, 1994: 2.480) Despite the appearances of royal power, the lack of independent revenues rendered the monarch a mere first among equals within his realm, and he was rarely a match for the combined force of his great barons. As kings were unable to enforce their commands without great exertion, the result was, as Hume noted, that "a kingdom was considered only as a great barony, and a barony as a small kingdom" (Hume, 1778: 1.462) This feudal hylomorphism was aptly summarized by Robertson (1827: 1.64): "The genius of the feudal government, uniform in all its operations, produced the same effects in small as great societies" so that "the territory of a baron was, in miniature, the model of a kingdom." Without the protection of centralized authority, the common people were prey to the violent depredations and anarchic rapine of the warrior elite (Hume, 1778: 1.350) In these circumstances, the vast bulk of the population had no choice but to seek the protection of some great lord and place themselves in a state of "serfdom, villeinage, or slavery." Without secure property, commerce and the arts practically disappeared and Europe descended into an extended age of darkness.

What ended the age of feudal anarchy was the revival of commerce. Robertson traced the moment to the crusades, while Hume saw it emerging more slowly and only gaining traction in the period between the rise of the Tudors and the settlement of the Americas. But both agreed that it was commerce that transformed Europe. Both also agreed that commerce had been enabled by the self-interested actions of monarchs who incorporated and privileged towns and cities as both a source of independent revenue and a political counterweight to the baronial aristocracy. It was the kings who first encouraged self-government in the towns and who first called for the boroughs to send representatives to what would become his parliaments.

As commerce grew, the great barons diverted their income from armed supporters to the conspicuous consumption of luxuries. This not only "gave subsistence to mechanics and merchants," it also "dissipated the immense fortunes of the ancient barons" and transferred land and wealth to the more rational and industrious gentry and middling sort (Hume, 1778: 4.384). As the industrious saw their wealth grow, they threw their strength behind their kings' attempts to establish their authority with standing armies that could institute the king's peace and secure the rule of law. "In some nations, the privileges of the commons increased" while in most the result was merely the rise of royal absolutism. In either case, Hume insisted, the condition of the common people "received great improvement, and they acquired, if not entire liberty, at least the most considerable advantages of it" (Hume, 1778: 3.80).

This new account of feudalism fundamentally challenged Adams's vision of European political history. The great danger to popular liberty had not come from royal prerogatives but from aristocratic license and anarchy. The modern age of liberty had emerged as the unintended consequence of monarchical striving for mastery that had fostered the growth of commerce and arts while transferring wealth and power to the common people. Implicit in this account was the sort of consequential or "invisible hand" argument of human progress found in Bernard Mandeville and Adam Smith; the greatest benefits come from the unintended consequences of selfish behavior (Cook, 1999). Indeed, Enlightenment itself was, for these philosophical historians, the consequence rather than the cause of this great commercial and liberating development.

The most obvious impact of Adams's new conception of feudalism was a near obsession with the power of aristocracy. While drafting the first volume of his *Defense* he confessed to one correspondent that "I have half a mind to devote the next ten years to the making of a book upon the subject of nobility" (C.F. Adams, 1850–1856: 8.370). In fact, that subject was central to both his three volume *Defense* and his subsequent *Discourses on Davila*. Behind all his mature writings was a profound fear of elites of all stripes, a fear informed by his awareness of the long history or aristocratic domination of medieval and early modern Europe. "The Aristocracy is always more sagacious" than either the people or their representatives, just as it "sooner or later proves an overmatch in policy" to both kings and people (C.F. Adams, 1850–1856: 4.354–355). This fear of aristocratic power was not limited to its hereditary or "artificial" form. The whole distinction between natural and artificial aristocracy now struck Adams as illusory. All aristocracy was natural insofar as it emerged from a universal process of social differentiation: "Was there, or will there ever be, a nation whose individuals were all equal, in natural and acquired qualities in virtues, talents, and riches? The answer of all mankind must be in the negative." Even in his beloved New England towns most political offices "have generally descended from generation to generation, in three of four families at the most" (C.F. Adams, 1850–1856: 4.392–393). Adams's new-found concern with aristocracy did not lead him to reject his belief in constitutional balance, but it did change his understanding of that doctrine. In his early writing, he had seen the ideal balance in terms of Montesquieu's notion of the separation of powers. "A Legislative, and Executive, and a judicial Power, comprehend the whole of what is meant and understood by Government," he informed Richard Henry Lee as he began drafting *Thoughts on Government*. "It is by balancing each of these Powers" that the dangers of tyranny could be checked (*Adams Papers*: 3.307–308). He championed bicameralism because unicameral assemblies were likely to be avaricious, ambitious, "liable to all the vices, follies, and frailties of an individual" and entirely incapable of handling the executive and judicial functions of government. This was reflected by the fact that in *Thoughts on Government* he proposed that the upper chamber of the legislature be chosen by the assembly and that both branches should then elect the governor (*Adams Papers*: 4.88–89). In his later writings, however, Adams came to see bicameralism as fulfilling the older ideal of mixed government, balancing the influence of the people against the social elite. These two groups were the primary source of political factions and rivalries and, as he argued in *Discourses on Davila*, "the essence of a free government consists in an effectual control of rivalries" (C.F. Adams, 1850–1856: 6.280). Indeed, without a clear separation of these groups in the legislature, Adams feared that the popular element would be effaced by the superior guile of the elite. "The rich, the well-born, and the able, acquire and influence among the people that will soon be too much for simple honesty and plain sense, in a house of representatives," he claimed. "The most illustrious of them must, therefore, be separated from the mass and placed by themselves in a senate," and that "this is, to all honest and useful intents, an ostracism" (C.F. Adams, 1850–1856: 4.290).

Ancillary to Adams's fear of aristocracy was a new appreciation of monarchical power. Where Adams had previously spoken of the executive, he now insisted on referring to elected chief magistrates as monarchical. His understanding of feudalism taught him that simply executing the law and vetoing those that were unconstitutional was an inadequate safeguard of popular republican government. "In every feudal country" the baronial elite had overrun their titular monarchs "under the pretense of limiting its authority" and thereby rendered both king and people politically impotent. This process ran unabated "until the kings, by incorporating cities and granting privileges to the people, set them up against the nobles, and obtained by their means standing armies, sufficient to control both nobles and commons" (C.F. Adams, 1850–1856: 4.362). Only in England had the people been able to support their kings without giving them standing armies, thus restoring political balance within the government and allowing public liberty to take root. The lesson Adams drew was that the American republican "elective monarch" needed to be an independent power within the state, balancing the factions that divided the legislature and restraining the inevitable struggle between the common people and the elite. All men and all factions sought power, after all, and "tyranny will be the effect, whoever are the governors" unless restrained by "equal laws, made by common consent, and supported, protected, and enforced by three different orders of men in *equillibrio*" (C.F. Adams, 1850–1856: 5.9–10).

If the new philosophical history of Hume, Robertson, and Gibbon deepened Adams's understanding of the principles of political architecture, his account of human nature – the raw material of political life – was transformed by the moral psychology he absorbed in Adam Smith's *The Theory of Moral Sentiments.* Adams had seen humanity as subject to both reason and passion or sentiment in his early writings. Unfortunately, the selfish passions were more powerful than their social counterparts. This represented a great challenge for republican government since "virtue alone is or can be the Foundation" of such a popular political system (*Adams Papers*: 3.295–296). Obviously religious establishments and sumptuary laws might help redress the imbalance in our moral nature, but Adams's chief strategy was a public and political appeal for virtue among the citizenry. "There must be a positive Passion for the public good, the public Interest, Honour, Power, and Glory, established in the Minds of the People," he wrote to Mercy Otis Warren, "or there can be no Republican Government, nor any real Liberty" (*Adams Papers*: 4.124–125). Since virtue, both public and private, was essential to republican self-government, "it must encouraged" by those government with "Rewards, in every Department civil and military" (*Adams Papers*: 3.295–296).

Adam Smith's moral psychology complicated Adam's conception of human motivation. In addition to our selfish and benevolent sentiments, Smith argued that humans had an inbred desire for the approval of others. Indeed, individuals regulated their behavior in light of how they thought an impartial spectator would judge their actions and intentions. When combined with the natural vanity inherent in all people, this desire for approval gave rise to the emulative desire for distinction. Adams seized on this desire repeatedly in his *Discourses on Davila*, arguing for its ubiquity among all social strata. "In a city or village," he claimed, "little employments and trifling distinctions are contended for with equal eagerness, as honors and offices in commonwealths and kingdoms" (C.F. Adams, 1850–1856: 6.241). Although this passion for distinction could spur the iniquitous pursuits of avarice and ambition, it could also prompt the individual "to excel another, by fair industry in the search of truth, and the practice of virtue." If the latter result was to prevail over the former, at least within the political realm, an Enlightened republic must channel the emulative passion into the paths of virtue. "It is a principal end of government to regulate this passion,"

Adams averred, and once properly regulated it "becomes a principal means of government" (C.F. Adams, 1850–1856: 6.233–234). Thus the honorable status of senator, or high executive position, could spur the elite to make themselves worthy of such offices, especially if they were accompanied by exalted titles and other marks of distinction. This would, in turn, keep such aspiring natural aristocrats out of the popular assembly, assuring a voice in government for the common people.

Like the philosophical history he absorbed, Adams's appropriation of Smith's spectatorial theory of morality pushed his thought in a more worldly, almost Mandevillean direction. Where he had previously called for virtuous exertion, he now agreed with Hume that "all projects of government, founded in the supposition or expectation of extraordinary degrees of virtue, are evidently chimerical" (C.F. Adams, 1850–1856: 6.415) Rather than appealing to virtue to overcome our selfish passions, Adams now sought to manipulate the inherent vanity in all men to promote virtuous behavior (Trees, 2001) Since vanity was, in Adams's mind, simply "self-love" or selfishness and "an universal passion," Adams was in fact pitting selfishness against itself to promote the very socially and politically beneficial consequences that virtue alone could not achieve (Schutz and Adair, 1966: 96). By such a policy, he believed, selfish and ambitious men could be "chained down to an incessant servitude to their fellow creatures," a servitude "constituted by their own vanity." Driven by their passion for distinction and manipulated by prudent statesmanship and political architecture, ambitious individuals would voluntarily undermine their own self-interest, for, as Adams wryly observed, "on a selfish system, what are the thoughts, passions, and sentiments of mankind to us?" (C.F. Adams, 1850–1856: 6.245). Adams's researches had left his constitutional and political principles largely intact, but they had certainly transformed his understanding of and justification for them.

2.3 Rejecting Radicalism

Adams's engagement with Scottish philosophical theory and moral psychology broadened and deepened his mature understanding of Enlightenment. But it was his exposure to the rising tide of radical philosophy of the French late or high Enlightenment that gave it focus and direction. In fact, much of Adams's mature publications and philosophical correspondence was written in direct response to the tenets he first observed in Paris during his diplomatic service in the late 1770s and 1780s. To be sure, Adams was sensitive to the domestic and diplomatic challenges facing the early republic in the years after independence, and troubled by the failure of both the states and the confederation to respond to them, concerns that undoubtedly informed his mature writings (Staloff, 2005:164–177). Yet it was reports of the spread of radical French doctrines, especially the unicameral proposals of Turgot and his supporters to "town and county meetings in Massachusetts" that inspired him to counter their baleful influence (C.F. Adams, 1850–1856: 9.622–623). And it was the prevalence of those tenets, especially among the philosophical champions of the early phase of the French Revolution, which filled him with fear at the unfolding of that world historical event. The most immediate context of his hostile reaction to philosophical radicalism was its near universal rejection of his constitutional architecture. Most radicals favored a thoroughly centralized administration under the control of a unicameral assembly. But, as C. Bradley Thompson has shown, what underlay that dispute was a deeper divergence over methods of political theorizing or "constitutional epistemology" (1996: 363). What hinged in that debate was a contest over the proper form of scientific inquiry into the human realm and its relation to political practice. At bottom, Adams's struggle against the radical Enlightenment was over the very nature of Enlightenment, a struggle that was vital to defending what he saw as a truly Enlightened republican order.

Adams was often hyperbolic in his denunciation of the dangers of French radicalism. Not only true radicals, but moderates like Voltaire and D'Alembert and even *anti-philosophes* like Rousseau were vilified as sharing the noxious doctrines of atheism, materialism, and unbalanced democracy. But the bulk of Adams's critiques were focused on three figures: Anne-Robert-Jacques Turgot; Marie Jean Antoine Nicholas de Caritat, the marquis de Condorcert; and Antoine Louis Claude Destutt, the comte de Tracy. Turgot was a high government official – he had served as Intendant of Limoges and Controller General of France – and a leading member of the physiocratic "sect." In 1778 he wrote a letter to the British radical Richard Price criticizing the majority of American state constitutions for slavishly copying the English model of bicameralism and checks and balances instead of embracing an unfettered unicameral legislature that represented the "general will." After Turgot's letter was published, Adams began preparing his reply, the three-volume work whose full title was a *Defense of the Constitutions of the United States of America, Against the Attack of Mr. Turgot, in his letter to Dr. Price, Dated the Twenty-Second Day of March, 1778.* Condorcet, a disciple of Turgot and a distinguished mathematician, responded to the first volume of the *Defense* in a series of published letters purportedly from a citizen of "New Heaven" attacking Adams's bicameralism (he also successfully colluded with Jefferson and other radicals to suppress a French translation of Adams's work: Appleby, 1968). Adams's 1790 *Discourses on Davila* was, in large measure, his reply to Condorcert (C.B. Thompson, 1996: 364). Adams's engagement with the works of Tracy occurred in the last decade of his life at the prompting of Thomas Jefferson. Tracy was a philosopher of the radical Enlightenment who founded the science of ideas he called "Ideology," a philosophy that Jefferson deeply admired. Indeed, Jefferson was so impressed with the Ideology of Tracy that he personally worked on the translation and publication of two of his works, *A Commentary and Review of Montesquieu's Spirit of Laws* (1811) and *A Treatise of Political Economy* (1817), both of which he installed as standard texts in the curricula at the College of William and Mary and the University of Virginia.

Turgot, Condorcet, and Tracy had much in common aside from the critical enmity of John Adams. All three frequented the salon of Madame Helvetius, a hotbed of radical philosophy, in the Paris suburb of Auteil. It was there that Adams – as well as Franklin and Jefferson – first encountered them. All three ascribed to the "sensationalism" of Ettienne Bonnot, the abbé Condillac, a reductive materialist account of human psychology and cognition that had informed Claude Adrien Helvetius's posthumously published and scandalously radical *A Treatise on Man*. Both Condorcet and Tracy, like many of the devotees of the Helvetius salon, supplied intellectual leadership for the revolutionary Girondin party, and those that survived the Jacobin terror participated in the subsequent Ideological movement during the Directorate (Staum, 1980: 16–17). Most critical of all, however, all three shared a common philosophical outlook and a common approach to social and political inquiry that was strikingly antithetical to that of Adams.

Where Adams's notion of philosophical inquiry was based on Baconian induction and Lockean empiricism, Turgot, Condorct, and Tracy embraced an *a priori* model. In this regard their style of thinking hearkened back to the geometrically inspired writing of seventeenth-century rationalists like René Descartes, Baruch Spinoza, and, to a lesser extent, Thomas Hobbes. Rather than appealing to facts and experience, they looked to pure reason to intuit undeniable first principles. Once these foundational principles were recognized, subsequent truths could be logically deduced in a rigorous fashion. The result would be a coherent system of truths, a broad and unified systematic body of knowledge, one whose science of man included the fields of political theory and ethics.

For much of the eighteenth century, French *philosophes* followed Voltaire in rejecting such "systems" as sterile throwbacks to the era before Locke and Newton had blazed the path of modern learning. But Turgot, like most physiocrats and sensationalists, broke with that "moderate" tradition. He argued that those who castigated systematic and rigorous rationalism were "prejudiced men" who were amazed to "meet with a man inwardly convinced of a truth, and deducing form in consequences with the rigor of an exact logic" (Turgot, 1895: 316, 244–245). For Condorcet (1795), such systematic thinking was particularly important in matters of ethics and political analysis. Unless one began from the metaphysical truth of human sensibility, a first principle arrived at by sensationalist analysis rather than empirical observation or experiment, there was no limit to the errors one might arrive at. Any reliable "knowledge of the true rights of man," he insisted, must be "deduced from this simple principle; that *he is a being endowed with sensation, capable of reasoning upon and understanding his interests, and of acquiring moral ideas*" (1795: 231). Those moral ideas in turn arose from "analising the faculty of experiencing pleasure and pain" as did "those general principles which form the necessary and immutable laws of justice" (1795: 242). Tracy agreed entirely. In fact, Ideology was not simply the foundation of political science and economics, it was the basis of all human inquiry. The very goal of formulating the science of ideas was "to deduce from that knowledge the first principles of all other branches of our knowledge" in a systematic fashion (Tracy, 1817: ix).

The deduction of social science from first principles not only simplified the process of theorization, it also simplified the theories themselves. Because Tracy analytically reduced all social struggles to the "movement and resistance and the general conflict of will," they could be easily surmounted by a policy of laissez-faire which allowed individuals to engage in free exchanges. This in turn was because such exchanges were the very stuff of society and were an inherently "admirable transaction, in which two contracting parties always gain" (E. Kennedy, 1978: 211; Tracy, 1817: 17). Tracy similarly jettisoned the cumbersome taxonomy of constitutions found in Aristotle, Polybius, and Machiavelli. There were really only two forms of government, those which were based on the legitimate foundation of the general will, and those which were not. (Tracy, 1811: 13–14). Perhaps most striking of all was the abandonment of the ornate bric-a-brac of tradition constitutionalism. Mixed government, the separation of powers and especially checks and balances were rejected as "erroneous and indefensible" (Tracy, 1811: 117–118). In their stead was a simple unicameral legislature bounded by the undisputable rights of man. Condorcet marveled at "how much more pure, accurate and profound, are the principles upon which the constitution and laws for France have been formed, that those which directed the Americans." The reason for this superiority was obvious. Abandoning the misguided empiricism that had led the Americans astray, the statesmen of revolutionary France had limited the power of the state by natural rights rather than "that specious balance which has so long been admired" (Condorcet, 1795: 268–269).

It was not merely the radical *philosophes*' rejection of his constitutional principles that troubled Adams. Equally disturbing was their deductive rationalism. Adams's own inductive method of social scientific analysis drew on the empirical observations of philosophical history and Scottish moral psychology. Condorcet derided this mode of inquiry as producing "a science rather of facts, and, if I may so speak, empirical, than a true theory." By contrast, such a "true theory" would be "founded on general principles, drawn from nature, and acknowledged by reason" (Condorcet, 1795: 89) Tracy concurred entirely. Only a purely analytic theory of politics and society, one divorced from the observation of the human past, could "establish a priori, the principles of a truly free, legal, and peaceable constitution" (Tracy, 1811: 108). Adams found this *a priori* methodology so troubling that he wrote an extended critique directed at both Turgot and Condorcet as he began drafting his *Defense* (C.B. Thompson, 1998: 110–125). The incipient Cartesianism of the radicals ignored the advances made by observation and experimentation by Newton. More pointedly, it rejected the political insights to be drawn from the analysis of human experience and history by philosophers from Aristotle and Machiavelli to Bolingbroke and Hume. This was all the more shocking in that, in almost every other field of study and endeavor, the methodology of empirical science had become the accepted mode of inquiry. As Adams complained to his old comrade Benjamin Rush, the experimental and empirical method was now "admitted in all other arts and sciences" except government and political theory where it "is wholly unheeded." This was indeed "a strange disposition," rather like the primitivist desire "to live in hollow trees and log houses without chimneys or windows" (Schutz and Adair, 1966: 31).

Every bit as troubling as this *a priori* methodology was the deterministic metaphysic that underlay it. Adams had, after all, accepted the natural-rights thinking of Locke, predicated as it was on faith in an equal creation of humanity. But radical *philosophes* like Condorcet and Tracy subscribed to the necessitarian account of human psychology and cognition prescribed by sensationalism, one that ultimately reduced all mental faculties and operations to the mechanical activity of the senses. Condillac had most famously illustrated this sensationalist account in his *Treatise on the Sensations* (1754) which showed how a soulless and mindless statue could execute all our mental operation by gradually having each of its senses illuminated. Psychologically, the presence of pleasure and pain triggered desires and passions, which in turn generated interests. These in turn determined all subsequent mental activity; "The different degrees of pleasure and pain are the law by which the germ of all we are is developed" and these ineluctable sensations "have produced all our faculties" (Condillac, 1930: 198, 200, 46). It was this reductive understanding of the human mind as a mechanism generated by its perceptual interaction with its material surroundings that underwrote the political, constitutional, and economic theories of radicals like Condorcet and Tracy. Because human behavior was ultimately the predictable response to sensual inputs and stimuli, changing those stimuli by rearranging institutions and rewards would necessarily transform that behavior.

For Adams, whose empirical skepticism precluded metaphysical knowledge, such abstruse reasoning struck him as absurd. To assume that both the world and the human mind were ordered along strictly deterministic lines was to claim to have limned the basic structures of being, a claim that was both hubristic and dogmatic because "the faculties of our understanding are not adequate to penetrate the Universe" (Cappon, 1959: 607). Adams acknowledged that there were points of value in radical French philosophy.

He admired much of Tracy's *Political Economy* as well as his larger Ideological project, but he felt that at bottom its steady "stream" of inferences and deductions "disembogues itself into the unfathomable gulph of liberty and necessity." Adams did not take the opposing metaphysical position in defense of free will, although he did insist that without such liberty "there [is] no merit or guilt, and there can be neither reward or punishment in the universe." Instead he argued that the entire metaphysical debate between liberty and necessity was beyond the range of human knowledge. "Human understanding will never dive in this state of existence to such depths" he argued, "and it is a vain and impertinent curiosity to think of it" (Cappon, 1959: 534–535).

Adams's alarm over the philosophical mode of radical thought was more than merely academic. By rigorously deducing their political theories from indubitable sensationalist first principles, they claimed to produce a body of knowledge whose truth was necessarily certain. Indeed, one of the remarkable implications of the sensationalist account of the mind reacting automatically to its impressions was that it led to the prospect of infallibility. "We are perfectly, completely, and necessarily sure of all the we actually feel," Tracy insisted, and "none of our judgments, taken separately, can be erroneous, since, for the very reason that we see one idea in another, it must actually be there" (Tracy, 1817: 2–3). As Emmet Kennedy has put it (1978: 144): "in maintaining that thinking is sensing, and that sensing is inerrant, Tracy seemed to eliminate the possibility of error." That error did occur was due to the ambiguity of natural language that left the precise signification or words indeterminate. Such error could be eradicated by refining language through sensationalist analysis, literally breaking each word/idea into its constituent sensual parts (Tracy, 1817: 5). Condorcet argued that such analytically refined language would give every "object that comes within the reach of human intelligence, a rigour, and precision" that would "render error almost impossible." This would make every science "as infallible as that of mathematics" (Condorcet, 1795: 366). A careful sensationalist analysis could not help but generate what Tracy called "opinions necessarily correct" (Tracy, 1811: 133).

It was precisely this epistemic posture that made the thought of materialists like Condorcet and Tracy so disturbing to Adams. Just as his skeptical doubts supported the value of moderation, the claim to certainty underwrote the contrary ethos of radicalism. An infallible *a priori* science of man could not help but raise the stakes of both political theory and practice. Because such a science was inerrant, it would necessarily produce a perfect constitution or what Tracy called "the democracy of enlightened reason" as well as perfectly just laws. More than that, however, the resulting Ideal political regime and wholesome legal code would transform humanity itself. The political order, "built upon the truths of the political sciences," Condorcet argued, would "naturally dispose men to humanity, to benevolence, and to justice." Just as advances in the natural sciences had improved the mechanical arts, so too would the perfection of "the moral and political sciences" have "a similar influence upon the motives that direct our sentiments and actions." Here lay the radical consequence of the *a priori* determinism of Condorcet and Tracy, namely that by transforming stimuli in the form of institutions and laws, the "moral goodness of man" was capable of "an indeterminate improvement" (Condorcet, 1795: 352–355). It was this "doctrine of the infinite perfectibility of the human mind," a doctrine Condorcet first attributed to Turgot, that had finally delivered the "fatal blow" to "the fabric of prejudice" of the ancienne regime that was "tottering to its foundations" (1795: 257–258). It was this doctrine, predicated on a flawless system of politics and laws, that assured radicals "that we are approaching the era of one of the great revolutions of the human race" (1795: 19). Given the chiliastic stakes at issue – the actual regeneration of the human mind and the perfection of the human condition – it is not surprising that those who shared such hopes eschewed moderation and talk of balance and caution. If the prospect offered was in fact a thoroughly scientific scheme of universal human emancipation, only a truly radical, indeed ruthless, use of means was morally defensible.

For Adams the Lockean moderate, such claims to certainty and perfectibilty were tragic and dangerous. To think that human nature could be fundamentally altered was to deny that the future will resemble the past, the very uniformity of nature that makes all scientific and practical knowledge possible. It was precisely such erroneous fantasies that had produced the fanaticism of the French Revolution and justified the Jacobin reign of terror. Adams compared the French revolutionaries to "sailors flushed with recent pay" who, drunk with enthusiasm and fanaticism, "mounted on wild Horses, lashing and spurring, till they would kill the Horses and break their own Necks." Such millennial effusions had not only halted the spread of human progress, they gave it "a retrograde course" (Cappon, 1959: 357–358). "Is the millennium commencing?" he asked in 1790, or will "the struggle in Europe be any thing more than a change of imposters and impositions? (C.F. Adams, 1850–1856: 6.411–412). The dogmatic rationalism of French radical Enlightenment filled him with fears, fears that, in his own mind at least, were tragically fulfilled in the course of events. "I leave those profound Phylosophers whose Sagacity perceives the Perfectibility of Humane Nature," wrote a sarcastic Adams in his retirement, "to enjoy their transporting hopes." That was, of course, "provided that they will not engage us in Crusades and French Revolutions, nor burn Us for doubting." Adams's own "spirit of Prophecy" could extend "no rather than, *New England* guesses" (Cappon, 1959: 462).

Adams did not, of course, deny the possibility or reality of human progress. From his earliest youth he had championed the process of Enlightenment and the reformation of institutions and practices. But he also saw both limits and threats to this process. "Our hopes of sudden tranquility ought not be too sanguine," he warned Jefferson. "Fanaticism and superstition will still be selfish, subtle and intriguing" and "will yet for a long time continue a Fermentation, which will excite alarms and require eternal vigilance" (Cappon, 1959: 435). But if the threat of superstition came from the reactionary defenders of the old regime, the dangers of fanaticism issued from the like of Turgot, Condorcet and Tracy. Adams saw very little to choose between them. "Have not philosophers been as honest and as mad as popes, Jesuits, priests" and other fomenters of superstition and credulity, and "has the Inquisition been more cruel than Robespierre or Marat or Napoleon?" (Haraszti, 1952: 179). Adams did acknowledge that some of the radicals, like the English divines Richard Price and Joseph Priestly, had been sincere in their hopes of human liberation, well-meaning "enthusiasts" who had been swept up in "the popular contagion of the times." But with most philosophical radicals he was not so generous. Rather they "prated about the perfectibility of man" solely to capture "the attention of the public." Once they had succeeded in "amusing and cheating the populace with promises of equality and levelism, which they knew were impracticable" they seized power and pursued the higher end of "present plunder" (Schutz and Adair, 1966: 74). But whether sincere or cynical, Adams saw such radical chiliasts as fanatics and enthusiasts rather than members of any Enlightenment he could recognize. Despite their claims to scientific knowledge and modern progressivism, they were a throwback to the previous age of religious zealotry and credulity despite their materialist assumptions. From Adams's perspective, they simply were not Enlightened at all. Men like Turgot, Tracy, and Condorcet, like any "Philosophers antient and modern," appeared to him "as Mad as Hindoos, Mahomitans and Christians," a view which Adams well knew was reciprocated. The gap between the moderate Enlightenment of John Adams and the radical Enlightenment of the party of progress had simply become to great to bridge. "For any thing I know this globe may be, the bedlam [madhouse] of the Universe" (Cappon, 1959: 437). Here lay the great irony of John Adams and Enlightenment in his final years. The modern republican order that he championed had survived and flourished. In his own eyes at least, the vision of Enlightenment that had produced it had not.

Guide to Further Reading

Despite a wave of popular biographies, there have been few recent scholarly studies devoted exclusively to the thought of John Adams. A notable exception is C. Bradley Thompson, *John Adams and the Spirit of Liberty* (1998) which, although devoted to his political thought, has excellent coverage of Adams's relationship to the Enlightenment. Among older works, Alfred

Iacuzzi, *John Adams Scholar* (1952) and Zoltan Haraszti, *John Adams and the Prophets of Progress* (1952) both have valuable information concerning Adams' reactions to various early modern thinkers as does, to a lesser extent, John R. Howe, Jr., *The Changing Political Thought of John Adams* (1966) and Peter Shaw, *The Character of John Adams* (1976). There are, however, a variety of books that have chapters devoted to Adams and his intellectual engagement with early modern philosophy. These include Joyce Appleby, *Liberalism and Republicanism in the Historical Imagination* (Cambridge, MA, 1992), Ernest Cassara, *The Enlightenment in America* (New York, 1975), Paul K. Conkin, *Puritans and Pragmatists: Eight Eminent American Thinkers* (Indianapolis, 1968), John Patrick Diggins, *The Lost Soul of American Politics: Virtue, Self-Interest, and the Foundations of Liberalism* (New York, 1984); John Ferling, *John Adams, A Life* (1992), Ralph Lerner, *The Thinking Revolutionary: Principle and Practice in the New Republic* (Ithaca, 1979), Darren Staloff, *Hamilton, Adams, Jefferson: The Politics of Enlightenment and the American Founding* (2005), Andrew S. Trees, *The Founding Fathers and the Politics of Character* (2004), and Gordon S. Wood, *The Creation of the American Republic, 1776–1787* (1969). Brooke Allen, *Moral Minority: Our Skeptical Founding Fathers* (New York, 2006) contains a provocative chapter on Adams' religious views.

For a good background on the American Enlightenment, see Henry May, *The Enlightenment in America* (1976) and Donald H. Meyer, *The Democratic Enlightenment* (New York, 1976). A more recent study of print culture in the American Enlightenment and its relation to political culture can be found in Michael Warner, *The Letters of the Republic: Publication and the Public Sphere in Eighteenth-Century America* (Cambridge, MA, 1990). David S. Shields, *Civil Tongues and Polite Letters in British America* (1997) offers an intriguing and alternative view that stresses the polite and private dimensions of the American republic of letters. A first-rate collection of articles on the Enlightenment in British America is Frank Shuffelton (ed.), *The American Enlightenment* (Rochester, 1993). The best recent works on the radical thought of the French high Enlightenment are Jonathan I. Israel's *Democratic Enlightenment: Philosophy, Revolution, and Human Rights 1750-1790* (2011) and *Enlightenment Contested: Philosophy, Modernity, and the Emancipation of Man 1670-1752* (Oxford, 2006). For more focused treatment on the origins of the Ideologues and their political role in the French Revolution, see Emmet Kennedy, *A Philosophe in the Age of Revolution: Destutt de Tracy and the Origins of "Ideology"* (1978); Martin S. Staum, *Cabanis: Enlightenment Medical Philosophy in the French Revolution* (1980), and *Minerva's Message: Stabilizing the French Revolution* (Montreal, 1996).

Chapter Three

The Revolutionary Politics of John Adams, 1760–1775

Colin Nicolson

John Adams was in his fortieth year when the Revolutionary War began in April 1775. He was a reluctant and seemingly unlikely revolutionary. A portly, middle-class lawyer of below-average height, Adams was widely respected in his home province, more for his intellect, learning, and professional acumen than for any actual achievements in politics. His principal contribution to the colonial protest movement, in the decade before the colonies went to war with Britain, was as a political writer. He was not a foot-soldier to radical activism, a single-issue campaigner, or a classic radical who bemoaned the loss of innocence. His revolutionary ideology was never an article of doctrine or faith, but always – at least, so he liked to suppose – the product of reasoning. Adams was a scholar who pored over the evidence, probing law and history for answers to the many questions that troubled him. Before he could become a revolutionary in the cause of American independence, Adams had to justify revolution to himself.

After the fighting began, Adams rarely practiced law again and made his living instead from public service. He served his countryfolk as an able and hard-working Congressional delegate at Philadelphia and as an American diplomat muddling through in places much further from home – Paris, Amsterdam, London. Posterity chiefly remembers Adams not as a revolutionary, but as a somewhat curmudgeonly Founding Father and second US president, and the progenitor of a political dynasty. Adams the conservative elder statesman seems far removed from

A Companion to John Adams and John Quincy Adams, First Edition.
Edited by David Waldstreicher.

the energetic middle-aged intellectual who had scrutinized the Patriot case and urged revolution on with his pen.

Historians have not subjected Adams's pre-war politics to the intense scrutiny expended on other Founding Fathers. Historical scholarship has generally focused on Adams's role as a national figure in the grand narrative of American history, from the onset of the Revolutionary War to the early nineteenth century. The fullest account of Adams's pre-Revolution politics, by Page Smith, excels in imaginative reconstruction and, like Catherine Drinker Bowen's earlier fictionalized biography, conveys the drama of Adams's life and times (Smith, 1962: 1.78–195; Bowen, 1950: 3–62). The commercial success of David McCullough's Pulitzer Prize-winning 2001 biography, and the more recent critically acclaimed television series of Adams's life, testify to the popularity of the subject; yet even here Adams's early politics remain largely untold – save his part in the Boston Massacre trial and his reaction to the Boston Tea Party (McCullough, 2001; HBO, 2008). John P. Diggins reduced Adams's pre-war years to a single chapter, while James Grant filled in some gaps with a straightforward narrative (Diggins, 2003; Grant, 2005). John Ferling alone provided a sustained detailed analysis of Adams's pre-Revolution politics, followed by an enriching comparison with Washington and Jefferson (Ferling, 1992: 36–151; 2000).

This chapter provides a historiographical map with which to negotiate what is potentially hazardous terrain. It discusses Adams's political education, political activities, and political writings to demonstrate his emergence as a revolutionary amidst the imperial crisis of 1760–1775; more briefly when reaching terrain familiar to students. John Adams was never the foremost polemicist in Massachusetts's Patriot movement – his cousin Samuel Adams was – but his numerous influential essays and letters probed the constitutional basis of British imperial authority. The editorial teams behind the magisterial *Adams Family Papers*, *Papers of John Adams*, *Legal Papers of John Adams*, and *Diary and Autobiography* have already undertaken much reparatory research required for investigating John Adams's politics of the pre-Revolution period. Their works have long informed what historians of the Revolution and Revolutionary Massachusetts say about John Adams. The best place to begin Adams's pre-Revolution politics is the first volume of the *Papers of John Adams* (R.J. Taylor et al., 1977) and the first volume of his *Diary and Autobiography* (Butterfield et al., 1961). The quality of editorial work is unsurpassed and the printed documents are accompanied by authoritative commentaries that link Adams's writings to his life and times. Using the *Legal Papers* requires some prior awareness of legal procedure (and the editors do their best to guide readers). Any research question pondering Adams's revolutionary politics needs to connect with these substantial tomes as well as Adams's Revolutionary Era writings, now widely available (C.B. Thompson, 2000; G. S. Wood, 2011a, 2011b).

3.1 The Education of John Adams

Historians tend to view the political education of John Adams as a rather straightforward process, with few twists and turns. And yet, it is not altogether clear why Adams became a revolutionary. Any Adams biography, such as McCullough's, or Joseph Ellis's impressive thematic study, examines the "Education of John Adams" yet with discussion of Adams's politics a poor second to analysis of his childhood, career, marriage, friendships, and social mobility (McCullough, 2001; Ellis, 1993: 26–55). Certainly, John Adams's great grandson, Henry Adams (1838–1918), provided John Adams's biographers with a delightfully convenient apparatus on which to hang their subject's formative experiences.

Yet the celebrated *Education of Henry Adams* remains instructional for John Adams's historical reputation. For Henry, an Adams's education meant coming to terms with the weight of the family's expectations. Henry "took for granted that any great-grandfather of his must have always been good," starting as he did from the feet of his own father, Charles Francis Adams Sr. (1807–1886), and grandfather, John Quincy Adams (1767–1848) (H. Adams, 1906: 9). Born two centuries to the year since the arrival in Massachusetts of his eponymous pioneer ancestor, Henry Adams felt that he could "scarcely have been more distinctly branded." He saw himself an "eighteenth-century child," "handicapped" by the achievements of five generations of Adamses in the law, in politics, in public service, and so on (1906: 3). "My venerable ancestor has at least me," Henry once wryly quipped (W.C. Ford, 1938: 323). Though Henry never knew his great-grandfather, what he knew of him – and affected to resent – spoke volumes for the historical reputation that Henry's father and grandfather had seemingly constructed for Henry's benefit.

Charles Francis Adams Sr., (Henry Adams's father and John Adams's grandson) wrote the first published biography of John Adams. Unlike Henry, of course, Charles Francis did know John Adams, and heard his grandparents' recollections of life in pre-Revolutionary Massachusetts. The ten-year-old boy, just returned from eight years in Europe with his father, came to know John Adams as the old man was publishing epistolary essays on the imperial crisis in *Niles's Weekly Register* and other periodicals during 1818, and later appended to the first joint edition of *Novanglus and Massachusettensis* (J. Adams and Tudor, 1819: 229–312). Otherwise, Charles Francis probably saw little of his grandfather's revolutionary writings until he edited the entire corpus of the president's public papers for publication as *The Works of John Adams* (1850–1856). The *Life of John Adams* was the first volume of this ten-volume series (C.F. Adams, 1850–1856); it offered some "Preliminary" matters "Respecting" family history and three chapters on John Adams's pre-Revolution days of which the final chapter was the editor's, the others having been composed by John Quincy Adams, between 1829 and 1839.

There are some striking differences in these accounts of John Adams's "education" – and in what they can tell modern historians about the making of a revolutionary. Harvard meant everything to John Quincy Adams and his descendants, and yet the pre-Revolution "distinction of ranks" that John Adams had to endure rankled still. John Adams had been placed fourteenth out of twenty-four in the Harvard class of 1755, in recognition of his family's Puritan lineage and middling social standing, rather than graded on merit as students were from 1773 – a change which John Quincy "considered ... a pregnant indication of the republican principles" that swayed his father's generation. To establish John Adams as an enemy of privilege was not the same as validating his revolutionary principles, but John Quincy's subsequent meanderings through the religion-laden revolutions of the sixteenth and seventeenth centuries nevertheless provided deep context for understanding why his father repudiated the "bigoted and gloomy doctrines of Calvinism," and subsequently embraced Unitarianism. More than any other historian, perhaps, John Quincy Adams established what courage it took for John Adams to pursue the law, and to defy his Calvinist father's zeal that his son should become a minister.

John Quincy's memoir provides an engaging profile of his father's public persona. The John Adams that his son knew and loved was a deeply principled man, espousing the virtues of social meritocracy and independent political thinking, and distrustful of anyone who might deign to tell him what to do or think. This was also the strong-willed man, perpetual enemy of injustice and intolerance, whom his 30-year-old son had seen elected to the presidency. But John Quincy had also learned much about the studious young man his father had once been: the devoted law student and scholar, who found self-improvement through a reading diet of law, history, classics, and government. It was a regimen all too familiar to John Quincy, of course; but where the son found enlightenment and escape in traveling with his father to Europe aged 10, it was his father's experiences and the friendships as a young lawyer that opened new vistas and life opportunities.

The continuation by Charles Francis Adams reinvigorated his father's flagging historical narrative (however clumsy the biographical apparatus). John Adams is near-invisible until Charles Francis's attempted reconstruction, (minus an extant court report) of John Adams's defense of the British soldiers for the murder of five civilians during the Boston Massacre of March 5, 1770. "Facts are stubborn things," said he, "and whatever may be our wishes, our inclinations, or the dictates of our passions, they cannot alter the state of facts and evidence."

The "perfect simplicity" of his grandfather's argument hints at intellectual purity. Through his grandson's eyes we see John Adams doggedly upholding the rule of law, standing alone against the lords of misrule whose bloodlust might have corrupted a cause ennobled by their ancestors' "scrupulous veneration for the sacredness of law .... Thus ended the first and the lightest of the four moral tests which occurred in the course of Mr. Adams's public life" (C.F. Adams 1850–1856: 1.113–115). The second "moral trial" constituted John Adams's support for American independence at the Continental Congress; his third trial was in bringing the Dutch Netherlands into the Revolutionary War against Britain; the fourth and "greatest" trial came late in his presidency when Adams defied fellow Federalists and kept the United States from war against France. The august John Adams that Charles Francis Adams created in a Bunyan-esque narrative was far removed from the rough and tumble of pre-Revolution politics; he was a guarantor of republican ideals and a conservator of morality.

It proved to be an enduring reputation. Adams himself would have warmed to his grandson's moralizing, for his several trials were indeed tangible political dilemmas that turned on questions of principle – as *The Works of John Adams* revealed. On this impossibly heavy burden, Gilbert Chinard in *Honest John Adams* heaped the expectations of historians (Chinard, 1933: 20–43): Chinard imagined Adams on the eve of the Boston Massacre trial feeling "that a revolution was impending which would imperil his good name and perhaps his life" (1933: 60). Honest John was about to embrace his destiny – the "difficult path" of defending the enemy, and so provide "courageous reaffirmation of the principles of law and order" (1933: 62) before he "started forth on his historic journey" (1933: 72) to the first Continental Congress at Philadelphia, in September 1774. In contrast – not least in its exposition of young Adams's rebellious instincts – Catherine Drinker Bowen's portrait of Adams's early years provided a clearer account of Adams's restlessness. To pursue the law not only did Adams have to defy his Calvinist father, he had to deny to himself the nobility of manual labor (Bowen, 1950: 3–62).

For this son of the soil – the first in the father's family to attend college or to become a professional – politics was neither a preferred option nor a calling. Early scholarly endeavors to exhibit the education of John Adams skirted round his political education, but identified life's enduring lessons. The family's politics fostered self-respect and gave John the courage to challenge received wisdom with his intellectualism and his commitment to principles. The struggle with his father induced not anti-authoritarianism, but Adams's determination to make his own way, voiced in his uncommon "hunger for fame" (Ryerson, 2004; see also C.B. Thompson, 1998: 26–31). Fame, he supposed, depended on what he might do to change the world. But the search for fame, according to Ferling, was Adams's way of trying to realize his father's "ambitious dreams for him ... without offending his father through self-serving or treacherous acts" (Ferling, 1992: 31).

Adams's punishing scheme of self-learning sought to acquire the knowledge he would require to succeed. Adams drank from an ever-deepening well of anti-Calvinism, replenished with the great works of the law, the Enlightenment, English Whig theorists, history, science, and the classics (including translations) (Haraszti, 1952; C.B. Thompson, 1998: 3–23). The impressive library that Adams collected was "an embodiment of his faith in the doctrine that knowledge is power." The law provided intellectual tools Adams would wield in public life. The court circuit brought him check to jowl with humanity of all classes, an accretion of experience in the politics of life, with privileged access to espy the political elite at work. The courthouse proved to be his "theatre," where he excelled not only as a public speaker self-tutored in Ciceronian rhetoric, but as a logician and forensic analyst (R.D. Brown, 1989: 99; Farrell, 1989: 505–528; 1992b: 55–72) Adams was the hardest-working barrister in the province of Massachusetts Bay, building from scratch a prosperous practice, studying interminably, and eschewing Crown office. Adams modernized by excelling as a professional lawyer, but often appears emotionally conservationist of the Puritan heritage and values of the provincial world that he knew and loved. (Breen, 1967: 501–520; Carroll, 1959).

The happiness that Adams realized in the pursuit of the law was matched by the joy and contentment in family life and personal friendships. By 1775, eleven years of marriage to Abigail, his loving and stimulating confidante, had delivered four healthy children (one other dying in infancy). Gender relations and the politics of this family had a profound bearing on Adams's own political development, as Abigail's famous injunction that he "Remember the ladies" testifies. Abigail drew her husband where she wished they travel together, and was often one or two steps ahead of him on the road to independence. The extent of her influence on and contribution to her husband's pre-war writings, including *Novanglus*, can only be inferred – but must have been profound (Holton, 2009: 39, 94).

If Abigail transmitted what her biographer calls the "soft power" of friendship, John Adams's political adolescence and maturity were also shaped by male personal friends, notably Jonathan Sewall (1729–1796), future attorney general and Loyalist whom Adams would confront in several literary jousts, and James Otis Jr. (1725–1783), the brilliant and unpredictable lawyer and Whig polemicist. Adams's friendships disclose (1) how social networks sustained politics, and (2) the intellectualism of the Revolutionary generation's politics. Sewall and Otis were Adams's political mentors, in rather different ways.

Any personal encounter with the moralistic, ambitious, and scholarly Adams was never dull – and sometimes potentially explosive. The root cause of many an ill-tempered outburst, Peter Shaw has suggested, was probably a "*suppression* of ambition," involving periodic withdrawal from public but not professional life. Adams reacted angrily to "*anticipated* enmity," usually in private, but when openly confronted responded in a measured, thoughtful manner; thus he broached contentious issues in public forums, notably the Congressional debates on independence (P. Shaw, 1976: 79, 89). This "passionate sage" (as

Joseph J. Ellis describes Adams) was often "gripped" by a syndrome of irascibility jeopardizing personal relationships; but while Adams made enemies with ease, his saving grace ennobled him with a desire for reconciliation, as Sewall, Jefferson, and Mercy Otis Warren all experienced (J.J. Ellis, 1993: 61–62). John Adams's emotions turned on love as well as ambition.

So, what was it that made John Adams a political writer? Adams's writings – his published essays, his correspondence, and his diary – constitute a conscious application of all that he was learning, just as he was already doing in his legal case work. The process of writing was cathartic as well as goal-driven. Potential enemies would draw a loud and luminescent broadside; actual enemies he assailed tactically and with ideas carefully worked out. Thus his beloved Cicero (read so uncritically by Adams's generation) had performed. And it was in the act of writing that John Adams discovered revolution.

3.2 Partisan Politics, 1760–1764

Adams learned his political craft in the rambunctious forum that was Massachusetts politics. Writing his *Autobiography* at his home in Quincy, between 1802 and 1807, Adams easily recalled the ghosts of this past and reacquainted himself with the imperial crisis. Though often unreliable when dating events, the *Autobiography* vitally identifies the key players in Adams's political life and his thoughts on them. Ten years later, Adams recreated cherished scenes for Otis's biographer William Tudor (1779–1830), and inevitably lionized James Otis as a forgotten champion of Liberty, above all in the Writs of Assistance case before the Massachusetts Superior Court in February 1761. Adams (then 25 years old and resembling "a short thick fat archbishop") watched in awe as his two early heroes, James Otis and Oxenbridge Thacher (1719–1765), protested the unconstitutionality of the general search warrants used by the Customs officers and law officers against colonial merchants; then, he famously recalled, "the child independence was born"(J. Adams and Tudor, 1819: 244–247). The legal challenge failed, but in Adams's view Otis and Thacher had started the intellectual process of questioning colonial subordination.

The octogenarian Adams might easily be forgiven for self-vindication, fearing, as he long had, that he would soon be forgotten. But Adams's efforts to recapture the vitality of the Revolution and to inspire future generations were a serious intellectual undertaking. His correspondence with Tudor tackled the ability of a participant in great events to write their history. And he supplied Tudor and others with advice and information about the revolutionary generation.

In 1760, the contest to succeed Stephen Sewall (1702–1760) as Massachusetts chief justice had unleashed a bitter partisan dispute, shaping the political landscape in which Adams matured. Adams was drawn towards James Otis Jr., whose father's ambitions for the vacant chair were thwarted when Governor Francis Bernard (1712–1779) fixed it for his lieutenant governor, Thomas Hutchinson (1711–1780). Jonathan Sewall turned against the Otises (according to the elderly Adams) because of the failure of the influential Colonel James Otis Sr. to aid Sewall in a family quest. What turned the Otises and the Whigs against Hutchinson (Adams continued) was Hutchinson's grasping for office, power, and status. Hutchinson (Adams fulminated) had seduced friends like Sewall, for which Adams would not forgive him while acknowledging his abilities (J. Adams and Tudor, 1819: iv). Adams's hatred of Hutchinson, a constant in his political career, showed his "central personality characteristics" molding his writing thence forward (Bailyn, 1992: 3–21).

But Adams's friend Sewall was a willing accomplice in defending both Hutchinson and Bernard from Otis's fusillade against the administration in the Boston newspapers. Adams took a while to accept that at the time. Adams was not oblivious to what was happening in the province, but blind to Sewall's predatory attempts to bring him over to the government side. Sewall's first foray into political writing as "J" in the *Boston Evening-Post* (Feb. 14, 1763), prompted Adams's first-ever piece on March 14 in the same paper.

Writing as "Humphrey Ploughjogger," Adams fabricated a faux-rustic dialect in humorous phonetic spelling to mock the pretensions of those "grate" men who thoughtlessly encouraged factionalism. It was a wryly simplistic performance, whose ideas came from no dim-witted ploughman (resurrected by Adams for five further public letters). Adams's targets were: Congregational and Anglican controversialists at odds over Anglican pressure for an American episcopate; partisanship envenomed by rival supporters of James Otis and Thomas Hutchinson; and the merits of planting hemp (for rope not dope). The task of replying to Sewall, unmistakably identified by Adams as "J" (it has been suggested), was not Adams's prime consideration: chastising and re-educating the province's entire political leadership was – including Otis as well as Hutchinson (Saltman, 1980: 125–135; R.J. Taylor et al., 1977–: 58–62). "Humphrey Ploughjogger" was thus an early demonstration of Adams's independent political thinking, yet shortly gravitating to Otis not Sewall. However, his relationships with Sewall, Otis, and other friends are far more complex and intriguing than this brief summary can possibly convey. The homage to Otis in *Novanglus* and in his later writings would be far from what Adams was thinking politically in 1763. Adams's early essays were a sincere plea for nonpartisanship, believing the most elusive political ideal of the age to be within the grasp of a society governed by the rule of law where reason negated passions. Otis, however, confounded everyone, Adams included, with his passionate admonitions on corruption and tyranny and stirring exhortations on liberty: at the time perhaps, the idealist in Adams distrusted the flame of passion burning so brightly in Otis.

3.3 The Stamp Act Crisis, 1765–1766

At first, Adams was largely a spectator to the great events that were unfolding around him. He had (Ferling concludes) only a "minor and inconspicuous" role (1992: 42) in the opposition movement to the Stamp Act and other British colonial policies (Ferling, 1992: 38–58). Living in Braintree, Adams was detached from the machinations of the Boston Sons of Liberty who were organizing the campaign, though he certainly knew who these men were. Adams's diary and correspondence show his firm embrace of the orthodox Whig position: direct parliamentary taxation was fundamentally unconstitutional if the colonists were to pay taxes without their formal consent. Friends of government such as Sewall urged caution and submission to the Act while the governor and legislature, along with the Massachusetts agents in London, sought its repeal. But the dispute over taxation posed conundrums for Adams and his friends, some legalistic in nature, others wholly political.

As a lawyer, Adams was overtly hostile to mob action such as the Stamp Act riot of August 26, 1765 that destroyed Thomas Hutchinson's mansion house and his invaluable library. Adams's open distaste for crowd action that threatened private property and his inward distrust of what Ferling calls the "netherworld" of Boston politics explain why he did not "fully commit himself" to the protest movement (Ferling, 1992: 49). Adams had praised the unity of purpose and moral authority behind the milder riot of August 14, which forced the resignation of the stamp distributor (as he did similar such actions throughout the colonies). Adams was especially wary of Samuel Adams (1722–1803), who had emerged as a local leader coordinating protests in the street and town meeting. While he appreciated his cousin's activism, he feared his excesses would push the colonies into conflict with Britain. John Adams did not question Samuel Adams for engineering disputes with the governors over imperial authority, or his suspected advocacy of independence; he lacked the moral weight to challenge Samuel, even if he had wished to. It took him ten years to share Samuel's radicalism.

Adams's first public action during the Stamp Act dispute firmly established his credentials as a moderate Whig. Adams drafted Braintree's instructions to its representative in the provincial assembly; approved on September 25, the instructions protested unconstitutionality of parliamentary taxation and – of particular interest to a lawyer – complained about the Act being enforceable in the juryless courts of Admiralty (R.J. Taylor et al., 1977–: 129–143).

The ecumenism of the Whigs' lists of grievances is manifest in some of the most polished essays that Adams ever produced – in what comprises his second public intervention. In four articles printed in the *Boston Gazette* between August 12 and October 21 (known today as *A Dissertation on the Canon and Feudal Law*), Adams deftly linked the Congregationalists' longstanding objections to an American episcopacy to widespread popular concerns about the Stamp Act. Adams railed at "Ignorance and Inconsideration" – which, he said, John Tillotson (the archbishop of Canterbury most acceptable to the Puritans), termed the "Ruin of Mankind." Adams conscripted the age of reason to eradicate absolutism and its servants: "the Papists, the Jacobites, and Tyrants who wouldst burden the colonists with taxes and Church of England bishops." Conflating religious liberty with political liberty ably demonstrated Adams's skill as a polemicist (Bailyn, 1967: 97–99), while the quirky historicism of the *Dissertation* became a trademark of Adams's political writing. The essays on the canon and feudal law (he declared much later), though sketched in draft, were "written at Random weekly without any preconceived Plan, printed in the Newspapers, without Correction." (R.J. Taylor et al., 1977–: 104). This quick-fire composition served Adams well in the future, right up to *Novanglus*, produced as a weekly series. Writing for Adams was often a hurried affair, whose ideas usually had had a long gestation.

Adams's third public act concerned a more complicated issue. Appointed counsel for the town of Boston, along with his legal mentors James Otis and Jeremiah Gridley (1706–1767), Adams appeared before the governor and council on December 20, 1765 to argue that officials in the province law courts should conduct public business without using stamped papers. The offices had been closed since the day the Stamp Act had taken effect (Nov. 1), for the governor (according to the counselors) had pointedly refused to direct officials to ignore the requirements of an Act – even though it was manifestly a dead letter. While the counselors' case required officials to act *ex necessitate* it also placed the onus on the governor to resolve the deadlock. He refused. It was two months before the judges themselves resolved a face-saving method of allowing the courts to reopen (Butterfield et al., 1961: 1.267; R.J. Taylor et al., 1977–: 151–153; Coquillette, 1984: 417).

In the interim, Adams, writing as "Clarendon" (*Boston Gazette* Jan. 13–27, 1766, printed in R.J. Taylor et al., 1977–: 155–170) and James Otis, writing independently as "Hampden" (*Boston Gazette*, Dec. 9, 1765–Jan. 27, 1766) both ridiculed arguments from British defenders of the Stamp Act. Otis and Adams wrote with verve and confidence, and Adams enjoyed the venture. They had already rehearsed the more difficult legalistic aspects of the Whig case. Ostensibly, Otis and Adams were replying to a series of essays penned by one "William Pym" for the *London Public Ledger* the previous summer. The mysterious Pym may have been a pseudonym, though the most likely living author was William Pym (1722–1788), a Bedfordshire landowner.

Adams relished the opportunity to consider the Stamp Act crisis in the context of English history. His pseudonym derived from Edward Hyde, first earl of Clarendon (1609–1674), a monarchist and popular historian of what his side termed the Great Rebellion. What might seem an odd choice was adroitly managed: where "Hampden" recalled anti-monarchical rebellion, Adams's "Clarendon" (we learn) found in the writing of history a release of sorts to explain his own political tergiversations, having abandoned the Parliamentarian side early on to preserve the institution of monarchy (only to flee Restoration England to escape a treason charge). Clarendon was exhumed by Adams to warn New Englanders of present England's indifference to the English past: and with the weight of history on their side who might gainsay the Americans' claims to embrace the rights of Englishmen?

History in Adams's hands thus provided both precedent and justification for popular rebellion against tyranny. "You of all mankind," "Clarendon" addresses Pym in the first letter, "should have been the last, to be hired by a minister to defend or excuse such taxes and such courts" as the stamp tax and the admiralty courts. (This implied Pym was another seventeenth-century polemicist: the parliamentarian John Pym.) By the third letter, Clarendon was explaining the English constitution with its "grand division of constitutional powers" and firmly taking the side of its democratical elements. Adams's lifelong fascination with constitutional history and constitution-making had certainly taken root, as had his attachment to popular politics. "Clarendon" left his readers with an inspiring plea for liberty and democracy (as then understood):

> The constitution is not grounded on "the enormous faith of millions made for one." It stands not on the supposition that kings are the favourites of heaven; that their power is more divine than the power of the people, and unlimited but by their own will and discretion. It is not built on the doctrine that a few nobles or rich commons have a right to inherit the earth, and all the blessings and pleasures of it: and that the multitude, the million, the populace, the vulgar, the mob, the herd and the rabble, as the great always delight to call them, have no rights at all, and were made only for their use, to be robbed and butchered at their pleasure. No, it stands upon this principle, that the meanest and lowest of the people, are, by the unalterable indefeasible laws of God and nature, as well intitled to the benefit of the air to breathe, light to see, food to eat, and clothes to wear, as the nobles or the king. All men are born equal: and the drift of the British constitution is to preserve as much of this equality, as is compatible with the people's security against foreign invasions and domestic usurpation. It is upon these fundamental principles, that popular power was placed as essential in the constitution of the legislature; and the constitution would be as compleat without a kingly as without a popular power. (R.J. Taylor et al., 1977–: 167–168)

"All men are born equal:" Charles de Montesquieu, in *De l'esprit des lois* (1748), had famously supposed that the equality of mankind could only truly exist in a state of nature – a time before government and society – but that it was the function and purpose of the law to recover as much of that equality as possible from the clutches of the governments mankind had created. While John Adams hedged his bets as to how much liberty he and his neighbors derived from natural law, he obligingly confirmed that the "drift" of British constitutional history was to preserve popular rights from further encroachment. This was the most conservative of "Clarendon"'s precepts: Adams's talk of egalitarianism and popular power, however, sounded as radical as it was possible to be in 1766. (Perhaps only Otis could have matched the panache with which Adams delivered his case.)

Adams's writings put him left of center in the spectrum of political opinion. In spring 1766, provincial elections created a major realignment effectively marginalizing the friends of government as a political force. There was little open support for British policies, but few colonists thought the governor could represent their grievances to London. They had even less confidence in the British government's willingness to listen, although the Stamp Act was repealed in March (Nicolson, 2001: 139–166). The politics of protest seemed the most effective way of influencing British policymakers, as Adams – for all his distrust of the mob – seems to have accepted (F. Anderson, 2000: 684–686). But the litmus test of radicalism was to become an active member of the movement – in some official capacity – and several years elapsed before Adams did that.

3.4 The Imperial Crisis, 1768–1774

In April 1768, Adams (temporarily) moved his family from Braintree to Boston. Living at the epicenter of the imperial crisis, the Adamses remained committed supporters of the Whig opposition, but John (according to Ferling) was obliged to "play a discreet role" in the movement between 1766 and 1770 (Ferling, 1992: 60). When the Townshend Acts reignited the dispute about Parliament's authority to tax, Adams greased wheels behind the scenes. He declined any leadership role or public office – whatever his yearnings – largely on account of his substantial professional commitments and personal concerns about crowd action (Ferling, 1992: 53–63).

Of all his encounters with Sewall, Adams's description of their discussion of the governor's offer of a Crown office has attracted most attention. We know, in sum, what was discussed, how the discussion was conducted, what it meant to Adams – but not when the meeting actually took place (M. Smith, 1906: 99–101; Ferling, 1992: 60–61; McCullough, 2001: 65). Adams's *Autobiography* suggests a mid-summer meeting (at least four weeks after the introduction of the first of the Townshend Acts on June 27)

Sewall, by then, had been attorney general for about six months and was still advocate general of the Vice Admiralty court; rapidly embroiled in the brouhaha surrounding the seizure of John Hancock's sloop *Liberty* on June 10 and unenviably saddled with compiling evidence of the townsfolk's treasonable proceedings. He came to dinner bearing the offer that Adams should replace him as advocate general. Sewall and Bernard probably discussed bringing in Adams in early July. But it was an offer Adams could not accept: his first duty would have been to prosecute Hancock with *in rem* libels against his property, while Sewall brought *in personam* libels against the person. Sewall, moreover, was threatening to resign from both offices, following a dispute with the American Board of Customs Commissioners – which would have left John Adams as the province's principal Crown lawyer.

That Adams was not for turning, both Sewall and Bernard well knew. Sewall promised the governor's toleration of his Whiggish views with Adams "at full Liberty to entertain my own Opinions." These were indeed empty words, as Adams would have realized (but did not say) since as advocate general, duty-bound to enforce the law, the people of Massachusetts would judge whether he was acting and thinking independently; and he could anticipate their judgments all too well. These many "restraints and Obligations" (he did not specify in relation to which side, but meant both) were such that, in all truth, "I could not in honor or Conscience Accept it" (Butterfield et al., 1961: 1.288). Three weeks later, Sewall called again; the answer was still the same.

Hancock's trial, which opened on November 28, 1768, and ran through to March 25, 1769, was sensationalized by the realization that the prosecution stood to gain enormously from any conviction. Hancock was facing penalties of £9000; Sewall, as prosecutor, was due one-third of any seizures and fines, with the governor and the Crown taking another third each. Adams was hired by Hancock. The Crown's failure to procure sufficient and convincing testimony of Hancock's smuggling and other crimes led to the trial's abandonment, but Adams had to persuade his adversary (in the absence of a jury) of its hopelessness.

Facing Sewall across the Vice Admiralty court room on February 24, Adams set out to destroy the credibility of a "key" Crown witness with another witness to testify that the key witness had committed a "heinous crime." While the judge refused to admit Adams's witness, it would have been abundantly clear to Sewall that the prosecution case – at this late hour – was seriously flawed. Adams's surviving legal papers, moreover, offer up in single draft a tantalizing glimpse of his probable arguments. Although he constructed a defense on technicalities and legal procedure, the Ciceronian flourishes, and profusion of political ideas were reminiscent of Otis's finest hour contesting the writs of assistance (Wroth and Zobel, 1965: 2.173–210), as his legal editors claim:

> [*Adams's*] argument in *Sewall v. Hancock* is ... a subtle and accomplished piece of craftsmanship. Here, political theory is manipulated within a legal framework in such a way that the case is presented both at the level of the court room and at the level of the public forum in which the broader constitutional issues are discussed. Whatever the purpose for which it was written, the argument deserves recognition as an unfinished contribution to the political literature of its time. (Wroth and Zobel, 1965: 2.193)

Adams had to remind his countrymen that Hancock had "never consented" to the Navigation Acts; that he had "never voted for it" or given his "consent" to any such trade law ... and that to oppose it he now risked everything, for "Construction has made Treasons where the law has made none": "Clarendon" had delivered much the same peroration when reminding Sewall's "Philanthrop" of what happened when Kings Jemmy and Charley had rejected criticism from their own peoples; how Adams must have relished being able to goad Sewall once more about the tyranny of kings, this time in a king's court and under the king's arms (Wroth and Zobel, 1965: 2.198–199).

On August 14, 1769, when 350 Sons of Liberty dined to celebrate their unity on the anniversary of the first Stamp Act riot, Adams was utterly at ease as an epicurean "cultivating the Sensations of Freedom" (Butterfield et al., 1961: 1.341). Adams had distinguished himself as a principled but cautious Whig, more realist than idealist. The previous May, he authored instructions for Boston's representatives in the General Court, articulating the townspeople's deep-seated resentment of the British soldiers sent to Boston the previous autumn as a pseudo-police force to protect officials. Yet politics, he determined, would not prevent him representing British soldiers against the Crown should justice require it, nor defending them from the popular furies. He proved a friend of the people – of ordinary people – whether British soldiers facing a murder charge or Massachusetts neighbors facing murderous soldiers. Adams was supremely aware of the stakes in everything he ever risked – his own family, his own reputation, and his meritocratic ideals. His commitment to principle enlivened all he did, and his guiding principle was the rule of law.

He agreed to represent Captain Thomas Preston and the British soldiers charged with murder after the Boston Massacre of March 5, 1770. Preston's trial, *Rex v Preston*, took place between October 24 and 30; that of the soldiers, *Rex v Wemms et al.*, between November 27 and December 4.[1] Was Adams persuaded to take the case by the promise of political office? The supposition rests on the not unreasonable assumption that Boston's radicals expected easy convictions, but with the defense having so respected a barrister as Adams they might exculpate themselves from future accusations of having intimidated judge and jury. In any event, Adams's brilliant defense achieved not-guilty verdicts for six defendants and their commanding officer, and reduced manslaughter convictions for two others (Ferling, 1992: 67–70).

Adams's greatest case unavoidably brought him into the political arena. His performance irritated those radicals hoping for retribution. In saving the soldiers' lives and the province's reputation Adams cut a statesman-like figure. In June 1770, he was elected to the province legislature (with a staggering 418 out of the 536 votes cast) as a substitute for one of Boston's representatives who had been elected to the governor's council.

Adams subsequently had a formative influence in advancing the Patriot case for colonial legislative independence within the British empire. Early in 1773, Adams conducted vigorous newspaper joust with councilor William Brattle (1706–1776) attacking proposed Crown salaries for colonial judges, and while arguing for judicial independence bolstered the Patriot case for legislative independence from Britain. The debate "galvanized" Adams into political action (Ferling, 1992: 78–79) when during 1773 he helped to draft, with Samuel Adams and Joseph Hawley (1723–1788), a series of position papers for the House of Representatives. Governor Hutchinson had protested that in dismantling royal prerogatives and claiming exemption from parliamentary authority, Whigs were creating a constitutional paradox, an *imperium in imperio*; Parliament's legislative authority was supreme, he insisted. The House claimed that the Province Charter of 1691 conferred legislative sovereignty on the colonies (Lord and Calhoon, 1969: 739). All of this helped to establish Adams's reputation as an intellectual heavyweight of the Whig side. On these ideological poles *Massachusettensis* and *Novanglus* were subsequently to pin their flags.

Adams missed the Boston Tea Party of December 16 (being out of town on legal business) and endorsed its resistance to what Americans were calling British "tyranny." That ideological commitment was demonstrated when the ministry of Lord North answered the destruction of £9,000 worth of tea with the Draconian Coercive Acts, closing Boston harbor with intent to reduce the provincial government to a cipher of the Crown. As J.P. Reid has shown (1977), the "conditions of law" in Massachusetts, unlike Ireland, simply did not allow the British to compel obedience. Yet this was the direction that British policy seemed to be taking. As Reid argues convincingly, there was no better demonstration of Parliament's power to regulate the empire than the Port Act and the Massachusetts Government Act (Reid, 1993: 9–26). Lord North, as *Novanglus* would show, had painted for Americans a terrible future within the British empire: that of conquered, subjugated provinces. In September 1774, Adams was one of four Massachusetts delegates dispatched to the first Continental Congress at Philadelphia, to organize inter-colonial cooperation. When he returned in December, he learned that the revolution in Massachusetts had begun without him: for over the late summer and autumn, the province's Patriots had successfully dismantled or disabled royal institutions outside of

Boston. When the British started fortifying Boston, John and Abigail Adams resigned themselves to the inevitability of conflict between General Thomas Gage's four thousand British Regulars and the thousands of ill-armed but determined volunteers of the colonial militia who moved to surround the town.

3.5 Novanglus

All in all, the decade before the Revolutionary War had been a personally fulfilling time for John Adams and his family. Even so, the disputation between the American colonies and Britain worried them no less than their Massachusetts neighbors. Adams's political lessons – whether in town meetings, in law courts, in the Massachusetts legislature, or at the Continental Congress – radicalized him. Ferling (1992: 80–85) suggests that by the summer of 1773, John Adams was starting to view the imperial crisis from Samuel Adams's vantage point, concluding that his cousin had been right – there *was* a conspiracy to deprive the colonists of their rights and liberties; in such circumstances, the colonists were fully entitled to rebel. Coming to terms with Samuel was not the last of John's personal tussles with the heroes of the Revolutionary generation – his commemoration of Otis and Sewall would be that – but it underlined how much Adams supposed that he himself was "exceptional" and how few others measured up to his standards (Pencak, 2001: 65). But while Samuel Adams was already committed to independence; John Adams was not. Perhaps it was not Samuel who converted John to the idea of revolution, so much as the writing of *Novanglus.*

On January 23, 1775, John Adams began a series of essays for the *Boston Gazette* – "To the Inhabitants of the Colony of Massachusetts Bay" – signed "Novanglus" (the New Englander). Conceived originally as a reply to the Loyalist letters by *Massachusettensis*, which denounced the drift to war, Adams wrote *Novanglus* on the mistaken assumption that "Massachusettensis" was his erstwhile friend, Jonathan Sewall (1729–1796), the king's attorney general. (It was in fact another lawyer, Daniel Leonard.) Adams's twelve published essays ranged widely over history, law, government, and politics and tackled abstruse and convoluted constitutional questions regarding the imperial–colonial relationship.

The central ideological message of *Novanglus* was that the colonists were combating a British and Loyalist conspiracy to deprive them of their rights and liberties (beginning with Letter II). Adams did not yet advocate independence, and in keeping with mainstream colonial aspirations envisaged rolling back a decade of colonial policies; even so, he proposed a much-altered constitutional relationship with the mother country indicative of revolutionary thinking, with power and authority centered on colonial rather than royal institutions. Adams, in short, made a compelling case for colonial autonomy under British monarchy drawing in depth on British constitutional law and the histories of England, Wales, Ireland, and Scotland (Letters VI–XII). While constructing compelling, if sometimes disjointed and abstruse, essays justifying colonial resistance, Adams ended up justifying revolution to himself. Adams's personal dilemma was that of colonial Americans writ large: whither independence and at what cost? He was profoundly disturbed by the twin specters of rebellion and civil war (Letter III onwards). But these nightmares he banished with the writing of *Novanglus*.[2] In one article reviewing Adams's political career, the editor of the *Papers of John Adams* concluded that

> … in their complexity and fullness they [*Novanglus*] served more to satisfy the intellectual needs of Adams than to advance an argument with the general public. The point is this: had Adams sought with a display of legal learning to conceal a desire for independence, for separation, as Massachusettensis charged against him and the Whigs generally, Adams need not have gone to such lengths. Rather, he was sincerely concerned with the rigor of his argument and could honestly deny, as he did twice in the letters, that an independent republic was his goal …. He wanted what he could justify – a commonwealth of states under the king. (R.J. Taylor et al., 1977–: 66–67)

The *Novanglus* series might have continued (the last appeared on April 17) if military hostilities had not commenced at Lexington and Concord on April 19, and in the following twelve months Adams emerged a firm advocate of American independence. He had long bypassed conservative Patriots like John Dickinson who shrank from urging the kind of military preparations that Massachusetts had taken (Knollenberg, 1963). Adams embraced revolution after concluding, as John Ferling argues, that independence from Britain was the only viable course of collective political action if Americans were to enjoy liberty to the full (Ferling, 1992: 154–155). In cultural terms, Adams's embrace of American independence did not entail a whole new set of values but rather the adaptation of familiar mores and a determination to resist unnecessary innovation. Yet independence also entailed new ways of thinking about government, and of how innovation would change society and people's behavior. It repudiated some of history's legacies – as when Adams, in *Novanglus*, came to the conclusion that the heirs of English liberty in London were doing their level best to corrupt the present. John Adams, as one historian put it, firmly belonged in the "cerebral wing" of the revolutionaries' camp (Grant, 2005: 5). Adams's revolutionism was not so much the product of a personal rebellion against authoritarianism or conformity, but the product of an honest inquiring mind and robust personality. He was neither the first nor the last intellectual to convert himself to the idea and prospect of revolution, though few others have left such a complete documentary record of their travails.

Notes

1 The trial proceedings are in Wroth and Zobel (1965), vol. 3; the best account is Zobel (1970: 241–294).

2 For *Massachusettensis* and Loyalist ideology see Nelson (1961: 69–72); Calhoon (1973: 90); Upton (1977); Potter (1983: passim). For *Novanglus* and revolutionary ideology see A.D. Morse, (1899: 298–299); G.S. Wood (1966: 4–5); Bailyn (1967, passim); P. Shaw (1976: 83–88); Coquillette (1984: 359–418). The best summary of the debate is R.J. Taylor et al. (1977–: 2.216–226).

Further Reading

While it is daunting for any scholar to contemplate writing about any one of the Founding Fathers, the resources available for studying John Adams are simply unmatched in their quantity and quality. John Adams has left more personal and public papers than any other eighteenth-century American. The best place to start an investigation of Adams's pre-Revolution politics is the first volume of the *Papers of John Adams* (R.J. Taylor et al., 1977–) and the first volume of his *Diary and Autobiography* (Butterfield et al., 1961). The quality of editorial work is unsurpassed and the printed documents are accompanied by authoritative commentaries that link Adams's writings to his life and times. Using the *Legal Papers* requires some prior awareness of legal procedure (and the editors do their best to guide readers). Ferling's biography is strong on detail but Ellis and McCullough will together provide a profile of the man and his personality (Ferling, 1992; J.J. Ellis, 1993; McCullough, 2001). There is also a useful, if somewhat dated, bibliographical guide (Ferling, 1994b). The principal manuscript collection is the *Adams Family Papers* at the Massachusetts Historical Society (the microfilm edition is a more convenient way to read many of the papers, but only a handful of research libraries have it). The new digital edition of the *Adams Family Papers* is freely available via the internet (http://www.masshist.org/publications/) and can be easily searched via the Online Adams Catalogue launched in 2011.

Chapter Four

John Adams in the Continental Congress

Karen N. Barzilay

John Adams left Boston for the First Continental Congress in the summer of 1774 as a thirty-eight year old provincial lawyer. His name, unlike that of his distant cousin, Samuel, was unknown elsewhere in the American colonies and abroad. He left New England and crossed into foreign provinces wanting only to restore the structure and traditions of the Massachusetts government that he had known as a child. The next four years radically changed John Adams's life, keeping him from his young family for extended periods of time but giving him a sense of purpose and importance that defined him and fulfilled his longing for a place in history. By the time Adams sailed for France in February 1778, he had become one of the leading statesmen of the Continental Congress and a man of national renown. His career and continental reputation grew up alongside the new nation he helped to create, intertwined with its successes and failures.

As historian Richard Ryerson has rightly pointed out, Adams's service in the Continental Congress has been the least controversial part of his long and illustrious career. Scholars have almost universally agreed that, whatever Adams's weaknesses as a diplomat or president, as a congressman he was highly effective – brilliant, even – and made an invaluable contribution to the eventual success of the American Revolution. Hindsight reveals that his judgment was usually accurate during his years in Congress; he recognized the wisdom of appointing George Washington commander-in-chief of the Continental Army, the importance of forming new state constitutions and building an American navy, and the timeliness of declaring independence in the summer of 1776 (Ryerson, 2001: 10–11). Serving on dozens

A Companion to John Adams and John Quincy Adams, First Edition.
Edited by David Waldstreicher.

of congressional committees, Adams also proved exceptionally efficient and skilled at administrative work in the continental government. He became one of the most vocal and courageous contributors to congressional debate and gained a reputation for his almost unparalleled learning and expertise in history, government, and the law. Interestingly, this widespread recognition of Adams's critical contribution to the Continental Congress stands at odds with the way Adams frequently has been characterized by historians. At times it is difficult to reconcile Adams's skill as a political strategist with scholarly portrayals of Adams as neurotic, mercurial, and tactless.

Ironically, because Adams's time in Congress has generated so little debate among historians, comparatively little has been said about it – in spite of the fact that it also happens to be one of the best-documented portions of Adams's life. During these years Adams frequently kept a diary and he wrote lengthy and candid letters to a number of correspondents, especially his wife, Abigail, and friend James Warren. His notes of debates taken at the First Continental Congress provide some of the only information historians have as to what occurred inside Carpenters' Hall, that gathering's meeting space. Adams also commented at length on his time in Congress when later writing his autobiography, although his recollections are sometimes inaccurate. The success of Adams and his allies in the Continental Congress was so absolute that the proceedings largely have gone unexamined (Ryerson, 2001: 10–11).

4.1 First Continental Congress

When John Adams heard in May 1774 that the port of Boston had been closed by the Coercive Acts – laws designed to punish the people of Massachusetts for dumping over three hundred crates of tea into Boston Harbor – he felt strangely elated. Writing to Abigail from Boston, he assured her, "Don't imagine from all this that I am in the Dumps. Far otherwise, I can truly say, that I have felt more Spirits and Activity, since the Arrival of this News, than I had done before for years" (Butterfield et al., 1963: 1.107). The Port Bill infused Adams with a sense of purpose and direction that energized him. The rest of the Revolution, as it unfolded, likewise continued to provide him with an outlet for his passions, intellect, and ambition.

The Massachusetts legislature elected Adams to the First Continental Congress on June 17, 1774, along with Samuel Adams, fellow attorney Robert Treat Paine, Thomas Cushing, Speaker of the provincial assembly, and merchant James Bowdoin, who declined to serve due to illness in his family. John Adams approached the gathering – at the time simply called a General Congress – as the diplomatic meeting that it was. He envisioned the Congress as a convention of deputies from distinct provinces: "I view, the Assembly … as I do, the Court of Ariopagus, the Council of the Amphyctions, a Conclave, a Sanhedrim, A Divan, I know not what" (Butterfield et al., 1961: 2.99). It was in his mind akin to ancient councils composed of powerful, wise men – representatives from confederated states coming together periodically to settle differences and confront shared problems. Though he expressed a hope that it would meet annually, he had no idea that the Congress eventually would become the permanent legislature of a new and independent nation.

Drawing a parallel to these historic councils, Adams revealed the high expectations he brought with him to Philadelphia in the late summer of 1774. He dreaded the idea that the Congress might disappoint the people of his province and fail to rise to the occasion, declaring that "When Demosthenes, (God forgive the Vanity of recollecting his Example) went Ambassador from Athens to the other States of Greece, to excite a Confederacy against Phillip, he did not go to propose a Non Importation or Non Consumption Agreement. !-!-!" (Butterfield et al., 1961: 2.109). Adams wondered about what the Congress might be capable of if Demosthenes and other historical figures he venerated – Cicero, Sully, Cecil – were there. Perhaps the caliber of men sent from the other American colonies would be as exceptional. He imagined joining a group of learned and sophisticated delegates to whom the Massachusetts' delegation would be "deficient in Genius, in Education, in Travel, in Fortune – in every Thing" (*D&A*: 2.97). In the weeks before his departure, Adams worried about his lack of familiarity with British and American leaders and the economics of the various provinces, lamenting "I have not that minute and accurate Knowledge … which an American Senator ought to have" (Butterfield et al., 1961: 2.109). Feeling unequal to the task, he nonetheless hoped "that We shall conduct our Embassy in such a manner as to merit the Approbation of our Country" (Butterfield et al., 1963: 1.158).

The truth was, Adams had comparatively little political experience compared to most of his fellow delegates from elsewhere in the provinces. While older congressmen such as Stephen Hopkins of Rhode Island or Richard Bland of Virginia had served in the governments of their respective colonies for several decades by 1774, Adams had served for less than a year in the Massachusetts House of Representatives. A number of the more eminent men attending the Congress, even young Edward Rutledge of South Carolina, had spent time in England at grammar schools or studying law at the Inns of Court. Most of the congressmen were extravagantly wealthy compared to Adams, the Southerners in particular owning huge plantations and hundreds of slaves. John Adams, although one of the most accomplished and highly respected lawyers in Massachusetts, was nonetheless the product of a provincial world that was far less genteel.

In other ways, however, Adams's anxiety prior to Congress was unfounded. Much of the wealth he did have was tied up in books – he confessed that he was "a little inclined to be extravagant, in that kind of Entertainment" – legal and historical texts that he had studied with care. By the early 1770s he was looking to buy from booksellers in London, as soon as they came out, "every Book and Pamphlet, of Reputation, upon the subjects of Law and Government" (Butterfield et al., 1963: 1.75). Adams, seeking to build his reputation as a lawyer "of distinguished Genius," forced himself to read dense, challenging texts about history, science, and law in Greek and Latin that few if any of his peers attempted to master (*D&A*: 1.78). Through this independent study, Adams's legal knowledge eventually went well beyond that of the average provincial lawyer. Historian C. Bradley Thompson (1998: xiii) claims that even Thomas Jefferson and James Madison were inferior to Adams in the extent of their reading and thinking about political science and constitutional theory. So although lacking in wealth, formal education, and political experience, Adams brought to Congress other strengths. Well-read and scholarly, Adams's exceptional legal mind – combined with his realistic approach to problems, deep commitment to the American cause, and willingness to work hard – ultimately made him one of the most valuable members of the Continental Congress.

The four Massachusetts delegates to the First Continental Congress gathered in Boston amidst a large crowd the morning of August 10, departing the city from Thomas Cushing's house in a coach drawn by four horses and accompanied by several servants (*D&A*: 2.97–98). The men embarked on a nineteen-day journey through Connecticut, New York, and New Jersey, where they met with local leaders and did some sightseeing. Once they left New England, Adams was in entirely unfamiliar territory, having traveled earlier in his life only as far as New Haven. Having completed a report for the General Court earlier that year on an ongoing boundary dispute between Massachusetts and New York, Adams crossed into what was from his perspective foreign territory, meeting for the first time prominent leaders from the Middle Colonies.

A group of local gentlemen and fellow congressmen met the Massachusetts delegation upon their arrival in Philadelphia. Benjamin Rush, who was to be Adams's lifelong friend, accompanied Adams and Robert Treat Paine in their coach as it traveled into the city that day. Rush would remember that Adams's "dress and manners were at that time plain, and his conversation cold and reserved." Adams was eager for information, Rush recalled, asking "many questions relative to the state of public opinion upon politicks, and the characters of the most active citizens on both sides of the controversy" (Corner, 1948: 110). The group proceeded to the genteel City Tavern to socialize before the Massachusetts delegation settled in rented rooms at Sarah Yard's stone boarding-house, conveniently located across the street. Apart from several days early on at a different boarding-house on Arch Street, these would be John Adams's lodgings in Philadelphia until the spring of 1777; he remembered in his autobiography that the place "was by some Complimented with the Title of Head Quarters, but by Mr. Richard Henry Lee, more decently called Liberty Hall" (*D&A*: 3.310).

During these early days in Philadelphia, Adams and the rest of the Massachusetts delegation spent considerable time with leaders of the opposition movement in Pennsylvania, particularly the young and wealthy merchant Thomas Mifflin – later Washington's chief aide-de-camp. It was Mifflin who gave the men from Massachusetts their first tour of Philadelphia the day after their arrival and hosted the men in his "grand, spacious, and elegant House" for an introductory meeting with soon-to-be secretary of the Congress, Charles Thomson. "This Charles Thompson is the Sam. Adams of Phyladelphia – the Life of the Cause of Liberty, they say," Adams noted in his diary (*D&A*: 2.115). Because of the leisurely pace of the First Continental Congress, Adams had ample time to form judgments in "out-of-doors" settings about fellow delegates' abilities, political positions, and personalities. Early on, Adams spent time with men like Thomas Lynch of South Carolina and Richard Henry Lee of Virginia, whom Adams called a "masterly Man" and "deep thinker" (*D&A*: 2.120). From these early conversations with Lee grew the strong personal and political alliance between the Adamses and the Virginian that eventually became known as the Lee–Adams junto.

With Benjamin Franklin still in England, John Dickinson was the only man Adams met in Philadelphia in 1774 who had a truly continental reputation. Something of a celebrity because of his widely reprinted "Farmer's Letters," written in the late 1760s, Dickinson's influence at the First Continental Congress was considerable in spite of the fact that he was not technically a delegate until October 17, about a week before the Congress adjourned. Adams was familiar with Dickinson's writings and at first seemed impressed by the refined, well-educated, and erudite "Farmer," calling him "very ingenious, as well as agreable" (*D&A*: 2.133). However, after a local election in October led to Dickinson joining Pennsylvania's congressional delegation, Adams grew disillusioned; probably in reaction to Dickinson's conciliatory revision of a petition to the king, Adams now criticized him as being too "delicate, and timid" (*D&A*: 2.157). Their relationship would continue to deteriorate at the Second Continental Congress, culminating in their leadership of opposing factions during the debates surrounding independence.

The First Continental Congress met for a little over seven weeks starting in early September 1774. Adams took notes on some of the debates he witnessed during the meeting and, because of the delegates' pledge to keep the proceedings secret, these are some of the only accounts historians have of what happened. He tended to record exactly what was said, and by whom, seemingly without interjecting his own opinion either in writing or on the congressional floor. In fact, it appears from extant documents that the Massachusetts delegates – John Adams included – kept a deliberately low profile at this Congress. In part, this may have been due to the feelings of inferiority that Adams expressed before joining the Congress; it also was a result of his status within the Massachusetts delegation. Although his role would expand markedly at the Second Continental Congress, in 1774 John Adams remained very much a junior delegate from his province. That year, according to former Massachusetts governor Thomas Hutchinson, King George III had reportedly heard of Samuel Adams but not of John; as late as 1778, when Adams arrived in France, people abroad still confused him with "the famous Adams" (Hutchinson, 1884–1886: 1.163; Morris, 1973: 72–73). Samuel Adams was older, better known throughout the continent, and certainly the more influential at the First Continental Congress.

However, the delegates from Massachusetts also played an outwardly passive role at the First Continental Congress for political reasons. Coming from an occupied city, their port blocked and local governments crippled by the Coercive Acts, the men from Boston urgently needed the help and support of the other colonies to deal with an increasingly volatile situation. At the same time, they confronted men facing far less dire circumstances with much more to lose – delegates who in many cases did not trust New England in the first place. Thought to be from a colony of "levellers" and troublemakers, the men from Massachusetts struggled to soften others' long-held stereotypes about the region. As Adams told William Tudor: "We have had numberless Prejudices to remove here. We have been obliged to act, with great Delicacy and Caution. We have been obliged to keep ourselves out of Sight, and to feel Pulses, and Sound the Depths – to insinuate our Sentiments, Designs, and Desires by means of other Persons, Sometimes of one Province, and Sometimes of another" (Butterfield et al., 1961: 2.177). Sectional jealousies and bias persisted – as late as April 1776, Carter Braxton argued that New Englanders eschewed reconciliation, wishing only to embrace their "darling Democracy" – but to some degree the Massachusetts delegates' efforts paid off (P.H. Smith, 1976–2000: 3.522). By the fall of 1774, Adams and the rest of his province's delegation had overturned pernicious stereotypes of Massachusetts enough to earn the other colonies' support for the strongly worded Suffolk Resolves and their participation in non-importation and non-exportation pacts to be enforced by a Continental Association.

John Adams served on several committees while attending the First Continental Congress. Named to the committee to prepare an address to the king, Adams was not actively involved in its drafting. His most important assignment was to represent Massachusetts, along with Samuel, on the committee to draft a statement of the colonies' rights and how they had been violated. Adams apparently was responsible for the wording of an important section of the final Declaration of Rights and Grievances. Involved in an extended debate regarding the extent of Parliament's authority over the American provinces, members of Congress strongly disagreed about whether to acknowledge Parliament's right to regulate colonial trade. Delegates such as Christopher Gadsden of South Carolina took the extreme position, arguing that a "Right of Legislation in one Case, is a Right in all." As Adams recorded Gadsden's point in his notes, he inserted an unusual editorial comment: "This I deny" (Butterfield et al., 1961: 2.147). In fact, Adams had taken great pains to counter the same argument when it was made by Thomas Hutchinson the previous year, arguing at that time that there was a middle ground in which Parliament could regulate matters affecting the empire while otherwise allowing the provinces self-determination. As a way to placate congressmen on both sides of the debate, Adams suggested framing the regulation of trade as something to which the provinces would consent – not submit. Thus the fourth article of the final document insisted that Americans had the right to govern themselves, but would "cheerfully consent" to Parliamentary regulation of trade (Butterfield et al., 1961: 2.147, 2.149).

After a month of sitting in Congress, Adams had grown weary of the same eloquence and careful deliberation among the delegates that had first impressed him. No longer comparing the Congress to venerable ancient councils, he grumbled, "This Assembly is like no other that ever existed. Every Man in it is a great Man – an orator, a Critick, a statesman, and therefore every Man upon every Question must shew his oratory, his Criticism and his Political Abilities." He added, "I believe if it was moved and seconded that We should come to a Resolution that Three and two make five We should be entertained with Logick and Rhetorick, Law, History, Politicks and Mathematicks, concerning the Subject for two whole Days, and then We should pass the Resolution unanimously in the Affirmative" (Butterfield et al., 1963: 1.166). At first in awe of the wealth and elegance of the homes where he dined, providing in his diary detailed accounts of the lavish meals he ate, by October Adams also had grown tired of formal, extravagant dinners. He complained to Abigail, "I have many Visits to make and receive – much Ceremony to endure, which cannot be avoided, which you know I hate" (Butterfield et al., 1963: 1.165, 1.166). Socially awkward, self-conscious, and unused to the ostentation of Philadelphia's high society, Adams struggled with these social obligations. As his once close friend Jonathan Sewall wrote many years later, Adams was a warm, honest, and generous man, but he was not skilled at small talk (Ferling, 1992: 203). Yet Adams, recognizing the usefulness of social settings in building sympathy and support for Massachusetts, felt he could not decline these neverending invitations.

When Adams finally left Philadelphia in the pouring rain on October 28, 1774, he thought he was saying goodbye for good. "It is not very likely that I shall ever see this Part of the World again," he recorded in his diary (*D&A*: 2.157). The members of Congress had agreed to meet again only if grievances were not redressed by the spring. Perhaps Adams trusted the optimistic view of Richard Henry Lee that the "same ship which carries home the Resolution will bring back the Redress" – that a coordinated and well-enforced trade embargo would lead to the immediate reversal of British policy (*D&A*: 2.120). Or, if the Congress did meet again, perhaps Adams thought another man would take his place. As he had suggested to James Warren before the Congress began, he supported making the Congress an annual event, "sending an entire new set [of delegates] every Year, that all the principal Genius's may go to the University in Rotation – that We may have Politicians in Plenty" (Butterfield et al., 1961: 2.100). Whatever he believed, he could not have known that he would spend more time in Congress over the next several years than he would at home in Massachusetts.

Arriving back in Braintree the second week of November, Adams spent a month with his family before serving in Massachusetts' Provincial Congress for several days in December. Re-elected to the Continental Congress on December 2, he devoted much of the winter to working on a series of newspaper essays he signed "Novanglus" – Latin for New England. These letters, in which he advanced the ideal of a commonwealth of independent provinces united under the king, ran weekly in the *Boston Gazette* from January 23, 1775, until interrupted by the events at Lexington and Concord in April. Writing in response to Daniel Leonard's well-written and persuasive newspaper essays as "Massachusettensis," Adams penned thirteen essays (twelve of which were published) that proved too intellectual, dense, and meandering to be appreciated by anyone but fellow lawyers with a scholarly bent.

Historians' reactions to the *Novanglus* letters have varied, with one scholar calling them "more polemical than profound" (Diggins, 2003: 27), while others have characterized them as important but disorganized and tedious (P. Shaw, 1976: 83–84; J.J. Ellis, 2010: 39). Robert J. Taylor contends (1977: 56–57) that, although Adams's position was not original, he was unique in "supporting his argument with a mind-numbing foray into legal authorities." With close attention to a number of historical sources, the lawyerly Adams sought to explain the history of Parliament's relationship with places such as Ireland, Wales, and Guernsey, establishing precedents for Britain's association with the American colonies. Whatever their weaknesses in style, the *Novanglus* letters are widely recognized as one of the earliest efforts to articulate the position taken by the First Continental Congress, denying Parliament's authority over the American colonies without their consent and arguing that there were constitutional grounds for the parallel sovereignties of Parliament and American provincial governments. Not written for or appreciated by a public audience, they were – unlike those of "Massachusettensis" – not widely reprinted, although English booksellers republished parts of the letters in 1775 and 1784; Adams had the 1775 edition translated into Dutch in 1782 (Butterfield et al., 1961: 2.223–224).

On April 19, 1775, events at Lexington and Concord irrevocably altered the political landscape. Adams later recalled that a few days afterward, he visited the battlefield at Lexington and inspected the army gathered in Cambridge, alarmed at its lack of organization and inadequate provisions (*D&A*: 3.314). On his way home he fell ill with a fever, leaving for Philadelphia in a small carriage instead of riding horseback as he planned. He caught up with the Connecticut and Massachusetts delegations, now including John Hancock, outside of New York. Upon leaving Manhattan with the congressmen from that colony, two hundred members of the militia marched with the delegations along roads crowded with onlookers. Hundreds of others, swords drawn, many riding in carriages, met them as they approached Philadelphia. Bells rang and it was, in the words of Caesar Rodney of Delaware, "verry grand" (P.H. Smith, 1976–2000: 1.343). Then, officially convening on May 10, the delegates got to work. "Such a vast Multitude of Objects, civil, political, commercial and military, press and crowd upon Us so fast," Adams soon wrote, "that We know not what to do first" (Butterfield et al., 1961: 3.11).

4.2 Second Continental Congress

On his way to Philadelphia for the Second Continental Congress, Adams reported to his wife that he had purchased books on military subjects and planned to buy more (Butterfield et al., 1963: 1.191). Several weeks later, he listed to Abigail the names of fellow congressional delegates in military service: "Mr. Dickinson is a Coll. – Mr. Reed a Lt. Coll. – Mr. Mifflin a Major … Coll. Washington appears at Congress in his Uniform and, by his great Experience and Abilities in military Matters, is of much service to Us." Adams exclaimed, "Oh that I was a Soldier! – I will be. – I am reading military Books. – Every Body must and will, and shall be a soldier" (Butterfield et al., 1963: 1.207). As historian John Ferling has argued, Adams had longed to be an officer since the French and Indian War, worrying at the time that he was cowardly for not enlisting. He greatly admired soldiers and, like others of his generation, associated military service with ideals of manhood and virility. However, unlike many of his peers in Congress – not to mention earlier generations of his own family – John Adams never did bear arms. That he remained a civilian bothered him, especially early in the conflict. Adams told himself that he was too old, infirm, and indispensable at Congress to justify becoming a soldier, but he struggled with ambivalence about his lack of military service until he became president of the Board of War (Ferling, 1992: 21, 132–133, 159–160).

Adams may not have served in the army, but during the American Revolution his contributions to the war effort were substantial and in some cases long-lasting. Throughout his tenure in the Continental Congress, Adams proved deeply committed to promoting the growth and professionalization of the American army and navy. One of his first contributions – and arguably his most significant – was his decision to nominate George Washington as commander-in-chief of the Continental Army in June 1775. Adams had been impressed by the Virginian since first meeting him at the First Continental Congress, and described him after his appointment as "the modest and virtuous, the amiable, generous and brave George Washington" (Butterfield et al., 1963: 1.215). However, the choice to have Washington lead the Continental Army had more to do with political strategy than personal affinity. It certainly was not an impulsive decision; both James Warren and Elbridge Gerry had expressed in letters to Adams their hope that Washington would be offered the position (Butterfield et al., 1961: 3.4). Gerry declared, "I should heartily rejoice to see this way the beloved colonel Washington, and do not doubt the New-England generals would acquiesce in showing to our sister colony Virginia, the respect, which she has before experienced from the continent, in making him generalissimo" (Austin, 1828: 1.79). Opposition leaders in Massachusetts recognized that if they were to build a truly continental army supported by Congress, and by extension all of the American provinces, it would be of the utmost importance to install a man from the powerful colony of Virginia at its head.

Adams's account of the circumstances surrounding Washington's appointment comes from his autobiography, a document notoriously full of errors. This portion was written in 1805 by an aging Adams with the benefit of hindsight and a tendency to get confused about chronology and occasionally mix up names. With that said, Adams's later recollections are all we have; he was not writing in his diary at this time and the details of the nomination are not revealed in contemporary letters. According to Adams's recollection, John and Samuel Adams took a walk around the State House yard one morning in June 1775. John recalled that he told Samuel, "I am determined this Morning to make a direct Motion that Congress should adopt the Army before Boston and appoint Colonel Washington Commander of it." Samuel was thoughtful, Adams remembered, but did not reply (*D&A*: 3.322).

When the congressmen were assembled, John rose to speak in favor of Congress taking over administration of the army and appointing a general. Adams remembered that he

> had no hesitation to declare that I had but one Gentleman in my Mind for that important command. … a Gentleman from Virginia who was among Us and very well known to all of Us, a Gentleman whose Skill and Experience as an Officer, whose independent fortune, great Talents and excellent universal Character, would command the Approbation of all America. (*D&A*: 3.322–323)

Washington quickly left the room and Hancock looked displeased that he was passed over for the position. Adams reported that several members rose to oppose Washington's appointment; they objected not to Washington personally, but to appointing a Virginian to lead an army of New Englanders. According to his account, a vote was postponed to a future date, during which time out-of-doors meetings persuaded those opposed to withdraw their objections to the nomination (*D&A*: 3.321–324). The congressional journal shows that the body voted to adopt the army on June 14 and that Washington was unanimously elected commander-in-chief the following day (W.C. Ford, 1904–1937: 2.89–91). On June 16, John Adams was placed on a committee with Richard Henry Lee and Edward Rutledge to draft a commission and instructions for the new general (W.C. Ford, 1904–1937: 2.92–93). This was one of nine committees on which John Adams served before departing Congress for a brief recess in early August 1775.

That summer, Adams's relationship with John Dickinson, so cordial initially, deteriorated markedly as the cautious Pennsylvanian continually advocated the use of conciliatory language when dealing with the British government. By July 1775 the more radical and fiery Adams was losing his patience, complaining about Dickinson in a letter to his wife as "one, whose Abilities and Virtues, formerly trumpeted so much in America, have been found wanting" (Butterfield et al., 1963:1.253). Another, written to James Warren the next day, declared "A certain great Fortune and piddling Genius whose Fame has been trumpeted so loudly, has given a silly Cast to our whole Doings." This second letter was to be carried to Massachusetts by a young Boston lawyer, Benjamin Hichborn; trusting the privacy of the conveyance, Adams complained openly to Warren that the colonies had not yet formed a Constitution, raised a navy, and opened their ports (Butterfield et al., 1961: 3.89). Adams paid for his indiscretion when this letter was intercepted by the British and published in a Boston newspaper in August 1775. The original letter does not survive, making it impossible to assess Adams's later claim that it had been altered – a charge that proved to be the case with another intercepted letter written by Benjamin Harrison (*D&A*: 3.319).

Benjamin Rush later remembered that, upon returning to Congress after his trip home in August, Adams was kept off important committees and shunned because of what he had said about the powerful Dickinson. However, according to the editors of the *Adams Papers*, the record does not bear that out (Butterfield et al., 1961: 3.92–93). Certainly, his relationship with Dickinson would never be the same. Adams described in his diary an encounter in mid-September:

> I met Mr. Dickinson, on Foot in Chesnut Street. We met, and passed near enough to touch Elbows. He passed without moving his Hat, or Head or Hand. I bowed and pulled off my Hat. He passed hautily by … I shall for the future pass him, in the same manner. But I was determined to make my Bow, that I might know his Temper. We are not to be upon speaking Terms, nor bowing Terms, for the time to come. (*D&A*: 2.173)

Adams did not seem to mind, writing to an apologetic Hichborn that he saw no harm in what had happened (Butterfield et al., 1961: 4.217).

Remaining at his post as absenteeism at the Congress reached over 30 percent, Adams served on thirteen committees between September 13 and December 9. An important assignment came in October, when Congress named Adams and two others to a committee charged with planning the interception of two British ships entering Canadian waters (W.C. Ford, 1904–1937: 3.277). This committee, later enlarged and ordered to fit out a small fleet of armed vessels, became known as the Naval Committee. It is now recognized as a crucial first step in the establishment of an American navy – something Adams strongly supported during his time in Congress and as president. Adams remembered his time on this panel as "the pleasantest part of my Labours for the four Years I spent in Congress," mostly because he enjoyed the wit and anecdotes of Stephen Hopkins of Rhode Island (*D&A*: 3.350). As a member of the committee, Adams was responsible for drafting a set of rules and regulations to govern the new navy. To write the articles, Adams sought out comparable British sources, such as "Rules of Discipline and Good Government to be Observed on Board His Majesty's Ships of War," often copying from them exactly while adapting other portions to the circumstances. For instance, Adams's draft included provisions that seamen be fed more meat than their British counterparts; it also lessened or eliminated punishments for all offenses except murder. Congress adopted Adams's document, with minor changes, in late November 1775. These "Rules for the Regulation of the Navy of the United Colonies" were left unchanged under the Constitution and have shaped the United States Navy throughout its history (Butterfield et al., 1961: 3.xx-xxi, 3.147–156).

Soon after completing this task, Adams asked for permission to return to Massachusetts; he left Philadelphia for home on December 9, exhausted. Serving on the province's council, as he had during his August recess, Adams learned that he had been re-elected to the Continental Congress almost unanimously. Massachusetts also returned Hancock, Samuel Adams, and Robert Treat Paine – although Paine received barely enough votes. Thomas Cushing, more moderate than the rest of the delegation, lost his seat to the radical Elbridge Gerry. Indeed, by late 1775, there were indications that public opinion in Massachusetts and throughout the American provinces was starting to shift, mirroring more closely Adams's personally held views. News arrived that the king would not consider the so-called Olive Branch Petition signed in July; Virginia's governor, Lord Dunmore, offered freedom to enslaved men who would fight for the king, infuriating white Southerners. Adams traveled back to Philadelphia later that winter with Gerry knowing that his delegation could now be counted on to stand with him on key policy issues (Butterfield et al., 1961: 3.378). As the Congress as a whole became more responsive to his political agenda, he also found himself with an even larger workload, serving on thirty committees between February and August 1776.

Adams first read Thomas Paine's *Common Sense* on his way back to Philadelphia in early February 1776. Afterwards, while acknowledging the pamphlet's popular appeal, he expressed disgust at Paine's advocacy of a unicameral legislature. He admitted to Abigail that he "could not have written any Thing in so manly and striking a style," but maintained that Paine had "very inadequate Ideas of what is proper and necessary to be done, in order to form Constitutions for single Colonies, as well as a great Model of Union for the whole" (Butterfield et al., 1963: 1.363). Paine was, in Adams's opinion, "very ignorant of the Science of Government" (Butterfield et al., 1961: 4.182). Adams, on the other hand, had long been intellectually interested in constitutional theory and political science. As C. Bradley Thompson has observed (1998: 40): "Adams had reflected on the subject for some time. Indeed, he had been preparing for this moment his entire adult life." In the spring of 1776, Adams produced a pamphlet of his own, titled *Thoughts on Government, Applicable to the Present State of the American Colonies. In a Letter from a Gentleman to His Friend*, in which he argued for a bicameral government and the importance of the balance and separation of powers.

The general framework for *Thoughts on Government* grew out of a conversation with Richard Henry Lee at Adams's lodgings in the fall of 1775. Following a discussion about the best way to convert the colonies' temporary governments into more permanent institutions, Lee asked Adams to write down the ideas he presented, which Adams promptly did in a letter to Lee of November 15, 1775 (Butterfield et al., 1961: 3.307–308). By February 1776, Lee had used Adams's letter to write a handbill that appeared in the *Virginia Gazette* (Selby, 1976: 393). In March, William Hooper and John Penn – two delegates from North Carolina about to return home to assist in framing their colony's government – likewise asked Adams to share his thoughts on the subject. Adams "concluded to borrow a little Time from his sleep and accordingly wrote with his own Hand, a Sketch, which he copied, giving the original to Mr. Hooper and the Copy to Mr. Penn" (Butterfield et al., 1961: 4.131). George Wythe of Virginia saw what Adams had written and requested a copy, which Adams wrote from memory sometime in late March or early April. Jonathan Dickinson Sergeant of New Jersey also asked for a duplicate; Adams later recalled that he elaborated his points most fully in that version, though Sergeant's copy is not extant.

When Richard Henry Lee asked for yet another copy of the piece in order to publish it, Adams apparently borrowed back Wythe's version. Adams and Richard Henry Lee were distributing the pamphlet by April 20, 1776, and a Pennsylvania newspaper advertised it for sale a couple of days later; the text also was reprinted in Boston in October. Wythe's version, much longer than the drafts penned for the delegates from North Carolina, expanded on some points and introduced others especially relevant to the more aristocratic colony of Virginia. It mentioned, for instance, that terms of office could be three or seven years – or even for life – though Adams himself strongly preferred annual elections. The pamphlet suggested retaining property qualifications for voting and did not attempt to bring about any other major social or cultural change. Adams recognized that keeping alterations to a minimum made the prospect of independence more palatable and increased the likelihood of successfully establishing permanent provincial governments, which to him was paramount.

Advocating a plan for each colony "as nearly resembling the Governments under which We were born and have lived as the Circumstances of the Country will admit," John Adams clearly did hope that the reorganized governments of the Southern colonies would more closely resemble those of New England (*D&A*: 3.356). His pamphlet described an ideal government that was nearly identical to the existing provincial government of Connecticut – or, in the words of T. H. Breen (1967: 512), "the charter government of Massachusetts with the royal element removed." Adams predicted that "in New England, the 'Thoughts on Government' will be disdained, because they are not popular enough. In the Southern Colonies, they will be despised and dissected, because too popular" (Butterfield et al., 1961: 4.182). He miscalculated, since the Southern provinces' constitutions ultimately proved more democratic than he anticipated (Butterfield et al., 1963: 2.42).

Never intended for the public, *Thoughts on Government* failed to reach a wide audience. However, the individuals who did read it were key players in framing new provincial governments, making this pamphlet one of Adams's more influential writings during the American Revolution. In fact, it has been called "a kind of handbook in several states for the drafting of new constitutions" (Elkins and McKitrick, 1993: 532). A number of Virginians, including Robert Carter Nicholas, Edmund Pendleton, and General Charles Lee, read Adams's pamphlet before attending their colony's convention. Patrick Henry wrote to Adams, "I'm not without Hopes it may produce Good here" (Butterfield et al., 1961: 4.200). *Thoughts on Government*, as well as Adams's letter to Richard Henry Lee of November 1775, influenced George Mason, primary author of the Virginia constitution of 1776. Hooper and Penn both were placed on the committee charged with preparing a constitution for North Carolina, though they were disappointed with the result – a more democratic structure than they preferred. Though it is unclear what influence the pamphlet had in New Jersey, it was Jonathan Dickinson Sergeant who penned an early draft of that province's constitution (Butterfield et al., 1961: 4.65–93).

In May 1776, the Continental Congress finally passed a resolution formally allowing all of the colonies to form their own governments. Exultant,

Adams declared to Warren that it was "the most important Resolution, that ever was taken in America" (Butterfield et al., 1961: 4.186). Adams believed that the resolve was, to all intents and purposes, a declaration of American independence. On a committee with Edward Rutledge and Richard Henry Lee to write the preamble, Adams himself authored the resolution's controversial preface, which stated that it was "absolutely irreconcileable to reason and good Conscience, for the people of these colonies now to take the oaths and affirmations necessary for the support of any government under the crown of Great Britain, and it is necessary that the exercise of every kind of authority under the said crown should be totally suppressed" (W.C. Ford, 1904–1937: 4.358). Several days later, Adams asked Warren:

> What do you think must be my sensations, when I see the Congress now daily passing Resolutions, which I most earnestly pressed for against Wind and Tide, Twelve Months ago? – and which I have not omitted to labour for, a Month together from that Time to this?... What do you think must be my Reflections when I see, the Farmer himself, now confessing the Falsehood of all his Prophecies, and the Truth of mine. (Butterfield et al., 1961: 4.196)

At last, Adams felt vindicated. The following month he began to keep letterbook copies of his correspondence, suggesting he understood the historical importance of what was unfolding (Butterfield et al., 1961: 1.xviii).

It is impossible to say at what moment John Adams began unequivocally to support the colonies' independence from Britain. Some historians have argued that he embraced the idea of independence shortly after the events at Lexington and Concord in April 1775; others see Adams as unsure of his position until much later that year. According to Robert J. Taylor (1977: 56), scholars have incorrectly assumed that Adams's opinion solidified earlier than was in fact the case, in part because Adams – benefiting from hindsight – portrayed his stance that way in his autobiography. This ambiguity about timing is also a result of extant documents; much of the political process leading up to independence evolved in ostensibly secret face-to-face settings, not through correspondence. Adams often held back in letters, knowing from experience how easily they could be intercepted. It appears that it took time for Adams to arrive at a firm, unwavering commitment to separation. His position fluctuated with the circumstances until he became fully committed to this perilous step. As he wrote to Abigail in early October 1775, "The Thought that we might be driven to the sad Necessity of breaking our Connection with G. B. exclusive of the Carnage and Destruction which it was easy to see must attend the seperation, always gave me a great deal of Grief" (Butterfield et al., 1963: 1.295). Taylor argues (1977: 67) that Adams's support for independence was "reluctant, tentative, even ambiguous, and subject to moods." In the end, Adams felt that the colonies had been given no other choice. By late 1775, he had made up his mind.

However, at the same time, Adams also fully understood the importance of building consensus and acting only as a unified confederation. "Like a Coach and six," he had written to Abigail during the summer of 1775, "the swiftest Horses must be slackened, and the slowest quickened, that all may keep an even pace" (Butterfield et al., 1963: 1.216).Thus Adams signed the Olive Branch Petition to the king that July, knowing that "Discord and total Disunion would be the certain Effect of a resolute Refusal to petition and negociate" (Butterfield et al., 1961: 3.62). He declared:

> The Colonies like all Bodies of Men must and will have their Way and their Honour, and even their Whims. These Opinions of Some Colonies which are founded I think in their Wishes and Passions, their Hopes and Fears, rather than in Reason and Evidence will give a whimsical Cast to the Proceedings of this Congress. ... We ought immediately to dissolve all Ministerial Tyrannies, and Custom houses, set up Governments of our own, like that of Connecticutt in all the Colonies, confederate together like an indissoluble Band, for mutual defence and open our Ports to all Nations immediately. This is the system that your Friend has aimed at promoting from first to last; But the Colonies are not yet ripe for it. (Butterfield et al., 1961: 3.61–62)

Perhaps this was Adams's first reference to his outright support for American independence. Adams continued to advocate for separation while acknowledging that the deliberative process could not be forced.

When Richard Henry Lee at last presented a motion to declare independence on June 7, 1776, resolving that "these United Colonies are, and, of right, ought to be, Free and Independent States," John Adams seconded it (W.C. Ford, 1904–1937: 5.507). Congress debated the issue for two days, those against the motion objecting primarily to its timing. For Adams, Lee, and others, the decision was necessary and long overdue. More moderate congressmen such as Dickinson, Edward Rutledge, James Wilson, and Robert R. Livingston did not necessarily oppose the resolution for independence personally, but they did argue that it was premature. The middle colonies were not ready, they said, and they awaited news from Silas Deane, who had left for France in April 1776 to assess the likelihood of receiving assistance from the French government. There were boundary disputes among the colonies that remained unresolved. Independence should follow the establishment of a confederation among the provinces and the promise of foreign aid, these men suggested. In early June, a vote on the question was destined to fail; five colonies still had not given their delegates instructions that would allow them to vote for independence. Thus the issue was postponed for several weeks to await further word from the various provinces and from Deane. However, Congress appointed a committee on June 11 to draft a declaration of independence in case it proved necessary, naming as members Adams, Thomas Jefferson, Benjamin Franklin, Roger Sherman, and Robert R. Livingston.

After that, the details become unclear. As Robert E. McGlone has shown (1998: 425–438), Adams's own version of what happened changed over time. Writing at age 86, Adams recalled that he and Jefferson had been named a subcommittee to prepare a draft of the declaration; each offered the task to the other, with Adams ultimately persuading Jefferson to pen the document. Historians sometimes have taken Adams at his word. However, Jefferson denied having this conversation with Adams, maintaining that he alone was chosen to write the Declaration.The memories of both men concerning the drafting process have proved inaccurate, so it is impossible to know for certain what occurred. As Adams wrote as an old man, "What are we to think of history, when, in less than forty years, such diversities appear in the memories of living persons who were witnesses?" (C.F. Adams, 1878b: 505). While Adams was a more senior member of Congress than Jefferson, and therefore more likely to be given the job, it was a Virginian who introduced the motion for independence. With Richard Henry Lee and George Wythe both away from Philadelphia at the time to assist with drafting the Virginia constitution, it followed that the responsibility for drafting the declaration fell to a more junior delegate (and gifted writer) from that colony, Thomas Jefferson. Moreover, Adams was already overworked, charged with preparing a Plan of Treaties and elected to chair the Board of War within days of being placed on the drafting committee. Adams called June 1776 "the busyest Month, that ever I saw" (Butterfield et al., 1963: 2.23).

Regardless of how the decision was made for Jefferson to write the document, it is clear that Adams had very little to do with its actual drafting. Jefferson did ask Adams and Franklin to review what he had written before presenting it to the rest of the committee (Butterfield et al., 1961: 4.343). Much later in life, Adams noted that there was language "which I would not have inserted if I had drawn it up, particularly that which called the King tyrant … I thought the expression too passionate, and too much like scolding, for so grave and solemn a document" (C.F. Adams, 1850–1856: 2.514). However, upon reading Jefferson's draft at the time, Adams only made several minor changes before making a copy for himself, which he sent to his wife on July 3. A draft of the declaration was presented to the Congress on June 28 and adopted on July 4, after it had been extensively edited by the members of Congress meeting as a committee of the whole. The actual signing of the Declaration of Independence took place on August 2, 1776.

No one at the time anticipated the importance of the Declaration of Independence or the fame that would be bestowed on its author. As Pauline Maier (1997: 48–49) has demonstrated, Congress's declaration was just one of approximately ninety similar pronouncements made by provincial legislatures and local communities throughout the colonies between April and July 1776. In fact, for fifteen years after its publication, it received little attention and was rarely read in public. When it became clear as the decades passed how sacred the document had become, Adams saw that his contribution to the independence movement had been overshadowed by Jefferson's authorship of the Declaration. He complained in a letter to Benjamin Rush written in 1811 that the drafting had been a "theatrical show," with Jefferson running away "with all the stage effect … and all the glory of it" (Schutz and Adair, 1966: 182).The real work, as Adams saw it, took place during congressional debates inside the walls of Congress.

The declaration itself was not nearly as important to John Adams as the actual resolution in favor of independence, which passed on July 2 following heated debate. John Dickinson gave an impressive prepared speech on the first of July using "all his Eloquence," which was answered by an equally impassioned extemporaneous presentation by Adams (*D&A*: 3.396). These speeches summarized arguments already made over and over again inside the walls of the State House, each man embodying one side of an historic and momentous debate. "That Debate took up the most of the day, but it was an idle Mispence of Time for nothing was Said, but what had been repeated and hackneyed in that Room before an hundred Times for Six Months past," Adams complained (Butterfield et al., 1961: 4.353). However, Adams's speech that day made an impact on at least one fellow congressman. A colleague from Georgia, George Walton, wrote to Adams fifteen years later: "I can truly assure you, that, since the 1st day of July, 1776, my conduct, in every station in life, has corresponded with the result of that great question which you so ably and faithfully developed on that day – a scene which has ever been present to my mind." The son of another fellow signer, Richard Stockton, remembered his father returning home in the summer of 1776 declaring that "The man to whom the country is most indebted for the great measure of independence is Mr. John Adams, of Boston. I call him the Atlas of American independence. He it was who sustained the debate, and by the force of his reasoning demonstrated not only the justice, but the expediency, of the measure" (C.F. Adams, 1850–1856: 3.56).

By early July 1776, nearly all of the colonies' instructions permitted a vote for independence; only New York abstained from voting until given formal authorization to support it several days after the fact. On July 2, Caesar Rodney's last-minute arrival from Delaware pushed that colony into support for the resolution, South Carolina finally agreed to vote for independence for the sake of unanimity, and Dickinson and Robert Morris deliberately did not attend Congress, allowing Pennsylvania also to vote yes. Adams was triumphant, declaring that "the greatest Question was decided, which ever was debated in America, and a greater perhaps, never was or will be decided among Men" (Butterfield et al., 1963: 2.27–28). He believed that it would be July 2, not July 4, that would be celebrated in the future:

> The Second Day of July 1776, will be the most memorable Epocha, in the History of America. – I am apt to believe that it will be celebrated, by

> succeeding Generations, as the great anniversary Festival. It ought to be commemorated, as the Day of Deliverance by solemn Acts of Devotion to God Almighty. It ought to be solemnized with Pomp and Parade, with Shews, Games, Sports, Guns, Bells, Bonfires and Illuminations from one End of this Continent to the other from this Time forward forever more. (Butterfield et al., 1963: 2.30)

He was wrong, of course. Even the following year a hastily planned celebration was held on the fourth of July, not the second (Butterfield et al., 1963: 2.274).

Not deeply involved in the writing of the Declaration, Adams was not even on the committee that produced the Articles of Confederation, although he clearly thought the Articles important and committed himself to being present on the congressional floor for most of the debates on the subject. In terms of the actual drafting of the three founding texts called for in Lee's resolution of June 7 – a Declaration of Independence, Articles of Confederation, and a Plan of Treaties to be used for establishing alliances with foreign powers – Adams was only influential in shaping the last. Formed on June 11, 1776, the committee to produce a Plan of Treaties included Adams, Dickinson, Franklin, Robert Morris, and Benjamin Harrison. Adams, seeing an alliance with France as integral to American success, had forcefully argued the need for such a document, which may have been how he came to write it. He relied on British texts, using two early eighteenth-century volumes of tracts and laws as a guide to constructing the first thirteen articles of the treaty. For roughly the second half, the final seventeen articles, Adams borrowed a helpful book from Franklin titled *A Compleat Collection of All the Articles and Clauses which Relate to the Marine, in the Several Treaties Now Subsisting Between Great Britain, and Other Kingdoms and States*, published in London in 1760. This volume allowed Adams to write more quickly, copying verbatim a number of its articles. From Article 14 on, the draft combines three separate agreements between France and England, particularly a commercial treaty of 1713. Thus based on Anglo-French agreements, France would find the language of the model treaty familiar and perhaps ratify it without objection (Butterfield et al., 1961: 4.263). Adams, distrustful of France, was careful to include in his draft the provision that France not be allowed to annex territories in North America. He was also very explicit about the importance of America maintaining its neutrality, nurturing an open commercial relationship with foreign nations while remaining uninvolved in military conflicts abroad.

The committee reported Adams's draft to Congress on July 18 and, after debating the plan in late August, Congress returned the document to an expanded committee that now included Lee and James Wilson. On September 17, Congress adopted the Plan of Treaties; it followed closely Adams's first draft. The Treaty of Amity and Commerce between the

United States and France of February 6, 1778, would depart from the Plan of Treaties in certain areas but reflected the overall principles and tone of Adams's original work. The editors of the *Adams Papers* maintain that the Plan of Treaties was, of all the documents Adams drafted in Congress, one of his greatest and long-lasting achievements. Almost entirely Adams's work, it guided foreign policy in the United States for well over a century (Butterfield et al., 1961: 4.260–265).

During his tenure in the Continental Congress, Adams served on a number of committees dealing with military matters and strongly advocated for the professionalization of the army, recognizing that inefficiency and disorganization hindered the American cause (Butterfield et al., 1961: 5.xv). He visited with Washington at his headquarters while on recess from the Continental Congress in August 1775 and again in early 1776, conferring with him at that time about General Lee's proposed plan to secure New York against the British and strategizing about recruitment problems (*D&A*: 3.325; Butterfield et al., 1961: 3.297, 3.395–396, 3.404–405). As a member of the Committee of Spies, Adams was part of the group that revised the Articles of War, adopted on September 20, 1776. Following closely the British Articles of War, it introduced more severe punishments for crimes such as desertion and clarified a number of administrative matters. That same month, Adams apparently was involved in instituting other changes in the army designed to entice soldiers to enlist for the duration of the conflict, offering more money and land grants as compensation (Butterfield et al., 1961: 5.38–40). In the fall of 1776, Adams also called for the establishment of an American military academy – although nothing came of it at the time. Military matters, strategy, and tactics are the predominant topics of discussion in Adams's congressional correspondence.

On June 12, 1776, the Continental Congress created the Board of War and Ordnance to handle administrative duties related to the military. To staff the Board, Congress selected Adams, Benjamin Harrison, Edward Rutledge, Roger Sherman, and James Wilson; Adams served as president from its inception until his departure from Congress in late 1777. John Adams accepted the position well aware that no one currently in Congress, including himself, was qualified to handle the job. He immediately wrote to several officers requesting advice, confessing to Brigadier General Nathaniel Greene, "It is a great Mortification to me I confess, and I fear it will too often be a misfortune to our Country, that I am called to the Discharge of Trusts to which I feel myself So unequal, and in the Execution of which I can derive no Assistance from my Education, or former Course of Life" (Butterfield et al., 1961: 4.325). To Abigail he called the presidency of the Board "an Honour to which I never aspired, a Trust to which I feel my self vastly unequal," but declared, "I am determined to do as well as I can and make Industry supply, in some degree the Place of Abilities and Experience" (Butterfield et al., 1963: 2.24). With characteristic vigor,

Adams continued his ongoing efforts to educate himself on military matters in his determination to handle with adequate knowledge and preparedness the Board's weighty responsibilities.

Thus five civilian members of Congress, along with a secretary – all knowing very little about military administration – were charged with keeping records of all American officers and their dates of commission and handling a multitude of managerial tasks related to recruitment, appointments, supplies, and enemy prisoners. The Board worked at a rented office on Market Street, its walls soon covered – at Adams's insistence – by as many maps of the colonies as the Board's members could find (Schaffel, 1986: 185). The Board was to receive reports each month from military commanders that would include accurate accounts of their soldiers and equipment. John Adams and his fellow Board members first requested this information in a letter to Washington and other officers written shortly after the War Office's formation in June.

> It will be necessary for you forthwith to furnish the Board with an exact State of the Army under your Command and everything relative thereto. It is expected that in future monthly Returns be regularly transmitted to the War Office that Congress may frequently have a full and general Knowledge of the true Situation of their military Affairs ... We must farther request that you will keep up a constant and regular Correspondence with us. (Butterfield et al., 1961: 4.321–322)

The expectation was that the Board would act as a mediator between Congress and the commanders, forwarding relevant congressional documents to army officers and reporting to Congress what was happening on the ground. Congress would then pass resolutions and take actions based closely on the Board's reports and recommendations.

The Board of War demanded many hours of Adams's day, before and after the daily congressional session, at a moment when he was simultaneously serving on over twenty other committees. His schedule during this time was grueling; he awoke before dawn to write letters, headed to the War Office at 6 o'clock in the morning, and was expected in Congress at 10. Following the day's session, Board members typically returned once again to the War Office and worked until late in the evening, overwhelmed by countless administrative tasks. Adams's obligations to the Board took up more time than the rest of his assignments combined. He later recalled, "the Duties of this Board kept me in continual Employment, not to say Drudgery ... Not only my Mornings and Evenings were filled up with the Croud of Business before the Board, but a great Part of my time in Congress was engaged in making, explaining, and justifying our Reports and Proceedings" (*D&A*: 3.342). Historians have argued that, as head of the Board of War from June 1776 to November 1777, Adams acted in many ways as the country's first "de facto secretary of war," as "a war department" and as "the rough equivalent of secretary of defense" (Page Smith, 1961: 1.289; P. Shaw, 1976: 101; J. J. Ellis, 2010: 32). Adams served in Congress until October 12, 1776, burdened not only by the demands of the War Office, but by many additional committee assignments concerning everything from how to get medicines to the Army, to issues related to currency, to preparing credentials for the commissioners to be sent to France (Butterfield et al., 1961: 5.10).

Adams was back in Congress for most of 1777, from January 2 to November 6, serving during this period on twenty-six committees and chairing eight of them (Butterfield et al., 1961: 5.58). In addition to considering petitions and sundry other matters such as post office regulations and potential rewards for destroying British ships, Adams continued throughout the year to lead the Board of War – a position that increasingly left him frustrated (Butterfield et al., 1961: 5.61–62). Officers failed to regularly provide the War Office with the information it requested, making it impossible for it to assemble complete and accurate records and respond accordingly. Adams grew particularly tired of handling personnel problems related to the relative seniority and promotions of army officers. Writing at 4 o'clock one morning to his wife, Adams complained, "I am wearied to Death with the Wrangles between military officers, high and low. They Quarrell like Cats and Dogs. They worry one another like Mastiffs. Scrambling for Rank and Pay like Apes for Nutts" (Butterfield et al., 1963: 2.245). Adams struggled with the unnecessary loss of so many soldiers to disease, finding himself profoundly depressed by a visit to an army cemetery in April 1777. Walking among the graves of thousands of war dead, he confessed to his wife that he had never before been "affected with so much Melancholly" (Butterfield et al., 1963: 2.209). More discipline was needed in the army, he cried, and a better plan to prevent sickness among soldiers. Soon before Adams left Philadelphia in November, Congress – at last recognizing the problems inherent in having inexperienced and overworked congressmen run a war department – reorganized the Board of War. Officers could now serve on the Board full time; replacing Adams would be Major General Horatio Gates, along with Thomas Mifflin and Timothy Pickering. Gates proved ineffective, holding the position for less than a year, and over time the Board of War's influence diminished. It had become virtually irrelevant by the time a third reorganization of the Board in late 1780 led to Benjamin Lincoln being named the first secretary of war (Schaffel, 1986: 186–187).

In July 1777, Adams – expecting to hear any day about the birth of another son or daughter – learned instead that Abigail had suffered a stillbirth. "Never in my whole Life," he wrote, "was my Heart affected with such Emotions and Sensations" (Butterfield et al., 1963: 2.292). Whether because of emotional anguish or just a busy schedule, around that time Adams stopped writing to anyone except his wife, recording no letters in his letterbooks after July 7, 1777 (Butterfield et al., 1961: 5.xix). The following month, Adams described himself as "condemned to the dullest servitude and Drudgery, seperated from all that I love, and wedded to all that I hate." He vowed to his wife, "The next Time I come home, shall be for a long Time" (Butterfield et al., 1963: 2.298, 299). That autumn, both John and Samuel Adams requested a leave of absence to spend time with their families; the men departed the city on November 11, 1777. John Adams would not return. In fact, he seemed poised to resume his legal career, accepting a court case to be tried in Portsmouth – although, according to Elbridge Gerry, he had some idea that a diplomatic appointment was imminent. In December, letters arrived announcing Adams's election by Congress to join Benjamin Franklin and Arthur Lee as commissioners to France; he was to replace Silas Deane, who had been recalled. Driven by a sense of duty, ambition, or the allure of a new challenge – perhaps a combination of all three – Adams accepted the post, sailing in February 1778 from Massachusetts with 10-year-old John Quincy for a dangerous passage across the Atlantic.

Adams returned to Massachusetts in August 1779 for just four months. His timing was fortuitous, for during this brief time he served as a delegate to the state's constitutional convention and participated in the framing of the Massachusetts constitution of 1780. It was fitting that Adams – with his lifelong intellectual interest in government and constitutions and his deep affection for his home state – was charged with producing the first draft of this founding document. Rereading *Thoughts on Government*, as well as the Virginia constitution of 1776, Adams set to work. Although the convention made substantive revisions to Adams's draft, including allowing the legislature to override the governor's veto, much of what remained came originally from his pen. Committed all along to the formation of permanent state governments, Adams helped craft what C. Bradley Thompson has called (1998: 41) "the most systematic and detailed constitution produced during the Revolutionary era." Later serving as a model for other states, as well as for the federal constitution, the Massachusetts constitution remains the oldest written constitution functioning anywhere in the world today. As Adams drafted the document, the Continental Congress again voted to send him abroad – this time as minister plenipotentiary to Great Britain. Before long Adams was crossing the Atlantic once more with his two older sons to embark on the next phase of his long career. He would not appear in Congress again until he began his term as vice president under the United States Constitution in 1789.

Further Reading

Adams, J. (2000). *The Revolutionary Writings of John Adams*. Indianapolis.

Hawke, D.F. (1976). *Honorable Treason: The Declaration of Independence and the Men Who Signed It*. New York.

Knollenberg, B. (1963). "John Dickinson vs. John Adams: 1774–1776." *Proceedings of the American Philosophical Society* 107: 138–144.
Morgan, E. (1976). *The Meaning of Independence: John Adams, George Washington, Thomas Jefferson*. Charlottesville.
Rakove, J. (1979). *The Beginnings of National Politics: An Interpretive History of the Continental Congress*. New York.
Ryerson, R.A. (1983). "John Adams' First Diplomatic Mission: Philadelphia 1774." *Massachusetts Historical Society Proceedings* 95: 17–28.

Chapter Five

John Adams's Political Thought

David J. Siemers

The best-known presidential scholar of the last fifty years, Richard Neustadt, concluded that the presidency "is not a scholar's job" (1990: 89). John Adams would have passionately disagreed.[1] He thought a genuinely scholarly approach to politics was indispensable and all too rare.

Adams was certain that in their studies of history the most discerning human minds had found political arrangements which worked; they had also warned against the political arrangements which would not work. Politicians needed to learn from these political theorists and historians. Accordingly Adams read political theory with gusto from his early adulthood to his old age, intentionally forgoing much other reading in the process. To a correspondent who asked Adams to read a book titled *Of the Anatomy of Caterpillars*, Adams wrote "I doubt not the Book is worth studying. All Nature is so. – But I have too much to do, to Study Men …" (Butterfield, 1966: 36). He knew classical political theory as well as anyone in the United States during his lifetime and applied what he learned to the work of state-building and governance.

Adams's scholarly approach to politics helped to distinguish him in Massachusetts and aided his advance to prominence. Yet as a mature politician he would be routinely ridiculed for the views he held, which seemed old-fashioned to many, out of step with the United States' more democratic ethos.

For his part Adams was consistently exasperated by both the public and fellow political leaders, most of whom either could not or would not understand the eternal truths about politics which had been discovered. Humans, Adams was certain, were selfish and vainglorious by nature. However, he

A Companion to John Adams and John Quincy Adams, First Edition.
Edited by David Waldstreicher.

hoped that politicians would choose to make their name by building up and maintaining a stable institutional system which encouraged compromises that would benefit all. Instead they dreamed of fantasy regimes which could not work in practice, and once situated in a regime they tended to pander to those they purported to represent. The general populace, largely ignorant, could hardly resist being misled.

The signature commitment which Adams gleaned from political theory was a version of the "mixed constitution," also often called the "mixed republic." This type of regime was characterized by a class or "estates"-based system of government institutions featuring checks and balances. Adams's favored version featured a "lower house" of the legislature which would represent the people, an "upper house" representing the nation's most capable and well-positioned, and a powerful executive, with a unilateral legislative veto. Each of these three institutions could stop laws being passed and thus all would have to compromise to effect legislation. This arrangement had roots going back to political theorists of Roman and Greek antiquity, and Adams was entirely convinced that this was the only arrangement which could produce an effectual, non-tyrannical government over a sustained period of time. Adams's devotion to this form of government allowed him to be portrayed by political foes as an apologist for aristocracy and monarchy, charges which Adams found silly and groundless, yet which severely irritated him for most of his political career.

Adams's politics gained purpose and direction from his understanding of political theory. His principles made him something of a Federalist but also distanced him from party politics and helped him to rise above partisanship at critical times when making key decisions. His devotion to theoretical principles also caused him to be considered stubborn and hindered his chances of getting re-elected as president. Adams's preference for classical political theory and theory which considered the long sweep of history came at a substantial cost as well: he believed that there would be no fundamentally new developments in politics. If a political arrangement had not yet appeared or worked, it would not do so ever. This blinded him to innovations in political thought and practice, some of which were occurring in the United States during his career. Yet Adams was a remarkably successful politician who consistently built his politics upon his theoretical preferences. For better and for worse "Adams's relationship to political philosophy defined who he was" (Siemers, 2009: 43).

5.1 Foundational Beliefs

In his youth Adams learned classical Greek and Latin. To him these languages helped unlock a trove of interesting works of political theory. Unlike Thomas Jefferson, Adams did not dismiss these old tomes out of hand as the worthless rationalizations of privilege through the ages. Many of these books were still valuable, he thought, because of their careful treatment of history. The young Adams entered Harvard with some idea of training for the ministry, but he very deliberately moved away from that plan, groping toward things he came to consider much more practical, including politics (Butterfield, 1966: 38). At Harvard Adams became enamored of science (Grant, 2005: 23), and he first and foremost considered his own approach to political theory to be scientific. The approach of most others was not and was therefore, he believed, guesswork at best.

Immediately after graduation Adams worked as a teacher in Worcester, Massachusetts. His intellectual restlessness soon prompted him to study law. While his course of study may not have been much more rigorous than others, Adams became unusually interested in and conversant with legal theory. Having moved to Boston to practice, he joined a book club called "the Sodality," through which he kept up a reading regimen in political theory (Butterfield, 1966: 22). Long after he stopped practicing law to serve as a diplomat and politician he kept reading political theory.

Adams read many texts repeatedly, and he usually wrote observations in the margins. He tended to react strongly, finding the conclusions of some authors true and worthy but denouncing others as utterly misguided.[2] By the time of the American Revolution, there was very little political philosophy, classical or contemporary, which had escaped his grasp. He continued to add books in this genre to his library (and add marginalia in them) even in retirement. Thus C. Bradley Thompson, the most thorough modern examiner of Adams's political thought, encapsulates his approach to politics by writing that "the primary context within which Adams' political thought must be viewed … is his confrontation with the Western political and philosophical tradition" (1998: 238).

Adams believed that he had gleaned a workable and consistent political theory from his reading. He borrowed from many different sources to cobble this theory together, but considered his own thinking or contribution to political thought to be unoriginal. Deep into his retirement he wrote Thomas Jefferson that "I can say and have said nothing new on the Subject of Government" (Cappon, 1959: 357). This admission was not a profession of modesty nor an admission of failure. Rather it was a reflection of how few fundamental axioms Adams believed existed, and his faith in their ironclad validity. The same psychological and political patterns repeated themselves over and over, and those who had turned a systematic eye to history before him had discerned them. For his own part, Adams felt immense pride in applying this true theory of politics to practice as well as he could. He also attempted to popularize these ideas – with only marginal success – but this was work that needed to be done because far too few recognized the truths of politics which had already been discerned.

Adams's supreme confidence in his conclusions derived from a logical premise. He believed in the dictum of Dionysius which had come down to him via Viscount Bolingbroke that "history is philosophy teaching by example" (Haraszti, 1952: 58). In other words, if we examine how politics has worked through history, we can discern the practices and structures which are beneficial. Of course, there were hundreds of societies and thousands of regimes across which to make observations. Yet human nature did not change. Nor did the most fundamental dynamics of social organization. Adams was convinced by several writers who used this empirical method, such as Aristotle, Machiavelli, and Montesquieu, that these eternal truths yielded hard-and-fast rules about how to construct a government.

Adams contrasted these empirical thinkers with *a priori* philosophers, who dreamed up ideal political orders springing from their own wishes rather than basing them on what worked in lived experience. He derided these latter thinkers as "ideologians" and believed that they caused humankind very grave harm despite having good intentions. Among this type of thinker he included Jefferson and others committed to democracy; Plato; and almost all the *philosophes*, the thinkers of the French Enlightenment, who were particularly exasperating to him. The *philosophes* were restless, driven by ideology and uninformed. As such they, like most ideologians, were much better at tearing an existing government down than building one up which worked.

The method of "political science" which Adams embraced seemed to yield favorable results. Montesquieu's suggestion for a separation of powers among government institutions was similar to Machiavelli's ideas, for instance, and both had much in common with Aristotle. Adams took this as confirmation that each had used the lessons of history to come to a similar conclusion. Though each had used different examples, the problem was that the later thinkers had read the former ones and been influenced by them. In truth Adams was the latest advocate in a long tradition of political thought which had built up enough intellectual credibility, but whose conclusions were hardly the only ones which could be derived from past history. And the thinkers in this tradition did disagree with each other sufficiently that Adams might have questioned whether one could really make such definitive inferences about politics based on past events. Despite rather easily slipping into quick judgments of individual thinkers, Adams was nevertheless willing to accept individual ideas from any quarter.

In practice Adams's political thought primarily revolved around what kind of institutions made for good government. Furthermore, he believed that the proper institutional structure was dictated by human nature and social dynamics. In these matters, Adams attempted to approach the subject pragmatically. He wanted to deal with human nature as it existed, rather than offering some idealistic vision about what human nature could be.

Adams perceived human beings to be driven by a thirst for distinction (Grant, 2005: 33). People want to be noticed and esteemed, in every society. What makes societies different – and often substantially different – is that the people in each society notice and esteem a different array of things. To work well, societies should mark out for notice and esteem constructive behaviors: inventing something useful, for instance, or creating an aesthetically pleasing work of art, or engaging in public service that benefits people. A dysfunctional society would notice and esteem problematic things, like committing daring criminal acts, or being able to keep up with the latest fashions most effectively. True to Adams's view of himself, these ideas were not original. They were adopted mainly from the thinkers of the Scottish Enlightenment (Thompson, 1998: 151–156).

Individuals strive to achieve that which is noticed and esteemed in their society, but there are massive disparities in individual abilities to accomplish this. Some people are simply much more capable than others. This is a natural occurrence, true in all places and at all times. This phenomenon can be seen in businesses, schools, families – in any grouping of humans and in any endeavor a few gifted individuals will tend to rise above others. Taken altogether, the exceptional people and their families in any society form a kind of aristocracy (e.g. Haraszti, 1952: 201). In noting this, Adams was not describing or promoting a hereditary aristocracy. On the contrary, he recognized that such an aristocracy could hinder the emergence of a true aristocracy of talent. Adams himself had not been born into wealth, after all. He was simply suggesting that the "best and brightest" are more successful than others in gaining notice, esteem, and property.

In any society members of the aristocracy of talent possessed a disproportionate share of the wealth and power. In fact, these two – wealth and power – inevitably coincided. In this he was a disciple of James Harrington, the English thinker who championed a version of the mixed republic. Harrington had pithily expressed his understanding of political dynamics this way: "power follows property" (J.R. Howe, 1966: 87, 141). Thus to Adams, as for Harrington, in any nation with a commitment to free exchange, property and political power were divided among two rough groups: a small group of wealthy individuals, and the remainder of the populace.

The key to good politics was to make sure that neither of these two groups predominated. The way to do this was by properly constructing government institutions. This, too, was hardly a new idea. Machiavelli had stressed that the most important clash in politics is between the well-off few and the more modest many and that each should be represented in government. Polybius and Aristotle had offered this idea in ancient times. More recent commentators like Harrington and Montesquieu echoed this thinking, as did current writers of political philosophy, most notably Jean Louis De Lolme, whose *Constitution of England* was first published in 1776.

Many of Adams's contemporaries who wrote in this vein were anglophiles. They viewed Parliament, with its House of Lords and House of Commons as a working model of a regime which properly "balanced" the concerns of the few and the many.

For Adams's part he viewed the post-Revolutionary governments in America as the best approximations of this mixed or balanced regime. All but Pennsylvania had an upper legislative chamber (which Adams argued were representative of a "natural aristocracy" rather than a hereditary one) and a lower legislative chamber that was highly democratic and representative of the people at large.

Thus Adams's political thought had a pretty straightforward and logical structure. Human psychology worked a certain way, which produced predictable social dynamics. In turn, these social dynamics had to be recognized in, but also contained and guided by a proper institutional structure which would produce authoritative laws which approximated the common good.

Some have argued that John Adams's political thought changed significantly during his lifetime, particularly his view of human nature (J.R. Howe, 1966). Even if that is true, he never departed from his belief that human nature dictated what societies looked like and that, in turn, necessitated the same specific checks and balances be set up in every government. Thus it is wise to take seriously John Adams's own insistence on his consistency. Adams had the habit of reviewing his own notebooks and marginalia, commenting on his own prior comments in the process. Finding an early notebook in which he wrote "no simple form of Government, can possibly secure Men against the Violences of Power," Adams wrote that this idea "has been the Creed of my whole life" (R.J. Taylor et al., 1977–: 1.83).

5.2 Major Writings

By habit and inclination Adams could not stop himself from writing and speaking about his ideas (Grant, 2005: 360). Our modern expectation of politicians is that they hedge their words to sound pleasing and to avoid fights. Adams did not do so. Since he believed he had found the truth, publicizing it to others was a great service to them. Adams's political writings thus do not merely hint at his political thought, they are a compendium of his understanding of political thought. They might even be called a political philosophy.

Adams was not a gifted writer, however. Jefferson and Lincoln have come down through the ages as admired figures partly because of their ability to turn a phrase that expressed commitments so meaningfully and elegantly as to help make their ideas part of the American *credo*. Adams had no such gift. If one scours Adams's written works for the equivalent of "we hold these truths to be self-evident ..." or "fourscore and seven years ago ..." the best that one can come up with is something like "as the happiness of the people is the sole end of government, so the consent of the people is the only foundation of it, in reason, morality, and the natural fitness of things" (proclamation adopted by Massachusetts Bay colony, 1774). John Patrick Diggins (2002), who otherwise greatly admires Adams, characterizes his writing as "dense, meandering, sprawling, disconnected ... a jarring blur of free association about Western political philosophy" (Diggins, 2002: 57). Adams himself was perfectly aware that his writings had not had the effect that he desired. In an 1820 letter he wrote to Charles Holt that "my plain writings have been misunderstood by many, misrepresented by more, and vilified and anathematized by multitudes who never read them. They have, indeed, nothing to recommend them but stubborn facts ..." (C.F. Adams, 1850–1856: 10.391).

Adams initially gained fame as a young lawyer for his opposition to the Stamp Act. He defended colonists against the British authorities when he felt their rights were threatened, but he also defended the British soldiers involved in the Boston Massacre. Adams showed a rock-solid commitment to the rule of law in doing so. Without it he understood that no regime could be stable. In the *Novanglus* letters of 1775, he protested British imperial policy suggesting that parliamentary control over the internal affairs of the colonies was an illegitimate innovation that did not square with the theoretical underpinnings of the colonies. The king had authorized the colonists to govern themselves in their internal affairs. The colonial legislatures were the true representatives of the American people. Only the monarch and not Parliament had authority in the domestic affairs of the American colonies.

Thoughts on Government, published anonymously in 1776, was Adams's advice to the newly independent states about how to govern themselves (C.F. Adams, 1850–1856: 4.193–200). In this short essay Adams insisted that the form of a government mattered a great deal (an Alexander Pope aphorism popular at the time suggested that form did not matter – it was how the form was administered that mattered). In short order Adams acquainted his audience with the idea that "the foundation of every government is some principle or passion in the minds of the people," an idea cribbed directly from Montesquieu, and then insisted that a representative assembly "should be in miniature an exact portrait of the people at large." He moved on to list the ways in which a single assembly would err. He then proposed a Council of Revision of twenty or thirty as a kind of quasi-senate – which would have a veto on proposals from the assembly. This was a form that existed in many states already and so did not raise many hackles for being too aristocratic. The governor, elected annually by the Council of Revision, would also possess a veto. Adams also suggested an independent judiciary and the outline of some basic laws.

A Defence of the Constitutions of Government of the United States (1787) was Adams's next major written work and it was his most comprehensive effort at explaining political theory. The three-volume set was written in the context of a radicalizing Europe, as Adams saw it. Many leading political thinkers, particularly in France, were writing in favor of unicameral legislatures, which they believed would be more democratic and better reflect the will of the people. Adams conceived the *Defence* as the definitive refutation of this idea.

Instead of using his own words to explain the success of the American states (with their bicameral legislatures), the *Defence* was largely a cut-and-paste job, incorporating huge swaths of text from the political philosophers with whom Adams agreed. In fact, three-quarters of the three volumes consist of quoted material, with much of it not even properly attributed (Thompson 1998: 308n3). Today this would be considered plagiarism, but there were no firm conventions about citations in Adams's day. The more egregious fouls were that the work did not proceed in a logical sequence and it taxed even the most patient of readers beyond what they could comfortably bear.

The first volume of the *Defence* is clearly the most carefully constructed. In it Adams considers modern regimes, ancient regimes, and a wide array of political theorists' ideas. The subsequent volumes offer three case studies of Italian republics from the Middle Ages and then a critique of a book that was already more than a century old: Marchamont Nedham's *The Excellency of a Free State*, published in 1656. Adams could have described his own understanding of political theory in a much shorter space and provided concise summaries and quotes from various political thinkers. In proceeding as he did, Adams squandered an opportunity (seized upon by Edmund Burke) to become the most prescient critic of the French Revolution, which began in the same year the *Defence* was published.

Adams's final major work was titled *Discourses on Davila*. It appeared in 1790 and Adams himself thought of it as a fourth volume of the *Defence*. The *Discourses* "recount the battles, intrigues, factions, and assassinations during forty years of French civil war" during the sixteenth century, but also crib Adam Smith's understanding of human nature described in his *Theory of Moral Sentiments* (Thompson, 1998: 126). This was another work so ponderous as to be almost laughable and Adams never did live down their reputation, despite the subject being very serious points of political theory. Though he was speaking only of his ideas on aristocracy, Adams admitted his own failure to communicate: "I have been so unfortunate as never to be able to make myself understood ..." (Cappon, 1959: 351–352).

5.3 The Mixed Republic in Theory

Very early in the first volume of the *Defence* Adams related that there were only three critical discoveries about politics made in human history (C. F. Adams, 1850–1856: 4.284).[3] The first was representation. Nations and societies were of such a size that workable regimes could not do without this mechanism. The second was the separation of powers. While earlier thinkers had made strides toward formulating the idea, John Locke deserved credit for placing the matter squarely at the center of political theory discourse. Locke emphasized the separation between the legislature and the executive. Adams insisted on Montesquieu's addition of the judiciary as a necessary counterweight to the possibility of legislative or executive tyranny. Adams also did not favor the way many interpreted Locke's idea: that there should be a strict legislative–executive division of power. He thought this would leave the executive vulnerable to the legislature's whims, rendering the entire system unstable. "Balance" could be had by constructing a mixed republic, which was the third major discovery in politics.

The premise behind the mixed republic is the idea that no "simple" regime is stable, but that a "compound" regime can be. There are three basic types of simple regime: monarchy, aristocracy, and democracy. The problem with each is that there is little keeping the person or group in charge from governing for their own benefit to the exclusion of others. This was a view first expressed by Plato and then elaborated upon by Aristotle. A king who is the sole ruler of a country has a great incentive to rule in ways which benefit himself. If an aristocracy is in charge, it makes laws favoring the wealthy. If the general public is in control, they are tempted to redistribute wealth, taking it from those who have a good deal to spread it broadly. To Adams this "simple democracy" was the worst kind of regime. At least aristocrats and monarchs had an interest in keeping order when they were in control to preserve their own fortunes. Democratic self-interest did not prompt an interest in stability but upheaval.

History showed, according to the theory, that where simple regimes were put in place, coups and wars were the norm, initiated by those who were shut out and disadvantaged. At its worst this produced a nearly endless cycling of unstable regimes and civil wars.[4] Thus the comment which Adams suggested had been the creed of his whole life was that "no simple Form of Government can possibly secure Men against the Violences of Power" (R.J. Taylor, 1977: 1.83).

The mixed republic aimed to replace instability with a government which could last, which was more fair to all, and which would allow a nation to prosper. The way it would do so is to force compromise to occur within government. The hallmark of any form of the mixed constitution is that it has one government institution representing the aristocracy and another representing the people at large.[5] Machiavelli believed that the Roman republic fit this description because its senate represented propertied citizens while the tribunes looked out for the interests of the people. Though Adams valued Machiavelli's revival of the idea, the more recent versions of the mixed republic which Adams preferred included a much more robust mechanism for popular input. Convinced by Harrington,

Montesquieu, and others, Adams believed that every government should have one legislative body which represented the people, which could not be done by proxy.

A bicameral legislature which would force compromise between the people at large and the aristocracy was insufficient of itself. There would be an accompanying executive and a judiciary applying the law in practice. Yet the executive had to do more. With only two lawmaking institutions there was the possibility of an immovable deadlock between the aristocratic "estate" and the people. Adding an official legislative role to the executive's portfolio would allow the executive to mediate between the two, weighing in against unreasonable ideas and leading the lawmaking process toward reasonable conclusions. Since he was not beholden to any constituency, the executive could independently press for good legislation. Thus in a way, "the executive … was the mainstay of the entire mechanism, the indispensible balancer, 'the essence of government,' that kept social forces in equilibrium" (G.S. Wood, 1969: 578).

To be effective, the executive had to be equal in power to each of the two legislative bodies in the lawmaking process. This had to be done formally, through a constitutional mechanism. Adams believed that the only viable way to do this was by granting the executive a unilateral veto. Thus no legislation could be enacted without the agreement of a majority in both chambers and the executive's assent. This allowed any of the three to stop a bad proposal from becoming law. It allowed the independent executive to force both the people at large and the wealthy to compromise, producing some approximation of the common good.

Given all this it is no wonder that Adams admired the British government of his time. The House of Lords effectively segregated the aristocracy from the people and the two lawmaking bodies were required to compromise to make law. The British monarch possessed a veto power as well (though the exercise of that power was very much on the wane during Adams's life) and since the monarchy was well established, it possessed the requisite independence to make sound decisions. Britain was the world's foremost economic and military power at this time with a remarkably stable political system. To Adams the British system of government seemed to be a resounding success.

Of course Adams's preference for the mixed republic and for the British constitution were deeply intertwined, like the two helices of a strand of DNA. The books Adams most admired each built their own understanding of politics from the British model. In admiring Britain as an example of their theories put into practice, Adams was in most cases actually admiring the practice that had inspired the theories. Adams's admiration for the British system was not blind, nor did it move beyond an embrace of its structure. Yet Adams's political opponents were happy to suggest that he was too much in love with Britain, as well as its monarchy and aristocracy, to be trusted.

5.4 The Mixed Republic in Practice

Since much of Adams's political thought was focused on institutional design, he was fortunate to live at a time when many new constitutions needed to be written. Selected to a drafting committee and then to a subcommittee, Adams wrote the bulk of Massachusetts' new state constitution singlehandedly in 1780. Despite many amendments, it remains in effect, the oldest written constitution in use. Adams began with a declaration of rights, proof that to him institutional design was a vehicle to achieve the desired outcome of human freedom rather than being primarily to bring stability or an end in itself. The Massachusetts constitutional convention decided to limit the powers he gave to the governor, predictably including the unilateral veto he proposed. Adams was not happy with this alteration, but in a curious way it suited his preferences: Adams was one of the first, if not the first person in the Americas to call for constitutions to be drafted in conventions expressly called for that purpose (Thompson, 1998: 40). They retained his suggestion for a property qualification on voting.[6]

Most of the newly independent states consulted Adams on framing their constitutions. Many states looked to Massachusetts' constitution as a model and "it was an important and influential model for the framers of the Federal Constitution of 1787" (Thompson, 1998: 41). It is not an outlandish claim that the United States might not be a land dominated by bicameral state legislatures without Adams (currently Nebraska is the only state with a unicameral legislature). However, we have left behind his justification for this architecture, replacing it with a more fuzzy general commitment to "checks and balances."

Adams was serving as US ambassador to Great Britain when the Philadelphia Convention forged the US constitution. Some delegates there favored the mixed republic, though, so ideas similar to ones that Adams would have voiced were offered. From his theoretical commitments, one can easily see what Adams would have advocated: a bicameral legislature; an upper legislative chamber with a selection mechanism which would populate the chamber with smart, impressive and accomplished individuals; a lower chamber with a highly democratic selection mechanism; and a relatively powerful president possessed of a final veto power (see Wirls and Wirls, 2004: 46–49, 57–61). The constitution that was framed was close enough to Adams's preferences that he strongly favored its adoption. His biggest disappointment was that the presidency was too weak. Writing to Roger Sherman he noted that "the house and senate are equal [in the legislative process], but the third branch, though essential, is not equal" (Carey, 2000: 449). With the Senate being granted certain exclusive powers he was also fearful that the Senate would encroach on both the president and the House of Representatives.

Confirmation abounded in American politics for the idea that political factions divided along the lines of wealth. The politics of most states, Massachusetts included, had one more popular political party and another which seemed to represent the upper class better. The 1786 debtor uprising in Massachusetts, called Shays' Rebellion, was a classic example of haves versus have-nots. It confirmed to Adams that effective mechanisms were required to force compromise between the well-off and the democratic majority. Shortly after the constitution was implemented, two national parties formed. Unlike some others in the founding generation, Adams thought that parties *would* form – parties were inevitable because the disproportionate distribution of wealth was inevitable. He hoped that politicians would stay aloof from active organization or promotion of such parties – the standard he held himself to, but as time went on he realized this would not be the case.

Adams himself was able to remain surprisingly aloof from party politics. A unique set of circumstances enabled him to do so. Because he was in Europe on diplomatic missions during most of the time between the Revolution and the implementation of the constitution, his ties to other politicians were relatively weak. He was selected as the nation's first vice president after several others declined. By his own admission this office made him largely irrelevant, but it also enabled him to remain above the partisan fray in Congress. While vice president, Adams suggested that Congress designate titles for political officials, including "His High Mightiness" or "His Majesty" for the president. Adams has been ridiculed for this ever since, but the suggestion fit his mindset. He hoped to cultivate public esteem for political offices, and the greatest esteem for the highest office. He was aiming to make the United States into a society which esteemed its government institutions and the president, enabling them to function.[7] Most felt the suggestion pompous and inappropriate in a popular republic.

President Washington viewed himself as a disinterested politician above political party. When he announced his retirement, Adams was a logical successor, because he shared the same outlook and had been a loyal Washington protege. Thus Adams was the only president besides Washington to make his way to the presidency without actively cultivating ties to a political party. Because of this John Patrick Diggins (2003: 173) characterizes Adams as the last honest man to be president, because he did not make promises or compromises to get elected. Adams would have had it no other way. He continued to act independently of party (though his views were much more similar to the Federalists' than the Jeffersonian Republicans') during his four years in office.

While we are accustomed to presidents who use the cabinet as a loyal support team and cultivate ties with Congress to effect legislation, Adams's view of the presidency would not allow this. The drawback was that there was little effective coordination. Several cabinet members were closer to

Alexander Hamilton, Adams's major rival within the Federalist party, and at times these men subverted Adams's work. For his part Adams did not attempt to win them to his side. He seemed happy to make decisions which contradicted their advice because it proved his independence. Nor did Adams care to coordinate with members of Congress. This was not part of his job as he envisioned it. His job was to judge what Congress did, not jeopardize the ideal of three independent branches by cultivating their support. The most important decision which Adams made independent of the Federalists was a good one – not going to war with France. Cabinet members were stunned at this decision and it probably cost Adams re-election, as going to war is usually popular in the short term. But his was also the right decision for a fledgling nation which could barely field an army.

In the mixed republic Adams had a well-thought-through political theory which had a long history and arguably explained empirical reality. Its prescriptions for political institutions were a fit, but hardly a seamless fit, with what Americans were accustomed to and would accept during the Revolutionary era. Mixed constitutionalists, Adams foremost among them, contributed a great deal to the formulation of the post-revolutionary American governments. This included the national government. Yet all the constitutions written during this period were imperfect approximations of their ideal. Formal executive power was not sufficient and in some cases the constitutions were much too democratic. This was especially the case with Pennsylvania's post-revolutionary government, which had a unicameral legislature. The Americans' experience with King George III had convinced the great majority during the revolutionary era that executive power needed to be curtailed. Only as the Philadelphia Convention met had most of the nation's political elite realized that this had been a mistake. They created a more powerful executive at the national level than most states had, but it still was not powerful enough for devotees of the mixed republic like John Adams and Alexander Hamilton. Those who favored the mixed republic prized stability and respected the rule of law. Adams, like the rest, would abide by these constitutions and do his best to make them work.

As the decades passed, it became increasingly clear that Americans were much more committed to democracy than Adams was. James Madison defended what we now call popular sovereignty – the idea that in a legitimate government *all* the nation's institutions have to represent the people. Thomas Jefferson went even further, suggesting that democracy itself was the standard of good government. The viewpoints of these men, whom most considered learned, frustrated Adams; they simply did not understand the lessons of history. Yet Adams's version of the mixed republic was hardly without holes. How could he expect the president, presumably one of the nation's most successful people, to remain independent, rather than identifying with the aristocracy? Adams himself had done so to a point, but he did not fully recognize how aristocratically friendly his own views were, particularly compared to what most American citizens believed. If two major parties almost inevitably form in politics, why would they not aim to select the president, who would then be a party leader and not independent? How could Adams be confident that the average citizen would be well represented by the lower legislative chamber?[8] Would a system which required three institutions to make law be overly cumbersome and prone to gridlock? Adams did not provide satisfying answers to any of these matters.

5.5 Borrowing Genius

Even if we know of Adams's well-developed views about a scientific method of politics, human nature, social dynamics, and institutional design, and we know the logical linkages he made between these items, we may not yet have a well-rounded view of his political thought. Adams seemed to have been fighting others more often than not. Because of this it might be tempting to think of him as outside of the mainstream among the Founders, or as someone with a negative outlook. These conclusions would do Adams a disservice. Clearly no other individual subscribed to the entire catalogue of Adams's ideas. Yet the same could be said for James Madison, Thomas Jefferson, Alexander Hamilton, and every other Founder who could be named. Because constitutions were being written in his time and because so many opposed the mixed constitution as not sufficiently democratic, Adams focused great attention on this matter – so much so that the sum total of his views are easily obscured.

So let us reflect on a more holistic picture of John Adams's thought. Adams was pragmatic and utilitarian in the generic senses of these words. As a young adult he had explicitly embraced "usefulness to man" as the standard for correct action. Among his earliest papers is a letter to an unknown correspondent that remarks "we are not therefore, to measure … Admiration of a man by the Number alone, but by the Utility and Number jointly of the Propositions that he knows, and his dexterity in applying them to Practice" (Butterfield, 1966: 71). This was a sentiment which animated Adams's actions for the rest of his life. The reason that Adams entered government service is that he believed that, of all things a human being could do, service in government could be the most practical and wide reaching. By his definition a satisfied populace defined whether a government worked and he endeavored to make that happen in Massachusetts and in the United States.

Adams believed in both rights and freedom. These were concepts that nearly every American then, as now, could subscribe to. Yet when one goes beyond using these words as slogans, there are distinctions to be made regarding them. Thomas Jefferson emphasized the "natural" character of rights – they were given to humans by God and it was the goal of every government to live up to them or that government should be dissolved. Dissolution did nothing to the right itself. Adams did not wholly disagree, but he de-emphasized the "naturalness" of rights. The more religiously orthodox Adams was more reticent to link God and politics on this matter, probably because he concluded that politics was something that God had largely left up to humans to figure out for themselves. Rights were justified by their utility rather than because of some supernatural quality they might be thought to have.

Jefferson seemed almost flippant about the possibility of tearing down one government and replacing it with another. This was not a matter that Adams would ever take lightly. Only because the British parliament had tried to usurp the lawfully established self-government in the colonies had Adams supported revolution (for the record he was neither a reluctant nor a late revolutionary). Jefferson made an easy but often false assumption: the less government there is, the more individual freedom there is, famously observing "that government is best which governs least" (Read, 2000: ch. 5). To Adams the relationship between government authority and liberty was not so simple. Balance was necessary in all things and government was no exception. Freedom needed to be tempered by authority. There could be too much freedom and too little authority. Poorly established governments allowed some people to get away with things that well-established governments would not, like harming someone who is innocent. Authority also was needed to allow liberty to prevail. A well-functioning government enhanced freedom in practice, because it granted security.

Adams's belief that liberty had to be tempered by authority led him to support the Alien Act and Sedition Acts. Crass accusations in the press could cripple the new government instead of allowing it to be held in public esteem. He supported prosecuting newspaper editors whose accusations were false and scurrilous as a means of safeguarding order (R.D. Brown, 2001). Adams may not have foreseen the problematic latitude with which Federalist prosecutors interpreted the law. Likewise he favored tightening immigration requirements in part because radical democrats were fleeing France's reign of terror and he did not want them to become full citizens quickly. They would vote for the Jeffersonian Republicans, of course, but worse, they might favor destabilizing the American regime to achieve democracy.

Though it might have been inconvenient in the long run, Jefferson could imagine and even idealize what life might be like without government. He and political theorists before him had called the time without or before government the "state of nature." Adams, by contrast, believed that the state of nature was not a literal concept. It was not even valuable conceptually. Government authority was a necessity and it was also a fact of life. When one government fell there was a power vacuum created which needed to be filled immediately or there would be dire consequences. Fortunately during the American Revolution the state governments never stopped working, the pleasant result of their being the true representative bodies of the American people. At times during and shortly after the French Revolution the world got a glimpse of what the absence of a functional government would bring: violent anarchy.

Though it is Jefferson's visage which has been carved into Mount Rushmore, Adams was the more realistic theorist of politics. It was he who suggested practical plans for government which had more of an impact. Jefferson, as an eloquent person and as a coordinating member of the nation's first and longest-lived political party, has a set of adherents to this day. Adams's more qualified and measured approach does not inspire followers, nor is there any political party which claims him. Only a few brave admirers serve as his public relations team, and their voices are typically overshadowed by the criticisms that people were making of Adams even in his own time – David McCullough's *John Adams* (2001) and John Patrick Diggins' (2003) book of the same name, for example. Though he defined himself in opposition to others, this opposition was always in service of a positive but difficult result that was arguably underappreciated during his time: establishing a stable regime after a revolution.

Adams spent a good deal of thought on international relations as well. Presidents Jefferson and Madison simply insisted that the United States be treated as an equal in the community of nations. In so doing they cited treaty obligations but also progressive international-law theorists like Hugo Grotius and Emmerich de Vattel. Adams wished the United States to be treated as an equal as well, but he was under no illusion that just insisting on it would make that happen. The theorists consulted by Jefferson and Madison may have described international law as it should be, but not as it was practiced. In practice the power disparities between nations mattered greatly. The weak could not insist that the strong treat them fairly just because Grotius and Vattel said so.

The United States was a small, relatively weak nation at the turn of the nineteenth century, a time when Britain and France, the world's foremost powers, were usually at war. This dictated to Adams that the United States should embrace neutrality, but it also meant that the nation had to come to grips with a permanent military establishment, something which Jefferson and Madison at best accepted very reluctantly.[9] A consistent proponent of American sea power, Adams successfully advocated for the establishment of the Navy and the creation of a separate cabinet level post to oversee it. When the French government seemed to be a threat and demanded tribute to remain in their good graces, Adams readily suggested a sharp increase in the number of troops in the regular army. His understanding of international affairs had been honed by his years of diplomatic service, but it was also something that he learned about from books which used an empirical method. History granted purchase on how nations related to each other.

Empiricists like Machiavelli described how power dynamics among nations worked better than Grotius or Vattel, even as Adams recognized that the United States should work to implement the latter theorists' humane visions through international agreements.

Adams had used legal theory to argue that the colonies had the right to govern themselves. Legal theory continued to be important to Adams after the Revolution. To him a sound government was really just a fair way of making laws which would reflect the common good and be respected by the populace. Thus Adams described his purpose as creating "a government of laws and not of men" (C.F. Adams, 1850–1856: 4.106). The mixed republic was the way to achieve that, but Adams combined this idea with other familiar Enlightenment era legal concepts, like public trials with juries of one's peers, proportionality in punishments (the worse the crime the harsher the punishment), the production of evidence, and the prohibition of torture.

All in all, Adams offered up a full basket of positions about government, most of which are quite measured and reasonable. That he did so having constructed his outlook out of political theory (though empirical political theory, to be sure) is highly unusual and noteworthy. He had explicitly borrowed so much that he did not think of himself as original, and yet the sum of these parts was a unique vision of government. In his life's work, Adams had lived out his own youthful ideal to be a "great political genius" by "combining" laws of human nature "into Rules for the Government of Society, to Procure Peace, Plenty, [and] Liberty" (Butterfield, 1966: 72–3). Richard Alan Ryerson (2001: 23) notes of Adams that "alone of the Founding Fathers, he provided an explicit link to nearly every writer who became a major source for America's political and legal traditions, from Plato and Justinian to Blackstone, Rousseau, and Beccaria."

Political theorists were valuable to the Americans partly because through them a vocabulary and rationale of resistance to the British was formulated, including the concept of "inalienable rights," and the necessity of "consent of the governed." Adams was among those who had used political theory to argue for a split from Britain. But theorists were also valuable *after* separation because they helped narrow the myriad possibilities about how to construct a government. Of the most prominent founders Adams most appreciated this nation-building aspect to political theory, and because of it he offered fellow citizens the wisdom of a conservative revolutionary.

5.6 Historiography

Adams has elicited fewer interpretations of his political thought than his contemporaries Thomas Jefferson and James Madison. This is not due to any objective disparity in how consequential each was or how interested they all were in the theory of politics – clearly each deserves study by these standards. However, Jefferson is usually thought to be more inspiring (not to mention more enigmatic), a free thinker whose commitment to democracy seems to put him on the right side of history. Madison did more to forge his own vision of political theory than either Jefferson or Adams. He displayed greater brilliance in doing so and he expressed himself more clearly than Adams (Siemers, 2009: 75–76, 84). But it is a problem if the primary matter keeping us from fully considering Adams's thinking is a lack of pizzazz. Because of his relative neglect by scholars, Stanley Elkins and Eric McKitrick observed in *The Age of Federalism* (1993: 530) that "there are not even any generally accepted conclusions on what a comprehensive statement of Adams's theories in summary would really look like." Thus there are competing emphases among those who have examined his political thought.

Modern scholarship on Adams's political thought begins with Gordon Wood's *The Creation of the American Republic* (1969). Wood describes American society as undergoing a substantial change in its approach to politics between the writing of the Declaration of Independence and the forging of the constitution. Starting as a relatively amorphous and premodern set of individual republics, Revolutionary leaders emphasized the concept of self-government in order to lead and inspire the public during the war. In so doing, the notion that "the people" should be in charge of politics took hold and the United States was placed on the trajectory that led to its embrace of democracy. Away in Europe, nose in books, John Adams did not quite realize what had happened. To the extent that he did, he strongly resisted the new American way of thinking.

Thus Wood emphasizes both the "relevance and irrelevance of John Adams" (the title of his chapter on Adams). Yes, he became president and had a significant effect on the nation serving in that role, but his devotion to the mixed republic was an anachronism even at the time he served. Wood recognizes that Adams was a formidable intellect and a learned man. He calls the *Defence* "the finest fruit of the American Enlightenment" (G.S. Wood, 1969: 568). The implication is that the Enlightenment had a humane vision, but not a democratic one as we understand it. Adams was America's exemplar of the Enlightenment's well-meaning paternalism. Perhaps he was also simply too honest (G.S. Wood, 1969: 568–569). Other leaders may not really have believed in popular rule as much as they implied, but they knew it was a way to rally the people to their side. Adams would play no such games.

Elkins and McKitrick (1993) hone in on Adams's pugnacious personality as the key to understanding him. Adams's obsession with personal independence meant that he felt "better if there were costs and obstacles" rather than a smooth road to easy agreements or a willingness to compromise (1993: 531). This tendency bordered on the self-destructive because "though he contended with everyone, his grimmest contentions were with himself" (533). His difficulties in getting along with others and his scholarly approach to politics went hand in hand. He turned to books instead of to people because books and ideas could be pure whereas people could not. "For Adams, there had to be a right way of confronting the problems of political order, and it could not be done without a full comprehension of correct principles" (1993: 534). Along with several other commentators, Elkins and McKitrick suggest that by the time he wrote *Discourses on Davila* Adams had turned pessimistic, seeing ever "greater danger in an unbalanced democracy (1993: 536)." Theirs is a grim, negative Adams.

C. Bradley Thompson presents a more complete and admiring picture of Adams in his full length monograph *John Adams and the Spirit of Liberty* (1998). He thoroughly catalogues Adams's immense debt to a great number of political theorists and excuses Adams's tedious writing by noting that it was not intended for a mass audience (1998: 258). Adams borrowed ideas, but he was not simply derivative. He adjusted them to fit new circumstances and combined disparate strands of political theory in new and innovative ways to make something even more workable than the original. Thompson calls Machiavelli Adams's "principal teacher in political affairs" both for his lessons on the empirical method of politics and for his devotion to the mixed constitution (1998: 42). Yet here was a prime example of how Adams borrowed but also adapted what he learned from books. He had hundreds of years of history to add to what Machiavelli knew and a much more nuanced or careful approach to the construction of institutions than the Florentine.

As in this chapter, Thompson illustrates Adams's place in the history of American political thought by referencing his contemporaries. He argues that Adams was in the mainstream among Federalists and not far from James Madison on most fundamental issues (1998: 260–265). He did have unorthodox ideas, some of which were far from the norm, but so did Madison and Hamilton and Jefferson. Of these four, Adams's odd ideas were more consistently publicized and ridiculed, however, in a deliberate attempt by Jeffersonians to "excommunicate" Adams "from the Revolutionary faith of 1776" (1998: 265–274). Thompson concludes that Adams deserves better, because he offers "a profound alternative to the democratic dogmas of our day" (1998: 277).

If anything John Patrick Diggins is a more ardent admirer of Adams than Thompson. However, instead of thinking of Adams's political philosophy as a viable alternative to current American practice, Diggins (2003: 5) figures that Adams "deserves a far more prominent place in intellectual history and social philosophy … [because] it is his theory of government that we live with today." The tripartite system of checks and balances written into the US constitution is Adams's legacy to us today. Already noted above is Diggins' description of the second president as the nation's last honest one. He and Washington alone among these luminaries did not have to sell their souls to serve. Diggins would add (2003: 7) that Adams's cautions about democratic excess and the perils of liberty make him much more perceptive and prescient about the modern condition than Jefferson.

Others add their own distinctive contributions about Adams's political thought. Daniel and Stephen Wirls (2004) note that Adams's conception of the upper legislative chamber developed significantly between 1776 and 1787. What had been a more fluid and realistic view in *Thoughts on Government* became "impracticable in the extreme" in the *Defence*, because he suggested life tenure for senators (Wirls and Wirls, 2004: 60). The editor of *The Political Writings of John Adams*, George A. Peek, Jr. (1954), asserts that Adams was probably the best American conservative thinker, potentially rivaled only by John C. Calhoun. John R. Howe (1966) stresses that Adams became much more pessimistic in his view of human nature through time, leading him to rely ever more heavily on institutional structure as the one thing which would make for a good society.

In their varied approaches these observers suggest enduring questions about Adams's political thought. How original was his thinking? Who influenced Adams and how? What, if anything, did he add that was distinctive in the history of political theory? How well did he explain how politics works? How worthy of emulation are his ideas? How influential or relevant is Adams? None of these questions have simple answers and there is significant scholarly work yet to be done on each one of them.

5.7 Conclusion

John Adams was not simply sympathetic to the American Revolution, he helped to lead it. He became one of the United States' foremost statesmen during the early republic because his was a learned voice on political affairs which helped lend credibility to the American argument for independence. Despite being a contrarian and frequently lecturing his fellow citizens about politics, Adams was an enthusiastic proponent of the cornerstone concepts that we associate with the American Revolution: self-government, freedom, and rights. His distinctive additions to these three came in the form of a warning and a method. He believed that "authority" deserved equal billing – a nation must be able to govern itself effectively through law. The method to achieve this vision of sustainable government was the mixed republic. Indeed, this was the model for all governments, because it was the only form which had consistently worked. Thus Adams could proclaim confidently from his early adulthood to his dying day that "the best Governments of the World have been mixed" (Butterfield, 1966: 58).

In taking this stance Adams believed he was being scientific, but in fact he was being needlessly rigid and at the very least mistaking what *had* been in human history for all that could be. More than two hundred years after he left the presidency, there are many working states which are without a tripartite scheme of checks and balances and many which are far more democratic than his ideal. In his commitment to the mixed republic Adams seems to have had one foot planted in modernity while another is off in some more ancient land, where privilege or wealth or birth held sway. Yet there can be no quick dismissal of Adams's view even regarding the mixed constitution. Wealth and education and opportunity are not evenly distributed anywhere. Perhaps the most fundamental political matter to solve in popular regimes is keeping those who have more of these from dominating. Adams proposed one way of doing this. Truly effective mechanisms to get this to occur, beyond the tenuous one of relying on people to care about others, have yet to be found.

Adams placed more faith in political theory than any other major political figure in US history. He sifted and winnowed what he found in this genre of writing, rejecting most of it but also discerning a well-integrated set of ideas which he believed to be true, most of which had been repeated over and over by empiricists. He did have "political theory blind spots," however. Adams never was able to bring himself to question the traditional idea that a single government had to be sovereign in any place. This meant that he never quite came to grips with how most others conceived of American government, as a federal system where the states and the national government shared sovereignty.

C. Bradley Thompson catalogues other areas where Adams's intellectual grasp of politics was not strong and where he did not make a contribution: political economy, theories of constitutional interpretation, and free trade versus protectionism (1998: 276). All of these matters were being vigorously discussed during Adams's middle age. This points to Adams not being a particularly lithe or imaginative thinker. He had a hard time placing things in his mental universe which he had not learned about as a young man. Even so the breadth of Adams's political thought is very impressive.

Adams was possessed of complex ideas. He paired mutually exclusive concepts to achieve balance. Freedom had to be balanced by authority; democracy was to be tempered by aristocracy, interests were to be weighed against expertise. This tendency did not lend itself to stirring slogans. In the end, these are the tradeoffs which define politics in most times and places. Even when we can articulate our ideals, they tend to clash in practice and end in absurdity if taken too far. Thus Adams's vision fits with the realities of modern politics as it is practiced in a fallen world. For this he has never quite received his due. Since he prized independence, he never gathered around him an ardent group of partisans who would "take care of me when dead," as Thomas Jefferson had put it to James Madison at the end of his life. What's more the pity is that the impenetrability of Adams's prose obscures one of the most important of American thinkers.

Notes

1 He would simultaneously have lamented that Neustadt disseminated this view to so many of the nation's future leaders at Adams's own *alma mater*, Harvard University (at the time Adams went there Harvard College – still the name of its undergraduate program).
2 Of all the books which Adams owned, the one in which he put the most marginal comments was Mary Wollstonecraft's *French Revolution*. Among his comments were "does this foolish woman expect to get rid of an aristocracy? God Almighty has decreed in the creation of human nature an eternal aristocracy among men … all that policy and legislation can do is to check its force by force" (Haraszti, 1952: 186, 201).
3 Adams actually wrote that there were only three critical political discoveries since the days of Lycurgus, Sparta's legendary lawgiver. Lycurgus – perhaps not even an authentic historical figure – supposedly lived in the eighth century BC and brought Sparta's austere, militaristically communal civic program to life. Lycurgus predates virtually all meaningful historical writing about politics that Adams would have known, including Plato, Aristotle, and Thucydides, whose lives spanned the fifth and fourth centuries BC. Since Adams was no great fan of Sparta and he does not mention any critical political discovery from before Lycurgus' time, one can only conclude that the list of three political axioms is definitive and complete in and of itself. There are no additional great truths in politics which he believed needed to be popularized.
4 Plato described a progression of regime types, each one becoming selfish and abusive in turn. Adams copied that whole section of Plato into the *Defence*. Aristotle and Machiavelli also borrowed (and modified) this idea from Plato. One of their observations was that democracy would be so chaotic that many would crave a single strong leader to restore order. Adams undoubtedly looked at the French Revolution's aftermath as this theory occurring in practice. Napoleon Bonaparte, a general who crowned himself emperor, followed the upheaval of the "Reign of Terror."
5 Naturally these regimes did not represent "the people" as we understand the concept today. Aristotle, himself a metic (someone not born exclusively of Athenian ancestry) and thus not a full citizen in Athens, offered a version of the mixed republic in which only citizens made decisions. In the United States, Adams favored a more broad-based representation. Yet there was slavery, which prevented African Americans from being considered part of the *demos*. Additionally there was the subordinate status of women – and Adams was quite orthodox for his time in believing that males quite effectually represented their mothers, wives, and daughters. Putting these issues aside for a moment, when a proponent of the mixed republic like Adams wrote about "the people," he did not mean every citizen. He meant every citizen who is not a member of the aristocracy or the executive.
6 Given his wish that an upper chamber should represent a state's elite and the Assembly should represent "the people" at large, one might think that Adams would have favored more restrictive voting requirements for Senate elections than for Assembly elections. This was not true. In each case the qualification to

vote was an annual income of at least £3 or property holdings valued at £60 (Carey, 2000: 517, 525–526). How did Adams expect to achieve his favored result? He apparently believed that the bigger districts of the Senate would allow only the well-known and well-placed to win. These were county-wide elections and only those of a certain reputation were likely to be well known outside their own towns. Each town of at least 150 eligible voters could elect someone to the Assembly and so friends would elect a trusted neighbor, regardless of their station in life. Adams believed, like many in his generation, that someone without any property had no right to vote. Being without property they had no permanent stake in what government did. Without articulating it in so many words, Adams likely thought along with many others that in most cases males without any appreciable income or property were too indolent, transient, or imbecilic to cast a meaningful vote.

7 Andy Trees notes that instead of thinking like many of his contemporaries, that it would take a virtuous populace would create a good government, Adams reversed the equation and thought that a well constructed government "would cultivate virtue in a people" (2001: 405).

8 This was one of the most frequent anti-Federalist laments about the new constitution. In state governments they were reasonably sure that the average citizen would be represented because there were many common people in state legislatures. With Congressional districts having 30,000 people (and now approximately 700,000) how could someone from the middle class get elected?

9 This characterizes Jefferson and Madison's ideal of foreign policy, one they implemented in 1801 when Jefferson became president. They relied almost exclusively on militias and defensive gun batteries in harbors for defense, thinking that a non-belligerent republic need not spend much money on military preparedness. The next decade would demonstrate that this was a very problematic assumption, as British and French ships (at war with each other) intercepted American ships, taking goods and even sailors off them. By 1810 Madison had come around to a much more Adams-like way of thinking: the United States needed to arm to protect itself.

Further Reading

Brown, R.A. (1975). *The Presidency of John Adams.* Lawrence, KS.

Iacuzzi, A. (1952). *John Adams, Scholar.* New York.

Kurtz, S.G. (1968). "The Political Science of John Adams: A Guide to His Statecraft." *William & Mary Quarterly* 25: 605–613.

Lerner, R. (1987). *The Thinking Revolutionary: Principle and Practice in the New Republic.* Ithaca, NY.

McCullough, D. (2001). *John Adams.* New York.

Ripley, R.B. (1965). "Adams, Burke, and Eighteenth-Century Conservatism." *Political Science Quarterly* 2: 216–235.

Chapter Six

John Adams, Diplomat

Wendy H. Wong

One does not readily think of John Adams when assessing the diplomacy and foreign affairs of the American Revolution and the emerging United States. On the whole, he arguably falls within the intersection of several historical lacunae. Although Adams was an active statesman and diplomat during his political career, in the popular consciousness, it is Benjamin Franklin's fur hat and his insinuation into the life and intrigue of the French court, and Thomas Jefferson's time in Paris, that tend to capture the imagination and thus receive most of the recognition and glory. Among historians of the United States, diplomatic history and "great men" have until relatively recently been far from the thoughts of those whose preferred methodology stresses "history from the bottom up." In the recent past, Early American specialists have largely ignored the history of foreign relations, and diplomatic historians, mostly concentrating with the twentieth century, have largely ignored the preceding eighteenth and nineteenth centuries as a backwater. Both, therefore, have been virtual ships passing in the night.

Perhaps more viscerally, as various historians for several generations writing about Adams have noted (and often baldly at that), the character and temperament of the elder statesman and second president was mostly unattractive, and often got in the way. In 2003, Rosemarie Zagarri observed in her review of Richard Ryerson's *John Adams and the Founding of the Republic* that as a founder, he seemed to "fall short": prickly, portly, paranoid John Adams is far better known for his aristocratic pretensions, for his vanity and prideful insecurity, and for being neither as dignified as George Washington, nor as intellectually brilliant as Thomas Jefferson, nor as

A Companion to John Adams and John Quincy Adams, First Edition.
Edited by David Waldstreicher.

politically savvy as James Madison. Perhaps even more intriguingly, Gilbert Chinard has noted earlier (1933) that Adams tended to offer an uncomfortable intellectual challenge to supposedly settled American orthodoxies: he was critical of eighteenth-century doctrines of progress and the perfectibility of human nature, and doubted whether simple democracy was a panacea for political ills. Also, in certain corners of the American historical memory (and psyche) the repressive nature of the Alien and Sedition Acts tends to loom large. For these reasons, Chinard suggests, the erstwhile Massachusetts lawyer and second president was far less popular than his contemporaries, therefore becoming "famous without being truly known in his own lifetime." Progressive narratives tend to cast long shadows in the study of American history. In contrast, to grapple with John Adams is to grapple with the tension between change and continuity, which he arguably embodied as he contemplated the complex relationship between Old World and New.

As such, it is not altogether surprising that one scholar should have remarked during the 2010 Annual Meeting of the Society for Historians of American Foreign Relations (SHAFR) that Adams tends to get short shrift in discussions of diplomacy and foreign relations. Moreover, as president, he is sandwiched between the same aforementioned Washington and Jefferson as a sort of half-way point or interlude in early American diplomatic history. More recent popular attention to Adams through the writings of Joseph J. Ellis (1993) and David McCullough (2001), however, has served to spark general interest in "founder chic." And so, John Adams, the forgotten Founder, returned to public consciousness in 2001–2002. Notably, McCullough's biography subsequently received the lush television-mini-series treatment. Not only had colonial America never looked so good on film, remarked Jill Lepore in a (2008) review in the *New Yorker*, but Adams is vividly depicted representing the United States abroad as a diplomatic actor in his own right, even if as somewhat of an awkward foil for the worldlier Franklin.

Despite general historical amnesia, Adams was connected with every political crisis from 1765 to 1801. Also, foreign affairs were front and center in the political life of the emerging republic as they have been at perhaps no time since. As the colonies felt the impact of the crisis of empire in the aftermath of the Seven Years' War, leading to open defiance and rebellion of the British Crown, Adams actively lobbied on the floor of Congress for American independence, realizing full well that European powers would not commit to the United States in its absence. He later joined Benjamin Franklin, Arthur Lee, and John Jay in Europe as an envoy, negotiating alliances and loans on behalf of the American cause. As president of the United States from 1796–1800, he managed to negotiate a difficult peace with France, certainly at the cost of his own re-election and the unity of his own party. On the whole, in the comfort of retirement, Adams looked back on his diplomatic career with satisfaction, deeming it, in his own opinion, the most humble and consistent service he had rendered.

Adams as a diplomat and student of foreign affairs was arguably astute. Unlike many of his contemporaries, he saw earlier than many of his contemporaries the possible danger that French interests might pose to the United States, acutely aware as he was of the vulnerable transatlantic existence of the emerging Republic and what he saw as the volatility of human nature itself. Specifically, he understood that French interests differed from those of the United States, and demonstrated an awareness of how too much dependence on France could be problematic. In addition, he keenly grasped the connection between diplomacy and military policy. He was also prudent, for as Greg L. Lint wryly notes, Adams "did not single-handedly deliver the United states into the hands of the British or destroy the Franco-American alliance" (Lint 2001: 105). To boot, Adams was also seemingly better in comparison with Washington and Jefferson on slavery, firstly for not having owned any slaves, and secondly for pursuing as president a far more liberal foreign policy regarding the former colony of St Domingue (later Haiti) at the close of the 1790s.

In general, accounts of his diplomatic career usually form a significant aspect of standard biographies of John Adams, from Gilbert Chinard's *Honest John Adams* (1933), Page Smith's very comprehensive two-volume work (1962), Peter Shaw's *The Character of John Adams* (1976), and John Ferling's *John Adams: A Life* (1992). Smith's work is especially useful to mine, both for detail on Adams's career as a diplomat and for references to primary material. The sole work dealing specifically with Adams's diplomatic role in the American Revolution has been James H. Hutson's *John Adams and the Diplomacy of the American Revolution* (1980). Adams as diplomat has also spawned more recent article treatments by Ferling (1994a) and Greg L. Lint (2001), both generally positive assessments of his performance. But on the whole, while his career and experience with diplomatic endeavors has been a staple of his biographers, they have only given rise to a handful of articles and have not formed the subject of monograph treatments for some time.

Diplomatic biography, though, is still potentially a rich subject for expanded treatment, as Samuel Flagg Bemis (1949) and James Lewis (2001) have demonstrated in their works on John Quincy Adams. Useful models for biographies such as these are those that treat the subject as an historical node or nexus from which to examine other connected and pertinent issues. For as even earlier biographies of John Adams show, foreign-relations matters tend to be multifaceted, touching as they do upon the exchange of goods and information and the movement of people. A notable example of such a biography is Camilla Townsend's *Pocahontas and the Powhatan Dilemma* (New York, 2004) which, while being about Pocahontas is also about Native American culture, diplomacy with the English, and the young woman's role in it. Other work that effectively uses the central subject as an historical node to address matters beyond it, though they are not diplomatic biographies *per se*, are David Waldstreicher's *Runaway America: Benjamin Franklin, Slavery and the American Revolution* (2004), and Woody Holton's recent work on Abigail Adams (2009).

The scholar seeking to assess John Adams (or anyone else) as a diplomatic actor, however, should be aware of the nature of foreign relations and diplomacy in the specific context of the eighteenth century. In earlier treatments of American foreign relations, particularly prior to the late 1950s, diplomatic historians such as Samuel Flagg Bemis, often relying on a plethora of foreign archives, have tended to emphasize international power politics and state-to-state relations. In such narratives of early American diplomatic history, the United States, in remaining aloof from European broils, was able to capitalize on foreign turmoil. Europe's pain was America's gain. But the reality is more complex. In contrast to Bemis, other scholars such as Alexander DeConde (1959), William Appleman Williams (1959), Paul Varg (1963), and Marie Jeanne Rossignol (2004) have long noted that early Americans did not draw the contemporary, largely twentieth-century distinction between the foreign and domestic spheres. In the eighteenth century, foreign and domestic were of the same fabric; what affected one affected the other. Furthermore, historians of foreign relations, who examine their subject in a more global context such as Jeremy Black (2010), have noted that the state-to-state relations approach is problematic. Such an approach is anachronistic, if not demonstrating a tendency toward outright whiggery, in privileging the nation state and its supposed inevitability. This is not so much a matter of denigrating approaches that examine power politics or those that focus on domestic matters as it is suggesting that the student of the eighteenth century can have it both ways by examining how the tenuous relationship between the two can be mutually illuminating.

As further illustration of these points, Peter Onuf has reiterated in *Federal Union, Modern World* that the domestic and the foreign were actually of the same fabric because in the British empire, the two tended to be conflated. This holdover naturally extended to the United States post-independence (Onuf and Onuf, 1993: 108), itself hardly a cohesive and centralized nation state. The union was beset by centrifugal forces from the outset, such that David Hendrickson (2003) has referred to it as a "peace pact." Furthermore, state-to-state relations for the eighteenth century tend to be more complicated by the fact that the nation state *was* relatively new in general, and hardly an accomplished or certain fact. Also, more broadly speaking, there did not yet exist a fully standardized diplomatic culture in Europe and elsewhere. This, in turn, served as an additional factor blurring the foreign and domestic. And since the seventeenth century, there had been a developing trend in international relations – that of public diplomacy where information was more explicitly designed for public consumption and "the public sphere" (Black, 2010: 79–80). In the post-Cold War era, historians of American diplomatic history and foreign relations have rightly decried any privileging of the nation state in that conflict's aftermath. And the problems of doing so are arguably all the more apparent to historians of the eighteenth. It is therefore useful to keep these realities in mind when contemplating the foreign affairs of the United States during Independence and immediately afterward, for it is this blurring and slippage that presents research opportunities for historians of ideas and culture, for example, to engage in the history of foreign relations.

Also, a study of diplomacy itself might well benefit from a reassessment of what it is and the range of activity it covers: while foreign policy is the statement of a nation's goals in dealing with other powers – and as such the way a nation understands itself – Peter P. Hill makes some useful observations about the differences between "foreign policy" and "diplomacy," both of which serve to make up the larger category of "foreign relations": diplomacy is the art of attaining the ends of foreign policy (Hill, 2003). In addition, Hill also writes that in the early period, the distinction between the major shapers and actors was often blurred because many were both. As such, Adams "might be said to have practiced the policy of war-avoidance and acted 'diplomatically' when he sent a second peace mission to Paris in the wake of the XYZ affair" (Hill, 2003: 50). More specifically, though, as Jeremy Black points out (2010: 13), diplomacy is "the implementation of policy through accredited persuasion." Diplomatic activity involves the collection and assessment of information, and is not restricted to negotiation, which often receives the larger share of scholarly attention (Black, 2010: 73). "Diplomacy," he also notes, "should be located, therefore, not only in terms of developments in international relations, but also of those in cultural representation and in intellectual thought" (Black, 2010: 9).

In light of the Atlantic turn in the history and literary studies of colonial America and the early American Republic, the untapped potential of exploring foreign-affairs issues tends to hover tantalizingly at the edge of the work of those historians undertaking such a framework in any case. That said, however, treatment of these issues within the realm of foreign-relations or diplomatic history is not always explicit. On the whole, assessments of Adams's activities that have relevance for the history of American foreign relations often suggest themselves as regards the following topics: his political thought, his authorship of the Model Treaty, his activities abroad as a minister representing the United States, and as president during the Quasi-War. And it is to those topics that this essay will turn. In assessing John Adams's engagement with foreign relations and matters diplomatic, scholars specializing in Early America and the history of United States foreign relations will find fruitful areas of possible research as well as a basis for much-needed dialogue.

6.1 John Adams, Political Thought, and Foreign Relations

In a letter to Benjamin Rush, dated September 30, 1805, Adams related that a suspicion of – and desire to avoid – European politics and wars had been "the invariable guide of [his] conduct in all situations" while minister in France, Holland, and England, and as vice-president and president of the United States. Throughout his life, it is fair to say that he generally entertained a healthy skepticism of Europe, both while at home and while abroad. As Samuel Flagg Bemis (1949) and others have noted, John Adams was a consistent advocate against close involvement in European wars and politics. Indeed, he had warned of "entangling alliances" as early as the spring of 1776, some time before independence. But there was a paradox in the way that Adams viewed the Old World, particularly France: Edward Handler notes that "perceiving the differences between America and Europe, Adams nevertheless applies American norms to Europe and transposes on America a set of fears derived from Europe" (Handler, 1964: vii). Try to distance himself from Europe as he might when inclined to do so, Europe was nonetheless intimately intertwined with his thoughts on America. Adams did not tend to see the United States as a country without a past. Well-read in the law and in history, he displayed a familiarity with Aristotle, Plato, Livy, Cicero, Sidney, Harrington, and Locke, and the details of what he read (and the notes that he made in the margin) have been commented upon by Zoltan Haraszti (1952). Furthermore, Joyce Appleby (1973) sees Adams's residence in Europe as influential, and as causing considerable changes in his political ideology.

In the light of Adams's critical distance from Europe, therefore, it was crucial that the emerging United States make only treaties of commerce. That the issue of commerce was one of great importance to Adams in his political and diplomatic thought has been noted by Gerard Clarfield (1979). And yet, Clarfield argues, it would be a mistake to classify Adams as either an isolationist or a free-trade liberal. Rather, his understanding of the role of commerce in foreign policy was an application of generally held mercantilist views. Adams believed that the key to a successful foreign policy was to deftly manipulate the marketplace. He assumed that Britain and France (and all of Europe's great states) would be eager to compete for American trade.

If commerce was an important consideration to Adams, so was the concept of divine providence, with which Adams wrestled. In contradistinction to Rousseau, Adams started out with the conviction that men are governed by their interests and their passions (Chinard, 1933: 206). It then followed, according to Gordon Wood, that if a government were to be based on the virtue of its citizens, it would be doomed to failure. There would be no "special providence" (G.S. Wood, 1969: 569) for Americans, who would do as did other people. Furthermore, the United States would do as did other nations (G.S. Wood, 1969). As a result, Adams tended to stress the need for a balanced government, which would channel men's natural greed and interests toward nobler ends, and which would restrain their passions. Accordingly, Peter Shaw (1976) notes that Adams's "Dissertation on Canon and Feudal Law" was a secular and political version of the Puritan conviction that America was a chosen land, where good government could free Americans from the dual dysfunctions of medieval government and "popery." Adams's thought on government and on Europe therefore constitutes a possible opening for religious historians to grapple with foreign affairs. To what extent does his understanding of America, government, and diplomacy constitute a nexus between the transatlantic histories of the Protestant Reformation and the subsequent Enlightenment? Henry F. May (1976) has noted the connection between the Reformation and the Enlightenment in his treatment of the latter's American manifestation, as has Michael McKeon (2005).

6.2 The Model Treaty of 1776

Early in 1776 Adams, in a series of speeches before Congress, stressed what he had thought for some time: that the colonies had little chance of carrying out hostilities against Great Britain unless they received outside assistance. Nothing could be done, however, until the colonies declared their independence and an end to British rule. Congress approved three committees: a committee for the Declaration of Independence, a committee to prepare the Plan of Treaties, and a committee to prepare a plan of Confederation. While Jefferson was given the task of drafting the Declaration of Independence, itself a document pertaining to foreign relations and an international context in its own right (namely, "a candid world"), Adams set to work on the Plan of Treaties, which he drafted with a treaty with France in mind. The goal of the Model Treaty, adopted by Congress in September 1776, was to dissolve the British monopoly of American commerce and to invite all nations to trade with the United States on equal terms, thus providing for American security while maintaining the European balance of power. The Plan of Treaties contained no provision permitting political or military ties. Rather, it was strictly commercial, proposing reciprocity between two nations.

The Model Treaty is largely recognized by historians as highly influential for, if not encapsulating the cornerstone of, American foreign policy. It was therefore a very significant contribution for Adams. Felix Gilbert (1961) has seen it as the precursor to Washington's Farewell Address, and evidence that Enlightenment thought played an important role in the formulation of Early American foreign policy: the Americans "wanted to establish a commercial system of freedom and equality which would eliminate all cause for tension and political conflicts" (Gilbert, 1961: 52). As such, Gilbert sees the Model Treaty as a break with Old World diplomacy. William Stinchcombe (1977) and James H. Hutson (1980) disagree, however, citing that it was self-interest and Old World balance-of-power politics that played more of a leading influence in the shaping of early American foreign policy. They therefore take issue with the interpretation that this was primarily an Enlightenment consideration. Further to the point, Stinchcombe argues (1977) that Adams's view of strictly commercial diplomacy was nothing new, and was, in fact, widespread in Europe. Also, he adds, the treaty did not so much reflect the practice of the Continental Congress in conducting foreign affairs, but instead reflected Adams's moral cast of mind – his moral interpretation of commerce and diplomacy. Peter Onuf (1998), however, cautions against historians being too quick to dismiss Gilbert's seminal essay and Enlightenment influences in American foreign relations.

Surprisingly, as Greg L. Lint (1978) relates, while Adams's authorship of the Plan of Treaties is well known to historians, the manner in which he drafted it is often ignored. Instead, Lint remarks that biographers tend to examine the content of the Plan, and "rarely go beyond noting that the draft of the plan was in his hand" (Lint, 1978: 313). In examining Adams's sources, the notations that he made in his drafts for the Plan of Treaties, and the remembrances that he makes in his autobiography, Lint finds that Adams was inexperienced: he was familiar with Hugo Grotius, Samuel Pufendorf and Emmerich de Vattel, but as authorities on natural law, not the law of nations. Furthermore, Adams had turned to three collections of European treaties for guidance – namely those pertaining to state tracts and sea laws (Lint, 1978: 313–315). From there, he transformed existing Anglo-French agreements into Franco-American ones, thereby representing for France a re-ratification for them in favor of the United States.

On the whole, beyond identifying the Model Treaty as Adams's handiwork and a template for future foreign relations, not many diplomatic histories view the Model Treaty in conjunction and comparison with the Declaration of Independence and the Articles of Confederation. Adams, after all, was on the committee to draft the Declaration of Independence, and he paid close attention to the deliberations of the committee to formulate a plan of confederation. Furthermore, if the Model Treaty represented Adams's moral interpretation on commerce and diplomacy, perhaps it presents an opportunity for scholars to place it further within the context of political economy, a subject where Drew McCoy (1980) has noted that in the eighteenth century, it was not common practice to separate economics and ethics. Americans during the colonial era and the early Republic, after all, had concerned themselves with the perversity of "luxury," and its adverse effects on republican stability.

6.3 France, Britain, and The Netherlands

From 1778 to 1788, Adams found himself abroad in Europe, tasked with negotiating treaties with France, Great Britain, and the Netherlands. By and large, Adams encountered both success and frustration. The two treaties of 1778 with France consisted a commercial agreement and an alliance contingent upon the breaking out of hostilities on the part of Great Britain. In the end, Congress did not hew to Adams's ideas outlined in the Model Treaty, whereby diplomatic aims would be restricted to economic considerations. In the Netherlands, Adams negotiated loans, first incurring difficulties for not being accredited as a minister plenipotentiary to the Dutch government. In appointing Adams minister to the Court of St James in 1785, Congress intended that he should protect American interests and obtain redress for wrongs committed by Britain after the conclusion of the peace treaty of 1783 – among which were the exportation of black slaves, the loss of American trade as a result of British restrictions, and the evacuation of British forts in Canada.

Traditional treatments of diplomatic history pertaining to Adams's activities in Europe such as those by Samuel Flagg Bemis (1956), Richard Morris (1967), and William Stinchcombe (1969) have tended to focus on the balance of power and the blow-by-blow negotiations between Adams and his French, British, and Dutch counterparts. On a more personal and intimate level, they also stress his relationships with fellow American ministers, especially that with Jefferson while serving as minister plenipotentiary in London, but most of all his progressively difficult relationship with fellow minister in France, Benjamin Franklin. As such, these works are a good reminder of the balance of power that Americans had to contend with, though they tend to stress the importance of negotiation to the neglect of other aspects of diplomatic activity, such as intelligence gathering and reporting.

Indeed, some of Adams's main activities as a minister abroad was to gather and place information. While in France, Britain, and the Netherlands, he kept Congress abreast of goings-on in Europe. Adams sent long reports on the political situation there as well as long dissertations on sea power. In addition, he cut and transcribed long articles from the newspapers, carefully listed all ships of the British fleet (complete with the number of guns for each vessel). Also, Adams was keenly aware of the importance of publicity and public opinion: in Europe he conducted an active propaganda campaign, writing essays for newspapers while in France and the Netherlands, in support of the American cause. For, as also evidenced in his *Dissertation on Canon and Feudal Law* (1765), he valued a free press and a well-informed public as essential to liberty, whereas ignorance would lead to Old World-style tyranny and slavery. Thus, he understood full well the significance of the flow of information, and wrote and published essays designed to counter the misinformation about the United States that he knew likely came from British sources. While in France he urged Edmé Jacques Genet (the father of future French minister plenipotentiary to the United States, Edmond Charles Genet), who was chief of the Bureau of Interpretation in the ministry of foreign affairs, to publish translations of American constitutions. The Bureau, after all, was a clearing-house of information on American affairs and acted a center for propaganda that justified the rebellion and stressed the commercial advantages that France would gain in supporting the American cause. Adams therefore acted as a conduit of information to Congress, informing it of the true situation of European affairs and distributing correct information on American affairs to the French public. To the comte de Vergennes, he wrote endlessly in order to inform him of the true state of American opinion. He engaged an agent in London in order to gain access to all of the political pamphlets as they were printed, whereby he carefully studied the English methods of influencing public opinion.

In addition, Adams's activities abroad and his observations tended to reflect yet another reality of eighteenth-century foreign affairs and diplomacy: style mattered. And Adams was untrained and inexperienced. The life of the diplomat at court was largely social, and Page Smith (1962) has chronicled in much detail the way Adams contended with the culture of European courts and the norms of European diplomacy. French aristocrats praised the American cause in the name of "republican simplicity." Franklin had created a personal style that Adams criticized if not outright rejected. Luxury unnerved Adams, and American ministers abroad largely tended to dress in a less showy manner. Furthermore, Greg L. Lint (2001) notes that in method and attitude, Adams brought to his diplomacy a "boldness" based on his understanding of Europe and America as Old World and New. Also, Lint argues, economics were not the usual focus of European foreign policies, whereas Adams put it front and center. But there was, however, the matter of communication, which could often be slow indeed in the eighteenth century, thus leaving the diplomat in question devoid of information, whereby he sometimes exceeded his instructions. As such, American envoys were in an inferior and unenviable position, which they hid under an exterior of brusqueness. Certainly in Amsterdam, to cite an example, Adams had no prestige, and often felt powerless against British agents and well-organized British propaganda (Chinard 1933: 155).

Clearly, there is room for historians studying Adams as diplomat to engage more directly with scholarship on the culture and style of diplomacy, an avenue that has been touched upon by Felix Gilbert, certainly, in his treatment of the Farewell Address, but also more recently by historians of Native–white relations such as James Axtell (1985), Richard White (1991), and Leonard Sadosky (2009). Jeremy Black (2010) has also pointed out a need to study diplomatic culture that stresses that in this period, there was no standardized diplomatic corps that ran according to models more familiar in the late nineteenth and twentieth centuries. Furthermore, since diplomatic culture must also take into consideration the tools of diplomacy, there is ample opportunity also to engage with the work of literary and media scholars, such as Michael Warner (1990), David Shields (1997), and Sandra Gustafson (2000), who assess print, rumor, rhetoric, and letter-writing and their relationship to political activity, with implications for diplomacy. Martha Elena Rojas (2003) has recently studied the relationship between Early American pamphlet wars and diplomatic culture, and thereby the diplomatic lessons that Americans learned.

Historians who point out that he was more aware than anyone else of the potential dangers of being too closely tied to France often note that Adams never felt completely comfortable at the various courts of Europe, where he struggled to advance the American cause. While diplomatic and political historians have largely tended to shy away from character in recent years, there is nonetheless an opportunity for research for those scholars dealing with emotion. James H. Hutson's work, *John Adams and the Diplomacy of the American Revolution* (1980) emphasizes Adams's character and personality (specifically, his "paranoia") as a factor in his diplomatic conduct. While character can be problematic, it is nonetheless a factor worth considering in light of others. While in France, Adams developed a suspicion of the French minister for foreign affairs, the comte de Vergennes, and his relationship with Franklin grew more and more tense. While in the Netherlands, Hutson notes that he shunned the French ambassador Vauguyon, and in the process, effectively isolated himself from sources of reliable information about French motives, by settling in Amsterdam and not in The Hague (Hutson 1980: 76–77). What role, then, did emotion play, not just in politics, but in diplomacy, in the early Republic? Such inquiries with import for studies of politics in eighteenth century America have been conducted by Nicole Eustace (2008). Eustace argues that emotion was just as important as reason in the coming of the American Revolution, and discusses how it constituted a power dynamic in rhetoric and politics. A similar inquiry can thereby be conducted about the period's diplomatic culture. And while difficult to assess, lest one impose twentieth-century categories of psychology on earlier time periods, Richard H. Immerman, who writes mostly about the Cold War, has often noted the potential for studying psychology as a factor in the study of US foreign relations (Immerman, 2004).

6.4 "A Qualified Hostility": The Quasi-War

During Adams's presidency, the highly tenuous and worsening relationship with France almost brought the two nations to war by the close of the 1790s. Upon being elected president of the United States, Adams pledged in his inaugural address to uphold his predecessor's policy of neutrality. But the tensions between the two nations resulted in an undeclared war with France, known as the Quasi-War, which dwarfed all else in the Adams administration. Indeed, it was because this war with France was undeclared that it caused not only problems abroad, but also domestic political instability.

On the whole, the 1790s in the lead-up to the Quasi-War were a time of foreign and domestic tension for the United States, much of which stemmed from the growing pains of an emerging nation further exacerbated by a deteriorating relationship with the French Republic in an Atlantic world at war. The federal constitution, which had replaced the Articles of Confederation, had only just been ratified, and not without much political controversy. Shortly thereafter, the French Revolution and the French Republic's declaration of war on monarchy everywhere led to a European war. During the presidency of George Washington, the United States had aimed to stay clear of European wars and "entangling alliances" by declaring a policy of neutrality. Neutrality, however, did not shield the United States from foreign pressure, and the crisis that it spawned dominated United States foreign affairs during the period. Aggravated by the American neutrality proclamation of 1793 and what it thought to be the subsequent betrayal of the Franco-American alliance with the Jay Treaty, France resorted to the seizure of American shipping. On March 2, 1797, the French Directory issued a decree that violated the Franco-American commercial treaty of 1778 by annulling the principle of "free ships, free goods." This meant that warships could bring into French ports all neutral vessels carrying British goods. For the United States in particular, it meant that any American found serving under an enemy flag would be treated as a pirate. Furthermore, all American ships that did not carry a list of crew and passengers in a form considered proper by French officials could be captured as a lawful prize. A refusal to receive American diplomats and to normalize diplomatic relations with the United States until a large bribe had been paid marked the start of the "qualified hostilities."

Most general accounts focusing on Adams's diplomatic career, however, usually do not mention the Quasi-War. In large part, this has been due to the fact that many of these earlier works – and even more recent ones such as John Ferling's "John Adams, Diplomat" (1994a) – stress the role of Adams as an envoy abroad and not, as Peter Hill (2003) has suggested, a maker of foreign policy also acting diplomatically. But although the larger Quasi-War and the troubled relationship of the United States with France was the mainstay of Adams's presidential term, the story of Adams's presidency has largely been overshadowed by the repressive nature of the Alien and Sedition Acts and their hostility both to foreigners (many of them French) and to Republican newspapers. The Quasi-War is important and deserves further consideration in discussions of Adams's diplomacy, if only because it is this diplomatic crisis that formed the context of the Alien and

Sedition Acts in the first place. Also, the French Revolution was a transatlantic phenomenon that had repercussions for France's West Indian possessions. The resulting turmoil in St Domingue especially could not but affect the United States. Moreover, Adams's decisions to release the XYZ dispatches, resulting in their publication, and to send another peace mission to France in 1799 in the wake of the XYZ affair, were examples of him acting "diplomatically."

Alexander DeConde argues in his classic and very extensive treatment of the conflict that "Adams wished to solve the Franco-American crisis through diplomacy" (DeConde, 1966: 11). He concludes that peace came not only because of Adams's efforts, but because France also desired peace just as much as the United States. But as his account demonstrates, those diplomatic efforts were hardly restricted to dealings between high-level diplomats and statesmen, in this case Adams, Elbridge Gerry, Charles Cotesworth Pinckney, John Marshall, and Talleyrand. Adams's diplomacy also concerned itself with what happened in the political arena at home, and so his pursuit of foreign policy had a decidedly domestic face. In sum, the president had to balance many considerations at once: geopolitical realities, public opinion, and unity within his own party.

Again, Adams possessed an awareness of the importance of publicity and public opinion. In 1798, when it became clear that the French Directory had attempted to bribe the American envoys in Paris, he released the XYZ dispatches, which marked the beginning of the undeclared war with France, and on the domestic front set off a wave of anti-French indignation and boosted the popularity of the president. When patriotic gatherings organized by Federalists involved addresses in support of the president's foreign policy, Adams devoted time to answering them. Since they were published in newspapers around the country, he was able to effectively disseminate his views to the public. As other work on this period such as James Morton Smith's *Freedom's Fetters* (1956) and William Stinchcombe's *The XYZ Affair* (1980) demonstrate, the president had to contend not only with the balance of power abroad, but also in domestic politics. In this regard, Stephen G. Kurtz's treatment of Adams's presidency (1957) provides much useful detail on the political wrangling in the press and related sectional issues leading up to the election of Adams and during his presidency. Adams's actions during the Quasi-War, then, are an example of how diplomatic action in effect straddled both the foreign and domestic spheres.

As with Adams's earlier diplomatic activities, communication and the gathering of information were important. In pursuing peace with France, Nathan Perl-Rosenthal (2011) argues that Adams relied on networks of information that helped him to evaluate and resolve the diplomatic crisis with France. Adams – as did many other American leaders in the early Republic – relied on private information networks, which did not work alone. Rather, they complemented and intersected with official channels.

Neutrality – and peace – abroad was also closely related to neutrality at home. Studies touching upon the politics, foreign policy, the public sphere and the political culture of the 1790s such as those by David Waldstreicher (1997), Jeff Pasley (2001), Marcus Daniel (2009) and Rachel Hope Cleves (2009) have often discussed the turbulent nature of the period, and have pointed out the prominent role of media, in particular the press, in the formation of parties and of nationalism. Adams and the peace with France, therefore, offer fertile ground for research for literary scholars and historians of political culture, for both have an opportunity to assess the importance of media and its impact on foreign policy and diplomatic conduct, as well as the relationship between foreign relations and the public sphere.

The Quasi-War, being fought largely in the Caribbean, also meant that the United States could not easily side-step relations with the former French colony of St Domingue. The American colonies had had an ongoing, long-term, if illicit, trade with the French possession in the West Indies. Beginning in 1791, however, the French Revolution transformed the island from colonial problem to a problematic chapter in the Age of Revolution: namely the existence of the first black republic in the Atlantic world. The abolition of slavery and the violent seizure of power by former slaves on St Domingue presented complications for the United States. Among American slave-holders in the South, St Domingue constituted an ill omen: it did not take Thomas Jefferson and others much imagination to conclude that in an Atlantic world that had in part been formed by slave revolt, what had happened on the island colony could well happen in Virginia or in South Carolina. As scholars of the Haitian Revolution often note, this chapter of the Age of Revolution later came to be thought of as "unthinkable," and was subsequently "silenced" (Trouillot, 1995). The American position toward St Domingue, as David Brion Davis (1990), Don Fehrenbacher (2001), Tim Matthewson (2003), Gordon Brown (2005), and Ashli White (2010) have noted, was at best uneasy. Slavery, as David Waldstreicher (2009) has recently argued and elaborated upon, had been a part of the American federal union and its balance of power, and written into the Constitution. For certain states in that union, slavery could be a matter of national security and interest. Moreover, slavery calibrated politics in the early republic. Balances of power could be internal as well as external, and powerful local interests necessarily competed with incipient national ones.

In contrast to Jefferson, John Adams, Douglas Egerton (2002) writes, took a far more liberal approach in his diplomacy toward Haiti – in trading and establishing diplomatic relations with St Domingue short of official recognition – in fact, far more liberal than any administration prior to 1861. While not openly advocating social equality for African Americans, Adams's diplomacy did not base itself on color or servitude. Rather, it was pragmatic, and based on economic considerations and geopolitical realities. As such, a North American, if not hemispheric, empire of liberty would have been better served by the re-election of Adams instead of the election of Jefferson and the "peaceful march westward" that his victory and "revolution of 1800" had wrought. This favorable assessment of the Adams administration's treatment of Toussaint L'Ouverture's regime has been echoed in Ronald A. Johnson's (2011) article-length treatment of American diplomacy toward St Domingue, which discusses how relations between the colony and the United States moved the former to the brink of nationhood. The historiography of the Quasi-War, therefore, suggests that future work on John Adams's approach to diplomacy would benefit from including a treatment of this episode that is more integrated with his earlier activities.

6.5 Concluding Remarks

With his defeat in the election of 1800, Adams retired from public life and settled into a long retirement. He read widely on various subjects – philosophy, theology, and history (and indeed the relationship between all three), often writing his comments and his thoughts in the margins of his books or recording them in his commonplace book. In 1802, he decided to write his autobiography in order to rescue his sullied reputation, whereby he intended to leave to posterity an account of the peace negotiations of 1782 and 1783. Adams kept well abreast of foreign affairs in the latter years of his life.

Page Smith (1962), David McCullough (2001), and John Ferling (1992) have related that in his retirement, Adams concerned himself with how his career would be portrayed in America's history. Specifically, they point out that it was the criticisms of his presidency by Alexander Hamilton in 1800 and by Mercy Otis Warren in her history of the American Revolution that put him on the defensive as regards his conduct as president and diplomat. Adams penned his rebuttals in numerous letters to friends and family (namely Benjamin Rush, Thomas Jefferson, and John Quincy Adams) and in print, whereby he published a series of essays in the *Boston Patriot*, complete with official documents. Upon resuming his relationship and correspondence with Jefferson, he chided the latter for his early support of the French Revolution, his handling of the neutral rights crisis, and for the Kentucky Resolutions. Furthermore, he concluded that it was Jefferson's weak foreign policy that had imperiled the union. Not only should an account of his thoughts on his own diplomacy and that of his successor be included in any diplomatic biography of Adams, but there is ample room for an analysis of Adams as an historian of the Revolution and its diplomacy.

The diplomatic career of John Adams is, on the whole, fertile ground for further research in both the history of American foreign relations and in Early American history. In particular, many such opportunities arise in using the methods of literary scholars and historians of political culture to address what have long been foreign-relations issues, the traditional stomping ground for diplomatic historians – namely, negotiation with foreign powers and the makings of American foreign policy – but for virtually no-one else. As foreign policy is a statement of how a nation makes sense of itself, this sort of undertaking necessarily involves assessing the very structures of the emerging nation and the larger international context. In tandem with structure, this larger endeavor needs to consider the relationship of political culture with ideology, its manufacture and its dissemination, both at home and abroad. A consideration of John Adams as diplomat necessarily touches upon all of these issues. Such work therefore has the potential to address anew the intellectual roots and culture of early American diplomacy, and subsequently, the overall history of the American Enlightenment as the young republic sought to join the European system of nations.

Guide to Further Reading

Several materials have been most useful in this study of John Adams's diplomatic career. Gilbert Chinard's biographical treatment, *Honest John Adams* (1933) is a good place to begin for overall detail on not only Adams's time abroad in France, Britain, and the Netherlands but his political thought. Also in this vein are Peter Shaw, *The Character of John Adams* (1976) and James H. Hutson's *John Adams and the Diplomacy of the American Revolution* (1980). For a more involved and in-depth account that is good to mine for detail on Adams's diplomatic career as well as his thoughts on foreign relations, Page Smith's rich, two-volume work, *John Adams* (1962), is highly recommended. Based as it is on Adams's papers, letters, and autobiography (edited by Lyman Butterfield), it is also a good guide to the primary literature on the subject. More recent assessments in regard to Adams as an envoy abroad consists of two articles: John Ferling (1994a) and Greg L. Lint, "John Adams and 'The Bolder Plan'" in Ryerson (2001). For a good, insightful historical overview of the particularities of diplomacy, Jeremy Black's *A History of Diplomacy* (2010) will provide a good initial introduction and jump-off point, and therefore much to ponder when it comes to understanding eighteenth-century diplomatic realities on their own terms and therefore rethinking Early American foreign relations. For the Model Treaty in particular, the best-known treatment is Felix Gilbert's *To the Farewell Address: Ideas of Early American Foreign Policy* (1961), while Greg L. Lint's (1978) article in *Diplomatic History*, "John Adams on the Drafting of the Treaty Plan of 1776," provides insight into the sources that Adams used to draft it. The most classic works on the Quasi-War are Alexander DeConde's very comprehensive *The Quasi-War* (1966) and William Stinchcombe's *The XYZ Affair* (1980). Slippage resulting from the close and blurred nature between foreign and domestic in the early Republic makes Stephen G. Kurtz, *The Presidency of John Adams: The Collapse of Federalism, 1795–1800* (1957) very useful reading. Recently, Nathan Perl-Rosenthal has made good use of this observation in his article-length treatment of Adams's use of information networks, "*Private Letters* and Public Diplomacy: The Adams Network and the Quasi-War, 1797–1798 (2011). Albert Hall Bowman, *The Struggle for Neutrality: Franco-American*

Diplomacy During the Federalist Era (Knoxville TN, 1974) is also useful for Adams and Quasi-War. For the nature of Adams's diplomatic relations with St Domingue (later Haiti) and their import for Jefferson's "Revolution of 1800," see Douglas R. Egerton, "The Empire of Liberty Reconsidered" (2002). More expansive treatment of the Founders' relations with St Domingue are the central subject of Gordon Brown's *Toussaint's Clause* (2005).

Chapter Seven

John Adams and the Elections of 1796 and 1800

David W. Houpt

John Adams had the dubious fortune of participating in two of the nation's most controversial elections. In 1796, the country faced for the first time the question of who would serve as the next president. George Washington had been the unanimous choice in 1788 and 1792 but declined to serve a third term. With Washington out of the running, emerging political parties competed against each other for the first time on the national stage. Four years later, the election of 1800 nearly tore the country apart. A vast body of literature on these elections exists. Focused monographs, biographies of candidates, and countless books and articles on the early American republic examine the personalities and events involved in the elections. Interestingly, despite being one of the two central candidates, historians have often portrayed Adams as a secondary player in the drama surrounding the elections. Alexander Hamilton, Aaron Burr, and Thomas Jefferson are usually presented as the primary actors. This is likely a byproduct of the tendency to focus on Hamilton's various schemes to undermine Adams and the tie between Jefferson and Burr. Adams had, however, deeply invested in the elections and his role should not be overlooked.

7.1 The Election of 1796: A Lesson in Partisan Realities

The nation's first contested presidential election was the product of a flawed constitution and the development of national political parties. As Jeff Pasley put it (2003: 96), "The 1796 presidential campaign was not supposed to

A Companion to John Adams and John Quincy Adams, First Edition.
Edited by David Waldstreicher.

take place at all." In part, the Founders designed the electoral college to prevent the type of national political organization that the election helped create. According to Noble E. Cunningham (1957: 109), "The contest between Jefferson and Adams revealed that nationally parties were rather sharply defined by 1796; and, in general, both state and national elections showed that parties had gained new strength and confidence." On the other hand, the election of 1796 can be seen as an example of the electoral college working perfectly. Arguably the two most qualified men were elected to the nation's two highest offices. As Susan Dunn points out (2004: 96), "In 1796, an election had taken place. It was neither a "succession" nor the anointing of another charismatic leader. It had been a contest ... In the new post-Washington age, the fatherless children had not run amok." Whether a failure or a success, the election of 1796 stands out as one of the most important elections in this nation's history (Page Smith, 1985: 59).

The Rules of the Game: the Electoral College

Technically Adams was a candidate for the nation's highest office in the first four elections. Because the founders did not foresee the development of parties, the electoral college did not differentiate between candidates for president and for vice president. Each elector simply voted for two candidates, the only stipulation being that at least one candidate must reside outside the elector's home state. Like much of the constitution, compromise was a hallmark of the process for electing a president. Once delegates to the Constitutional Convention agreed on a single executive, the debate centered on whether the president would be elected directly by the people or indirectly by the states. After an exhaustive discussion of different methods, the framers settled on the creation of a special legislature that would meet for the sole purpose of selecting a president. The allotment of electoral votes followed the earlier compromises over representation and gave each state the same weight it had in Congress. Significantly, this meant an acceptance of the three-fifths clause that granted slave states extra representation. The delegates left the decision of how to choose presidential electors up to each state (Kuroda, 1994: 15).

Adams and the Growth of Parties

The elections of 1796 and 1800 were the culmination of a nearly a decade of simmering political tensions. Only George Washington's presence at the helm had prevented partisanship from boiling over. As Cunningham put it (1957: 115), "The retirement of Washington cleared the way for uninhibited party development, and the history of the next four years is the story of the struggle between two opposing parties for the control of the government." Historians disagree over how to characterize the political battles of the 1790s. Many historians have concluded that by 1796 two political parties divided the nation. Political historians such as William Nisbet Chambers, Noble Cunningham, and Paul Goodman (1967) see 1796 as a major milestone in the development of parties. The presidential election encouraged national coordination and helped clarify political differences. Other scholars are skeptical of the degree of party development. James R. Sharp points out (1993: 95) that the clear partisan divide portrayed by some historians "would not have been recognized by the participants themselves". Partisan divisions were, he argues, a reflection of "sectional strife" (Sharp, 1993: 158). In a similar vein, Stephen G. Kurtz (1957: 158) finds that "eighteen-century political life was still predominantly local in both outlook and operation." Others argue that factions of the 1790s lacked the necessary infrastructure to be considered true political parties (Freeman, 2001a: xviii). Whatever terminology is used to describe the opposing groups, the nation's politics had clearly become polarized by 1796.

Like most of the Founding Fathers, Adams had a deep suspicion of political parties. His readings of authors such as Bolingbroke, along with his familiarity with British history, convinced him that factions were one of the greatest threats to liberty. More so than many of his colleagues, Adams actually practiced what he preached. Although he was clearly aligned with the Federalist party, Adams was notoriously independent and partisans could never fully trust him. In some respects, this independent streak earned him the respect of his fellow countrymen. However, this same stubborn refusal to adhere to a party line eventually contributed to his downfall.

During the first years under the Constitution, divisions emerged over economic policy, foreign relations, and political style. Of the three subjects, Adams's only real impact occurred in debates over style. Adams, despite being the vice president, was shut out of most major policy decisions. Washington chose not to include him in cabinet meetings and rarely sought his council. As president of the Senate, Adams did his best to make his presence felt. He rarely missed the opportunity to share his opinion and he cast the tie-breaking vote on a record twenty-nine pieces of legislation. His position on titles, however, earned him the greatest recognition.

Shortly after the first Senate came into session, the question of how to address George Washington arose. Many senators assumed that "George Washington, President of the United States" would suffice. Adams, who attended the Senate in a powdered wig and ceremonial sword, believed that the president needed a more formal and dignified title, one that was not reminiscent of "Presidents of Fire Companies and of a Cricket club." "What will the common people of foreign countries, what will the sailors and the soldiers say" if he was simply known as "President," Adams fretted? "They will despise *him* to *all eternity*" (Bowling and Veit, 1989: 29–32). The

Senate ultimately agreed to "His Highness the President of the United States of America, and Protector of their Liberties," but the House of Representatives rejected the title outright. Adams's role in the title debate earned him the ire of many former antifederalists and future Republicans. His obsession with titles was evidence, they claimed, that Adams was a closet monarchist. After suffering near-constant ridicule during his first term, Adams decided to simply hold his tongue. He played a much less conspicuous role during his last years as vice president (Warren, 2001: 117–135).

The End of the Beginning or the Beginning of the End: Washington's Retirement

As George Washington's second term came to an end, most observers believed that the country's first president would step down. Reluctant to take the office in the first place, Washington had seriously considered retiring in 1792. He stayed on at the behest of both Alexander Hamilton and Thomas Jefferson – one of the few subjects the two men could agree upon. By 1796, however, few arguments remained that could convince Washington to continue. Although he was still the most revered man in the nation, he was no longer seen as impartial. His decision to sign the Jay Treaty and his refusal to share diplomatic papers with the House of Representatives resulted in a steady barrage of attacks from the Republican press. He was likewise criticized for modeling his behavior after the king and accused of trying to establish a monarchy (Dunn, 2004: 70). By early 1796 the general assumption was that he would not seek a third term. But, until he made a public announcement, any overt electioneering could be seen as disrespectful – not something most men were willing to do publically (Pasley, 2003: 205–208).

Adams first learned of Washington's decision in January 1796. At first he seemed unsure what would happen next. "The consequence to me is very serious, and I am not able, as yet, to see what my duty will demand of me," he wrote to his wife. Two weeks later, however, Adams happily reported that he was "as you say, quite a favorite" and the "heir apparent" (quoted in Kurtz, 1957: 79). But, until Washington made his decision public, Adams, like everyone else, was forced to wait.

Washington first approached Alexander Hamilton in May of 1796 to discuss his retirement and ask for an updated draft of a farewell address (Madison had written one in 1792). The original plan was to publish the address at the end of the congressional session. Hamilton urged Washington to delay his announcement as long as possible. He argued that the real possibility that war with France could erupt at any minute meant that Washington was needed at the helm for as long as possible (Sharp, 1993: 139). Republicans, and some historians, argue that this argument was a ploy to prevent the opposition from organizing (Kurtz, 1957: 83–87). As the Republican operative John Beckley said, "the short notice is designed to prevent a fair election, and the consequent choice of Mr. Jefferson" (quoted in Cunningham, 1957: 90; Kurtz, 1957: 80–85; Pasley, 2003: 205–212).

Washington's Farewell Address finally appeared in the Philadelphia newspaper *American Daily Advertiser* on September 19 and by the first week in October it had been reprinted in papers throughout the country. The address was drafted by Hamilton with an eye towards the upcoming election (Pasley, 2003: 100). Looking back at his time in office, Washington had a lot to be proud of. He had overseen the establishment of a stable central government, helped put the nation's finances in order, and avoided war. He was, however, concerned for his country's future. Partisan and sectional divisions coupled with the vicious debates over foreign policy threatened to tear the young country apart. Washington warned specifically against the "insidious wiles of foreign influence" and "permanent alliances," a not-so-subtle reference to Republican support for France (Pasley, 2003: 101).

The Non-Candidates, Candidates

Washington's Farewell Address was, according to the arch-Federalist Fisher Ames, "a signal, like dropping a hat, for the party races to start" (quoted in Ferling, 2004: 85) The identity of the two top candidates was clear from the start and partisans wasted little time in promoting their respective candidates. Despite his uneasy relationship with some members of the Federalist party, Adams was the logical successor to Washington. His service during the Revolution, diplomatic work, and position as vice president more than qualified him for the nation's first office. Although he initially expressed some skepticism about the job, Adams became "downright giddy" as the election neared (Ferling, 2004: 83). Adams also benefited from a few vocal supporters. "Compared to other Federalists, Adams advocates were much more disposed to move in public and openly appeal for popular support"(Pasley, 2003: 229).

On the Republican side, Thomas Jefferson was the obvious choice. Jefferson had retired from his position as secretary of state in 1793 and vowed to spend the remainder of his life at his beloved Monticello. During his time away from Philadelphia, Jefferson claimed to pay no attention to national politics (Dunn, 2004: 76; Pasley, 2003: 212–218). Somewhat ironically, Jefferson's position as the leader of the opposition was solidified during this time by Alexander Hamilton. By filling the newspapers with vivid descriptions of Jefferson's secret ambition and clandestine dealings, Hamilton unintentionally established Jefferson as the top Republican (Pasley, 2003: 218).

Unlike Adams, Jefferson was a reluctant candidate in 1796. When first approached about the idea of running for president by James Madison, Jefferson denied any interest in ever serving in government again. The "question is forever closed with me," he wrote (quoted in Ferling, 2004: 76). Politics was, however, in his blood. He was horrified by the Jay Treaty debates and generally feared that the nation was sliding back toward a monarchy. Thus, as the country turned its attention towards the election, Jefferson remained silent – a tacit nod toward his willingness to serve if called. To ensure that Jefferson did not change his mind at the last minute, Madison simply stopped writing him in the months before the election, effectively preventing Jefferson from backing out (Sharp, 1993: 114; Dunn, 2004: 78–79).

While the selection of candidates for president was clear, neither party had an obvious frontrunner for vice president. A general sense existed in both parties that sectional balance was needed on the ticket. Federalists, therefore, honed in on the South, and Republicans focused on the North (Kurtz, 1957: 100). But an established procedure for officially nominating candidates did not exist. Making matters more complicated, public declaration of interest in office was seen as improper. Thus many Americans remained unclear about who was actually running. This ambiguity coupled with the fact that, when voting, electors did not specify which candidate they wanted as president and which one for vice president, opened the door for intrigue (Sharp, 1993: 156; Freeman, 2001a: 216–217; 2001b: 148–149; Ferling, 2004: 87–88).

With no established procedures in place, the selection of a vice president fell to a few influential men (Kuroda, 1994: 64) For the Federalists, Alexander Hamilton appears to have taken charge. Hamilton only begrudgingly accepted an Adams candidacy. His few interactions with the vice president had left a bad impression and convinced him that Adams could not be trusted. For his part, Adams saw Hamilton as an over-ambitious nuisance. As one historian put it, "Adams liked to lead, and Hamilton liked to lead. Compromise between the two was rendered unlikely where viewpoints clashed, owing to mutual jealousy and suspicion" (Kurtz, 1957: 99) For vice president, Hamilton therefore wanted someone he could rely on, if not control. He first considered the aging hero of the Revolution, Patrick Henry. Although Henry had begun his life a radical, he had grown more conservative with time. Henry was, however, content with his life as a private citizen and did not relish the idea of being thrust back into the limelight (Kurtz, 1957: 103; Dauer, 1953: 95–97). With Henry out of the running, attention turned to Thomas Pinckney of South Carolina. Pinckney was on his way home from Europe after signing a treaty with Spain that granted Americans access to the Mississippi. Unlike Jay's treaty, Pinckney's treaty was met with widespread approval. His South Carolina roots made him all the more attractive as a vice presidential candidate. The Palmetto state was one of the few areas in the South where Federalists might have a chance of winning. Once he received word that Henry had refused to run, Hamilton quickly threw his support behind Pinckney (Kurtz, 1957: 105–113).

Republican selection of a vice president was an even more confused and convoluted process. Agreement on a candidate failed to materialize even after Republican members of Congress held caucus in the spring of 1796. Aaron Burr of New York emerged as the candidate with the most support, but he had certain drawbacks. Chief among them was a general sense that his Republicanism was superficial. But Burr had important allies in New York and his presence on the ticket would balance Jefferson's. Thus, somewhat halfheartedly, Republicans accepted Burr as their vice presidential nominee (Cunningham, 1957: 91–92; Kurtz, 1957: 93–94).

Strategies for Victory

Neither Adams nor Jefferson overtly campaigned on behalf of their election. Both men remained secluded at their respective farms. This does not, however, mean the campaign lacked excitement. Like any good political drama, the election of 1796 was filled with intrigue, backroom deals, and questionable tactics. The biggest controversy surrounding the election of 1796 is the so-called Hamilton–Pinckney Plot. It was no secret that Hamilton wanted to see Pinckney elected president. As Washington's closest advisor, Hamilton had grown used to exerting a significant amount of influence over the executive branch. The stubbornly independent Adams could not be manipulated in the same way. Pinckney, on the other hand, was seen by Hamilton as more malleable. Additionally, if Pinckney believed he owed his presidency to Hamilton's scheme, Hamilton might be able to act as a virtual shadow president (Dunn, 2004: 82; Ferling, 2004: 88).

The plan was fairly straightforward. Knowing that Adams was likely to receive one of the votes cast by every Federalist elector in New England and that Pinckney would get one from every Southern Federalist, Hamilton sought to convince every Northern elector to cast their second vote for Pinckney and let the Southern electors scatter their second vote. Pinckney would, therefore, sneak past Adams and win the presidency. In an attempt to scare some of the Massachusetts electors into voting for Adams and Pinckney, Hamilton even had an article inserted into the Boston *Centinel* that warned that the Vermont vote would be declared invalid due to voting irregularities. If this was indeed the case (it was not), the vote for Pinckney was the only way to prevent Jefferson's election (Dauer, 1953: 96–105; Kurtz, 1957: 105–113; Kuroda, 1994: 65; Ferling, 2004: 88).

An impressive degree of partisan unity would have been necessary to ensure that all Northern electors cast their votes for Adams and Pinckney respectively. Not even Hamilton could accomplish such a feat at this point.

Additionally, in order for his plot to succeed, Northerners would have had to be completely unaware of the consequences of their actions. Adams's friends were quick to see that, unless they scattered the second votes, Pinckney could easily pull ahead (Dunn, 2004: 82; Kurtz, 1957: 110–113).

Adams received reports of Hamilton's machinations from various sources. He wrote to his wife that "There have not been wanting Insinuations to make me believe that Hamilton and Jay have insidiously intrigued to give Pinckney a Sly slide over my head. …" (quoted in R.A. Brown, 1975: 20). While he was willing to believe that Jay was innocent, Adams was rightly suspicious of Hamilton. Abigail Adams fumed that Hamilton was "as ambitious as Julius Caesar, a subtle intriguer," and added that "His thirst for fame is insatiable" (quoted in Wesiberger, 2000: 166) The president-elect, however, chose to remain silent on the topic in order to maintain partisan unity. As Ralph A. Brown suggests (1975: 20), Adams "did not want to jeopardize his administration, at the very start, by recognizing and thus widening the schism within his party."

Hamilton was not the only one who conspired against an Adams presidency. Under Washington, America had steadily moved closer to Great Britain and away from France. Washington's decision to remain neutral in the war between France and Great Britain, followed by the Genet affair, severely damaged the relationship between the two republics. The Jay Treaty was the final straw for the French Directory and French ships began attacking American vessels (Kurtz, 1957: 114). Early in 1796, French Minister Pierre Adet came to the conclusion that a Jefferson election was the only sure way to restore the friendship. Adet was a keen observer of American politics and saw that Jefferson had to make inroads in New England if he hoped to beat Adams. After a brief tour of New England, Adet concluded that the merchants could only "be led by fear" (quoted in Kurtz, 1957: 126). Following instruction from the Directory, Adet published a series of diplomatic notes just weeks before the electors met that announced the suspension of full diplomatic intercourse and called on all French citizens of the United States to oppose the Federalists. The implication was that Jefferson's election was the only way to prevent war. As Pasley points out (2003: 105), "[t]his was a blatant attempt by a foreign power to interfere in the internal affairs of the United States, and it was shocking in its frankness." (See also Kurtz, 1957: 126–128; Cunningham, 1957: 101; Weisberger, 2000: 165; Ferling, 2004: 93.)

Whether Adet's actions had a direct effect on the election is impossible to discern. Contemporaries of Adet's believed that the threat of war helped push some pacifist Quakers into the Republican column (Kurtz, 1957: 189–190; Ferling, 2004: 93). Perhaps the more important consequence of Adet's decision to intervene was that the Republicans became even more intertwined with the French in the eyes of voters. This impression arose despite the fact that Adet had acted without the knowledge of either

Jefferson or Madison. As Madison quickly realized, if relations with France continued to deteriorate, this connection could cost Republicans votes (Kurtz, 1957: 132).

In addition to these private schemes to undermine Adams, the newspapers were filled with attacks on his character and reputation. Republicans accused him of being a closet monarchist who was obsessed with titles. Some went so far as to suggest that Adams sought to establish himself as king (Dauer, 1953: 99) Using portions of his *Defense of the Constitutions of Government of the United States of America* as proof, they presented Adams as a man who believed the common man incapable of self-government (Cunningham, 1957: 98). A Philadelphia broadside summed up the differences between the two candidates: "Thomas Jefferson is a firm REPUBLICAN – John Adams is an avowed MONARCHIST" (quote from Ferling, 2004: 89–90) Even some Federalists pitched in, claiming that when it came to the economy, Adams was no better than Jefferson (Dauer, 1953: 99).

Going to the Polls

No two states voted for the president in exact same manner, and the level of interest in the election differed widely. Furthermore, states cast their votes at different times, which made any national strategy difficult. In ten states, the legislature selected electors, four used districts, two held statewide elections, and one relied on a town meeting (Kurtz, 1957: 409). In general, more interest existed in states that allowed voters to select the electors. By today's standards, however, only a small number of voters actually went to the polls (Kurtz, 1957: 145). Though it is impossible to calculate exactly the percentage, turnout never topped 40 percent, and in most states it hovered in the twenties. Considering the fact that most states limited the vote to property-holding white men, the election was decided by only a fraction of Americans (Ferling, 2004: 86) As Pasley concludes (2003: 102): "While the first contested presidential election was a milestone in the development of American democracy, not much democracy was actually involved in the 1796 presidential election."

Most states witnessed little, if any, overt electioneering. Adams was the clear favorite in New England and Jefferson easily won much of the South and West (Kuroda, 1994: 66–67) Campaigning occurred in Maryland and Virginia, states that selected electors by districts, but the contests "revolved around Jefferson's personal character rather than the larger issues of the 1790s" (Pasley, 2003: 103). As is the case today, the election hinged on a few closely contested "swing" states.

New York, a state that could have gone either way, voted early and Federalists won the state legislature, thereby ensuring the state would go for Adams (Pasley, 2003: 104). Both Federalists and Republicans singled out Pennsylvania as a "must-win" state (Kurtz, 1957: 147). Federalists had controlled Pennsylvania since the ratification of the constitution, but Republicans had been steadily making inroads. A growing base of urban radicals along with the coalition of rural voters was primed to seize power. The state selected electors on a statewide basis. To help ensure a Republican victory, partisan operative John Beckley launched an unprecedented get-out-the-vote campaign. After amassing an all-star team of high-profile Republicans to run for electors, Beckley blanketed the state with handwritten ballots and printed handbills. "Like most campaign literature since," Pasley points out, the handbills were "terribly distorted and simplistic" and designed to sway undecided voters. Voters were cautioned that the future of the republic depended on this election. "Will you, by neglectfully staying at home," one handbill read "permit others to saddle you with Political Slavery?" (quoted in Pasley, 2003: 105). Pennsylvania Federalists were caught off guard, and Jefferson took fourteen of the state's fifteen electoral votes (Dunn, 2004: 81–82; Cunningham, 1957: 101–106; Kurtz, 1957: 107–191).

Despite the loss in Pennsylvania, when the results were finally announced in December Adams had narrowly bested Jefferson by a vote of 71 to 68. Pinckney ran third with 59 while Burr managed to get only 30 votes. Adams swept every state north of Pennsylvania. He also won a majority in Maryland and received one vote in Pennsylvania, Virginia, and North Carolina. A survey of the votes for vice president reveals the weakness of the national parties. Only 60 percent of electors voted for both candidates nominated by their party. Thirteen different candidates received votes in the electoral college. As Joanne B. Freeman points out (2001a: 223; 2001b: 154), regional loyalty, personal friendship, electoral trickery, and "stubborn persistence" played just as much of a role in the outcome of the election as partisanship did.

Observers disagreed over why Adams won. James Madison believed that the popularity of the Jay Treaty in the North ensured a Federalist victory. Jefferson thought Adams benefited from his association with George Washington (Ferling, 2004: 54) Historians lack consensus as well. Kurtz argues that Adams won due to a combination of New England sectional pride and missteps by the Republicans. New Englanders refused to go along with Hamilton's plan and remained steadfast in their support of Adams. The only person harmed by Hamilton's plot was Hamilton himself. His deception further convinced Adams that Hamilton could not be trusted. Kurtz (1957) also maintains that Republicans helped Adams when they took their criticisms of George Washington too far and ended up alienating many potential supporters. Had Republicans graciously accepted their defeat during the Jay Treaty debates, Kurtz believes, Jefferson would have won (1957: 203). John Ferling contends (2004: 93) that Adams won the election in the South. He points out that, had Adams not won the two

Southern votes, Jefferson would have become the second president Whatever the cause, the consequences were clear – the two highest offices in the nation would be held by men from opposing political parties.

7.2 Round Two: The Election of 1800

The vitriol and passion evoked by the election of 1796 paled in comparison to the feverish reaction generated by the rematch between Jefferson and Adams in 1800. Sharp (1993) suggests that "the political differences in 1800 were of a different magnitude" than those of 1796. "The XYZ affair, the undeclared naval war with France, the Alien and Sedition Laws, the defense buildup, and the Virginia and Kentucky resolutions all had created an unprecedented political crisis in the new republic" (1993: 228). Other than a brief interlude when it appeared that Jefferson and Adams might cast aside their differences and work together to move the country forward, Adams's four years in office were marked by increasing partisanship. On the eve of the election, Federalist clergymen warned that the election of Jefferson would result in an American reign of terror, and New Englanders buried bibles in fear that Republicans meant to purge the nation of Christianity. Republicans pointed at the recently passed Alien and Sedition Acts as evidence of what another Adams re-election would bring.

Although "neither the Federalists nor the Republicans could confidently assumed victory," Republicans entered the election season with the momentum (Sharp, 1993: 227). After an undeclared naval war with France erupted and the French government insulted American diplomats by demanding a bribe, voters had punished Republicans for their previous support of France. Federalists sought to capitalize on the Republicans' misfortune by passing the Alien and Sedition Acts, which were designed to weaken the Republican base of support. Instead of crippling the Republicans however, the laws provided them with a cause to rally around. As the presidential election approached, Jefferson remained the obvious choice for Republicans. Despite his professed distaste for politicking, Jefferson had taken on the role of party leader during his tenure as vice president and did nothing to dissuade Republicans from nominating him (Dunn, 2004: 95–120; Cunningham, 1957: 116–143).

The first-ever Republican nominating caucus for president convened in Philadelphia on May 11, 1800. The forty-three members of Congress unanimously agreed on Jefferson as their candidate for president (A.W. Robertson, 2003: 114). For a running-mate, Republicans once again looked to New York. The choice came down to either George Clinton, the former antifederalist governor, or Aaron Burr. When first approached with the idea, neither Burr nor Clinton appeared particularly interested. Although he would agree to serve as Jefferson's vice president in 1804,

Clinton did not trust Jefferson. Clinton saw Jefferson as a "trimmer" – a modern-day flip-flopper – "who would change with the times and bend to circumstances for purposes of personal promotion" (quoted in Dunn, 2004: 177). Burr remained resentful that Virginia and North Carolina Republicans had not supported him in 1796. Nevertheless, after receiving assurances that the South would stand behind him this time, Burr acquiesced and threw himself into the campaign (Dunn, 2004: 177; Sharp, 1993: 234).

Conversely, Federalists were in the midst of a schism. Much to the chagrin of Hamilton and his allies, Adams had decided the make another attempt to avoid a full-scale war with France. Against the advice of his cabinet, Adams sent a commission to negotiate a treaty (Sharp, 2010: 75). The move, which was widely supported by the public, deprived Federalists of a key campaign strategy – fear. Federalists had become proficient in the art of fear-mongering over the past few years and had used the prospect of a war with France to win elections and generate support for controversial pieces of legislation. Hamilton, who had never been particularly happy with Adams, was livid.

Despite Hamilton's misgivings, a Federalist caucus that met in May of 1800 agreed to support Adams's re-election. Hamilton did, however, make sure he had an ally nominated as vice president. Charles Cotesworth (C.C.) Pinckney of South Carolina, the brother of Thomas Pinckney, was selected to run with Adams. As Edward J. Larson points out (2007: 120), "[p]arty insiders knew that Pinckney's loyalties ran toward Hamilton rather than Adams." Pinckney's nomination also made strategic sense. Not only would his help Federalists in the South but his participation in the "XYZ" affair earned him strong anti-French credentials (Ferling, 2004: 131–132; A.W. Robertson, 2003: 116). Notably, as had been the case in 1796, the Federalist caucus did not specifically state that Adams was running for president and Pinckney vice president. The door was once again left open for intrigue (Sharp, 2010: 90).

The Federalist Party Splits

Adams was well aware of the plot against him in 1796 and quickly came to the conclusion that Hamilton was once again scheming (Elkins and McKitrick, 1993: 735) Adams responded by firing secretary of war James McHenry and secretary of state Timothy Pickering. Both men had served in Washington's cabinet and had remained loyal to Hamilton. At a routine cabinet meeting only two days after the Federalist caucus, Adams unleashed a tirade of abuse and scorn on McHenry. Not only did he accuse McHenry of ineptitude and deceit, the president lashed out at Hamilton, calling him "a man devoid of every principle – a Bastard" (quoted in Ferling, 2004: 133).

McHenry submitted his resignation the next morning. Five days later, Adams demanded Pickering's resignation. As an exclamation point to his break with Hamilton, Adams proceeded to sign orders disbanding Hamilton's beloved standing army (E.J. Larson, 2007: 128).

Although this tongue-lashing may appear to be an act of blind rage, it was actually a calculated move designed to appeal to moderates (Ferling, 2004: 133) By 1800 Adams had concluded that he had more to fear from the Hamiltonian High Federalists than from the Republicans, and that his reelection depended on his ability to distance himself from some of the more unpopular Federalist positions (Dauer, 1953 [1968]: 254). Kurtz goes so far as to claim (1957: 395) that "Adams attempted to present himself to the voters in 1800 as an independent or third party candidate." While Adams was not, as some Federalists feared, looking to join forces with Jefferson, he was certainly aiming to separate himself from the extreme elements of his party (Sharp, 2010: 94–95). McHenry and Pickering epitomized the High Federalists. Their dismissal, in conjunction with the renewed attempt at peace with France, signaled that Adams would attempt to govern from the middle. Firing them also allowed Adams to appeal to Southerners by appointing the popular Virginian John Marshall to head the State department. Samuel Dexter, a moderate senator from Massachusetts, was selected to replace McHenry as secretary of war (Larson, 2007: 128; Cunningham, 1985: 112–113). Although he may have acted with forethought, Adams clearly let his temper get the better of him. Even some of Adams's allies feared he had gone too far. No one doubted that McHenry would give Hamilton a full report of the events. Republicans, meanwhile, praised the move and happily watched as their opponents attacked one another.

Hamilton reacted with predicable scorn, but few observers were prepared for just how far his anger would take him. "My mind is made up," Hamilton wrote. "I will never more be responsible for [Adams] by my direct support, even though the consequences should be the election of Jefferson." If his party was going to support a man as unhinged and reckless as Adams, Hamilton felt he was left with but one option: to "withdraw from the party" (quoted in Dunn, 2004: 161–162; see also Elkins and McKitrick, 1993: 740). Hamilton eventually backed away from this threat, but could not remain silent. Over the protestations of fellow Federalists, he penned a scathing 53-page pamphlet entitled "Letter from Alexander Hamilton Concerning the Public Conduct and Character of John Adams" in the fall of 1800. Hamilton claimed that the document was meant to be circulated privately, but a copy was quickly leaked and reprinted across the country. As Joseph Ellis points out (1993: 28), the pamphlet was simply a printed version of what Hamilton had been saying about Adams for years. It portrayed Adams as a vain man who was driven by ego and unfit for public office. At the end of the harangue, Hamilton somewhat contradictorily concluded that Federalists should still rally around the president (Elkins and McKitrick, 1993: 737–739; Larson, 2007: 213–218).

> To refrain from a decided opposition to Mr. Adams's re-election has been reluctantly sanctioned by my judgment; which had been not a little perplexed between the unqualified conviction of his unfitness for the station contemplated, and a sense of the great importance of cultivating harmony among the supporters of the government. (Alexander Hamilton, quoted in Dunn, 2004: 164)

The tepid endorsement did little to soften the attack, as Republicans gleefully pointed out. William Duane, the editor of the *Aurora* – a rabidly Republican newspaper – claimed that Hamilton's Letter did "more mischief to the parties concerned, than all the labors of the Aurora" (quoted in Haraszti, 1952: 346).

Opinions vary on Hamilton's motivations for authoring the pamphlet. Some Federalists feared that Hamilton was losing his mind. Sharp agrees that Hamilton was "suffering a severe crisis of self-doubt and despondency" and had "simply lost his moorings" after the death of Washington (Sharp, 2010: 115). Other historians have reached different conclusions. Kurtz (1957: 401) believes that "Hamilton's rash behavior in 1800 was the product of a realization that he had been deserted by the rank and file of his own party" and "was deeply concerned of the loss of leadership." Other scholars have suggested that Hamilton truly did prefer Jefferson to Adams. He did, after all, write that, "If we must have an enemy at the head of the government, let it be one whom we can oppose, and for whom we are not responsible" (quoted in Dunn, 2004: 162). Ferling, on the other hand, views the pamphlet as part of grand plot to advance the election of C.C. Pinckney. Knowing full well that he had lost the support of Adams, Hamilton recognized that his political future depended on electing someone else. Seen from this perspective, the pamphlet, along with a summer trip through New England, was designed to weaken Adams's base of support. Meanwhile, Hamilton planned to quietly promote Pinckney's qualifications. This approach could result in either Pinckney pulling ahead or, more likely, in no candidate securing the necessary number of electoral votes, thereby throwing the election into the House of Representatives where Hamilton could wield his influence (Ferling, 2004: 142–143).

Though furious, Adams chose not to respond publicly to the pamphlet. He would later write that Hamilton "was in a delirium of ambition; he had been blown up with vanity by the tories, had fixed his eyes on the highest station in America, and he hated every man, young or old, who stood in his way or could in any manner eclipse his laurels or rival his pretensions. …" (Adams to Benjamin Rush, Jan. 25, 1806, in Shutz and Adair, 1966: 48.). A public response was, however, beneath him. "I will not write in newspapers nor in pamphlets, while I am in my present station against that pamphlet," he declared. "I dread neither [Hamilton's] menaces of pamphlets nor the execution of them... The public indignation he has excited is punishment enough" (quoted in Brown, 1975: 185–186). Once out of public office, however, Adams did take up his pen to refute some of the charges levied by Hamilton. Shortly after the election, he prepared a response to Hamilton's pamphlet but did not actually publish it until 1809 when he (and his son John Qunicy Adams) came under fire from the Federalist press for supporting Jefferson's embargo against France. Published first as a series of articles in the *Boston Patriot* and later as a book, Adams defended his decision to seek peace with France and viciously attacked Hamilton's record and character (Haraszti, 1952: 7; Freeman, 2001a: 199–200; Freeman, 2001b: 148–149).

Electioneering Strategies

In the midst of the Federalist intra-party fights, states began casting their votes. The parties were fairly evenly matched, so the election would clearly come down to a few key states. The first major state to vote was New York. John Adams had carried all twelve of the state's electoral votes in 1796, but Republicans had made significant inroads since then. Despite an attempt by Republicans to divide the state into districts, the state legislature voted to select electors on a winner-take-all basis. Aaron Burr worked tirelessly in the weeks before the April elections for the state legislature. Taking a page out of the Pennsylvania play-book, he cajoled some of the state's most prominent figures to run for the legislature, and then kept the ticket secret until after the Federalist candidates were announced. On election day Burr appeared in person at polling places to lobby voters. He also dispatched an army of supporters to ensure that every Republican cast his vote (Sharp, 1993: 233).

Alexander Hamilton and his allies were taken completely by surprise by Burr's maneuvers. Instead of recruiting well-known candidates, Hamilton had packed the Federalist ticket with individuals loyal to him. The blunder cost him dearly (Elkins and McKitrick, 1993: 732–733; Dunn, 2004: 176–181; E.J. Larson, 2007: 93–106). Republicans, in large part thanks to a huge turnout in New York City, swept the elections thereby ensuring the state would go for Jefferson. Although Burr's electioneering certainly contributed to the Federalist's loss, Republican success was also symptomatic of a larger shift in the electorate. More and more urban artisans and laborers were coming to identify with Jefferson and the Republican party, an ominous sign of what lay ahead for the Federalists (Ferling, 2004: 128–131, 166–167) Adams, however, placed the blame squarely on the shoulders of Hamilton (Haraszti, 1952: 7; Ferling, 2004: 168).

Hamilton was enraged and embarrassed by the defeat. Politically bested by his personal rival, Hamilton frantically wrote the governor of New York, Federalist John Jay, and proposed a plan that would prevent Republicans from their rightfully won prize. In a now infamous letter, Hamilton warned Jay that extreme measures were required to prevent "an *Atheist* in Religion and a *Fanatic* in politics from possession of the helm." Jay, he pressed, should call the outgoing Federalist-controlled legislature back into session and force passage of a district election bill. Though outside "a strict adherence to the rules," Hamilton assured Jay that "the reasonable part of the world will, I believe, support" the move (quoted in Cunningham, 1957: 184–185). The idea, nevertheless, struck Jay as extreme, and he concluded that such a plan "would not become me to adopt" (Dunn, 2004: 181–182; Weisberger, 2000: 239–240).

Historians have condemned Hamilton for his suggestion and praised Governor Jay's rejection, but the manipulation of election laws for partisan purposes was, in fact, a common occurrence. In January 1800, Republicans in Virginia voted to select presidential electors through a general ticket instead of by districts as had been done in prior elections. Their motivation was clear: to prevent a repeat of 1796, when Adams was able to steal one electoral vote. Massachusetts Federalists retaliated by switching the choice of their electors from district elections to selection by the state legislature. Georgia Republicans did the same. In short, both parties sought to "maximize their turnout" by manipulating the rules of the game (Cunningham, 1957: 144–147; A.W. Robertson, 2003: 118–119).

The loss of New York and intra-party fights put the pressure on the Adams campaign. According to Kurtz (1957), in the months leading to the election Adams made no public statement "without what appears to have been careful consideration as to its probably effects upon public opinion." Adams chose to focus on winning the support of the people rather than the backing of Hamilton – a bold move, particularly when "his re-election would have been assured had he followed the Hamiltonian line" (Kurtz, 1957: 394). In May, in an overt attempt to win support, Adams rejected the advice of his cabinet and pardoned Pennsylvanians who had participated in Fries Rebellion. The pardon infuriated Hamilton and his allies but proved popular in Pennsylvania (E.J. Larson, 2007: 129). Adams then began a long, circuitous journey from Philadelphia to the new seat of federal government in Washington, DC. Along the way, he paused in York, Frederick, and Baltimore and gave a series of speeches that highlighted his role in the American Revolution and stressed the importance of remaining independent from both France and Great Britain. Adams's public defense of his record was unprecedented and signaled his willingness to engage in popular electioneering (Kurtz, 1957: 397–399; E.J. Larson, 2007: 142–150). Adams received a warm welcome in most places, but his appeals to the Revolution and promises of neutrality exasperated High Federalists. On his way back to Massachusetts, Adams was virtually ignored when he passed through areas loyal to Hamilton (Ferling, 2004: 137–139). Even in Boston High Federalists boycotted a reception after Adams toasted the Anti-federalist heroes John Hancock and Samuel Adams (E.J. Larson, 2007: 148).

Print in general, and newspapers in particular, continued to play an integral role in the nation's politics. As Andrew W. Robertson (2003) has shown, the election of 1800 saw "new forms of vivid typography – emphatic punctuation, woodcuts, boldface type" designed to catch "the attention of readers" and convey "the vividness of oral speech in print" (A.W. Robertson, 2003: 117). Both parties utilized the press to mobilize supporters and warn of the consequences of defeat. Republican newspapers, which had been steadily increasing in number despite a series of prosecutions under the Sedition Act, teemed with attacks on Adams and the Federalists. Pointing to the Alien and Sedition Laws and the standing army as proof, Republicans once again charged Adams with being a closet monarchist bent on chipping away at the people's liberties.

Although the Federalist press was lukewarm at best in many places toward Adams, it was unified in the belief that a Jefferson election would be disastrous. Many Federalists honed in on Jefferson's religion (or lack thereof) as his most dangerous quality. "In 1800," Edward Larson writes (2007: 165), "the United States remained a fundamentally Christian nation." Furthermore, the French Revolution had exacerbated religious divisions and put American clergymen on the offensive. Although the specifics of Jefferson's religious beliefs remain uncertain, he was clearly outside the mainstream. Federalist orators seized on various statements Jefferson had made throughout his life and frantically warned that, if elected, Jefferson would launch an attack on Christianity. Federalists also "proudly pointed to Adams's public support for religious institutions: The president attended church, invoked God's name in his speeches, and declared days of prayer and fasting" (E.J. Larson, 2007: 176). As one newspaper succinctly put it, the election came down to whether one would side with "GOD – AND A RELIGIOUS PRESIDENT or impiously declare for JEFFERSON – AND NO GOD" (quoted in Dunn, 2004: 148; see also Cunningham, 1985: 121–125; Ferling, 2004: 145–151). For his part, Adams never attacked Jefferson's religion and believed the strategy actually cost him support. But, as Larson claims (2007: 176–177), Adams "did nothing to protect Jefferson or to reign in the Federalist press" and therefore shoulders at least part of the responsibility.

The publication of a letter penned by Jefferson to Philip Mazzei, a former neighbor who moved to Italy, provided Federalists with another line of attack. In the letter, Jefferson rehashed a standard set of criticisms of the Federalists and characterized them as "an Anglican, monarchical and aristocratic party." Had that been all he wrote, the letter would not have been particularly noteworthy. Jefferson, however, continued that "It would give you a fever were I to name to you the apostates who had gone over to those heresies, men who were Samsons in the field and Solomons in the council, but who have had their heads shorn by the harlot England" (quoted in Ferling, 2004: 153). The consensus was that Jefferson was referring to George Washington. Washington had become even more revered since his death in 1799, and Federalists seized on the letter as proof that Jefferson was a radical bent on upending tradition; (Kurtz, 1957: 232–233).

Federalists in the Senate also discussed a bill that would have allowed them to oversee (and possibly influence) the selection of presidential electors. The "Ross Election Bill" called for the creation of a "Grand Committee", composed of members of both the House and the Senate, which would decide any question concerning a presidential election. The Grand Committee would consist of thirteen men selected by the Federalist-controlled Congress. Not only would the committee have an enormous influence over contested elections, it would be invested with the power to decide whether any "irregularity" existed in the first place. This power meant that the committee would potentially have the ability to overturn any election. Thankfully for the future of the country, the measure did not pass (Elkins and McKitrick, 1993: 730; Kuroda, 1994: 78–82; E.J. Larson, 2007: 78–83; Sharp, 2010: 87).

Election Day(s)

In 1800 the legislature selected electors in eleven states, meaning that only five states allowed the public to vote directly for the president. This led Sharp to conclude that "[t]he election of 1800 was actually less democratic than 1796" when voters in eight states chose the electors (2010: 116). Voting occurred at different times between March and December. As results from the different states trickled in it became clear that the election was extremely close. Despite some scattered Republican opposition Adams easily won in New England, New Jersey, Rhode Island, and Delaware. Jefferson took Virginia, Kentucky, Tennessee, and Georgia. A spirited campaign in Maryland that witnessed "advanced" election techniques to mobilize voters resulted in a split vote – five for Adams and five for Jefferson (Cunningham, 1957: 189–191; Sharp, 1993: 245). The North Carolina vote was likewise divided with eight votes awarded to Jefferson and Burr and four to Adams and Pinckney (Sharp, 1993: 246).

Meanwhile, Pennsylvania's legislature was in a tense standoff over how to select electors, and the possibility that the state would not participate in the election was moving toward reality. Republicans, who controlled the lower house, sought to repeat their success in 1796 by using a general ticket. Federalists, who controlled the upper house, knew full well they would lose a statewide election and so backed a district system that might lead to a few Federalist electors. The legislature remained deadlocked throughout the summer and early fall while the newly elected Republican governor Thomas McKean desperately worked to broker a compromise. Republicans had been counting on a majority of Pennsylvania's votes. After the victories in New York, a Jefferson presidency seemed inevitable. The possibility that Pennsylvania would not vote threw the election into turmoil (Kuroda, 1994: 91, 96; Weisberger, 2000: 232–235; Dunn, 2004: 186–187).

With the situation in Pennsylvania uncertain, both parties turned their attention to South Carolina. Like New York, the state's legislature selected the electors. The fate of the election would be settled in the fall elections. Federalists were confident that C.C. Pinckney's presence on the ticket gave them the upper hand. Their hopes were dashed when Tench Coxe, a former Federalist who now backed Jefferson, published a letter written by Adams in 1792 in which the president denigrated the Pinckneys. "Were I in any executive department," he wrote, "I should take the liberty to keep a vigilant eye on them" (quoted in E.J. Larson, 2007: 179). The Pinckney family wielded enormous power over South Carolina politics and the letter further alienated some Federalists who were already unhappy with the president. It seemed to validate some of Hamilton's accusations that Adams was vindictive, vain, and an unreliable Federalist. Adams quickly sent off a letter to Thomas Pinckney, C.C. Pinckney's cousin, claiming to have no recollection of ever writing the letter. Pinckney seems to have accepted the explanation but the damage had been done (R.A. Brown, 1975: 187; Sharp, 2010: 124).

Although Coxe's letter weakened Adams, the work of Charles Pinckney sealed his defeat. Second cousin to Thomas and C.C., "Blackguard Charlie," as he was known by his enemies, had turned his back on his family and the Federalist party and been elected to the Senate as a Republican. During the election of 1800 Blackguard Charlie worked around the clock to promote Jefferson's election. Despite winning Charleston, Federalists failed to mobilize enough rural voters to retain their majority in the legislature (Cunningham, 1957: 231–239; Elkins and McKitrick, 1993: 742–743; Dunn, 2004: 187–189; Ferling, 2004: 158–160). The final result of the election remained uncertain: electors might vote regionally, as had been the case in 1796, and split their votes between the two Southerners Jefferson and C.C. Pinckney. As Freeman points out (2001a: 227), partisan boundaries were still fluid and regional loyalty and bonds of honor could easily trump party labels. A split Jefferson–Pinckney ticket in South Carolina could, depending on the results from a few other states, lead to a Pinckney presidency.

Counting the Votes

With electoral-college deadline approaching, neither party felt confident of victory. Then, on December 1, the Pennsylvania legislature reached a compromise that gave Republicans eight electors and the Federalists seven. On

December 2, the day before the electoral college convened, South Carolina announced that all eight of its delegates would be voting for Jefferson and Burr. The election was over, and Adams and Pinckney had lost. As details began to trickle in, however, Republicans realized that any celebration would be premature – Jefferson and Burr had received the same number of votes.

Jefferson and Burr each received seventy-three votes, while Adams secured sixty-five and Pinckney sixty-four. Not one Republican elector broke ranks or threw away a second vote. Party discipline appeared – at least on the surface – to have improved greatly since 1796. Cunningham (1957: ch. 9) calls the election a "triumph of party." Ferling points out (2004: 166) that "[w]hereas roughly 40 percent of electors had not adhered to the decisions of the party caucuses in 1796, only one of 138 broke ranks in 1800." On the other hand, Freeman, who is highly skeptical of the existence of political parties before the 1820s, argues that "no Republican had dared drop a vote because each assumed that others would prove disloyal. ... Indeed, regional distrust and personal differences only increased during the course of the election" (Freeman, 2001a: 242–243).

The drama, of course, did not end with the counting of electoral votes. The constitution stipulates that any time the electoral college fails to produce a winner the House of Representatives decides the election. Each state, regardless of size, is given one vote and a candidate needs to receive a majority in order to be elected president (Kuroda, 1994: 99–100) Even though Republicans had captured the House of Representatives in the election of 1800, the presidential contest would be decided by the lame-duck, Federalist-controlled Congress. This meant that Federalists could decide whether Jefferson or Burr became the next president. Thirty-five ballots were cast over the course of a week but neither candidate could claim victory. Although Jefferson had obviously been the nation's top choice, Burr remained coy and refused to publicly declare Jefferson as the president. Tensions rose with each successive ballot. Rumors circulated that the governor of Pennsylvania, Thomas McKean, was prepared to call out the militia if Jefferson did not win. There were backroom deals and intrigue on all sides. Disgusted and dejected, Adams remained above the fray and "took no part in the final phase of the presidential election." Although he preferred to see Jefferson win, Adams chose to leave the outcome to the House and focus his energy on ensuring that the Senate ratified the peace treaty with France (E.J. Larson, 2007: 251). The election was finally settled on February 17, 1801, on the thirty-sixth ballot when Delaware representative James A. Bayard agreed to support Jefferson (Dunn, 2004: ch. 10; Ferling, 2004: ch. 12)

Opinions vary on why Adams lost. Thomas Adams, the president's son, held Southerners and supporters of C.C. Pinckney responsible. Pinckney, after all, had not even managed to win his home state of South Carolina (Freeman, 2001a: 237) John Adams went to his grave convinced that

Hamilton had cost him the election. Not only did Hamilton's Letter surely cause some voters to hold back, Adams believed, but Hamilton was directly responsible for the initial losses in New York (Dunn, 2004: 193) This assumption is not irrational, and many historians have reached similar conclusions. Other scholars, however, believe different factors were at work. Dunn, for example, stresses the role of geography. Adams received every vote cast in New England while Jefferson took 85 percent of the South's total vote. Ferling (2004) acknowledges that Hamilton was at least partially responsible for Jefferson's election, but not for the reasons Adams espoused. Instead, Hamilton and his supporters' "sulky and treacherous obstruction" of Adams's efforts to make peace with France resulted in Jefferson's election. "Had the envoys sailed when Adams first wished them to go … word of the accord with France likely would have reached the United States at least by midsummer 1800, and it might perhaps have turned the heads of enough electors to alter the outcome of the vote" (Ferling, 2004: 168). News of the peace did not arrive until the middle of November, well after the majority of states had voted. Manning J. Dauer (1953), on the other hand, sees Adams's defeat as the product of "the step-by-step loss of the agrarian elements from the [Federalist] party." Despite Adams's best efforts, by 1800 commercial interests controlled the Federalist Party, which drove moderates into the arms of the Republicans (Dauer, 1953: 7.259). R.A. Brown (1975: 190–191) believes that the army and the heavy taxes levied during Adams's administration cost him support in critical parts of the country. Cunningham (1985) dismisses the argument that splits in the Federalist party cost Adams the election. After all, "[t]he divisions in Federalist ranks were the most serious in New England, but Adams lost not a single vote in any New England state" (1985: 130). In fact, Cunningham suggests that Adams's split with the Hamiltonian wing of the party may have actually helped him in Southern and Western states.

Federalists also blamed Adams's defeat on the Constitutional provision that counted a slave as three-fifths of a white man for the purpose of representation. Pickering even called Jefferson the "Negro President" (Dunn, 2004: 208). There is some truth to the charge that Jefferson owed his election to the three-fifths clause. "Had slaves not been counted in the apportionment of state representation in the electoral college," Ferling finds (2004: 168), then "Adams would have edged Jefferson by two votes, sixty-three to sixty-one" (see also Larson, 2007: 250). Additionally, some historians have argued that Adams lost because of the last minute changes to election districts. Had Virginia kept the district system, for example, Adams could have won up to additional eight votes (Ferling, 2004: 168). John H. Aldrich (2005: 34), however, finds that the final electoral vote would have remained the same even if the five states that selected electors with a general ticket had awarded electors proportionally.

Some historians argue that the closeness of the electoral votes masks the size of the Republican victory. Available election returns for those states that allowed voters to select electors show huge Republican majorities. The results of the congressional elections likewise show that voters overwhelmingly sided with Republicans. Republicans won 46 out of the 106 seats in the House of Representatives in 1798; in 1800 they won 67. Additionally, many of the Republican victories in 1800 were quite lopsided. In Pennsylvania, for example, where the electoral votes were split, with Jefferson receiving 8 and Adams 7, Republicans running for the House of Representatives received 24,108 votes while the Federalists garnered only 8,964. Republicans had become competitive in every part of the country. Even John Adams's home state of Massachusetts, a bastion of Federalism, sent six Republicans to Congress (Dauer, 1953: 257). Republicans also captured the Senate for the first time.

Ferling is more skeptical of the argument that the election was a major defeat for Adams and the Federalists. After surveying the available voting returns, he concludes (2004: 170–171) "that the Republicans received about 52 percent of the votes cast in various national and state races in 1800." While these figures do not include votes from Kentucky, Tennessee, and Georgia, where Republicans likely won by large margins, it does suggest that the nation was still fairly evenly split. Ferling also points out that Adams "had run a considerably better race than that conducted by his Federalist Party." Sharp (1993: 171), who is likewise unconvinced that Republicans received a mandate, points out that even with Republicans' sizeable majorities, "the election was not a national political victory for the Republicans." The country remained geographically divided and Federalists retained majorities in New England (1993: 248).

The Revolution of 1800?

Ever since Jefferson wrote that his election was "a real revolution in principles of our government as that of 1776 was in form" (quoted in Sharp, 2010: 169), historians have debated the significance of the election of 1800. Richard Hofstadter (1969: 139) saw the election as "a decisive step ... toward constitutional recognition of the role played by parties in the federal government." Similarly, Dunn (2004) argues that "It was a revolution in the modern – not the astronomical – sense: a transformation" that led to the creation of the modern party system. Additionally, Dunn asserts that the election was "transformational because it proved to be a democratizing revolution – socially, economically, and politically." More Americans gained access to land and the franchise. At the same time, however, the country was "moving backward toward exclusion and inequality" (2004: 276). Along with the election of 1860, Sharp (2010: 169) considers the election of 1800 as one of "the two most critical elections in American history." Adams's defeat "marked the beginning of the end of the Federalist party and began a twenty-four year period of national political domination by Virginia Republicans" (Sharp, 2010: 177).

Other historians disagree with Jefferson's assertion. Henry Adams, John Adams's great-grandson, mocked Jefferson's claim and argued that "it was hard to see how any President could be more Federalist than Jefferson himself" (H. Adams, 1984a: 145–147). Kurtz (1957) contends that "the election of 1800 was not a political and moral revolution because Adams had inaugurated the return to responsible government by his peace decision in February 1799. He had closed the wide gap between what the Republican party stood for and what his administration represented" (1957: 407). He likewise denies that Jefferson's election represented any major shift in the electorate. "It seems highly unlikely that the American electorate was choosing between the underlying political philosophies of Adams and Jefferson when they voted.... It seems more likely that the voters were concerned with the record: with the Alien and Sedition Acts, high taxes, the standing army, and the possibility of future peace" (Kurtz, 1957: 404).

John Adams never accepted that the election of 1800 signaled a revolution. In his mind, the election had been too close to be considered a significant rejection of his policies. Moreover, Jefferson's election had nothing in common with the many violent, bloody, and tumultuous revolutions the world had seen. The election did, however, mark the end of John Adams's prolific political career and is, in this sense, truly consequential.

Further Reading

Brown, R.A. (1975). *The Presidency of John Adams.* Lawrence, KS.

Cunningham, N.E. (1985). "Election of 1800." In Schlesinger, ed. (1985): 101–156.

Dauer, M. J. (1953). *The Adams Federalists.* Baltimore. (2nd revised edn. 1968.)

Dunn, S. (2004). *Jefferson's Second Revolution: The Election Crisis of 1800 and the Triumph of Republicanism.* Boston.

Elkins, S. and E. McKittrick (1993). *The Age of Federalism: The Early American Republic, 1788–1800.* New York.

Ferling, J. (2004). *Adams vs. Jefferson: The Tumultuous Election of 1800.* New York.

Freeman, J.B. (2001). "The Presidential Election of 1796." In Ryerson, ed. (2001): 142–167.

Hofstadter, R. (1969). *The Idea of a Party System: The Rise of Legitimate Opposition.* Berkeley, CA.

Horn J., J.E. Lewis, and P.S. Onuf (2002). *The Revolution of 1800: Democracy, Race, and the New Republic.* Charlottesville, VA.

Kurtz, S. (1957). *The Presidency of John Adams: The Collapse of Federalism, 1795–1800.* Philadelphia.

Larson, E. J. (2007). *A Magnificent Catastrophe: The Tumultuous Election of 1800, American's First Presidential Campaign*. New York.
Pasley, J. (2003). "The Election of 1796." In Shade et al. (2003): 96–109.
Robertson, A. W. (2003). "The Election of 1800." In Shade et al. (2003): 113–127.
Ryerson, R. A. ed. (2001). *John Adams and the Founding of the Republic*. Charlottsville, VA.
Schlesinger, A. M. (1985). *History of American Presidential Elections, 1789–1968*. New York.
Shade, W. G., B. Campbell, and C. Coenen. (2003). *American Presidential Campaigns and Elections*. Armonk, NY.
Sharp, J. R. (1993). *American Politics in the Early Republic: The New Nation in Crisis*. Yale University.
Sharp, J.R. (2010). *The Deadlocked Election of 1800: Jefferson, Burr, and the Union in the Balance*. Lawrence, KS.
Smith, P. (1985)."Election of 1796." In Schlesinger (1985): 59–98.
Weisberger, B. A. (2000). *America Afire: Jefferson, Adams, and the Revolutionary Election of 1800*. New York.

Chapter Eight

The Presidency of John Adams

Douglas Bradburn

Political careers of American presidents can end in glory, but John Adams's did not. Beaten by a rival he had come to despise, mocked and ridiculed by former political allies, Adams slipped out of Washington, DC, on the early morning of March 4, 1801, Thomas Jefferson's day of inauguration. Adams believed that the power of the presidency stemmed from popularity, and he left the office as a deeply unpopular man, although not perhaps as unpopular as his party. Three years earlier he had been toasted throughout the country as the leader of a great and free people, the focus of an enthusiastic national popularity that had only been matched by George Washington. America's pride was "her Adams" – insisted Robert Treat Paine's popular song "Adams and Liberty"– and over the spring and summer of 1798 Adams received hundreds of letters and petitions of support from thousands of citizens. But by 1799 he was reviled in equal measure, with members of his own political party eventually leading the calls for his replacement (Bradburn, 2009: 139–205).

His fall was precipitous, caused partly by self-inflicted wounds, but ultimately complete because of heavy opposition from both inside and outside his party. He would lose his bid for re-election, and policies he supported helped to destroy the national power of his political party. Within two years of his dismissal from office, nearly all the importance pieces of legislation that he signed had lapsed or had been repealed. He never exercised his veto power. But he would defend his actions as president to his death as "deliberate, virtuous, and disinterested" (J. Adams, 1823: 39), an opinion supported by a very small segment of his contemporaries, but

A Companion to John Adams and John Quincy Adams, First Edition.
Edited by David Waldstreicher.

largely accepted by his enthusiastic biographers. In the capricious polls of experts that "rank" the presidents, John Adams invariably makes the top third, and even sometimes cracks the top ten (Schlesinger, 1997).

He was America's first one-term president, and was the father of America's second one-term president. Both of the Adams presidents suffered from a lack of party support, not only because their political power was not born of adherence to party, but also because they tended to independence in thought and action. To say that John Adams really belonged to a party is a bit of an anachronism: he saw himself as the representative of the American people, and the parties themselves were still in their infancy for most of his time in political office. His presidency has been described as a failure, but most historians have come to think of Adams more as a victim of the times and of his enemies, and as a figure of great political courage, who averted a war that might have saved his political career. It is a typical fallacy of scholarship on John Adams to begin by asserting that he has not "gotten his due," for in fact there are numerous books that are extremely favorable to him and this includes at least three serious studies of his presidency and multiple biographies. John Ferling, for example, considers Adams's movement towards peace to be "courageous" and "fraught with political dangers." (Ferling, 1992: 3; see also McCullough, 2001; Diggins, 2003; Kurtz, 1957; R. A. Brown, 1975; Dauer, 1953). But Adams was ultimately a weak executive. He underestimated the power he could command and overestimated the role of popularity in his ability to shape the character of his own administration. Slow to gain control of his office, by the time he had men he could trust around him, it was too late. By refusing to confront the rivals in his cabinet and party he was governed by them. By spending too much time away from the seat of power, he wielded little. Competent politics on a national scale eluded him, as his vision for his role matched neither the reality of his office, nor the necessities attendant on an emerging party system.

The themes of Adams's presidency, transcendent in their historical importance and controversial to historians, relate fundamentally to the place of the young country in a world racked by war and revolution, the relationship between untested political parties and the practice of politics, and the limits of acceptable dissent in a popular government. These issues were all connected, since Adams's domestic policies were dictated by events in Europe and the West Indies, and the party dynamic that Adams confronted took its cues, symbols, and passions from transatlantic influences and the tensions of foreign affairs. The policies he supported helped cause a small rural riot, and helped bring the country to an extreme state of discontent which might have sparked a civil war. But while he bears responsibility for helping to cause and inflame a war scare and the resulting political crisis, he also merits credit for resolving the crisis, and negotiating a peace that secured a clear path for American relations with France for the next decade – none of which endeared him to an inflamed electorate, but all of which have allowed historians to view his political failures with great sympathy. Biographers of Adams are universally forgiving in their assessments of his political skill, and both Stephen G. Kurtz and Ralph Adams Brown, who studied the administration carefully, are apologists for Adams's political behavior, with Brown hopelessly biased in Adams's favor. Kurtz is more interesting and more correct in his assessments, but ultimately reads too much initiative in Adams's politics. Adams was essentially reactive, and too often over-reactive – and he had very little involvement in choosing men or shaping measures.

Adams came to the presidency after two terms as vice president with limited regional support, few political allies, and an extraordinary resumé. As one of the early proponents of independence at the Continental Congress, Adams had first stepped onto the "national" stage more than twenty years earlier – a fact he was quick to mention – and had rarely been without a public office of honor. Yet despite his experience in local and national politics, his expertise in diplomacy, and his recognized learning in political theory, Adams was not understood as the natural successor to Washington until the winter of 1796, and Washington did not make public his intentions to retire until September of 1796. Adams lacked executive experience – he had never run anything, and had never served as a military commander. The vice presidency, as it existed in the early 1790s, was not an office of leadership. And Adams, by his early behavior as the president of the Senate, had alienated many of the active politicians in the capital. Nevertheless, Adams cast a tie-breaking vote in the Senate on more than thirty occasions, moments in which he showed himself to be a dependable supporter of Washington, and by default a member of the Federalist party, which had been organized as a party-in-government to support the policies of Treasury secretary Alexander Hamilton (Guerrero, 1982). Washington never brought Adams seriously into his counsel; Adams spent a large amount of time away from the seat of government, complained often about the office, whined about his own lack of popularity, and lacked the confidence of much of the cabinet. He was never enthusiastically supported by Alexander Hamilton – secretary of the Treasury until 1794 and national leader of Federalist party – and it is unlikely that he would have gained the support of Washington for the presidency if Hamilton had remained in Philadelphia.

Hamilton's animosity to Adams stemmed from distrust and a deep philosophical disagreement about the direction the country should take. Adams, for his part, although he had been impressed with Hamilton's drive and intelligence, considered him too prone to intrigue, and ultimately came to fear his intentions – although perhaps only after it was too late. In the election of 1796, Hamilton played a deep game. Publicly professing and extolling the virtues of John Adams, he privately sought a scheme that would place Adams in the second spot again, this time to the

South Carolina "Great Man" Thomas Pinckney, recently returned to the United States from his successful negotiation of the treaty of San Lorenzo, with Spain. But Hamilton's plan, which attempted to have Southern electors support Pinckney over Adams, failed to convince New England electors, contributed confusion to the Federalist cause, and only succeeded in exposing the regional distrust of the American electors. It ensured that Thomas Jefferson would garner the second most votes, becoming vice president. The regional nature of the voting, which saw Adams gain only two electoral votes south of the Mason–Dixon line, revealed the reality of the partisan divide over the outspoken New Englander. In fact, Adams's election was almost dumb luck. A few random electors voted for him; if two had changed their minds there would have been no majority candidate. There was no one to replace Washington as a national figure, and the fantasy that the president could somehow stand above region – without an aggressive engagement in the nascent party system – should have been clear to Adams. Mocking Adams's margin of victory, his enemies would brand him the "president by three votes."

In the abstract, Adams understood his power as president to be "monarchical" in character, a presumption that would rankle his opponents, and weaken his own ability to navigate political controversy. As an executive with "monarchical" authority, Adams thought he could serve as a patriot king – stand above party, and rule in the national interest. He considered the United States to be a limited monarchy – like the United Kingdom – but with too many limits on the executive. He was pedantic in his definitions and so therefore found himself constantly having to clarify his notions of "aristocracy, monarchy, republics," and so on (Schutz and Adair, 1966; G.S. Wood, 1969: 567–592). It was a naïve thought, and quickly fell prey to the party commitments that had elected him. Even Washington had ceased to have diverse opinions around him by 1795, and the cabinet had become an important arm of party government. But while the tall, commanding Washington – who spoke little in public, disliked argument, and encouraged consensus – could effectively stand above the fray early in his presidency, the loquacious, passionate Adams could not. In neither his public behavior nor his private inclinations did he have much patience to heal political differences; rather he seemed to enjoy exposing the hypocrisy and foolishness of all who disagreed with him. Although a brilliant observer, he was not a leader of men. Once Adams began to act without the advice of his cabinet, he was effective – in short bursts of activity. Adams always prided himself on his independence, but as president his independence too often translated into isolation. He needed more allies to give consensus to his decisions and afterwards, to explain his actions. But his independent moves greatly weakened his party, by exposing and exacerbating a great rift in Federalist allegiances, a breakdown that ultimately insured that he would serve only one term.

As president, Adams was reinforced in his own prejudices and hampered in his perspective by his wife Abigail, whom he relied upon for advice and companionship. As he took the reins of power, he wrote to Abigail to come at once: "I never wanted your advice and assistance more in my life," he wrote, and his presidency would be marked by his earnestness to be with Abigail, and away from the storms of politics. Edith Gelles (2001) argues that Abigail was the original First Lady of politics, and she certainly was, but however much she aided Adams in his process of working through a problem, she was an ineffective political advisor since she indulged John Adams's worst instincts. While her political opinions largely mirrored his own, her political instincts tended towards defensive paranoia, and her private letters, while brilliant in themselves, are filled with the extravagant rhetorical flourishes of a partisan leader. She considered Adams's enemies nothing more than dupes of France and pure "Jacobins." The brilliant Albert Gallatin she called the "Jesuit" Gallatin, hated him as a "foreigner," and considered him a "subtle," "artful," and "designing" enemy. Matthew Lyon, the obnoxious congressman from Vermont, was "the beast Lyon." Even her good friend Elbridge Gerry she thought had a "kink in his head." Added to this she was particularly prickly about her rank and the continuing adoration of George Washington, which created embarrassment for the first couple in the Philadelphia social scene, when she flatly refused to attend a dinner in honor of Washington's birthday. Of course, in her rhetorical excesses Abigail was no worse than the opponents of the president, or even Thomas Jefferson, but she was not a moderating influence on Adams's judgment, and in fact, with her willingness to invoke Providence on the side of her cause, more likely had a tendency to inflame his vanity. She certainly contributed to his enthusiasm for war with France in the spring of 1798, as she celebrated his "manly" stance, openly accused vice president Jefferson of being in league with the French, circulated pamphlets calling for the expulsion of immigrants, and demanded some sort of "sedition bill" to use the "wrath of the public" to destroy the political writers who attacked the president. In June she would complain to a close friend that Congress was "dillydallying about passing a bill enabling the president to seize suspicious persons and their papers."[1] It was during her illness and indisposition that President Adams would decide to send another peace mission to France.

So Adams as president was hampered by his own lack of political acumen, by his isolation, and by a lack of moderate advice. He could see only ambition and foreign influence all around him. He alone – as he and Abigail noted often – seemed to stand against the inevitable perversion of the interests of the country. Within two weeks of his inauguration he wrote to Abigail that he could "see how the thing is going." At the next presidential election, he argued, the British would support John Jay and the French would put up Thomas Jefferson – and the country would experience "all the Corruption of Poland" (John Adams to Abigail Adams, Mar. 17, 1797,

Adams Papers, reel 386). These are ridiculous flourishes, and they reveal a man indulging in self-pity and already resigned to a failed presidency. His willingness to accuse highly regarded men of collusion with a foreign government – even men of his own party like John Jay, who would become a stalwart supporter of Adams – would eventually weaken his party, and his own reputation. As president, he needed to be more discreet.

And yet, while Adams began his term in office thinking the worst of his allies and his enemies both, he made little effort to remove them from influence, either by replacing untrustworthy ministers, or by attempting to set up his own avenues of influencing public opinion by working closely with pro-administration newspapers.[2] He simply refused to behave like one of the leaders of a political organization, insisting that he stood above party for the nation. But he relied on party men to help him govern. The three most important officers of the executive branch – secretary of state Timothy Pickering, secretary of the Treasury Oliver Wolcott, Jr., and secretary of war James McHenry were kept at their posts, a decision that would ultimately cripple his presidency. With hindsight, Adams's retention of these Secretaries is an obvious blunder but at the time he came to office there was no precedent for removing people from high offices, as long as they were willing and competent to continue, and Adams looked to maintain the integrity and continuity of the government. He also was aware that he would have a difficult time replacing these major officers of state. The pressures of office, the growing scurrility of the public debate, the lack of financial compensation, and the health risks of Philadelphia in the summer were pushing people away from serving. Even George Washington struggled to fill the most eminent office – the secretary of state – asking six other men before offering Timothy Pickering – who had no diplomatic experience – the post (Kurtz, 1957: 239–60). Good men were hard to find. But as they were not beholden to Adams for their office, they did not extend their loyalty to him but to the men who were responsible for their appointment – George Washington and Alexander Hamilton. While Washington remained informed but aloof from any direct influence on the cabinet, Alexander Hamilton took the whip hand whenever it was offered – and it was offered regularly. Keeping these men in place proved a tremendous blunder, and their influence touched the main crisis of Adams's presidency – what to do about the French (DeConde, 1966).

As Adams ascended to the presidency in March of 1797 the threats and posture of the expansionist French Republic dominated the scene of events. Unsatisfied with the bargains made between the British and the Americans in Jay's treaty, particularly the abandonment of the principle of "free ships and free goods," and having failed to stop ratification and the election of John Adams to the presidency, the French Directory began a policy of open belligerence against the United States. First, they refused to recognize the American minister plenipotentiary Charles Cotesworth Pinckney, insulted him, and forced him to leave French soil. Second, they announced a policy of open warfare against American merchant shipping, and began seizing and condemning ships in the Caribbean. They promised to hang any American sailors found on British ships. Adams confronted the crisis by calling an emergency session of Congress, and asking his cabinet for advice. Without informing the president, Wolcott, McHenry, and Pickering sent Adams's queries to Alexander Hamilton for comment. All three men received extensive notes from Hamilton outlining what he thought the "actual government" should do (DeConde, 1966: 386n36). In fact, the course of the administration was initially set by policies recommended by Hamilton, in terms originally framed by Hamilton and unknowingly repeated by President Adams.

So the stance towards France represented a defiant belligerence, and combined a suite of defensive measures with the creation of a special commission to attempt to negotiate a new relationship with the Directory. The policies included the creation of a stamp tax to pay for an enlarged navy. Merchant ships trading in the Mediterranean and the East Indies were armed. The opposition to Adams immediately believed the policy to be the one advocated by a "pro-British" wing of the Federalist party, and began attacking Adams as little more than a puppet of British merchants, speculators, and Hamilton. In this posture the first year of Adams's presidency passed, the debate over whether the country should pursue war or peace became a party issue, and the stage was set for the dramatic events of 1798 and 1799, which would mark the beginning of the end of the Federalist party.

The three ministers appointed for the special commission were C.C. Pinckney of South Carolina, John Marshall of Virginia, and Elbridge Gerry of Massachusetts. Gerry had no Federalist credentials to speak of, and although loathed by Hamilton's faction, he was the personal choice of Adams, being one of the few Republicans with whom he could still work. His participation gave the commission an appearance of cross-partisan participation, and ultimately proved essential for maintaining negotiations after the formal process had fallen apart. The amateur character of American diplomacy was on exhibit in Directory France. The French minister of foreign affairs, Charles Maurice de Talleyrand-Périgord, had no intention of treating with the Americans on equal terms. He perceived the Adams administration as little more than a tool of Britain, and intended to string the American ministers along as long as possible. Through his agents – known eventually as Messieurs X, Y, and Z – he requested bribes for access, his typical practice, but the Americans believed the price was too high. Even worse these requests for bribes and "loans" were accompanied by threats, particularly threats to revolutionize the American government using supporters already in the country. Outraged, Marshall and Pinckney made plans to leave the country while Gerry stayed behind to attempt to salvage something from the mission.

The dispatches from the commissioners reached Adams in March of 1798 and quickly transformed the dynamics of American politics. Adams took a long view of the breakdown in relations with France and the crisis that faced the nation. At first he thought the behavior of the French meant that war existed or was inevitable. And when he attempted to place the state of affairs before the nation, he clearly believed French threats of internal subversion were not only possible, but visible in the party strife that had dominated his presidency. Adams was something of an analytical historian in his political analysis, and he placed the causes of the crisis upon foreign interference and Americans who had been misled or confused. But now the true tendency of the course of events was revealed, and America needed to be roused to a warlike posture to face this threat to national existence.

Adams did not work with the legislature directly; he allowed other men to write the laws and guide the policy. He considered the executive branch wholly separate from the process of legislation (in fact he considered the separation a great weakness of the design of the constitution) so he would only have an indirect impact on the direction that Congress took in the midst of this war scare. But although he wrote no bills, his attitude and argument through the spring of 1798 had an important impact on the mood and character of the Congress. In fact, Adams was far ahead of the bulk of his party in his eagerness for war preparations, laws to control sedition and dissent, and the inevitability of open war. Even Hamilton would later admit that Adams should get credit for the "manly and courageous lead" that he took to "rouse the pride of the nation" (Hamilton, 1800: 22–23). Abigail fueled his enthusiasm, which was in turn stimulated by the dramatic public response to Adams from April and into the summer. He was feted and celebrated throughout the United States. Rousing songs were preformed and sung in his favor. He took to wearing his military uniform at public events. And as hundreds of addresses of support streamed into Philadelphia, Adams answered each of them in turn, putting his particular voice at the forefront of the nationalist frenzy (Bradburn, 2009: 139–167).

The triumphant Federalists in Congress pushed through a breathtaking series of bills, which promised to transform the relations of the United States with France, and the relationship of the citizenry to their national government. The treaties with France were abjured, the use of force was authorized against the French at sea and an embargo was placed on all French commerce. A navy department, a marine corps, funding for arsenals and port defenses, and substantial funding for new warships were passed. An Act authorizing the president to raise a provisional army, an Act allowing the president to borrow five million dollars from the National Bank at his discretion, and a direct tax to pay for anticipated costs were also passed. The Federalists created a series of laws to exorcise all foreign elements from the American citizenry. A new Naturalization Act extending the wait for citizenship to fourteen years, the Alien "Friends" and "Enemies" Acts, and the Sedition Act, represented a break with past efforts to deal with immigrants and political dissidents in the United States. No longer sure that the American character could remain inviolate against the perceived dangers of foreign influence – despite the numerous memorials of loyalty – the Federalists in Congress strove to regulate immigrants and aliens and legally deny all legitimacy to any opposition to the Federalist government (Bradburn, 2009: 162–167).

At the end of the exciting term, Adams retired to Quincy, to the seclusion of his farm. He continued to spend a large amount of his time responding to patriotic addresses, a responsibility that he took seriously. But from Massachusetts he failed to control his administration, which became clear as the question of the rank of the major generals needed to be finally determined. After Washington, Adams had nominated Alexander Hamilton, Henry Knox, and C.C. Pinckney, and Adams believed that Knox possessed seniority over Pinckney and Hamilton. But his cabinet officers were friends of Hamilton, and had already secured a promise from Washington that he would only serve with Hamilton as his second-in-command. Adams did not know, or pretended not to know, of Washington's preference, and loathed the idea of Hamilton in the second spot. After a series of long letters of explanation, excuses, and justifications between Adams and his secretary of war James McHenry, Adams began to see that he would not get his way. At the same time Hamilton moved behind the scenes to get Washington involved in the debate. Ultimately, Washington threatened to resign if Hamilton was not placed in the second spot, and Adams knew such a move would create a political firestorm. He gave in (Smith, 1962: 2.980–983). So at the height of his popularity – popularity that Adams wrongly assumed gave him influence – he stumbled into a foolish fight with Alexander Hamilton, a fight that ultimately led to a collision with George Washington, and from Adams's perspective, humiliation. And the whole tendency and momentum of his presidency was transformed.

The squabble over the command structure in the army marks the moment when Adams's ardor for war disappeared. Only two weeks before he gave in to Washington's demand he expressed desire for a possible temporary British alliance. But as he lost his fight over control of the command structure of the army, he could finally see that his cabinet served another master. And if war actually came, he would be president in name only. If Hamilton would command the army, then there would be no war – if Adams could help it – and if there had to be a war, then it would be best to restrict it to the navy. Benjamin Stoddert, the first secretary of the Navy, appointed in the heady spring of 1798, was not beholden to Hamilton. Besides, as Adams noted, rejecting the need to begin recruiting troops for the new army, there was "no more prospect of seeing a French army here than there is in Heaven" (John Adams to James McHenry, Oct. 22, 1798,

Adams Papers, reel 389). This became particularly true after news of the battle of the Nile (August 1–3, 1798) reached the United States. With the destruction of a major French fleet in the Mediterranean, the French could not even retrieve their army from Egypt, and there was no chance of an invasion across the Atlantic. In some ways the fall of 1798 marks the end of Hamilton's surrogate presidency. As Adams began moving alone to find a way out of war, he never used the advice of his cabinet again – and so never again heard or heeded Hamilton's secondhand advice.[3] It would take a year at least for the final break to happen, but when it did the rift destroyed the Federalist party as a national force.

For a president looking for a reason to justify sending a new mission to France, despite having insulted the French publicly in every possible way, there were numerous positive signs. By late summer, there were clear formal assurances, and numerous informal suggestions that France did not desire open war with the United States. Talleyrand himself ensured that guarantees of French good behavior would reach the Adams administration. By the spring of 1798 the wily minister recognized that he had overplayed his hand. The United States could not be bullied in the same fashion as European states, because the threat of the French army was never quite real. He had intended simply to delay the American ministers, extort some money, buy some time, and wait for a new American election. The abrupt departure of C.C. Pinckney and John Marshall threatened a real break, something Talleyrand did not intend, as it could have lead to a war from which France had nothing to gain and much to lose, including its Caribbean colonies, any chance of regaining Louisiana, and a general strengthening of Britain's power. Successful in persuading Gerry to remain, Talleyrand nearly lost control of the situation when the XYZ dispatches were published and became known in France. In the face of a public outcry Talleyrand immediately began rescuing himself – denying knowledge of everything, arguing that his agents had acted without his control, attacking the Americans for gullibility and naiveté, and engaging in series of mock conferences with Gerry in which Gerry named names, while Talleyrand pretended to be astonished. Perhaps most importantly, Talleyrand sent Louis André Pichon to reignite an old friendship with William Vans Murray, the American minister at The Hague. Through Pichon Talleyrand would communicate his earnest desire for peace and good relations with the United States, including an important letter that assured that America would be treated as a "free, independent, and powerful nation," the very terms Adams demanded in his addresses to Congress in the spring (Talleyrand to Pichon, Sept. 28, 1798, in C.F. Adams, 1850–1856: 8.690–691). Murray was not only the representative of the United States at The Hague. He was also the intimate friend of John Quincy Adams, American minister at Berlin. The Directory, for its part, released American seaman held as prisoners and lifted embargoes on American ships in French ports.

Talleyrand also instructed French colonial courts to release American merchant ships and restrain the activities of corsairs and privateers. He would eventually consider his ability to keep the United States from actually declaring war, and therefore thwart the intrigues of the British as one of his greatest diplomatic triumphs (DeConde, 1966: 226).

The news of these peaceful actions and sentiments flowed into the United States from numerous quarters, both official and unofficial: from Murray in The Hague and Adams's sons John Quincy and Thomas Boylston in Berlin;[4] from private individuals like George Logan, who secretly visited France over the summer of 1798, and returned with official word of the French actions; from the Polish patriot Thaddeus Kosciuszko, who was asked by Thomas Jefferson to meet with the Directory on behalf of peace. And of course from Gerry himself, who met with Adams in private in Braintree, Massachusetts, and whose letters from his mission were published in the United States in January 1799. Finally, Adams heard the opinion of George Washington, who had received an extensive letter from Joel Barlow suggesting that France did not want war, a letter which Washington believed was written with the full knowledge of the French government. Importantly, Washington also asserted that the American people wanted peace – an opinion that could not be found in the Federalist newspapers, but which Washington could not fail to hear in Virginia, where the opposition to war, and war measures, was broad and loud. In fact, the popular agitation against the Alien and Sedition Acts, the direct taxes, and the standing army, was still spreading in the spring of 1799, and played a crucial role in assuring that Adams would attempt to negotiate peace and a new treaty with France.

While many historians have considered Adams's decision to send a new mission to France as an act of great political courage that ruined his chances for re-election – an opinion insisted upon by Adams after he left the presidency – they overstate the case, and misinterpret the impact of the peace overtures on Adams's chances for re-election. Political decisions that are popular with at least three-quarters of the voting public are not courageous, or difficult. War with France made no sense by February of 1799, and very few people were in favor of war when Adams announced that he would nominate William Vans Murray as minister plenipotentiary to France. Given all the evidence – much of which was available to the public – it was the only responsible course of action to pursue. He not only had the support of the opposition, but of a substantial body of Federalists, including much of the merchant community, and some of the most important Federalist leaders including John Jay, John Marshall, C.C. Pinckney, Benjamin Lincoln, Henry Knox, and George Washington, in addition to his own secretary of the Navy Benjamin Stoddert and the attorney general Charles Lee. From this nucleus of leadership, representing all the regions of the Union, Adams could have built a powerful coalition. The new Federalists who came to power in the elections held shortly after the announced mission to France also tended to be outside of the mainstays of Federalist power, and therefore willing to follow Marshall more the Hamilton.[5] Once Adams made his decision to send a new mission to France, he should have seized the initiative in his party, built a new ruling coalition around support for a strong but small navy, and ceased all efforts to create a large army.

But Adams took a more passive approach, seemed to second-guess himself, and eventually fled the scene. First he expanded the commission to include high federalist Oliver Ellsworth, and North Carolinian Willie Davie in response to pressure from Federalist senators, with support from secretary of state Timothy Pickering, who threatened to block Adams's nomination. Second, although he nominated the ministers to treat with the French, he delayed sending them, until more evidence that they would be received could be amassed. Finally, he kept his cabinet intact, despite their clear distain for Adams's decision. Frustrated with their opposition to his plans Adams threatened to resign the presidency to Thomas Jefferson if they would not follow his guide. Wolcott, McHenry, and Pickering, for their part, behaved as if nothing had changed, and continued to hope to draw the French into open war, prosecute enemies under the Sedition Act, and sniff out French conspiracy and perfidy.[6] The Federalists in Congress continued to follow the suggestions of Hamilton, and the policy of the anti-French wing of the Federalist party. Pressed by Hamilton, they would continue to attempt to constitute the army – in fact recruiting only began in earnest in the spring of 1799 – and they succeeded in postponing the commission to France. Delaying the commission was relatively easy as John Adams fled Philadelphia for his farm at Quincy from late April until October of 1799. Despite repeated entreaties from his allies, Adams refused to leave Quincy. As Uriah Forrest complained, "The people elected you to administer the government. They did not elect your officers" (Uriah Forrest to John Adams, Apr. 28, 1799, in C.F. Adams, 1850–1856: 8.637–638). The absence of Adams was critical, as it meant that he would not lead the Federalist party in the cause of peace through naval strength, but would instead continue to allow the Hamiltonian faction to pull the party further away from the trends of mainstream opinion. With the election year of 1800 looming Adams had completely lost control of his party, and only succeeded in pushing moderates into the lists for Republicans.[7]

The problem with continuing the policies of the spring of 1798, even with the prospective launch of a new peace commission, was that the legislation was tremendously unpopular, and had outlived its purpose. Not only had tens of thousands of people petitioned the Congress to repeal the Alien and Sedition Acts by early 1799, but from every indication there was no need for a large standing army – as Adams himself admitted. Even worse, the British behaved badly throughout the summer and into the fall and winter of 1798–1799, impressing sailors from American ships and seizing American merchant ships ostensibly carrying contraband goods for the

French. So the persistence of the army, and the taxes to pay for it, weakened support for Adams and his party. It also raised serious questions about what the army was built to do, and numerous Federalists were not shy in noting that the army would be useful in putting down popular dissent – an idea that was anathema to the vast majority of the American citizenry, Federalist and Republican alike.[8] The grumblings even in areas of traditional Federalist strength had begun in the fall of 1798, with the first appearance of tax collectors, and would continue even to open insurrection in the spring of 1799. Jacob Fries's rebellion was a relatively puny affair, but it was a significant harbinger of things to come. Fries himself and his neighbors, the men who assaulted tax collectors and freed their men from jail, had always considered themselves Federalists. John Adams declared Fries a traitor, mobilized both militia and new federal forces, and quickly put down the rioting. But as Adams retreated to his sanctuary at Quincy, Pennsylvania Republicans conducted a well-organized campaign that would culminate in a Republican triumph. Winning the governor's office and a majority in the legislature with a campaign focused not on local issues but on the Alien and Sedition Acts, peace with France, and federal taxes, Pennsylvania Republicans anticipated the direction of the country in the elections of 1800.[9]

The last year of Adams's presidency was marked by his increased frustration with his cabinet, and the complete collapse of his relationship with the Hamiltonian wing of his party. With Adams at his farm at Quincy, Pickering, Wolcott, and McHenry were able to delay the peace mission throughout the summer of 1799 and into the fall as news of instability in France reached the United States. Finally returning to the seat of government in the fall, Adams insisted that the ministers leave in early November despite the continued opposition of Hamilton, who told the president that Britain might declare war if the commission was actually sent to France, and predicted that the French monarchy would be restored before the end of the year. Adams kept his own counsel and further infuriated his cabinet by rejecting their advice, hiding his own plans until they were already in motion. The Ellsworth mission was eventually a success, aided by the fact that the ministers arrived after the fall of the Directory and the rise of Napoleon to First Consul. Napoleon retained Talleyrand and hoped to enlist the Americans in the creation of a new armed neutrality against the British. The convention eventually negotiated by the Americans in Môrtefontaine permanently abrogated the old American–French treaties, and ended the Quasi-War – although as many opponents to ratification noted, it did not indemnify American shipowners for French depredations, and played into Napoleon's European politics (DeConde, 1966: 223–293).

The actual provisions of the Convention would have no impact on the presidential elections of 1800, however, as the outcome of the mission was still uncertain when electors were chosen in the fall of 1800. Adams had strengthened his position with the American voting public over the course of the year, but his party had nearly collapsed in the face of an open and public breach between Hamilton and Adams. The year began with the death of Washington, the only man who might have been able to heal the breach in the Federalist party. The enthusiasm for an expanded military establishment died with him, and Adams refused to promote Hamilton to the first place in the army. Although Congress had not taken an opportunity to repeal the Alien and Sedition Acts in the face of warming relations with France, a coalition of Republicans and moderate Federalists successfully cancelled recruitment for the army, and began to dismiss officers and earlier enlistments. Plans for heavy frigates were delayed, and by the spring of 1800 it became clear that war with France was unlikely (Bradburn, 2009: 168–205).

The president's relationship with his cabinet degenerated over the course of the 1799–1800 session of Congress. While it was finally clear to Adams in the fall that his three most important ministers were disloyal and plotting behind his back, he did not dismiss them because he did not want the politics of his cabinet to dominate the session of Congress. Unfortunately, Adams could not bury his resentments and began what his cabinet would consider to be extremely erratic behavior, grumbling openly about that "alien" Hamilton and the British faction in the country, and refusing to speak with them for long stretches of time. In early May, news that the Republicans had carried elections in New York – assuring that the state would go for Jefferson in the presidential election – seemed to have relieved Adams of any need to retain Hamilton's help, and he dismissed his cabinet in dramatic fashion. James McHenry, secretary of war, was pushed out after an angry tirade from the president in which Adams insulted McHenry for his ignorance in issues of foreign affairs, accused him of plotting with Hamilton, and attacked Hamilton's questionable parentage, calling him "a bastard, and as much a foreigner as Gallatin." McHenry was shamed and humiliated, and weakly left the room noting that he would offer his resignation. A few days later Adams abruptly asked for the resignation of Pickering (Page Smith, 1962: 2.1027–1029).

There was nothing politically courageous about the way Adams managed his cabinet. Pushing out both the ministers was popular with everyone but the Hamiltonian faction, and they were already resigned to supporting Adams in the election, despite Hamilton's wish to put C.C. Pinckney in the first spot.[10] His hectoring and bullying of McHenry was shameful and absurd; he should have jettisoned the incompetent McHenry at least a year before he did. In the month of May Adams also pardoned John Fries and all remaining rebels, and began the first direct politicking of any American president. On his inspection of the new capital at the District of Columbia, Adams went hundreds of miles out of his way to rally supporters, including multiple trips to Baltimore. In these speeches he was conciliatory, talking up the prospects of peace, complaining about British trade policy, and emphasizing his own role in the American Revolution (Kurtz, 1957: 387). Adams was anticipating the movement of numerous moderate Federalists into the Republican party – a journey eventually taken by John Quincy Adams. Meanwhile, Republicans circulated a letter Adams had written years earlier to Tench Coxe, complaining that the Pinckney brothers were part of a British faction in American politics.

As Adams moved further away from the Hamiltonian leadership of his party, Hamilton attempted to move Adams to the second rank in the election. He wrote an infamous diatribe against Adams over the summer of 1800, a letter that eventually made its way into print (Hamilton, 1800). The first published versions of the letter were only circulated after most of the electors had already been chosen. While historians favorable to the Federalists have seen the letter as of major importance, by the time the letter was published the damage had already been done by the policies the Federalists supported (Elkins and McKitrick, 1993: 726–743). The split in the party became clear in the spring of 1799, when Adams decided to move towards peace, and therefore Adams lost the presidential election because he lost New York and South Carolina, and he lost those states because of the policies of the Federalists, and the organization of the Republicans. But Adams ran better than his party in 1800, which is not surprising, given his more popular behavior in the late spring of 1800. Adams stood for peace, while the party still was perceived as the party of war, taxes, and the Sedition Act. The rejection of Adams in the election of 1800 is important, but the real transformation was the Republican victories in the House of Representatives, the Senate, and numerous state houses. In the elections of 1799 and 1800, Republicans won majorities in the state houses of New Jersey, Pennsylvania, New York, and South Carolina. In Massachusetts, one of the strongest Federalist states in 1798, the delegation elected to Congress was evenly split between Republicans and Federalists in the elections of 1800, and the Republican candidate for governor, Elbridge Gerry, lost by only 200 votes of nearly 35,000 cast. But Gerry ran as a friend of Adams in Massachusetts, and his near victory owed much to the New Englander's continued sympathy for the president.[11]

Adams learned of his defeat in the presidential election in December of 1800, as news of the outcome in South Carolina reached the infant capital at Washington. He took his defeat personally, as he should have. Hamilton had made it personal from the start, and Hamilton had damaged his own credibility by trying to push his frustrations on to his party. Jefferson had once been an intimate friend and political ally – and Adams's own conception of politics placed a heavy emphasis on the personal dynamic. He strove for the smiles of lasting glory, personal fame, and honor – despite his insistence that he did not. These abstractions possessed meaning to Adams, as they did to many of the men who hazarded their fortunes in rebellion, and his failure to win re-election ranked as a devastating blow in his quest for lasting fame. To his credit he refused any part in the intrigues which surrounded the deadlocked presidential election of 1800, and concentrated on getting the Convention of Môrtefontaine through the Senate, after its initial rejection. He also appointed John Marshall chief justice of the Supreme Court to replace the ailing Oliver Ellsworth.[12] The appointment of Marshall was one of Adams's significant legacies, given that Marshall would serve till his death in 1835. Adams also supported the Judiciary Bill of 1801, the lame-duck Federalist measure to increase the power of the federal judiciary. With the bill came the creation of numerous new federal judgeships – these positions became the infamous "midnight judges" that Adams appointed up to his last days in office. Adams clearly believed that Jefferson and his allies could not be trusted to uphold the Constitution – as Adams wrote, the revamped Judiciary was essential to "save the nation" from "visionary schemes or fluctuating theories" (John Adams to John Jay, Dec., 19, 1800, in C.F. Adams, 1850–1856: 9.91–92).

Ultimately the Judiciary Act would be repealed, as would the majority of important bills that Adams signed as president. Marshall would remain, as would the United State marine corps – created in the heady days of 1798. Efforts to redeem the presidency of Adams emphasize the vision and integrity of the man but fail to recognize to role he played in enflaming the pro-war spirit, and encouraging the malicious prosecutions of his political enemies in the spring and summer of 1798 – actions which he never disavowed. His belief that a large portion of the opposition would hand the country over to the French was absurd, certainly more so than the complaints of Jefferson and Madison that there was a faction in US politics who desired a war with France and an alliance with Great Britain. Adams realized both of these truths too late, but he had ridden high in the spring and early summer of 1798. In his retirement Adams would defend his Quasi-War as a noble thing, a policy of peace through strength. He also argued that he alone kept the country from an open and devastating war with France, and historians have been too quick to believe him (J. Adams, 1823). War with France made no sense, and the country definitively voted for peace in 1800 – as they would have whether or not Adams sent another mission to Europe.

Notes

1 Abigail Adams to John Quincy Adams, Apr. 3, 1798: *Adams Papers* reel 388; A. Adams to Mary Cranch, May 10, 1789, June, 19, 1798 in A. Adams (1947), 170–172, 193.

2 It is clear that the Federalist political leaders worked less closely with the most important newspapers than their rivals. Of Federalists in tune to the importance of newspapers in the political debate, Hamilton was certainly the most forward, often writing essays to attempt to shape opinion, control debate, and attack his enemies. On the relationship between the opposition party and the newspapers see Pasley (2001).

3 Hamilton castigated Adams at a later date for never using the advice of his department heads, and considered it one of his great weaknesses as a leader.

4 Thomas Boylston returned in early 1799, and delivered first hand the opinion of John Quincy, who was heavily influenced by Murray's relationship with Pinchon at The Hague.

5 New, but moderate, Federalists were elected in the spring of 1799 throughout the Southern states (Kurtz, 1957: 379–83).

6 The finest study of the prosecution under the Sedition Act remains that by James Morton Smith (1956). Historians have often assumed that the Alien Act was never enforced because no alien was arrested under the act. But the Act also contained extensive provisions for the registration, description, and surveillance of aliens, and evidence, still in need of close study, shows Timothy Pickering as the secretary of state eagerly collecting information on immigrants in these years. See Timothy Pickering to Philip Moore, Esq., Nov. 1, 1798, National Archives. *Domestic Letters of the Department of State*, June 30, 1798–June 29, 1999, vol. II.

7 Kurtz (1957) attempts to argue that Adams was an adroit politician, who used the peace initiative to France to better his chances for election. But the evidence seems to undermine his assertions. Adams was an inept politician, who loathed playing politics. There is little doubt that his peace initiatives were popular, but he failed to capitalize on the popularity of the move by allowing the country to wait the entire summer before the mission was actually sent, creating insecurity, and allowing Federalists opposed to his policies room to advocate against the measure and further split the party. Adams eventually returned to Trenton after Benjamin Stoddert implied that plots were in place to ruin peace overtures.

8 Kurtz (1957: 307–333) makes a case that Hamilton and his allies intended to use the army to put down dissent. Scholars continue to be mixed in their assessment of Federalist intentions. In addition, if actual war were to come, numerous Federalists believed the army would be useful in seizing the Floridas and New Orleans.

9 Harry Marlin Tinckom (1950: 237–238) notes that the rhetoric of the elections in Pennsyvania reflected the belief "that the very existence of the nation depended on the selection of the Pennsylvania Governor". On the election, see also Rowe (1978: 285–309).

10 A caucus of Federalist leaders supported Adams ahead of C.C. Pinckney in both December of 1799 and, after the defeat in New York, in May of 1800. Hamilton also failed to convince the rank and file Federalists of New England to abandon John Adams.

11 Republicans captured approximately 69 House seats and the Federalists won 39 – from numbers nearly the opposite, and the Senate was controlled for the first time by the Republicans. New Jersey, Georgia, Kentucky, and Tennessee sent complete Republican delegations to Congress, Virginia sent only one Federalist, Pennsylvania and New York sent majority Republican delegations. Elkins and McKitrick (1993: 741) list the number at 65 and 41; J.C. Miller (1960: 274) has "approximately" 65 and 40.

12 For the reasoning and politics behind Marshall's appointment, see Turner (1960).

Guide to Further Reading

For a recent study that frames itself around the notion that John Adams has been neglected see David McCullough, *John Adams* (2001). A better, more nuanced biography, also meant to finally give Adams fair recognition is Page Smith, *John Adams*, 2 vols. (1962). Studies of Adams's presidency, all of which are favorable to the perspective of Adams, are Steven G. Kurtz, *The Presidency of John Adams: The Collapse of Federalism* (1957), Ralph Adams Brown, *The Presidency of John Adams* (1975), Manning J. Dauer, *The Adams Federalists* (1953). John Wood, *The History of the Administration of John Adams, esq., Late President of the United States* (1802), is a Republican polemic, useful in seeing how Adams was perceived by his fierce opposition. General studies of the era, such as John C. Miller, *The Federalist Era, 1789–1801* (1960); Stanley Elkins and Eric McKitrick, *The Age of Federalism: the Early American republic, 1788–1800* (1993), and James Roger Sharp, *American Politics in the Early Republic: The New Nation in Crisis* (1995), tend to write very little from Adams's perspective, not surprisingly considering that Adams was a fairly passive president.

In addition to the numerous biographies, a useful study of Adams's time as vice president is Linda Dudik Guerrero, *John Adams' Vice Presidency, 1789–1797: The Neglected Man in the Forgotten Office* (1982). The best study of the American French diplomatic crisis of Adams's presidency remains Alexander DeConde, *The Quasi-War: The Politics and Diplomacy of the Undeclared War with France, 1797–1801* (1966). It is also an extremely balanced and useful history of John Adams's presidency. Studies of the election of 1796 are notoriously lacking, but Stephen Kurtz, provides an extensive history from Adams's perspective, in Kurtz (1957: 78–208). See also Joanne Freeman, "The Presidential Election of 1796" (2001), which emphasizes the lack of parties, and David Houpt's chapter (Chapter 7) in this volume. A good study of the international context remains Alexander DeConde, "Washington's Farewell, the French Alliance, and the Election of 1796" (1957).

Chapter Nine

John Adams and Religion

John Fea

In an 1811 letter to Philadelphia physician Benjamin Rush, John Adams described himself as a "churchgoing animal." Indeed, he always believed that he was a Christian. He was raised in a Christian home. He worshipped God in a Congregational church founded by seventeenth-century Puritans. He even considered a career as a clergyman. A cursory reading of his private writings reveal a man who strove to live in accordance with the teachings of the Bible, placed his life in the hands of providential God, and was a loving husband and father who cared for the spiritual well-being of his family. Adams dreamed of living in a godly society. He once imagined a "nation in some distant region" that would "take the Bible for their only law Book, and every member should regulate his conduct by the precepts there exhibited" (John Adams to Benjamin Rush, Aug. 28, 1811, quoted in Schutz and Adair, 1966: 209). Such a society, he wrote, would consist of people who would "be obliged in Conscience to temperance and frugality and industry, to justice and kindness and Charity towards almighty God." (Diary, Feb. 22, 1756, *Adams Family Papers*).

While such a description of Adams's religious life may be enough to satisfy modern-day evangelical Christians who want to claim him as one of their own, scholars who have taken a deeper look into Adams's public and private writings have found a complex figure informed by multiple streams of seventeenth- and eighteenth-century religious thought. Unfortunately, those scholars are few in number. Adams's religious beliefs have been under-explored by early American historians. Benjamin Franklin, Thomas Jefferson, and George Washington are the subjects of scholarly books devoted to their

A Companion to John Adams and John Quincy Adams, First Edition.
Edited by David Waldstreicher.

public and private faith, but there is no book-length study of Adams's religion available. The most thorough treatment of the subject – Philip Kevin Goff's (1993) University of North Carolina doctoral dissertation, "The Religious World of the Revolutionary John Adams" – has yet to be published. Moreover, Adams biographers give cursory attention to his religion. John Ferling's (1992) *John Adams: A Life* has little discussion of his religious beliefs. The same might be said for Joseph Ellis's (1993) *Passionate Sage: The Character and Legacy of John Adams*. David McCullough, author of the best-selling popular history *John Adams* (2001) and the source where most Americans turn to learn more about the second president of the United States, is content with simply calling Adams a "Christian."

Historians who *have* tackled Adams's religion have offered a myriad of descriptive terms to describe it, a further testimony to its tangled nature. Writing mostly in articles, book chapters, and dissertations, scholars have called Adams "Puritan," "Latitudinarian," "liberal Protestant," "deist," "Christian deist," "theistic rationalist," "Unitarian," "devout Unitarian," "Calvinist," "enlightened Puritan," and "angry Unitarian." Whatever historians decide to call him, John Adams lived in an eighteenth-century world where religion – particularly Christianity – was important.

9.1 Early Religious Influences

Most historians agree that John Adams's religious beliefs were shaped by the New England Puritanism of his youth. His parents – John Adams, Sr. and Susanna Boylston Adams – were regular churchgoers. His father was a deacon in the Braintree (later Quincy), Massachusetts Congregational church. As an heir to a Calvinist heritage, John grew up believing that God was sovereign over all of his creation, human beings by nature were depraved, and God, as an act of grace, chose to redeem some of his sinful creation through the sacrificial death of Jesus Christ. As a Congregationalist, the Adams family believed that local congregations had the right to govern themselves without interference from a supervising ecclesiastical body. Congregationalists exercised their own church discipline, chose their own ministers, and erected their own meeting houses.

While we know very little about the religious rituals of the Adams household, young John would have imbibed the religious culture of his parents and the Braintree church. Ellis, for example, has suggested that Adams's law career was infused with older Puritan values related to the importance of religion in public life. Adams understood the law as a vocation or calling and made every effort to "inform his law practice with religion and morality." Adams's intellectual life was defined by a practice of "introspection and self-doubt" that reflected the Puritan custom of spiritual self-examination. Lester Cappon (1959: xxxv) has linked Adams's practice of self-discipline to some of the more stoical dimensions of New England Calvinism. He approached politics with the same kind of zeal and self-discipline that, if he chosen a ministerial vocation, "he would have brought to the sacred" (J.J. Ellis, 1993: 52, 53, 228).

Puritans were deeply committed to education. All truth and knowledge belonged to God. This meant that New England Calvinists did not shy away from studying the belief systems of different cultures and religions, even if their primary purpose in doing so was to refute them. Edwin Gaustad (1987: 89) has suggested that Adams's intellectual curiosity, support of free inquiry, and belief in religious toleration were influenced by this Puritan defense of the life of the mind. A pessimistic view of human nature was another part of Adam's Puritan theological heritage that he carried with him during the course of his life. Though, as we will see below, Adams came to reject the Calvinist belief in original sin and total depravity, he never seemed to abandon the belief that humans beings, when left to their own devices, would act in ways that were not conducive to the common good or the moral fabric of society. As Philip Goff (1993) reminds us, Adams was not an optimist. His belief in balanced government – which would inform his work on the 1780 Massachusetts constitution – reflected a deeply held conviction that government "checks" were necessary to curb man's innate propensity toward selfishness (Goff, 1993: 8).

Throughout his public career, as well as in his private life, Adams upheld a traditional Puritan belief in the providence of God over the affairs of men and women. According to Goff, Adams presumed that major historical events – such as the Protestant Reformation and the American Revolution – were directed by the hand of God. He took for granted the idea that England was a nation chosen by God and that the British American colonies benefited from this special relationship. As heirs to the Reformation, God would fulfill his Protestant plan for the world by using the colonies to fight against liberty and tyranny wherever it reared its ugly head (Goff, 1993: 145, 152, 163, 165). At some point in his intellectual and theological journey, Adams came to think that God's blessing was removed from England and applied solely to the United States. According to Charles LaFontaine, he affirmed a belief in a "transcendent deity" who governed the universe through natural law and divine intervention. Adams's God could "select certain people for a special purpose and make a covenant with these people," making America a "set apart nation" with a "special destiny and obligations of obedience" (LaFontaine, 1976: 54–55).

Most accounts of Adams's childhood and young adult years mention his thoughts, which he recorded in his manuscript autobiography in 1804, concerning a religious controversy in the Braintree church that reached a boiling point while he was a student at Harvard. Adams's childhood minister at Braintree, Lemuel Bryant, was constantly under attack by orthodox Calvinists in the congregation for his embrace of Arminian theology that denied traditional Puritan doctrines such as original sin, divine election, and salvation by arbitrary grace. Briant's preaching and writing on individual freedom (as opposed to Calvinist determinism) and moral striving, and his skepticism concerning the Christian doctrine of the Trinity, led to much division in the congregation. Adams wrote that the controversy over Briant's theology "broke out like the Eruption of a Volcano and blazed with portentous aspects for many years." Adams's uncle, Ebenezer Adams, called for Briant's removal from the Braintree pulpit. His father was one of Briant's supporters, but he thought that because the congregation could not heal the wounds caused by the controversy the divisive pastor had to go. In the end, the Braintree church voted to retain Briant. Though the people of Braintree would remain committed to a congregational form of church government, the theological and religious sensibilities of the congregation would, from this point forward, be Unitarian.

Nearly all Adams historians concur that the Braintree religious controversy had an impact on John's religious beliefs and vocational choice. David Holmes (2006: 76–77) maintains that the incident pushed Adams from a "liberal Congregationalist" to a Unitarian. The Braintree incident explains his lifelong criticism of those churches that sacrificed congregational unity and moral community on the altar of a rigidly defined theological orthodoxy. Though Adams's embrace of Unitarian faith was also in keeping with his education at Harvard University, where he learned to evaluate religious experience based upon scientific reason and observation rather than on what Frank Lambert has called (2003: 175), "blind acceptance or bigotry," this local congregational dispute certainly had something to do with it. For some historians, the Braintree controversy convinced Adams that he would not pursue a career in the ministry despite his father's wishes. Lambert argues that his decision to become a lawyer was based on his growing disgust with church politics and Puritan theology and his newfound passion for reason and natural law (Lambert, 2003: 170). John Ferling (2004) offers one of the few interpretations of Adams's decision to pursue a career in the law that does not dwell on the Braintree conflict. Ferling suggests that Adams pursued the law for purely selfish means, realizing that such a profession "would offer him the greatest chance to obtain recognition" (2004: 19). Such an interpretation fits with Ferling's biography, which downplays the role that religion played in Adams's life.

9.2 Mature Religious Beliefs

There is universal agreement among historians that John Adams's religious beliefs were shaped by a mixture of orthodox Calvinism and Enlightenment rationalism. Historiographical debates (there are few) occur over minor points of emphasis rather than the overall substance of his faith or the ideas that informed it. Whether it was his experience in the Braintree congregation or his training in liberal religion at Harvard, the mature John Adams would eventually come to reject many of the most cherished tenets of Calvinist orthodoxy. In 1799, while serving as vice president of the United States, he told his wife Abigail that his religious beliefs were "not exactly conformable to that of the greater Part of the Christian World" (John Adams to Abigail Adams, Jan. 28, 1799, in *Adams Family Papers*). Adams had much respect and reverence for the life and teachings of Jesus Christ and described the ethical teachings of the Gospels as the "most benevolent and sublime, probably that has been ever taught and more perfect than those of any of the ancient Philosophers" (Adams to Thomas Jefferson, Nov. 4, 1816, in Cappon, 1957: 509). Yet he could not accept the historic Christian belief that Jesus Christ was God or that his death atoned for the sins of the world. In denying the deity of Christ, Adams was also casting aside the traditional Christian belief in the Trinity. Indeed, he thought that anyone who believed in the Trinity violated the first commandment, which forbids the worship of but one God. His son, John Quincy Adams, was considerably more conservative and orthodox in his Christian beliefs, a fact that often drove his father crazy. As Gaustad (1987) notes, John Adams could not fathom how his son could possibly embrace the teaching of the Athanasian creed, the first ancient Christian confession to affirm the deity and equality of the three persons of the Trinity (Gaustad, 1987: 90). Adams's devout belief in one God and his disdain for the Christian doctrine of the Trinity made him a Unitarian. New England Unitarianism grew out of the premise, which had already influenced Briant at Braintree and many of the faculty at Harvard, that God was understood best through the power of reason. Since the Trinity could not be explained rationally, it was discarded in favor of a unitary God.

Because of his commitment to this rational form of religiosity, several historians interpret Adams's faith in the context of the American Enlightenment rather than that of New England Calvinism. Frank Lambert claims that Adams and all the so-called Founding Fathers were shaped by an "Age of Reason" rather than an "Age of Faith." Adams was a product of the "New Learning" that originated in Great Britain and made inroads at most American colleges in the mid-eighteenth century. The New Learning was not incompatible with Christianity, but it did teach students to find answers to religious and moral questions from sources outside the Bible. It affirmed that the learning of moral lessons was one of the fundamental aims of religion and a virtuous life could be attained through the development of what Scottish moral philosophers called "the moral sense." The moral sense, when trained through reading, education, sociability, and the general application of reason to everyday life, enabled persons to arrive intuitively at ethically correct assumptions. In this sense, the New Learning, as it pertained to morals, was as much a "science" as natural philosophy; it was practiced through an experimental and rational analysis of the human condition. In adhering to the idea that personal virtue could be attained through rational and natural means, ethical thought became firmly rooted within a British, and consequently American, Enlightenment that made the science of morals a focus of attention.

Moral behavior would not contradict the teachings of the Bible – God was the author of both the Scriptures *and* moral principles. However, the New Learning taught that morality could be constructed through *inductive* experimentation. By embracing the New Learning and current trends in moral philosophy, Adams was departing from an approach to ethics in which morality was *deduced* by systematizing the revealed commands of divinely inspired Scripture. Jonathan Edwards, the great Northhampton divine and the eighteenth-century guardian of New England orthodoxy, taught that "true virtue" was impossible without a personal relationship with God, the ultimate source of all good works and public morality. By suggesting that the human will was strong enough to overcome the sin nature, thus allowing unbelievers to lead morally upright lives, Adams was embracing a moral revolution that was taking ethics in a new, more Enlightened, direction.

C. Bradley Thompson, the author of *John Adams and the Spirit of Liberty* (1998), is the most forceful proponent of the view that Adams belongs firmly with the Enlightenment camp. The influence of Puritanism on Adams's life could certainly be found in his work ethic or practice of self-examination, but Thompson argues that the Harvard graduate went through a profound intellectual transformation that led to a complete break from his Puritan childhood and into an adult life defined by "modern philosophic rationalism." Adams was influenced more by the Enlightenment views of John Locke, Francis Bacon, and Issac Newton than he was the Scottish moral philosophers or Puritan divines. His decision to choose a career in law was motivated by his utter rejection of Calvinism. Based on a close reading of Adams's personal library, Thompson (1998) concludes that it was reason, not revelation or Providence, that served as the starting point for all of Adams's religious and moral inquiries. Adams viewed the passions as a threat to a rational religious faith and spent much of his private life trying to keep them under control through the practice of self-discipline (C.B. Thompson, 1998: 4–5, 11, 19–23).

Similar to Lambert and Thompson, Gregg Frazer (2012) argues that Adams combined a faith in an active God with a belief in the power of reason that made it impossible for him to accept the tenets of either eighteenth-century deism or Christianity. Like both deists and Christians, Adams believed that God created the world and should thus be worshiped. Yet his belief in a God who has the power to regularly intervene in human affairs through answers to prayer and miracles separated him from much of contemporary deist thought. At the same time, his rejection of core doctrines such as the Trinity, the deity of Christ, and the full inspiration of the Bible has prevented some scholars from describing him as a "Christian." In order to make sense of Adams'sreligion and for that matter the religion of all of the major American Founders, Frazer introduces the label "theistic rationalist." This belief system, which Frazer suggests was "at the center of the American founding," was a "hybrid belief system mixing elements of natural religion, Christianity, and rationalism, with rationalism as the predominant element" (Frazer, 2012: 14, 107–124). David Holmes (2006) has suggested something similar. Because Adams attended church, prayed, and placed his life in the hands of a God who was active in the affairs of men and women, yet at the same time believed that the ultimate purpose of religion was to make ethical members of society, Holmes has described him as a "Christian Deist" (Holmes, 2006: 73). Goff (1993: 135) contests that Adams always sought a "middle, balanced, and synthesized" approach to his religious convictions.

Adams's liberal religious commitments and his propensity for independent thinking often resulted in harsh attacks on the champions of Christian orthodoxy. Throughout his life he maintained a strong distrust of the clergy. He despised the authority that ministers held over the lives of their congregants and remained suspect of their intricate theological systems. Adams believed that the purpose of religion was to make good citizens, leaders, family members, masters, and servants. He thought that the New England clergy were well-schooled at solving theological "riddles," but failed in fostering a more benevolent, moral, and harmonious society. He accused the clergy of being too motivated by selfish ambition and power to take seriously the self-effacing teachings of Jesus and thought that ministers had a power over ordinary people that bordered on tyranny.

On several occasions Adams described his personal religious creed. While serving as vice president of the United States he wrote: "The Christian Religion is, above all the Religions that ever prevailed or existed in ancient of modern Times, The Religion of Wisdom, Virtue, Equity, and Humanity… It is resignation to God – it is Goodness itself to Man."[1] A few years later he described his convictions more succinctly and personally: "Benevolence and Beneficence, Industry, Equity and Humanity, Resignation and Submission, Repentance and Reformation are the Essence of my Religion" (John Adams to Abigail Adams, Oct. 27, 1799, in *Adams Family Papers*). In 1816 Adams informed Thomas Jefferson, "The Ten Commandments and the Sermon on the Mount contain my Religion" (Adams to Thomas Jefferson, Nov. 4, 1816, in Cappon, 1959). As these statements make clear, Adams was interested primarily in the way religion was practiced in everyday life. A godly person cultivated benevolence, performed good deeds, and obeyed the moral law as set forth in the Bible.

This socially utilitarian approach to religion was consistent with New England Unitarianism, which stressed ethical living over strict adherence to religious dogma. But it was also compatible with liberal Protestantism or the "Latitudinarian" religion popular in eighteenth-century England. Latitudinarianism downplayed doctrinal differences between Christians and emphasized ecumenical unity in the body of Christ. The latitudinarian emphasis on human love and societal harmony meant that its adherents tended to stress religion's contribution to the improvement of society over the eternal rewards it provided to the believer. G.J. Barker-Benfield (2010) has argued that both John and his wife Abigail were heavily influenced by latitudinarianism. Instead of presenting Adams as a stoic rationalist, as Thompson (1998) has portrayed him, Barker-Benfield suggests that he was often attracted to forms of religion that celebrated the passions and always promoted the kind of loving relationships among fellow human beings that ultimately produced a more benevolent world (Barker-Benfield, 2010: 25–39).

Calvinism and Catholicism took the brunt of Adams's attacks on religion. He understood Catholicism to be the ultimate form of superstitious and irrational religion. Throughout the course of his travels in Europe he visited Catholic shrines and monasteries, rarely portraying his visits in a positive light. Adams believed that Catholics were deceived by the pope, the bishops, and especially local priests. He had particular contempt for Jesuits and feared that the worldwide influence and superstitious doctrines of this Catholic order would eventually penetrate the British American colonies. Like most American politicians of his era, Adams thought that the teachings of Catholicism were incompatible with political and religious liberty. Catholics, he believed, were not permitted the freedom to read or interpret the Bible for themselves and were required to submit to the religious teachings of the church with little opportunity for dissent or independent inquiry. Catholicism, of course, was the established religion of some of the most tyrannical political regimes in Europe, especially France, England's most powerful military and economic rival.

Very few students of Adams focus extensively on his anti-Catholicism despite the fact that his beliefs in this area are essential for understanding his politics and commitment to religious freedom. Adams believed that a providential God intervened in human history during the Protestant Reformation in favor of a brand of Christianity (Protestantism) that championed religious liberty over a brand of Christianity (Catholicism) associated with what he perceived to be religious tyranny. In Adams's understanding, it was a natural love of liberty that led his ancestors to flee England for America in order to escape the Catholic-style tyranny imposed upon them by the seventeenth-century Anglican church. In his pamphlet, *A Dissertation on the Canon and Feudal Law* (1765; C.B. Thompson, 2000: 22–24, 33), Adams applied this history lesson to the relationship between the colonies and the English Parliament, directly tying political freedom to religious freedom. He informed his readers that any consent to political slavery was sacrilegious because God had created human beings to be free. Religious establishments reeked of Catholic tyranny and any attempt at unifying church and state was equivalent to the tyranny of Rome.[2] A thorough history of anti-Catholicism among the American founders, including Adams, has yet to be written. Until that happens, the best places to turn are Steven Waldman's *Founding Faith* (2008), Mark Massa's *Anti-Catholicism in America* (2005), John Fea's *Was America Founded as a Christian Nation* (2011: 194–197), and Elizabeth Fenton's *Religious Liberties* (2011).

Adams's was a lot less strident in his criticism of Calvinism. He respected the teachings of John Calvin and tended to follow some of Calvin's views on human nature, the links between biblical morality and a flourishing society, and the providence of God. It was the Calvinist doctrine of original sin and total depravity that made Adams particularly hostile to the religion of his youth. Though Adams, as we have seen, never abandoned his pessimistic view of human nature, he could not reconcile the doctrine of original of sin and total depravity, as taught by New England Puritans and their heirs, with the necessity of performing good and virtuous acts in society. He struggled with the Calvinist notion that humans were so sinful that they could not do good deeds without a special dose of God's grace. Though Adams believed that human beings could and did sin against God, he also had too much faith in a loving God to believe that individuals pursuing a moral life, without a conversion experience, could be chosen to spend eternity in perpetual state of punishment.

9.3 Religion and Politics

Writing about Adams's regular use of providential language in his public statements, particularly as President of the United States, historian Arthur Scherr has suggested that he practiced "providential politics" (1991: 26). Indeed, one cannot understand John Adams's vision for a healthy and flourishing American republic without some knowledge of his views on the relationship between religion and public life. Adams's devout Unitarianism influenced his patriotic activity during the American Revolution. As a believer in God's providential care for the United States, he was convinced that God was an American patriot, or at least was on the American side in this struggle for freedom. He affirmed that the only way the newly established nation would be victorious in the War for Independence was if they depended on Providence. Adams always upheld a sense of wonder about the settlement of America. He consistently fused his Enlightenment belief in human progress with his providential understanding of the world. His God was a god of American and Enlightenment progress.

Philip Goff (1993) suggests that Adams may have never relinquished the Puritan idea that God had a providential plan for New England. If this was indeed the case, then this view of New England exceptionalism was, by 1776, transferred to the burgeoning United States. He described America, in the words of Goff, as a "divine tool … analogous to Israel in God's providential plan" (1993: 14–15) and thought that he had a mission to make sure this part of God's will for the nations was carried out. Like all good Calvinists, Adams had a calling. And in revolutionary America this calling had political implications. This explains his dedication to the Continental Congress as the vehicle for which such a divinely inspired movement for independence could be achieved (Goff, 1993: 227). In this sense, Adams, like many of the heirs of seventeenth-century Puritanism, maintained what historian Harry S. Stout (1986) has described as a "New England Soul." Despite his heterodox religious views, he consistently carried forth the idea that God had a special covenant with Massachusetts's seventeenth-century governor John Winthrop's original "city on a hill."

In the wake of the Revolution, Adams was on the front lines in promoting a virtuous republic. The American republic would only survive, he believed, if people acted in an ethical way that enabled them, at times, to place the interests of others over their own selfish needs and wants. Selfishness, Adams believed, was at the heart of British taxation policy during the years leading up to the Revolution. He characterized the British as materialistic sinners who were deserving of God's punishment. Now, he feared, the American people were facing a similar temptation to replace virtue with greed. Adams was convinced that religion was the only true foundation of moral happiness in the American republic. "There is no such thing [morality], Adams wrote, "without a supposition of a God. There is not right or wrong in the universe without the supposition of a moral government and an intellectual and moral governor" (marginal note in Condorcet's *Outlines of an Historical View of the Progress of the Human Mind*; see Hutson, 2005: 146). While serving as president he told the officers of a Massachusetts militia brigade, "Our Constitution was made only for a moral and religious and people. It is wholly inadequate to the government of any other."[3] In 1811 Benjamin Rush encouraged Adams to deliver a public address arguing that "national happiness" could only be found in religion (Rush to Adams, Aug. 20, 1811, in Schutz and Adair, 1966: 205–206). Adams never delivered the speech, but he did speculate about what he might say in such a proclamation. He envisioned speaking about how "religion and virtue are the only foundations not only of republicanism and of all free government but of social felicity under all governments and in all combinations of human society" (Adams to Rush, Aug., 28, 1811, in Schutz and Adair, 1966: 208–209). He believed that the preservation of the Sabbath and regular church attendance would go a long way toward the nation's moral and social improvement.

Historian John Charles Evans (2006) argues that Adams's vision for a moral republic was informed by "coherent synthesis" of liberal, republican, and Christian ideals." He thus joins scholars such as James Kloppenberg, Mark Noll, John Murrin, and John Fea who have argued for the interrelatedness of these schools of eighteenth-century virtue. Indeed, Adams's moral beliefs had much in common with the ancient notions of public life that historians have described as "civic humanism" or "republicanism." Though there was nothing particularly Christian about the idea that good citizens should sacrifice their own interests for the good of their country, the sacrificial spirit that republican civic duty required did overlap a great deal with both the biblical virtue of selflessness and the ethical lessons of the civic humanists. As Evans argues, Adams believed that the country could be nourished from the wells of both reservoirs of virtue. He rarely embraced a form of political liberalism "absent of Christian and classical values." In fact, Evans maintains that Adams's ability to merge Christian and classical conceptions of virtue may have been his "most unique and important contribution to American political thought" (Evans, 2006: 60–61, 65, 70, 80). Like Evans, Goff (1993) argues that Adams combined an "Enlightened Puritanism" with a view of history and politics informed by Whig political principles. His pessimistic view of human nature and his embrace of a rational Puritanism led him to reject a government that was ruled completely by the people, but he doggedly defended the right of the people to rebel against tyranny and defend individual liberties (Goff, 1993: 128).

Frank Lambert (2003) compares Adams to the Connecticut minister and Yale College president Ezra Stiles in the sense that both men thought that the American Revolution was tied up with both religion and politics. Like Evans and Goff, Lambert argues that Adams always understood religion as central to the ordering of public life, but he prefers to draw more heavily on contemporary studies in "civil religion" to explain Adams's convictions in this area. Lambert notes that Adams's public religious expressions upheld the existence of a "powerful, intelligent, beneficent, foresighted, and providential divinity," a belief in an afterlife where human beings will be judged based on their behavior in this world, and the "sanctity of the social contract," but rarely did his words venture into anything that could "be construed as specifically Christian." (Lambert, 2003: 254, 282). C.B. Thompson (1998) is in general agreement with Lambert on this point, but he described Adams' public religion with the label "civil morality" (1998: 23).

Historians point to Adams's draft of the Massachusetts constitution of 1780 as a fitting window into his beliefs on the relationship between church and state. The Massachusetts constitution affirmed that all members of society had the "right" and "duty" to worship God and, at least by today's standards, had a limited view of what constituted the religious rights of its citizens. The people of Massachusetts had the right to worship the "Supreme Being," the "Creator," and the "Preserver of the Universe." By implication, religious rights were not afforded to those who did not worship this God. The emphasis on "duty" reflects the historical New England Puritan ideal that individual rights must always be understood within the context of the responsibility one has to the larger Christian community.

The Massachusetts constitution did, however, affirm liberty of conscience in matters of religion. It states that "no subject shall be hurt, molested, or restrained, in his person, liberty, or estate, for worshipping GOD in the manner and season most agreeable to the dictates of his own conscience." Citizens of the state could freely, without any government interference, practice their religious faith, but the wording of this clause suggests that such religious freedom applied only to those who worship God. And unlike many of the states outside of New England, the Massachusetts constitution required the government to collect taxes to support ministers and religious teachers. The Congregational church would remain the state's established religion, but those who were not part of this church would be permitted to use their tax dollars for the support of a teacher of their own Christian denomination. Adams called this "a most mild and equitable establishment of religion." Adams and other framers also made sure that anyone serving in the Massachusetts state government was a Christian. This applied to the governor of the state and anyone else elected to public office. Though the days of removing dissenters from the colony were long gone, the established Congregational church was not. The Massachusetts constitution, written under Adams's leadership, was designed to maintain a distinctly Christian state.[4]

John Witte, Jr. has argued that Adams, in drafting the Massachusetts constitution of 1780, put forth a distinct model of religious liberty that sought to balance the freedom of individuals with what he called a "Publick Religion" necessary for maintaining moral order and public peace. This fits with what Barker-Benfield (2010) has described as Adams's "latitudinarian" faith, what Lambert (2003) has called "civil religion," and what Thompson (2000) refers to as "civil morality." Witte (1999) prefers to see the public religion of the Massachusetts constitution as "ceremonial" and "institutional." He maintains that Adams, unlike his seventeenth-century Puritan ancestors, was sensitive to the spiritual needs of Massachusetts dissenters, as long as they upheld their civic duty to worship God. He thus paints a picture of a "tempered" John Adams, a statesman who sought to balance conservative and liberal approaches to the relationship between church and state. Adams believed that "too little religious freedom … is a recipe for hypocrisy and impiety. But too much religious freedom is an invitation to depravity and license" (Witte, 1999: 215–217, 237–240, 252).

A second example of the way Adams applied his religion to government and politics was his practice of calling for days of fasting and prayer. As Charles Dickson notes (1987), these special days of religious observance provide a link between Adams's Puritan roots and "what has since become the politically sanctioned relationship between God and the American people." Public days of fasting and prayer, of course, were common in colonial New England. They were designed to call attention to the individual and collective sins of Puritan society and have been interpreted as part of a larger tradition of Puritan "jeremiads," sermons and public declarations written to strengthen what the leaders of society believed to be God's covenant with the Calvinist settlers of New England. While Adams's proclamations as president were generally generic in terms of their use of religious language, it is noteworthy that they did include references to more specific Christian concepts such as the "Holy Spirit" and divine grace (Dickson, 1987: 188, 206).

Adams issued two such days of fasting and prayer during his presidency, the most controversial being his declaration on March 6, 1799, in the midst of the United States's undeclared naval war with France. The focus of this special day, which was to be observed by all citizens of the country, was to seek God for the protection of American troops and to ask for his blessing on the nation's foreign endeavors. Many perceived Adams's call for a day of fasting and prayer as a political tool to win support for his own political party, the New England-centered Federalists. The Federalists believed that government had the responsibility of enforcing public morality rooted in the Christian faith. His call for national supplication was endorsed by the Presbyterian church, a denomination suspected by many to have secret ambitions of creating a national religious establishment. The fast-day declaration was thus criticized by his Republican political enemies, including Thomas Jefferson, his eventual opponent in the next presidential election. According to Adams, American religious denominations and sects, especially those who guarded their religious liberties against the possible threat of tyranny and thus tended to vote Republican, feared that Adams was indeed trying to establish a Calvinist nation or, at the very least, a nation governed by the moral codes (and Congregational establishments) of New England. Political historians have treated the controversy over Adams's days of fasting and prayer as a political episode. In this view, these proclamations were little more than a political tool. They are often interpreted in the context of Thomas Jefferson's victory over Adams in the election of 1800. (Common people who supported Jefferson's views on religious freedom feared Adams was trying to create a quasi- or unofficial religious establishment and thus threw their support behind Jefferson.) Dickson (1987) embraces the political nature of Adams's call for prayer and fasting, but he does not dismiss the fact that Adams truly believed that the practice of these Christian disciplines would be good for the nation. He writes, "Clearly, he wanted his two fasts to be national acts which would 'teach and inculcate' important truths, truths denied by the opposition party." Adams thought that the new republic needed help from God and he found a model for seeking this kind of outside aid in one of the most important traditions of his spiritual ancestors (Dickson, 1987: 20–24).

9.4 Conclusion

It is safe to say that John Adams was a Godly man, or, as I have described him elsewhere, a "devout Unitarian" (Fea, 2011: 191). As a "church-going animal" he always believed that the teachings of the Bible needed to be applied to everyday life in order to sustain a healthy republic. He tried to balance his obvious ambitions with a life committed to "Justice, Kindness, Piety, and Charity." One could easily argue that despite his flaws he often succeeded in living by these standards. His relationship with Abigail was characterized by love, mutual respect, and honor. In fact, he often fretted over how his entrance into politics would affect the general well-being of his family. Adams believed in forgiveness – even for the British government during the American Revolution. He railed against the luxury and materialism of the society in which he lived and worried about what the self-interested inclinations of ambitious men would do to the country he loved so dearly. Based upon the way he conducted his life and his own understanding of his religious identity, Adams appeared to have been a Christian.

But as we have seen, and as the historical interpretations we examined above have made clear, Adams's religious and theological sensibilities were complicated. Adams lived in a world at the intersection of New England Calvinism and the American Enlightenment. He showed little tolerance for those with whom he disagreed, especially Catholics, Calvinists, and members of the clergy. He had very little patience for Christian beliefs that could not be explained by reason. And he believed that the United States of America, a country he helped to found, was a "Christian nation," but only if we use that time-worn phrase to describe a country with a moral system supported by the teachings of Jesus and a belief in a providential and unitary God who blesses America, but did not send his son to become the savior of the world.

Notes

1 John Adams diary, July 26, 1796; various loose folded sheets, Aug. 6, 1787 to Sept. 10, 1796 (with gaps). *Adams Family Papers.*

2 Adams, *A Dissertation on the Canon and Feudal Law* (1765) in C.B. Thompson (2000: 22–24; 33).

3 Adams to the Officers of the First Brigade of the 3rd Division of the Massachusetts Militia, Oct. 11, 1798, *Adams Papers*, reel 119; cited in Hutson, 2005: 76.

4 Massachusetts constitution, Jan. 1780, accessed Oct.21, 2012 at http://www.nhinet.org/ccs/docs/ma-1780.htm.

Further Reading

Barker-Benfield, G.J. (2010). *Abigail and John Adams: The Americanization of Sensibility* Chicago.

Dickson, Charles Ellis (1987). Jeremiads in the New American Republic: The Case of National Fasts in the John Adams Administration. *New England Quarterly* 60: 187–207.

Ellis, Joseph J. (2001). *Passionate Sage: The Character and Legacy of John Adams.* New York.

Fea, John (2011). *Was America Founded as a Christian Nation? A Historical Introduction.* Louisville, KY.

Ferling, John (1992). *John Adams: A Life.* Knoxville, TN.

Frazer, Gregg L. (2012). *The Religious Beliefs of America's Founders: Reason, Revelation, and Revolution.* Lawrence, KS.

Gaustad, Edwin S. (1987). *Faith of Our Fathers: Religion and the New Nation.* San Francisco.

Holmes, David Lynn (2006). *The Faiths of the Founding Fathers.* New York.

Lambert, Frank (2003). *The Founding Fathers and the Place of Religion in America.* Princeton.

Larson, Edward (2007). *A Magnificent Catastrophe: The Tumultuous Election of 1800.* New York.

Scherr, Arthur (1991). John Adams, Providential Rhetoric and Party Warfare: A Note on Massachusetts Politics in the Late 1790s. Mid-America 73: 7–27.

Thompson, C. Bradley (2002). *John Adams and the Spirit of Liberty.* Lawrence, KS. (Originally pub. 1998.)

Waldman, Steven (2008). *Founding Faith: Providence, Politics, and the Birth of Religious Freedom in America.* New York.

Witte, John Jr. (1999). "A Most Mild and Equitable Establishment of Religion": John Adams and the Massachusetts Experiment. *Journal of Church and State* 41: 213–252.

Chapter Ten

Abigail Adams and Feminism

Elaine Forman Crane

It is tempting to admonish Abigail Adams by invoking the March Hare: "You should say what you mean," he advised Alice during one of history's most famous tea parties. "I do," responded Alice, "at least I mean what I say." To Alice, the semantic turnabout seemed a simple redundancy. "Not the same thing a bit," retorted the Mad Hatter who was following the discussion with some interest. This fictional reprimand might apply to Abigail Adams as well, because although she usually meant what she said, she was frequently reluctant to say what she meant. Since Adams was an articulate woman with the ability to fine tune what she wrote, it is likely this was a deliberate strategy on her part to play fast and loose with women's most potent tool: words. Confined by contemporary gender mores, Abigail employed conventional language to fashion a persona acceptable by eighteenth-century standards. At the same time, she drew on literary allusions to cloak what she hesitated to reveal openly. Notwithstanding this creative manipulation, most of Adams's biographers have been inattentive to her ambiguous word play (Crane, 1999).

Adams accurately quoted a variety of writers, sometimes with attribution, sometimes without. She modified, misidentified, or distorted others. She plagiarized with impunity, employed *double entendres*, and left thoughts unfinished or vague to conceal her intentions. As a result of Adams's occasional unwillingness to say unequivocally what she meant, her biographers have reached conflicting conclusions as they try to unravel her copious correspondence. Nowhere is this sparring more evident than in the

A Companion to John Adams and John Quincy Adams, First Edition.
Edited by David Waldstreicher.

controversy over Abigail's stand on women's rights and whether she may rightly be called a feminist.

The problem, of course, is whether it is appropriate to invoke a word that did not exist in the eighteenth-century Anglo-American world. Neither "feminist" nor "feminism" had thrust their way into the English language during Abigail's lifetime, making it a somewhat questionable tactic to apply or deny the label to anyone. Nevertheless, historians have spent little time considering the implications of this linguistic lacuna, even as they contentiously debate her credentials as a member of the sisterhood. Yet they have a point: despite the lack of a contemporary word to define Abigail's outlook, it is difficult, if not impossible to analyze her position on women's rights without a nod to words invented many decades after her death.

On the most elementary level, feminism is a doctrine based on the belief that women should possess the same economic, political, and social rights as those enjoyed by men. Yet this definition raises provocative questions: is mere *belief* in equal rights for women equivalent to feminism? Or must one be a vocal *advocate* for the positions it espouses in order to earn the badge? Taking the question a step further, does feminism require *action* on those beliefs (beyond speech)? In any case, can one be a partial feminist – that is, someone who favors certain conditions of equality but not others? As applied to Abigail, how central was feminism to her life – if at all? Does it make a difference if she thought, wrote, or acted on feminist principles only rarely or intermittently rather than consistently? Since we cannot know how often she mentally sifted feminist ideas or discussed them with other like-minded people, are the last two questions superfluous?

As far as Abigail Adams is concerned, her biographers have evaluated her commitment to women's rights in the context of eighteenth-century customs and cultural standards, and have judged her credentials accordingly. It is hard to fault such a method, even if a close analysis of her voluminous correspondence by a dozen historians provides little consensus about Abigail's feminist proclivities. In short, Abigail's biographers come to agreement in only two areas of her many pronouncements about women: education and domesticity. On these two subjects Abigail is both clear and unambiguous.

Historians rightly conclude that Abigail's platform for female improvement consistently contained one proposal that was amenable to a growing number of her contemporaries: female education. Because Abigail not only meant what she said but indicated quite clearly what she meant, there is no dispute among biographers about Abigail's dedication to the cause. From Janet Whitney's semi-fictional narrative written more than six decades ago to the latest biographies by Woody Holton, Edith Gelles, and Joseph Ellis, every author has noted Abigail's unwavering support for female education. Among all of Abigail's biographers, Holton (2009) explores Abigail's comments on the disparities between male and female education in greatest detail, pointing out how often Abigail referred to the constricted education of American women, how deprived she felt about her own lack of formal learning and how educated women improved marriage, motherhood and, more grandly, the culture of the United States. Yet at the same time that Abigail pleaded for learned women – indeed, as Lynn Withey (1981) notes, for female education as a right – Adams positioned herself squarely within the perimeters of eighteenth-century gender roles. She insisted that a woman should never "shine at the expence of her Husband" (Abigail Adams to John Quincy Adams, May 20, 1796, in Withey, 1981: 234). She should be able to learn Latin and Greek as well as any other subject that would improve the mind, but as Phyllis Levin reminds us, Adams also cautioned intellectually savvy women not to incur "the jealousy of the men and the envy of the women" (Levin, 1987: 237–238; Abigail Adams to Mary Cranch, April 28, 1787, in Kaminski, 2009: 361).

Abigail's appeals for female education were made privately in the form of persuasive or even angry comments to her wide circle of correspondents. Moreover, she admired educated women who could claim a public pen; as her biographers note, Catherine Macaulay and Mary Wollstonecraft ranked high in Abigail's estimation. But despite her admiration of published female writers, Abigail's own foray into public authorship, Woody Holton maintains, was limited to an introductory note to an essay by Mercy Otis Warren (Holton, 2009: 159). Notwithstanding their recognition of Abigail's appreciation of education, however, Adams's biographers fail to note that Abigail's unique position as the wife of the president of the United States offered a chance to act as an advocate for the expansion of female education. She had badgered John before he became a nationally recognized political figure. As Rosemary Keller (1994) and others remind us, in August 1776 Abigail implored him to prod Congress to equalize educational opportunities (Keller, 1994: 135). Nevertheless, no extant letters have surfaced, and no biographers suggest that when it was politically feasible she pressed John to take a public stand on the improvement of female education. If she influenced him on so many other matters, why not the one that was integral to her sense of equality? Perhaps she tried privately. If so, no evidence survives of the attempt. Yet Abigail felt deeply about the educational gap between men and women and never deviated from her progressive stand on female education even if that stand had limits. As Edith Gelles points out (1992: 48), the issue "preoccupied" her "throughout her life".

Furthermore, if Abigail's position on female education was progressive, it was progressive within a conservative framework to the extent that education was not an end in itself or a stepping stone to a career. In short, she argued her case without extracting women from the domestic sphere, a social role that, according to her biographers, was a mantra among Abigail and her contemporaries. All of the authors who have taken on Abigail as a subject readily agree that from her earliest pronouncements on the subject to the end of her life, she firmly believed that "women by nature were fundamentally different from men and best suited to be wives and mothers." Moreover, Withey maintains that "Abigail did not herself aspire to anything more than being a good wife and mother," a debatable proposition that seems at odds with Withey's assessment about her unwavering advocacy of female education (1981: xi, 45–46). Joseph Ellis (2010) agrees that Abigail's "primary focus, what defined her daily life," were her children and "demanding domestic duties," although the division of labor within the Adams's marriage was not "absolute" (J.J. Ellis, 2010: 16, 17). Gelles also argues that Abigail's belief in separate spheres arose from her religious and cultural upbringing. It "revealed a divinely prescribed patriarchy in which it was her destiny to live in the domestic sphere" (Gelles, 1992: 26). Abigail's assertions late in life leave little room for doubt about her understanding of proper gender roles: "I believe nature has assigned to each sex its particular duties and spheres of action" (Abigail Adams to François Adriaan Vanderkemp, Feb. 3, 1814, in Kaminski, 2009: 361).

Notwithstanding Abigail's apparent commitment to female domesticity and separate spheres, however, there is ample reason to believe she was not as devoted to the hierarchical organization as eighteenth-century domesticity (and her biographers) imply. In fact, this may be one of those instances where Abigail meant what she said, but demurred from saying what she meant. In 1796, shortly before John was elected to the presidency, Abigail needled patriarchal government in a letter to their son, John Quincy. "Government of States and Kingdoms, tho God knows badly enough managed, I am willing should be solely administered by the Lords of Creation, nor would I object, that a Salique Law should universally prevail. I shall only contend for Domestick Government, and think that best administered by the Female" (Abigail Adams to John Quincy Adams, May 20, 1796, in Kaminski, 2009: 360). The last sentence is curious. Is her reference to domestic government a throwback to Robert Filmer? If so, she has turned Filmer's male administration of the family on its head. Did the perks of domestic government include female acquisition of property? Did it imply enhancing household income through business ventures? Did it involve investment in bonds or devolving real estate? All this Abigail had done and more – relegating the law of coverture to a legal footnote. Where in the real world did domestic government end and state (public) government begin?

Abigail's use of the word "contend" is also curious. Contend is not a neutral word; it signifies strife, vigorous efforts, conflict, and struggle. Why would Abigail need to "contend" for domestic government if she meant the arrangement of the contemporary early American household? Interpreting her words at face value, Abigail's phraseology suggests that she was contending for a social institution presumably already in existence. Clearly she meant what she said, but it would have been nice if she had explained what she meant.

Three years later, in a letter to her sister, Elizabeth Peabody, Abigail struck an even more ambiguous and potentially radical tone. She still exhibited a belief in divinely inspired separate spheres, but insisted that "if man is Lord, woman is *Lordess*." She realized that women did not hold "the Reigns of Government," but, she went on, "I see no reason for her not judging how they are conducted" (Abigail Adams to Elizabeth Peabody, July 19, 1799, in Kaminski, 2009: 360). How did Abigail expect a *Lordess* to judge a Lord and the government he created? She meant her words to be taken seriously. But was she saying women were entitled to criticize government in private conversation or was she covertly campaigning for female suffrage? By 1799, she might well have been urging the latter, without daring to say so openly.

If all biographers agree that Abigail favored female education and gendered spheres, they are hopelessly divided about her commitment to and advocacy for female political rights, which they have equated with the franchise or even more expansive participation in the operation of government. Charles Akers insists that Abigail "never advocated that women vote," although Abigail clearly expressed her willingness to do so if opportunity presented itself (Akers, 1980: 49; Abigail Adams to Mary Cranch, Nov. 15, 1797, in Kamenski, 2009: 369). Withey suggests that Abigail "hinted" women had the right to vote, although she admits such an interpretation is "risky" (Withey, 1981: xi, 82). Keller (1994: 92) takes a less ambivalent position: "another benefit Abigail sought for her sex was a congressional law granting women the vote." Since the franchise eventually became the heartbeat of the feminist agenda in the later nineteenth century, if Abigail actually stimulated that drive, then Levin is not far wrong when she argues (1987: xv) that Abigail's life "illustrates feminism in the most comprehensive, Websterian significance of that electrifying word." Yet Gelles strongly disagrees, calling twentieth-century feminist efforts (such as Levin's) that attempted to place Abigail in the feminist camp "anachronistic" (Gelles, 1992: 10).

Why the dispute? Although Abigail said so much about so many things in a correspondence that extended over six decades, one letter has become the basis of the historical debate over Abigail's feminist proclivities. Written to John at the end of March 1776 when Abigail was 32 years old, this so-called "Remember the Ladies" letter contains ideas that were either radical or conservative, serious or satirical, private or public, banter or challenge. Abigail's biographers have been unable to agree about what she meant – never mind whether she meant it.

Although Janet Whitney resorts to fictional conversations between John and Abigail in her 1947 biography, her discussion of the letter in question contains accurate quotations from it. Whitney's interpretation classifies Abigail as a forward-thinking radical who "audaciously" pointed out that women were a "neglected multitude." Abigail had "broken a lance for their liberty" (J. Whitney, 1947: 129). Consistent with his opinion about the vote, however, Akers (1980 [2000]) maintained that the "bold paragraphs were not a declaration of the principle of sexual equality for which nineteenth-and twentieth-century feminists would contend. Abigail Adams did not call for a revolution in the roles of men and women" (Akers, 1980: 48). Instead, Akers' biography of Adams argues that her letter of March 31, 1776, had a more limited goal in mind. Abigail sought legal protection from abusive husbands whose rights were almost absolute. Yet if male rights to the person and property of married women were the bedrock of English law, as Akers implies, Abigail's call for legislative change would have been no less than "a revolution in the roles of men and women," despite Akers' assertion to the contrary.

It is interesting that Lynn Withey, writing at the height of the modern feminist movement, would take a moderate position on the meaning of Abigail's most famous letter. According to Withey (1981: 82), Abigail was not "politically or temperamentally inclined to favor social revolution," any more than she was "prepared to advocate a radically different position for women in society." Conversely, Phyllis Levin, writing six years later, gives Abigail credit for having "launched, unwittingly, the timeless campaign for women's rights," although Levin does not expand on this sweeping statement (Levin, 1987: 81).

Paul Nagel published his biography of Abigail in the same year that Levin's appeared. He calls the letter of March 31, 1776, "perhaps the most famous comment by an American woman on the relation between male and female." Surprisingly, however, Nagel did not give it a radical twist, in contrast to the many authors who had cited it approvingly in their campaigns for women's rights. Instead, Nagel, like Akers, proposed that Abigail's concern was more restrictive: she wanted to "protect women from men" (Nagel, 1987: 79). That being the case, it is puzzling that Nagel did not think that legislative protection was a radical idea at a time when Anglo-American law had done little to prevent married women from being physically abused and divested of property by their husbands.

In 1994, Rosemary Keller picked up where Phyllis Levin left off seven years earlier. According to Keller, Abigail's "Remember the Ladies" missive reveals her "acute perception, deep concern, and style of advocacy of women's rights." Keller suggests that Abigail's ploy, "a humorous undertone," was contrived to convince John that "legislative enactments ensuring justice to women were the only solution" to male tyranny. Since Abigail was already convinced that men would not voluntarily bestow rights upon women, her letter was "the first direct advocacy of women's rights by an American female." Having said that, however, Keller admits to the contradictory nature of Abigail's position. On the one hand, Abigail was steadfastly opposed to male domination of a power structure that led to gendered inequities, even as she "playfully coaxed" John to consider her argument "by overstating the subjugation of females." On the other hand, Keller backtracks by insisting that Abigail did not seek autonomy or the "right of self-determination for women, as later feminists did" (Keller, 1994: 89–90, 102). Which is it? Direct advocacy of women's rights or an unwillingness to seek female self-determination?

Edith Gelles also exhibits ambivalence about the content and meaning of Abigail's words in her famous March 1776 epistle. Gelles discussed the letter in three books about Abigail and John Adams. In the first, award-winning book, *Portia: The World of Abigail Adams* (1992), Gelles unequivocally asserts that Abigail's appeal to her husband to remember the ladies "has been used to support a (false) picture of her as a radical feminist." According to Gelles, Abigail was content with an inegalitarian sexual hierarchy, "and only occasionally did she chafe at the injustice of her submissive condition" (Gelles, 1992: 1, 71). Yet, if, as Gelles says, "Abigail disapproved of women who breached the prevailing code of female behavior," surely the "remarkable request" contained in the letter of March 31, 1776, was just such a breach. Gelles admits that Abigail displayed "unusual gender awareness for her time," and that her proposal for "legal guarantees" to safeguard "just gender relations" was "a daring step" (Gelles, 1992: 48). In this context, does daring differ from radical? And if feminism strives for equality between the sexes, how is it that Abigail cannot claim that intellectual label?

By the time Gelles published *"First Thoughts": Life and letters of Abigail Adams* in 1998, she had moved Abigail to the Left where "her thinking about the rhetoric of human freedom and equality had taken her in a direction that not many people of her time … had contemplated." While Gelles's perceptive comments and graceful writing have few parallels among Abigail's biographers, this last comment, as well as a similar one quoted above, is questionable. It is hard to believe that at a time when such words as liberty, rights, and independence were freely circulated, other women (and men) failed to question the gendered implication of such ideas. That they did not act on such ideas is a story for another time.

Confessing that Abigail had indeed engaged in a "radical … outburst" (albeit cloaked in a joke), Gelles went on to discuss the "revolutionary ideas" her letter of March 31 contained (Gelles, 1998: 15). While letter-writing has become a private matter over the centuries, this was not true during the 1700s, when letters were often shared and discussed. Thus, it is debatable whether Gelles's claim that Abigail "did not intend for it to become public" can be sustained. The ideas would certainly become public if, as Abigail hoped, John passed them on to Congress. And surely no-one who knew Abigail would accuse John of pressing Congress about this matter on his own account. Indeed, Abigail may even have hoped for a public airing, and it is entirely possible that somewhere in the summer sky over Braintree she is smiling, satisfied that her "radical" words eventually became the "rallying cry" for American women (Gelles, 1998: 16).

By the time *Abigail and John: Portrait of a Marriage*, the third volume of Gelles's trilogy, appeared in print in 2009, Gelles had come full circle. Abigail's call to remember the ladies was "an audacious move." No longer was the letter a joke: "Abigail was serious, very serious." Indeed, Gelles asserts, "it is the boldest statement written by an American woman in the eighteenth century, and for much of the nineteenth, as a demand for political rights" (Gelles, 2009: 77–78).

The three most recent biographies of Abigail Adams were written by men. Woody Holton's (2009) focus on Abigail as a financial mover and shaker has won a Bancroft Prize. Holton's approach to Abigail's famous letter is moderate, even conservative: she wrote the letter "for an audience of one," and of all the inequities that women suffered, Abigail "only called attention to one: marriage." Her plea was "vague," but Holton concurs with Akers and Nagel that Abigail's intention was to stifle "physical abuse," a conclusion based on a specific request that she hoped would reach Congress – presumably without attribution if the letter was for John's eyes alone. In Holton's estimation, Abigail slipped in "the serious observation that male Patriots prohibited their wives from exercising the very right to self-government" that was central to their "own dispute with Parliament." Contradictions aside, Holton describes the March 31 letter as a "protofeminist statement" (Holton, 2009: 99–100, 39). More recently, Joseph Ellis has weighed in, acknowledging Abigail's "playful" tone, but maintaining that John did not realize Abigail was seriously promoting an argument based on her belief in natural rights and popular consent" (J.J. Ellis, 2010: 49–51).

Finally, G. J. Barker-Benfield considers Abigail's letter in a striking book on the language of sensibility applied to Abigail and John's correspondence (2010). The combination of gender and sensibility leads Barker-Benfield to conclude that Abigail's "potential feminism was inflected by the culture of sensibility" and that her letter of March 31, 1776, paralleled the long-term transatlantic call for a "reformation of men's manners." Furthermore, Abigail was not an innovator: she merely "called for the same reform" found in other sentimental novels, and that it did not approach the "feminism" of Mary Wollstonecraft's treatise, which took gendered sensibility to task (Barker-Benfield, 2010: 8, 195).

It is surprising that many of Abigail's biographers fail to connect John's letter to James Sullivan of May 26, 1776, with the flurry of letters between husband and wife that preceded it. John's frivolous response to Abigail in mid-April indicates, as Keller suggests, an "unwillingness to examine her ideas seriously because they threatened the accepted roles of men and women within society and the family" (Keller, 1994: 99). It is likely that Keller is closer to the truth than Ellis: an unwillingness to consider Abigail's plea is quite different from not realizing that she was promoting an idea. But Abigail's sulky rebuke on May 7 must have struck a chord. Shortly after receiving her retort, which admonished him for "insisting upon retaining an absolute power over Wives," John defended his negative opinion about female political participation in a letter to James Sullivan, a colleague from Massachusetts. In so doing, he not only expressed his conviction that Abigail was calling for political rights, but he inadvertently substantiated Abigail's accusations. John perceived it would be "dangerous" to modify voter qualifications since it would open the vote not only to women, but to propertyless men. Although John Adams strongly believed that only the consent of the governed legitimized authority, it was inconceivable to him that such consent was required of women. John may have replied to Abigail facetiously, but that was because her words rang true. Abigail refused to retreat from the universal principles of natural law upon which rebellious Americans rested their case. John had no such scruples (Abigail Adams to John Adams, May 7, 1776; John Adams to James Sullivan, May 26, 1776; Keller, 1994: 100–101).

Two of Abigail's biographers dispute whether she continued to express her displeasure about the ongoing absence of women in the political world and their lack of rights. In *First Thoughts* (1998), Gelles concludes that after apprising Mercy Otis Warren of her efforts in the spring of 1776, "Abigail then dropped the topic. No other statement by her survives on the subject of women seeking legal recourse against men to protect themselves from abuse or subordination. She complained a lot about her own situation and sometimes about women's status, but she never again proposed legislative protection of women" (Gelles, 1998: 18–19).

Yet Holton subscribes to the idea that a call for greater rights was implicit in Abigail's letter to John written on the seventh anniversary of Bunker Hill – that is, on June 17, 1782. According to Holton, this letter was, perhaps, "more radical" than Abigail's more famous denunciation in her Easter Sunday letter of March 1776. Although devoid of a specific demand for redress, Holton points out that in the later letter Abigail still complained of being "Deprived of a voice in Legislation," and of being "obliged to submit to those Laws which are imposed on us." Since John was in Holland at the time and absorbed with business at The Hague, he would have been neither able nor willing to influence a Congress three thousand miles away on matters not relevant to finance or national independence, his opposition to Abigail's imprecations notwithstanding. Abigail surely knew this, and the fact that she continued to remind John of women's inability to vote and hold office is significant in itself (Holton, 2009: 172).

If, in 1992 when Gelles published *Portia*, she believed that "there is little evidence to show that Abigail thought inventively about politics," Holton, writing in the first decade of the new century, thinks otherwise. Abigail "held fast to her insistence upon women's right to be politicians as her era defended that term: active participants in the conversation about America's future." Or as Abigail herself admitted in 1797: "My mind has ever been interested in publick affairs" (Holton, 2009: 318). Indeed, she was addicted to it: "I cannot wean myself from the subjects of politicks" (Abigail Adams to Catherine Johnson, May 9, 1800, in Kaminski, 2009: 289). While the difference between these two assessments of Abigail's political interests may simply be the way in which Gelles and Holton "read" Abigail, Holton's construction may also reflect the newer interpretations of women and politics in the early republic (see Zagarri, 2007; Branson, 2001).

Abigail was politically inventive as well, despite the fact that the subject itself was theoretically off limits to women. Ever more outspoken as time went on, her understanding of politics, and her willingness to display that understanding, is nowhere more evident than in the astonishing dialogue she initiated in 1804 with Thomas Jefferson (without John's knowledge). Despite her age and the fact that she was a former First Lady, it was cheeky to take on, much less fault, the president of the United States. Interestingly, it is Janet Whitney (1947) who engages in the most extensive analysis of these letters, which began as a condolence note and eventually evolved into a confrontation about midnight appointments, James Callender, political authority, and separation of powers. In the correspondence, as Whitney demonstrates, Abigail shows a grasp of constitutional theory beyond most public writers, male or female (1947: 306–318).

Women have always been political actors, although many scholars have surrendered the word "political" to a definition that relegates women to the sidelines of the polity. Nevertheless, even if feminism and politics have a symbiotic relationship, they are not chained at the hip. Thus, engaging in discourse about "publick affairs" does not necessarily transform a woman into a feminist. If politics in its broadest sense consists of taking sides, making decisions, or supporting ideas, conservative women (*à la* Phyllis Schlafly, for example), have taken political positions that conflict with feminist goals. But if an eighteenth-century woman who is denied political rights above and beyond the "conversation about America's future," overtly protests such exclusion, she has combined political behavior with feminist advocacy. Abigail's politically motivated (not to mention intimidating) attack on a sitting president was a far cry from her culturally permissible appeal in 1778 for political news "which may be communicated to a *Woman*" (Abigail Adams to John Thaxter, Feb. 15, 1778, in Holton, 2009: 138).

Two other issues that captured Abigail's attention or in which she was involved are connected to a feminist agenda. The first relates to married women and their lack of economic independence, and the second to a woman's control – or lack thereof – over her body and childbearing. Until recently, historians have paid scant attention to Abigail's abilities and achievements concerning the first, and to her attitude regarding the second.

Most of Abigail's biographers recognize that she was engaged in mercantile activities during the Revolutionary era. Connecting her trading ventures with the economic conditions that prompted them, Janet Whitney is not the only historian who felt that although "Abigail became a businesswoman, and showed she could do it well," she would rather not have assumed the role (J. Whitney, 1947: 153). Akers mentions Abigail's successful management of their farm and in a few paragraphs quickly discusses the means by which Abigail paid bills. He also points out that Abigail recognized early on that "European goods were her best hedge against inflation" (Akers, 1980: 76–77). Withey adds more details to the story about Abigail's mercantile enterprise, indicating that it was John who instigated the trade in 1780. Yet Withey admits that Abigail told John "exactly what she wanted" and he responded by sending her the goods. According to Withey, John eventually "suggested that she simply write to the merchants herself," leaving Abigail to conduct foreign trade with prospective suppliers. Similarly, she acquired land, "acting with the advice and assistance of Cotton Tufts, but relying mostly on her own judgment" (Withey, 1981: 121–123). In other words, Abigail initiated successful transactions but she worked in tandem with other (male) family members. All this is to say that these historians have bestowed upon Abigail a half-hearted agency.

Gelles's emphasis is on John as well. She maintains that John began to send goods to Abigail from Europe "to supply family needs," and that "Abigail quickly grasped the opportunity," a timeline that slightly distorts the sequence of events by reversing the genesis of the trade. Gelles goes on to say that "the business may have had simple beginnings," but in time "Abigail's enterprises became more complex," which is true to the extent that her trade network expanded over time. And as Gelles concludes, "so it was that Abigail became a modest merchant, selling items which came from Europe through the good offices of her diplomat husband" (Gelles, 1992: 42–44).

Gelles does not give Abigail her due. It was Abigail who capitalized on the potential of a transatlantic trade, and whose "horizons" did in fact reach further than Gelles suggests. If Abigail "did not express ambition to go into the public sector," it was unnecessary for her to do so. She was already there. Gelles is more generous to Abigail as a land speculator. She possessed "ability and foresight" in this regard, and Gelles applauds her for becoming "a confident businesswoman and manager of property" without seeking John's permission for the variety of transactions in which she engaged (Gelles, 1992: 44–45).

Keller, whose book was published long after twentieth-century feminists had tumbled out of the home into public work space in ever-increasing numbers, is less willing to distribute the credit for Abigail's efforts. Abigail "was responsible for maintaining the economic stability of the home." Giving exclusive kudos to Abigail for her efforts while John was away, Keller concludes that she "became the family breadwinner." Keller sees Abigail as more independent of John than do previous biographers, arguing that although "Abigail saw herself as John's substitute, her strict policy was to assume responsibility for family business without his advice or assistance unless absolutely necessary." In fact, according to Keller, "Abigail was the businesswoman in charge of her enterprise. Her husband, on the other hand, was in the subordinate role of taking orders from her" (Keller, 1994: 107–108, 114–116).

If it sounds as though Keller overstates the case, Holton credits Abigail with even more responsibility and perspicacity. He sets the beginning of Abigail's mercantile career in July 1778, with her initial request for salable goods. In Holton's estimation, Abigail, not John, showed courage at a time when British privateers were scouring the Atlantic and two vessels carrying cargo shipped by John had been captured. Knowing that scarcity would enhance the demand for (and price of) consumer goods, she decided to favor profit over risk and persuaded John to continue sending merchandise. Moreover, when the goods did not meet her exacting standards, she did not hesitate to complain to John and her suppliers in words that gave notice she would not be trifled with.

In a lengthy discussion about her extraordinary ability to manage the family finances, Holton points out that Abigail had to combat both depreciation and inflation. Among her strategies for the present, she began to buy bonds. For the future, she speculated in Vermont land, despite John's reluctance. She manipulated the law to take advantage of large tracts in an area she knew little about except by word of mouth. If John continued to be hesitant about his wife's ventures, Abigail plunged ahead nonetheless. When John instructed her about a loan involving paper money, Abigail ignored him. "Abigail could easily have implemented her husband's directive by calling in the loan, but she chose not to do so" (Holton, 2009: 144–145, 154, 178).

When Abigail closed out her importing business at the end of the war, Holton calculates that she had made "stupendous profits" (2009: 185). As a result of her success, Abigail – either consciously or unconsciously – underwent a marital metamorphosis. She began to think of herself as an economic entity rather than a married woman subject to the rules of coverture, which stipulated that she could neither buy, sell, nor possess property independent of her husband. Circumventing these restrictions, she began to use the singular word "my" in reference to the rent she collected instead of "our." "In so doing," posits Holton, "Abigail demonstrated just how far the reality of her household had diverged from legal theory" during the Revolutionary years. She had retreated "from the ideal of the submissive wife," once she claimed the right to funds that were legally his. Furthermore, her proposal to buy "depreciated government bonds from private individuals on the open market would transform her into a full-scale securities speculator" (Holton, 2009: 186–189).

Holton calls Abigail's possessive language about money "extraordinary," asserting that "it was quite rare for a wife to insist upon her ownership rights (2009: 213). This being the case, Abigail was demonstrating the economic independence that later feminists sought for married women. No strident words accompanied her deeds. Instead, as Holton indicates (2009: xx), "she turned her own household into a laboratory where she imagined what the emancipation of women might look like." True enough, although it is difficult to calculate how many other women might have done the same thing in their husbands' absence during the Revolutionary years.

If Abigail's biographers have only lately caught up with her financial acumen, they have been even slower to appreciate and analyze the one document that places her firmly on the side of female economic independence: her will. The 1816 document, written two years before her death and with John's consent, is strong evidence that her "Remember the Ladies" appeal was more than a passing whim. Abigail's will was a document created by a woman who carefully listed, designated, and distributed her property among the female members of her extended family.

Paul Nagel, one of the few historians who even mentions the will, remarks on Abigail's single-minded approach to the allocation of clothing, cash, jewelry, stock, and real estate. "When the names of granddaughters, nieces, cousins, and other females were called to receive something, Abigail's concern for womankind was never clearer" (Nagel, 1987: 156). Both Phyllis Levin and Joseph Ellis briefly refer to Abigail's will, but overlook its strongly gendered content (Levin, 1987: 477–478; J.J. Ellis, 2010: 243–244). Woody Holton, however, engages in a longer, in-depth analysis and concludes that the "material circumstances" of the overwhelmingly female legatees played a substantial role in determining who would get what. Each granddaughter received a bequest "depending on how wealthy she was." And as Holton pointedly notes, Abigail's grandsons, nephews, and male servants "received nothing at all." Why would Abigail exclude all her male relatives except her sons John Quincy and Thomas? Holton suggests that Abigail may have been aware of the decline of women as producers and thus "believed that the need to provide for her female relatives was greater than ever" (Holton, 2009: 407–409).

The final and most perceptive statements about Abigail's will were written by a graduate student whose Master's thesis focused on the document. In just under fifty pages, Efrat Namerode (2011) traces the means by which Abigail accumulated the wealth she claimed for herself, as well as her long-term connections with the various recipients of her largesse. As she examined the bond between Abigail and each legatee it became clear to Namerode that Holton was wrong to assume that financial circumstances dictated the devolution of Abigail's property. After careful consideration of the financial situation of the heirs, Namerode concludes that "Abigail bequeathed her property according to her relationship with each specific heir," rather than with regard to their needs. Ignoring custom and precedent, Abigail designed a will that was "a gender statement" as well as "a declaration of female solidarity" (Namerode, 2011: 48).

If only a few of Abigail's biographers have analyzed her willingness and ability to control family finances, even fewer have considered her willingness and ability to take control of her body. This was an eighteenth-century woman who eschewed the command to increase and multiply beyond a certain number, and she offered to her sisters unsolicited opinions about the drawbacks of excessive childbearing. As Gelles indicates, between 1765 and 1772 Abigail gave birth to five children, four of whom survived: Abigail junior (b. 1765), John Quincy (b.1767), Susanna (b. 1768, d. 1770), Charles (b. 1770), Thomas (b. 1772). Then, in 1777 Abigail delivered her last child, a stillborn infant, Elizabeth (Gelles, 1992: 28). She was 33 years old and had apparently avoided pregnancies during the prior five years.

If feminism does not require family planning, it does insist that women should have control over their bodies to the extent that they can choose when and if to bear children. Given the importance of this issue, it is surprising that so few of Abigail's biographers discuss the Adams's decision to limit the size of their family. While most authors talk of her pregnancies and the children she bore – and lost – only a handful mention what is clearly an attempt to control procreation. The long hiatus between the birth of Thomas in 1772 and Elizabeth in 1777 should have been a tip that Abigail and John were deliberately managing the size of their family, as was the absence of additional children while she was still in her childbearing years. Although the distance between the couple when John was traveling acted as an effective barrier to conception, he was home often enough between 1771 and 1774 for Abigail to have conceived. Even long stints in Philadelphia after mid-1774 were punctuated by occasional respites in Braintree and Boston, one of which between Oct 1776 and January 1777 produced the pregnancy that ended in a stillborn child.

Paul Nagel indicates that similar ideas about female fertility were shared by Abigail and her sisters. They considered an over-abundance of children a form of slavery, although as Nagel points out, "Nothing in the surviving letters indicates what means, beyond self-control, these sisters considered useful for avoiding pregnancy" (Nagel, 1987: 80). Nevertheless, the actions of Elizabeth Shaw spoke louder than her words, and even though her sister Abigail hoped she was "not in the increasing way," Elizabeth had a baby at age 40, despite Abigail's untactful warning that "she was too old" (Akers, 1980: 61; Abigail Adams to Elizabeth Shaw, Feb.–Mar. 1782, in Kaminski, 2009: 87).

Akers indicates that Abigail confirmed her words with her deeds. After the birth of Thomas in 1772, he suggests that "Abigail and John may have agreed that four living children made a sufficient family. In any case – and by whatever means – she went five years without another pregnancy." It may be too much for Akers to say that after 1778 Abigail "resolved to have no more pregnancies," but in fact no evidence survives to suggest otherwise (Akers, 1980: 29, 69). Without reading Abigail's mind, it is also impossible to determine whether the couple "had planned to have another child" in 1777 or that they "wanted the baby very much," despite circumstantial evidence in support of these statements. Perhaps they did, but neither admitted to it in so many words. Withey agrees that "after Tommy, she and John had clearly decided to have no more children for the time being," although Abigail's reticence does not permit Withey to speculate on the method used to achieve that end (Withey, 1981: 86).

Woody Holton writes at greater length and more candidly about birth control and the Adams's attempt at family planning. At the same time, he is less confident about Abigail's and John's intentions. The 1777 pregnancy, Holton suggests, "may in fact have been planned," but his choice of words hints at a reluctance to say so definitively. Similarly, after explaining the state of knowledge about contraception in the 1770s, Holton admits "it is impossible to know for certain whether the Adamses used any of these birth control techniques," even if "there is tantalizing evidence that they did." That evidence – a promise extracted from John to be present at the birth – does not persuade that they used birth control techniques, although there is enough circumstantial evidence to assume they probably did (Holton, 2009: 120). Whatever means Abigail and John used to space their children and limit their family size, the more important point is that Abigail acted on her own principles, which were surely progressive at a time when family limitation was only beginning to trump fecundity (Klepp, 2009: 6). She also sought to influence other women in her family. Holton notes that Abigail thought her daughter Nabby was "having children way too fast," and she hoped her niece, Elizabeth, "would wean her first child" before embarking on a second round (Holton, 2009: 270–271).

Although Abigail would not have expressed her ideas about family planning in anachronistic feminist language, she clearly believed that women should assume control of their bodies. Since this issue has become a feminist concern, Abigail deserves some credit for raising it at a time when most people avoided words having anything to do with intimate matters. As far as we know, she advocated family planning only within a small circle that included her sister and husband. Yet she not only advocated birth control, she and John took measures to implement it – although we cannot be sure of their methods. Such behavior surely places Abigail among the more progressive women of her era. If the word "feminist" had existed in the eighteenth century, Abigail might have earned the label on this ground alone.

But not every issue is as intrinsically feminist as family planning. An educated woman in the eighteenth century was not necessarily a feminist even if feminism promoted education. A woman who was politically inspired was not always a feminist, even if feminism urges political activism. Feminism does not advise domesticity, but household labor is not antithetical to the feminist movement. All this is to say that the test of Abigail's feminist proclivities is closely correlated with how she translated her beliefs about education, politics, or the marital experience into action. Should all women be better educated? Yes. Should women, especially married women, have more egalitarian legal rights? Yes. An independent means of providing for themselves? Yes. *Voilà*.

There is one small area of Abigail's life, however, that remains curiously ambiguous even if almost all historians regard the identity of Abigail's *alter ego*, Portia, as a closed subject. Abigail adopted the name in a letter to John in May, 1775. That name, claim Withey, Gelles, Barker-Benfield, and Holton (among others), was surely a classical throwback to Cato's daughter and Brutus's wife. She was, Withey reminds us (1981: 6), "a favorite example of womanly virtue in classical times." Gelles (1992) explains that Abigail took this nom de plume "during the dark years of the Revolutionary war," because it was the name of the "Roman wife of the great statesman Brutus" (1992: xviii). And Philip Hicks, in an insightful article about female political identity during the Revolutionary era (2005: 281) concurs: "her pen name referred to Brutus's Portia."

Although agreeing with these authors as to the source of the reference, Holton notes how strange it was that Abigail and others "would take inspiration from the wife of an assassin" (Holton, 2009: 74). It is more than strange. While some may see Brutus as a senator-statesman who resisted tyranny, others point out that he participated in an assassination. At the very least he was guilty of disloyalty and treason, a traitor to one who trusted him. At worst, he was guilty of regicide. Furthermore, if Abigail was Brutus's spouse Portia, does it not imply that John was Brutus – a murderer? John may have said some unkind things about George III, but he never wished the king a violent demise. Not only was Brutus's Portia implicated in the assassination of Caesar, she was so distraught after hearing of the death of her husband that she committed suicide. Does this sound like a profile the avid Shakespearean reader, Abigail Adams, would claim?

In 1776, nearly a year after John and Abigail's close friend, Dr Joseph Warren, was killed in battle, Abigail still grieved over the death of this ardent patriot. On the occasion of his reinterment ceremony she adapted a passage from Julius Caesar:

> Woe to the Hands that shed this costly blood;
> A curse shall light upon their line.

Among the hands that shed the blood was, of course, Brutus's. Would Abigail, even as a literary device, invoke a curse upon John's line (which, of course, was hers as well)? Not likely (*Adams Family Papers*, Abigail Adams to John Adams, April 10, 1776).

Abigail's biographers may be wrong. She may not have taken her pseudonym from *Julius Caesar*, but rather from another Shakespearean drama, *The Merchant of Venice*. In this play, Portia's suitor and prospective husband,

Bassanio, extolled her by saying that she was "nothing undervalu'd to Cato's daughter, Brutus' Portia," an accolade that in context would have resonated with Abigail. Shakespeare's Portia in *The Merchant of Venice* described herself as "an unlesson'd girl," much as the erudite Abigail did. But this dramatically deferential Portia was, in fact, a learned woman – a mirror image of Abigail. As Shakespeare's plot thickens, this fictitious Portia disguised herself as a young male lawyer and argued brilliantly as well as successfully for the life of her husband's friend, Antonio, who owed money to the merchant, Shylock. She deceived her husband with her disguise and in the course of events, tested his fidelity. In the end, she revealed the ruse to her astonished husband. We will never know which of the two Portias Abigail identified with – which is what Abigail may have had in mind to begin with. Yet in her soul of souls perhaps Abigail believed she could have been as effective an attorney as Shakespeare's Portia or even as her lawyer husband. Portia might have been a secret expression of her ambition – or an unspoken aspiration, a longing hardly irreconcilable with feminism.

What to make of Abigail and feminism – or whatever word applies to the way she envisioned the role of women in American society? Two points need emphasizing. First, although some aspects of her worldview were clear, others are shrouded in obscure language and contradictory ideas. Second, some of her opinions, beliefs, and actions evolved over time, a casualty of war and distance from John. She seized opportunities unavailable to most other women and moved on.

According to Holton, John's absence during and beyond the long war years gave Abigail the chance to assert herself "in a way she never had before." It was not revolutionary rhetoric but distance that gave Abigail's self-confidence a boost and encouraged her independence (Holton, 2009: 69, 186). Akers also points out that as the war years progressed and distance continued to be a barrier between Abigail and John, her written expressions became more and more self-assured. In 1774, at the onset of their years apart, "she had written not of *my* affairs or *ours* but of *yours*" (meaning John's) (Akers, 1980: 78). Yet as she began to incorporate complex financial decisions within her domestic sphere, Abigail's correspondence more accurately reflected the role she had assumed. Distance became power, and she never relinquished control over assets she believed she had accumulated and that were rightfully hers – coverture notwithstanding. She apologized to John for using the possessive word "my," but her actions are more convincing than her words. She may have pacified John by telling him that "the desires and requests of my Friend are a Law to me," but if those desires and requests were incompatible with her own predilections, Abigail's deference succumbed to her own will (Abigail Adams to John Adams, Feb. 11, 1784; J.J. Ellis, 2010: 104).

Although, as Ellis observes, Abigail was "an extremely well-read woman who had traveled much in Braintree," at age 40 "she had never left the

Boston area." Her foreign education began when she joined John in Europe after the war. His appointments forced her "to stay abreast of diplomatic issues," and allowed her to reveal her own formidable intelligence, something Abigail had previously cautioned other women against (J.J. Ellis, 2010: 104, 107–108). She became a colleague and advisor as well as a wife. Given the unusual circumstances that upended the world of this Braintree housewife and stripped away some of the inequalities that governed her life, there was no need for Abigail to voice her disapproval of female inequality or to invoke feminist principles. On a personal level, there was even less reason to do so when she returned to the United States. Abigail had achieved equality on a number of levels. She acted out feminist principles instead of stressing her discontent through the written word.

Besides, both Joseph Ellis (2010) and Keller (1994) agree that at the end of the war, Abigail believed Congress would not "carry out the personal implications of freedom" as far as women were concerned and that the liberation of women would take place only in the future (J.J. Ellis, 2010: 130; Keller, 1994: 122). This does not mean, however, that as she aged "some of Abigail's positions appear to have become more conservative ... particularly on the subject of women's social role." Neither does Abigail's unwavering belief in women's discrete domestic role indicate that she "no longer expressed interest in women's political status" (Gelles, 1998: 170).

Holton also argues (2009) that Abigail's persistent commitment to social hierarchy is evidence that she "remained in many ways, an archconservative in her final years." Having pointed to her distaste of racy literature as an example of her conservatism, Holton nonetheless parts company with Gelles. He concludes that "Adams never detected any inconsistency between her conservatism in some areas ... and her desire for a radical transformation in relations between the sexes. And she continued to advise women to exploit every loophole in the doctrine of coverture." Among other things, she offered financial advice to women (Holton, 2009: 402–403). Based on her own experience, Abigail was well positioned to show that domesticity was not necessarily antithetical to female advancement.

To the end of her life, Abigail fervently believed in separate spheres for men and women, although exactly what that meant to her is unclear. The twenty-first century may see separate spheres (or its incarnation as the doctrine of separate but equal) through a hierarchical lens focused on the discredited case of *Plessy versus Ferguson*, but Abigail did not. With more than half a century behind her, she refused to have women "considered in an inferior point of light," and she never deviated from the equal value she placed on her half of humankind (Abigail Adams to Elizabeth Peabody July 19, 1799; in Kaminski, 2009: 360). Her opinions may not always correspond with modern feminist priorities, but considered from an eighteenth- or early nineteenth-century perspective, her advocacy of female education, economic independence, family planning, and perhaps even political participation are reasons enough to make room for Abigail Adams in the American feminist pantheon. Would she be pleased with a place among the worthies? It is hard to predict her response – clarity was not always her strong point.

Further Reading

Akers, C. (2000). *Abigail Adams, An American Woman.* 2nd edn., New York. (First pub. Boston, 1980).

Barker-Benfield, G. J. (2010). *Abigail and John Adams: The Americanization of Sensibility.* Chicago.

Branson, S. (2001). *These Fiery Frenchified Dames: Women and Political Culture in Early National Philadelphia.* Philadelphia.

Butterfield, L., Friedlaender, M., and Kline, M. (1975). *The Book of Abigail and John: Selected Letters of the Adams Family.* Boston, MA.Massachusetts Historical Society. (2nd edn. Boston, 2000.)

Crane, E. (1999). "Political Dialogue and the Spring of Abigail's Discontent," *William and Mary Quarterly* LVI: 745–774.

Crane, E. (2007). "Abigail Adams, Gender Politics, and the History of Emily Montague: A Postscript," *William and Mary Quarterly* LXIV: 839–844.

Ellis, J.J. (2010). *First Family: Abigail and John Adams.* New York.

Gelles, E. (1992). *Portia: The World of John Adams.* Bloomington.

Gelles, E. (1998). *"First Thoughts": Life and Letters of Abigail Adams.* New York.

Gelles, E. (2009). *Abigail and John: Portrait of a Marriage.* New York.

Hicks, P. (2005). "Portia and Marcia: Female Political Identity and the Historical Imagination, 1770-1800," *William and Mary Quarterly* LXII: 265–294.

Holton, W. (2009). *Abigail Adams: A Life.* New York.

Klepp, S. (2009), *Revolutionary Conceptions: Women, Fertility, and Family Limitation in America, 1760–1820.* Chapel Hill, NC.

Levin, P. (1987), *Abigail Adams: A Biography.* New York.

Keller, R. (1994), *Patriotism and the Female Sex.* New York.

Nagel, P. (1987), *The Adams Women: Abigail & Louisa Adams, Their Sisters and Daughters.* Oxford.

Withey, L. (1981), *Dearest Friend: A Life of Abigail Adams.* New York.

Zagarri, R. (2007). *Revolutionary Backlash: Women and Politics in the Early American Republic.* Philadelphia.

Chapter Eleven

Abigail Adams: The Life and the Biographers

Margaret A. Hogan

In the summer of 1777 John Adams wisely commented to his wife Abigail, "I think I have sometimes observed to you in Conversation, that upon examining the Biography of illustrious Men, you will generally find some Female about them in the Relation of Mother or Wife or Sister, to whose Instigation, a great Part of their Merit is to be ascribed" (Butterfield et al. 1963–: 2.306). Any consideration of the Adams family would not be complete without due attention to its matriarch, Abigail Adams. Best known as the wife of one president and the mother of another, her influence extended beyond those immediate connections, through personal contact but especially through her letters, thousands of which have survived down to the present day. Her writings reveal her to be a thoughtful critic and insightful observer of the world around her. They also show her to be a woman of great emotional capacity eloquently facing extraordinary personal changes at a pivotal moment in American history.

Since Abigail's death in 1818, biographers have found her a fascinating if sometimes contradictory character. Some authors have struggled to disentangle her life from that of her husband – whose public presence naturally far outstripped her own – while others have seen fit to only notice her in relation to the man she married and supported for over fifty years. Others seeking to emphasize her interest in women's rights wrestle with her as an essentially private figure, committed to the domestic sphere. Historians have yet to come to a clear consensus regarding Abigail's significance in American history, but all seem to agree that the joy of reading her writings makes the search to understand her a uniquely compelling project.

A Companion to John Adams and John Quincy Adams, First Edition.
Edited by David Waldstreicher.

11.1 "The Best of Women": The Life of Abigail

Abigail Smith was born in 1744 into a comfortable household as the daughter of William Smith, the pastor of the First Church of Weymouth, Massachusetts, and his wife, Elizabeth Quincy, a descendant of one of the leading families of the commonwealth. The second of four children, Abigail, along with her two sisters, received no formal education outside her home. Nonetheless, she was in many ways extraordinarily well-educated for a woman of her time. She had access to impressive collections of books, particularly at her grandfather John Quincy's home, Mount Wollaston, which contained what was widely believed to be one of the finest libraries in eastern Massachusetts. She received encouragement to read widely and regularly, and had the opportunity to participate in wide-ranging conversations at her father's home, the Weymouth parsonage. She taught herself how to read French and proved comfortable with basic mathematics, though she never quite mastered spelling or punctuation. She told her son Thomas Boylston in 1803, "as to points & comma's, I was not taught them in my youth, and I always intend my meaning shall be so obvious as that my readers shall know where they ought to stop" (Jan. 27, 1803, *Adams Family Papers*). Despite such limitations, Abigail eventually proved herself equal to far better educated people of her time, demonstrating her literacy by quoting from a wide array of authors and showing a capacity for letter-writing second to none for her time.

Without question the most significant figure in her life was her husband, John Adams. They met for the first time in the summer of 1759 at her father's home; John had accompanied there his best friend Richard Cranch, who in turn was courting Mary, Abigail's older sister. Their first encounter was not auspicious: John described Abigail in his diary as "Not fond, not frank, not candid," meaning in eighteenth-century language that she was too outspoken, lacking the "Tenderness" he sought in a female companion (Butterfield et al., 1961: 1.108, 1.109). She was not yet 15; he was 23, an aspiring lawyer, and perhaps she teased him about his pompous manner or some other foible. When exactly the relationship warmed is not clear but by 1762, John was addressing Abigail as "Miss Adorable" and ordering "as many Kisses, and as many Hours of your Company after 9 O'Clock as he shall please to Demand" (Butterfield et al., 1963–: 1.2). They married in October 1764.

Over the next nine years, Abigail bore five children – Abigail (Nabby, 1765–1813), John Quincy (1767–1848), Susanna (1768–1770), Charles (1770–1800), and Thomas Boylston (1772–1832) – while John continued to build his legal career and launched a political one. They split their time between Boston and John's home town of Braintree, though John spent much of each year away, riding the circuits to practice law at courthouses throughout Massachusetts and Maine. Well before John left to begin his great national service in the Continental Congress, Abigail had already begun to learn to manage a household on her own.

Despite this previous experience of separation, the Adamses' lives were nonetheless changed dramatically by the Revolution. John's departure for Philadelphia and the First Continental Congress in 1774 marked the beginning of a full decade in which he and Abigail were only together for brief periods at a time, and not at all for the final five years of that stretch. Abigail became fully responsible for the education of her four surviving children and for the management of the household, its servants and tenants, and the assorted pieces of property John had acquired. Abigail took to these tasks with some trepidation – she told John at one point, "I really am cumberd about many things and scarcly know which way to turn my-self. I miss my partner, and find myself uneaquil to the cares which fall upon me; I find it necessary to be the directress of our Husbandery and farming" – but she proved herself an able "Farmeress." Likewise she reported, "With regard to the Education for my own children, I find myself soon out of my depth, and destitute and deficient in every part of Education" (Butterfield et al., 1963–: 1.375, 1.420, 2.94).

These reservations notwithstanding, Abigail fully believed in the importance of education for her children – her daughter in particular as well as her sons – and did her best to offer all of them the schooling she had been denied. She encouraged John to develop "some more liberal plan … for the Benefit of the rising Generation" to support education. "If we mean to have Heroes, Statesmen and Philosophers," she wrote, "we should have learned women. … If much depends as is allowed upon the early Education of youth and the first principals which are instilld take the deepest root, great benifit must arise from litirary accomplishments in women" (Butterfield et al., 1963–: 2.94). When possible Abigail found tutors or schools for the children to attend, but given the uncertainty of the time, much instruction she handled on her own. The French she had learned earlier she passed along to her children. Likewise, John wrote on one occasion to ask that Abigail teach all of the children "Geometry, Geography, and the Art of drawing. … No doubt you are well qualified for a school Mistress in these Studies." On another, he reminded her "to compose Descriptions of Scænes and Objects, and Narrations of Facts and Events, Declamations upon Topicks, and other Exercises of various sorts" to give to their children. John had confidence in Abigail's abilities even if Abigail was uncertain (Butterfield et al., 1963–: 1.285–286, 2.40).

Abigail also turned her deft touch to household management and especially to the subject of the family finances. Far better suited than her husband to developing what financial resources they had – John never met a piece of property he did not want to own, no matter how useless it might be – Abigail found ways to invest their money profitably, giving the family far greater security than they might otherwise have known. When John was abroad in

Europe, she arranged for him to ship her goods, which she in turn re-sold for a profit. She invested her extra cash in securities that yielded impressive returns and negotiated advantageous contracts with tenants and farmhands. She described debts as "my abhorrance. I never will borrow if any other method can be devised" and kept the family solvent despite economic turmoil and the reluctance of the Confederation government to pay John's salary and expenses in a timely fashion (Butterfield et al., 1963–: 3.61).

Abigail's life was deeply shaped by the Revolution. Not only did her husband's service as a politician and diplomat leave her a single parent for long stretches of time, but the conflict affected her directly in the middle of the first year of the war. The siege of Boston limited Abigail's access to the main port in her region, and she routinely encountered soldiers marching past her home en route to encampments outside the city. She noted to John, "We live in continual expectation of allarms. Courage I know we have in abundance, conduct I hope we shall not want, but powder – where shall we get a sufficient supply?. ... Every Town is fill'd with the distressd inhabitants of Boston." From the top of Penn's Hill near her home she watched the Battle of Bunker Hill with her son John Quincy; her letter to John describing it was the first report on the battle to reach Philadelphia. When the British army finally evacuated Boston in March 1776, Abigail expressed her relief – but also her fear for the broader Revolution: "Tho we felicitate ourselves, we sympathize with those who are trembling least the Lot of Boston should be theirs. But they cannot be in similar circumstances unless pusilanimity and cowardise should take possession of them. They have time and warning given them to see the Evil and shun it" (Butterfield et al., 1963–: 1.217, 1.370). She lacked confidence that the slave-owning South would stand up to the British in the way Massachusetts had.

John's service in the Continental Congress ended in 1777, but he was only home briefly before receiving the call to diplomatic work in Europe. John's time abroad, beginning in 1778 and continuing until 1788 with only a brief return home in 1779–1780, presented new challenges for Abigail. They were separated by a far greater distance for a longer continuous period than ever before. His appointment removed Abigail's eldest son from her care, and her second son for a time as well. And those separations could not be relieved by regular correspondence, as had sustained Abigail through early periods apart. Abigail reported receiving only two short letters from John during the first five months of his absence in 1778, and their pace improved only marginally over the following years. "You could not have sufferd more upon your Voyage," she told John, "than I have felt cut of from all communication with you. My Harp has been hung upon the willows, and I have scarcly ever taken my pen to write but the tears have flowed faster than the Ink" (Butterfield et al., 1963–: 3.108–109). Still Abigail perservered, handling the household and farm with little input from John, embracing economic opportunities to shore up the family's precarious finances, continuing to oversee her children's education, and even navigating the tricky shoals of Nabby's first serious courtship.

Late in 1783, after considerable back and forth on the subject, Abigail and John finally reached agreement that she should come over and join him in Europe. She decided to bring their daughter Nabby as well (Charles and Thomas Boylston would continue their education with Abigail's sister Elizabeth and her husband John Shaw), and the two of them arrived in England in the summer of 1784. Abigail found the voyage unpleasant – she believed "A Lady cannot help being an odious creature at sea" – but, in usual fashion, improved the situation as best she could by demanding that the sailors clean the boat from stem to stern and instructing the cook in better preparation of the meals (Butterfield et al., 1963–: 3.242). John Quincy met them in London and John himself joined them shortly thereafter – reuniting the couple after five years' separation.

The Adamses spent their first nine months in France then moved on to London in mid-1785, after John was named US minister to Britain. Abigail had been somewhat reluctant to come to Europe at all, fearful that she would present an "awkward figure" in European diplomatic circles, but she proved more than capable of managing her social duties. Initially mystified by the extravagance of Parisian life – the home they rented in Auteuil had scores of rooms, a far cry from their small saltbox cottage in Braintree – she eventually found it commonplace. Writing to her sister Mary, Abigail sheepishly admitted, "I have found my taste reconciling itself to habits customs and fashions, which at first disgusted me. The first dance which I saw upon the Stage shoked me" but "seeing these Dances has worn of that disgust which I first felt, and that I see them now with pleasure" (Butterfield et al., 1963–: 5.280; 6.67). When the time came to leave France, Abigail expressed sadness at leaving.

England perhaps felt more familiar but carried great challenges too, as Abigail would now be the wife of a resident minister, the first such appointee by the United States since the Revolution. She endured the tedious rituals of court etiquette, including standing for four hours while waiting to be presented to the royal family, and other uncomfortable situations caused by lingering animosity toward all things American. But she also came to appreciate the "mother country," enjoying a pleasant routine of social calls, garden walks with Nabby, and theater performances and concerts. Together she and John explored the English countryside and visited the Netherlands for several weeks, and Abigail and Nabby traveled to Bath, along with Nabby's new husband, William Stephens Smith, to see that noted vacation spot. While abroad, Abigail continued to have primary responsibility for the family finances, a real trial given the high costs of living and meager salary provided by Congress.

Abigail and John returned together to the United States in 1788. John paid lip-service to retirement but only Abigail and a few others were fooled into believing this was truly the end of his public career. Only a few months after the couple settled into their new home in Braintree, the former Vassall-Borland estate (later called Peacefield or the Old House, and now owned by the Adams National Historical Park), John learned that he was to be elected the first vice president under the new constitution. Thus began twelve more years of service in the federal government, which introduced yet another new pattern into the Adamses' lives. Until 1792, the couple traveled together between wherever the federal government was then sitting for congressional sessions and returned together to Braintree each summer. But illness in 1792 kept Abigail from joining John in Philadelphia that year, and she remained in what was now the town of Quincy (having separated from Braintree in 1792) until 1797 and John's election to the presidency. During his presidency, Abigail once more entered society, embracing the role of First Lady despite her considerable fears that she would be a poor substitute for the much-esteemed Martha Washington.

Never lacking for political opinions, Abigail served as John's unofficial advisor during his tenure in the federal government and especially during his presidency. This was not a new role for her – she is justifiably famous for urging John to "Remember the Ladies" during discussions of a new plan of government in 1776 – but it carried more weight given John's greater power as the chief executive of the nation. She read the newspapers faithfully (despite her distaste for their highly partisan nature), kept herself well informed on the issues of the day, and offered John her insights. She urged him, for example, to support the Alien and Sedition Acts, outlining her thoughts in a letter to her sister:

> I wish the Laws of our Country were competant to punish the stirer up of sedition, the writer and Printer of base and unfounded calumny. This would contribute as much to the Peace and harmony of our Country as any measure, and in times like the present, a more carefull and attentive watch ought to be kept over foreigners. This will be done in future if the Alien Bill passes, without being curtaild & clipt untill it is made nearly useless. (Mitchell, 1947: 179)

She likewise critiqued John's speeches, suggesting ways to clarify ideas or improve sentences. Her role was well known and some office-seekers even approached Abigail rather than John in search of posts.

Abigail was, if anything, far less forgiving than John of political attacks and consequently found the increasing vitriol of federal politics difficult to stomach. She wrote to John in January 1796, "The Scripture tells us that we must pray for our Enemies, but it does not say that we must pray, that they may not be punished according to their deserts," and lamented to her nephew William Cranch, "The callumny issues unmolessted and almost uncensured from so many of our Presses upon some of the wisest ablest and most virtuous Characters is a very great disgrace to our National Character" (Hogan and Taylor, 2007: 400; Dec. 3, 1797, *Adams Family Papers*). She found it especially difficult to forgive Thomas Jefferson, at one time a close friend, for what she considered a personal betrayal. "How different is the Situation of the President from that of Washington?" Abigail asked rhetorically of her cousin William Smith. "The vice-president never combined with a party against him, and his administration, he never intrigued with foreign Ministers or foreign courts against his own Government & country."[1] By the time John had lost the election of 1800 and come to the end of his political career, Abigail was equally ready.

In one of his last letters to Abigail, John thanked her for coming down to join him in Washington, DC, where he would soon be turned out of office. He noted, "it is fit and proper that you and I should retire together and not one before the other" (Hogan and Taylor, 2007: 473). He spoke correctly. The retirement was not his alone, though his life would change far more than Abigail's would. It was a retirement for both of them and Abigail would have to adjust accordingly. She retreated to Quincy a few weeks before John and they spent nearly all of their remaining years together in residence there.

Over the next seventeen years, Abigail faced an array of difficulties. Her son Charles had died of alcoholism in 1800, and daughter Nabby would succumb to breast cancer in 1813 after several long years of suffering with the disease, including undergoing a grueling double mastectomy at her parents' home in Quincy. Both of Abigail's sisters predeceased her. A bank failure in 1803 put the Adamses' financial well-being in jeopardy, and they were rescued only by contributions from John Quincy. Abigail endured a variety of illnesses though always seemed to bounce back.

Despite these sorrows and growing infirmity, retirement offered many blessings. She was frequently surrounded by grandchildren and put as much energy into raising them (sometimes against the wishes of their parents) as she had her own children. Abigail also found more opportunity for reflection. She had once lamented, in 1776, at the height of the Revolution and during one of the busiest periods of her life in terms of family responsibilities, "I always had a fancy for a closet with a window which I could most peculiarly call my own" (Butterfield et al., 1963–: 2.112). Thirty years on, she had that space – and the time to enjoy it. Her correspondence with John was at an end but she continued to write to many others, including hundreds of letters to her children and grandchildren, her sister Elizabeth, and numerous friends and family. She played no part in John's mission to preserve the family papers but happily continued to add to the trove.

When Abigail died of typhoid fever on October 28, 1818 she was surrounded by family, friends, and of course John. He reported to John Quincy, "The bitterness of Death is past. The grim Spector so terrible to human Nature has no sting left for me." He was consoled by "the sympathy and Benevolence of all the World," and believed that this "Seperation cannot be so long as twenty Seperations heretofore" (Hogan and Taylor, 2007: 479). Although he lived nearly another eight years, he was ready to join his beloved partner who had gone before.

11.2 "My Pen Is My Only Pleasure": Abigail's Letters

All biographies of Abigail Adams begin and end with her correspondence. Although she was the wife of a Founder and second president of the United States, and the mother of the sixth, her greatest legacy has always been her writings. As one of the premier – arguably the best – American letter-writers of the eighteenth century, she left a tremendous trove of correspondence showing her to be a thoughtful and incisive observer of the world around her, which also reveal much of her private thoughts and activities. John recognized his wife's facility as a letter-writer, commenting to François Adrian Van der Kemp in 1809:

> It is a little remarkable that you never heard the Litterary Character of my Consort. There have been few Ladies in the World of a more correct or elegant Taste. A Collection of her Letters for the forty five Years that We have been married would be worth TEN times more than Madame Sevignés, though not so perfectly measured in Syllables and Letters: and would or a[t] least ought to put to the Blush Lady Mary Wortly Montague and all her Admirers.

Abigail herself found great solace in her letter-writing. She noted to John that "There are perticuliar times when I feel such an uneasiness, such a restlessness, as neither company, Books, family Cares or any other thing will remove, my Pen is my only pleasure, and writing to you the composure of my mind" (Butterfield et al., 1963–: 1.xxxii, 2.133).

One of the great legacies John Adams left for his children and succeeding generations was the dictat to save the family's papers: "Whatever you write preserve," he implored his grandsons in 1815.[2] And the family for the most part complied. Members of the family dutifully saved their papers with each generation adding to the collection. John himself began the work of organizing them, first to better respond to perceived political slights in histories of the Revolution and later for the benefit of posterity. He carefully docketed letters in his increasingly shaky handwriting, reporting to his son John Quincy in December 1818, a mere month after Abigail's death:

> Your favour of the 14th. found me deeply immersed in researches … after old Papers. … Every scrap shall be found and preserved for your Affliction [or] for your good. … I shall leave you an inheritance sufficiently tormenting, for example, The huge Pile of family Letters, will make you Alternatly laugh and cry, fret and fume, stamp and scold as they do me. (Dec. 24, 1818, *Adams Family Papers*)

Ironically, Abigail did not share John's enthusiasm for saving their correspondence. She in fact begged him on more than one occasion to destroy her letters, out of embarrassment at her poor handwriting and spelling or concern that she had written too frankly and that, in the wrong hands, her letters could become ammunition for John's enemies. Fortunately, John refused to comply. He wrote to Abigail on one occasion, "The Conclusion of your Letter makes my Heart throb, more than a Cannonade would. You bid me burn your Letters. But I must forget you first" (Butterfield et al., 1963–: 1.400). Abigail no doubt appreciated the sentiment but it did not stop her repeating the request in future correspondence. She was likewise horrified by the prospect of her letters being published. She told a friend who suggested the possibility, "No. No. I have not any ambition to appear in print. Heedless and inaccurate as I am, I have too much vanity to risk my reputation before the public" (C.F. Adams, 1840: lix).

The first attempt to document Adams' life was made by her grandson, Charles Francis Adams. The only son of John Quincy and Louisa Catherine Adams to survive into later adulthood, Charles Francis assumed the role of family historian, taking over from his father responsibility for organizing the family's papers and beginning the long-term process of editing them for publication. His initial effort in this direction appeared in 1840 with the publication of *Letters of Mrs Adams, the Wife of John Adams*, which subsequently appeared in three additional revised editions over the next eight years. In these books, Charles Francis presented scores of Abigail's letters dating from 1761 to 1816. A large percentage of the correspondence was Abigail's to John, though Charles Francis also included letters to children, friends, and other family members such as Abigail's sisters Mary Smith Cranch and Elizabeth Smith Shaw Peabody. While thoughtfully including letters from a range of time periods and on a variety of topics, to demonstrate the breadth of Abigail's interests, Charles Frances unfortunately also edited the letters with a heavy hand, silently redacting large portions referencing matters of health, personal finance, and other topics he deemed inappropriate. Nonetheless, his edition was for many years the only collection of Abigail Adams letters available to the public; it consequently provided a first glimpse into her extraordinary skills as a correspondent and heavily influenced her early biographers.

In his introduction to these volumes, Charles Francis recognized that Abigail's letters provide a counterpoint to more traditional papers documenting the American Revolution.

> The heroism of the females of the Revolution has gone from memory with the generation that witnessed it, and nothing, absolutely nothing, remains upon the ear of the young of the present day, but the faint echo of an expiring general tradition. … It is the purpose of this volume to contribute something

> to supply the deficiency, by giving to tradition a palpable form. The present is believed to be the first attempt, in the United States, to lay before the public a series of private letters, written without the remotest idea of publication, by a woman, to her husband, and others of her nearest and dearest relations. Their greatest value consists in the fact, susceptible of no misconception, that they furnish an exact transcript of the feelings of the writer, in times of no ordinary trial. (1840: xx–xxi)

He hoped to use Abigail's correspondence to provide a history of "feeling" rather than of action in the Revolution (1840: xviii).

Charles Francis subsequently moved on to the writings of his father and grandfather but returned to Abigail's letters in 1876 when he prepared *Familiar Letters of John Adams and His Wife* to mark the centennial of American independence. This collection, focused explicitly on the revolutionary years, includes letters between John and Abigail dating from 1774 to 1783. Of the nearly 300 pieces in the volume, some fifty, over thirty by Abigail, had not previously been published in Charles Francis' earlier editions of his grandparents' correspondence. These would be the last to appear in his lifetime and they did little to transform knowledge of Abigail's life though the book has remained enduringly popular for the dialogue it presents between two such capable letter-writers who also happened to be important observers of monumental events in American history. Charles Francis sadly continued his habit of omitting large sections of material he considered unsuitable for public consumption so the collection today must be approached with care.

Little further systematic effort was made to publish Abigail's writings until the mid-twentieth century. The Adams family tightly controlled access to the papers still in its possession, restricting use to a mere handful of individuals even as it put them on loan at the Massachusetts Historical Society (MHS) in Boston and formed the Adams Manuscript Trust to decide the ultimate disposition of the papers. No family member took upon him- or herself responsibility for continuing the legacy of Charles Francis Adams to make these materials more widely available until 1954, when the Trust decided finally to release the material to the public. In a rather extraordinary turnabout from earlier attitudes among the family, this group committed themselves – through the MHS – to drastically increase access to the papers. Not only were the manuscripts deeded outright to the MHS but, in return, the Society had to promise to support a documentary edition whose express purpose was (and is) to publish the papers of the three generations of Adamses from the 1760s to 1889.

Since the 1950s, the Adams Papers editorial project has published some 45 volumes of Adams materials, including ten volumes of *Adams Family Correspondence* in which Abigail's letters appear. Lyman H. Butterfield, the first editor in chief of the project, established this particular series explicitly to showcase the letters of the women of the Adams family, a novel approach that recognized the importance of their writings to the overall story of the Adamses. In the introduction to the first volume, he noted that the policy of separating the family correspondence from the public papers of the Adams statesmen "enables the women of the family, both those born into it and those who married into it, to take their places beside the Adams men instead of being obscured by them" (Butterfield et al., 1963–: 1.xxiv). The series continues to showcase Abigail's letters, with letters written by her routinely constituting more than 25 percent of the contents in recent volumes.

Apart from this ongoing work to print systematically the full range of Adams materials, smaller sections of Abigail's letters have appeared in various published collections throughout the twentieth century, slowly opening up her writings to a broader audience. The first such effort occurred between 1917 and 1925 when letters among John and Abigail Adams and James and Mercy Otis Warren contained in the *Adams Family Papers* at the Massachusetts Historical Society (MHS) and privately owned at the time by the Warren family (since donated to the MHS) were published in that organization's *Collections*. The editors included only about twenty of Abigail's letters, all to Mercy Otis Warren, but this represented the first time a non-family member oversaw the publication of any of Abigail's writings.

In 1942, 250 letters from Abigail to her sister Mary Smith Cranch were donated to the American Antiquarian Society in Worcester, Massachusetts, 141 of which were subsequently printed in Stewart Mitchell's 1947 *New Letters of Abigail Adams 1788–1801*. This was by far the largest collection of new Abigail letters to be published to that date and the first of its size to be published without substantial editorial intervention. They offer considerable insight into Abigail's mindset during the early federal period, with sharp political commentary on international events such as the French Revolution. They also give Abigail's rich observations on day-to-day life, from the difficulty of keeping servants (and keeping servants sober) to the dangers of smallpox to the beautiful vistas from the Adamses' home in New York City looking out toward the Hudson River. Finally, these letters show the lively conversation that continued between Abigail and her sisters throughout their lives. Abigail's correspondence with her husband is justly famous, but these letters – and later publication of other letters between Abigail and both Mary and her other sister Elizabeth – demonstrate how much she relied on her sisters as sounding boards and confidantes. Happily, also around the middle of the century, a large collection of Shaw family papers was given to the Library of Congress, making Abigail's letters to Elizabeth publicly available, if not published, for the first time.

Lester J. Cappon's (1959) *The Adams-Jefferson Letters* includes all of the roughly fifty letters Abigail exchanged with Thomas Jefferson between 1785 and 1817. Cappon describes Abigail's correspondence as "an integral part of the record," with her helping to facilitate Jefferson's social connection with the family and welcoming him into their home in France (Cappon, 1959: 1.xxxix). Abigail's and Jefferson's lively exchanges once the Adamses left Paris for England in 1785 further cemented the relationship, and Jefferson even entrusted Abigail with the care of his younger daughter Mary upon her arrival in Europe. But if Abigail's warmth toward Jefferson initially outpaced her husband's, her ire at Jefferson's perceived political betrayal in the 1790s and especially during the election of 1800 exceeded John's. An attempted reconciliation in 1804 that Abigail initiated to offer condolences on the death of Mary Jefferson Eppes sputtered quickly on Jefferson's refusal to acknowledge his role in earlier political attacks on John. They finally reconciled in 1813, piggybacking on John's and Jefferson's correspondence, but Abigail and Jefferson only exchanged a few additional letters with little of the spark of their earlier correspondence. Still, this collection offers the interesting perspective of Abigail as a letter-writer to a male friend, someone from outside of New England, and a politician of quite different views from her own.

To commemorate the bicentennial in 1976, the staff of the Adams Papers editorial project, led by former editor in chief Lyman H. Butterfield, prepared in 1975 *The Book of Abigail and John: Selected Letters of the Adams Family 1762–1784*. Designed to highlight Abigail's and John's correspondence, interspersed with material from other family members, this volume made these materials easily available to a popular audience for the first time in a century – since Charles Francis Adams had marked the centennial with his *Familiar Letters*. *The Book of Abigail and John* seeks to present "the *best* letters of John and Abigail Adams," including many never printed by Charles Francis, in a format "to be read rather than studied" (Butterfield, 1975: 10, 13).

Thirty years later, Adams Papers editors Margaret A. Hogan and C. James Taylor undertook the work of updating this popular edition, eventually producing a wholly new volume, *My Dearest Friend: Letters of Abigail and John Adams*, in 2007. Limiting themselves exclusively to correspondence between Abigail and John, the editors included material from the entire corpus through 1801, rather than creating a chronological cut-off after the Revolution. These decisions allowed Hogan and Taylor to include nearly three hundred letters in total, over seventy of which had never before been published. It also gives readers a foretaste of Abigail's and John's extensive correspondence from the 1790s, which will eventually appear in *Adams Family Correspondence* (Butterfield et al., 1963–). Unlike earlier times, Abigail's life in this period was essentially stable. Without children to raise or military threat from the British, Abigail could manage the family homestead in relative tranquility, marred only by the vitriolic nature of politics and her concerns for John's place in the government. And with no fear of letters being intercepted or waylaid, she could write regularly to John and he could respond in kind, giving their 1790s correspondence a routine nature quite distinct from those of previous years. Neither this work nor its predecessor, *The Book of Abigail and John*, seeks to supplant the scholarly edition but both have contributed to keeping the letters of Abigail Adams – and her husband – in the public eye.

11.3 "A Life I Know You Value": Biographies

Scholars who have sought to tell the story of Abigail's life consistently find themselves torn between certain benefits and limitations. Her letters provide rich documentation of her day-to-day activities and considerable insight into her interior life throughout her adult years. But because Abigail herself did comparatively little on the public stage, her biographers have struggled to separate her own story from that of her husband. Even recent biographies, schooled in women's history and social history to argue for Abigail's personal significance – as a feminist icon, as John's most important advisor, as a model of female economic activity, and so on – frequently find themselves organizing Abigail's life more by John's actions than her own. The difficulty was at one time further compounded by the lack of source material written by Abigail herself, as compared to that from John, though this disparity has diminished with the ongoing publication of *Adams Family Correspondence*. In general, the biographies can be seen along a continuum of ever-greater recognition of Abigail as her own person with her own complicated character.

Upon Abigail's death in 1818, Rev. Peter Whitney, minister of the First Church in Quincy of which the Adamses were long-time members, eulogized Abigail in what would be her first biography. Taking as his text Proverbs 14.32, "The righteous hath hope in his death," Whitney offers the usual celebrations of her piety and virtue. But he also highlights several characteristics of Abigail less commonly associated with women in the early nineteenth century. "Madam Adams possessed a mind elevated in its views and capable of attainments beyond the common order of intellects," he believes. "Her discernment was quick, her judgment solid, and all her faculties so happily adjusted, as to form at once the intelligent, discrete and captivating mind." He goes on to note, "Her acquaintance with men and with events, with the civil and political interests of her own nation, from the sphere in which she was called to act, was deep and extensive." He recognizes Abigail's "spirit of patriotism" and "lively concern into every thing relating to the national welfare" (P. Whitney, 1819: 7–8). Similarly, in one of the obituaries that accompanied the published eulogy, it was reported that "her acquaintance with public affairs, her discrimination of character, her discernment of the signs of the times, and her pure patriotism made her an excellent cabinet minister" (1819: 18).

Charles Francis Adams included in his editions of Abigail's letters a "Memoir" giving a short overview of her life designed to justify the items selected for his volume. He emphasizes her early lack of formal education as well as her abiding interest in the popular writers of the day and affinity for letter-writing. Portraying her as a woman of unusual "presence of mind and accuracy of judgment," Charles Francis celebrates her domestic pursuits, commenting that "there was no time when she was more usefully occupied" than managing the household in John's absence in Europe (1840: xxxiv, xli). But he is also keenly aware of the complexity of such tasks and of Abigail's great skill in approaching them:

> She is a farmer cultivating the land, and discussing the weather and the crops; a merchant reporting prices-current and the rates of exchange, and directing the making up of invoices; a politician speculating upon the probabilities of peace or war; and a mother writing the most exalted sentiments to her son. All of these pursuits she adopts together; some from choice, the rest from the necessity of the case; and in all she appears equally well. (C.F. Adams, 1840: xli)

While shying away from any negative comments on his grandmother – she is a model wife and mother in Charles Francis's eyes, a saintly woman nobly assisting her husband and defending him against all enemies, foreign and domestic – Charles Francis's memoir provides early acknowledgment of the myriad responsibilities Abigail undertook in her life and her impressive skill at managing the duties of wife to an American statesman.

Early twentieth-century biographies, such as Laura E. Richards's *Abigail Adams and Her Times* (1917) and Dorothie Bobbé's *Abigail Adams: The Second First Lady* (1929), follow a similar path albeit while allowing Abigail somewhat more complexity of character. As much histories of John as they are about Abigail, their focus is on major events in his life – the trial following the Boston Massacre, time spent in the Continental Congress, dangerous transatlantic crossings, election to the presidency. Abigail is largely left to endorse John's actions and prove her endless courage in the face of whatever adversity he (or occasionally she) must face. Thus, when John accepts a post in the Massachusetts General Court in 1770,

> Abigail, was by no means insensible of the danger to herself and her children that this turn of fate might bring, while for John her fears were endless, though she would not show them. They thought alike on the main project. He had done as he ought; and she was willing to share in what might come, and to place her faith in Providence. (Bobbé 1929: 33)

Part of the difficulty these authors face is a necessarily reliance on published sources. Simply put, far more of John Adams's writings were available at the time. Richards laments these limitations, commenting on her lack of knowledge of domestic affairs: "What was home life like, when Johnny and

Abby Adams were little? It would be pleasant to see something of it in detail; if Mrs. Adams had only kept a diary!" (1917: 124). She then goes on to speculate, based on knowledge of eighteenth-century life, but with little specific reference to Abigail's own experiences.

Still, these works cover events in Abigail's life apart from John, such as her attendance at the first reading of the Declaration of Independence in Boston or her own transatlantic crossing, and make clear that her life was not spent solely waiting for John to return. And by quoting substantially from Abigail's own letters – at least, those that were publicly available in the first decades of the twentieth century, a limitation important to bear in mind for all works on the Adamses published before the middle of the century – both Richards and Bobbé place them in historical context and counter any notion of Abigail's passivity. Thus, Bobbé's comment that Abigail in November 1800 "had journeyed to stand by the President in the hour of his disillusionment" is juxtaposed against her letter to Thomas Boylston sagely evaluating the political realities of the election of 1800 and commenting thoughtfully on her and John's future prospects as they entered retirement (1929: 303–304).

By 1947, when Janet Whitney published her *Abigail Adams*, considerably more material was available to the author. Adams family descendants granted her access to some of the papers held at the Massachusetts Historical Society, greatly broadening the scope of her work and allowing her to paint a much more complex picture – substantially in Abigail's own words – of her subject. Thus Whitney gives considerably more weight than earlier biographers to Abigail's own activities, describing at length her efforts managing the farms in John's absence, commenting on the challenges of childbirth and childrearing, and recounting her mercantile transactions during John's years abroad. She describes Abigail's own voyage to Europe in detail and offers a thorough review of Abigail's views on European life and society.

Yet Whitney does not completely break free from the trope of Abigail as paragon.

> John Adams could easily have become a domestic autocrat [she writes]. A meek woman would have been crushed by him, a woman of average intelligence would have been reduced to silence, an assertive woman … would have found life a misery of continual battle. But Abigail's lively and natural self-confidence, her deep and wide intelligence, and her feminine softness made the ideal combination. (1947: 29)

Still, Whitney portrays Abigail in a more nuanced fashion. The author recognizes, for instance, that Abigail's interference in John Quincy's romantic life did not lead to his happiness or contribute his well-being: "So little did [John Quincy's] mother understand his deep, repressed, mature suffering" over her insistence that he break off an understanding with his first love,

Mary Frazier, that "her sympathetic concern was curiously beside the point." Abigail mistakenly assumed he was pining for lack of work, not for the relationship (1947: 244). Overall, Whitney envisions Abigail as a remarkable woman but not a perfect one.

Charles W. Akers' 1980 biography *Abigail Adams: An American Woman* was the first to appear following the formal opening of the Adams Papers manuscripts at the Massachusetts Historical Society. It was also the first to be published in the wake of the development of social history and women's history as meaningful approaches to historical research, and he uses both to elucidate Abigail's life and examine her as a model of "republican motherhood" in the eighteenth century. He argues that "[t]he life of this one woman forms a large window on society during the three-quarters of a century that saw the birth and political maturation of the United States" and uses his book to show Abigail as a woman of significant note beyond her connection to John and John Quincy (Akers, 1980: 1). At pains to emphasize Abigail's activities, Akers admirably avoids retelling John's life, as was common in earlier biographies, instead providing merely enough information on John's work to explain Abigail's own actions. But Akers sometimes overreaches in his efforts to demonstrate Abigail's independence. His repeated emphasis, for instance, on the equality of their marriage masks the reality of John's legal authority over Abigail. Abigail herself might have wanted "to insist on the equal importance of the male and female roles or on the right of a woman to judge how well her hsuband and sons met their responsibilities" but she also ultimately deferred to John's decisions regarding his acceptance of diplomatic appointments and public office (Akers, 1980: 189). Even in the realm of finances, Abigail's choices may have prevailed but that was because John wisely allowed them to. Nonetheless, Akers' book was at the time of its publication a welcome corrective to earlier Abigail biographies and remains a readable and thoughtful treatment of its subject.

Focusing on what the author sees as the ambiguities and contradictions in Abigail's character, Lynne Withey's *Dearest Friend: A Life of Abigail Adams* (1981), which was published at nearly the same time as Akers' book, argues for her essential conservatism despite Abigail's outspoken nature, seemingly radical ideas, and tendency to press the boundaries of the accepted place for women in the eighteenth century. Withey believes that, fundamentally, Abigail "feared revolution; she valued stability, believed that family and religion were the essential props of social order, and considered inequality a social necessity" (1981: x). Withey challenges the picture of Abigail the radical demanding equality for women, rightly recognizing that Abigail operated within an eighteenth-century mindset where "improved legal and social status for women was not inconsistent with their essentially domestic role" (1981: 82). This argument, however, undermines Withey's belief in Abigail's contradictory nature. Abigail's press for rights for women within the home appears far less conservative or contradictory in a world where women's scope was limited to the home. Withey's tendency to project her twentieth-century ideals onto Abigail creates the occasional jarring note in an otherwise well-constructed volume.

The journalist and author Phyllis Lee Levin began studying the life of Abigail Adams in the early 1970s but published her *Abigail Adams: A Biography* in 1987. Influenced by the women's movement of the 1960s and contemporary (if timeless) debates over the balance of family and career, Levin believes Abigail's "life illustrates feminism in the most comprehensive, Websterian significance of that electrifying word. Abigail did, indeed, have the vision to support (if not invent) the principle that women should have 'political, economic, and social rights equal to those of men'" (1987: xv). Yet Levin, in contradiction, focuses far more heavily on Abigail as John's partner, a dutiful, domestic wife assisting her husband to further his political career, than as an independent woman promoting equal rights. Levin writes, without irony: "In the very first letter John wrote to Abigail on his way to Philadelphia he outlined precisely the primary areas of responsibility in their partnership" (1987: 40). John makes the decisions and issues the orders; Abigail obeys. Furthermore, Levin's attention often strays from Abigail to John, who sometimes seems the subject of the volume. Well written but not always as carefully researched as it might have been, Levin's book is entertaining reading but fails to grapple with the complexity of Abigail's character, preferring convenient tropes to more thorough analysis.

The only biographer to date to break out of the traditional chronological telling of Abigail's life is Edith B. Gelles, whose *Portia: The World of Abigail Adams* (1992) and *First Thoughts: Life and Letters of Abigail Adams* (1998) both eschew that format for one based on examining discrete episodes in Abigail's life – what Gelles describes as a "collage" (1992: xv). In *Portia*, Gelles covers such topics as Abigail's flirtatious relationship with the Massachusetts congressman James Lovell, her evolution as a businesswoman during the Revolution, and even what she calls "the Abigail Industry," a recounting of the use of Abigail in biographies and other histories for myriad different agendas (which any reader of this chapter would be well served to peruse for Gelles' analysis of many of the same works considered here). Her second book focuses on Abigail the writer, seeking "to highlight Abigail's letter-writing persona while acknowledging her other accomplishments." Gelles rightly acknowledges that Abigail's letters "deserve to be the primary source of her historic reputation" and proceeds to explore the different ways Abigail used her letters and the different genres into which they fall (1992: 3, 4). Thus Gelles offers an entire chapter to fully explore Abigail's "Remember the Ladies" letter, another on her travel-writing en route from the United States to Britain, and yet another on "Historic Letters" that unpacks her writing as First Lady.

Gelles' approach has the considerable strength of focusing her writing on issues and events of importance to Abigail, without succumbing to the need to tell John's story as well, except of course as it intersects with Abigail's. Thus, for example, Gelles is able to examine in considerable detail Abigail's economic activities during the Revolution, including her management of tenants and the farm and the growth of her business reselling European goods in Boston, all to better understand Abigail's growing responsibility for the support of her family. The lack of a traditional cradle-to-grave narrative, however, leaves gaps that may mystify readers unfamiliar with her basic biography. Still, Gelles' approach effectively points the lens squarely at Abigail, making her unquestionably the center of her own biography.

Rosemary Keller launches her (1994) study of *Patriotism and the Female Sex: Abigail Adams and the American Revolution* with one of Abigail's most famous quotations: "Patriotism in the female Sex is the most disinterested of all virtues" (1994: xix). Keller seeks to consider the intersection of women's lives with the Revolution, especially how Abigail "extended the arguments for independence to envision new rights for women" and how the Revolution, in turn, "penetrated Abigail Adams's mind and life" (1994: 2). After an extended introduction to Abigail's ancestors, designed to show the Puritan milieu out of which Abigail emerged, followed by a discussion of her courtship, highlighting women's place in marriage in the eighteenth century, Keller focuses on Abigail's "intellectual conversion" from loyal colonist to committed patriot over the period from the mid-1760s to 1776 (1994: 44). She then discusses how Abigail came to use these new-found ideas in her own life, even if she did not explicitly recognize her own independence, concluding with Abigail's decision to venture to Europe in 1784, which Keller interprets as an act of "bold, courageous exploration" (1994: 167).

Keller places Abigail on the broader continuum of feminism, a "link in the evolving role of women in American history. ... Abigail Adams's life represents an effort to prepare the way for enlightened feminism, the autonomy of women through development of reason and serious intellectual advancement" (1994: 185–186). While offering a thoughtful assessment of Abigail's evolving ideas, however, Keller ignores the reality that Abigail was not a public figure during the Revolution; John was. Abigail has come down to us as one because her once-private papers are now public, not because she played a significant public role in the 1770s. This does not diminish Keller's legitimate interest in Abigail's intellectual journey but does raise questions about the uses to which it can be put in the broader realm of women's history. How much influence did Abigail wield beyond the (not insignificant) circle of her own family and friends? And to what extent was her maturation paralleled by other women at the time?

The most recent contribution to the growing library of Abigail biographies is Woody Holton's *Abigail Adams*, published in 2009. Initially intrigued by her participation in bond speculation in the 1780s, which he researched as part of an earlier project on the origins of the constitution, Holton expanded his work into a full-length book on Abigail. But Holton has retained his interest in Abigail's financial dealings, focusing on her business activities as an expression of her independence and autonomy – regardless of the limitations placed on women under the law. He argues that her investing in government securities, using money she herself had earned re-selling European goods, constituted "the first of her own declarations of independence" and that "she turned her own household into a laboratory where she imagined what the emancipation of women might look like" (2009: xii). Holton is not the first to consider Abigail as a businesswoman or to see the connection between economic independence and personal freedom, but he examines it in the most sustained fashion to date, tracing these qualities through the entirety of Abigail's adult life. His analysis of Abigail's "Disposition of Her Property" – her will by another name, though it had no authority as a legal document – is particularly thoughtful. Holton highlights it as the culmination of Abigail's own thinking on the subject of women's rights and property but wisely also recognizes the extent to which Abigail's ability to distribute her own goods was contingent upon the consent of her husband. Abigail's forty-year "laboratory" was only possible because John wisely tolerated it, a conundrum to challenge all scholars who want to promote Abigail's "emancipation."

Finally, in 2009 and 2010, respectively, Edith B. Gelles and Joseph J. Ellis – both writers well familiar with the Adamses – chose to tackle Abigail and John in joint or double biographies, seeking to examine them explicitly as a couple. John and Abigail often used the term "partner" to reference one another, and biographers have frequently acknowledged the difficulty of relating the story of one without also devoting substantial time to the other. Gelles entitles her work *Abigail & John: Portrait of a Marriage*, emphasizing that "Only by seeing the Adamses in tandem, as a couple, can we fully understand John or Abigail Adams and their lives and times." She argues that theirs was "a marriage of equals" in terms of the qualities each individually brought to the relationship, but also that it was "a typical eighteenth-century marriage" where each partner embraced a Puritan-inspired understanding of their duties in the world, separate but equally important (Gelles, 2009: ix–x). Joseph J. Ellis's *First Family: Abigail and John* (2010), in turn, is the story of Abigail and John's "long-standing conversation" within their letters, which Ellis hopes to tell "within the context of America's creation as a people and a nation" (2010: ix). Both books cover similar ground, providing strong introductions to the Adamses written in Gelles's and Ellis's usual polished fashion, and both strikingly end with the evocative image of Abigail and John lying together in death at the First Church in Quincy. While neither work offers the analytical insight one would expect from these authors, readers could do far worse than to use them as introductions to an extraordinary couple.

Better documented than virtually any other eighteenth-century American woman, Abigail's life defies easy categorization. The sheer quantity of her writings, produced over more than fifty years across a period of significant personal and national change, makes it possible for biographers to find her saying almost anything they could wish to support a particular interpretation. And the time in which she lived, her proximity to major political and diplomatic figures, her interest in women's roles, and her own active life all give ample material for scholars seeking to discuss myriad historical topics from a range of perspectives. What is certain is that Abigail's life continues to fascinate readers and provide a special challenge to historians.

Notes

1 March 24, 1798, in Massachusetts Historical Society, Smith-Carter Papers.

2 John Adams to George Washington Adams and John Adams, May 3, 1815 (*Adams Family Papers*).

Guide to Further Reading

The discussion above provides information on the major book-length biographies of Abigail Adams including two recent joint biographies of Abigail and John, and should serve as a guide to those seeking fuller treatments of Abigail's life.

For further information on the history of her papers and the Adams Papers generally, along with plans for their publication, see the introductions to the *Diary and Autobiography of John Adams* (Butterfield et al., 1961) and vol. 1 of the *Adams Family Correspondence* (Butterfield et al., 1963–), along with L. H. Butterfield, "The Papers of the Adams Family: Some Account of Their History," Massachusetts Historical Society *Proceedings* 71 (1953–1957): 328–356. The introductions to each volume of *Family Correspondence* (introductions appear in vols. 1, 3, 5, and in every book from vol. 7 forward) frequently focus on Abigail and should be consulted as useful guides to and overviews of her correspondence in the context of the wider family's writings. As Butterfield intended, with John's public writings appearing elsewhere, *Adams Family Correspondence* puts Abigail's letters front and center, and the introductions are designed to aid the reader in better appreciating them.

Abigail also appears prominently in collective biographies and histories of women in the revolutionary and early federal periods of the United States, due in large measure to her richly descriptive letters. See, for example, Cokie Roberts, *Founding Mothers: The Women Who Raised Our Nation* (New York, 2004), and Pauline Schloesser, *The Fair Sex: White Women and Racial Patriarchy in the Early American Republic* (New York, 2002), among many others.

Finally, Abigail has inspired fictional treatments, notably Irving Stone's *Those Who Love: A Biographical Novel of Abigail and John Adams* (1965), a highly readable account of the Adamses' lives up to 1783 heavily based on the Adams Papers volumes. Barbary Hambly creates fictional biographies of Abigail, Martha Washington, Sally Hemings, and Dolley Madison in *Patriot Hearts: A Novel of the Founding Mothers* (New York, 2007). And most recently, Abigail appears – improbably – as a fictional detective in a series of historical mysteries by Barbara Hamilton, beginning with *The Ninth Daughter* (New York, 2009) and in two others to date.

Part II

The Second Generation

Chapter Twelve

John Quincy Adams: The Life, the Diary, and the Biographers

David Waldstreicher

As a subject of biography, John Quincy presents us with two persistent dilemmas in the writing of American history, a braided paradox that delights as much as it provokes scholars. These are the superabundance of primary source materials and the not unrelated challenge of interpreting them. Like his father, John Quincy kept a diary, saved his letters, and wrote numerous reports and documents as well as producing a family that did the same. Like his father, too, John Quincy had a long life and a long career in which he confronted – some would say sought – controversy. Consequently, tackling an Adams is no small matter, and arguably gets harder with each generation.

12.1 Family Matters

The problem goes back to his parents, who shaped the reputation as well as the life of John Quincy Adams. And it is related to the special burdens of the second and later generations of Adamses, who felt so deeply the tugging compulsions of preserving tradition in a country that seemed to thrive on the rejection of traditions. To the Adamses – with their acute sensitivity to history and, not incidentally, their own good reputations – the records that they left could determine how they and their times would be viewed in hindsight. In 1874 Charles Francis Adams introduced his *Memoirs of John Quincy Adams*, a twelve-volume edition of his father's diary, by observing: "It may reasonably be doubted whether any man has ever left behind more abundant materials for the elucidation of his career,

A Companion to John Adams and John Quincy Adams, First Edition.
Edited by David Waldstreicher.

from the cradle to the grave, as John Quincy Adams." The diary could epitomize both the man and the times (C.F. Adams, 1874–1877: 1.1).

Charles Francis was the "good son," the only one of four who survived the burdens of being an Adams and had a notable public career of his own. Preserving and presenting his father's and grandfathers' papers was among the duties he owed both them and the country for his advantages. As both the honest exemplar and the maintainer of the legacy, he hoped that by presenting the best sources for understanding his forebears, the family's legacy would be better understood. As he had done with other family papers since he published some of Abigail's letters in 1840, he did, however, edit his father's diary with a heavy hand (Gelles, 1988: 656n2). He deleted parts of the diary in a process he described as merely a necessary subtracting out of the everyday dross and repetition which, he insisted, past editors of great diarists like Voltaire had mistakenly failed to perform. At the same time, he was captivated by the insights in the diaries and other manuscripts, the confirmations of virtue and the correctives which they provided to partisan attacks and misunderstandings of his father. Perhaps this is why he did not worry too much whether he had managed to penetrate what he had described, as a young man, as his famous father's iron mask, the poker face that made it impossible to discern his true feelings and motives (L.L. Richards, 1986: 4).

Charles' three sons differed among themselves about their grandfather. Charles Francis Adams II identified with him, and in 1901 made him sound like the epitome of Victorian manliness and accomplishment: "His courage was unconquerable; his ability great; his moral force admirable; his will abounding." Brooks Adams tried to write a definitive biography of the man he called "the most interesting and suggestive personage of the early nineteenth century," but he hoped his version would demonstrate that grandfather Adams's decidedly un-whiggish history was also that of the country: "a tragedy, ending with Civil War." Brooks's John Quincy Adams was a modern hero who had come to understand his role in the historical process, and adapted to it. He knew he was complex, that reality was complex; this explained why his contemporaries did not understand him (Nagel, 1983: 351–353; Nevins, 1928: xi; B. Adams, 1919a: vi).

But when Henry Adams – the first professor to teach a seminar in US history at Harvard – read his brother's manuscript, he was appalled. For him Brooks's homage would not do, even in the service of explicating the tragedy of America's failure to follow or even re-elect its Adamses. Moreover, Henry identified with Louisa Catherine Johnson Adams, whose abundant loyalty to, and appreciation for, her husband had not prevented her from making clear, to family members, her ambivalence about his career and, sometimes, his character. To Henry Adams, his grandfather's story may have suggested the old man's victimization at the hands of democracy, and some of the tragedy of American history, but he was not interested in that kind of morality tale. Better to keep some distance from his own feelings about his grandfather – at least when wearing the historian's hat: Henry Adams, tellingly, focused his masterwork on the years 1800 to 1816, between the two phases of Adams family leadership in the halls of the nation's capital (Hofstadter, 1968: 30–31).

John Quincy Adams's own failures to successfully instruct his countrymen suggested to Henry that historians, like politicians, could not expect to impart simple lessons from the past. In this he epitomized the contemporary professionalization of American history. Moreover, his grandfather had sacrificed his family's happiness on the altar of his career. And for what? It wasn't just that he had neglected spouse and children. He had served the slave power, only to be thrown over by them in 1828. His grandfather was not an exemplar, except perhaps late in life, trying to reverse the trends of a history he had sought to ride to power and fame. He was, in short, a typical career politician who became a somewhat bitter, all too wise and all too ineffectual old man. And Henry Adams knew the breed. Better to keep an ironic, knowing distance from a figure who talked morality and practiced power politics.

Even the self-knowledge depicted in an 1837 letter, in which John Quincy reflected on how Southern planters had sunk internal improvements and with it his own presidency, suggested to Henry a historical and political failure, rather than the redemption Brooks had found: "As I read, between its lines, the bitterness of his failure, an the intensity of his regret at having served the Sable Genius of the South, are immensely tragic – so much so that he shrank from realizing its whole meaning even to himself" (M. O'Brien, 2005: 6; see also Nagel, 1983: 352–353; Wills, 2005: 12–28). To Brooks Adams, John Quincy Adams's late battle with the slave-power was a lesson about both his grandfather's unparalleled dedication to the public good and the failings of "the democratic dogma": its tendency to produce greed, which produced slavery and war. He had a point. But so did Henry. After all, John Quincy himself had stated in the same 1837 letter that the "great object of my life therefore, as applied to the administration of the government of the United States, has failed" (John Quincy Adams to Rev. Charles Upham, Feb. 2, 1837, in Koch and Peden, 1946: 389).

When John Quincy Adams opined about the meaning of his life in 1837, he may have been telling it as he had come to see it, and perhaps he "shrank from realizing its whole meaning," as a fascinated Henry speculated; but he was also a sitting congressman rallying the faithful, even in his private letters. Indeed, historians are coming to realize that a former leading diplomat and Harvard professor of rhetoric and oratory who becomes president knew very well how hard it could be to separate his statesmanship from stories about the self. It might not even be useful to do so. Part of the ironic success of Adams's post-presidential second career lay precisely in his ability to make himself and his words the issue, eloquently and at length, more effectively than he had been able to do during his presidedncy, for purposes that were indeed larger than himself. In this context, even narratives of failure, and pronouncements about the constitution having become a "menstruous rag," (C.F. Adams, 1874–1877: 12.171) could spell a kind of recovery, even success. In this sense, the admiring historians who wrote his life in the wake of that second career were not far out in suggesting that John Quincy Adams had ultimately found – and in his diary written – the role of a lifetime.

The grandsons' debate set the stage for all future biographies to date. To evaluate John Quincy Adams's life, and even just to tell the long story, has often been to take sides in an on– off controversy about the nature of American statesmanship and politics and who may be said to have typified its core values. The partisanship, the voluminous documentation, and the fact that the Adamses – including John Quincy himself – have already been there, has inspired – or is it discouraged? – more biographers than one might expect. Perhaps as much as any other figure, Adams reminds us that the popular, seemingly straightforward genre of presidential biography remains both a literary and political enterprise.

12.2 Writing His Life in Order to Live It

In mining John Quincy Adams's diary and proclaiming it "the best of all records for the famous author's life and times" (Bemis, 1949: 17), historians and Adams biographers have rarely paused to consider precisely how much the diary itself as a work of history prefigures the themes of John Quincy Adams scholarship – including the conflicts within that body of work. Of course, as the best source for his viewpoint as it emerges, and often for the events of his life, the diary is front and center in the biographies, though usually submerged in the footnotes in those works that focus on Adams as a political actor – mined and quoted rather than treated as a source requiring careful scrutiny. Increasingly, though, the diary is coming to be understood as part of the process of creating the self he described as difficult to know. The diary became a way of managing the gap between desire, intention – or we might say, great expectations – and reality, including mixed success, inevitable failures, and the problem of others' perceptions.

In other words, John Quincy Adams's diary illustrates, and occasionally reflects on, seemingly paradoxical aspects of his public persona and personality – the paradoxes that have bedeviled biographers and tempted his fans and detractors at least since 1806 and perhaps earlier. In other words, the diary was at once a private and a public document even as it was being written – as one would expect from the ambitious son of a public man who also kept a diary. Lyman Butterfield, the editor of John Adams's diary, concluded that the elder Adams "regarded his diary as a private and impermanent record." (Allen et al. 1981: xxii). For Samuel Flagg Bemis, his most important biographer, the diary was "a secret tuning fork for his pent up emotions," "a process of self-disipline and introspection" that might guide descendants in writing his biography; the diary itself would never be published, or so he thought (Bemis, 1949: viii). Lynn Parsons, a more recent biographer, states that he "came to grips with himself and the world" through it (Parsons, 1998: 18). But in 1981 the editors of the first portion of John Quincy Adams's diary came to a different conclusion: "To the young John Quincy Adams, however, a diary's usefulness was not alone as a 'means of improvement to myself,' but as a source of interest and entertainment to others" (Allen, 1981: xxii). Part of this comes from the travel-journal nature of the earliest entries; the pendulum may have swung in the direction of privacy later. But it also swung back. There is every reason to believe, as Leonard L. Richards (1986) has argued, that the diary became a workshop for Quincy Adams's self-fashioning in every sense (1986: 5–6). For George Dangerfield (1965), one of the most perceptive historians of the "era of good feelings," Quincy Adams's heyday, the diary was a place where Adams rehearsed public arguments, at least for these periods of public service (i.e., most of the rest of his life). Ultimately, he "intended it for publication" (1965: 29).

Not least because he was John and Abigail Adams's son, he imagined himself under his parents' *and* the public's critical and appreciative observation. He expected a rich and complicated private or inner life and an extensive, cosmopolitan public life. He craved both solitude and attention – the solitude in part to prepare for attention. He made study and writing – manuscript book, desk, and pen – into a source of his public eminence.

The kind of contrariness that resulted should not be surprising. Eventually, the diary itself would be pulled into the process: on several occasions he copied out extracts from the diary for others to consult during legal and political controversies. This process culminated in his use of the diary in 1844 to combat the accusation that he had sold out Texas intentionally when negotiating the Florida boundary as secretary of state a quarter-century earlier. The mixed character as well as the length of the diary helps explain Charles Francis Adams's commitment both to publication and to what has been called (sympathetically and appreciatively) a careful abridgement and (more critically) a typically Victorian expurgation of private matter – a third of the text, according to Bemis; half of it according to Paul C. Nagel (Allen et al., 1981: xxiv–xxv, xxx–xxxi; Bemis, 1949: viii; Nagel, 1997: 424).

Certain other patterns are apparent from the early diaries. Just as his parents simultaneously praised him and held him to exacting standards, John Quincy Adams used the diary to increase and document his studious habits. Yet he also found ample reason to bewail his own laziness, not least in diary-keeping. From the early years, we see intimations of the Puritan legacy but also criticisms of excessive Calvinism. There is solitude and delight in others' company, including parties and, especially, women. There is intellectual ambition, even arrogance, coupled with frustration at the limits of his own learning, genius, and originality. There is every reason to accept, and good reason to celebrate, the multidimensionality of the self that Adams recorded. In editing his one-volume edition in 1928 Allan Nevins stressed the contrast between the public persona and the diarist:

> To his contemporaries he was a frigid and icy New Englander; but we who have his diary can perceive that at heart he was really of a hot and passionate nature, volcanic in his hates, intense in his loves, compact of fervent feelings, and sometimes wrought up to the most extreme emotional pitch. The emotionalism of the diary is indeed one of its most appealing qualities. (Nevins, 1928: xii)

Adams, in short, fashioned a modern self through his diary: cultivating, controlling, regulating his inner needs and desires, managing appearances to himself and, sometimes, to others. The diary has helped historians appreciate that self. But as with Benjamin Franklin's famous autobiography, it conceals as it reveals, and makes even the private self a public phenomenon. Adams's diary, rightly called a great work, can paradoxically seem to erase a stable, core, private self in creating and elaborating the public persona (Seavey, 1988). If it does not completely dissolve his son and editor's "iron mask," neither is it an open book. It has left room for different interpretations.

12.3 Starting at the End: Whig History

With John Quincy Adams's death in 1848, and to a certain extent before with his rising popularity in the North during his Congressional "second career," his admirers began a tradition of singling him out as a very special figure: he represented the epitome of the Revolutionary generation, an "old man eloquent" who brought the Founding Fathers' saving graces with him into the nineteenth century. These histories were truly whiggish: not merely in the contemporary partisan sense of the Whig party, but in the sense that the signature of a whig style of history has always been the establishment of continuities and progress. William Henry Seward, a standard-bearer of the Whig party, gave one of the eulogies and got some ghostwriting help from John M. Austin in completing his *Life and Public Services of John Quincy Adams, Sixth President of the United States* in 1855 (Seward, 1855; D.W. Howe, 1979: 198–199). Seward's *Life* started a trend by beginning with a story that JQA liked to tell, of his very public spirited and accomplished great-grandfather Quincy dying as he himself was being born in 1767. He cited fellow Whig Edward Everett's funeral oration in noting that John Quincy Adams seemed to have had no boyhood in the conventional sense, since it was never a possibility that he would not be in training to be a Quincy as well as an Adams.

Seward's Adams displayed a remarkable "purity"; his public life evinced "elevate and patriotic principles of action" (Seward, 1855: xi). As a teenager abroad he learned more than the subtle arts of the diplomat; in England he "learned from Wilberforce [the English antislavery leader] the principles of political philanthropy." His newspaper writings of the early 1790s advocating neutrality drew the attention of George Washington and Thomas Jefferson and really made him the "first" to advance a vision of real American independence. Still, despite the remarkable achievements of his early to mid-twenties, Seward could quote a March 16, 1792 diary entry to the effect that John Quincy thought himself obscure, and had not been seeking preferment. Elected to the Massachusetts senate he quickly displayed his "superiority to the policy of the mere politician" in resisting party measures for their own sake (Seward, 1855: 43–44, 54, 81).

Later, he became the source of the good, moderate politics of the Monroe years. While the "stern integrity" of John Quincy Adams came to be turned against him by disloyal cabinet members, he remained "high and pure in all his aims," the president of all the people, "not a section or a party." The Adams presidency constituted not a political crisis or the birth pangs of "democracy," as some would later describe them, but rather the seed-time of national greatness. The premium on ideals, on American nationality, and on the public good culminated in his return to Congress, where he "eclipsed all his former services." He had hated slavery all along, but as a statesman bid his time – to good effect. Adams linked the politics of the Revolution and the War of 1812 with the struggle against the slave power. As Theodore Parker had recently reminisced in his own eulogy, John Quincy Adams had crossed party lines to chair a Boston meeting against impressments, and then forty years later did the same at a meeting about the recapture of a fugitive slave. To northern antislavery Whigs, these efforts were indeed "the same object" (Seward, 1855: 202, 271, 326).

A similar desire to to combat skeptics informed the prolific and skilled biographer John T. Morse's volume for his *American Statesmen* series (1882). Adams had never received the praise he deserved; in light of his personal unpopularity, the biographer could and should risk "exaggeration in the service of truth." Actually, there was "only a little of the prig and nothing of the hypocrite in his nature." His "obstinate courage" made a virtue of his remarkable "confidence in his own judgment." Adams revealed the limits of the democracy that had in fact emerged during his era: he exhibited more "freedom of thought, speech and action" than any politician since the rise of parties. For Morse, the lesson of the diary, first published as he was writing his book, was that Adams was motivated by, and acted upon, principles. There was no smoking gun of self-interest. Nobody believed the story of the "corrupt bargain" of 1824; everyone but Andrew Jackson understood it as a partisan smokescreen. The absence of derogatory statements by Adams about Jackson "up to the last moment, and when Jackson became his most dangerous competitor," shows his lack of enmity at heart and his appreciation for the accomplishments of even potential rivals, so long as they too served the nation (Morse, 1882).

Morse did not see prevarication in Adams's path to the White House; he saw wisdom. Adams's integrity is revealed in his gradual shift on the politics of slavery. While stating unequivocally that the diary showed how Adams had "always" abhorred slavery and slaveholders, Morse kept that fact back until a late point in his narrative, probably to avoid leaving the door open to accusations of trimming during the senatorial, cabinet, or presidential years. Instead, Morse was the first to use the diary to demonstrate Adams's strikingly "intense repulsion to slavery" at the time of the Missouri crisis and his prescience in writing, albeit privately, that antislavery might cause – and be worthy of – disunion. The professional fixer of the "corrupt bargain" becomes a prophet. The consolidation of the South "as a political unit" around 1825 – "in opposition to" Adams – revealed the president as "really the first leader in the long crusade against slavery." His Congressional career as a result formed "the most striking and distinguished portion of his life." Morse's Adams grew, "both his mind and his character developing in strength, even in these years of his old age, and his traits standing forth in bolder relief than every before" (Morse, 1882: 163, 189, 243–244, 226). It wasn't so much great rhetoric and oratory as the knowledge and honesty of a senior statesman, combined with hard fighting and hard work.

In dialogue with Charles Francis Adams, who had presented materials to the Massachusetts Historical Society on the subject, Morse developed the thesis that as Congressman, in 1836 and 1841–1842, "he was the first to declare the doctrine, that the abolition of slavery could be lawfully accomplished by the exercise of the powers of the government," through the treaty-making and war-making powers ultimately rooted in the law of nations (Morse, 1882: 261–63), a far-seeing argument that history seemed, after 1863, to have proven correct, and which subsequently became standard in later biographies. In the end, history had proven John Quincy Adams right: about the nature of the national union, about government, about slavery, and about the relationship among them.

In this sense Morse applied to Adams biography the common sense of his generation of historians, the first professional historians of the United States. Hailing disproportionately from New England, or working there, many Gilded Age historians saw the worst aspects of the United States as having their origins in the Jacksonian ascendancy; they were open to the Adams counternarrative (Cave, 1964: 14–17). As Brooks Adams would put it (ignoring his brother's counsel not to be didactic) John Quincy Adams forwarded a vision of consolidated union *à la* George Washington; invented internal improvement as national public policy; and came to fight slavery when it became a clear obstacle to the public good. The Jacksonians did the reverse and plunged American democratic politics and public policy into ineffectiveness, and the country into Civil War (B. Adams, 1919a). Nevertheless, even Adams's most unpopular ideas were later realized. In the words of Hermann Von Holst, whose *Constitutional and Political History of the United States* (1879–1888) was standard reading for at least half a century, "in the person of John Quincy Adams there passed from the White House the last statesman who was to inhabit it for a long time" (quoted in Bobbé 1930: 237, 242.).

These arguments continued to be a motivating factor for those who wrote about John Quincy Adams. Whether the emphasis was personal or political, purity of motives reflected high vision and accomplishment. For James Truslow Adams, writing in 1933, the Senate years were "a sort of martyrdom." The son was like the father, a rock of integrity who "stuck to his principles" in refusing to campaign for the presidency in 1824. His presidency occurred in a time of peace which had been partly his own creation; the history of his administration could be reduced to the "machinations of his political enemies." It was hardly his fault, and it hardly mattered much. Henry Clay's affection and loyalty, coming after their rivalries and conflicts from the time of the Treaty of Ghent, proved that the high principled Adams was not at all impossible to work with. Above all, Adams "believed profoundly in God" and "in his country." (J.T. Adams, 1933: 134, 179, 191–192, 198, 211) In a relatively balanced treatment based on original sources, Senator Bennett Champ Clark (1932) depicted "one of the greatest Americans" who had the virtues of his minor flaws. "Excessively opinionated, dogmatic, egocentric, cold, yet at the same time honest, conscientious, patriotic, and fearless.... He was cold, aloof, self-centered, suspicious and censorious in his relations with all the world, but accounts agree that in his family relationships he was one of the most affectionate and devoted of sons, husband, and fathers." While the former legislator chafed at the "amazing political ineptitude" of President Adams's refusal to play the patronage game, he pronounced the man "consistent" in his constitutional scruples and in his sense of the politically possible on the slavery question. Clark drew a direct line between Adams's doctrine of the war powers and slavery, and both Garrison and Lincoln's use of it during the Civil War (Clark, 1932: 9–10, 364–365).

Editing a selection of the writings of John and John Quincy Adams, including selections from the diary, in 1946, Adrienne Koch and William Peden described the younger Adams as having put into practice the republican understandings of leadership that the older Adams theorized. Both were nationalists; both were moralists and yet also realists (Koch and

Peden, 1946). In his bestselling *Profiles in Courage* (1956), another senator, John F. Kennedy, and his ghostwriter Theodore Sorensen picked up the theme, though carefully (and perhaps for the sake of Kennedy's own career in national politics, astutely) avoiding the antislavery part of the story in favor of the younger Adams's stand against Federalist elites on the Louisiana Purchase and embargo. Adams's Puritanism was key: "Harsh and intractable, like the rocky New England countryside which colored his attitude to the world at large the Puritan gave meaning, consistency, and character to the early days of the American republic." Kennedy picked up on Adams's "almost morbid sense of constant failure," revealed in the diary, but suggested that somehow it made possible his willingness to stand "out of tune with the party intrigues an political passions of his day." Adams led off *Profiles in Courage* because he displayed "an integrity unsurpassed among the major political figures of our history." As with John Adams, his "failures, if they can be called failures, were the result of their own undeviating devotion to what they considered to be the public interest and the result of the inability of their contemporaries to match the high standards of honor and rectitude that they brought to public life" (J.F. Kennedy, 1956: 28–29, 31–32).

12.4 Downplaying the Middle of the Story: Nationalists and Professionals

Kennedy's treatment registered a certain change in professional as well as popular history. The postwar era saw the emergence of willingness to take on *less* of the story. One aspect of Adams's career could be enough to stand in for the whole. Such is to be expected from history professors and dissertation writers seeking to make an original contribution, especially in the wake of the fine complete biographies published from Morse to Clark. The decision of the Adams Trust to make the entire Adams family archive available in microfilm beginning in 1952 also made a difference. From the 1910s to 1951 access to the materials not available in Charles Francis Adams's edition of the diary, or Worthington C. Ford's edition of the letters and public writings, had been routinely denied by Brooks Adams and Henry Adams II, administrators of the Adams Trust (Allen et al., 1981: xxxiv–xxxv; Lipsky, 1950: ix, 5n4).

But the new trend to start somewhere other than at the end of the story may also have had something to do with the resurgence of Andrew Jackson and Jacksonism in the historiography, traceable to Frederick Jackson Turner and the Progressive historians and culminating in Arthur M. Schlesinger, Jr.'s *The Age of Jackson* (Schlesinger, 1945; Cave, 1964; L.L. Richards, 1986: 208n4). For Schlesinger, Adams and his presidency were at best the "last chance" of the "business community" – a version of Herbert

Hoover before the advent of Franklin Delano Roosevelt. He showed "immobility in the face of crisis" and "few evidences of statesmanship" (Schlesinger, 1945: 35). Adams's fight against the gag rule did not require more than a brief acknowledgement, quoting the diary, that Adams had foreseen the irrepressible conflict in 1820, which allowed him to play a not terribly significant Nestor-like, prophetic-old-man role in a politics that, for Schlesinger, was ultimately *not* about slavery. Adams's complicity, Schlesinger implied, made him an ineffective if not irresponsible spokesman against slavery when the matter "occasionally flare[d] up for a moment in an exchange on the floors of Congress (often around Adams, who knew his responsibility)" (Schlesinger, 1945: 424).[1]

The neo-Jacksonian interpretation of the period raised questions about Adams's nature as a politician, about the presidency, about his ideas, and about how to interpret his Congressional second career – previously seen as a triumph, suddenly hardly seen at all. Staughton Lynd (1967) has described how the Progressive ascendancy in US historiography went hand in hand with a downplaying of the slavery issue and a forgetting of the earlier, antislavery historiography that had celebrated figures like Adams (Lynd, 1967: 3–24, 135–84). The debate remains alive today, pivoting around the Adams presidency and the bitter election of 1828. To neo-Jacksonian historians, Adams's failings as a president serves as a convenient pivot; they seem to delight in Jacksonian touches like depicting Adams as out of touch with the people, quasi-foreign and aristocratic, and politically "inept," in the words of eminent Jackson biographer and defender Robert Remini, whom Arthur M. Schlesinger chose to write the John Quincy Adams volume in the new *American Presidents* series of short biographies (Remini, 2002: 76). Even Lynn Hudson Parsons (1999, 2009), a sympathetic and sensitive biographer of Adams, cannot resist the Jacksonian narrative of *The Birth of American Politics*; Sean Wilentz (2005) replays these themes in his prize-winning *The Rise of American Democracy*, where Jackson – rather than Adams – gets us "from Jefferson to Lincoln," and in his own "Andrew Jackson" entry in the *American Presidents* series that Wilentz now edits (Wilentz, 2007). Yet the neo-Jacksonian syntheses have been countered by Daniel Walker Howe, a careful student of the Whigs, in his Pulitzer-winning entry in the *Oxford History of the United States*, "What God Hath Wrought," which is dedicated "to John Quincy Adams," which covers 1815–1848 (thus including Adams's greatest political and diplomatic triumphs) and which explicitly refuses to name its period Jacksonian (D.W. Howe, 1979, 2007).

So much for the dueling doorstops of the historiographical present. In the immediate postwar era, with Schlesinger's interpretation dominant, it was left to a specialist in diplomatic history, Samuel Flagg Bemis (1949), to counter the Progessive-Turnerian-Jacksonian narrative, and he did so by getting access to the Adams manuscripts and putting Adams's diplomacy and his nationalism at the center of the story. If the Turnerians, "a captivating school of historical scholarship," as Bemis put it with a careful, typically professional faint praise, were right in positing expansion as the "central dynamic of American history," then "the handling of American foreign affairs during John Quincy Adams's life-span ought to have major meaning for the general historian" (Bemis, 1949: 300). Bemis's biography carefully and appreciatively described how, precisely because of his early and extensive diplomatic experience, and because he always put the nation before sectional and partisan politics, Adams laid "the foundations of American foreign policy," which included "self-determination, independence, non-colonization, nonintervention, non-entanglement in European politics, Freedom of the Seas, [and] freedom of Commerce." He was also a late convert to "suppression of the African slave trade" and "Pan-Americanism" (Bemis, 1949: 300, 569).

Bemis developed a canny response to those who would make the one-term presidency the epitome of Adams's career and life. Adams had two brilliant careers: the first in the Department of State and the second in Congress. The presidency had been a mere interlude. The timing could not have been better for such a revision. From the perspective of the early Cold War, a limited, careful nationalist internationalism – neither isolationism nor a crusade to remake the world by force – seemed not only central but also a distinctive and arguably beneficial American institution. Bemis justified his extended biographical approach by noting at the outset that "there is a lot of the man in the foundations of American foreign policy." A "chip off the old block" of John Adams in his suspicion of Old World diplomats, he learned early the importance of both national power and American neutrality *vis-à-vis* European conflicts. Bemis makes a strong case that the very young Adams, through his letters and newspaper essays, actually influenced Washington's Farewell Address, and generally helped forge a healthy middle ground between Hamiltonian and Jeffersonian politics. Whether he realized it or not, diplomacy – or diplomacy as national politics – became his "real profession." Rather than being out of touch, Adams had perspective, method, and real effectiveness.

Bemis won the Pulitzer prize for biography in 1949. At the time, he confessed in his preface, he was not sure he would or could handle the domestic aspects of the presidency, much less the second career. But for the period up to 1824 and the diplomacy during the presidency, the subject and the documents suited both Bemis's thesis and his method. Adams's careful reconstructions of conversations in his diary appealed to the diplomatic historian's need to analyze subtle and consequential negotiations – a tradition of analysis using the diary that the next generation's leading diplomatic historian, Ernest R. May, would take in a more critical direction in another prizewinner, *The Making of the Monroe Doctrine* (1975). In Bemis's hands, diplomatic history became biography as high art. Adams's letters to family had already in the 1790s taken on a dispatch-like quality, and Bemis brilliantly brought out a theme suggested by Morse and others earlier: John Quincy Adams had thrived in the world of early-republic politics precisely because he was scholarly, fairly judicious, and built a reputation for probity, wisdom, and skill – on the page as well as in interactions with major political players at home and abroad – over time. What the Jacksonians and Jacksonian historians castigated as flaws (being scholarly, calculating, and worldly) could be seen as great virtues, once it was clear that Adams was a republican, nationalist politician, not merely or mainly an anti-democratic one. He "kept to his political creed" for the good of the country, invented the Monroe Doctrine, and "stamped the metal" of the Manifest Destiny that Jacksonian Democrats later trumpeted as their own. Bemis found Adams "a competent, reliable, agreeable man to do business with," "one of the most entertaining dinner companions of his day in a select group," someone who most people found impressive and patriotic. The diary entries in which he criticized himself should not be taken literally: "a man who knows his defects was more likely to control them" (Bemis, 1949: 253, 569). The diary revealed and epitomized a great and good man at his best.

In the first sustained, scholarly analysis of Adams's thought, with an introduction by Allan Nevins, and praised in the *New Yorker* and the *New York Times* (by Bemis), George A. Lipsky (1950) came to similar conclusions. Adams was above all "a nationalistic American" whose "tendency to undue severity" and self-righteousness in dealing with others, including diplomats, was curtailed by his own awareness of it, evident in the diary (Lipsky, 1950: 25, 31). For Lispky, the quintessential politician Martin van Buren's respect for Adams was most telling. Unlike most politicians, Adams "made few concessions in theory and practice to necessity and opportunity," but he was at heart a moderate. He tended to deny class differences (except eventually, and rightly, in criticizing the planter aristocracy), yet kept his distance from the wealthy as well as the poor. Private property was sacrosanct, but the rich had duties to their country. His positive view of government was tempered by a sense of natural, God-given rights: "his sovereignty was limited." His political theory was "essentially a system of balances between extremes of power and limitations" (Lispky, 1950:156, 205).

In such a light, Adams's hesitations about democracy, if somewhat "behind the times," could be seen as a virtue, especially in light of his "ahead of the times" understanding of federal power and the balance of executive and legislative powers. Adams saw Congress exerting too much control over foreign policy, which simply had to be an executive office because of the need for speed and secrecy in diplomacy. Strong executive leadership was necessary for American power abroad. Anticipating later scholarship, Lispky admitted the presence of "contradictions" with respect to war and imperialism, but like Bemis stressed the importance of Adams's stance against European colonialism as an aim of US policy. Expansion was simply different from colonialism (a distinction that scholars today are more apt to see as illusory, though the issue remains controversial). Adams's United States was a new world leader in an ultimately successful search for liberal nationalism. Adams, in short, was a Cold War hero. The primacy of good values *and* realism in his politics was then demonstrated by the side he took in the slavery controversy. The slave power had, indeed, gotten out of hand and was trampling on the constitution and the Declaration of Independence; the meaning of America was at stake (Lipsky, 1950: 121–127, 212, 278, 316–317).

Lipsky helped solidify the "foundations" upon which Bemis would complete his monument to *John Quincy Adams and the Union* in 1956. The emphasis here was on Adams's

> spectacular Second Career: as Minority President with visions of a consolidated Union of Liberty with Power, then in Congress as a crusader in crescendo for human rights against the expansion of slavery – abolitionist at heart but constitutionalist in practice – until he fell at the climax of his life a dying gladiator on the floor of the House of Representatives. (Bemis, 1956: ix)

Looking forward, Bemis now found himself fully able to assimilate the seemingly failed presidency to a larger second-career story. In 1824 no one was better qualified for the presidency, as Adams rightly realized. He kept quiet on slavery; his discretion on this issue and on the tariff helped him get elected by the House of Representatives in "an implicit but certainly not corrupt bargain." The union had to be preserved and expanded before anything could be done about slavery (Bemis, 1956: 11, 58, 63).

But the election itself, and Adams's policies, changed things. The opposition to him was sectional. His plan for a great national government was a threat to slavery, and understood as such by Southern leaders like John Randolph (1956: 70–71, 88, 90–91). This shaped his presidency and his defeat. In a passage that seems to be ignored by recent historians of the election of 1828 (Parsons, 2008; Cole, 2009), and even in recent scholarship on the politics of slavery, Bemis insisted that "The most significant issue on the Presidential campaign of 1828 was the hidden issue … the issue of slavery." While neither candidate said anything about it for fear of antagonizing real or potential supporters, "the hidden issue silently transformed the Presidential Question of 1828 into an underlying sectional contest." Van Buren successfully courted "the vested interests of the slavery capitalists" and created the Jacksonian cross-sectional coalition (Bemis, 1956: 150, 152).

Adams, though, came to understand that the sovereignty of the national government, and the larger legacy of the Revolution, were at stake. By 1833 he had developed the doctrine that war powers – Congressional or executive – could ultimately end slavery. The next year, the Gag Rule debates "gave healthy vent to John Quincy Adams's compulsive character" (Bemis, 1956: 348). His work to cloak antislavery in petition rights paralleled his scholarly yet confrontational diplomatic work. He came to see himself as a leader of the antislavery movement, especially as slavery issues and diplomatic issues in Congress converged in the Texas annexation controversy – a perfect storm that was not only Adamsian in its nature but which included debates over his actions as secretary of state. Bemis ultimately delighted in Adams's refusal to be diplomatic and compromise, as if he had compensated, in his second career, for the limits or flaws of his first. He did not adjust to his times: "Adjustment can mean surrender." In light of the happy ending, Bemis could admit that Adams, in his life, had displayed the sins of self-righteousness, "personal contrivance" over political conscience (in 1824–1825), and a "pedagogical attitude" (1956: 544) because Adams, in his second career even more than his first, still represented the nation and its statesmen at their best:

> The historical figure of John Quincy Adams stands behind that of Abraham Lincoln in this Union. Both men were abolitionists at heart. Both believed that the Union could not long live half slave and half free. Both were practical statesmen. Both stood as long as they could by the bargain of the Constitution. Neither would propose to abolish slavery in any state where it was protected constitutionally, or in the District of Columbia, without the consent of the people thereof. But both were set against the expansion of slavery in the territories and against the acquisition of more territories in which slavery might extend an perpetuate its power and interest within the Union. Both opposed the War with Mexico. Both looked forward to the ultimate extinction of slavery through the democratic process by constitutional amendment. If the people of the South, bowing to the peculiar an powerful interest of slavery, should resist that process, both Adams and Lincoln were prepared to use force to break own that resistance, to go to war if necessary. Adams took his followers to Mount Pisgah and showed them the Promised Land. Lincoln led them through the valley of the shadow into the sunlight of freedom for the continent where still dwells in national unity the government of the people by the people for the people. (Bemis, 1956: 545–546)

This kind of rhetoric had earned its author the nickname "Wave the Flag" Bemis. But no one has approached Bemis's mastery of the sources and breadth of concern where it comes to Adams's politics.

12.5 The Inside Story

Bemis set the tone for late twentieth-century assessments of Adams's politics, including those that, like Lipsky, have portrayed him as a principled moderate to conservative who mostly made the right choices (Clarke, 1964; Russell, 1995), and those who have assessed postively his progressive, even radical "last crusade" (L.L. Richards, 1986; W. L. Miller, 1996). These studies – particularly those by Leonard Richards (1986), William Lee Miller (1996), and subsequent historians of the *Amistad* affair like Howard Jones (1987) – have added greatly to our understanding of Adams and his times. Yet the still more recent popularized versions seem to lack an appreciation for irony and contradictions, and the tragic dimensions so apparent to Brooks and Henry Adams (Wheelan, 2009). If not a "John Quincy Adams industry" to parallel the overproducing John and Abigail industry (Gelles, 1988), there is little doubt that a gap has appeared, or reappeared, between scholarly and popular versions. More recent scholarship has sought in Adams's personal life a deeper appreciation of how the seemingly negative and positive aspects of Adams might be reconciled. The opening of the manuscripts after 1951 accelerated this trend, underway in some quarters even in Bemis's time.

Robert A. East wrote a highly regarded monograph, published in 1962, on the connection between the nation's "critical years" and those of the young Quincy Adams between 1785 and 1794. East recaptured the contingency of the young Adams's experience without losing sight of the almost crushing sense of expectation which surrounded him as a young patriot. While East's focus remained the development of a statesman who "made his mark" in these years, he relied to a great degree on Adams's correspondence with his parents. As such, East's work serves as a bridge from the politics-focused work of the first century of biographers to the revised portrait that emerged from a closer scrutiny of the entire Adams family.

Dorothie Bobbé (1930) set a new tone and may have invented a new genre: the biography of the presidential couple as a study of a marriage and character, with implications for the evaluation of statesmanship. The view here is the sunny side of both the personal and the political. Her portrait of Louisa Catherine Johnson Adams is of a person who played as much a role in the making of the second President Adams as did his mother. By contrast, writing two decades later, Bemis was interested in none of this. Placing his chapter on the marriage at the crucial moment of 1824 (where he is otherwise cleaning up issues of the transition from the first to the second career), Bemis admitted John Quincy's "irascible" tendencies, but described Louisa as harsh, "hysterical," and "almost enjoying [her] ill health." He rarely consulted her, according to Bemis; she worried that she was somehow a political liability (Bemis, 1956: 113). The death of their son George brought them together a few years later; in sum, John Quincy Adams "adjusted" and persevered in marriage as in so many things.

By the 1970s, the public and historians alike had greater appetite for marital strains and ambivalence as a subject of history. Jack Shepherd's *The Adams Chronicles*, later made into a mini-series for public television (see Chapter 24 in this volume), found in Adams's ambitions the seeds of "inevitable" conflict between the spouses. The early death of two sons led

Louisa and Charles Francis Adams to accuse John Quincy of sacrificing his children to his career (Shepherd, 1975: 217, 322). In Shepherd's follow-up dual biography, *Cannibals of the Heart: A Personal Biography of Louisa Catherine and John Adams* (1980), it becomes apparent that a real change in historical and biographical perspective comes directly from a closer encounter with the manuscript writings of Louisa Catherine – not a diary *per se*, but letters, a memoir and thinly veiled autobiographical novel, and other literary experiments which Henry Adams had clearly read and preserved.[2]

Shepherd saw Louisa Catherine as an extremely intelligent and accomplished woman who was caught between an Enlightenment and late colonial era of expansive possibilities for women, and the domesticating impulses of the early republic, which historians of women were just beginning to highlight when he wrote in the late 1970s. She was "a victim of her husband's ambition," yet she pushed him to attain and became a "major player" on the political stage by 1824 – only to be "bored, isolated, and angry" in the White House (Shepherd, 1980: 263). Attuned to the limits of the time, Shepherd is refreshingly comfortable with the ambivalence in the Adams's arguably modern (or typical) marriage, and his work had the effect not so much of taking Quincy Adams down a peg but of humanizing him and helping explain why he could be both compelling and frustrating to the same people.

Yet Shepherd also found a way to make the second career a triumph for them both. In an argument little noticed by historians, Shepherd has Louisa Catherine and her daughter-in-law Mary Hellen acting as the equivalent of Adams's congressional staff, logging and tallying antislavery petitions. In Shepherd's view, Adams's fight against the Gag Rule extended into a battle for women's rights (as petitioners), in part because both he and his wife had read Charles Francis's 1840 edition of Abigail's letters. John Quincy was also "listening, for perhaps the first time, to his wife" (though Shepherd doesn't reflect on what this remark implies for his version of the argument that Louisa Catherine functioned as a campaign manager in 1824). The era of John Quincy Adams's revival was a period of growth and reckoning for his wife, as in some ways she underwent even more of a reformer's transformation. Consciousnesses raised, the tensions between the demands of the public and the private were, in the end, resolved. Both died, in a real measure, fulfilled (Shepherd, 1980: 358, 355–410).

Jean Marie Hecht sought and achieved a similar balance of the public and the private, the tragic and the triumphant, in her capacious and well-written one-volume biography (1972). She noted Louisa Catherine's sense of victimization, and her critiques of her husband in her private writings, but commented that they "defy analysis," leaving it up to the reader how seriously to take them. At the very least, "feeling sorry for oneself" was after all as much "a kind of Adams mannerism" as it was characteristic of Louisa

Catherine Johnson, and so we ought neither dismiss nor take too literally their emotional scribblings. Perhaps better than any biographer before or since, Hecht moved effortlessly between the private demons and inspirations (like JQA's "deep, subtle and complex" relationship with his mother and his "lack of confidence" in his own social behavior) and his equally complex political career. For example, in 1824 Hecht's Adams shows "a natural aptitude for political maneuvering and diplomacy" – but one that sets him up to fail, because, as Louisa Catherine herself pointed out to him, as president he needed to "lend himself a little to the usages and manners of the people without hiding himself and too modestly rejecting their civilities, no man could be more popular because his manners are simple, unostentatious and unassuming" (Hecht, 1972: 118, 24, 289, 294, 465, 459). Hecht's openness to Louisa Catherine and the family's view from the inside helped her to provide the most balanced portrayal to date, in which we really begin to see John Quincy Adams's virtues and flaws as two sides of the same coin.

Every good historiographical development deserves, and usually gets, its characteristic exaggeration, and the "inside story" of John Quincy Adams is no exception. Paul Nagel's bracing and fittingly titled *Descent from Glory: Four Generations of the John Adams Family* (1983) continued the trend of putting the women and family dynamics closer to the center of the story. But since the transition from John Quincy to his sons, two of whom died tragically, is the moment of "descent" which provides the overall structure and drama, Nagel gives much explanatory weight to the high aspirations and heavy emotional burden of expectations that John Quincy passed on, and even magnified, in dealing with his sons.

Illuminating as this was in an inter-generational story marked by love, achievement, and loss, it had its costs when Nagel wrote *The Adams Women* (1989) and sought to produce a definitive biography of *John Quincy Adams: A Public life, a Private Life* (Nagel, 1997). While sometimes now cited as the standard one-volume biography, Nagel's later book has rightly been criticized for privileging the private at the expense of the public. For Nagel, the public story of Adams derived from his inner demons, which he diagnoses as repeated episodes of depression. Building on earlier articles by David F. Musto (1969), Nagel places the blame on Abigail Adams, an "aggressive person" with a "need to dominate," a "calamity as a mother" who is condemned without any sense of contradiction or engagement with other scholarship, on the very evidence that has led others to celebrate her: the remarkable letters preserved by the family (Nagel, 1997: 31; Gelles, 1988: 667–669, 674–680). Given his reliance on his subject's emotional testimony, it is not surprising that Nagel asserts that Adams "did not play games in his diary"; rather he was communing with his soul" when writing there (Nagel, 1997: 31, 87–88). This is probably why Nagel reads the second career less as a conversion to antislavery than a battle with proslavery

Southerners – that is, as therapy. As such, the second career earns only a chapter, and some grudging praise (at least the patient learned to treat himself). While full of original insight and useful detail (for example, Nagel uncovers a moment in 1797 when Adams imagined that marrying Louisa Catherine would enable him to retire to a Georgia plantation, and even said as much to his parents), Nagel's biography often seems more a testament to the modes of twentieth-century psychology than even twentieth-century historiography – which is a shame, since Nagel himself had done such useful work on union and nationalism, the central themes of Adams's politics. In the end, his "Adams was never content." At best, "his all-consuming desire for political vengeance" led to his greatest triumph (Nagel, 1997: 97, 414, 419; Nagel, 1964).

12.6 Toward a Balanced Assessment: Character, Action, and Politics

By the time Nagel finished his biography, other historians had already begun to succeed better at crafting a balance of the private and public, the positive and the negative, in the John Quincy Adams story. A particularly fine and influential example is Leonard L. Richards' *The Life and Times of Congressman John Quincy Adams* (1986). Richards devotes much of his first chapter to the demons that may have driven Adams down this unusual second career path: the loss of his sons, a "shaky marriage," and most of all his awareness that the sectional politics of slavery had cost him the presidency. The Southerners were partly right: "until the 1830s his position on slavery was hard to fathom," but he had become more hostile to planter interests , more willing to make trouble, because of his losses. Richards sees the tragedy, in other words, but his Adams is a more self-conscious and canny actor in the drama than Nagel or Henry Adams would allow. Adams publicly developed an analysis of Jacksonian politics, including Indian removal, as driven by the slave power, and the effort, as Bemis (1956) and Nagel (1983) and before them Louisa and Charles had noted, did indeed function like therapy: "the more he needled his opponents, the better he felt." Richards wrote against a still-regnant Jackson-centered historiography, but proved to be prescient in building on Bemis and taking the "slave power" thesis, and the debate about it, seriously (L.L. Richards, 1986: 83, 122, 125, 159).

During the early 1990s, heightened sensitivity to US imperialism swung toward a more critical, or we might say "balanced," assessment (and perhaps toward relative neglect of the subject, as the prophet of a "tortured empire" seemed less inspiring than the daring scourge of the slave power; Immerman, 2009: 59–97). In a somewhat controversial interpretation, William Earl Weeks (1992) built on even while diverging from

Bemis in positing the second career as a repudiation of the first. Weeks focused mostly on the diplomacy and politics of 1817–1819 and found that the intertwined issues of slavery, sectionalism, and international finance led Adams to "compromise his personal integrity" in pushing America (and Andrew Jackson's) expansionist aims. Weeks noted a striking "Hispanophobia" in Adams's writings that paralleled his racism toward Africans and Native Americans. His suspicions of the results of both the Haitian and Spanish American revolutions need to be taken seriously as part of why he recommended non-involvement in these revolutions as well as non-colonization by Europeans. In his crucial letters of instruction to George W. Erving, the minister to Spain, Adams laid out a version of Manifest Destiny that ultimately defended Indian removal and the expansion of slavery. Adams, in short, took the wrong side in the First Seminole War, even if he was more sympathetic to southern Indians later on. He played fast and loose with facts and did not stand for peace. Consequently, the roots of his Southern problem lay not just in geopolitics he could not control, but in a situation he helped create – to advance American interests and his own career. Revealingly, Weeks finds that in this era his "hectoring" language to Spanish minister Onis paralleled the tone in his letters to his sons, and that Louisa Catherine was as disgusted by his politics during this period as favorite grandson Henry would be decades later. Weeks insists that the "corrupt bargain" of 1824 was corrupt by Adams's political standards, and that even in his Congressional second career Adams "flipflopped" on key issues like Texas. Charges of hypocrisy are justified – making Adams not so much a failure, however, as typical of America's imperial history. Jacksonian America was John Quincy Adams's America (Weeks, 1992: 90, 139, 76, 196–197; for a similar, contemporaneous analysis of a "National Republican" thesis forwarded by Adams and a Jacksonian "antithesis," see Saxton, 1990).

In recent years, the biographies have turned short, responding perhaps to a need for a comprehensive yet accessible view but perhaps also to the still-waving shadow of Samuel Flagg Bemis. Lynn Hudson Parsons sought and largely achieved a middle ground between Bemis and Weeks, depicting Adams as brilliant, but wrong, in his defense of Jackson (Parsons, 1998: 143), a success in two careers but a failure as a president. And in 2001, in an even shorter work similarly aimed at students but with a focus on foreign affairs, James E. Lewis, Jr. sensitively applied emerging understandings of the primacy of federal union in early national politics to Adams's career. Lewis's Adams, like Bemis's, valued union above all, but understood and profited from the distinctively American version of federal union, in light of which the diplomat Adams could defend against accusations of American weakness – the national government's inability to tell the states what to do on the borders for instance – as an example of New World freedom that simply had to be accepted. His diplomacy was more poker than chess – it was making the most of a bad hand, and it did involve some specious arguments that would come back to haunt him and the nation, as Weeks suggested.

Adams continued the Founders' American style of diplomacy, trying to make a virtue, as his father had, of American weaknesses, or recasting limits to power as freedom and internationalism. Fittingly, Lewis sought to have his academic sophistication and his diplomatic-biographical genre too: while the successes of 1817–1819 actually resulted from a lack of control over events, "a recognition of this irony should not lessen Adams's achievements" as a great secretary of state. Nevertheless, Lewis concluded that Adams's great achievements did not ultimately strengthen the union. The Transcontinental treaty worsened the Missouri crisis: more was at stake. The triumphs of the Monroe years cannot be separated from the enervating cabinet conspiring for the presidential mantle between 1821 and 1824: Adams has to take some of the blame for this situation, and perhaps his awareness of this helps explain his seeming "depression" and unwillingness to even try to build a constituency as president (Lewis, 2001: 53, 112). A more far-seeing Adams (and Clay) might have found in the idea of union a less hierarchical vision of American independence and leadership in the hemisphere (here Lewis, 1997, builds on his earlier work on the Panama congress and the collapse of the Spanish empire). As the most recent biography, though now more than a decade old, Lewis provides a fine road-map for the kind of fine-grained, engaged yet ironic approach to the life and the politics, one that perhaps even Henry Adams would have appreciated.

12.7 Conclusion

It seems clear that the main barriers to a rounded view of Adams lie in the length and breadth of his career, which transcends the specializations of US historians, who tend now to separate the earlier early republic from the "antebellum" period," domestic and foreign policy history (though there are signs of change here), and both of the latter from the politics of slavery. Just as important, however, are the challenges posed by the long diary, and similarly what happens when the ample record of Adams's private and family life is taken as an important part of the story.

The lack of an up-to-date view of the entire John Quincy Adams story reveals not only professional academic trends but also some of the limits of popular biography. The desire for heroic founders militates against the kinds of irony, much less tragedy, that Adams himself and his own family perceived in his career. We can take solace, though, in the sense that the arguments about Adams's intentions, effects, and meanings existed in his own time. It is not anachronistic to pursue them. Based on the scholarship of the past century, I would predict that the publication online by the Massachusetts Historical Society of the full manuscript diary, and the inclusion of Louisa Catherine's writings in the *Adams Family Papers*, will encourage deeper analyses of the constitutive relationships between the triumphs and tragedies, public and private.

Notes

1 "Looking back, I think I did Hamilton, Adams and Clay a good deal less than justice in *The Age of Jackson*," Schlesinger wrote in a 1989 essay he incorporated into his memoirs in 2000 (Schlesinger, 1989: 50; Schlesinger, 2000: 366).

2 These are about to be published in 2013 as part of the *Adams Family Papers*.

Further Reading

Adams, Charles Francis, ed. (1874–1877). *Memoirs of John Quincy Adams Comprising Portions of his Diary from 1795 to 1848*, 12 vols. Philadelphia,

Adams, John and John Quincy Adams (1946). *Selected Writings of John & John Quincy Adams*, ed. Adrienne Koch and William Peden. New York.

Allen, David Grayson, Robert J. Taylor, Marc Friedlaender, and Celeste Walker, eds. (1981). *Diary of John Quincy Adams*, 2 vols. Cambridge, MA.

Bemis, Samuel Flagg (1949). *John Quincy Adams and the Foundations of American Foreign Policy.* New York.

Bemis, Samuel Flagg (1956). *John Quincy Adams and the Union.* New York.

East, Robert A. (1962). *John Quincy Adams: The Critical Years, 1785–1794.* New York.

Hecht, Jean Marie (1972). *John Quincy Adams: A Personal History of an Independent Man.* New York.

Lipsky, George A. (1950) *John Quincy Adams: His Theory and Ideas.* New York. (Repr. 1965.)

Lewis, James E., Jr. (2001). *John Quincy Adams: Policymaker for the Union.* Wilmington, DE.

Morse, John T., Jr. (1882). *John Quincy Adams.* Boston, MA. (Repr. 1898.)

Nagel, Paul C. (1997) *John Quincy Adams: A Public Life*, A Private Life. New York.

Nevins, Allan, ed. (1928) *The Diary of John Quincy Adams, 1794–1845.* New York. (Repr. 1951.)

Parsons, Lynn Hudson (1998). *John Quincy Adams.* Madison, WI.

Richards, Leonard L. (1986). *The Life and Times of Congressman John Quincy Adams.* New York.

Weeks, William Earl (1992). *John Quincy Adams and American Global Empire.* Lexington, KY.

Chapter Thirteen

John Quincy Adams and National Republicanism

Andrew Shankman

From the end of the War of 1812 to the close of his presidency in 1828 John Quincy Adams was one of the most significant figures in the National Republican movement, which eventually became the National Republican party. In many ways the movement mirrored Quincy Adams's considerable strengths and weaknesses. By discussing National Republicanism and Quincy Adams's role within it, this essay will examine why such a bold and coherent movement that enjoyed such able leadership must, in the end, be understood by its own terms of measurement to have failed. The National Republicans' inability to shape the Republic as they wished doomed Quincy Adams to one largely unsuccessful presidential term.

John Quincy Adams abandoned the Federalist party for Thomas Jefferson's Republican party in 1807 just as the Republic entered a prolonged period of crisis. By 1807 it was clear that the United States could not assert its rights on the ocean as an independent and neutral nation. Britain, in particular, harassed American ships, impressed American sailors, and sought to dictate in which foreign ports the nation could trade. In response, Jefferson's administration sought to demonstrate the critical importance of American agricultural exports by imposing a national embargo for one year on all imports and exports. The Jefferson administration expected to show that the European nations at war could never hope to feed themselves unless they earned access to American agriculture by acknowledging the Republic's international rights (McCoy, 1980).

The Federalist party denounced the Embargo Act but by 1807 John Quincy Adams, senator of Massachusetts, had concluded that the future lay

A Companion to John Adams and John Quincy Adams, First Edition.
Edited by David Waldstreicher.

with the party of Jefferson not that of Washington, his own father John Adams, and especially the Federalists' current leaders such as Timothy Pickering. Quincy Adams's change had most likely begun during the Louisiana Purchase of 1804, which every Federalist in Congress opposed but that he (absent from Congress during the vote) privately supported. Unlike virtually all other New England Federalist leaders, by the early years of the nineteenth century Quincy Adams had concluded that westward expansion and full access to the Mississippi River were critical to the Republic's future. Adams's drift from the Federalists made it easier to disagree with his party about British aggression, especially after the British ship *Leopard* fired on the American vessel *Chesapeake* – the immediately precipitating cause of the Embargo Act. In response, Quincy Adams helped write the embargo legislation and was the only Federalist to vote for it (Remini, 2002). In spring 1808 Quincy Adams attended the Republican caucus, which chose James Madison as its presidential candidate. In June 1808 he resigned from the Senate knowing the Federalist-dominated Massachusetts legislature would never re-elect him. Henceforth, John Quincy Adams either served in or headed only Jeffersonian Republican administrations.

The Embargo Act began the process of events that led to the War of 1812. The war years 1812–1815 were tremendously difficult for the United States. The war deeply divided the nation causing many to fear that Federalist-dominated New England might leave the Republic and rejoin the British empire (Buel, 2005; Taylor, 2011). In addition, the war forced Americans to give up their long-expected goal (stated explicitly in the Articles of Confederation) to extinguish the British presence from North America by adding Canada to the Republic (Stagg, 1983). The war clarified that the United States would not be conquered. But it also showed that Britain did dominate the oceans, that it could inflict tremendous harm on the Republic, and that the nation was divided and disorganized enough that alliances of Spanish, Indians, and British could make its borders south, west, and north, dangerous and vulnerable. Indeed, the war could be said to have intensified a prolonged anglophobia, and even something of a national inferiority complex, that continued to influence the nation's politics and culture during the first half of the nineteenth century (Haynes, 2010).

The most frightening period of the war was between April 11, 1814 and March 1, 1815, the dates of Napoleon's first defeat and exile to Elba and his escape and dramatic landing at Antibes. During these months the nation faced Great Britain alone and confronted the undistracted fury of the preeminent fiscal-military state, a nation capable of servicing an £800 million debt and of spending as much as £100 million per year on its military efforts (Wright, 1995; Bonney, 1995: 383). It was during these alarming months, when the British occupied Washington, DC, burned the Capitol, and forced President Madison to flee, that the followers of Jefferson, at times, seemed truly to despair.

Republicans who would become National Republicans, and who had been or would be allies and supporters of John Quincy Adams, feared the worst during this period. Albert Gallatin, former secretary of the treasury under Presidents Jefferson and Madison and now a chief diplomat, wrote to Madison that Britain's "superabundant naval forces" and "very formidable army" would quite likely force "the restriction of our commerce and fisheries ... the curtailment of our northern boundary and an exclusive right to navigate the [Great Lakes] ... and even a division of the union" (Ferguson, 1967: 333, 336–337). Henry Clay, who would join Gallatin and John Quincy Adams as a negotiator at Ghent seeking an end to the war with Britain, described Napoleon's defeat and the isolation of the United States as "astonishing." Clay wrote to James Monroe that he thought "a new epoch ha[d] arisen ... ." These months for Clay "put the mind more in a state of amazement which attends a deep dramatic performance or an agitating dream, than belongs to the sober conditions of real transactions." Yet it was not an agitating dream; the conditions of 1814 were terrifyingly real and Clay, like so many other nationally minded Republicans, implored that "we must not despair for the Republic" (Hopkins, 1959: 885, 896–897, 899).

John Quincy Adams spent the war years in Europe, primarily as minister plenipotentiary to Russia, but as he joined Gallatin and Clay at Ghent he was exposed at close quarters to the grave concerns for the Republic's future that had reached him even at a great distance. At Ghent, though they might not have similar personal habits or style, the two future leading figures of the National Republican movement, Quincy Adams and Clay, worked feverishly together to secure that future. Key to their negotiations was United States access to the Great Lakes, full control of the Mississippi River, and essentially a free hand for westward expansion south of Canada.

The Embargo Act and the subsequent curtailment of oceanic commerce from 1808 to 1815 had already encouraged a turning inward and a real effort to develop the nation's domestic economy. At Ghent, Quincy Adams and Clay sought to consolidate this development, believing that the Republic's strength and safety lay with a shift from near total reliance on foreign markets to a domestic market with the concomitant development of internal commerce and manufacturing. Yet if the Republic was to avoid what Jeffersonian Republicans viewed as the pernicious social conditions of Europe – extreme disparities in wealth and poverty, overcrowded often urban populations, and the degradation of many – policy would have to ensure that a steady westward expansion supplemented dynamic and diverse internal economic development.

At the Ghent negotiations Quincy Adams, the most experienced diplomat, became the chief negotiator. He more clearly than anyone insisted that the United States must emerge from the war committed to and with the means to pursue a policy of full economic and political independence, national union, and westward expansion. The nation must conduct its affairs so that it never again faced the vulnerability of 1814. In particular, Quincy Adams was clear that the United States could countenance no Indian client state of Great Britain as a buffer between the United States and Canada. During the negotiations Quincy Adams's stance revealed one of the many instances where a bold and even noble vision of opportunity, freedom, and prosperity for all citizens of the Republic would come only at the direct expense of other residents of North America.

Quincy Adams believed that westward expansion was the key to promoting economic development without experiencing European social conditions. Therefore he had no doubt that it was inexcusable to "condemn vast regions of territory to perpetual barrenness and solicitude that a few hundred savages might find wild beasts to hunt upon ..." (A. Taylor, 2011: 414) Quincy Adams's fears that the British planned to support an Indian state that could prevent or at least sharply limit westward expansion were very real. As Clay reported to secretary of state James Monroe on behalf of the negotiators at Ghent, the British sought a "definite boundary" between their Indian allies and the United States and a prohibition on all future purchases of Indian land, but with the Indians free to sell to a third party. The negotiators "clearly understood [this demand] in all its enormity – a proposition to sever our country – made under the guise of a generous and disinterested attention to the welfare of their allies, amounting in effect to a cession of territory by the U. States to G. Britain" (Hopkins, 1959: 964, 967).

In the end Britain abandoned the demand, but the shared concerns expressed by Quincy Adams and Clay at Ghent pulled together many of the developments since 1807 and pointed the way to the full articulation of National Republicanism after the war. Beginning in 1816 Clay and Quincy Adams solidified their positions as leaders of an emerging movement. Initially the relationship was rocky. President Monroe chose the far more experienced Quincy Adams to be his secretary of state, the usual stepping stone to the presidency, and a position Clay coveted. Though at times in 1817 and 1818 Clay's resentment showed, in essentials the work Quincy Adams did in the cabinet and that Clay did in Congress reinforced the other's and launched the National Republican moment.

National Republican ideals and values were grounded in the interlocking system of policies that Clay called the American System, one that Quincy Adams's diplomatic achievements in the Monroe Administration did a great deal to promote. The series of policies that comprised the American System were enacted in 1816 by the Fourteenth Congress, of which Clay was a leading figure. In 1816 Congress passed the nation's first protective tariff, and in the waning months of Madison's administration sent him a bill to recharter a national bank, which the president signed. Congress also committed to internal improvements at the national level while encouraging the states to follow suit. President James Monroe, who took office in 1817, and his secretary of state Quincy Adams made these policies the cornerstone of the new administration.

The American System was intended to produce a sizable domestic market by diversifying the nation's economy. Emerging National Republicans such as Quincy Adams and Clay took seriously the notion that they were living in a new epoch. They reasoned that peace in Europe would restore European agriculture and lead to a decline in demand for American agricultural surpluses. Unless the Republic could create a sizable domestic demand, agricultural prices would plummet; farmers would face indebtedness, and possibly even lose their lands. The solution was to create a vibrant domestic manufacturing sector. Non-agricultural producers could purchase domestic agricultural commodities and find ready markets among American farmers. Internal improvements (roads and canals) would connect various domestic producers and significantly lessen the Republic's dependence on foreign markets and the oceans controlled by Britain (Shankman, 2011; McCoy, 1987, 1989).

Commitment to the American System was the hallmark of National Republicanism. Yet National Republicans faced entrenched ideological concerns and real challenges as they sought to persuade many of their fellow citizens to embrace their bold measures. Many critics of the American System, such as traditional Republicans like John Randolph, senator from Virginia, and younger critics like Martin Van Buren, congressman from New York, associated the American System with the policies of the Federalist party, and even worse with Britain and a culture of monarchy (Shankman 2008). The Federalist party of the 1790s had sought to promote domestic manufacturing, had chartered the first national bank, and had tried to augment the power of the national government so that it could energetically mobilize the nation's resources and provide a guiding (critics said overweening) hand to the nation's economic development. Indeed, the party of Jefferson, to which Clay and Quincy Adams claimed allegiance, had emerged in response to the Federalists' policies promoting manufacturing, a national bank, and a more energetic nation state. The Jeffersonian Republicans throughout the 1790s had insisted that such policies, drawn from the British example, would produce social conditions of extreme disparities in wealth and power and the degradation and dependence that allowed for a few to abuse and overawe the many – as far as the Republicans were concerned the quintessence of monarchy (Banning, 1978).

It was, therefore, quite easy for critics of the emerging National Republican movement to make the same charges against Quincy Adams, Clay, and the rest. There was now a new national bank in Philadelphia, only blocks from the First Bank of the United States. The protective tariff would create a growing population of landless citizens seemingly dependent on the patronage of their wares for their livelihoods. And worst of all, according to critics, these developments were not occurring naturally. Instead, an aggressive nation state promoted policies that artificially pushed the nation's economy and society away from its natural pastoral and agricultural condition, and so in the process placed republican institutions in grave jeopardy (Sellers, 1991; Watson, 1990; R.E. Ellis, 2007; Brooke 2010; Latner, 1993).

These were serious charges. And yet National Republicans quite fairly felt that they were groundless, and distorted what were in fact policies that would save not destroy the Republic. Followers of Jefferson becoming National Republicans first pointed to the new epoch. In the post-1815 conditions of declining European demand, they had no doubt that a primarily agricultural political economy would actually ruin American farming families. Yes, there was a bank and there was a protective tariff to promote manufacturing and diversify the economy. Nevertheless, National Republicans quite fairly insisted that the American System could fit completely within the Jeffersonian ideal of a society of producer citizens in a growing empire of liberty.

Comparing Federalist and National Republican political economy shows that the National Republicans had every right to insist that they were not neo-Federalists and were not violating the spirit of their Jeffersonian Republican ideals. Equating Federalist and National Republican political economy was superficial and specious. Under the direction of Alexander Hamilton the Federalist party had pursued a top-down approach to economic development intended to reinforce and, where necessary, to restore a social hierarchy disrupted by the American Revolution. Federalists funded the national bank and their most ambitious manufacturing project primarily with public debt, a debt whose ownership was highly concentrated in the hands of the nation's wealthy elite. Financial and manufacturing institutions that held public debt in exchange for their own stock were owned by public creditors and received a direct public subsidy in the form of interest payments funded by taxes.

Significantly, this method required regular revenue, which came primarily from tariffs on foreign manufactured imports. The need for revenue to fund the debt and their ambitious financial and manufacturing projects meant that the Federalist party did not wish to discourage foreign imports. Craftsmen, especially in the mid-atlantic region, pleaded for protective tariffs, duties on foreign manufactured goods that were so high that the corresponding price it would be necessary to charge would discourage their consumption. Tariffs at such levels were called protective because they protected the domestic market for domestic manufacturers. Tariffs that reliably raised revenue by taxing foreign imports could never also function as protective tariffs because revenue came only if goods continued to be imported. The Federalist party's prime need was revenue to fund the debt, the Bank of the United States, and manufacturing companies supported primarily by their holdings of public debt securities. Therefore, the Federalist party opposed protective tariffs, an opposition led by Alexander Hamilton (Shankman, 2003).

National Republican methods and policies were profoundly different from Federalist ones. The foundation of the American System was a protective tariff, something American craftsmen had called for since the American Revolution, and something the Federalists had never enacted. Unlike the top-down methods of the Federalists, the protective tariff directly assisted actual craftsmen by significantly raising the price of foreign goods and therefore by creating an immediate demand for craftsmen's wares. The protective tariffs passed in 1816, 1820, 1824, and 1828 by nationally minded Republicans, and then by the National Republicans once that name formally attached to the movement, were intended to recreate something of the conditions of the embargo years, when domestic manufacturing had flourished.

The rechartering of a national bank in 1816 was also by no means a restoration of Federalist party finance. The new Bank of the United States, capitalized at $35 million, was 3.5 times larger than the first bank had been. Yet by 1816 it was literally unthinkable to imagine the second bank functioning as the first one had. Between 1791 and 1816 the number of banks at the state and local level had increased from a mere handful to over 400. Proportionally the second Bank of the United States controlled far less of the nation's banking capital than the first bank had. Indeed, for the most part the First Bank had been virtually the sole source of banking credit in the nation, a condition that would never be recreated. National Republicans did not want the second bank to control or limit access to credit but rather to stabilize and make more dependable the hundreds of paper currencies circulating in the nation. Since every bank issued its own notes, it was difficult to know how much to value a bank's notes without personal knowledge of the bank of origin (Mihm, 2007). But through public land sales and other business conducted with the national government using local bank paper, supporters of a new Bank of the United States reasoned that over time the national bank would accumulate a portion of the notes issued by the most active local and state banks. The new Bank of the United States, then, could regularly exchange those notes for specie, and the knowledge that the demand would come would force local and state banks to be judicious in their issuance of notes and not print notes at values far beyond their actual specie holdings. Under this system, by definition, a bank in business would have sound currency since it would have proven that it could make specie payments when asked.

This conception of finance coordinated but not controlled by a Bank of the United States fit well within the broad democratizing of economic opportunity that the National Republicans sought. The protective tariff would foster manufacturing and so reduce the nation's unfavorable balance of trade. A more favorable balance of trade would reduce specie drain and so allow banks to issue even more paper, which would lubricate the economy and increase credit possibilities for producers able to take advantage of growing markets. The commitment to internal improvements would bring all the producers together, facilitate commercial exchange, further increase the size of markets, and so allow for the further expansion of the financial system. Unlike Federalist party political economy, the American System was based on placing resources in the hands of actual producers and on connecting the nation's economic growth to widespread access to markets and credit. The American System of the National Republicans was a profound democratization of American political economy (Shankman, 2003).

The National Republicans' position on westward expansion underscored this democratization and their stark differences with the Federalist party (Van Atta, 2001). The best way to prevent European social conditions, National Republicans argued, was to ensure widespread access to resources, and even the American System could not do that if the availability of productive property diminished. Federalists (virtually the only exception being the young John Quincy Adams) had feared westward expansion since they viewed great distance from the center as synonymous with being ungovernable. For that reason leading Federalists had opposed the Louisiana Purchase (Hamilton, 1804). But National Republicans organized the American System around the assumption of constant westward expansion and no policymaker was more significant in ensuring that expansion than Quincy Adams.

As President Monroe's secretary of state, in 1818 and 1819 Quincy Adams negotiated key treaties with Britain and Spain respectively, the two great European nation states that still claimed a presence in North America. In the Convention of 1818 negotiated with Great Britain, Quincy Adams secured the border of the United States and Canada at the forty-ninth parallel from the Lake of the Woods to the Rocky Mountains. The convention also established the Oregon territory west of the Rockies and allowed for joint British–US governance for the next decade, which helped consolidate the United States presence on the Pacific coast. In agreeing to the ten years of joint settlement, Quincy Adams was not giving up on his goal of United States dominion in the Pacific Northwest. Quincy Adams believed that people not governments would largely shape the character of the North American West and that regardless of what the United States and Britain negotiated, American settlers advancing west would come in numbers to overwhelm both Canadians and Indians. There was no need for formal hostile posturing when peaceful compromise would inevitably produce US hegemony. The decade of joint settlement, Quincy Adams was confident, would produce an irreversible process of movement by the Republic's citizens "until all possibility of [Great Britain] preventing [United States possession of Oregon] shall have vanished" (Lewis, 2001: 59). In addition to the long-range plan to acquire Oregon, as part of the convention the

United States secured full rights to the Mississippi River, which was absolutely essential for western markets and so vital for successful westward expansion. In addition, Quincy Adams secured a crucial territory in Michigan and Minnesota, which included the Mesabi Range rich in iron ore, a precious resource for a nation on the verge of industrializing (Remini, 2002: 53–54).

In 1819 Quincy Adams negotiated with Spain what he considered an even more significant treaty than the convention, a treaty which solidified the nation on its southern border. The Adams–Onís, or Transcontinental, Treaty finally consolidated a stable western border for the Louisiana Purchase territory. Quincy Adams believed the Transcontinental Treaty would move Spanish–United States relations "from the highest of mutual exasperation and imminent war to a fair prospect of tranquility and a secure peace" (Lewis, 2001: 60). The negotiated border began at the present border between Louisiana and Texas and then extended north and west along the Red and Arkansas Rivers to the forty-second parallel, the present-day border of California, Nevada, and Utah, and from there continued to the Pacific coast. By extending the border that far west, in the long term the treaty also encouraged settlement in Oregon since it reinforced the expected outcome of the negotiated joint settlement with Great Britain. In addition, the United States gained Florida while giving up any claims to Texas, which the Jefferson and Madison administrations had argued was part of the Louisiana Purchase. Together the two treaties paved the way for the Republic to become a transcontinental power and made it much more likely that rapid westward expansion would proceed unimpeded (Remini, 2002: 56–57; Stagg, 2009).

Quincy Adams's efforts to consolidate the United States as the leading North American state were part of a larger effort to remake relations in the western hemisphere as a whole. The National Republicans' belief that westward expansion was essential to preserve republican institutions and a social order comprised of autonomous and free republican citizens also led them to seek to reduce the influence of monarchy and aristocracy in the Americas generally, particularly after 1815 when so many former Spanish colonies in the Americas fought their own wars for independence and embarked on republican revolutions. As secretary of state under President Monroe, Quincy Adams sought a coherent policy that would assist an international republicanism while also further establishing the central place of the United States in the western hemisphere. These efforts culminated with the Monroe Doctrine of 1823 that Monroe and Quincy Adams hoped would force Spain and its allies, the Holy Alliance that also included Russia, Austria, and France, to give up their hopes that the Americas could remain a place of colonial conquest.

The Monroe Doctrine was intended to encourage neutral and peaceful commerce among republican nations in the hemisphere without European intervention. By 1823 the United States had recognized the new republics, and so the increasing likelihood that the Holy Alliance would seek to restore the Spanish monarchy and its empire would have exposed the United States as a weak and even worthless ally if it offered no response to the threat. The Monroe Doctrine announced that the western hemisphere was a place of free republican states that could no longer be colonized. It further stated that any effort to conquer former Spanish colonies would be viewed as a threat to all republics, including the United States. Quincy Adams insisted that the Latin American republican revolutions had to be understood as irreversible and that they had made it "impossible that the old exclusive and excluding colonial system should much longer endure anywhere" (Lewis, 2001: 94).

And yet the successful implementation of the American System, Quincy Adams's North American diplomatic triumphs, and the articulation of the Monroe Doctrine did not produce conditions of harmony and plenty. Instead the years 1819–1820 produced the worst economic crisis to that point in the nation's history – the panic of 1819 – and the bitterest national conflict over slavery the nation had ever experienced – the Missouri crisis. The years of panic and crisis were an ominous portent, a foreshadowing of the terrible difficulties and complexities Quincy Adams would face as president from 1825 to 1828. The panic showed that the outcomes of policies could turn out very far from their authors' intentions.

The years after the War of 1812, to a great extent encouraged by expansive national policies, produced a giddy period of economic boom, dangerous credit overextension, much debt, and grandiose assumptions about future economic opportunity. Most galling to National Republicans, the new Bank of the United States, rather than provide sober guidance and financial management, fueled the boom by irresponsibly issuing its own notes far beyond its specie holdings and by not overseeing the paper emissions coming from the state and local banks. By 1818 there was tremendous anxiety about the actual value of paper notes. Creditors began to call in loans and note holders began to seek specie repayment. As a result most currencies collapsed when in response banks failed to provide full specie repayment or suspended specie repayment altogether. As the value of property and currency plummeted, and foreclosures and job losses mounted, critics of the American System felt vindicated that they had opposed the system from the beginning (Rothbard, 1962; B. Hammond, 1957; Sellers, 1991).

The Missouri crisis was at least as frightening as the 1819 panic and probably more so. Though it had taken a great deal of wishful thinking, into the early nineteenth century many Jeffersonians north and south had clung to the old Revolutionary-era insistence that slavery would gradually diminish over time and finally disappear. Indeed, many had even claimed that westward expansion would hasten that development (Davis, 1999; L.K.

Ford, 2009: 54–76). Yet the first two decades of the nineteenth century showed that westward expansion meant slavery's expansion too. Most citizens seemed to accept this expansion in areas where slavery was firmly established, and Mississippi and Alabama entered the union as slave states without incident in 1817 and 1819 respectively. Yet when Missouri sought entrance as a slave state as well, it showed that slavery could spread west and so quite possibly continue to spread even further as the nation expanded.

The Missouri crisis was a bitter conflict over where slavery should be and about the future of the institution itself. But the crisis also showed how seemingly disparate concerns could be brought together to challenge the vision of the National Republicans. Proslavery advocates identified Missouri legalizing slavery with states' rights generally and the efforts to restrict slavery's expansion with an overweening national government that claimed an authority that was nowhere expressly granted in the constitution. It was this same alleged overreach, charged the National Republicans' critics, which allowed them to claim that the national government could charter corporations, erect internal improvements, and levy duties for purposes other than raising revenue. These constitutional fears were connected to deep anxiety about the society that the American System might produce, and they brought those opposed to the American System and those fearful of potential antislavery legislation together. As Congressman Nathanial Macon of North Carolina explained "examine the Constitution of the U.S. … and then tell me if Congress can establish banks, make roads and canals, whether they cannot free all the slaves in the U.S." Increasingly for proslavery critics of the National Republicans such as Macon it was pointless to deny that "If Congress can make canals, they can with more propriety emancipate" (Mason, 2006: 162–163). But Southern concerns could also resonate with those outside the slave states who were fearful of the world wrought by the panic of 1819 and the rapid transformation of society and economy brought on by banks, a protective tariff, and internal improvements. This confluence of concerns was assisted by the fact that proslavery values and hostility to the American System often went together. But at the very least, the constitutional concern provided a way to bring voters of different sections and backgrounds together, a process that began and continued to grow throughout the 1820s.

In such a volatile context even Quincy Adams's diplomatic triumphs could intensify sectional debate and conflict over the future of slavery. The treaties with Britain and Spain had all but guaranteed future westward expansion, but Missouri suggested that westward expansion might perpetually go hand in hand with conflict about the place (if it had one) of slavery in the west. Already Quincy Adams noted in 1820 the conflict in Missouri was making expansion of the nation's borders controversial, though acquiring new territory for the nation's citizens should have been a grand, unifying project. Nevertheless noted the secretary of state "the

Missouri question and its compromise [gave] the northern and eastern state interest a distaste even for Florida, because that would become another slave state" while the crisis encouraged "the greediness of the southern states to make more slave states" (Lewis, 2001: 63). Suddenly in this climate Quincy Adams's sensible diplomatic decision to give up United States claims to Texas as part of the Transcontinental Treaty negotiations could appear sinister to those who were opposed to slavery's restriction in Missouri and determined that slavery's future remain connected to future westward expansion. Giving up Texas in exchange for all that the United States did receive in the treaty had been entirely uncontroversial before the blow-up over Missouri. But during and after the Missouri crisis the notion that Texas had been abandoned, and with it the interests of slave states, became a rallying cry in the South and Southwest.

When John Quincy Adams won the hotly contested presidential election of 1824 there was only embryonic potential for a national party drawing support from both slave and non-slave states, and organized around a constitutional vision that was hostile to the American System while allowing questions concerning slavery to remain state issues. Though Andrew Jackson of Tennessee received more popular and electoral votes, he did not garner enough support to win the election outright. In the House of Representatives Speaker of the House Henry Clay helped to secure Quincy Adams the presidency. It made perfect sense for Clay to support Quincy Adams over Jackson, just as it made perfect sense for Quincy Adams to name Clay his secretary of state. There were few more qualified than Clay for the position and none more committed to Quincy Adams's vision of the Republic's future. But the emerging opposition, soon calling itself the Democratic party, charged a "corrupt bargain" and the election campaign of 1828 began as soon as Quincy Adams had been elected in 1825.

As president, Quincy Adams worked closely with Clay to consolidate the National Republicans' vision for the nation. He spelled out this vision, bravely if perhaps rashly, in his first annual address to Congress in December 1825. In this wide-ranging address, perhaps the best distillation of National Republican values ever provided, President Quincy Adams promised to build on the work he had begun during the Monroe administration. He charged the nation to work with its fellow republics in Latin America to shore up the Monroe Doctrine. A good start, announced Quincy Adams, would be sending representatives to the conference of American Republics in Panama occurring in 1826. In addition, in the address Quincy Adams called for a national bankruptcy law, sustained westward expansion, a massive internal-improvements initiative, and national institutions of higher learning and research including a national observatory to rival what he called the European "lighthouses of the skies." Each of these proposals, argued Quincy Adams, would organize and mobilize the nation's resources and fulfill the American System's promise of a vibrant national economy of, by, and for the Republic's producer-citizens. Yet with a deeply suspicious opposition already forming and already fearful that such an expansive vision threatened their most vital interests and ideals, Quincy Adams was surely too rash to conclude the address

> ... let us not be unmindful that liberty is power ... while foreign nations less blessed with that freedom which is power than ourselves are advancing with gigantic strides in the career of public improvement, were we to slumber in indolence or fold up our arms and proclaim to the world we are palsied by the will of our constituents...? (Remini, 2002: 80)

The statement "palsied by the will of our constituents" was all that furious political enemies such as Andrew Jackson and crafty political adversaries such as Martin Van Buren needed to hear. Aristocratic corrupt bargainers (as the Democratic party would have it) would of course ignore democratic majorities, seize as much power as they could, and would then produce the European social and political conditions that robbed citizens of their independence and freedom. Virtually every idea in the address offered ammunition to the Democratic party. At the Panama conference the United States would treat with abolitionist republics, even, potentially, with former slaves. In such a meeting those already fearful for their slave property could only imagine the worst-case scenarios. As the South Carolina congressman Robert Hayne – proslavery and staunchly anti the American System – explained: "with nothing connected with slavery can we consent to treat with other nations" (Remini, 2002: 83).

The domestic vision sketched by Quincy Adams in the address was possible to enact only within the constitutional vision of expansive power in the name of liberty that had so alarmed Nathanial Macon. The Democrats charged that such rapid and disruptive economic development was the very political economy that had caused the panic of 1819. Despite the opposition's determination, Quincy Adams's administration did have some modest successes. During his years in office the federal government spent more than twice as much on internal improvements as had all previous administrations combined. Yet a Congress increasingly dominated by the opposition Democratic party prevented the central coordination of policy that was the hallmark of National Republicanism. Instead, the public money had to be allocated to private internal improvement companies. The increased commitment to road and canal building did not yield the centralized or nationally planned system of policies that Quincy Adams and Clay had hoped would forge connections within the nation among citizens and so begin the process of reducing, and ideally extinguishing, sectional mistrust.

Tariff policy produced the same frustrations. The Quincy Adams administration did manage to continue the trend begun in 1816 of raising tariff levels to sufficiently protective levels. Yet in the hands of the Congress the tariff policy did far more to assist sectional interests and the tariff of 1828 even worked to undercut some New England manufacturing. Quincy Adams signed the tariff bill into law believing it the best he could hope for. But he did so acknowledging that "it was certainly not what I should have thought the best measure ..." (Lewis, 2001: 108). From the start of his administration, then, Quincy Adams was on the defensive. Rarely has a presidency possessed such a clear and coherent (and compelling) vision and set of policy priorities and yet been so ineffectual at persuading enough of the nation to allow it to be successful.

Quincy Adams's administration certainly tried to win over its critics. secretary of state Clay gave explicit instructions to the United States envoys to the Panama conference (who never arrived while it was in session anyway) to do nothing to undermine the nation's commitment to slavery. The administration also sacrificed the Monroe Doctrine and republican ideals and institutions for the sake of slaveholders' concerns and a political economy that needed the commodities produced by slave laborers. On behalf of his president, secretary of state Clay made it clear to the new Latin American republics that they must never seek to liberate Cuba from Spain. Should they try the United States would side with Spain and its European allies in a war against the other American republics since the effort, almost certainly, would also mean liberating Cuban slaves. The prospect of a possible second Haiti, this one even closer to the slave populations of the United States, was simply not to be borne by the Quincy Adams administration (Shankman, 2011). As recently as 1821 Quincy Adams had proudly articulated the role the United States would play in bringing an end to monarchical and aristocratic institutions in the western hemisphere, and quite possibly everywhere. Yet by 1826 that commitment did not extend to assisting republicanism in Cuba since revolution also meant supporting blacks' efforts to move from slavery to freedom. Though of course the motivations for such a reversal and such a collapse of principle were varied, the need of Quincy Adams's administration to prove that it was not hostile to the interests of slave-owners played a crucial part.

Yet despite the diplomatic efforts, abandonment of principles, and the insistence that the American System created markets for commodities produced by slaves as much as for anything else, there seemed nothing the Quincy Adams administration could do to convince those savaged by the panic of 1819 or terrified by imagined possible future assaults on slavery that National Republicanism was anything other than toxic, antidemocratic, antislavery, and un-republican. The rapid rise of the Democratic party as a nationally prominent intersectional political force was rather ironic. National Republicans had always assumed that their political economy would create a harmony among regions as agriculturalists and manufacturers produced a mutually profitable and symbiotic relationship. A harmony of interests across region, section, and social class would create the conditions to sustain a national political party led by men of sober and judicious vision such as Quincy Adams and Clay. Instead the National Republicans' efforts provoked an opposition that became a successful national party in ways the National Republicans did not, and that was held together by an intense commitment to localism and provoked a profound distrust, even hatred, of the values embodied in Quincy Adams's address.

In that address Quincy Adams had explained his view of the nation state and national power and had asked the nation to let him use both. Andrew Jackson and Martin Van Buren, in effect, argued that they should be given national power because they could be trusted largely not to use it. It was these two very different visions of the nation state and the Republic that competed during the mid-1820s, and the broad, ambitious future offered by the National Republicans simply could not overcome the twin legacies of the panic of 1819 and the Missouri crisis. The National Republicans tried to convince slaveholders that they had nothing to fear from their expansive political economy just as they tried to convince all citizens that the solution to the panic was a full commitment to the American System. In 1828 they could not persuade enough of their fellow citizens and that year, like his father had before him, John Quincy Adams became a one-term president.

Too often Quincy Adams had appeared tone deaf to the effect his words and actions had on his fellow citizens. Too often he seemed unwilling to engage in what he viewed as the less than dignified activities necessary to counteract the democratizing tactics of innovative political strategists such as Van Buren. A fine example of Quincy Adams's inability to compete adequately on the Republic's ever-democratizing political terrain occurred at the height of electioneering for a second term as president. When he was asked to attend a celebration of internal improvements in central Pennsylvania, a region dominated by German-speakers and a state crucial to his hopes for re-election, Quincy Adams declined the invitation to address a largely German-speaking crowd on the occasion of the opening of a new and very popular canal. Here was a quintessential policy of the American System that Quincy Adams could claim as the essence of his vision. And of course Quincy Adams, the highly accomplished former diplomat, spoke fluent German. But Quincy Adams stuck to his principled dignity and rather than address the crowd did not attend at all (Remini, 2002: 102).

Certainly behavior of this sort conveyed Quincy Adams's ambivalence towards the democratic and party politics that Jackson's supporters thrived upon. Quincy Adams's aloofness has even led some historians to characterize him as a president above party and to question whether there really was a National Republican party in 1828, at least to the extent that there clearly was a Democratic party (Ketcham, 1984). Yet when compared not to the Democrats but to the state of affairs in 1824, the National Republicans were clearly moving in the same direction as the supporters of Jackson, albeit more slowly. National Republicans knew each other and shared and articulated a policy worldview distinct from the values of the Democrats. In addition, the administration of Quincy Adams coordinated his re-election effort through a national campaign. Clay clearly functioned as a campaign manager in 1827 and 1828, carrying out almost daily correspondence with supporters in states in all regions. Clay also first suggested the series of conventions to support internal improvements and domestic manufacturing that took place in several states and that culminated with a meeting in 1827 in Harrisburg, Pennsylvania, then as now the capital of a key battleground state. Newspapers supporting Quincy Adams's re-election covered the convention, and the policies embraced by the convention it was clearly understood, depended on a second term for President Quincy Adams.

It is fair to say that the National Republicans lagged behind the Democratic party in organization and in the tactics of learning how to think and function like a political party, and much of that was due to their ambivalent leader. Certainly when Clay ran for president in 1832 he ran much more openly as the leader of the National Republican party. Nevertheless, given the coherence of their policy positions, the coordination from Washington, and the regular connection between members of the administration and supporters and activists at the state level in all regions, it is absolutely the case that the first campaign of the National Republican party was Quincy Adams's re-election effort in 1828.

And yet, despite (or was it because of) Quincy Adams's unwillingness to fully embrace the partisan conflict that came with the Republic's democratic politics, he was one of the most earnestly honest and public-spirited presidents in the nation's history. Nevertheless, between 1828 and 1840 Presidents Jackson and Van Buren thoroughly dismantled the American System and Quincy Adams's presidential legacy. The conclusion of a prominent modern Quincy Adams biographer is profoundly apt: "It is really impossible to think of any other President quite like John Quincy Adams. He seemed intent on destroying himself and his administration. By the same token, it is difficult to think of a president with greater personal integrity" (Remini, 2002: 110).

And it was that integrity that led Quincy Adams to have the greatest second act in the history of the American presidency, possibly in the history of American public life. Quincy Adams became the only president in the nation's history to accept a lower elected office after serving as president. In the 1830s and the 1840s he became the most prominent voice in mainstream politics against slavery in the nation, earning the sobriquet "old man eloquent" (L.L. Richards, 1986; W.L. Miller, 1996). Yet in this admirable second act he could never be the leader of a party or have substantial national influence, despite his prominence. Thus with his defeat in 1828, Quincy Adams's usefulness to the National Republican party came to an end. None recognized that more clearly than Quincy Adams himself. Towards the end of Jackson's second term Quincy Adams reflected on a nation without a Bank of the United States, without a national internal-improvements policy, and with a tariff rapidly returning to a non-protective rate. All had come with Quincy Adams's defeat. "I fell," wrote Quincy Adams, "and with me fell, I fear never to rise again, certainly never to rise again in my day, the system of internal improvements by National means and National energies" (Lewis, 2001: 116).

In assessing John Quincy Adams's legacy as a leading National Republican one must be as tough-minded about his years at the apex of power as one is laudatory about the moral courage of his final years in the House of Representatives. Clearly during his two terms in office Andrew Jackson did more to spread slavery west and to slaughter or forcibly remove Indians than had any previous president (Wallace, 1993; D.W. Howe, 2007). Yet drawing a clear distinction on these matters between Jackson and Quincy Adams as policymakers and as presidents is harder to do than it would first appear (Saxton, 1990: 41–42, 54–59). Quincy Adams saw little place in the Republic for those he described as "savages" during the negotiations at Ghent. Quincy Adams did as much as anyone to secure the west and to consolidate the hegemony of the United States while reducing the power of the Indians and their European allies.

In addition, when Quincy Adams's negotiations with Spain in 1819 all but ensured a vast expansion by the Republic into the North American Southwest, those negotiations came after almost three decades of the forced movement of slaves across the Appalachians (R. Kennedy, 2003; Rothman, 2005; J.C. Hammond, 2007). Quincy Adams was simply too shrewd a statesman to fail to see by 1819 that expansion into the Southwest would also mean the vast expansion of slavery. Indeed, it took very little imagination (and Quincy Adams had a great deal) to view the future of Texas being shaped by the same popular forces as the future of Oregon, to see Texas like Oregon as a place likely to be dominated by the citizens of the United States who settled there and reflecting their most vital interests, regardless of what the diplomats decided in the short term. The fortunes of slavery improved rapidly during the Quincy Adams administration while the fortunes of Indian peoples began their serious decline.

In every way Andrew Jackson was rasher, more violent, and less thoughtful than John Quincy Adams. He also despised the national institutions and commitment to coordinated national policymaking that was Quincy Adams's ideal. Certainly by dissolving the second Bank of the United States, by ending the protective tariff, and by ending nationally sponsored internal improvements projects within the borders of states, President Jackson and the Democratic party trumpeted their profound differences from Quincy Adams and the National Republicans. The Republic relentlessly achieved westward expansion after Quincy Adams's presidency. But it did so without the coherence and without any of the potentially unifying national institutions that Quincy Adams considered essential to establish a common sense of purpose among the Republic's sections and to keep them from turning on each other (J.L. Larson, 2001).

Jackson and the Democrats obliterated much about which Quincy Adams cared. But during his presidency Quincy Adams and the National Republicans in no way departed from a constant and vicious *leitmotif* in early United States history. Regardless of president or party, during the first half of the nineteenth century the needs and aspirations of the Republic's white citizens virtually always were pursued at the direct expense of North America's people of color, whether the indigenous or the descendants of the forcibly introduced, who were in general denied citizenship. In brutally removing Indians and relentlessly expanding slavery into the American West, Andrew Jackson and the Democrats built on a firm set of policy achievements that must be credited to John Quincy Adams and the National Republicans.

Guide to Further Reading

For a general overview of the period see, in addition to Daniel Walker Howe and Charles Sellers, Sean Wilentz, *The Rise of American Democracy: Jefferson to Lincoln* (2005). For issues of political economy, in addition to Drew McCoy and John Lauritz Larson (2001), see John Lauritz Larson, *The Market Revolution in America: Liberty, Ambition, and the Eclipse of the Common Good.* On the War of 1812, in addition to Allan Taylor and Richard Buel, see Donald Hickey, *The War of 1812: A Forgotten Conflict* and Roger H. Brown, *1812: The Republic in Peril.* For social and legal change see Christopher Clark, *Social Change in America from the Revolution to the Civil War*, Morton Horwitz, *The Transformation of American Law, 1780–1860*, and Tony Freyer, *Producers versus Capitalists: Constitutional Conflict in Antebellum America.* For the Missouri Crisis and the Political Conflicts of the 1820s, see Robert Pierce Forbes, *The Missouri Compromise and its Aftermath: Slavery and the Meaning of America* (2007), Richard E. Ellis, *The Union at Risk: Jacksonian Democracy, States Rights, and the Nullification Crisis*, and William H. Freeling, *Prelude to the Civil War: The Nullification Crisis in South Carolina, 1816–1836.* For diplomatic issue and particularly the United States response to the Latin American Revolutions, see James Lewis, *The American Union and the Problem of Neighborhood: The United States and the Collapse of the Spanish Empire, 1783–1829* (1998).

Chapter Fourteen

John Quincy Adams, Diplomacy, and American Empire

John M. Belohlavek

In April 1794, a troubled Vice President John Adams reproached his 26-year old son for a perceived lack of ambition. "You come into life with advantages which will disgrace you if your success is mediocre, if you do not rise to the head not only of your profession, but of your country, it will be owing to your own Laziness, Slovenliness, and Obstinacy." In historical hindsight, it is difficult to believe that such a biting admonition was aimed at John Quincy Adams, arguably the most successful diplomat in United States history, a man whose lengthy service in foreign affairs included ministries to four European nations and tenure as a remarkably successful secretary of state (Nagel, 1997: 76).

What qualities comprise the successful diplomat and to what extent does Adams meet those requirements? Intelligence and vision seem essential. Determination and toughness might also be on the list, as well as resourcefulness. After all, emissaries were often asked to function at great distances with little guidance or communication from home. Good character would be helpful, but with the caveat that the ability to manipulate, or even deceive, may be necessary.

Unfortunately, official Washington rarely considered these qualities. Political appointees dominated in the nineteenth century, selected for their support of a particular candidate or party. Others won their place overseas perhaps rather cynically, because a rival chose to remove them from the country. More benignly, family or personal bonds prompted the appointment of individuals who sought to build their resumes or fortunes abroad.

A Companion to John Adams and John Quincy Adams, First Edition.
Edited by David Waldstreicher.

Even so, presidents did choose talented secretaries of state and the United States dispatched competent men abroad to represent national security and commercial interests. Throughout the pre-Civil War era, secretary of state was considered the stepping stone to the presidency. Before 1817, Thomas Jefferson, James Madison, and James Monroe had occupied the post and moved on to the White House. Yet appointment was no guarantee of success, as the selection of Timothy Pickering (Adams) and Robert Smith (Madison) demonstrated. Concurrently, experienced Americans such as Rufus King and Thomas Pinckney served ably at the courts of Great Britain and Spain respectively. However, later under Thomas Jefferson, both Charles Pinckney in Madrid and William Pinkney in London struggled to achieve American goals.

Since the selection of diplomats and achievement of US objectives were uneven in the early republic, the rise and successful career of John Quincy Adams assumes a greater luster. His formal duties spanned more than twenty years – with time out for a term in the US Senate from 1803 to 1808. He initially regretted the appointment as minister to the Hague in 1794, but concluded his diplomatic tenure with the satisfying departure from the State Department into the presidency in 1825.

John Quincy Adams had been raised as a New England gentleman, imbued with a strict moral code and a belief in the value of education and religion. The importance that he placed upon learning, for himself, his sons, and his nation was unending. He believed that religion formed a critical part of his personal and professional life: not only should Christian principles determine his behavior, but divine providence offered a steady hand in guiding the destinies of the country. Adams viewed the United States as a "redeemer nation" whose prospects for global greatness had been ordained by God. His career fostered the expansion of American trade and territory as well as republican ideals.

Abigail and John Adams, first and foremost, raised a dutiful son. Their desire for his success as a high-profile public servant dominated his thinking. In spite of their lofty ambitions, however, at twenty-seven he had not yet married and increasingly seemed to reject his legal practice in favor of a life of the mind, possibly in a literary or academic career. When President George Washington nominated John Quincy for the post of minister to Holland in May 1794, the hand of the father was writ large in the appointment. The young barrister had no interest in journeying overseas and was angry that he had not been consulted, yet he could not refuse either the honor or the $4500 annual salary (Weeks, 1992: 9–21).

The new republic needed well-traveled, intelligent, unencumbered, single men to represent its interests. On all grounds, John Quincy qualified. The adolescent Adams had been educated at academies in France and Holland, trekked to Russia, and spent time in England while his father served abroad through the 1780s. By the age of 14 he had developed a fluency in French that would serve him well throughout his career. When Francis Dana, the first American minister to Russia in 1781, needed an interpreter/personal secretary, he eagerly accepted the services of the young, dedicated John Quincy. The mission to achieve recognition from Catherine the Great failed badly, but Adams expanded the foundation of his boyhood knowledge and garnered impressions of cities, courts, and cultures from London to St Petersburg. In 1787, after returning to the United States, he continued in the family tradition and earned a degree from Harvard.

By 1794, an empowered Adams prepared for his return to the Hague, committing the month of July in Philadelphia to receiving instructions and preparing for his post. Fortunately, as some compensation for leaving his Boston friends behind, he persuaded his youngest brother, Thomas Boylston, to join him as his private secretary. After a harrowing four weeks at sea, the two young men arrived in London in mid-October. The timing was perfect. US envoy and Supreme Court justice John Jay in conjunction with minister Thomas Pinckney had negotiated a treaty with Great Britain intended to resolve a number of troublesome issues, including violations of American rights on the high seas by British ships engaged in a war with France. The fortunate Adams was included in the conversation about the pact and determined that the merits outweighed the liabilities. Some gains were made concerning formalization of trade and evacuation of British troops from posts in the old Northwest, but the Americans surrendered on the principle of "free ships, free goods," and failed to deal with the infuriating impressment of Yankee sailors by the Royal Navy.

While the Jay Treaty, narrowly approved by the Senate in 1795, did maintain US neutrality and avoid a costly war, its concessions to Britain sparked a political furor that contributed to the rise of the Jeffersonian Democratic-Republican Party by 1796. Yet, for his part, John Quincy Adams, a novice diplomat, had been intimately involved in analyzing the most critical treaty of the Washington presidency. His voice had been heard, and he conveyed his reflections back home. For two weeks John Quincy absorbed the sights, sounds, theater, food, and culture of London, and was duly impressed. But duty called, and by early November 1794 he arrived in The Hague to begin a three-year mission that marked the start of an exceptional career in foreign affairs (Nagel, 1997: 75–87).

Holland was one of only five US diplomatic posts (Great Britain, Spain, France, and Portugal the others), thus the honor for John Quincy was great. The new American republic had historically enjoyed good relations with the Dutch, many of whom had been sympathetic to the Revolution of 1776. The existing harmony therefore provided few challenges or problems to be resolved, other than the repayment of old debts. Instead, the younger Adams found himself monitoring the European scene and reporting swiftly moving events and his views to his family, in addition to the State

Department. His observations were taken quite seriously, since the Napoleonic Wars had recently commenced and French armies would move triumphantly across Prussia, Spain, Austria – and the Netherlands.

The United States maintained a tentative alliance with France signed in 1778, but the Americans hoped to trade with both sides in the conflict. John Jay had compromised those bonds of friendship by the recently signed Jay Treaty with Great Britain, which the French viewed as an act of betrayal. The situation was complicated. Would the United States hold to its neutral posture, as designated by President Washington in 1793, or would the nation engage more vigorously in support of an old ally? Any such pro-French action would probably endanger budding Anglo-American ties.

Intelligent, astute, and conscientious, Adams quickly earned plaudits from the Washington administration. In recognition of his efforts, the president dispatched him to Britain in October 1795 to handle the formal exchange of ratifications of the Jay Treaty. Storms detained him in Holland, and he arrived too late in November for that purpose, but he took the opportunity to serve as acting minister in the absence of Thomas Pinckney and to spend several months in London enjoying the social and cultural whirl. The formal duties did not go well. Adams felt ill-prepared and, for the first time, out of his element. Wary and insecure, he struggled to find his diplomatic voice. Fortunately, solace could be found at the lavish home of American consul Joshua Johnson where he had the pleasure of meeting the consul's attractive and eligible daughters. John Quincy was especially drawn to Louisa Catherine, a 22-year-old beauty, who possessed a sharp mind, spoke French, and played the piano. Over the next eighteen months, Adams courted Louisa Catherine somewhat awkwardly, tempestuously, and at a distance. He appeared increasingly reluctant to surrender his bachelorhood. Their relationship ebbed and flowed, and appeared to rely more on circumstance, shared values, and affection than on genuine passion. Abigail Adams opposed the marriage, denouncing "the Siren" as a half-British seductress. But Abigail, who had done her best to ruin John Quincy's previous engagement with Mary Frazier in Newburyport in 1790, would likely never endorse a proper mate for her eldest son. John Quincy wisely ignored her counsel and wed Louisa Catherine in London on July 26, 1797 in a brief Anglican ceremony with only family members in attendance (Remini, 2002: 24–31; Shepherd, 1980: 77–83).

Adams enjoyed his time in The Hague and the light diplomatic load, a routine of scholarly books, fine food, spirited conversation, and good cigars. He found himself as an individual along with a degree of independence unknown in Boston, surrounded as he was in Massachusetts by expectant friends and family. But he had labored during those early months of 1796 in London, uncomfortable in a role for which he was not ready. Adams questioned his future. Perhaps public service was not for him. More and more he fell back upon a preference for the academic lifestyle. As John

Quincy deliberated his role, both as husband and diplomat, word arrived in the summer of 1796 regarding a change of assignment – as the new minister to Portugal.

At double his salary ($9000) and with marriage impending, Adams could not refuse. No doubt the continuance of minimal responsibilities and the hope for a prolongation of his previous lifestyle influenced his decision. In fact, John Quincy was on his way to marry Louisa Catherine and assume his new post in Lisbon in July 1797 when he received word that his assignment had been changed to Berlin by the newly elected chief executive – John Adams. The Federalists had narrowly triumphed (by three electoral votes) over the Democratic Republicans of Thomas Jefferson in the first contested presidential election in American history. John Quincy's ensuing appointment created the strong odor of nepotism, which nettled the principled son. However, the president did choose perhaps the most able man available as the newly created minister to Prussia (Nagel, 1997: 87–106).

John Quincy, his bride, and his brother arrived in the German capital in October 1797; the challenges here would be greater and the experience invaluable. France and the United States had broken diplomatic ties and were locked in a virtual undeclared naval contest, a "Quasi- War" that continued until 1800. In the midst of this conflict Adams was instructed to re-negotiate outstanding treaties with Prussia and Sweden that would result in the abandonment of American demands for neutral rights in international commerce ("free ships, free goods") and realign US trade with Europe along the lines of the Jay Treaty with Great Britain. John Quincy dutifully pursued this objective, signing a treaty with Prussia in July 1799. Close ties between Sweden and France prohibited a similar pact with Stockholm (Bemis, 1949: 93–95).

With his major goal accomplished, John Quincy and Louisa Catherine devoted several months in 1800 to touring the southern provinces of the country. In his element, John Quincy wrote extensive commentary on their travels, remarking on the people and culture. The *Letters on Silesia* was published to much acclaim; however, the idyllic days soon came to an end. John Adams's narrow defeat in his re-election bid by Thomas Jefferson resulted in the president recalling his son in late April 1801. Losing to the Virginian was humiliating enough; surely there would be no room for an Adams in the reconstituted diplomatic corps of the Sage of Monticello (Nagel, 1997: 107–132; Remini, 2002: 30–32; Lewis, 2001: 8–13).

John Quincy no doubt shared some of the bitterness that seemed to consume his family over the course of the next several decades. Both Abigail and John resented and disdained Republicans large (Jefferson) and small (Madison) whom they blamed not only for John's premature exit from the White House, but also for hindering their son's budding career as a public figure. John largely withdrew from public life for his remaining quarter-century, emerging in our historical consciousness in a welcome reunion of minds and spirits, through his thoughtful and engaging correspondence with Jefferson between 1812 and 1826. Even so, John and Abigail neither forgave nor forgot the brutal nature of politics during his term in office. A president willing to place himself above party, John Adams nevertheless remained a man of Federalist philosophy and sympathies throughout his life.

John Quincy differed. Recognizing that the opposition to the Federalists did not inherently represent the forces of evil, he sympathized with the Republicans on a variety of issues during the Jefferson administrations. Adams had been abroad when the two parties formed in the 1790s. Perhaps that absence, combined with his commitment to broader principles of union and expansion that transcended party, encouraged him to be less partisan and more eclectic in choosing his positions. While indeed idealistic and even noble, such a stance was not necessarily wise in a heated political environment.

Elected to the US Senate in 1803 by the Federalist legislature of Massachusetts, John Quincy quickly found that his views on foreign policy coincided more often with the Republicans than with his own party. He had determined that the Union was indeed in jeopardy. Sectionalism, party divisions, and commercial rivalry threatened the nation from within while warring Britain and France posed a threat to American neutrality and independence from without. As a man of republican principles who viewed the maintenance of the nation as the first imperative, he recoiled at the provincialism of his New England colleagues who opposed territorial expansion and talked of secession. He also believed in an energized federal government that would expand the nation's borders and protect its commerce. Although arriving in Washington too late to cast a vote, Adams supported the Louisiana Purchase, the only Federalist senator to do so. Likewise, he endorsed a variety of measures introduced by the Jeffersonians in 1806–1807 to condemn British attacks on American vessels and limit US trade, specifically the Non-Importation Act of 1806 and Embargo of 1807. Adams' s sanction of these measures, which he knew might be problematic for Bay State shippers and merchants if continued for any length of time, prompted his demise. So did his attendance at the Republican presidential caucus in January 1808. Massachusetts Federalists held little patience for a man of independent thought and action. In May, the legislature sent a clear message by choosing Adams's replacement months before his term ended. Not insensitive to such signals, Adams promptly resigned. Once a rising star in the foreign service, his career had been cut short by partisan politics. Seemingly, events were repeating themselves in domestic politics as well (Lewis, 2001: 13–26).

Adams returned briefly to what he knew best – his scholarship and the law. Harvard granted him a position as a professor of rhetoric, but he needed the supplementary income from his legal practice to maintain a wife and three young sons. A valiant Louisa Catherine endured numerous miscarriages and troubled pregnancies during her lifetime, ultimately giving birth to surviving sons George (1801 in Berlin), John (1803), and Charles Francis (1807) in the USA.

John Quincy enjoyed considerable success for a man who felt no particular passion for his vocation. In February 1809, he traveled to Washington to argue several cases before the Supreme Court, including the celebrated *Fletcher v. Peck* involving land grants and fraud in Georgia. Although Adams succeeded in pleading for defendant John Peck, clearly his trip had a broader purpose. He took pleasure in a cordial visit with outgoing President Jefferson, attended the inauguration of incoming President James Madison, and several days later was invited to the White House. The Republican hierarchy knew of Adams's diplomatic experience and surely noted his courageous support of many of their measures in the Senate. Having abandoned his Federalist ties, Adams presented an intelligent, savvy, experienced option for a vital mission – minister to Russia. Predictably, his mother frowned upon the post, but John Quincy now relished a return to public life. The $9000 salary and financial stability no doubt offered an added incentive. For the family, the lengthy appointment posed difficulties: the remoteness of St Petersburg, the cold climate, and the separation from his parents and sons George and John, who John Quincy insisted remain in Boston to be educated.

The Madison administration, however, made an ideal choice. The president promptly offered the job to Adams on March 6, 1809. The Senate, weighing the value and financial costs, delayed approving the mission until June 27. Hastily preparing for their departure, the Adams entourage – which included Louisa's younger sister Catherine as companion and John Quincy's nephew William Smith as personal secretary, sailed from Charlestown in early August, finally arriving in St Petersburg in late October. John Quincy faced not only a brutal Russian winter, but a Tsarist regime beset by its own international problems (Nagel, 1997: 182–188; Remini, 2002: 39–41).

Adams could indeed be prickly and condescending. Lacking the skill of easy social conversation, he had few friends. Yet, the scholar had become a Renaissance man in the classics, history, literature, and science through his relentless accumulation of knowledge in the liberal arts. Both John Quincy and Louisa Catherine spoke fluent French – the language of the court – and he had braved St Petersburg as a youth in 1781–1782. US relations with England and France remained tentative, sometimes bordering on open conflict, and the president sought to build a relationship with Tsar Alexander I. Russia, too, found itself in an awkward position – nominally allied with France, but seeking to break free from that relationship (Saul, 1991: 50–63; Bolkhovitinov, 1975: 187–217).

The combination of national circumstance and the personalities of the principals promptly produced a positive framework for discussion. Adams, seeking a balance between mind and body, enjoyed exercise, but the Russian climate posed certain obstacles. He was an extraordinary swimmer; his relaxing workouts in the Potomac River as president became legendary. Obviously, swimming in the Neva River posed formidable challenges, and he rejected the notion of playing indoor tennis. The 32-year-old Tsar, however, possessed both an inquisitive mind and a love for long walks around the city. Amazingly, Alexander found a soul mate in the older John Quincy. An odd couple: the absolute monarch and the republican crusader. Adams lamented that he did not have time to learn Russian, so the two men took frequent strolls and conversed freely in French about matters important and pedestrian: American society, politics, and international affairs. The strong personal bond between them built political capital for John Quincy at court and gave him access and advantage that few other diplomats shared. Even so, after four long winters, he developed few personal bonds. "We have formed no social attachments that can make us regret the Country," he told his mother in May 1813, "and I have no employment here which can afford me the consolation of being useful to my own" (Saul, 1991: 63; Crosby, 1965: 150–225; Bolkhovitinov, 1975: 218–253).

In spite of the climate and physical isolation, John Quincy enjoyed some level of satisfaction with the post, a gratification most easily detected in his response to his nomination and confirmation to the Supreme Court in 1811. Justice William Cushing of Massachusetts died, and Bay State Republicans championed Adams as his successor. The choice seemed less than obvious, since his credentials in politics and foreign affairs far superseded his triumphs in the law. A lifetime on the bench must have appeared as a death sentence. A decade later, the frustrated writer and poet reflected on his inadequacies in the courtroom. "I have been a lawyer for bread, and a statesman at the call of my country. In the practice of the law I never should have attained the highest eminence, for the want of natural and spontaneous eloquence. The operations of my mind are too slow, my imagination sluggish, and my powers of extemporaneous speaking very insufficient" (Nevins, 1928: 248, Dec. 26, 1820).

Regardless of his reservations, a seat on the Supreme Court was a high honor and would have prompted a return to the United States, a move that would have delighted his parents. Possibly, Adams reflected on the joy and fulfillment of his own self-engineered success in St Petersburg, the challenges that still remained, the reality that he could have become a Republican partisan; or the rather meager $3500 salary of a justice. In any case, he graciously and gratefully refused, citing Louisa's "peculiar circumstances" (pregnancy) as the causal factor.

For her part, Louisa appeared ready to depart Russia. Amidst the unrelenting parties, theater, balls, and dinners, she and her attractive sister Catherine thrived at the center of court life. Yet Louisa never fully embraced St Petersburg or its society. Part of the problem stemmed from John

Quincy's $9000 salary, which seemed adequate at a distance, but not when applied to the realities of the demands of entertaining, gaming, dressing, and dining. Housing posed its own set of problems, as the Adams scurried about searching for sizeable and affordable apartments for the family and staff. Health issues, exacerbated by the forbidding climate, appeared as a constant source of debilitation for both Louisa Catherine and John Quincy. While Charles Francis remained with them, Louisa felt guilt at "abandoning" her other two sons in Massachusetts. She had miscarried several times before giving birth to a daughter, Louisa, in August 1811. Tragically, the baby contracted dysentery and, despite the best efforts of the doctors, died in September 1812. The loss predictably devastated both parents (Shepherd, 1980: 129–172).

As the tiny Louisa battled for her young life in the summer of 1812, Tsar Alexander battled for the survival of his nation. Once an ally of the French, Alexander had turned his back on them over issues of free trade. An unforgiving Napoleon massed an imperial army of over half a million men and invaded Russia in June, arrogantly anticipating an easy conquest of his last remaining continental foe. John Quincy had earlier observed the success of Gallic arms when the French occupied The Hague in 1795 and established the "Batavian Republic." But this new invasion was markedly different, as witnessed by a ravaged Russian countryside and the death of hundreds of thousands of soldiers.

Meanwhile, in June, a frustrated and angry US Congress had declared war on Great Britain – the War of 1812 began with a whimper rather than a bang. President Madison outlined the causes of the conflict, laying the burden at the feet of the English for their repeated violations of American national honor and rights on the high seas. Britain, of course, also continued its war with France which made the English and Russians natural allies. John Quincy found himself in a unique and uncomfortable position. Fortunately, his relationship with the Tsar and their common cause transcended the potential difficulties. Alexander hoped that his country might profit from US exports and embraced the American notion of neutral rights. Moreover, he offered to mediate the Anglo-American war. Adams had no power to accept such a proposition, but he recognized its potential and readily agreed (Nagel, 1997: 189–211).

The American minister expressed deep disappointment in the ability of his countrymen to unite and pursue the conflict. American naval vessels performed well on the high seas in 1812, but the army faltered in a multi-theater invasion of Canada. Federalist opposition in New England – the heart of the war effort – persisted. Consequently, the Madison administration was pleased to learn of the Tsar's diplomatic gesture. Wasting no time, the president dispatched two talented statesmen to join Adams – Jefferson's Secretary of the Treasury Albert Gallatin, and Federalist senator James Bayard. They reached St Petersburg by the end of July 1813. The

European power balance had once again shifted as the French army encountered disaster in Russia. Moscow fell to the French in mid-September 1812, but the Russians burned the capital, leaving Napoleon with neither resources nor peace. He wisely decided to retreat back into Europe in October, but freezing cold and heavy snows combined with Alexander's forces to destroy the French army (Crosby, 1965: 230–272; Bolkhovitinov, 1975: 279–333). Napoleon would fight on through 1813, but his shield of invincibility had been cracked. After a year of unrelenting combat against an almost united Europe, the emperor abdicated in April 1814 and was exiled to the island of Elba off the coast of Tuscany. From the English vantage point, the pressure for peace with the United States now lessened – especially if negotiations involved mediation that might damage Britain's control of European commerce. The British sought a more neutral site for talks than St Petersburg. They first considered Gothenburg, Sweden, and, after some negotiation, changed the location to Ghent in the Netherlands (Remini, 2002: 41–43).

Clearly, European priorities now focused upon the realignment of the continent with the most able and experienced diplomats from each of the victorious nations meeting in Vienna. Prime Minister Lord Liverpool and his Foreign Secretary Lord Castlereagh rightfully regarded talks with the Americans in Ghent as a sideshow. They dispatched an unheralded delegation consisting of Henry Goulburn, an under-secretary in the Colonial Office, Dr William Adams, an admiralty lawyer and expert on international law, and Vice Admiral Lord Gambier, a Napoleonic naval hero. The Americans countered with the original trio of Adams, Gallatin, and Bayard, and then the president added Republican Speaker of the House Henry Clay and minister to Sweden Jonathan Russell, who had previously served as chargé in London. A talented and generally balanced commission, it contained Federalists and Republicans, moderates and War Hawks.

The 47-year-old Adams, with his degree in statecraft, intellectual capacity, and orderly mindset, assumed he would lead the delegation. The administration obligingly complied. Leaving Louisa Catherine behind in St Petersburg, John Quincy appropriately sailed with Russell on the *John Adams* from Gothenburg, reaching Ghent on June 24, 1814. When the Tsar's mediation proposal collapsed by January, Gallatin and Bayard departed St Petersburg and headed for London and the possibility of direct talks with the English. They remained there for six months watching events turn in favor of the British. By the end of June, Bayard and Clay arrived in Holland and on July 6 Gallatin appeared to complete the American delegation. The Crown's representatives were distressingly absent for the next month.

In the United States the war was not going well. Freed from military constraints in Europe, the British could now bring the full might of their army and navy against the seemingly hapless Americans. They commenced a blockade of Atlantic ports, attacked Maine, and began to raid systematically up and down the coastline. Redcoats landed near Washington, DC, and, after token resistance, burned the White House and other public buildings in the capital on August 25. The English challenged aggressively on the Niagara frontier, and on Lake Champlain a third force launched a campaign into New York state. On the southern frontier, the British planned a series of maneuvers designed to reveal Spain's tenuous hold on Florida and perhaps seize the territory. The US treasury was bare and Federalist criticism of the war escalated dramatically. As the grim Americans in Ghent waited anxiously for talks to begin, only Clay believed the timing was auspicious for a treaty (B. Perkins, 1964: 35–38).

The hiatus provided an opportunity to deliberate their approach and talking points. Between April 1813 and April 1814, the administration crafted instructions that were lengthy (50 pages) yet generally vague. For the United States, the humiliating question of impressment of American sailors had drawn the nation into war and must be resolved. President Madison, motivated by both politics and principle, had insisted upon the termination of this policy. However, by mid-June 1814, a rather desperate secretary of state James Monroe informed the delegates that they might back off on the issue if necessary. This course of action demonstrated both the weakness of the American position at the time and the abandonment of a key ideal. The new flexibility coincided nicely with the viewpoint of the representatives at Ghent who recognized that such a stance was a "deal breaker." They had already practically abandoned the demand at the outset of the talks (Perkins, 1964: 54). Madison determined that the naval blockade, violations of neutral shipping rights, indemnities for damages, and the cession of Canada to the United States (a very unlikely objective) merited attention. These "soft goals" had no firm demands attached to them. Ever the nationalist and expansionist, Adams hoped the situation would also allow for the discussion of the longstanding boundary dispute with Canada and the confirmation of fishing rights for New Englanders in Newfoundland waters.

John Quincy considered himself – and maybe rightfully so – better able to define these matters than his colleagues. They, in turn, resented his presumptiveness. His hair-trigger temper combined with smug arrogance, all the while lacking a sense of humor, did not help. Russell, in particular and for unclear reasons, detested Adams. Clay could also be easily sparked into disagreement. All four men utilized passive-aggressive behavior to pick apart and then reconstruct virtually any provision Adams drafted. Within a month he determined, "if any one member objects to anything I have written, all the rest support him in it, and I can never get anything through" (Nevins, 1928: 129–136, Aug. 23, Sept. 25, 1814). As historian Robert Remini (2002: 45) accurately observed, "Intellectual pride. One of JQA's towering problems in life."

Lifestyle issues made matters worse. At night, the restless Americans engaged in prolonged rounds of smoking, drinking, and card-playing at the Hotel d'Alcantara that lasted well into the morning hours. Adams took exception to the noise, but his inherent Puritanism also resented the undisciplined habits of his compatriots. John Quincy's regimen leaned towards arising at 5: 00 a.m., lighting the fire in his room, and then getting on with the business of the day. He relaxed at night by frequent visits to the theater or playing whist with the local genteel ladies. He retired by 11: 00 p.m. Ultimately, the squabbling would not damage the US position. While principle may well have been involved, just as often the petty bickering and flaring tempers reflected conflicting egos. Although the delegates were not unified, they eventually found consensus on the major points of concern. Concord became critical since, as time passed, the Americans increasingly negotiated from a position of weakness, rather than strength (Perkins, 1964: 39–57; Nevins, 1928: 120, 133, 142, July 8, Sept. 8, Oct 31, 1814).

When the British delegates finally arrived on August 8, the important differences of opinion manifested themselves. Unlike the Americans, who operated at great distance with some latitude in terms of their instructions, the Crown kept its delegates just across the Channel on a rather tight leash. Lord Castlereagh recognized the sensitivity of the impressment issue, but hoped that question, as well as neutral rights, would be resolved later in European conference. As reward for their support and to provide greater security for Canada, an Indian buffer state in the Midwest became a *sine qua non* for the Crown. Two additional matters, a Canadian boundary adjustment and the discussion of the fisheries would be welcomed by the ministry (Nevins, 1928: 122–125, Aug. 8, 9, 13, 1814; Perkins, 1964: 58–80).

The absence of warm personal relationships exacerbated communications. The English neither particularly liked nor respected their American counterparts, or the upstart nation they represented. Adams observed that the more he conversed with Henry Goulburn "the more the violence and bitterness of his passion against the United States disclosed itself" (Nevins, 1928: 130, Sept. 1, 1814). Not to be outdone, in his diary the anglophobic John Quincy referred to the "uniting of our whole country in support of the war against our eternal and irreconcilable foe" (Nevins, 1928: 139, Oct. 12, 1814). While the two delegations talked regularly and dined occasionally, the absence of real understanding seemed evident, compounded by an ongoing demand by the British public, press, and politicians for a punitive war and vengeful peace (Perkins, 1964: 62–64).

Consequently, discussions dragged on through the fall months with little progress. The routine consisted of the exchange of notes and proposals on various issues between the delegations, interspersed with a periodic face-to-face meeting. Each draft drew the sides further apart and the the Americans remained gloomy about the long-term prospects. John Quincy advocated tough talk deriding the British notes as "arrogant, overbearing, and offensive" (Nevins, 1928: 138, Oct. 12, 1814). The Crown feared for the security of Canada and thus seemed adamant on the subject of an Indian barrier state and exclusive control of military posts on the Great Lakes. Adams – intent on advancing American continental empire – was no less strident, chiding Goulburn in a private conversation, "To condemn vast regions of territory to perpetual barrenness and solitude that a few hundred savages might find wild beasts to hunt upon it, was a species of game law that a nation descended from Britons would never endure" (Nevins, 1928: 132, 126–127, Sept. 1, 1814; Aug. 19, 1814). He rejected the notion that Canada was in any ongoing danger of American invasion, and the United States would not be humiliated by allowing the Union Jack to fly solely over the Great Lakes. For almost four months such exchanges typified the talks (Perkins, 1964: 81–101).

By mid-November the tide began to turn. Adams, as usual, found his colleagues had red-lined three-quarters of a proposed draft. At an ensuing meeting, he argued forcefully, and ultimately successfully, for the reincorporation of the following language: "the proposal *to conclude the peace on the footing of the state before the war*, applied to all the subjects of dispute between the two countries, leaving all the rest for the future and pacific negotiation" (Nevins, 1928: 142, Nov. 10, 1814; my italics) Two weeks later, the British delegates sent back the American draft with notes scribbled in the margins. Adams observed, "They have rejected all the articles we had proposed on impressments, blockade, indemnities, amnesty, and Indians." However, the Crown abandoned the Indian buffer state, exclusive domination of the Great Lakes, and control of any US territory they presently occupied. A measured sense of relief filled the room, as the Americans realized the road to a peace treaty had been cleared. Nettlesome issues remained, and provincialism emerged as the Americans wrangled over insisting on guarantees of North Atlantic fishing rights and prohibiting British use of the Mississippi River. The delegates agreed to say nothing in the treaty about either subject (Nevins, 1928: 144–150, Nov. 27, Dec. 1, 11, 22, 1814). On Christmas eve, the Americans made their way to the British Residence where all the participants signed multiple copies of the accord. As Adams departed, he expressed the hope that this "would be the last treaty of peace between Great Britain and the United States" (Nevins, 1928: 151, Dec. 24, 1814; Remini, 2002: 43–47; Perkins, 1964: 102–127).

The critical question, of course, is *why* the British performed a diplomatic about-face in November. The answer lies substantially in changing royal concerns over events in two hemispheres. The much-anticipated summer campaign in the United States had stalled. Washington had fallen, but Fort McHenry in Baltimore stood fast against a heavy bombardment, inspiring observer Francis Scott Key to write his now-famous hymn to American patriotism. Meanwhile, as a force of 10 000 English soldiers, many Napoleonic veterans, threatened Plattsburg, New York, in September, the defeat of a companion British flotilla on Lake Champlain prompted the army commander to withdraw his troops. In spite of these setbacks, His Majesty's military continued the fight as the navy was about to commence an assault in the Gulf of Mexico. The wisdom of pouring additional resources and energies into the American conflict, however, now seemed almost counterproductive to the ministry. Would British interests not be better served by neutralizing the Americans, rather than perpetuating a policy of alienation? In Europe, Napoleon had not returned from exile, but discord plagued the talks at Vienna. Both Liverpool and Castlereagh recognized that a now needless war with the Americans would divert their attention at a time when the European continent should be their primary focus (Lewis, 2001: 27–30).

John Quincy Adams had dedicated seven months to the peace talks at Ghent – he referred to it at the time as "the most memorable period of my life." Regrettably, the settlement had not produced results that accomplished any of the goals defined by the administration. The delegates themselves anticipated that they were more likely to be pilloried than praised by a disappointed public and president. Instead, the Senate overwhelmingly ratified the agreement and the reputations of Adams and his compatriots remained intact. Naysayers might mutter about the terms of the treaty, but Adams lamented from afar the inability of his country to unite politically against a common foe, to properly fund the war, or to organize a capable fighting force. American hearts beat with pride over Andrew Jackson's dramatic victory at the Battle of New Orleans on January 8, 1815, an extraordinary triumph that, of course, did not affect the already concluded peace negotiations. They also could take satisfaction in the news from Ghent that while their delegates gained nothing, neither did they surrender anything to the mighty British Lion. As historian Bradford Perkins emphasized, the American delegates "made no major mistakes and held the fort until London made the key decisions which led to peace." In the flow of world events in the fall of 1814, that was sufficient (Nevins, 1928: 156, Jan. 26, 1815; Perkins, 1964: 128–131).

His primary mission accomplished, Adams headed to Paris in February where Louisa Catherine and Charles Francis, after a month-long, dangerous and arduous overland voyage from St Petersburg, joined him. On March 19, Napoleon returned to Paris, King Louis fled the country, and Europe went into an uproar. John Quincy distanced himself diplomatically and emotionally from these events. He saw the emperor at a distance, but had no official reason to meet with him. Adams restricted his political commentary to somewhat mocking remarks on the rather transitory loyalties of the French people. Instead, he relaxed, dining with old friends and attending the theater and opera. By this juncture, the weary John Quincy had notified both the Tsar and the president of his plans to come home. Clear evidence that Madison bore him no ill-will for the Ghent talks arrived on May 7 – the appointment as minister to Great Britain. The administration hoped to follow up on the peace with a new commercial treaty. Surprised, but flattered at the honor and responsibility, Adams could hardly refuse. In little more than two weeks the family was ensconced in a flat near Cavendish Square in London (Nevins, 1928: 160–161, 163, March 19–21, 25, 1815).

While Adams savored the distinction attached to his new post, meeting in June with Lord Castlereagh and the Prince Regent, he was once again placed in harness with his Ghent comrades, Henry Clay and Albert Gallatin. As they drafted their proposals to the Crown, old enmities rose to the surface and tempers flared once again. As troubling, the ministry selected Henry Goulburn and William Adams to the English delegation. Surely, John Quincy endured an annoying sense of *déjà vu*. International affairs ultimately overrode any personality issues. While the Americans were anxious to quickly resolve many of the residual commercial issues from Ghent (blockades, impressment, and trade with British colonies), the ministry was understandably distracted by Napoleon on the march with a massive and menacing new army. Extensive concessions were unlikely to be made in such an environment. The Anglo- American treaty of July 3 was, again, perhaps the best that could be achieved. The United States received "most favored nation" status, the right to trade with the British East Indies, and a prohibition against discriminatory duties. Adams remained in Britain until the spring of 1817, enjoying the social life, but his hopes for additional productive talks bore no fruit (Nevins, 1928: 164–168, June 1–July 1, 1815; Remini, 2002: 47–8).

In spite of the recent war, he soon realized that the United States and its representative did not command uniform respect. His evenings were filled with dinners and levees, including invitations from the highest levels of the English gentry, and he developed solid relationships with both prime minister Liverpool and foreign minister Castlereagh. Yet the furrow of respectability appeared shallowly plowed. To some degree, he blamed himself. Self-critically, he noted following one meal that he had said several silly things and been "altogether stiff and dull beyond my usual measure" (Nevins, 1928: 172, June 2, 1816). Following an embarrassing dinner introduction to the Duke of Wellington, a disappointed Adams declared, "This is one of the many incidents from which I can perceive how very small a space my person, or my station, occupies in the notice of these persons, and at these places" (Nevins, 1928: 174, Aug 8, 1816).

With the treaty negotiations concluded in the summer of 1815, the remainder of Adams's sojourn in Britain evolved into a genuinely joyful period in his life. He took pleasure in being reunited with his two older sons, George and John, whom he had not seen in six years and in guiding (in his often overbearing manner) all aspects of their education. Financial limitations and family concerns obliged the Adamses to move seven miles out of central London to Ealing, but the transition did not seem to hinder their night life. He and Louisa Catherine enjoyed a steady diet of dinners, theater, opera, and political conversation. He could claim social reformers Jeremy Bentham and William Wilberforce among his new acquaintances. Adams even took time to return to a first love – writing poetry. Ever the keen observer, he wandered London remarking on topics large and small; the gas street lights bothered him by their odor, but he accurately predicted they would soon replace similar oil lamps. (Nevins, 1928: 169, Dec. 18, 1816; Nagel, 1997: 223–232).

These near-idyllic days of family, friends, and fishing came to an end rather abruptly in the spring of 1817. James Monroe had soundly drubbed his Federalist opponent, Rufus King, in the presidential contest the previous November. For months rumors had circulated that Adams was to succeed Monroe in the State Department, and the letter of invitation to join the cabinet finally arrived on April 16. Abigail and John saw this post – the stepping stone to the White House – as a natural and rightful progression for their son. John Quincy knew he must accept the offer, but also recognized that his obsessive behaviors regarding public office would seriously compromise his flourishing relationship with his wife and sons. There was neither choice nor middle ground. On June 15, after eight years abroad and two months of packing and goodbyes, he bid Europe farewell for the last time. The *Washington* finally touched American shores on August 6, and Adams reveled for the next month in the celebratory receptions held in his honor. Proud parents and family matters in Boston had to be hastily dealt with – the nation's business awaited – as John Quincy and Louisa Catherine boarded a stagecoach for Washington, DC, on September 11, 1817 (Nagel, 1997: 233–241).

John Quincy Adams was about to embark on the most critical role and period of his life – for himself and the country. He clearly deserved the appointment as secretary of state. Who could rival his intellect or experience – not Speaker of the House Henry Clay who believed *he* should have been selected. On the surface, Adams's diplomatic record was impressive – fifteen years in four different countries. He had been involved in the negotiation of key treaties and helped cement ties with several nations. Most of his efforts had focused on building trade or mediating commercial problems, not advocating territorial expansion. However, the results were mixed at best, though the astute, but sometimes volatile Adams bears little blame for this. In spite of his dedicated efforts, trade with Prussia and Russia failed to materialize at a significant level. He played a part in the two treaties with Great Britain in 1814–1815, but, while honor was preserved and modest progress made, major issues remained unresolved. In addition, his earlier term in the Senate witnessed a controversial shift in loyalty that earned him the enmity of Bay State Federalists and virtually compelled a temporary exile from political service. Had John Quincy Adams retired from public life in 1817, both historians and his contemporaries may have judged his career as successful, but hardly brilliant.

James Monroe recognized Adams's talents, plus he needed a capable New Englander in his cabinet. The Virginian, who served as secretary of state during the War of 1812, certainly planned to play a major role in diplomatic policy during his own presidency. Monroe intended a "top down" leadership style in which he would manage the agenda and make the important decisions. Historian William Weeks argues that "the three guiding principles of the Monroe administration's foreign policy – reciprocity treaties and commercial retaliation, reconciliation with Great Britain, and a strengthened military – constituted a blueprint for global expansion" (Weeks, 1992: 47).

John Quincy, given to controlling events and individuals himself, faced an ongoing contest to advance his policies in cooperation with the White House. Concurrently, Adams battled other members of the cabinet, particularly secretary of the treasury William H. Crawford, and Speaker of the House Henry Clay, both of whom hoped to use foreign affairs to advance their own presidential ambitions. Try as he might, Adams could not avoid hearing the rumors of his name bandied about as Monroe's heir. Adams believed, however, that seeking public office was unseemly, and while he maintained a quiet interest in the nation's highest honor, the people would be obliged to come to him. He would stand, but never run, for office.

During the first Monroe administration, Adams energetically built his resumé. Two treaties with Great Britain helped to round off problems nagging Anglo-American relations since the Revolution. Soon after John Quincy's departure from London, his successor, Richard Rush, joined the British minister Charles Bagot in signing an agreement in April 1817 that demilitarized the Great Lakes. The following year, Adams facilitated the talks for the Convention of 1818, a treaty that continued the boundary line between Canada and the United States from the Lake of the Woods in northern Minnesota to the Rocky Mountains at 49°N. Possession of the vast Oregon territory that extended from northern California to Alaska, however, remained unclear and open for settlement and commercial development by both nations. Much to Adams' s delight, the nettlesome issue of the opportunity for New Englanders to fish off the Canadian maritime provinces was also confirmed. In sum, with the exception of the seemingly insoluble questions of neutral rights and impressments, a number of matters that had divided the two countries were resolved and tensions lessened.

Adams's greatest triumph was yet to come in 1819 – the Transcontinental Treaty with Spain. Florida and a new western boundary constituted the prizes. Spain had lost "the Floridas" and then reclaimed them from Great Britain in 1783. Concerned about matters of national security, expanding the plantation economy, and controlling the Southern Indians and runaway slaves, the United States had expressed a sharp interest in obtaining Florida during Jefferson's presidency. The Virginian's efforts proved unsuccessful, and since that time, the region had increasingly become a middle ground for pirates, filibusters, traders, and rogue operators. Madrid remained preoccupied with the Napoleonic Wars and rebellion in its Latin American colonies, thus making law and order on the Florida frontier a low priority. US settlers in Baton Rouge took advantage of the chaos in 1813 and separated "West Florida," – Pensacola and the Perdido River into Louisiana – from "East Florida." Madison recognized this illegal action, but was unable to secure the valuable peninsula from Spain. Acquiring East Florida became a major priority of the Monroe administration and talks began to that end in 1817 between Spanish Minister Don Luis de Onis and John Quincy Adams. The Americans had little to offer and negotiations moved at a snail's pace until the fateful and controversial invasion of General Andrew Jackson in the spring of 1818. Jackson was instructed by the White House to deal with meddlesome Seminoles and their runaway-slave allies who raided plantations and farms in Georgia and Alabama. His incursion, while rather successful in dealing with the problem, also sparked an international brouhaha when "Old Hickory" boldly occupied Spanish outposts at St Marks and Pensacola and executed two British subjects who he viewed as collaborators with the Indians.

Predictably, ministries in London and Madrid – and not a few congressmen in Washington – called for an apology and Jackson's head. They would get neither. As tensions rose, Adams brilliantly considered the options of the major players and concluded that Britain would not risk a war with the United States over two dead subjects. Without support from the mighty British navy, Spain would not challenge the Americans. Adams converted international outrage into opportunity, and emerged as a lone voice in the cabinet and in the press defending "Old Hickory" against cries of courts-martial. In late November 1818, Adams drafted a letter to US minister to Spain George W. Erving. The missive somehow leaked to the press. Adams persuasively argued that Jackson's invasion mirrored self-defense and demonstrated clearly that Spain could no longer control the Florida frontier, an embarrassed Madrid was brought to the bargaining table. Biographer Samuel F. Bemis deems the Erving letter "the greatest state paper of John Quincy Adams's diplomatic career" (Bemis, 1949: 326; Weeks, 1992: 105–126).

Despite their wounded pride, and resentment of provocative American actions, the Spanish felt obliged to cut their losses. This meant a surrender of the Floridas in exchange for a definitive boundary separating the Louisiana territory from Spanish-held lands in the West and Southwest. The Americans agreed to a line at the Sabine River, conceding that Texas was *not* part of the Louisiana Purchase, and at 42°N, dividing the American claim of Oregon from Spanish-held California. Washington also agreed to assume up to $5 million in claims of American citizens against the Spanish government. On February 22, 1819, the Adams–Onis or Transcontinental

Treaty was signed and two years later ratification finally took place in Madrid and Washington. The acquisition of the Floridas, a goal of Thomas Jefferson, was a signal accomplishment of the Monroe administration and the capstone to a successful first term in foreign affairs. The president deserves credit for his leadership, Jackson for providing the kindling needed to fire the talks, and Adams for his steady and determined negotiations with the Spanish minister. Attaining Florida not only meant securing the coast of the Gulf of Mexico against foreign invaders, but also allowed for the legal pursuit of the Seminoles and ultimately for their removal and exploitation of their lands by white planters (Weeks, 1992: 147–175).

As implications of the treaty were debated in 1820, several key events occurred concurrently. Americans re-elected James Monroe to a second term with no opposition and only one dissenting electoral vote. The so-called "Era of Good Feeling" came to a crashing end as the nation suffered an agriculture depression, the "Panic of 1819," and a mighty quarrel in Congress over the issue of slavery in the territories that resulted in the Missouri Compromise (1819–1821). While domestic tranquility had seemingly given way to sectional rancor, the administration could take credit for the two treaties with Great Britain (Rush–Bagot and the Convention of 1818) as well as the recent Florida agreement.

A problem did emerge, however, in the form of revolutions in the Spanish Latin American colonies. Taking advantage of the chaos in Europe, these colonies – from Mexico to Chile – had launched rebellions against Madrid that proved ultimately successful. Monroe and Adams found themselves in a very awkward situation. Should the United States, as the world's leading republic, take a leadership role in encouraging and perhaps even aiding these aspiring nations south of the border in their crusade? Adams felt his republicanism deeply, but was reluctant to disrupt the talks with de Onis over Florida or the later ratification process. Timing was critical, since recognition of the colonies as independent countries, which may well have contributed to United States' political and commercial influence in the region, could be a dangerous course. The final signing of the Florida treaty in February 1821 gave Washington greater flexibility in dealing with Latin America.

For a time, the administration remained cautious and hesitant. Skeptical about the ability of the Latin Americans to create functioning democratic republics, Adams did not want the United States either to recognize their independence or to intervene in their affairs. In his mind, the United States could function as a lighthouse of republican principles, a beacon to inspire and educate, but "should not go abroad in search of monsters to destroy" (Lewis, 2001: 86). Henry Clay disagreed. He pressed for a more aggressive policy of recognition. Ultimately, the president aligned with Adams and the United States watched events from the sidelines until 1822. By then, independence was a *fait d'accompli* and Adams and Monroe rushed to recognize Mexico, Colombia, Peru, Chile, and Buenos Aires (Argentina). The United States, they believed, must establish itself in the southern hemisphere or face the feared alternative: the real presence of continental powers (France, Russia, and Great Britain) and the emergence of European-style monarchies rather than republics in the region. Neither was acceptable. As historian James Lewis emphasizes, "Republican government, diplomatic isolation from Europe, and liberal commerce would be pressed upon Spanish America in order to secure independence, republicanism, and prosperity in the United States" (Lewis, 2001: 89).

The Adams–Monroe strategy received an added jolt in October 1823 when US minister in London Richard Rush informed the administration that the Holy Alliance – Austria, France, and Russia – planned on cooperating with Spain to regain her lost colonies in Latin America. The rumor had credibility, since the Holy Alliance had invaded Spain in the spring and established Ferdinand VII as an absolute monarch. In a fascinating turn of events, the English, who had developed strong commercial bonds with the newly independent colonies, shared a common concern with the Americans over an invasion promulgated by the Holy Alliance. Foreign Secretary George Canning suggested an Anglo-American declaration that clearly stated the opposition of both nations to the recolonization of Latin America.

The proposition put the Americans in a quandary. Monroe sought the sage counsel of his Virginia predecessors, Jefferson and Madison. They reinforced his own predilection to accept Canning's offer of a joint statement. The Americans had their eyes on Cuba, and particularly feared its loss, possibly even to Great Britain. When the cabinet met to discuss the alternatives, in November 1823, Adams emerged as the leading voice of opposition to an Anglo-American declaration. He doubted the reality of a European invasion, but agreed that a statement needed to be made. However, that statement must be made as a proud, independent power, and not have the US appear "as the cock-boat in the wake of the British man-of-war" (Sexton, 2011: 47–62).

The President read the resulting document, commonly referred to as the Monroe Doctrine, as part of his annual address to the Congress on December 2, 1823. Its well-known principles declared US opposition to new colonization in the western hemisphere, rejection of European systems of government in the New World, and a "hands off" policy regarding American involvement in European affairs. The authorship has been widely debated, but Adams must be given extensive credit, as well as Monroe. Historian Jay Sexton sums the issue up nicely (2011: 53): "The secretary of state did not dictate policy to the President, but he nonetheless played a central role in the creation of what later become the 'Monroe Doctrine'. Of the three paragraphs of the Doctrine, Adams solely authored one (the non-colonization paragraph) and deeply influenced the other two (the nonintervention paragraphs)." (Ammon, 1971: 476–492; Cunningham, 1996: 152–163).

The administration's rather bold, "go it alone" strategy was declared without the knowledge that the crisis had already eased in Europe – as Adams had predicted. In October, the French minister in London, Prince de Polignac, assured Canning that France would not support a reconquest. The information was not relayed to minister Rush until December – days after Monroe had already made his position clear to the Congress. That statement did not close the door to a later joint policy with Britain, and the leadership in Washington hoped and expected that a mutual resolution would be forthcoming at some point. It never happened. Widely hailed in the United States in 1823 and lauded by Latin revolutionaries and European liberals, the "doctrine" was quite unenforceable in the event of a genuine invasion. Even so, it evolved, as did US military strength through the nineteenth century, to form the bedrock of Washington's policy towards Latin America (Lewis, 2001: 92–95).

Somewhat ironically, the Monroe Doctrine, while not immediately utilized in South America, found application in the Northwest. Adams had successfully resolved claims in the disputed region between latitude 42°N (California) and 55°N (Alaska) with Britain through a temporary settlement in 1818 and with Spain through a permanent one in 1819. Russian claims, however, extended south from Alaska to the northern border of California, and the Tsar appeared eager to advance his influence in the region. Alexander I issued an executive degree (*ukase*) in 1821, which closed the coastline and fishing waters north of 51° to foreigners. As Adams objected, claims and settlement in the area were muddled and the Americans had little leverage to effectively challenge the Russian position. Adams futilely attempted to orchestrate a three-nation arrangement that would more clearly define territorial hegemony: the Russians would control land north of 55°, the British between 55 and 51°, and the Americans everything between 51 and 42°. Such a resolution would have given the United States the area of Puget Sound, the Juan de Fuca Strait, and Vancouver Island. Already, Yankee merchants and traders were eyeing the potentially lucrative Pacific trade, and control of the rivers and deep-water harbors along the west coast would facilitate that commerce. Not surprisingly, neither London nor St Petersburg had any interest in furthering Washington's economic agenda in the Orient and nothing came of the proposal.

Adams was obliged to wait until 1824. With his commercial agent, the Russian-American Company, struggling, the Tsar became more amenable to negotiations. In April 1824, both nations signed a convention giving the Americans their desired rights: freedom of the seas and the right to trade along the unsettled parts of the coastline. The treaty adjusted the boundary slightly southward from 55°N to 54°40′N. Some months earlier, in July 1823, Adams had warned the Russians that the United States would strongly object to any new colonization in the Oregon country. The Russians did not formally reject that principle in the pact. As historian William Weeks conjectured (1992: 177): "The agreement of April 1824 represented a Russian capitulation to American demands. Seen from this perspective, the Monroe Doctrine was less a hollow threat to the European powers, than a formal announcement to Congress of a policy already in place" (Lewis, 2001: 93–94, Bemis, 1949: 523–527; Saul, 1991: 96–105).

John Quincy Adams secured his final diplomatic victory with the conclusion of the Russian– American Treaty. While others may argue that his presidential administration pressed on with foreign policy offensives in the Panama congress (a failed endeavor to engage the United States in a cooperative relationship with Latin America) and attempts to treat with Great Britain, we remember Adams most profoundly for his successes prior to the White House. Perhaps no other American has held positions of diplomatic responsibility as prestigious and timely as Adams before 1817. He made the most of those opportunities, negotiating treaties and developing ties when possible to the betterment of his nation while realistically keeping an eye on his own career. Arguably, his successes were mixed, highlighted by the Ghent talks where Adams battled his colleagues, the English delegation, and a marginal American war effort. As in most of his diplomatic situations, on that occasion he achieved the possible.

As secretary of state, however, he reached a zenith. While obstacles, both foreign and domestic, often appeared in his line of vision, he rarely lost focus on his goals of extending republican principles, and advancing American territorial and economic boundaries. Adams was indeed fortunate to serve with James Monroe, a president who largely shared and respected his views, and gave him maximum latitude to advance their dream of a burgeoning America. Both men were realists more than idealists. They recognized the limits of American power, as well as the internal threat to the Union posed by slavery and sectionalism.

Adams's historical legacy has been secured in part by his own hand. His multi-volume, decade-spanning diary looms as a compelling source for historians to dissect the personalities and events that affected the lives of John Quincy and his compatriots. While unquestionably at times self-critical, Adams ultimately offers a narrow lens. While letters exist, we have no rival diary from Clay, Calhoun, Monroe, or other contemporaries to provide balance. Samuel F. Bemis established the benchmark more than half a century ago with his pioneering work on Adams as the "father of American foreign policy" and the man who first attempted to establish many of its principles. Most historians have followed suit in their praise of Adams's intellect, talents, and successes – if not revealing a resounding affection for the man himself. While a general consensus lauds Adams for his accomplishments, some have pointed to inconsistencies in his thinking, noting, for example, that the anti-imperialism which formed a hallmark of Adams's thought did not stop him from becoming an advocate of global empire (Murphy, 2005: 32–34). The revisionist criticism, however, has thus far barely left a mark on Adams's reputation.

In recent years, the reputation of John Quincy Adams, the eldest son and scion of the eminent Adams family of Quincy, Massachusetts, has been reinvigorated. Historian Bemis brought John Quincy to life after World War II in a lengthy and sympathetic two-volume biography (1949, 1956). While not forgotten, Adams was soon marginalized as scholars engaged in heated debate over the merits of rival Andrew Jackson. The Adams presidency (1825–1829) and his controversial congressional career (1831–1848) have drawn considerable positive attention in recent decades; an admiring Daniel Walker Howe dedicated his Pulitzer Prize-winning volume, *What Hath God Wrought* (2007), to "Old Man Eloquent." Even as we are drawn to reconsidering Adams as a visionary chief executive and champion of free speech and antislavery in the House of Representatives, his service as a distinguished diplomat and advocate of American expansion continues to be the high-water mark of a long and notable public life.

Guide to Further Reading

John Quincy Adams has made it impossible to ignore his voluminous and thoughtful diary (Nevins, 1928). It remains a starting point for his thought and observations on a host of topics and individuals. Exploration of his early diplomatic career in Holland and Prussia are best found in biographical works, especially good are S.F. Bemis, *John Quincy Adams and the Foundations of American Foreign* (1949) and the more recent Paul Nagel, *John Quincy Adams: A Public Life, a Private Life* (1997). The lengthy Russian sojourn and Russian involvement in the Northwest have been extensively analyzed by both Russian and American historians including N. Bolkhovitinov, *The Beginnings of Russian-American Relations, 1775–1815* (1975), Alfred Crosby, *America, Russia, Hemp, and Napoleon: American Trade with Russia and the Baltic, 1783–1812* (1965), and Norman Saul, *Distant Friends: The United States and Russia, 1763–1867* (1991). The best volume on his ongoing relations with the English remains Bradford Perkins, *Castlereagh and Adams: England and the United States, 1812–1823* (1964). An important and interesting aspect of his life is his courtship and marriage to Louisa Catherine. The standard volume, J. Shepherd, *Cannibals of the Heart: A Personal Biography of Louisa Catherine and John Quincy Adams* (1980) has been recently supplemented by Michael O'Brien's fascinating *Mrs Adams in Winter: A Journey in the Last Days of Napoleon* (2010) which details her perilous travels from St Petersburg to Paris. Adams's tenure as Secretary of State has been extensively examined. William Weeks offers the best study of the acquisition of Florida in *John Quincy Adams and American Global Empire* (1992). More than a hundred years ago, Worthington C. Ford persuasively argued for Adams's influence on the Monroe Doctrine in his article "John Quincy Adams and the Monroe Doctrine," *American Historical Review* (1902). The Doctrine and its impact have been repeatedly analyzed with most scholars, led by Dexter Perkins' pioneering monograph, *The Monroe Doctrine, 1823–1826* (1964), heavily crediting Adams. Monroe has his champions as well, particularly Noble Cunningham in *The Presidency of James Monroe* (1996). Jay Sexton offers a very readable recent synthesis in *The Monroe Doctrine: Empire and*

Nation in Nineteenth-Century America (2011). The approaches to the Doctrine have also expanded: from the political (Ernest May, *The Making of the Monroe Doctrine*, 1975), to the philosophical (Greg Russell, *John Quincy Adams and the Public Virtues of Diplomacy*, 1995) and the cultural (Gretchen Murphy, *Hemispheric Imaginings: The Monroe Doctrine and Narratives of US Empire*, 2005). Those readers who desire a brief, but enlightened look at Adams would be well served by reading James E. Lewis, *John Quincy Adams: Policymaker for the Union* (2001) or Robert E. Remini, *John Quincy Adams* (2002).

Chapter Fifteen

John Quincy Adams and the Elections of 1824 and 1828

David P. Callahan

John Quincy Adams "was a political person," Daniel Walker Howe observed, and "his actions had political objectives" (1979: 46). Few historians have shared Howe's cogent assessment. Adams, Mary W. M. Hargreaves maintained, lacked "the will or the skills" to play the game of politics and always resisted political compromise (1985: 252, 321). No president ever had "less aptitude or inclination" for the political side of the job, Samuel Flagg Bemis insisted (1956: 11). Donald B. Cole opined that the puritanical New Englander "could not bring himself to put politics ahead of morality and duty" (2009: 24). "Avoiding the black arts of political maneuver became for him almost a kind of puritan trial of virtue," Richard Hofstadter colorfully suggested, "a political hair shirt of his own devising" (1969: 231). In short, Adams was an "inept politician" with demonstrated "inadequacies as a leader," Robert V. Remini asserted (2002: 76, 102). An analysis of John Quincy Adams's performance in the elections of 1824 and 1828 fails to sustain these negative appraisals. In those contests, Adams showcased a considerable amount of political acumen as a "politician who wanted very much to win" (Howe, 1979: 46).

15.1 The Election of 1824

Historians have situated the election of 1824 in a transitional period in American political culture. With one of the nation's first two political parties, the Federalists, in the midst of a long decline, the remaining party,

A Companion to John Adams and John Quincy Adams, First Edition.
Edited by David Waldstreicher.

the reigning Republicans, faced factional fissures and struggles for power between its leaders (Hargreaves, 1985: 39). Indeed every candidate in the 1824 election, despite their ideological differences, claimed to represent Republican orthodoxy. As the Republicans slowly fractured, the new political ideologies that would later preoccupy the Whig and Democratic parties began to tentatively emerge. Some Republicans advocated a more powerful central government to effectively address national problems on a national scale, while others wished to limit consolidated federal planning in favor of state rights (Dangerfield, 1965: 222; Hargreaves, 1985: 25). Though national ideologies may have been coalescing, equally powerful sectional tendencies still dominated the electorate. Candidates both represented and reflected regional or geographic voting patterns and attitudes (McCormick, 1982: 123, 128; Hargreaves, 1985: 33). Simultaneously, politicians faced an increasingly democratic political culture. As property qualifications for voting and office-holding declined and public participation in national elections escalated, successful candidacies required ears better attuned to the public voice (Dangerfield, 1965: 218; Parsons, 2009: 41). As democracy blossomed, public offices, and in particular the presidency, were to be bestowed by the people as a reward for superior public service, not crudely sought after by campaigning candidates. Though overt electioneering, factional intrigue, and political deal-making remained taboo, ironically the partisan, ideological, sectional, and democratic pressures of the period actually *encouraged* electioneering, intrigue, and deal-making (McCormick, 1982: 124, 142; Heale, 1982: 4, 42–43). Successfully navigating through these swirling political cross-currents would prove enormously challenging for the presidential candidates in 1824.

In this complex political environment success appeared unlikely for John Quincy Adams. As a former Federalist with a reputation for nonpartisanship, he was not a lifelong Republican like his fellow nominees. Adams's unabashed nationalism and New England regional roots might not appeal to Southern or Western voters. An egalitarian electorate, sometimes subject to bouts of anti-intellectualism, might reject a candidate known for his patrician bearing and scholarly interests. Still, Adams chose to enter the fray. Historians have argued that several factors motivated this decision. Personally ambitious, Adams also strove to burnish the family name since his father had served as the nation's second president (Bemis, 1956: 18; Nagel, 1997: 285). With his long record of superlative diplomatic service, Adams believed he possessed the exact type of "virtues and talents" that the public should reward with the presidency (Hecht, 1972: 375; Heale, 1982: 42; Parsons, 2009: 76). Since the last three presidents had also previously served as secretary of state, Adams's current job seemingly branded him the heir apparent to President James Monroe; the nation's highest office represented an appropriate culmination to his lengthy career in public service. Committed to nonpartisanship, Adams watched the factional strife that beleaguered the Monroe years with disdain. Ironically, he engaged in partisanship to win the presidency and prevent the office from falling into partisan hands (D.W. Howe, 1979: 48; Ketcham, 1984: 133–137). Finally, the secretary of state believed that his presidency, sustained by a record of family service, led by a meritorious man, and erected on a foundation of nonpartisanship, would best serve the general good and provide historic benefits for the Republic (D.W. Howe, 1979: 48; Hargreaves, 1985: 322; Nagel, 1997: 285).

Though Adams desired and felt he deserved the presidency, several other ambitious men also coveted the job. Speaker of the House Henry Clay, secretary of war John C. Calhoun, treasury secretary William H. Crawford, and war hero-turned-senator Andrew Jackson each sought to succeed Monroe. To defeat this array of formidable contenders, Adams exploited his considerable political gifts. He assembled an organization and newspaper network to promote his candidacy, exploited the patronage available to a secretary of state, and developed a few innovative electioneering techniques. When the 1824 campaign commenced almost immediately after Monroe's second inauguration, Adams proved eager and ready to capture the presidency.

Although often dismissed as "a few gratuitous workers feebly organized" (Bemis, 1956: 21) and admittedly less coherent than the future Whig or Democratic parties, Adams assembled a fairly powerful group to support his candidacy. The loosely-affiliated organization of thirty-two Adams partisans, concentrated in the crucial states of New York, Massachusetts, Pennsylvania, and Virginia but with representatives scattered throughout the Union, included port collectors, postmasters, state legislators, jurists, former cabinet secretaries, and, most importantly, editors. They established a Committee of Correspondence to promote Adams's campaign, while preparing and publishing complimentary newspaper articles about his tenure at the State Department. A core group of four men in Washington, all government employees appointed by Adams, supplemented the larger organization. These supporters kept him informed about political developments and spread his opinions about the capital, but allowed Adams to maintain a discreet distance from open electioneering. His organization also disseminated the first-ever campaign biography for a presidential candidate; only the Jackson and Calhoun camps produced similar documents in this election (Heale, 1982: 50). Ultimately, the Adams machine secured four presidential nominations for the secretary of state, from the legislatures of Massachusetts, Maine, and Rhode Island, as well as a Republican mass meeting in Boston. Adams's organization rivaled Crawford's, eclipsed Jackson's, and dwarfed the tiny Clay and Calhoun groups.

While some historians insist that Adams only haltingly exploited patronage to advance his electoral bid (Hecht, 1972: 337; Remini, 2002: 65), the secretary proved adroit at capitalizing on the advantages of office by routinely assigning State Department clerks to campaign-related duties. He also tried to use patronage in reverse by suggesting that Monroe appoint his rivals to diplomatic missions abroad. Adams floated Calhoun's name as minister to France, while touting Clay for three separate South American assignments in Columbia, Chile, and Argentina. Almost comically Adams recommended Jackson – the notoriously hot-headed general as an ambassador! – for posting to Mexico. Each man refused the proffered position, effectively foiling Adams's transparent scheme to remove three competitors from the presidential contest. Late in the race Adams insisted that Monroe appoint Martin Van Buren, Crawford's highly skilled campaign manager, to a Supreme Court vacancy. The wily Van Buren rejected this honor, correctly surmising that Adams hoped to eliminate his influence over the critical New York legislature's presidential vote.

Newspaper networks assumed increasing importance in 1824 once the race proved far more competitive than the previous two presidential elections. Each of Adams's cabinet colleagues could claim the loyalty of a central newspaper in Washington that generated stories for dispatch and reprinting in strings of local papers, with a special focus on the press in the battleground Middle Atlantic states. Without requesting a subscription, influential politicians often received free copies of these highly partisan newspapers. Adams established his own press network that easily matched his rival's efforts. His friends purchased the Washington *National Journal* which passed on favorable coverage of the secretary of state's activities, most prominently to the New York *American*, the Philadelphia *National Gazette and Literary Register*, and the Baltimore *American*. Adams anonymously penned highly favorable editorials about himself for diffusion throughout the network. Though an especially nasty press battle erupted early in the race between Crawford and Calhoun, Adams tried to remain serenely above the fray. His early stories mainly trumpeted his long record of public service and numerous diplomatic achievements. With so many candidates in the race none seemed likely to capture an electoral vote majority. Since that destined the 1824 contest for resolution in a House of Representatives vote, where today's enemy might be tomorrow's ally, personal attacks against rivals never reached the truly scurrilous levels achieved in 1828. Still, as the election neared, Adams participated in an increasingly vitriolic press war with the other contenders. Opposition pieces disparaged Adams's diplomatic achievements, blasted his aristocratic pretensions, and criticized his slovenly appearance. The prudish secretary of state was even accused of attending church in bare feet. Highlighting his notoriety as a party-switcher, partisan editorials denounced Adams both as a closet Federalist and as an apostate Federalist. Adams's organization responded with equal ferocity. His papers pilloried Crawford as an unscrupulous king of patronage unfit for public service, condemned Jackson as a military chieftain temperamentally unsuited for high office, and airily dismissed Clay and Calhoun as junior candidates too inexperienced to be president. The level of Adams's direct involvement in these attacks remains uncertain. However, Paul C. Nagel observed that "as an avid reader of the national press, he [Adams] had to know about the tactics of his supporters" (1997: 289).

In conjunction with an effective organization, a newspaper network churning out positive propaganda, and the utilization of the patronage at his command, Adams also actively campaigned to succeed Monroe. Certainly, from the start of the race he had publicly and privately renounced open or covert electioneering for the office he so desperately desired. "I will take not one step to advance or promote pretensions to the Presidency," Adams dutifully wrote to a supporter, while virtuously recording in his Diary that, "If that office is to be the prize of cabal and intrigue ... I have no ticket in that lottery" (J.Q. Adams, *Memoirs* 4.193, 5.298–289, quoted in Bemis, 1956: 19). Many historians have similarly concluded that at most Adams only "reluctantly" engaged in electioneering (Quincy, 1859: 69; Hecht, 1972: 372; Heale, 1982: 68; Remini, 2002: 63; Parsons, 2009: 76). As Adams's pre-election activities demonstrate however, the secretary of state discovered several novel and politically-astute ways to promote his candidacy within a political culture that discouraged overt electioneering.

On the fourth of July 1821 Adams fired what most contemporary politicos and the British diplomatic corps regarded as the opening shot of the 1824 presidential election. Invited to deliver a routine Independence Day address in the capital, Adams chose "What has America done for Mankind?" as his theme. After extolling his country's accomplishments and including a ceremonial reading of the Declaration of Independence, the sitting secretary of state turned to flaying Great Britain. He sarcastically excoriated America's former colonial rulers as "Ye chivalrous knights of chartered liberties and the rotten boroughs! Ye improvers upon the sculpture of the Elgin marbles! Ye spawners of fustian romance and lascivious lyrics!" (J.Q. Adams, July 4, 1821 address: APM #452, quoted in Hecht, 1972: 331). While many of his fellow Americans applauded Adams's widely published remarks, the secretary probably harbored ulterior motives beyond proving his patriotism to prospective voters. As a former Federalist, subject to charges that he still entertained pro-British proclivities, Adams used this address to distance himself from his Federalist past and burnish his Republican bona fides.

Employing another electoral tactic, Adams spiritedly defended himself against slanders. As Paul C. Nagel argued, "Defending the Adams reputation became his surrogate for overt campaigning" (1997: 283). Adams energetically displayed this strategy during an imbroglio surrounding the Ghent correspondence. In 1822, possibly inspired by a tip from Henry Clay as a means to discredit Adams, Congress began scrutinizing documents associated with the Treaty of Ghent that ended the War of 1812. The House of Representatives investigation turned up an 1815 letter from American commissioner Jonathan Russell to then secretary of state Monroe. The letter, marked "duplicate," charged that Russell's fellow commissioner Adams had been willing to grant Great Britain Indian trade rights south of the Canadian border, as well as offering the British navigation rights on the Mississippi, in exchange for New England's fishing privileges. If true, these charges seriously threatened Adams's presidential campaign in the West. Unfortunately for Russell, now a congressman and Crawford supporter, Monroe had retained Russell's original letter, which conclusively demonstrated that Russell had doctored the duplicate letter by embellishing the charges against Adams. Though the president resisted sending his personal copy to Congress, Adams secretly arranged for one of his congressional allies to call for Monroe's letter. Once the letters entered the public domain, including a *third* version that Russell had imprudently printed in the press – a "triplicate," Adams sneered – the furious secretary of state went to work (Hecht, 1972: 340). He issued a pamphlet with the letters printed side by side, effectively revealing Russell's deception and defending his own actions during the peace negotiations. While the spirit of Russell's accusations *were* correct, Adams had successfully redirected the controversy from an analysis of the original charges into an investigation into the forged document – and he handily won that contest. In the six months following the exposed fraud, though he continually carped that it interfered with official business and Russell had already been utterly disgraced, Adams published a series of newspaper articles justifying his Ghent activities and disparaging Russell. His defense culminated in a book-length account entitled *The Duplicate Letters, the Fisheries and the Mississippi, Documents Relating to Transactions at the Negotiations of Ghent.* Clay, also a commissioner at Ghent, hoped to salvage the original charges against Adams without seeming a participant in a malicious smear campaign against the secretary of state. He opined in the press that Adams's account contained "no doubt unintentional" errors and promised publication of his own version of the Ghent negotiations in the future. Adams quickly responded with a sarcastic letter promising to "vindicate contested truth" should Clay's account ever materialize and the Speaker wisely dropped the matter (Henry Clay to Joseph Gales, Jr., and William W. Seaton, Nov. 15, 1822, in Hopkins and Hargreaves, 1963: 323). Most observers agreed that Adams's popularity and presidential prospects had been enhanced by the affair. Adams had kept his name before the public and polished his reputation for probity without ever overtly electioneering.

Adams exploited social occasions to increase his chances for victory. Early in the race, despite grousing in his diary about the "perpetual" public events he was "obliged" to attend, the secretary of state dined at a series of banquets in Boston and Quincy designed to solidify his New England base (Nagel, 1997: 258). While in Washington he attended three church services every Sunday, diplomatically splitting his time between different denominations and conversing avidly with the congregants after worship had ended. As the election approached, Adams attended more dinners in New England, reminding supporters that only he represented their interests and promising administration appointments should he become president. The secretary's canniest use of a social occasion however originated with the candidate himself. To commemorate the ninth anniversary of Jackson's victory over the British at New Orleans, Adams hosted a ball for the general at his Washington residence in January 1824. Over one thousand guests attended this glittering soiree, watching Adams's wife Louisa escort her husband's gracious presidential rival through the festivities. Adams himself had planned the event. He had supervised the occasion down to the smallest detail, even closely monitoring the placement of party decorations. To his surprised spouse, Adams admitted that he had watched Jackson's increasing popularity – even in New England – with growing alarm. He intended the ball as an opening gambit in a campaign to harness the general's electoral power for his own purposes. Adams planned to open negotiations with Jackson's forces aimed at securing the general as his vice-presidential running mate. Jackson, Adams claimed, would make a worthy Vice President and he might increase Adams's own popularity with Western voters (Nagel, 1997: 287). Despite the secretary's shrewd ploy, the general recognized that he stood a legitimate chance of winning the race outright and rejected Adams's overtures to accept the lesser spot on the New Englander's ticket.

The secretary of state skillfully deployed departmental policy to further his electoral ambitions. When the Holy Alliance, formed by Prussia, Austria, and Russia to defend monarchism, authorized military action to restore Bourbon rule over Spain and ultimately its American colonies, the Monroe administration felt compelled to react. Adams's original draft response included direct criticism of the Holy Alliance, which he deemed "the cream of the paper," but the other Secretaries labeled it a "hornet of a paragraph" for its offensive potential (Hecht, 1972: 331). At Monroe's behest Adams eliminated the objectionable section. The secretary of state claimed that his gracious concession simply recognized Monroe's authority over his own government's foreign policy, while his fellow cabinet candidates fumed that his surprisingly reasonable compromise represented a crude attempt to win Monroe's endorsement in the 1824 election. Adams's draft paper undergirded Monroe's seventh Annual Message to Congress in 1823. Known popularly as the Monroe Doctrine, the president's message rejected further European colonization in the Americas and declared that any interference with Latin American independence represented aggression towards the United States. Ernest R. May (1975) dissected the role that Adams's presidential candidacy played in cabinet debates over formulating the Monroe Doctrine. More strongly than any of his cabinet colleagues, Adams resolutely rebuffed a British offer to jointly protect the Latin American republics. May argued that Adams's Federalist past and therefore potentially pro-British views necessitated that a unilateral declaration be placed before the voting public (E.R. May, 1975: 181). Since the United States lacked the military power to enforce the policy, most European diplomats believed that the cabinet candidates produced the Monroe Doctrine as a political ploy, hoping to generate electoral popularity by courageously challenging European monarchs.

As Adams's actions during the Independence Day speech and the Monroe Doctrine debates had demonstrated, the New Englander's Federalist past shadowed his presidential bid. While the other candidates, all true-blue Republicans, could openly pursue Federalist voters while simultaneously tarring Adams with the Federalist label, the secretary shrewdly realized that any association with Federalists might seriously weaken his support among Republicans. Shaw Livermore maintained that Adams, while accepting the support of individual Federalists, wisely distanced himself from the Federalists as a group before voters cast their ballots (1962: 139–142). Adams demanded the exclusion of all Federalists from the Massachusetts legislative caucus that nominated him for president in 1823. He discouraged prominent Federalists Joseph Hopkinson and Robert Walsh from openly working for his election, while declining the endorsement of a Federalist newspaper in Baltimore. He even challenged Federalist icon Timothy Pickering during the Cunningham correspondence affair. In a scheme to dampen any Federalist electoral enthusiasm for John Quincy Adams, twenty-year-old letters from John Adams to William Cunningham, in which the candidate's father had excoriated the Federalists, mysteriously surfaced. When Pickering composed a pamphlet about the letters that vilified both father and son, the secretary of state defied his advisors and publicly lambasted the old Federalist lion. Adams's perspicacious analysis proved prescient. Crawford's blatant courting of Federalists seriously depressed his Republican support in New England (Livermore, 1962: 150).

While Adams maintained his distance from the Federalists to retain his Republican appeal, some of his fellow partisans labored to deliver the presidency to Crawford via the time-honored party caucus. The last three Republican presidents had each been nominated for the office by a caucus of congressional representatives, but the method had been increasingly criticized since 1816. With the decline of the Federalist party, the Republican caucus nomination now appeared tantamount to a undemocratic coronation. Lacking any popular participation, such nominations seemed highly susceptible to manipulation by the scheming politicos in Washington. Since Crawfordites dominated Congress, however, the treasury secretary pushed forward with his intention to secure this orthodox *imprimatur* of party favor. Initially, Adams had supported the caucus. He deemed the device constitutionally acceptable, less subject to intrigue than other forms of electioneering, and probably believed he might capture the traditional nomination (Hecht, 1972: 379). However, once Adams discovered that caucus-goers planned to shunt him into the vice president slot on a Crawford ticket, he switched sides. The other contenders had also realized that Crawford would snare the nomination, so their newspaper networks predictably began railing against the undemocratic caucus. The Adams press joined this noisy chorus, denouncing potential caucus participants as "the dupes of intrigue … acting under the influence of caballers." Crawford's papers testily responded that none of the objecting candidates, Adams included, had refused their nominations by state caucuses. Undeterred by the opprobrium the Crawfordites, whipped onward by Van Buren, convened their ill-fated conclave on February 14, 1824. The group of congressman assembled by Van Buren, mostly New Yorkers, Virginians, and Georgians, nominated William Crawford for president by a vote of 64 to 4. Attended by the smallest percentage of congressional Republicans ever, Crawford was nominated by a minority of his own party's representatives in the last national caucus ever held. Adams's public stance against the caucus may have helped polish his credentials with an increasingly democratic-minded electorate.

Although he lost the official nomination to Crawford, Adams's four years' worth of organizational efforts and unique electioneering tactics paid off handsomely as balloting results trickled in from around the Union during the last three months of 1824. The constitution permitted states to select their method of choosing presidential electors. In the eighteen states that held popular elections, candidates and their supporters bore responsibility for assembling and printing the actual presidential elector tickets that voters cast. Despite Adams's historical reputation for political ineptitude, he clearly ran the most national campaign in the field. He competed in sixteen of those states, surpassing Crawford's fourteen, Jackson's thirteen, and Clay's meager nine state tickets. Calhoun, after a disastrous showing at a Republican nominating convention in Pennsylvania, had decided to run for vice president, so he no longer figured in the presidential sweepstakes. Adams easily carried six New England states, and received a portion of the electoral vote in Maryland and Illinois. Though he received no electoral votes from states he lost, Adams finished a respectable third behind Westerners Clay and Jackson in the hotly contested Ohio race, a surprisingly close second to Jackson in the Mississippi race, and almost edged out the general to take New Jersey. Astonishingly, Adams even received seven times more votes than native-son Clay in a losing bid for Virginia's votes. In the six states where state legislatures picked the electors, Adams performed even more successfully. He captured Vermont, while garnering a minority share of Delaware's and Louisiana's tally. Adams managed his greatest coup however in electorally rich New York. In a vote marked by backroom chicanery, proposed deals, and shifting alliances, the Adams machine, guided by "tactful but constant" correspondence from the secretary of state, overwhelmed the Van Buren-led Crawford machine (Bemis, 1956: 28; Hecht, 1972: 392–396).

The New Englander snared 26 of New York's 36 electoral votes. In some respects, Adams had defied the regional limitations of his candidacy. His enthusiastic support for internal improvements and cautious endorsement of protective tariffs attracted voters in the Northwest and in commercial seaboard cities. While Yankee emigrants outside his home base backed Adams, his sterling record of public service and support for national expansion appealed to some voters everywhere (Dangerfield, 1965: 218).

Still, Adams lost the election. He trailed Jackson by almost 39,000 popular votes, and finished second in electoral votes 99 to 84. However, since no candidate had received a majority of electoral votes, the Twelfth Amendment to the constitution mandated that the election would be decided in the House of Representatives. Each state's delegation, regardless of size, would cast one vote for one of the three top finalists from the general election: Jackson, Adams, or Crawford. The winning candidate still required a majority of states in the House vote to become president. Since maneuvering by the other candidates and their supporters to win the House vote commenced immediately, Adams's political skills faced a demanding test. He proved amply up to the challenge.

Since the tremendously influential Speaker had captured three states in the popular election but would not participate in the House vote, many observers branded Henry Clay the kingmaker and every candidate sought his support. While dismayed by his alternatives, Clay quickly decided to back Adams. Since both men shared similar ideological convictions, Clay realized that an Adams presidency offered the brightest future for his beloved American System – a national bank, federally funded internal improvements, and a protective tariff. The onus of a rapprochement between the two men however rested with Adams. The secretary of state had detested Clay both personally and professionally for many years. The Kentuckian had irritated Adams during the Ghent negotiations; as the conscientious diplomat arose at 4.00 a.m. to begin his workday, he would disgustedly discover that the card party in Clay's room was just breaking up. As Speaker of the House, Clay had bedeviled Monroe by contesting various administration policies, which Adams linked to his presidential ambitions rather than to sincere ideological differences. For Adams, reconciling with Clay meant overcoming his longstanding antipathy toward the Speaker. To win the presidency however, Adams dismissed ten years of sincere animosity in three hours. After negotiating through intermediaries, Adams and Clay met directly on January 19, 1825. Once Clay received Adams's assurance that he would support Clay's policy priorities as president, the Speaker promised to cast his vote – and presumably influence the vote of others – for Adams. Stephen Skowronek termed Adams's reconciliation with Clay his crowning political "masterstroke" (1993: 116). Snaring Clay's support helped Adams overcome the regional limitations of his candidacy.

Though Clay represented the top prize captured by Adams in his bid to win the House election, the would-be president's deal-making remained far from complete. Despite his historical reputation for unsociability, Adams met with dozens of congressmen before the final vote. Realizing that his support for the protection of manufacturing had irritated many Southerners and in particular Virginians, Adams informed Virginia senator James Barbour that he supported a conciliatory tariff for promoting commerce but not at the expense of agriculture. He promised John Scott, the lone Representative from Missouri and therefore solely responsible for that delegation's vote, that printers designated by Scott would receive all contracts to publish laws in the newest state. Jackson's supporters approached Daniel Cook, Illinois' sole representative and an Adams supporter, dangling a coveted appointment as governor of the Arkansas territory in exchange for his vote. Still, Cook remained loyal to his patron and as president, Adams rewarded him with "a confidential diplomatic junket to Cuba paid for out of the contingent secret-service fund" (Bemis,1956: 42). As Shaw Livermore (1962) demonstrated however, Adams's true political virtuosity emerged in his treatment of the Federalists.

Just as Adams had shied away from his former party before the general election vote so as not to damage his electoral prospects with Republicans, he now embraced the Federalists to prevail in the House vote. Six days before the election, Adams promised Federalist Daniel Webster that his fellow party members would receive appointments in the New Englander's government. In response, Webster produced a pre-written letter to Henry Warfield, a Federalist congressman from Maryland, that urged Warfield to join Webster in supporting Adams for president. The missive stated that Webster's backing of Adams arose "not from any understanding or communication with him." Adams read and approved the letter, thus endorsing a document that disclaimed electioneering and deal-making while he was in the middle of electioneering and deal-making! Webster's letter was aimed at securing Maryland for Adams, as well as Louis McLane, the sole representative from Delaware, and Stephen Van Rensselaer, a New York Federalist. Later, Adams met with McLane and Van Rensselaer directly (Livermore, 1962: 174–177).

Adams's political machinations reached their triumphant dénouement amidst a snowstorm on February 9, 1825. The House convened and presidential balloting began shortly after noon. Each state had one vote with a majority of 13 required for victory. For the secretary of state the suspense was brief. The House elected John Quincy Adams as the nation's sixth president on the first ballot. Unsurprisingly, Adams carried the six New England states. Maryland, Illinois, and Louisiana, states that had given Adams a minority share of electoral votes in the general election, also voted for him in the House. In a close vote, Adams carried New York's delegation over Crawford, with Van Rensselaer casting his critical vote for the former

Federalist. Van Buren later claimed that the pious Van Rensselaer, after praying for divine guidance, opened his eyes and spied an Adams ballot on the floor which he picked up and tossed in the ballot box. In all likelihood, Van Rensselaer's vote probably owed more to Adams's pre-balloting promises than to any act of God. Van Buren's colorful tale could not conceal a hard truth. The supposedly non-political Adams had bested the crafty New Yorker *twice* – once in the New York legislative vote and now in the House. Finally, Adams's vote included three states that had not given him a single electoral vote in the fall elections. Those states – Kentucky, Ohio, and Missouri – had voted for Clay. Kentucky's own state legislature had instructed the Speaker to cast the state's vote for Jackson, but Clay remained true to his ideological convictions and backed the secretary of state. Adams's triumph, Daniel Walker Howe observed, "marked him as a master of what might be called the political 'old-boy network'" (1979: 46). He had reached his long-cherished goal in 1824, but would success with the "old boys" in a House election translate into future success? Adams's imminent minority presidency would truly tax his political talents and ultimately influenced his bid for re-election in 1828.

15.2 The Presidential Interlude

In one of his first official acts as president-elect two days after the House vote, Adams tapped Clay to be his secretary of state. Since the last four chief executives had once held that position and many presumed the State portfolio to be a stepping stone to the presidency, Adams appeared to be designating Clay as his heir apparent. Jackson and his allies, already furious that the popular winner of the general election had been cheated out of his victory in the House, screamed that a "corrupt bargain" had occurred. They claimed that Adams had secretly offered Clay the desirable cabinet post in direct exchange for the House votes of the three states the Kentuckian had won in the fall election. Most historians disagree. Although Adams's normally thorough diary remains curiously vague about the details of his January meeting with Clay, most scholars suggested that the two men simply arrived at an implicit understanding to support each other rather than a vulgar office-for-votes horse-trade. As he publicly declared, Adams deemed Clay the most qualified candidate to fill the important post and as the first Westerner ever to serve in the cabinet, Clay's appointment provided well-earned recognition for that region (Ketcham, 1984: 137; Parsons, 2009: 105). Ideologically similar, the pair believed that working together would benefit the American System that they both supported (Bemis, 1956: 58; Dangerfield, 1965: 225; Hargreaves, 1985: 38; Remini, 2002: 70; Parsons, 2009: 110). Most importantly, adding Clay to the cabinet made enormous political sense for Adams; the Kentuckian brought regional balance to his administration and might ultimately secure western support for his re-election bid (Hargreaves, 1985: 45; Skrownek, 1993: 117). Some historians even argue that the scheming Jacksonians never truly believed the "corrupt bargain" charges. Instead, their claims amounted to little more than a crass political ploy cooked up to undermine Adams's legitimacy (Quincy, 1859: 74; Hargreaves, 1985: 47). Whatever the truth, the charges that Adams and Clay had conspired to make the New Englander president figured prominently in the 1828 campaign.

Adams would face a united opposition in 1828 as the forces of three 1824 losers, Jackson, Crawford, and Calhoun, consolidated behind the general as their standard-bearer. Historians diverge over the precise moment this combination emerged. Some suggested that the "corrupt bargain" produced the Jacksonian coalition (Quincy, 1859: 74; Ketcham, 1984: 137; Hargreaves, 1985: 40, 45; Remini, 2002: 70), while others maintained that it materialized gradually during the Adams administration (Bemis, 1956: 71; Livermore, 1962: 193; Cole, 2009: 53; Parsons, 2009: 120). Scholars have suggested that several factors influenced the formation of this bloc dedicated to Adams's defeat. Pro-slavery southerners feared the power of a potentially anti-slavery northern president (Quincy, 1859: 78; Hargreaves, 1985: 44). Westerners remained angry that their favorite had been denied his deserved office (Ketcham, 1984: 137; Hargreaves, 1985: 44). Republicans objected to Federalist influence within the Adams administration (Livermore, 1962: 193). Finally, supporters of state rights opposed the vigorous central government programs that Adams envisioned (Cole, 2009: 45; Parsons, 2009: 115, 120).

Indeed, many historians insisted that Adams's dynamic responses to the issues he faced as president helped generate the party that defeated him in 1828. When Adams tried to protect the rights of Creek Indians in their treaty dispute with Georgians who were determined to eject all Native Americans from state soil, he drove Southerners sympathetic to Indian removal – and Georgians particularly – into the arms of Jackson (Bemis, 1956: 87; Remini, 2002: 100). Adams proposed sending delegates to the Panama congress, a conclave of Latin American nations convened to address issues of mutual peace and security from European intervention. Strict constructionists opposed to entangling alliances and Southerners repulsed by any meeting that included former slaves as delegates opposed Adams's proposal. Both groups applauded Jackson's public condemnation of the Panama congress (Remini, 2002: 79, 82; Parsons, 2009: 115). When Missouri senator Thomas Hart Benton advocated the inexpensive sale of Western public lands to settlers – even squatters – to the point of actually giving away unsold land, the president objected. Instead, Adams wished to sell public lands at a higher price – often to speculators – and use the proceeds to pay off the national debt and finance internal improvements, a position that cost him Western votes, especially in Missouri, Illinois, and

Indiana (Hargreaves, 1985: 199; Remini, 2002: 87). Adams embroiled the nation in a trade dispute with Britain that ultimately resulted in an embargo of commerce between the West Indies and the United States. Agriculturalists in the Southern and Middle states shrieked that Adams had sacrificed their interests so as to secure favorable British commercial concessions for his New England shipping constituents and they turned to the Jacksonians for redress (Hargreaves, 1985: 109; Remini, 2002: 102). Finally, Adams signed legislation enacting the tariff of 1828, the so-called "Tariff of Abominations," that raised duties on a host of items including molasses, distilled liquor, sail duck, hemp, flax, irons, and woolens. The tariff proved highly appealing to farmers and manufacturers in the Western and Middle states, moderately unpopular in New England, but was utterly loathed in the South. While Adams received little credit from Northerners for passing the package, Southerners vilified him for it in the 1828 election (Remini, 2002: 111; Parsons, 2009: 158). Historians predisposed to underestimate Adams's political skills have deemed his stances on these issues as further signs of his political ineptitude.

Adams's appointment policy added fuel to this historical assessment. Despite the pleas of some cabinet members, the president rigorously maintained a nonpartisan patronage policy. He retained the bulk of Monroe's civil servants, filled vacancies only when they occurred, and appointed qualified individuals – even prominent Jacksonians – regardless of political affiliation. During his entire term Adams removed a mere twelve individuals and then only after receiving overwhelming evidence of their incompetence. Even postmaster general John McLean, despite openly working for Jackson's election, remained safely ensconced in the Adams cabinet. Most historians suggested that Adams carried his devotion to non-partisanship to politically self-destructive lengths (Hargreaves, 1985: 55; Remini, 2002: 110; Cole, 2009: 24; Parsons, 2009: 116). Seemingly, Adams never employed patronage to strengthen his congressional position, fashion a party that backed him, or to support his re-election bid.

In fact, there was partisan method behind Adams's seemingly political madness. The results of the 1824 election demonstrated that Adams had run well in New England, achieved only moderate success in the Western and Middle states, but trailed badly in the South. To win re-election the president needed to craft a coalition, combining his New England bloc with augmented support in the Middle and the West. Adams's espousal of tariffs might very well lure Western and Middle voters, while his position on public land sales and British trade would hopefully mollify his Northern and Eastern base irritated by his stance on the tariff. Further, the president's unwavering support for internal improvements appealed to every sector of his coalition. His "anti-Southern" positions mattered little. Adams knew he stood virtually no chance of winning in the South once the opposition had unified behind Jackson; moreover, his hostility to Southern interests might even appeal to Northerners and Westerners. Unfortunately for Adams, a patronage policy meant to facilitate the coalition he tried to construct proved almost impossible to follow. The political tactics he had used to win the 1824 election circumscribed his partisan activities. As Stephen Skowronek noted, since deal-making had helped make Adams president, building a party based on patronage would "fuel the already devastating charges of intrigue and corruption" that the Jacksonians unremittingly hurled (1993: 125). As for postmaster McLean, by the time Adams realized his duplicity the opposition controlled Congress. Had Adams removed McLean, it would have only confirmed the truth of the "corrupt bargain" charge and the Jacksonian Senate would never have approved a replacement anyway (Bemis, 1956: 139). The Federalists further complicated Adams's political life. He repaid their support in the House vote with a few high-profile positions, but his nonpartisan actions pleased no one. Federalists grumbled at the paucity of their appointments while Republicans groused that Adams had compromised their party's purity (Livermore, 1962: 187–190). Clearly, Adams's presidential actions seemed aimed at forging a North–Middle–West political coalition to bring victory in 1828, but one pleasingly dressed in nonpartisan clothing meant to undercut the damaging "corrupt bargain" charges. Adams's partisans even coined a new name for their coalition – the National Republicans.

15.3 The Election of 1828

Historians have long deemed the presidential election of 1828 a pivotal moment in American history. The results of the contest initiated "if not an earthquake, at least the rearranging of the old landscape and the configuration of a new one" (Parsons, 2009: xviii) that ultimately "contributed greatly to the rise of democracy and mass political parties" (Cole, 2009: 1). Adams trudged through these accounts of the election as a rather quaint eighteenth-century relic – a statesman representing "a lost era" of American political culture (Parsons, 2009: xvii) who "was never comfortable dealing with politics" (Cole, 2009: 58). The president, many historians insisted, played only a minimal role in his own re-election campaign. Despite the furious electoral battle swirling around him, the oblivious Adams focused on his official duties and his hobbies, poring over state papers, cultivating silkworms and planting live oaks while his re-election chances burned (Quincy, 1859: 83; Dangerfield, 1965: 289; Hecht, 1972: 473; McCormick, 1982: 152; Ketcham, 1984: 140; Nagel, 1997: 320; Cole, 2009: 58; Parsons, 2009: 152). Some scholars have maintained that a guilty conscience tortured Adams. The president, deeply remorseful over the scheming intrigues he had employed to win the 1824 House vote, scrupulously determined to make no effort to retain office (Dangerfield, 1965: 229,

289; Parsons, 2009: 153). Certainly, Adams once again avoided overt electioneering, since the electorate still rejected blatantly campaigning presidential contenders. More importantly, the Jacksonians' incessant "corrupt bargain" mantra demanded that Adams run a discreet campaign to prevent substantiating the opposition's charges. The resolution of the 1824 election, M. J. Heale has observed, "had made it even more necessary than ever for Adams to sustain the role of the patriotic and disinterested statesman" (1982: 69). The president's decision to keep his own re-election efforts at arms' length made a great deal of political sense. The New Englander was far from an inactive candidate, however. Adams formed an organization, sponsored a newspaper network, made selected "non-political" political appearances, and adopted ideological positions all aimed at fashioning a North–Middle–West political coalition and gaining that coveted second term.

Adams assembled an impressive re-election team. While the president maintained his deliberate public pretense of indifference, he established an informal central re-election committee in the White House and authorized an array of activities in his behalf. Clay, the *de facto* party chairman, directed operations from the capital. The Kentuckyian maintained a robust correspondence network with elite politicians in key electoral states, directing a quite successful campaign for state legislature-sponsored resolutions endorsing the president's re-election (Cole, 2009: 66–70). Clay summoned a national convention of supporters in the key battleground state of Pennsylvania that renominated Adams, and National Republicans even brazenly held nominating conventions in Virginia, North Carolina, and Louisiana, supposedly "hopeless" Southern states safely in Jackson's pocket. Webster, with his extensive New England and New York commercial contacts, came aboard as unofficial party treasurer. Clay shifted federal printing contracts and Webster funneled donations from wealthy backers into the hands of pro-administration printers. Though Adams avoided overt electioneering trips, he sanctioned campaign travel by his high-profile cabinet secretaries despite howls of protest from the opposition press. Navy secretary Samuel Southard made a highly effective swing through Maryland, Delaware, and New Jersey, all key Middle states that Adams needed to win. In the president's greatest strategic maneuver however, he anointed treasury secretary Richard Rush as his running mate. With the addition of Rush, an ardent protectionist from Pennsylvania, Adams had assembled an organization that appealed to each of the constituencies in his sought-after North–Middle–West political coalition. Clay should carry the West, Rush the Middle, and Webster would bring in the Federalists – Adams himself secured New England (D.W. Howe, 1979: 50).

Adams's organization supported a press campaign on the president's behalf. Both contenders employed newspaper networks and pamphleteering presses that far surpassed 1824's activities. Correspondingly, the venomous libels that the forces of both men hurled at each other became more slanderous than those in the previous election. These attacks contained a mixture of truths, half-truths, and outright lies. Adams was accused of pimping for the Russian tsar, which explained his diplomatic successes. He had opposed the Louisiana Purchase and tried to trade Mississippi navigation rights to the British to protect New England fishing privileges during the Ghent negotiations; both claims were meant to undercut his support in the West. He conducted business on Sunday, had engaged in premarital sex, and he hated Dutch Americans. In the East Adams was accused of anti-Catholic bigotry and in the West of favoring Catholics over Protestants (Remini, 2002: 119–120). "King John II," like his monarchical father, lived in regal splendor, installing a billiard table and other "gambling apparatus" in the White House all at public expense. Jacksonians charged that the president had abused executive power and indulged in wasteful spending. They even calculated every penny that he had earned in government service, concluding that Adams had gobbled up the "exorbitant" sum of $105 000 from the public trough over the years. The National Republican press hardly spared Jackson. With anti-masonic furor sweeping western New York, they luridly trumpeted Jackson's masonic membership. The "Coffin Handbill" blared that he had cruelly executed six innocent militiamen during the Creek War and he was accused of participating in the Burr conspiracy. The headstrong general had mistreated Indians and executed British subjects during the First Seminole War, while his tenure as territorial governor had been calamitous for Floridians. Jackson was an adulterer and married a bigamist, which was scarcely surprising since his mother was a prostitute.

While the National Republican newspaper and pamphleteering efforts attempted to undermine Jackson's image in the public mind, they also tried to paint a positive portrait of their standard-bearer. Adams, his press suggested, was an intellectual, morally upright, and experienced man. The president remained above partisanship and factional intrigue, and was utterly committed to public service and the nation's welfare. While historians have highlighted Jackson's use of the hickory pole as a symbolic evocation of his character, few have noted that Adams's forces employed the sturdy oak to represent the solid dependability of their candidate (Heale, 1982: 73). Unfortunately for Adams, the Jacksonian press turned his own image against him. For an electorate given to bouts of anti-intellectualism, the Jacksonians twisted Adams scholarly gifts into a simple, pungent aphorism – Adams who can write versus Jackson who can fight (Dangerfield, 1965: 294). They poisoned Adams's reputation for moral probity by tying it to the Yankee stereotype – "religious fanaticism, calculating stinginess, and, above all, a dangerous meddlesomeness in private affairs" (Parsons, 2009: 171). Adams's claims to longstanding meritorious public service simply validated the Jacksonian caricature of the president as a scheming insider with enough knowledge and influence in the corridors of power to cheat a non-political Western hero out of the presidency. In the battle of dueling public images, Adams seemed “a pale, far less dominant” figure than the larger-than-life General who had – almost single-handedly! – defeated the British in the Battle of New Orleans (Cole, 2009: 194).

Adams probably played little direct role in formulating the most malevolent press strikes against Jackson. His calculated pose of non-involvement allowed the president to stay out of the gutter, but as an inveterate newspaper reader he certainly knew the nature of his party’s press campaign against his challenger. While historians have generally portrayed the National Republicans as less energetic than the Jacksonians, in 1828’s press war the president’s party “could and did assume the offensive” (Bemis, 1956: 140). Adams’s forces initiated the personal attacks that became a hallmark of the race (Hecht, 1971: 479–480). While Jackson expressly forbid his partisans from criticizing women, Adams never restrained his forces from issuing their brutal slanders against Rachel Jackson’s character. Still, Lynn Hudson Parsons has argued that while the Jacksonians often refuted opposition smears of their candidate, the less responsive Adamsites played offense but ignored defense, so the damaging charges against the president remained unanswered (2009: 151). Additionally, National Republican assaults against Jackson’s “dangerous” military record only tended to remind voters of the general’s “glorious” military record that had attracted them to Jackson in the first place. In the 1828 campaign, while both sides were resourceful and malicious, the Jacksonians won the press battle.

While Adams remained in the background amidst his campaign’s organizational and newspaper activities, he engaged in several high-profile “non-political” political appearances. Adams’s notorious discomfort when speaking before crowds certainly produced a few political missteps at these events. At a celebration in Baltimore commemorating the city’s valiant defense against British attack during the War of 1812, the president offered a bizarre toast. “Ebony and Topaz, General Ross’s posthumous coat of arms, and the republican militia men who gave it!” Adams declaimed. Confronted by puzzled stares, he sheepishly explained that he had borrowed the expression from Voltaire’s *Le Blanc et Le Noir*. “Ebony” symbolized the spirit of evil, personified in this case by General Robert Ross, commander of the British troops that had besieged Baltimore. The king had modified Ross’s coat of arms after he had perished in battle. “Topaz” symbolized the spirit of good, personified by the brave American militiamen that defended Baltimore. “For the Jacksonians,” Donald B. Cole observed, “the president’s supercilious toast was a gift from the gods” since it fit perfectly into their caricature of Adams as an out-of-touch academic (2009: 150). Still, Adams sometimes exploited public occasions with real political finesse. On the Fourth of July 1828, only a few months before the election, the president eschewed the customary Independence Day celebrations in the capital in favor of speaking at the ceremonial ground-breaking for the Chesapeake and Ohio canal. After a speech reminding voters of his steadfast commitment to internal improvements, Adams wielded a spade to extract the traditional first shovelful of dirt. Instead, he hit a tree root and came up empty-handed. Undeterred, the august president of the United States tossed off his coat, rolled up his sleeves, and hacked at the root until he triumphantly raised that shovelful of dirt. The crowd roared in approval. Not only had Adams smuggled a political message into an ostensibly non-political event, he managed to demonstrate a common touch clearly at odds with the Jacksonian's parody of his personality. While Adams made fewer public appearances than Jackson, he judiciously employed those occasions to prove that he was "the far-sighted president of the whole nation" (Heale, 1982: 73).

Indeed, Adams's organization, press campaign, and public appearances reinforced an ideological message that the president hoped a North–Middle–West political coalition might find appealing. He claimed that his support for internal improvements, protective tariffs, credit-restricting banks, commercial treaties, and nationally oriented public land policies, all under the aegis of the federal government, would benefit the country as a whole. While the Western and Middle state voters Adams wished to attract enthusiastically supported some of these policies, especially internal improvements and tariffs, they wanted the benefits conferred locally and specifically (Hargreaves, 1985: 247). Though Adams may have been correct that his programs would ultimately profit the whole nation, in the short term they created conflict between localities and regions. Voters cared less about building canals or protecting commodities in the abstract than they did about support for their specific local road or particular regional industry. If one region in his proposed coalition received improvement or protection from Adams's government, it might come at the expense of another region in his coalition. The president's ideological positions tended to fracture the very political coalition he attempted to assemble. In contrast, the Jacksonians could run a simple opposition campaign. In standing against national solutions and a corrupt central administration, they attracted voters irritated that their local and specific needs remained unmet.

Despite Adams's competitive campaign efforts, politically wise electioneering strategy, and ideological stance on the issues, his proposed North–Middle–West political coalition failed to materialize. Jackson handily defeated Adams in the election of 1828. Twenty-two states held popular elections and only two selected electors in their state legislatures. Predictably, Adams carried the six New England states by fairly wide margins, although Jackson came uncomfortably close in New Hampshire and even snared one electoral vote in Maine. With the exception of the tight race in Louisiana, Jackson prevailed by significant pluralities in the seven Southern states as expected. Although Adams put up some fight in three, all six Western states ultimately supported his opponent. In the end, even Clay's beloved Kentucky fell to the Jacksonian onslaught. Returns in the Middle states were mixed. Adams and Jackson split the New York and Maryland electoral votes, the general trounced the president in Pennsylvania, but Adams captured New Jersey and Delaware. Defeated by almost 140,000 popular votes, Adams could not redeem himself in any deal-making House election. Jackson received an easy electoral vote majority, 178 to 83. The 1828 results mirrored those in 1824. The prior election, George Dangerfield analyzed, represented "a solid defeat for the American System and for consolidated, as compared to piecemeal, federal planning" (1965: 222). Despite four years of cheerleading, Adams's ideological positions simply remained less popular with the electorate than Jackson's less centralized approach to governing.

More importantly, the political abilities that Adams had exercised in 1824 seriously compromised his re-election effort. Adams had needed the Federalists to win the House vote. This allowed the Jacksonians in 1828 to tar the president with a Federalist brush, even though Jackson openly wooed the Federalists himself. In reaction, Adams backed away from crafting an official alliance with his former party. He appointed only six Federalists during his tenure, which included three after he lost the election. Webster's 1825 letter to Warfield, which had endorsed Adams's candidacy and predicted Federalist appointments from his administration, became public knowledge in 1827. The Jacksonians eagerly condemned Adams's "Webster Pledge" in their literature. Shaw Livermore has argued that National Republicans treated the Federalists as a bloc, hoping to amalgamate the two parties, whereas the Jacksonians recruited the Federalists as individuals (1962: 223). In 1824 Adams had attempted to recruit Webster as an individual, but it had inspired Jacksonian accusations of deal-making. Ironically, this led to the bloc approach in 1828, which allowed the Jacksonians to denounce a reputed Adams–Federalist alliance. The Jacksonian indictment of Adams's Federalist connections dangerously resonated with Republican voters. Desperately, Adams made one final attempt to sever his Federalist ties in the public's mind. With voting imminent in October 1828, Adams published an article in the *Washington National Intelligencer* charging that Massachusetts' Federalists had contemplated disunion during the Jefferson administration. Furious at the president's accusations, denied the appointments they expected, proudly unwilling to be amalgamated into the National Republicans, and receptive to Jackson's blandishments, many Federalists cast their vote for the general in 1828 (Livermore, 1962: 199, 217, 241–242). Clearly, Adams's 1824 Federalist deal haunted his 1828 re-election bid.

Similarly, Adams's 1824 bargains with House members cost the president's party seats in the 1826 congressional elections. As Lynn Hudson Parsons has noted, "for the first time in American political history many [1826] contests were conducted with an eye toward the presidential election two years down the road" (2009: 124). Some voters, angry that their representatives had denied the general election winner his just victory in the House vote, expelled pro-Adams congressmen. Illinois' voters sacked Daniel Cook, their sole representative who had backed Adams in the House despite Jackson's popular triumph in the state; Missouri's lone congressman John Scott suffered the same fate. With the Senate controlled by Vice President Calhoun, both houses of Congress passed into the hands of the Jacksonian opposition. The House of Representatives summarily dumped their pro-Adams Speaker and handed the gavel to Andrew Stevenson, a Jackson devotee from Virginia. Committee assignments flowed to dependable and competent supporters of the general. The Jacksonian House subsidized internal improvements and land grants, but only in "important or swing" states and then blamed the president for squandering government funds on wasteful spending programs (Remini, 2002: 110). Under the guise of a retrenchment investigation aimed at reducing the national debt, the new House harassed the administration. They demanded a seemingly endless series of documents and reports from the president, while arguing that he needed to reduce his staff but increase their hours of congressional access. These investigations, Mary W. M. Hargreaves insisted, "center[ed] in partisan-slanted criticism of disparate incidents rather than in debate upon coherently defined programmatic issues (1985: 246). Jacksonian congressional maneuvers dovetailed with their newspaper and pamphlet propaganda, mutually reinforcing both (Bemis, 1956: 134). Adams's 1824 political bargains had helped the Jacksonians gain control of Congress which they used effectively as a political tactic to defeat the president in 1828.

Finally, Adams had needed Clay to win the Western states in 1824, so he reconciled with his former enemy. His deal with the Kentuckian prompted the "corrupt bargain" charges that unified the opposition (Bemis, 1956: 131) and tainted his administration's legitimacy from the outset (McCormick, 1982: 126). Unable to employ patronage to forge his desired political coalition lest he substantiate the corruption charges, Adams "frequently alienated the sectors he was seeking to woo" since they never received the "plums" they expected (Hargreaves, 1985: 247). Jackson fashioned his campaign as a crusade against dishonest intriguers and his stance as the champion of anti-corruption became central to his identity as a candidate (Heale, 1982: 80). Clay's prominent position in the cabinet and the re-election campaign only reminded voters that Adams's presidency rested on a "corrupt bargain" and effectively validated Jackson's attack. Adams tried to counter with a campaign and image based on national, nonpartisan issues, but this approach proved ineffective while the "corrupt bargain" simply seemed too plausible. The superb political arts that Adams had used to win the election of 1824 sowed the seeds of his defeat in the election of 1828. Adams's political skills, though considerable, proved unable to solve this conundrum.

15.4 John Quincy Adams the Politician

Though he displayed significant political talent in the elections of 1824 and 1828, historians have often minimized the political side of Adams based on an authoritative source – the man's own words. In Adams's monumental diary, justly recognized as a treasure trove of early nineteenth-century political history, the notoriously self-critical candidate frequently disparaged both his political gifts and electoral chances. Daniel Walker Howe has argued however, that Adams's diary should not be taken at face value. Since it served as part of his program for developing self-control, within the journal Adams constantly denigrated the "unseemly" political side of his character. Further, he hoped for "vindication by posterity – specifically, his own posterity, for the diary was written principally for his descendants" (Howe, 1979: 45). Since Adams expected that it would be read by future generations, he proved less than candid when recording his own electioneering practices. Indeed, Adams excoriated William Crawford in the pages of his journal, arguing that Monroe's treasury secretary was "a worm preying upon the vitals of the Administration within its own body" (J.Q. Adams, *Memoirs*: 5.315, quoted in Bemis, 1956: 16). Despite eight years of unflagging insistence in his diary that Crawford's unscrupulous, unbridled, and unprincipled ambition rendered him quite literally unfit for public service, once Adams had safely defeated Crawford for the presidency he asked the Georgian to remain at the Treasury post in his own administration. Adams the diarist remains a problematic source for historians analyzing Adams the politician.

Paul C. Nagel best explained the ostensible contradiction between Adams's highly political public actions and the sharp criticisms of politics that he leveled in his diary. Based on a close reading of the complete journal, including the unpublished portions, Nagel offered a detailed psychological profile of the New Englander. A "deep schism" divided Adams's character, Nagel maintained: "one side detested politics while the other found it irresistible" (1997: 233). The two sides of Adams's reaction to politics actually complied perfectly with the reigning political culture, one that simultaneously disdained but required overt electioneering, factional intrigue, and political deal-making. Rather than some anachronistic eighteenth-century political fossil, Adams adroitly exploited his divided approach to politics to navigate the roiling political tides he encountered during both of his presidential campaigns.

Indeed, Adams's performance in the elections of 1824 and 1828 matched the political astuteness he displayed throughout his career. As Stephen Skowronek observed, "it was certainly no accident that this Federalist apostate rose to the highest office in the land along the traditional line of Republican advance" (1993: 112). As a Federalist member of the Massachusetts legislature in 1802, Adams bargained his way into a US

Senate seat. He arranged for members of his faction to back Timothy Pickering – a hated Adams family enemy – for a Senate seat in exchange for the Pickering bloc's support for his own Senate bid (Remini, 2002: 35). One of the first Federalists to recognize that his party seemed destined for a steep national decline, Adams nimbly switched sides, immediately nurtured a political base within his new organization, and unexpectedly rose through the Republican ranks to become a "formidable national figure in his own right" (Skowronek, 1993: 114). While usually depicted by historians as principled stands, even Adams's acclaimed post-presidential accomplishments, fighting against the Gag Rule and arguing the *Amistad* case before the Supreme Court, arose primarily "from his all-consuming desire for political vengeance" against Southerners (Nagel, 1997: 419). Recognizing John Quincy Adams as a capable politician should facilitate any historian's analysis of the statesman's long career.

Further Reading

Cole, Donald B. (2009). *Vindicating Andrew Jackson: The Election of 1828 and the Rise of the Two-Party System*. Lawrence, KS.

Dangerfield, George (1965). *The Awakening of American Nationalism, 1815–1828*. New York, .

Heale, M.J. (1982). *The Presidential Quest: Candidates and Images in American Political Culture, 1787–1852*. New York.

Howe, Daniel Walker (1979). *The Political Culture of the American Whigs*. Chicago.

Ketcham, Ralph (1984). *Presidents Above Party: The First American Presidency, 1789–1829*. Chapel Hill, NC.

Livermore, Shaw, Jr. (1972). *The Twilight of Federalism: The Disintegration of the Federalist Party, 1815–1830*, 2nd edn. New York.

May, Ernest R. (1975). *The Making of the Monroe Doctrine*. Cambridge, MA.

McCormick, Richard P. (1982). *The Presidential Game: The Origins of American Presidential Politics*. New York.

Parsons, Lynn Hudson (2009). *The Birth of Modern Politics: Andrew Jackson, John Quincy Adams, and the Election of 1828*. New York.

Skowronek, Stephen (1997). *The Politics Presidents Make: Leadership from John Adams to Bill Clinton* 2nd edn. Cambridge, MA.

Chapter Sixteen

The Presidency of John Quincy Adams

Padraig Riley

The president of the United States was drowning. Or so a passerby might have thought on the afternoon of June 13, 1825, as 57-year-old John Quincy Adams struggled to reach the far bank of the Potomac River. He had set out with his son John and his valet, Antoine Giusta, to cross the river in an old boat, with the intention of swimming back to the other side. His son had wisely abandoned the boat partway out, doubtful of its safety, while Adams and Antoine continued on their venture, until the boat began to fill with water. "Just at that critical moment," wrote Adams, "a fresh breeze from the northwest blew down the river as from the nose of a bellows … and set the boat to dancing till the river came in at the sides. I jumped overboard, and Antoine did the same." As he made out for the shore, his shirt sleeves "filled with water and hung like two fifty-six pound weights upon my arms," pulling the president toward the river bottom. He managed to make it to the far bank, where he spent the next few hours with his son, swimming "or sitting naked basking on the bank" until Antoine arrived with a carriage to take him home. Upon reflection, he determined that the "incident gave me a humiliating lesson and solemn warning not to trifle with danger." That lesson was reinforced just over a week later when Adams encountered a group of men dragging the river for a drowning victim. They pulled up one Mr Shoemaker, a clerk in the post-office and, by all accounts, an "excellent swimmer" (C.F. Adams, 1874–1877: 7.27–29, 35–36).

The scene is a good metaphor for Adams's tenure as president, which began boldly, but in a ship of state deeply compromised by political intrigue and of questionable popular ballast. Disaster soon followed, and Adams

A Companion to John Adams and John Quincy Adams, First Edition.
Edited by David Waldstreicher.

spent much of his presidency weighed down by the cares and pressures of political life, unable to find an independent course through the snags of personal and party competition in Washington. Yet in the end, Adams did reach the other shore, as he had that summer afternoon in June. From there, he would begin perhaps the most remarkable chapter of his long political life.

John Quincy Adams termed his own presidency a failure, and he was correct in his assessment. But it was also a sort of prolonged rebirth, a period of personal and national transition. Although he failed to consolidate authority or complete the bold plan of national improvement laid out in his first address to Congress, the trials of his presidency led to a last great act of personal improvement. In his post-presidential years, as the conscience of the North, he would give voice to sentiments that he had held in check for years, as he challenged the power of slavery in the American government. A minority president, Adams attempted to govern from the center and transcend partisan difference; in failing to do so, he prepared himself, at first only half-consciously, for a brilliant retirement of minority dissent.

In terms of national politics, historians have tended to treat Adams's term as an accident or an interruption, in their haste to arrive at Jacksonian democracy. But in fact, Adams's presidency was a critical period in American political development, a hinge between the early national and the antebellum eras. His presidency witnessed the initial formation of the second party system, which helped accommodate the rising class tensions of a developing capitalist economy, as well as the discordant sectionalism brought to life by the Missouri crisis. The 1828 contest between Quincy Adams and Jackson, like the contest between his father and Jefferson in an earlier epoch, represented a distinct conflict between two different paths of national development. As had happened in 1800, Americans took a contradictory road defined by democratic and geographical expansion and the growing power of slavery. They left behind Adams's vision of careful national planning and government-directed economic growth, married to the expanding capitalist economy of the Northeast (D.W. Howe, 2007: 279).

Quincy Adams' presidency likewise remains a critical historiographical problem, subject to considerable debate. While scholars tend to agree that Quincy Adams did not succeed as a president, few are certain just what his lack of success indicates. For some, Quincy Adams is an elitist New Englander, out of touch if not opposed to the major democratic reforms of his day; for others, Adams is a symbol of a conscientious public servant (so much so that one historian – D.W. Howe, 2007 – has dedicated his magnum opus to "J.Q.A.") who fought a noble if losing battle against political venality and the power of slavery. He was not quite either of these men – he was willing to compromise with slavery in the name of national power throughout his career; he was an early proponent of continental expansion, matching Andrew Jackson's frontier aggression with a militant diplomacy;

and he broke politically with New England Federalism in the name of nationalism during Jefferson's second term. He was above all a unique figure in American political history, perhaps the most national and least regional of all American presidents; an elite by training and to an extent by disposition, but also a man of ordinary passions (swimming and billiards occupied much of his free time as president) who could spearhead populist causes, from anti-masonry to antislavery.

Quincy Adams took office as a nationalist without a national mandate. The election of 1824 had resulted in no decisive winner, and while Adams had worked hard to win the contest in the House of Representatives, his coalition was uncertain from the outset. Adams famously won the election by the providence-inspired voting of New York's Stephen Van Rensselaer, but his rise to power depended far more on the political support of Henry Clay, who had come in fourth in the presidential balloting, and was therefore kept out of the balloting in the House. Clay soon threw his votes to Adams, an alliance which quickly became a liability for both men. Anticipating the Clay–Adams partnership, Jacksonians charged Clay with peddling his influence to obtain the office of secretary of state. Clay denounced the rumors, and briefly considered a duel with their principal author, one George Kremer, a representative from Pennsylvania (Hargreaves, 1985: 45). Kremer was an unimportant figure (and thus, in the culture of Southern honor, not worth exchanging shots with), but through his agency the Jacksonians had set a complicated trap. In one of his first acts as president, Adams appointed Clay his secretary of state and thus, by tradition, presumptive heir to the presidency. The appointment made perfect sense ideologically: Clay and Adams supporters shared a commitment to internal improvements and national economic development, and Clay was particularly interested in diplomacy with Latin America, a key issue due to the recent success of independence movements throughout the old Spanish empire. But the appointment, now termed the "corrupt bargain" by Jacksonians, became an albatross for both men, a sign that each defied popular sentiment in favour of their own elite interests. Clay had rejected the instructions of the Kentucky legislature by throwing the state's vote in the House to Adams in 1824; soon thereafter he assumed the role of secretary of state. Jackson supporters saw only backroom dealing and intrigue; Jackson himself termed Clay the "Judas of the West." According to John C. Calhoun, Clay had made himself "miserable for life" by accepting the cabinet position (Sellers, 1991: 272). When it came to Clay's presidential aspirations, he turned out to be correct.

While allying with Clay left Adams vulnerable, he lost other potential allies at the same time. One, of course, was Andrew Jackson. Before Jackson entered the contest in 1824, he was Adams's first choice for a vice president, and although the two men had clashing temperaments and lifestyles, they shared key objectives. Adams had been one of Jackson's strongest defenders when he invaded Florida on suspect authority in 1818; he used Jackson's extra-legal conquest as an opportunity for a signal diplomatic triumph, compelling Spain to surrender Florida and agree to the Transcontinental Treaty of 1819. At heart, both men were Jeffersonian nationalists, committed to the continental expansion of the United States. But Jackson, though he appeared to accept Adams's election, congratulating him politely at a Washington party in early 1825, quickly chose to accept the role of populist hero and wronged partisan, the electorate's true choice in 1824 and the embodiment of democratic renewal. When the Tennessee legislature nominated him as their candidate for the next presidential election in October of 1825, he resigned his seat in the Senate to begin the campaign of 1828.

Adams faced dissension within his administration as well as without. He attempted to heal the fissures of the 1824 electoral contest by perpetuating the policies and personnel of the Monroe administration, in a vain attempt to continue the one-party (and persistently acrimonious) "Era of Good Feelings." Calhoun, Monroe's secretary of war, became vice president, but he entered the office already in competition with Quincy Adams, plotting his own path to the presidency. Calhoun was replaced by James Barbour of Virginia, a former governor of the Old Dominion with a clear Republican pedigree, but without the growing state's rights radicalism of men like John Randolph of Roanoke and John Taylor of Caroline. As a senator during the Missouri crisis, he had been a key ally of Monroe's, and helped craft the Missouri compromise. Other Monroe appointees remained in their offices, notably William Wirt as attorney general and John McLean as postmaster general. Adams even considered keeping on William Crawford as secretary of the treasury, the senile Georgian who ran against him in 1824, and who had used his appointment powers to build up a coterie of loyal sub-officers. Fortunately, Crawford declined, and Adams replaced him with Richard Rush of Pennsylvania, who was far more sympathetic to the administration's objectives. This mixture of sectional and political loyalties reflected Adams's belief that he could govern beyond partisanship, as a symbol of national unity. He was doomed to fail: his appointment of Clay tainted him with charges of favoritism and corruption, Calhoun and McLean worked against him from the outset, and his high-minded refusal to play politics when it came to almost all other appointments meant that he could not maintain a national political coalition.

And yet, despite these severe limitations and questionable popular support, Adams forged boldly ahead. In his first message to Congress, on December 6, 1825, he outlined an ambitious program of national development, led by the federal government. He called for a national bankruptcy law, a uniform national militia system, "a permanent naval peace establishment" to defend American commercial interests abroad, a general expansion of internal improvements, a national university, national programs of geographical and astronomical discovery, a uniform system of weights and measures, revisions to federal patent law, and a national system of internal improvements funded by the orderly sale of public land. "Liberty is power," said Adams in closing, and the United States, possessed of the greatest share of liberty among the nations of the world, was therefore also the most powerful. But with power came responsibility, to oneself and God, to use power for "ends of beneficence, to improve the condition of himself and his fellow men." Adams therefore wished the United States to be the premier nation in scientific and commercial advancement, to exceed France and Britain in the discovery of new knowledge and the exploration of the world. Here Adams's political views dovetailed with his personal ethics. Reared to be a conscientious national servant, he likewise listened to his father's injunction to attend his conscience first and foremost, "the minister plenipotentiary of God Almighty in your breast" (John Adams to John Quincy Adams, May 13, 1782; Bemis, 1949: 8). He improved himself through rigorous self-examination in his diary and constant schemes to make the most of his time. He would attempt to apply the same rigor to governing the nation (D.W. Howe, 1979: 43–68).

At first, despite his fragmented cabinet, Adams had some chance of success. His friend John W. Taylor of New York was elected Speaker of the House in 1825, ensuring some support for the administration in Congress; in the Senate, Calhoun was far less reliable, but due to the fragmentation of the 1824 presidential race, there was no concerted national opposition to Quincy Adams's program. Yet he immediately faced challenges to his authority, from two principal quarters: a sectional challenge from the South, where many saw his plans for national development as a threat to local prerogatives and slaveholder power, and a political challenge from the North, where democratic culture was in a state of foment and renewal. Newspaper editors and urban artisans, especially after the panic of 1819, began to develop a new attack on political and financial elites, updating old Jeffersonian arguments to contend with the dynamic market society of the North. Meanwhile, New York's Martin Van Buren, who had backed William Crawford in the 1824 election, schemed to find a way back to power by organizing a national political coalition that could unseat Adams. He worked to unite Northern egalitarians and Southern slaveholders, two otherwise discordant groups that found unity through ideological attacks on Adams's nationalist ambitions.

Dissidents North and South pilloried Adams's 1825 address as the idle dream of a Federalist aristocrat, a charge which Adams only encouraged with his foolish recommendation that Congress "not be palsied by the wills of our constituents." Adams was never a truly democratic character, and he had close ties to the economic and political elite of the Northeast. In later life, he wrote that government was founded on the representation of property as much as it was on persons; he was skeptical of abolishing imprisonment for debt, lest creditors be left in the lurch; and he was a friend of Nicholas Biddle and a strong supporter of the National Bank of the United States (Bemis, 1956: 252–257). Yet it would be wrong to cast him merely as the henchman of an "unconstrained capitalist state" (Sellers, 1991: 270). Adams viewed governmental institutions as public goods, and he envisioned economic development as part of a widespread movement of political and social "improvement," beneficial to nation and citizen alike (D.W. Howe, 2007: 244). Southern elites, some of the most economically and politically powerful men in the United States, rightly perceived in this program a threat to their interests. In a private letter to William Branch Giles, Jefferson condemned Adams's address as indicative of the federal government's trend "towards the usurpation of all the rights reserved to the states and the consolidation in itself of all powers foreign and domestic."[1] Anticipating such objections, both Clay and Barbour had recommended that Adams curtail the nationalizing tone of his first major address (Clay asked that he only recommend objects which were popular and guaranteed of success); while Wirt of Virginia, though he agreed with the president on almost every count, predicted that Adams would lose significant support in the Old Dominion, where he would be seen as an advocate of Patrick Henry's nightmare: "a great, magnificent, government." Only Richard Rush backed Adams wholeheartedly. In the end, Adams chose to deliver the address with minor modifications, casting political considerations aside. It was his "duty" to present his grand vision before Congress, said Adams, and he would rather say his piece in his first message, lest he die before having the chance to deliver another. And so, Adams concluded, "the perilous experiment must be made" (C.F. Adams, 1874–1877: 7.61–65).

Peril waited around almost every corner, but Adams faced his gravest difficulties in the South. Southerners had long had mixed feelings about national power – many supported the federal government when it served their interests, but a powerful minority remained skeptical about the role of the federal government and its potential threat to slavery. Their voices only became more strident after the Missouri crisis of 1819–1821. John Randolph of Roanoake enunciated the old fear in an 1824 speech opposing a national survey of roads and canals: "If Congress possesses the power to do what is proposed by this bill they may not only enact a sedition law – for there is precedent – *but they may emancipate every slave in the United States.*" (Bemis, 1956: 64). His friend Nathaniel Macon agreed: a national power to build canals was a clear precedent for abolishing slavery (Bemis, 1956; Sellers, 1991: 142). These minoritarian views were exacerbated by a sense of economic resentment, particularly in South Carolina, that was directed at the federal tariff, a tax on imported goods. During the War of 1812, merchants had shifted capital towards domestic manufacture given the pitfalls of international trade on hostile oceans. Simultaneously, artisans began to transition towards intensive production of goods for commercial exchange. The growth of manufacturing stoked demands for government protection, to ensure that domestic industry would not be undersold by foreign imports. The tariff found broad support across the North, as even New England shifted from mercantile to manufacturing pursuits, while the Western states backed protectionism because of self-interest in particular articles (hemp and raw wool) or because they believed in the economic promises of protection: a burgeoning home market for agricultural commodities and increased revenues for internal improvements (Sellers, 1991: 289–290). Quincy Adams had never been a defiant protectionist, but he followed the transition in New England, and saw the tariff as an important part of his program for national development (Hargreaves, 1985: 189–190). The South remained a region of opposition, especially as cotton prices bottomed out after the panic of 1819. Southerners blocked an 1820 increase in tariff rates, and Carolinian planters began to criticize the federal tariff as benefiting manufacturers far more than agricultural exporters like themselves. Men like Thomas Cooper, an English radical turned Pennsylvania democrat turned educator of the slaveholding gentry at South Carolina College, began to develop a concept of state's rights that would later support the movement to nullify federal tariff law. Calhoun, once an outspoken nationalist and ideologue of federally supported economic growth ("Let us conquer space," he famously implored, in support of internal improvements) soon followed Cooper's path to become the high priest of Southern dissent.

Such defiance was always deeply rooted in the political autarky that slaveholders demanded when it came to their chattels. Quincy Adams knew this well, from his years of service in the federal government and, most recently, from the diplomatic fallout from South Carolina's Negro Seaman Acts, passed while he was secretary of state. Contrived in response to Denmark Vesey's failed rebellion, the first Act required all free black seamen to be jailed while their ships were in port, which both trumped national law and caused an ongoing diplomatic crisis with Great Britain. According to South Carolina state senators, the right to defend themselves against potential slave insurrections was "paramount to all Laws, all Treaties, all Constitutions" (Hamer, 1935: 11). A judicial decision declaring the Acts unconstitutional in 1823 did little to check slaveholding prerogative, and although the controversy died down during Adams's presidency, it would return with fervor in the late 1820s (Hamer, 1935; Forbes, 2007: 155–173). Secretary of state Adams had likewise put himself at odds with slaveholders by agreeing to a treaty with Great Britain defining the slave trade as piracy (thereby allowing the British right of search on America vessels), which Southerners in the Senate effectively blocked (Fehrenbacher, 2001: 157–160). Adams had little patience for state's rights radicalism, and he expressed his frustration with South Carolina in his diary and in conversation with his secretary of war. But in public, he attempted to maintain the tone of neutrality he had developed through years of service to a nation where slavery was powerful and protected.

Adams was mostly silent on slavery matters during his presidency, although some men, like Calhoun, knew of the opinions he had expressed during the Missouri crisis, when he dreamt of the great moral cause of opposing slavery and the possibility of a Northern party devoted to that end. But Adams had openly supported the Missouri compromise, to the dismay of some of his Northern admirers, and he attempted to strike a similar politics of balance in his own administration. Yet even as most men in Washington attempted to ignore the subject, there was little doubt that the politics of slavery remained a crucial determinant of alliance and partisan conflict. Speaker of the House and Adams comrade John W. Taylor almost immediately offended Southern members when he presented to Congress a memorial from a crazed Frenchman, "who invited Congress to destroy all the States which should refuse the emancipation of slaves" (C.F. Adams, 1874–1877: 8.103–104). The fact that Taylor was the Northern leader during the Missouri crisis did not help his cause in Southern eyes. But this was a mere trifle – the sectional and partisan dispute escalated over the administration's plans to send two representatives to an inter-American conference at Panama, in order to build commercial and diplomatic relationships to newly independent Latin American states. In Congressional debate, South Carolina Senator Robert Hayne trumpeted Southern prerogative, claiming that slavery was a purely "domestic question" which could not be subject to question by non-slaveholding states or the federal government. To participate in an international congress which might address subjects such as the African slave trade or the independence of Haiti would be to wantonly sacrifice this right. Furthermore, said Hayne, the new Latin American nations contained "men of color" in their armies and legislatures, and Adams had recommended "an acknowledged abolitionist" (Pennsylvania's John Sergeant, who had fought for slavery restriction during the Missouri crisis) to represent the United States in Panama. The anti-Southern prejudice of the president could not be more clear.[2]

Hayne's protest was a typical piece of Carolinian posturing (if the federal government interfered with slavery, he warned, "we will consider ourselves as driven from the Union"), but it represented a wider threat. Hayne acted in collusion with Martin Van Buren, who opposed the mission on political grounds, as an example of executive overreach; other administration critics considered the conference a prelude to an entangling alliance and loss of neutrality and national autonomy. In other words, in the Panama congress, Van Buren had found an issue that could unite Southern slaveholders with Northerners skeptical of an activist federal government. Adams was well aware of the political stakes of the debate, noting in his diary that the Panama congress presented "the first measure in which the opposition are endeavoring to array themselves." He was mostly right that his antagonists were "bitter, and rancorous ... [and] discordant among themselves," but

Van Buren clearly had begun to carve a path to national power (Remini, 1959: 105–113; Wilentz, 2005: 261–62; C.F. Adams,1874–1877: 7.103).

In the end, Congress approved the mission to Panama, but it did so too late to be of any use. By the time Congress appropriated money to send delegates to the congress, the tropical fever season was underway, and John Sergeant held off departing until it had passed. The other representative, Richard Anderson of Kentucy, was already en route, but died on his way to Panama. So the United States did not end up participating in the congress at all; with only four nations in attendance, it became a non-event rather than the platform for inter-American unity that Adams and Clay had sought. The entire episode was a debacle of partisanship and fury. In Senate debates over the mission, John Randolph of Virginia had reissued charges about the corrupt bargain between Adams and Clay, who, he claimed, were now poised to lead the nation into a disastrous foreign entanglement. He termed the Adams–Clay partnership "the coalition between Bilfil and Black George, the combination, unheard of till then, of the puritan with the blackleg," a typically arcane insult referring simultaneously to Henry Fielding's *Tom Jones*, Adams's New England hauteur, and Clay's reputation as a gambler. The secretary of state challenged Randolph to a duel, and after formalities, the two met in early April, 1826, outside of Washington. They managed to avoid killing each other, although Randolph took a bullet through the coat. Honor restored, they shook hands and returned to Washington, to continue the political contest of the Adams presidency (Greenberg, 1996: ch. 3).

Dueling was a sign of Southern militance and power, an engagement between gentlemen that preserved their social and political authority. As Randolph put it, "there were cases where gentlemen must fight, like gentleman," lest "blackguards" seize the day. "Abolish dueling," he told his friend Joseph Nicholson, "& you encourage bullies as well in numbers as in degree, & lay every gentleman at the mercy of a cowardly pack of scoundrels. In fine, my good friend, the Yahoo must be kept down, by religion, sentiment, manners if you can – but he must be kept down."[3] Condescension and control thus defined the dueling gentleman as much as grit and violence. Andrew Jackson represented both sides of this Southern character, as the pre-eminent warrior and symbol of Southwestern expansion, which meant, above all, the expansion of slavery. He likewise expressed the violent character of the militant South – he fought Missouri senator Thomas Hart Benton in a vicious bar-room brawl; he ordered the execution of six deserters during the War of 1812; and he killed a man in a duel in 1806, after being hit in the chest by his opponent. "I should have hit him if he had shot me through the brain," Jackson reputedly said. As Benton warned South Carolina's Hayne, in the midst of the nullification crisis, "when Jackson begins to talk about hanging, they can look out for the ropes" (Freehling, 1990: 264, 278). To his opponents, Jackson's character as a slaveholder and a man of violence made him a dangerous choice for the presidency. Anti-dueling Northerners found the political atmosphere increasingly dangerous leading up to the election of 1828. In March of 1827, Quincy Adams noted "four or five challenges to duels, all of which, however, happily ended in smoke" (C.F. Adams, 1874–1877: 7.239); by November, Speaker Taylor was less (or more) sanguine: "slander and personal combat seem to be the order of the day," he told his wife, recording the deaths of two Southern politicians on the dueling ground. "I know not where these things will end."[4]

They ended, of course, with the election of Jackson, whose record of violence was embraced by his supporters as part of his militant patriotism. The stakes in this contest involved far more than simply the *code duello* – as events during the Adams presidency made clear, the election of 1828 depended on sectional tension over expansion, slaveholder power, and Indian removal, three key areas of expertise on Jackson's resume. This was most obvious in a dramatic showdown between the Adams administration and the state of Georgia. In February 1825, federal commissioners had signed a treaty known as the Treaty of Indian Springs with a section of the Creek tribe headed by William McIntosh, a cousin of Georgia governor George Troup, who had fought with Andrew Jackson during his wars against the Seminoles. Influenced in part by open bribery, McIntosh effectively signed away all the Creek land in the state of Georgia, as well as a good part of Alabama. The treaty was quickly ratified by the Senate, and signed by Adams during his first days in office. But when the treaty was discovered to be fraudulent (McIntosh and his key supporters were executed by decision of the Creek National Council), Adams worked to abrogate it and negotiate a new treaty with Creek representatives in Washington. Signed in January 1826, the Treaty of Washington modified the Creek cession to create a boundary line at the Chattahoochee River, leaving the Creeks a remnant of their Georgian homelands. It was far less than they wished for, but it was a far more legitimate treaty than the previous compact made at Indian Springs. Back in Georgia, Troup decided to defy the federal government, and send surveyors out to lay claim to Creek land under the Treaty of Indian Springs. He had maintained power in state politics by promising expansion through seizure of Native lands, and he was not about to sacrifice his chief point of popular appeal. (In Georgia, Indian dispossession was married frankly to white equality, as new lands were allotted by lottery to ordinary citizens.) Now Troup joined open resistance to the federal government to his plans for expansion by force and fraud. In response, Adams used firm language but resisted open conflict with Troup, turning over the matter to Congress with the promise that if Georgia persisted in resistance, "the arm of military force will be resorted to" (Green, 1982: 133). But in the end, Adams wanted the matter resolved and he was not prepared to take a firm stand for Creek rights. Nor was he willing to provoke armed conflict with the state militia of Georgia. Ultimately, a third treaty in 1827 ceded all the remaining Creek lands in Georgia. Adams's patient resistance to Troup ensured that Georgia would turn against him in the ensuing election, while Jackson would come to embody the Southern demand for universal Indian removal. Jackson was no admirer of Troup and he thought the Treaty of Indian Springs a fraud, but he had forced punitive treaties on the Southwestern Indians after the War of 1812, and his national reputation was built on his career as frontier warrior. Georgians certainly saw Jackson as representing their best interests, and he swept the state in the election of 1828 (Green 1982; Wilentz, 2005: 262–265; D.W. Howe, 2007: 256).

Adams was not a friend to Native peoples – he thought that the North American continent (all of it, including Canada and Mexico) was the "proper dominion" of the United States, by a fixed law of nature (C.F. Adams, 1874–1877: 4.438–439) In cabinet discussions over the Creek issue, Henry Clay took a racist tack, declaring that Native Americans were "destined to extinction," and that they would simply be replaced by a superior Anglo-Saxon people. "They were not an improvable breed," he declared "and their disappearance from the human family will be no great loss to the world." In private, Adams thought that Clay's views might be correct, but in public, he decided that backing Georgia would amount to "gross injustice." Secretary of war Barbour suggested acquiescing to Troup in order not to lose support in Georgia; Adams characteristically threw such political questions out the window (C.F. Adams, 1874–1877: 7.89–92). Yet it was unclear where he stood personally on the question of Indian removal. He was an expansionist who had backed some of Andrew Jackson's more rash campaigns, and he subscribed to a prevailing theory of civilization in which nomadic "savages" gave way to civilized agriculturalists (Bemis, 1956: 84). But despite joining the growing racial consensus of his day on some matters, John Quincy Adams also questioned American Indian policy in retrospect, and determined that the United States had treated Native Americans extremely poorly. At the very least, he objected to Troup's willful actions, which, like South Carolina's before him, openly asserted a state sovereignty beyond federal control.

Southern sectionalism was thus alive and well throughout Adams's presidency, as it had been since the formation of the United States back in 1776. But it was not, by itself, powerful enough to unseat Adams or deter his entire agenda. In the election of 1828, the South held only 40 percent of the national electoral vote, "seemingly a hopelessly minority share" (Freehling, 1990: 261). A national presidential candidate required cross-sectional appeal in order to achieve victory. If Adams could maintain Northern support comparable to the reliable Southern backing for presidents Jefferson, Madison, and Monroe, he could presumably maintain office. Yet Adams faced an even more difficult problem in the North. It was arguably twofold, rooted in his inability to articulate a populist appeal and his frank unwillingness to play pragmatic politics in order to advance his own cause. The generic portrait of

Adams as a curmudgeonly man with few social skills has been overdrawn, but he did have some obvious limitations. When asked to appear in public, he typically refused, and he found the countless personal interactions required of his office a thankless task. A characteristic lament: "the succession of visitors from my breakfasting to my dining hour, with their variety of objects and purposes, is inexpressibly distressing" (C.F. Adams, 1874–1877: 7.200–201). Finally, despite possessing a rhetorical (and, arguably, a literary) power far greater than his predecessors or opponents, he found himself consistently humiliated in public for his oratorical gaffes. His constituents, it may be said, were often palsied with laughter at his expense. His grand call for national astronomical observatories, "lighthouses of the skies," was mocked as a foolish and absurd request for "lighthouses *in* the skies." On one public occasion, Adams managed to demonstrate his capacity for popular appeal. At the ceremonial opening of the Chesapeake and Ohio Canal on July 4, 1828, he at first struggled to remove a shovelful of earth when his spade hit a root. Stripping off his jacket, he dug with renewed intensity as the crowd cheered (Bemis, 1956: 102). The scene reflected his mettle and stubborn commitment, qualities which would endear him to New England (and render him anathema to the South) in his post-presidential years. But such moments were all too few during his presidency, and they were often countered by Adams's tendency to appear condescending, disinterested in popularity, and unfortunately awkward.

At a celebration in Baltimore the previous fall, Adams rose to give a toast in honor of the military exploits of American militiamen during the War of 1812. "Ebony and Topaz," he proclaimed, "General Ross's coat of arms and the Republican militiamen who gave it." The audience was mystified, as were those who heard of the toast secondhand. Martin Van Buren wondered whether the president was referring to the slave and the free states, and noted that the president was "fond of obscure but bitter allusions." As Adams explained to his audience, he was making an allusion to a work by Voltaire, identifying the British general Ross with Ebony, or the spirit of evil, and the militiamen with the good, symbolized by topaz. Even on explanation, no one quite understood him – but the fact that he had to add instruction to what should have been a simple rousing salutation indicates the substantial limitations on Adams's charismatic powers (Bemis, 1956: 101). He was aware of his own weaknesses, remarking straightforwardly in his diary that his election to the presidency had not occurred "in a manner satisfactory to pride or to just desire," since he had not received an electoral majority. "Perhaps two-thirds of the whole people," Adams estimated (with just a hint of resentment) were "adverse to the actual result. Nearly one year of this service has already passed, with little change of the public opinions or feelings" (C.F. Adams, 1874–1877: 7.97–98). In a popularity contrast with "Old Hickory," "Old Ebony" (a sarcastic moniker employed by opposition editors) was at a distinct disadvantage.

The irony, of course, was that slaveholders like Jackson, whose lives were founded on power, authority, and control, appeared as egalitarian heroes, while the much more ordinary and far less imperious Adams was cast as an insufferable elitist. John Randolph of Roanoke, who likewise turned towards the arcane in his speechmaking (usually to berate his opponents rather than champion American patriotism) and who was, by the 1820s, a consistent opponent of democracy, could still treat Adams as the scion of a New England monarchy. "I bore some humble part in putting down the dynasty of John the First," he declared, "and by the Grace of God, I hope to aid in putting down the dynasty of John the Second" (Bemis, 1956: 132). The paradox of being charged with aristocratic tendencies by a raving slaveholder must have been galling, yet Adams did little to help his own cause. Like his father during the 1790s, he was mostly disconnected from the new egalitarian political movements in the antebellum North. In John Adams's day, Jeffersonian democrats had turned against a New England president because of their opposition to the Alien and Sedition laws and Federalist distrust of democracy. In Quincy Adams's time, ideologues like Pennsylvania's Stephen Simpson updated these old Jeffersonian arguments by focusing their ire on economic power in addition to political hierarchy. Simpson, a protégé of the Jeffersonian printer William Duane, helped spark the Jackson movement in 1824, and he would define one of the critical issues of Jacksonian democracy in the urban North: the exploitative power of an emerging capitalist class, and the evils of a national banking system, particularly the Bank of the United States, based in Philadelphia (Wilentz, 2005: 210–213, 245–247, 282–287; Phillips, 1989: 548–589). To such men and their supporters, Adams, with his quasi-Hamiltonian vision of economic development (not to mention his hesitation about abolishing imprisonment for debt) had little to offer, beyond bourgeois promises that the American System would secure manufacturing jobs and a bountiful domestic economy for all. So, as had been the case in the 1790s, Northern democrats looked southward for a political hero to realize their egalitarian dreams.

There was one obvious area where Adams could have spoken plainly in a populist vein: as a Christian. Portraits of Adams as a hackneyed Puritan, then and since, are very mistaken. In his religious reflections, Adams expressed a due respect for providence, and he was a firm advocate of self-control, but he was above all an Arminian who had a very open sense of religious faith. Like Jefferson, he was skeptical of the miracles in the Bible, but he believed that it had an "irresistible power over the heart." He constantly read the Bible and biblical commentaries, and he attended multiple sermons on the sabbath. He had little patience with a Calvinist insistence on inevitable human perfidy, which "degrades men in their own estimation" (C.F. Adams, 1874–1877: 7.268). His latent antislavery views, his belief in human progress, and his firm Christian faith made Adams an ideal candidate for a growing evangelical constituency across the North. With the subsequent rise of the anti-masonic movement, Adams had an obvious opportunity to connect his developmental policies to a popular upsurge in New York state, a critical locale in the looming election of 1828. After one William Morgan was kidnapped and likely murdered by freemasons in upstate New York because he threatened to reveal the secrets of the order, a powerful social and political movement sought to expose and uproot masonic influence on American life. The young Thurlow Weed supported the anti-masonic cause as part of a wider movement to challenge Martin Van Buren's power in New York state, building connections that would later sustain the Whig and Republican parties. Andrew Jackson, a masonic grandmaster, eventually became a target of the anti-masons, suggesting the possibility of using anti-masonic paranoia to energize a national populist campaign. Adams did eventually affiliate with the movement, as a gubernatorial candidate in Massachusetts after his retirement from the presidency. But during his presidential years, he kept his distance (in part because Henry Clay was himself a high-ranking mason), and he never developed strong relationships to Weed. His inability to use the anti-masonic movement to his advantage reflected his reticence as a popular politician and his frequent inability to seize a pragmatic political opportunity (Wilentz, 2005: 272–280; D.W. Howe, 2007: 266–270).

Adams's aloofness towards Weed was a grave mistake, because Van Buren was not to be trifled with. Had Adams held New York, he might have had a chance of building an electoral coalition to challenge Jackson in 1828. Instead, the "Little Magician" won a far too easy victory. From the beginning of the Adams administration, Van Buren sought to develop a national opposition party that could challenge the president and eventually bring Jackson, and Van Buren himself, to power. In the first place, he would have to work to bring together the disparate sections of the Republican party that had been divided in 1824. In the South, this entailed an alliance between men loyal mostly to Crawford's old Republicanism, Calhoun's complex blend of nationalism and emerging sectionalism, and Jackson's aggressive and popular Southwestern patriotism. Nationally, it meant, as he told Crawford supporter and Virginia editor Thomas Ritchie in January 1827, an alliance between "the planters of the South and the plain Republicans of the North." For Van Buren too, the election of 1828 would bring about a return to Jeffersonian principles. But he was less interested in an ideological conflict between "aristocracy" and "democracy" than he was in a partisan alignment that would stabilize national political competition and keep threatening sectional issues off the table. Not all Southerners supported Van Buren's agenda. In South Carolina, elite slaveholders and ideologues had commenced a retreat from Republican nationalism to Southern sectionalism; by 1832, they would openly challenge the charismatic leader of Van Buren's coalition, Andrew Jackson. But in combination with Jackson's personal popularity and reliable Southern roots, many saw the Jackson movement as an artful way to protect slavery from democratic challenge and return the South to a preponderant position in national politics (R. Brown, 1966; L.L. Richards, 2001).

To deliver the North, Van Buren first of all had to consolidate power in New York, where the intricacies of state politics bedeviled men at the time and historians since. Going into the election of 1824, his Bucktail adherents had temporarily lost power by blocking the popular election of New York's presidential electors, in order to control the state's votes for Van Buren's candidate, Crawford. In addition, a Bucktail supporter foolishly stripped DeWitt Clinton of his title as a commissioner of the Erie Canal, the central achievement of his tenure as governor of New York. These combined injustices gave rise to the People's Party, a movement that sought to drive Van Buren's men from the legislature, support popular government, and restore Clinton to power. With James Tallmadge, instigator of the Missouri crisis, running as Clinton's lieutenant's governor, the movement had a clear sectional edge, and it succeeded wonderfully in state elections in 1824. The bulk of New York's electoral vote went to Adams, as Clintonians joined Adams men in opposition to Van Buren. There was a natural affinity between Adams's and Clinton's objectives: Clinton's Erie Canal was the signal transportation project of the era, a powerful example of the economic power of internal improvements. His presidential campaign back in 1812 had suggested the possibility of realigning national politics so that the expanding commercial society of the North became the political center of gravity, rather than Virginia and the slave states of the South. But Clinton was infamously fickle, shifting allegiances when it suited his purpose, and he had long admired Andrew Jackson. Van Buren played on this weakness by running an Adams man against Clinton for the governorship in 1826. Clinton saw Adams as behind the plot, and struck back at Adams candidates, including Speaker John W. Taylor (C.F. Adams, 1874–1877: 7.146). Dissension between the Clintonian and Adams forces left a clear path for Van Buren to take power in New York. The political situation remained confusing, as Clinton was soon openly backing Jackson's election in 1828, and thus supporting the candidate of his arch-rival, Van Buren. But this difficulty was soon alleviated by Clinton's death, leaving Van Buren in command (D.W. Howe, 2007: 237–241; Remini, 1959: 119–122, 167–169).

Van Buren exercised his power at the national level in the Speakership contest of 1827 in the House of Representatives. The mid-term elections had returned a Congress with a majority opposed to the president for the first time in American political history. "We are defeated," Speaker Taylor wrote to his wife; "about 20 of the New York members voted against me."[5] The anti-Adams coalition elected Andrew Stevenson of Virginia as Speaker, and he filled congressional committees with men opposed to the administration, including John Randolph of Roanoke, who had returned to the House after losing his Senate seat. Van Buren could now check the administration for the next two years, while he campaigned to bring Jackson into power. Quincy Adams should not have lost control of New York so easily. Lieutenant Governor James Tallmadge wrote frequently to his friend Taylor to ask Adams to take a firmer hand in building support within the state, but to no avail. Weed, who had helped catalyze the anti-masonic movement, likewise reached out to Adams unsuccessfully. These rebuffs were of a piece with Adams's refusal to use patronage to bolster his own cause. The Philadelphia printer John Binns asked the president to remove officers he considered hostile to the administration, but Adams demurred, and said he would remove "no public officer for merely preferring another candidate for the presidency." Binns later complained that "the Administration does not support its friends." Clay likewise suggested "confining henceforth appointments to our friends," but Adams was "averse to giving any public pledge" on such matters. He was not uniformly objective in granting appointments – nepotism counted in his administration as it had in previous ones, and he did take into account partisanship on occasion. Yet overall, he attempted to remain remarkably neutral when it came to political loyalties, even as other officers, particularly John McLean, used their appointment powers to work against the administration. According to one estimate, he only ever removed twelve federal officers during his presidency (Spann, 1957: 352–355; C.F. Adams, 1874–1877: 7.154–155, 163–164, 262, 257; Hargreaves, 1985: 50–61).

In many ways, Adams had given up on re-election long before 1828. When his father died on July 4, 1826, Adams entered a prolonged period of self-reflection, pondering the purpose of his life and his eventual mortality. He began to make plans for his eventual retirement from public life, and his own death. "The duty of weaning myself from the world and all which it inherits is that which impressed itself most forcibly upon my mind," he wrote, "not without the consciousness of my own frailty, and of the need of assistance and support from the Spirit of Truth." He decided to maintain his father's house as a "safe and pleasant retreat" for the future, and he officially joined the local church in Quincy. "My fathers for nearly two centuries have been members of this church," Adams told himself. "My purpose is, if my life should be spared till the end of my term of public service, to return and be gathered to my fathers here." On a visit to Massachusetts that summer, John W. Taylor informed Adams that Clinton was breaking with the administration in New York. The information should have called Adams into battle, but instead he responded by noting that New York was "utterly uncertain, and my only course is to prepare for retirement, as I hope I am now doing." Later proffers of reconciliation from men close to Clinton were mostly ignored; Adams decided that "it is my duty to link myself to the fortunes of no man." He was right to give Clinton a wide berth, but doing so at the expense of his own fortunes in New York state left him vulnerable as the presidential election approached. To judge by the tone of his diary, Adams both knew this and did not much care (C.F. Adams, 1874–1877: 7.128–129, 146–147, 184–186).

Adams even lost ground on his own key issues: economic development, commercial expansion, and internal improvements. His trade policy was hamstrung by a dispute with Great Britain over American access to British territories in the West Indies; after a British decision to bar American merchants, trade plummeted in 1827 and 1828, leading to partisan attacks against Adams for limiting American commerce. Adams was more successful in promoting internal improvements, and he expanded the nation's network of roads and canals throughout his presidency. But he could only obtain Congressional support for individual projects, since his original vision for a national system of internal improvements never gained widespread political support. Major projects, like the Chesapeake and Ohio canal, likewise failed to achieve the ambitious goals of the administration: by the time it was finally completed, it had been surpassed by the Baltimore and Ohio Railroad (although today the old canal path is a national historical park, an appropriate testament to Adams's ideological vision). Adams's plan for national development depended on a scientific attitude towards internal improvements, connected to the expansion of knowledge and the rational sale of public lands. These measures were met with skepticism, as Congress blocked plans for a national university and a naval academy, and refused to expand funding for the army engineering corps. Meanwhile, Westerners, led by Thomas Hart Benton, challenged Adams's land policy, by demanding lower prices for land sales and protection of squatter's rights. All of this dissension ensured that Adams would never build an integrated national network of internal improvements (D.W. Howe, 2007: 254, 367–368; Bemis, 1956: 75, 78).

When it came to tariff protection and economic development, Adams was once again outflanked by Van Buren. With eloquent spokesmen, like Matthew Carey and Hezekiah Niles, the tariff seemed like an issue on which the administration could build support, particularly in Pennsylvania, New York, and the Northwest. In 1827, tariff supporters, backed by Clay, held a convention at Harrisburg, Pennsylvania in support of protection. Van Buren's response was to engineer the infamous "Tariff of Abominations" in 1828, which raised rates on articles essential in Mid-Atlantic and Western states to protect producers, while likewise raising rates on products crucial to New England manufacturers, to punish Adams supporters. The bill did little for the South, calculated to be safely in Jackson's hands, and last-minute modifications ensured enough Yankee support to get the bill through Congress and obtain Adams's signature. Now Jacksonians in the Mid-Atlantic and the West could claim that they had backed protection to benefit their constituents, while counting on Jacksonians in the South to continue to attack Adams as a protectionist opposed to Southern interests. Had Adams opposed the bill, he would have lost ground with protectionist constituencies, while gaining next to nothing from the South, where distrust of New England ran deep. Van Buren's political genius was arguably never on better display (D.W. Howe, 2007: 274–275; Remini, 1959: 148–155, 170–185).

Despite Adams's resignation, and the seemingly invincible combination of Jackson's charisma and Van Buren's cunning, the election of 1828 was bitterly fought. Clay used what power he could to support printers in favor of the administration, who lashed out at Jackson. Adams himself remained relatively aloof from campaigning, as did Jackson. Adams had earlier maligned opposition editors, like Duff Green of the *United States Telegraph*, who "work by slander to vitiate the public opinion, and pay for defamation, to receive their reward in votes" (C.F. Adams, 1874–1877: 7.262). But such high-mindedness did not dictate a chaste campaign, as the election of 1828 was marked by scurrility and scandal on both sides. Adams was libeled as a pimp for Tsar Alexander of Russia, Jackson as a murderous, adulterous, half-breed son of a prostitute. The turn towards personal slander reflected both the rampant growth in partisanship and the partisan press since 1824 – electoral turnout was more than four times greater than in the previous election – but it also filled a vacuum created by Jackson's tendency to campaign on generalities ("reform" was his central message) and Quincy Adams's tendency not to campaign at all.

Historians continue to see Jackson and Van Buren's triumph as heralding the rise of democracy in the United States, even if they are more and more willing to acknowledge the powerful racial and gender limitations that made the Jacksonian polity what it was. Yet the Tennessee general and slaveholder remains the icon for his age, as Jefferson was before him, while Van Buren is persistently cast as the principal innovator of democratic politics. There is merit to such notions, since Jackson did triumph in 1828, and Van Buren did create the political realignment that resulted in the Second Party System. But Adams would not go down quietly, and after his return to Congress in the 1830s, he repeatedly challenged Jacksonian democracy, by assaulting the "slave power" in the United States government. In doing so, he helped begin an even longer-term realignment in the American political system, one that would eventually create a national political party devoted not, like Van Buren's Democratic party, to maintaining slavery, but to restraining and, eventually, destroying it.

That Adams returned to Washington at all, after a fairly devastating loss in 1828, was remarkable. That he returned to become an outspoken critic of Southern slavery reflected a powerful personal transformation from a centrist, neutral, nationalist president into a moral advocate who would always speak his mind. Since the beginning of his political career, John Quincy Adams had devoted himself to fulfilling what he saw as the destiny of the United States: to become a large and powerful nation, expanding until it became the preponderant power in the western hemisphere and a rival to Great Britain and other European states. Such ambitions caused

Quincy Adams to break with New England Federalism early in his career, so that by the time he assumed the presidency, he was a confirmed nationalist. But his patriotism had a dark side – most obviously, in his willingness to sanction Indian removal and cultural genocide to the benefit of American power. In a more complex way, nationalism proved a check on Quincy Adams's antislavery sentiments and his firm belief, which took form during his first years in national politics, that slaveholding power was the principal check on the expansion of political equality in the United States. He was more than willing to accommodate slavery when it served his vision of the national interest. But national development, Quincy Adams claimed, had died during his presidency, brought down by "the Sable Genius of the South." Henceforth, he noted bitterly in 1837, "The American Union as a moral person in the family of Nations, is to live from hand to mouth, to cast away, instead of using for the improvement of its own condition, the bounties of Providence" (Bemis, 1956: 150–151). Consumed with resentment, Adams overlooked perhaps the most salutary outcome of his defeat: the failure of his nationalist platform left him free to fulfill the mission he had articulated during the Missouri crisis, "to lay bare in all its nakedness that outrage upon the goodness of God, human slavery." He spent his final years working with like-minded colleagues to reorient American politics against Van Buren's Democratic coalition, in order to create a new Union, founded not on slavery but "on the fundamental principle of emancipation" (C.F. Adams, 1874–1877: 4.524–525, 531) He failed as a president, in the end, because he could not agree with the nation over which he presided. Unable and unwilling to retire quietly, he returned to Washington to make a better one.

Notes

1 Thomas Jefferson to William Branch Giles, Dec. 26, 1825, Jefferson Papers, Library of Congress.
2 *Register of Debates*, 19th Cong. 1st Sess. Senate, 165–166.
3 Randolph to Joseph Nicholson, June 24, 1811, Joseph Nicholson Papers, Library of Congress.
4 John Taylor to Jane Taylor, Nov. 29, 1827, Taylor Papers, New York Historical Society.
5 John Taylor to Jane Taylor, Dec. 3, 1827, Taylor Papers, New York Historical Society.

Guide to Further Reading

Robert V. Remini has written a good popular history of John Quincy Adams's presidency: *John Quincy Adams* (New York, 2002). Biographies of Adams include Paul C. Nagel, *John Quincy Adams: A Public Life, A Private Life* (New York, 1997) and Lynn H. Parsons, *John Quincy Adams* (Madison, 1998). To understand the ongoing historiographical conflict over the Adams years, readers should compare the accounts in Wilentz (2005), Sellers (1991), and Howe (2007) cited throughout the text. Finally, the *Memoirs*, correspondence, and writings of John Quincy Adams make for excellent reading. In addition to the published version of the *Memoirs* edited by Charles Francis Adams, one can consult the original pages of John Quincy Adams's diary thanks to the Massachusetts Historical Society. (Online at www.masshist.org/jqadiaries/, accessed Nov. 17, 2012.) A selection of Quincy Adams's correspondence and writings can be found in *Writings of John Quincy Adams*, ed. Worthington Chauncey Ford, 7 vols. (New York, 1913–1917).

Chapter Seventeen

John Quincy Adams, Internal Improvements, and the Nation State

Sean Patrick Adams

John Quincy Adams made several decisions which did not have the intended result over the course of his long political career; within his first year out of the presidency his run of bad luck continued. As many popular accounts of the American railroad industry are eager to point out, President Adams did not attend the ceremony opening the Baltimore and Ohio (B&O) Railroad on July 4,1828. Instead, the last remaining signer of the Declaration of Independence, Maryland's Charles Carroll, broke ground on the project. Adams turned over the first shovel of dirt on another Maryland endeavor, the Chesapeake and Ohio (C&O) Canal, on the same day that Carroll ceremoniously launched the B&O. Both projects aspired to link their respective cities – Washington, DC,and Baltimore – to the Ohio River. The C&O, in many ways, was a perfect symbol for the Adams administration. It blended federal, state, municipal, and private funding all together with the aim of integrating the federal district with the growing markets of the American West. George Washington himself had originally conceived of the plan, thus giving a Potomac–Ohio waterway the symbolic imprimatur of the founding generation. When President Adams championed the general notion of "improvement" across a number of areas and wanted to channel federal administrative and financial support for its progress, then the C&O could serve as a physical monument to that ideal. The B&O, on the other hand, represented a riskier approach to transportation. Not only were railroads a brand new technology, prone to breakdowns and organizational hurdles, but they also were expensive. The promoters of the B&O drew upon state and municipal funding for their venture, but did not carry the venerable ties

A Companion to John Adams and John Quincy Adams, First Edition.
Edited by David Waldstreicher.

nor the faith that the C&O enjoyed at its onset. A betting person would have placed their money, just like President Adams offered the gravitas of his office, on the future of the Chesapeake and Ohio.

This anecdote appears from time to time in the pages of history; more often than not it is used to illustrate the fallacies of conventional wisdom, the strange twists of history, or more specifically, the shortcomings of John Quincy Adams. We all know how the story turned out: the B&O reached the Ohio River in 1852 and from there blossomed into one of the most influential and powerful railroad corporations in American history. The C&O only made it to Cumberland, Maryland and although it saw quite a bit of coal traffic along its nineteenth-century waterway, the canal is now better known for providing excellent hiking and biking trails run by the National Park Service than its contributions to the American economy. The story fits into a powerful narrative of transportation history as well. Railroads replaced canals, which had replaced turnpikes, which had replaced cart paths. The march of progress moved on and Americans continued to move goods and people across their vast nation with ever increasing speed and efficiency by 1860. This is the vision of internal improvements put forward in George Rogers Taylor's sweeping history entitled *The Transportation Revolution, 1815–1860* (1951). "No longer were more than nine tenths of American agriculture and industry concentrated within a narrow strip extending no farther inland than a hundred miles from the Atlantic coast," Taylor proclaims of 1860, "nor was dependence upon foreign trade and European markets the almost universal characteristic of the economy." Instead, Taylor asserts, internal improvements "had resulted in the creation of a new and really national economic orientation." (G.R. Taylor, 1951: 396)

But the contrast between the C&O and the B&O offers more than a quaint story about the grand sweep of technology or the foibles of historical actors; the history of internal improvements, moreover, did not always follow the whiggish path outlined by Taylor's vision. It provides a real contrast that moves beyond the actual projects themselves and reveals a larger struggle that gripped the EarlyAmericanrepublic. What role would the federal and state governments play in economic development? Would cooperation or competition provide the driving force behind internal improvements? This chapter will attempt to shed light on these questions and others using the story of internal improvements policy during the era of John Quincy Adams. The choice between the C&O and the B&O, it argues, is not a quaint reminder of the quirks of history, but instead stood for more momentous questions of political economy that private entrepreneurs and public policymakers grappled with throughout the Early American republic. Would federal or state authorities actively direct a national transportation system in the United States? Or would government institutions leave initiative and execution to private actors? The contrast between a state-dominated command economy and a laissez-faire one is a false dichotomy, of course, as American historians have been careful to note elements of both public and private initiative at work throughout the history of American political economy. But as the distribution and responsibility for internal improvements policy danced among federal, state, municipal, and private actors, the responsibility for building a turnpike or digging a canal came to represent more than simply who would pay for the nation's transportation network. Instead the locus of "improvement" was no less than a struggle to determine the future course of American political economy. John Larson's 2001 study emphasizes the political conflicts that accompanied the growth of internal improvements in the early republic, as evident in the extended title, *Internal Improvement: National Public Works and the Promise of Popular Government in the Early United States.* Whereas Taylor depicted a national identity and economy fused together by roads, canals, and rails, Larson describes the many false starts and empty promises provided by federal and state authorities struggling with the implications of state coordination upon a republican society. "The problem that a system of internal improvements always raised was the specter of consolidation;" he argues, "the vision that so exercised its enemies was the rise of a design that could shape, limit, and control the prospects – the liberties – of freemen in states, villages, and farmsteads across the country" (J.L. Larson, 2001: 253).

So, when John Quincy Adams maintained in 1825 that, "no government, in whatever form constituted, can accomplish the lawful ends of its institution but in proportion as it improves the condition of those over whom it is established," he signaled a particular view of state action. "Roads and canals," he continued, "by multiplying and facilitating the communications and intercourse between distant regions and multitudes of men, are among the most important means of improvement" (Richardson, 1897: 311). By fusing the idea of coordinated government action in the service of "improvement" to the physical project of building a transportation system in the United States, the second President Adams articulated a vision that would become one of the most controversial themes in the history of American political economy. As generations of historians have discovered, the debates over internal improvements hinted towards larger discussions of the appropriate balance between public and private actors in the American economy; this debate continues today long after the individual roads and canals themselves faded into history.

John Quincy Adams was not the first chief executive to demonstrate passion for internal improvements; President George Washington promoted them both before and during his time in the office. Consider, for example, that in one of the discarded elements of his famous – and famously brief – First Inaugural Address, Washington encouraged publically funded internal improvements. This endorsement didn't make it into the final version of the address, but it is illustrative in revealing Washington's thoughts on the matter. "While the individual States shall be occupied in facilitating the means of transportation, by opening canals & improving roads," he nearly declared in 1789, "you will not forget that the purposes of business & Society may be vastly promoted by giving cheapness, dispatch & security to communications through the regular Posts" (Crackel, 2008: 158). Washington's vision of a national network of roads and canals began, not surprisingly, with his enthusiastic support of two private canal companies that would benefit his native Virginia: the Potomac Company and the James River Company. Both of these firms sought to link the tidewater regions of the east with the emerging markets of the west. The Potomac project would tie Virginia, Maryland, and even Pennsylvania interests together in the prospect while the James River Canal provided a potential avenue from Richmond to the Ohio River that lay completely within the boundaries of the Old Dominion. Both endeavors faced major physical hurdles, as they sought to carve waterways out of mountainous terrain at a time when canal technology was in its infancy. But more central to the story of John Quincy Adams and his notion of "improvement" were the political tensions inherent as far back as Washington's pet projects. Assuming that public money would be committed in some form to the construction of these canals, could Maryland, Virginia, and Pennsylvania interests act in concert to support the Potomac Company? Conversely, why would any actor outside of Virginia – public or private – show enthusiasm for a project contained within the boundaries of a single state? The answer to the first query lay in the federal government, while the key to the second seemed to place the responsibility for internal improvements into the hands of individual states. This divided responsibility for coordinating, financing, and constructing internal-improvement projects proved a thorny problem in the age of Washington, John Adams, and beyond.

First, let us consider the issue of federal responsibility. Many Early American policymakers shared Washington's private enthusiasm for federally supported transportation networks, but like the jettisoned portion of his First Inaugural, internal improvements fell by the wayside amidst wider ideological struggles to clarify what was "necessary and proper" under the newly ratified constitution. Some national economic institutions, like Alexander Hamilton's Bank of the United States, emerged from this early battle; a federally directed program of roads and canals did not. It is perhaps tempting to sort internal improvements, like the federal excise tax or the Bank of the United States, into the Federalist–Republican dichotomy. But this would not be accurate. John Larson's thoughtful and provocative (2001) look at the early history of internal improvements depicts most early American policymakers as sold on the idea of water and land transportation projects. These could link farmers to markets, bring isolated Western regions into the political fold of the nation, and offer new opportunities for the American economy. Even Thomas Jefferson, he notes, "enthusiastically embraced the concept of internal improvement: the hand of enterprise must intervene to keep opportunities unfolding according to nature's implicit design" (J.L. Larson, 2001: 41). Instead, the method and scope of these projects proved to be the stumbling block for early debates in the federal government. Republicans in Congress – and Jefferson himself once he ascended to the presidency in 1801 – applied a kind of wholesale skepticism toward Federalist programs. But the idea of an "American system," in which the federal government provided oversight and financial support for roads and canals, emerged from young Republicans like Kentucky's Henry Clay and South Carolina's John Calhoun. It is difficult, therefore, to use party affiliation or region as an accurate predictor of a politician's support of or resistance to federally funded improvements. As a senator from Massachusetts, for example, young John Quincy Adams supported the "American system," even as he broke partisan ranks with his father's Federalist roots.

The early history of federally supported internal-improvement networks is one of fits and starts. Federal authorities did plan, fund, and construct some postal roads and continued to allocate federal funds to assist turnpikes and canals during the early republic. For the most part, though, wholesale attempts to coordinate a national system failed. The postal system, for example, relied heavily on private contractors to build and maintain mail routes. Postal officials sometimes allocated additional funds to contractors for road maintenance, but this hardly constituted a strong guiding hand. The National Road was a federally planned and funded turnpike that would ultimately stretch from Baltimore to St Louis. The first major section connecting Cumberland, MD, and Wheeling, VA, opened in 1818 and the National Road reached Columbus, Ohio, by 1833. But the author of a recent study of the project argues that it "became an anachronism" and fell victim to "constitutional issues and sectional rivalries," and eventually was "overtaken by technology before America completed it" (J. Wood, 1996: 121). The federal coordination of water and land transportation projects also floundered in the early republic. In 1808 the secretary of treasury Albert Gallatin responded to President Thomas Jefferson's inquires about public improvements with a $20 million plan to integrate the eastern seaboard in a system of intercoastal waterways and cross the Appalachian Mountains with federally funded roads – the National Road was to be an important part of this national system. Gallatin's ambitious plan fell by the wayside during the War of 1812, but National Republicans led a second charge to fund a national system of internal improvements with the money coming in from the Second Bank of the United States following its charter in 1816. Known commonly as the "Bonus Bill," it was championed by a figure not commonly associated with a strong federal hand in the affairs of everyday life. South Carolina's John C. Calhoun, who later would be more skeptical of federal action, was among the National Republicans leading the charge to use the bank bonus in order to "bind the Republic together with a perfect system of roads and canals" (Peterson, 1988: 79). The Bonus Bill passed Congress, but President James Madison vetoed it. "National purpose drifted dangerously," John Larson (2001: 69) writes of the fallout from Madison's veto, "while the kind of minimal caretaker governments promised by the Spirit of '98 struggled to meet the demands of a changing world."

Without federal support, then, the impetus for constructing transportation projects in the Early American republic fell largely into the hands of individual states and private investors.This was not necessary a startling transition. In turnpike construction, for example, private capital had been long at work. Turnpikes usually provided an immediate benefit to communities along their routes, although profit margins proved notoriously thin for most turnpike companies. For this reason, state authorities generously bestowed corporate charters on investors willing to construct roads. When federal authorities debated Gallatin's plan, states had already chartered nearly 400 private turnpike firms. In states like Pennsylvania, Andrew Schocket (2007) argues, the reluctance of state authorities to fund internal improvements in the 1800s and 1810s led to great consolidations of corporate power and influence. "The larger the corporation, the less its supporters asked of the Pennsylvania legislature," Schocket argues, "and the more fiercely it guarded its financial independence from public authorities" (Schocket, 2007: 147). Once improvements to rivers and canals entered the picture, the need for well-capitalized ventures increased; yet profitability still remained elusive. In his comparative study of internal improvements in Pennsylvania and Virginia, John Majewski cites the importance of "developmental corporations," which "successfully mediated economic self-interest with community norms"in the construction of early transportation projects in both states (Majewski, 2000: 57). Although Majewski ultimately judges these entities incapable of raising the vast amounts of capital necessary to build railroads – hence Pennsylvania's later success in the endeavor and Virginia's failure – the "developmental corporation" provided a politically palatable solution to an economic challenge. The need for vast amounts of capital to excavate land, construct locks and loading facilities, and maintain waterways pushed most canal projects outside of the private sector's capacity. Corporations could not build an extensive canal system on their own.

Without the federal government to coordinate the nation's networks of roads and canals, state governments jumped into projects with a different sense of purpose. For example, policymakers in Virginia created a Board of Public Works in 1816 to support the construction of roads and canals in the Old Dominion. The board would support various projects through the commitment of state funds to purchase stock in existing ventures, blending public and private initiative in order to build an intrastate network of improvements. The jewel for ambitious Virginians, however, remained the east–west connection between tidewater and the Ohio River, the thoroughfare envisioned by George Washington that had long floundered in private hands. By 1820, Virginia's General Assembly committed state resources to an improved waterway along the James River, across the Appalachians, and then down along the Kanawha River to the Ohio. State surveyors and commissioners thus overtook the old James River Company and made it into the commonwealth's responsibility. This centerpiece project captured the imagination of ambitious policymakers, yet the political divisions between tidewater planters in the East and the aspiring mining and manufacturing interests in the West played out in Richmond much as sectional and ideological discord doomed federal internal improvements a decade earlier. "It was the old story of sectional prejudice and jealousy," Wayland Fuller Dunaway wrote back in 1922, "with here and there a man of broad and statesman-like views rising to stand for the interests of the whole state and of the Union" (Dunaway, 1922: 76). The James River and Kanawha Canal saw uneven funding throughout its existence as a state-controlled entity; by 1832 the General Assembly chartered the James River and Kanawha Company, a private corporation that enjoyed state assistance, but private direction. Virginia's ambitions echoed up and down the eastern seaboard, as states from South Carolina to New York all envisioned a centerpiece project that could realize this ambition.Nearly all of them failed to capture the flood of traffic that a western route to the Ohio and Mississippi valleys would generate. That is, all except New York's Erie Canal.

Historians have elevated the Erie Canal to a legendary status. For that reason, it is tempting to view the Empire State's state-funded project in a triumphalist light. Popular histories like Peter Bernstein's *Wedding of the Waters* (2005) announce in breathless terms that the Erie Canal was the culmination of Washington's vision of "the vast inland navigation possible in the United States and the significance of that transportation system to the future of a country so large and varied" (Bernstein, 2005: 377). Here again we see the old (and rather tiresome) account of the foibles of historical actors, particularly those who labeled the attempt to construct a 363-mile waterway connecting Albany on the Hudson River to Buffalo on Lake Erie "Clinton's Big Ditch," after Governor DeWitt Clinton's political support for the project resulted in a $7 million commitment by New York. When the canal opened in 1825, the naysayers were dispelled and the Erie Canal transformed upstate New York into a dynamic commercial and manufacturing region, with cities like Rochester and Lockport accommodating a stream of merchants, migrants, and factory workers who traveled along the route. Even preachers and reformers loved the canal enough to make it the central byway of the "Burned Over District," so named because of the frequency of their emotionally charged meetings in the 1820s and 1830s. It's a great story, to be sure. The history of the Erie Canal, however, reveals a mixed legacy in the overall story of internal improvements in the era of John Quincy Adams. On the one hand, it offered the best possible example of the transformative effects of internal improvements by making upstate New York a dynamic region of economic and cultural significance in only a few short years. But the political legacy of the Erie Canal proved less positive as it migrated from Albany to the nation's other state-houses. For most of the nation, the frustrations plaguing the James River and Kanawha venture would have seemed more familiar than the unparalleled success of New York's Erie Canal.

That said, the economic accomplishments of the Erie Canal were myriad and historians across generations have noted the many ways in which it made New York into the Empire State. New York City's emergence as the major port, manufacturing, and commercial center of the nineteenth-century United States, for example, owed a great deal to the Erie Canal. Historian Noble Whitford recognized this trend back in 1906 when he explained why New York City, not Philadelphia, became the nation's premier city: "Money gathers at New York because the products are there, and the products go there because they are cheaper to carry them there than to Philadelphia." "Transportation is king," he concluded (Whitford, 1906: 832–833). Subsequent historians chronicled the Erie Canal's economic impact with less boosterism, but no less enthusiasm. When the canal opened, the travel time from New York City to Buffalo dropped from six weeks to ten days, which revolutionized the transport of both people and goods. Once statistical measures became a mainstay of historical scholarship, the Erie Canal's accomplishments became even more impressive. George Rogers Taylor (1951: 161) estimated that $10 million worth of goods were shipped westward on the canal in 1836; this amount increased to $94 million by 1853. Ronald Shaw provides copious evidence of the Erie Canal's impact in his (1966) seminal study, *Erie Water West*. Over the course of a few pages, Shaw estimates that the population of New York's counties west of the Mohawk tripled from 1810 to 1835; shows that farmers sent 2 million barrels of flour and 1.5 million bushels of wheat to market via the canal in 1840 and that by 1847 this amount had doubled; and demonstrates the profound impact of the canal on urban growth in upstate New York. In 1820 Syracuse, with 1,814 residents, Rochester (1502), and Buffalo (2095) were small towns. By 1850 Syracuse, with 22 271 residents, Rochester (36 403) and Buffalo (42 261) were cities of some import (R. Shaw, 1966: 262–263). There is a good reason that the project basks in a triumphalist light, particularly when measuring the economic impact of the Erie Canal on New York, the North, and the West.

The Erie Canal transformed lives beyond the balance sheet, though, and its role in antebellum America has been the subject of several excellent studies that contrast the economic benefits of the canal with its more unsettling social impact. John Quincy Adams believed fervently in a holistic kind of "improvement," in which moral, political, and physical shortcomings dropped away in the face of American energy and resolve. The Erie Canal allows historians to explore how Adams' broad notion of "improvement" found expression during the early American republic. Paul Johnson, for example, deftly reconstructed the linkages between religious revivalism and nascent industrialism in his classic 1978 case study of Rochester entitled*A Shopkeeper's Millennium*. Johnson opens the book by describing the evangelical superstar Charles Finney's path from the canal landing to the center of town in 1830, passing both the familiar farmers and merchants of a small town, but also "what Finney may have felt was an uncomfortable number of urban workingmen," thus signaling Rochester's rapid change at the hands of the Erie Canal (Johnson, 1978: 16). The arrival of Finney's style of evangelical Christianity was a direct response to the unsettling nature of economic change, or, as Johnson argues, "a middle-class solution to problems of class, legitimacy, and order generated in the early stages of manufacturing" (P. Johnson, 1978: 138). As towns like Rochester or Lockport matured, they became urban centers with many of the same problems faced by their brethren on the seaboard. Canals thus brought new challenges along with new markets. In his study of canal laborers, Peter Way (1993) notes that many of the same workers who built and maintained canals took up residence in the towns they helped transform – in Lockport nearly half of the workers on the Erie Canal stayed there once it was built. "The working-class neighborhoods to which many ex-canallers were drawn," Way argues, " were fragile worlds of transiency, work shortages, ethnic bigotry, substandard living and working conditions, little hope of advancement, violence, crime, disease and death" (Way, 1993: 272). Carol Sheriff's (1996) history of the canal introduces what she labels "the paradox of progress" to describe the Erie Canal's impact on daily life. An evocative demonstration of this paradox occurs when Sheriff describes the response that an average merchant might have to the sights, sounds, and smells of the Erie Canal each morning. "The first sensual bombardment represented a social nightmare," she argues, of an army of workers "many of whom never even had a chance at 'respectable citizenship' because of their accents, skin color, sex, or age." But another, simultaneous response to the canal "represented the dream of the market revolution: the creation of unlimited possibilities for commercial expansion within the older context of a family-centered, socially stable community" (Sheriff, 1996: 167). Balancing the dread and promise of the Erie Canal thus forms an important theme in the reconstruction of antebellum American society at a time of momentous change. It is perhaps fitting that John Quincy Adams was inaugurated as president of the United States in 1825, the same year that the Erie Canal was completed.

Although John Quincy Adams was not personally involved or enriched by internal improvements in his private life, he spent much of his public career supporting their proliferation. Once might expect, then, that as chief executive he would attempt to reawaken the call for federal action in this area. President Adams, though, failed to push through any grand vision of a national university, a national observatory, and a union-wide system of internal improvements. His famous first message to Congress outlined this fervent belief in improvement – transportation was just one element of a complete reworking of American society in his mind. Not only did Adams evoke the success of the Erie Canal; he aspired to repeat its success at a national level. His biographers, however, have not been kind in assessing the success of Adams's expansive view of improvement. More specifically, they often cite the hard-headed nature of his personality, as well as his forceful intellect, as political liabilities in getting a successful response from Congress. "It would have been better if President Adams had not mentioned the subject of internal improvements at all," Samuel Bemis wrote in the 1950s (1956: 76). "His message's reception was devastating to Adams," Paul Nagel argued four decades later. "No one appeared to share his vision for America" (1997: 302). From the biographer's perspective, highlighting failure in this case seems logical. The image of John Quincy Adams marching steadfastly up the aisles of the House chamber to present an antislavery petition in the 1830s offers a much more favorable response to late twentieth-century sensibilities. His post-presidential work as an abolitionist, moreover, seemed to gain more purchase than any grand idea that he brought to the White House in 1825.

But Adams did have an impact upon the nation's internal-improvement network. Using a more realistic measure, Daniel Walker Howe sheds a positive light on John Quincy Adams in his sweeping survey of the early American republic entitled *What Hath God Wrought* (2007), and provides ample evidence of the one-term president's fervent belief in improvement at all levels and his political will to enact it while serving in the White House. More importantly, Howe breaks from the traditional view of the Adams presidency as a quixotic failure in this regard. "Adams celebrated the benefits of improved transportation and communication," Howe argues, "and undertook to marshal the resources of the federal government to further them" (D.W. Howe, 2007: 251–252). The rise of advocates of an energetic federal government, led in Congress by Kentucky's Henry Clay, served as the political force behind this "American System" and emboldened Adams to act strongly towards this goal. In regards to internal improvements, Adams and his political allies in Congress drew up a number of bills that drew upon federal funding to construct turnpikes and canals. Although the comprehensive planning inherent in Gallatin's plan did not reappear, the advocates of the American System revived the sponsorship of the federal state in internal improvements through piecemeal appropriations to various road and canal projects across the nation. Early advocates of a national transportation found the political hurdles high, yet with Adams in the White House, advocates of improvement pursued what one historian referred to as a "back door strategy" to revive Gallatin's vision, if not his explicit plan(Baker, 2002: 448). "By 1826," Howe argues, "the federal government had become the largest entrepreneur in the American economy" (D.W. Howe, 2007: 254).

The "spirit of improvement" emanating from the White House was shortlived, as Adams fell victim to the rising popularity of Andrew Jackson in the elections of 1828. The new administration did not share Adams's enthusiasm for federal action, even while it outdid its processor in spending money on internal improvements. George Rogers Taylor, for example, notes that Adams's notoriety as the "champion of internal improvements" does not add up fiscally, as his administration allocated $702,000 annually on transportation projects, whereas Andrew Jackson's average annual allocation exceeded $1.3 million (G.R. Taylor, 1951: 21). Yet, Andrew Jackson and his political allies represented a qualitative, if not a quantitative shift in the federal patronage of internal improvements. Andrew Jackson's 1830 veto of the Maysville Road project, which ran from Lexington, KY, to the Ohio River, offers quite a different perspective on the subject. In his veto message, Jackson does not attack the idea of internal improvements in general, nor does he deny the role of local and state authorities in sponsoring them. Instead, he argued that a project solely within the boundaries of Kentucky did not merit federal aid – and any other project that did not meet this "national" character should expect the same result from his administration. "The Maysville Road Veto Message," Howe argues, "had been crafted to endorse what we would call the transportation revolution while condemning what we would call big government" (D.W. Howe, 2007: 359).

Jackson's critics could argue that the Maysville Road was actually a component of a larger interstate system of roads (it was) and question (with justification) Jackson and his political allies in Congress on their commitment to fiscal restraint in funding internal improvement projects. But to be fair to Jackson, he sought to balance the longstanding ideological concerns – tracing back to Jeffersonian doctrines and Madison's veto of the Bonus Bill – over federal patronage of internal improvements, with the desire of his strong supporters in the South and West to develop their regions. The rise of South Carolina's John C. Calhoun – no longer as interested in binding the nation together with roads as he was defining the sovereign rights of individual states – as a counterbalance to Jackson's influence in those regions also injected a new political dynamic into the old debate over federally coordinated internal improvements. John Larson interpreted the Maysville veto as "an alternative national position, less consolidationist than Clay's American System yet less disintegrative than Calhoun's new doctrine of nullification" (J.L. Larson, 2001: 184). Whatever the impetus, Jackson's veto sent a message that was strong and clear: the spirit of improvement would receive little direction from Washington. In his impressive survey of the early republic, Sean Wilentz (2005) finds Jackson's position more reasonable and grounded in the politics of the moment than Howe's pro-Adams account. "Having bolstered his Old Republican southern supporters," Wilentz writes, "some of whom were leaning dangerously toward Calhoun's more extreme state's rights views, the president, his political circumstances precarious, made clear that he did not oppose all government-aided economic development." As to the doctrine that this politically expedient decision created, Wilentz found that Jackson "would adhere to that position fairly consistently for the rest of his presidency" (2005: 328).

On the heels of Jackson's symbolic veto of the Maysville project, internal improvements fell into the purview of private and state interests again, but this time the success of the Erie Canal inspired a "canal boom" across the nation in which state legislatures ponied up their own funds to build internal improvement networks. The Erie Canal demonstrated the potential of internal improvements to kick-start an economy. Pennsylvania, for example, embarked on an expensive project of their own that blended canals and gravity-powered railroads to cross the Allegheny Mountains and link Philadelphia to its emerging western metropolis, Pittsburgh. State-level organizations, like the Pennsylvania Society for the Promotion of Internal Improvements, acted as boldly as any modern-day interest group in boosting the primary and secondary benefits that would arise from such a project. In 1826, the society reported that they had circulated essays in several newspapers across Pennsylvania and had even sent an agent abroad to collection information not only on the expected "canals – locks – sluices – aqueducts – canal boats – breakwaters and artificial harbours," but also wider improvements such as "cranes and hoisting machines – tunneling – railways and locomotive engines – turnpike roads – the manufacture of oil and coal gas, and iron – coking bituminous coal – making cast and blister steel – and on the manufacture of copper rollers for the printing of calico."[1] Thus, the program to build internal improvements took on a zeal much beyond the simple movement of goods and people and instead became an economic panacea. With the federal government tangled up in competing ideological visions of national authority and political intrigue, it fell to the states to pick up the slack in the construction of ambitious canal projects modeled on the Erie's success.

Try as they might, other states floundered in their attempt to replicate the singular success of the Erie Canal. Each state's experience in building transportation networks took a distinct path, yet failures seemed to be the most common result. Virginia's James River and Kanawha Canal simply stalled as funding for the western section withered under the stewardship of Virginia's planter-dominated legislature. "Virginians east of the Alleghenies," Sean Patrick Adams (2004: 102) argues of the James River and Kanawha project, "feared that the enhanced economic prestige of the western counties would, at the very least, lead to greater spending on improvements beyond their immediate interest and increases in the taxation of slaves." As a result, the James River and Kanawha Canal project stalled and never provided Virginia's main thoroughfare to the West. In Ohio, Harry Scheiber (1969) described a system with a main trunk line that could have resembled the Erie Canal in forming an economic backbone for the state, but political sensibilities quickly overcame economic imperatives in the construction of local branch lines. During the 1830s, Ohio doubled its debt to build a statewide system based on a political calculus, failed to combat corruption in its canal administration, and continued to exert rate-making authority through the 1850s. These factors all combined to spell doom for the Ohio system, but the flaws of employing a political logic in its construction were present at the onset. "From the beginning," Scheiber argues (1969: 19), "the quest for a politically workable plan was linked with the task of scientific inquiry, and the [canal] commission itself was the arena in which local interests were taken into account and molded into a policy for the commonwealth." In Indiana, the legislature passed a "Mammoth Internal Improvement Bill" in 1836 that laid out an impressive system of canals, but their funding of the system "began a nightmare of financial ineptitude, fraud, and confusion" that pushed the state's debt to $15 million while failing to deliver on its promise to supercharge the Hoosier State's economy (J.L. Larson, 2001: 211).

Few states could replicate the spectacular failure of Pennsylvania's "State Works," which offered a most depressing contrast between the giddy highs of the "canal boom" and the fiscal hangover that followed. In 1826 the legislature created the "Pennsylvania Canal," at state expense, in order to link Philadelphia and Pittsburgh. This project, eventually dubbed the "Main Line," was an alternate system of canals and railway, which required three changes in order to negotiate the 359 miles completed by 1835. Like in Virginia, eastern and western interests in Pennsylvania demanded that the Main Line serve their own interests and like Ohio, the branch canals followed political, rather than economic routes.The Main Line itself cost Pennsylvania $12 million; legislators spent $6.5 million on 314 miles of branch canals. Like their counterparts in Indiana, Pennsylvania's legislators recklessly spent money that they did not have and could probably never pay back. The belief that the transformative experience of the Erie Canal would repeat itself again and again was an unrealistic, but all too common assumption in Harrisburg and other state capitals. Pennsylvania's debt ballooned up to $33 million by the early 1840s, and corruption and mismanagement racked the State Works. After a popular referendum decreed that the commonwealth sell the system, canal officials put the Main Line up for sale for $20 million. They had no takers and continued to cut the selling price, until the Pennsylvania Railroad purchased the Main Line for $7.5 million in 1857. The failure of the State Works created a backlash against public enterprise in Pennsylvania that reverberated for the rest of the nineteenth century. Louis Hartz argued in 1948 that the result was no less than the invention of the laissez-faire doctrine in American political economy and that "a new philosophy had emerged to blacken the entire principle of public enterprise" in Pennsylvania (Hartz, 1948: 180).

What do we make of the rapid lurches and stops in federal, state, and private influences on the internal-improvement networks? To get a sense of the wrenching change, consider the career of the James River and Kanawha canal project over the first fifty years of its existence. Washington's pet project was first conceived as the James River Company, a private corporation, in 1785. In 1820 the commonwealth of Virginia, via the Board of Public Works, reorganized the company into a state-run operation. In 1832, the James River and Kanawha Company replaced the state-run entity with a kind of mixed-form corporation blending public and private money. All of these iterations failed to build an effective east–west thoroughfare in Virginia, but they did link many of the Old Dominion's local agricultural and urban regions nonetheless. This incomplete legacy reverberated across the nation. Ohio's system may have lacked economic coherence, yet it still provided much-needed waterways in a state whose significance grew during the antebellum era. Pennsylvania's State Works must be considered a fiscal disaster, yet its branch canals tapped into valuable bituminous coal regions in the West, and the Main Line did see enough traffic to convince the directors of the Pennsylvania Railroad to purchase this completion in the 1850s.

What is the lesson to be learned from the incomplete legacy of state-run internal improvements, repeated throughout the nation in the 1830s and 1840s? The historical interpretation of state-fueled internal improvement over the course of the twentieth century has, not surprisingly, often addressed contemporary problems. Writing in 1902, Guy Stevens Callender sought to explain to his early Progressive Era audience the "conditions which gave rise to this remarkable movement towards State enterprise here in America, where of all places in the world we should least expect to find it" (Callender, 1902: 6). Callender's astonished tone suggests that he considered his readership steeped in laissez-faire assumptions and was aware how peculiar early twentieth-century audiences might find John Quincy Adams' faith in the state. This context would all change, of course, with the rise of Theodore Roosevelt's rejuvenation of federal authority, Woodrow Wilson's progressive influence in Washington, and finally the New Deal's aggressive management of capital and labor markets. But the interest in state-fueled internal improvements remained relevant to this earlier generation as well. Louis Hartz's (1948) study of antebellum Pennsylvania defended this new political paradigm by championing the idea of "mixed enterprise," in which public and private interests blended under a single corporate entity, "embracing both profit and control objectives" (1948: 290). Hartz's study made him part of a larger group of scholars known as the Commonwealth School, in which state-level studies of Massachusetts, Pennsylvania, Georgia, and Missouri sponsored by the Social Science

Research Council all attempted to justify a heavy state hand in business enterprises. By normalizing state action as a longstanding historical tradition, the Commonwealth School suggested that the laissez-faire assumptions of the Gilded Age were an anomalous chapter in the story of America, and not the natural order of things.

This positivist view of the Commonwealth School saw yet another revision during the Cold War, when a school of thought led by Carter Goodrich (1968) gravitated towards a "state in, state out" – shortened to "SISO" in those acronym-heady days – model in which a careful student of history could see the value of state action at the onset economic growth, but that eventually public policymakers should withdraw and allow private actors to take over. Using the "canal boom" of the 1820s and 1830s as the premier example of this dynamic, Goodrich argued that many countries employ the "state in" strategy, but the United States is unique in adding the "state out" component. For Goodrich, the most important element – and lesson to be extracted – from internal improvements in the early republic was timing. "A satisfactory return on the investment would therefore be delayed," he theorized in 1968, "and under these circumstances public policy, contrary to the orthodox assumptions of modern welfare economics, was often based on the assumption that government should act on the basis of a longer time span than private investors" (Goodrich, 1968: 378). It is easy to see how SISO could transform the history of internal improvements into a nice blueprint for the economies of emerging nations struggling with the Cold War rivalry between global capitalism and communism.

More recent works on the subject tend to view the state presence during the era of John Quincy Adams as less an all-or-nothing case study from which current policymakers should take heed. The most recent comprehensive study of the phenomenon, John Larson's (2001) *Internal Improvement*, depicts these years as a missed opportunity to realize an authentic republican vision of economic growth, rather than a blueprint for domestic and foreign policymakers. And yet, Larson is convinced that John Quincy Adams's vision of improvement was not an aberrant one. Rather, it represented the vast potential of republican government. "It is my contention," he states early in his work (2001: 3), "that the positive use of government power for popular constructive purposes, such as public works of internal improvement, never was proscribed by American republicanism but lay well within the presumed legislate authority of revolutionary governments." Other historians have lengthened the time frame of their studies to include the rise of railroads and the telegraph – previously considered decidedly non-state entities – to trace the continued, not abbreviated, role of federal and state authority in internal improvements. Colleen Dunlavy's (1994) comparative study of Prussian and American railroad development, for example, refers to a continuing "structuring presence" of the American state in the growing railroad network of antebellum America, even as private corporations built and operated those lines. Steven Usselman's (2002) sweeping study of railroad technology finds that technological changes in the industry from the very beginning "occurred within a complex framework of public and private institutions ecompassing a broad array of Americans in many capacities," and those changes "at once reflected and influenced issues residing at the very core of American politics and political ideology" (Usselman, 2002: 4). Richard John (2010) finds the role of the state significant in the circulation of information across the early postal service, then telegraph, and finally, telephone networks of the nineteenth century. "The federal government's mandate to circulate information was seldom questioned," he argues of the early American republic in his recent work on the origins of the telecommunications network, "on only rare occasions was it even debated" (John, 2010: 19). These studies extend the provocative case that Larson made in *Internal Improvement*: that state authorities in the early American republic not only demonstrated the potential to build valuable and progressive systems of transportation and communication in the United States, they continued to contribute to those systems even after the trials of the "canal boom" and rise of private actors in the world of internal improvements.

So we come full circle again to John Quincy Adams, the Chesapeake & Ohio Canal, and the Baltimore & Ohio Railroad. One historian of the latter argues that the Baltimore investors who built the B&O sensed a larger purpose in their work. "They were following George Washington's plan of binding together a young nation, commercially and politically," James Dilts writes (1996: 4), "and they were tracing a route Washington himself had picked out." Like the supporters of the James River and Kanawha Canal, the creators of the B&O believed that they were following a mandate from the founding generation. However, they did so largely with the backing of private capital and municipal subscriptions to their stock. One could argue that the C&O was the true inheritor of republican ideals; indeed that might explain John Quincy Adams's presence at the groundbreaking. What is often presented as a foible or weakness of character on the part of Adams thus deserves a new interpretation, one in which the broader contours of his vision of "improvement" is taken into account. By simply reimagining the ways in which Washington's vision of a national system of improvements was realized by either the state-fueled Erie Canal or privately funded railroads, the larger point about the appropriate role of state actors in the economic growth of the United States is suppressed in favor of a triumphalist account of progress. Doing so mutes an important controversy that contemporaries in the early American republic took quite seriously and reduces what could be an important, informative, and relevant debate for our own times to a mere curiosity or antiquarian relic.

The newspaper reports of Adams at the groundbreaking, as well as the text of his speech, speak to the sincerity of his vision. According to the edition of Washington's *Daily National Journal* for July 7, 1828, Adams accepted the ceremonial spade and demonstrated an "animation of manner and countenance which showed that his whole heart was in the thing." When he spoke to the assembled crowd, he began, not with the nation's founding, but with the idea that the Creator had imbued humans with the task of subduing nature. The United States, in the mind of Adams, offered the world's best chance for improvement. His view of internal improvement was expansive, and although many of his biographers choose to emphasize Adams's poor choice of breaking ground on a canal rather than a railroad, his Fourth of July 1828 speech tells us otherwise.

> In praying for the blessing of Heaven upon our task,we ask it with equal zeal and sincerity upon every other similar work in this confederation; and particularly upon that which on this same day and perhaps at this very hour, is commencing from a neighboring city.... It is one of the happiest characteristics in the principle of Internal Improvement that the success of one great enterprize, instead of counteracting, gives assistance, to the execution of another. [2]

After he finished the speech, Adams rammed the shovel into the ground in order to get the ceremonial shovelful of earth, but he hit a root. Rather than abandon the quest, Adams shrugged off his jacket and, drawing great cheers from the crowd, hammered on his chosen spot until he succeeded in his task.

As with his message to Congress in 1825, another eloquent and articulate Adams speech once again encountered an unforgiving terrain; the vignette of the president struggling to even break ground at the C&O ceremony is one of those delightful instances in which historians can construct metaphors in order to make small occurrences stand for larger themes. Perhaps predictably, biographers prefer to emphasize the hardheaded nature of Adams's character in lieu of his ideas. Samuel Bemis noted (1956: 103) that "Quite by accident he had made a little hit – with the spade, not the speech!" But a more fair-minded approach to internal improvements in the era of John Quincy Adams might highlight a different result. Yes, the grand federal vision failed, but the plethora of internal improvements did not. Moreover, the idea that one improvement enhances the other found perfect expression during the 1820s and 1830s; even as state-fueled programs in Pennsylvania, Indiana, and Ohio failed miserably, the idea of investing in the nation's physical infrastructure was unsullied. Even had he vetoed the Maysville Road project, Andrew Jackson never doubted the significance of internal improvements to the nation's economic future. The origins of that investment gradually shifted into the private sector and false hopes for the untrammeled efficiency of "laissez faire" may have arisen in the wake of failed state investments, but the "transportation revolution" never abated. In this regard, Adams' broad vision of improvement must be viewed not as a failure, but as a success.

There are still some unresolved issues. When John Quincy Adams outlined a vision for the federal government's leading role in promoting internal improvements, was he tapping into the established traditions of the Revolutionary generation? Or was he creating a new approach to governance, one that was *revolutionary* in its own right, but not consistent with the *Revolution*? Did the mixed legacy of the state-funded programs fulfill this vision or destroy it? These are some of the many questions that this rich literature on the subject has generated over the past century; no doubt future historians will generate new questions that will reflect the urgency and importance of internal improvements to our understanding of the early American republic. John Quincy Adams would have appreciated these arguments, even as he realized that attending the B&O's groundbreaking ceremony back in 1828 might have produced a more positive legacy. Knowing what we now know about his indomitable intellect and force of will, it might please Adams to know that his short-term mistake might have led to a long-range discussion over the proper role of the state in the American economy.

Notes

1 Pennsylvania Society for the Promotion of Internal Improvements, *To the Citizens of the Commonwealth of Pennsylvania*. Philadelphia (1826: 2).

2 *Daily National Journal*, July 7, 1828.

Further Reading

Adams, Sean Patrick (2008). The Tao of John Quincy Adams. Or, The New Institutionalism and the Early American Republic. *Common-place* 9, at www.common-place.org/vol-09/no-01/, accessed Nov. 5, 2012.

Friend, Craig Thompson (2005). *Along the Maysville Road: The Early Republic in the Trans-Appalachian West.* Knoxville, TN.

Goodrich, Carter (1960). *Government Promotion of American Canals and Railroads, 1800–1890.* New York.

Goodrich, Carter (1970). Internal Improvements Reconsidered. *Journal of Economic History* 30: 289–311.

Gray, Ralph (1967). *The National Waterway: A History of the Chesapeake and Delaware Canal, 1769–1965.* Urbana, IL.

Handlin, Oscar, and Handlin, Mary Flug (1947). *Commonwealth: A Study of the Role of Government in the American Economy, Massachusetts, 1774–1861.* Cambridge, MA.

Heath, Milton (1954). *Constructive Liberalism: The Role of the State in the Economic Development of Georgia to 1860.* Cambridge, MA.

John, Richard (1998). *Spreading the News: The American Postal System from Franklin to Morse.* Cambridge, MA.

Jordan, Philip (1948). *The National Road.* Indianapolis.
Miller, Nathan (1962). *The Enterprise of a Free People: Aspects of Economic Development in New York State during the Canal Period, 1792–1838.* Ithaca, NY.
Murphy, Brian (2008). Empire State Building: Interests, Institutions, and the Formation of States and Parties in New York, 1783–1845. PhD thesis, University of Virginia.
Seelye, John (1991). *Beautiful Machine: Rivers and the Republican Plan, 1755–1825.* Oxford.
Shaw, Ronald (1992). *Canals for a Nation: The Canal Era in the United States, 1790–1860.* Lexington, KY.

Chapter Eighteen

John Quincy Adams: Apostle of Union

David F. Ericson

John Quincy Adams's political career poses two major puzzles. First, why was Adams so late in publicly attacking slavery and, second, why did he never become an abolitionist.[1]

In treating these two puzzles, Samuel F. Bemis's early work on Adams's political career remains exemplary. In what became a two-volume political biography of Adams, the central theme of the first volume is his devotion to the Union during his first political career as a foreign minister and secretary of state, while the central theme of the second volume is his crusade against the Gag Rule and the annexation of Texas during his second career as a United States congressman (Bemis, 1949, 1956).[2] The "why so late" puzzle is a recurrent motif in the first volume and the "why not an abolitionist" puzzle dominates the second. The interface between Adams's two careers is, however, somewhat of a mystery in Bemis's work. The "why so late" and "why not an abolitionist" puzzles are also central to J. David Greenstone's chapter on Adams in his highly influential (1993) work on early American political thought. But again, Greenstone resolved neither puzzle,and his lesson was that Abraham Lincoln succeeded where Adams failed in combining strong unionist and antislavery stances through a particular "reform-liberal" conception of the Union (Greenstone, 1993: 192, 205–12).[3] The key to unlocking these two puzzles is to dig deeper into Adams's political thought. It requires us, as Greenstone did, to think of Adams's conception of the Union and his views on slavery together. It also requires us, as Greenstone again did, to think of Adams's views in relation to those of the other leading figures of his political generation.

A Companion to John Adams and John Quincy Adams, First Edition.
Edited by David Waldstreicher.

But going beyond both Greenstone and Bemis, we need to re-think Adams's conception of the Union and how the relationship between this conception and his views on slavery changed over time.

18.1 Adams on Slavery and Union

Adams was an apostle of Union because his conception of the Union carried a proselytizing element. In Adams's view, the Union was a moral entity dedicated to the cause of human freedom with a mission to spread the nation's unique liberal republican principles across the continent as well as around the globe. In an 1821 Fourth of July oration, he articulated this American sense of mission.

> Wherever the standard of freedom and independence has been or shall be unfurled, there will her [America's] heart, her benedictions and her prayers be. But she goes not abroad in search of monsters to destroy. She is the well-wisher to the freedom and independence of all. She is the champion and vindicator only of her own. She will recommend the general cause, by the countenance of her voice, and the benignant sympathy of her example. (J.Q. Adams, 1821: 32)

Adams's conception of the Union included a strong element of territorial expansion. He was one of the early proponents of manifest destiny and a transcontinental American empire. His conception of Union, however, involved a process of expansion by acquisition rather than military conquest and by example rather than direct intervention. Adams always drew the line on expanding southward into Latin America or northward into British Canada, even before the slavery issue complicated public debates over national expansion. In his 1825 inaugural address, he thus counterposed the fact that "the Floridas have been peaceably acquired; and our boundary has been extended to the Pacific Ocean" to the fact that "the independence of the southern nations of this hemisphere has been recognized and recommended by example and by counsel to the potentates of Europe" (J.Q. Adams, 1825a: 54).[4] Adams's conception of the Union, finally, included an element of qualitative development. Adams was a longstanding advocate of internal improvements but he thought of those improvements in both physical and moral terms. In his first annual message to Congress, he expounded on this dual sense of internal improvements.

> Roads and canals, by multiplying and facilitating the communications and intercourse between distant regions, and multitudes of men, are among the most important means of improvement. But moral, political, intellectual, improvement, are duties assigned, by the Author of our existence, to social, no less than to individual man. For the fulfillment of those duties, governments

> are invested with power; and, to the attainment of the end, the progressive improvement of the condition of the governed, the exercise of delegated power, is a duty as sacred and indispensable, as the usurpation of power not granted is criminal and odious. Among the first, perhaps the very first instrument for the improvement of the condition of men, is knowledge; and to the acquisition of much of the knowledge adapted to the wants, the comforts, and enjoyments of human life, public institutions and seminaries of learning are essential (J.Q. Adams, 1825b: 6).[5]

The continued existence of slavery in the United States was a potential burr in Adams's conception of the Union because it could conceivably subvert all these senses of mission. With Southern slave interests in the saddle, the American exemplar might well come to mean the spread of slavery, not freedom; disunity, not unity; and ignorance, not knowledge. Adams was always confident that this worst-case scenario would never come to fruition; that over time the spirit of slavery would wane rather than wax. After spending another agonizing day debating a series of proslavery resolutions offered by various Southern members of Congress, Adams wrote in his diary "that the fall of slavery is predetermined in the counsels of the Omnipotent I cannot doubt; it is but a part of the great moral improvement in the conditions of man, attested by all the records of history." But the short term was a cause of great concern. Indeed, Adams immediately tempered the optimism of his diary statement by adding that "the conflict [between freedom and slavery] will be terrible, and the progress of improvement perhaps retrograde before its final progress to consummation" (C.F. Adams, 1874–1877: 10.63, Dec. 13, 1838). Over the course of his nine terms in Congress, the progress of improvement did seem to retrograde as Adams became convinced that a slave-power conspiracy was monopolizing national councils and subverting the cause of freedom. (On the "slave-power conspiracy" trope, see Richards, 2001.)

According to this interpretation of Adams's political thought, Adams was so late in publicly attacking slavery because during his first, executive career he did not believe that the continued existence of the institution threatened the American mission. He only became convinced to the contrary during his second, congressional career, as the sectional disputes over slavery escalated in the early 1830s with the rise of William Lloyd Garrison's antislavery immediatism in the North and the vocal, and sometimes violent,responses to that development in the South. From that point onward, Adams became increasingly alarmed not only that the continued existence of slavery threatened the American mission but that it threatened the very existence of the Union, without which that mission was impossible. He, however, never became an abolitionist because he believed that Garrison's call for immediate, uncompensated emancipation also threatened the Union, given the extremely negative reaction to the advocacy of even gradual, compensated emancipation in most of the South. In Adams's mind, the fact that both the

Northern abolitionists and the Southern advocates of slavery became more disunionist over time confirmed the triple threat to the American mission posed by the continued existence of slavery, a radical group demanding its immediate abolition, and a reactionary group defending its indefinite existence. By the end of his life, Adams had become obsessed with a slave-power conspiracy to destroy that mission and less worried about the threat from the other side, if for no other reason than that the Northern abolitionists seemed so politically impotent, certainly when compared to the Southern advocates of slavery. Yet even as Adams vehemently attacked the latter, he kept the former at arms' length.

18.2 Alternative Explanations

Before more fully explicating this interpretation of Adams's political thought, let me admit the power of two alternative explanations for why Adams was so late in publicly attacking slavery and never became an abolitionist. The first explanation prioritizes his two political careers. During his first, executive career, it was natural that he should keep his antislavery views to himself because the political offices he held strongly encouraged him to act as a representative of the whole nation, especially because such a strategy offered him his best hopes of being elected president and, once elected, of being re-elected. At this time, he negotiated the acquisition of the slave territory of Florida from Spain, attempted to purchase the slave territory of Texas from Mexico, and assiduously pursued the claims of Southern slaveholders who "lost" their slaves during the War of 1812 with British officials.[6] As a "disjunctive president" and someone who had himself held prominent offices under two Democratic Republican presidents, Quincy Adams was, in particular, caught in the "double bind" of being unable either to fully embrace or to repudiate the policies of his predecessors. His determinationto send envoys to an 1825 Pan-American conference perfectly illustrates this double bindin light of Southern fears that the mission would represent a departure from traditional Democratic Republican strictures against negotiating multilateral slave-trade conventions and recognizing the black republic of Haiti (Skowronek, 1993: 111, 122–123). During his second, congressional career, Adams was then able to more freely express his antislavery views, especially because he now represented a strong antislavery constituency in a strong antislavery state in a strong antislavery region of the country. At that time, he was a vociferous critic of the annexation of the slave nation of Texas, opposed the claims of Southern slaveholders for "lost" slaves in a variety of domestic and international disputes, and argued powerfully for the freedom of the *Amistad* rebels before the United States Supreme Court.[7] As a member of Congress, Adams nonetheless recognized that he still faced some institutional restraints which limited the ways he could "responsibly" attack slavery. While he colluded with individual abolitionists, as in the Texas annexation (Joshua Leavitt and Lewis Tappan) and *Amistad* (Simeon Jocelyn and Tappan) cases, he always disclaimed being one of them.[8]

The second explanation is that Adams simply became more antislavery over time, as did his congressional district, state, and region, similar to the ways various Southern politicians and localities became more proslavery over time. According to this explanation, Adams never became an abolitionist because, in their growing opposition to slavery, both he and most of his constituents stopped short of accepting the abolitionist creed of immediate, uncompensated emancipation and its underlying premise that slaveholding was a sin and slaveholders sinners.

Again, these two explanations are very powerful.[9] They both place Adams's views in a temporal context. They also recognize how institutional, societal, and personal contexts can change over time as well as how political institutions themselves can be cyclic so as to become more or less amenable to ideologically charged initiatives. But neither explanation is sufficient alone in solving the two major puzzles of Adams's political career, nor are they together. With respect to the first puzzle, the "role model" explanation is not sufficient because other leading figures of Adams's political generation followed similar career paths and yet ended up taking quite different stances on slavery. John C. Calhoun, for example, followed a very similar career path to Adams from executive to congressional offices and yet ended up taking a quite different stance on slavery. Obviously, the proponents of this explanation must assume some baseline position on slavery to explain why Calhoun took a more explicitly proslavery stance during his congressional career and Adams a more explicitly antislavery stance, but that assumption only underscores the fact that a politician's official role cannot by itself explain his stance on slavery or any other issue. This view also does not explain why when Calhoun briefly resumed an executive career as President John Tyler's lame-duck Secretary of State he tooksuch a stridently sectional, proslavery stance in overseeing the annexation of Texas (C.N. Wilson et al., 1959–2003: 18.273–278, "To Richard Pakenham," Apr. 18, 1844).

The "sectional polarization" explanation forms a natural supplement to the "role model" explanation in working out why Calhoun and Adams might have taken more explicitly proslavery or antislavery stances later in their political careers than they did earlier. The reason was not only that they were no longer under executive constraints against taking more sectional stances on the slavery issue than they otherwise might have but also that both they and their constituents had become more polarized on the issue over time. Yet, the problem remains of how to explain why Calhoun and Adams ended up taking the exact stances they did on slavery as opposed to similarly situated politicians. For example, in South Carolina Robert

Barnwell Rhett was subject to the same increasing sectional polarization on the issue as Calhoun but he ended up taking a more radical stance on slavery than Calhoun did (Rhett, 1838). Similarly in Massachusetts, Daniel Webster was subject to the same increasing sectional polarization that Adams was but he ended up taking a more moderate stance on slavery than Adams did (Wiltse, 1974–1989: 2.130–131, "Reception at New York," Mar. 15, 1837).

Similar problems emerge when we turn to the second puzzle, of why Adams never became an abolitionist. Here, the "role model" explanation is of some use. As a member of Congress, he, again had to show some restraint in attacking slavery in a way that radical abolitionists who eschewed "normal" politics, such as Garrison and Leavitt, did not. But then the differences between him and other antislavery congressmen, such as Joshua R. Giddings, become difficult to explain. Although neither Giddings nor Adams ever became an abolitionist, Giddings took more radical antislavery positions than Adams did and showed less restraint in attacking slavery in Congress. For instance, Giddings supported the abolition of slavery in the District of Columbia and Adams did not. The "sectional polarization" explanation also does not fully make sense of the Giddings–Adams differences because there is no reason to believe that either Giddings or his constituents harbored more radical antislavery sentiments than Adams and his constituents did. In fact, Adams regularly presented petitions from his constituents praying for the abolition of slavery in the District of Columbia. He, however, always made clear that he dissented from the substance of their prayers, not because he agreed with the "gag rulers" that Congress had no power to abolish slavery in the nation's capital but because he agreed with them that the discussion of the issue would only "lead to ill will, to heart-burnings, to mutual hatred, where the first of wants is harmony" (C.F. Adams, 1874–1877: 8.454, Feb. 10, 1832).[10] Giddings, in contrast, was not dissuaded by such doubts, publicly staking out a "slavery local, freedom national" position against "the power of Congress to adopt, continue, or to uphold slavery here [in Washington] or anywhere else" (Giddings, 1853: 67, "Rights of the States Concerning Slavery," Apr. 18, 1844).

Of course, the career paths and political constituencies of the leading figures of Adams's political generation were not exactly the same. Calhoun and Webster were long-time senators and presidential hopefuls; Adams was (very narrowly) elected president and most of his congressional career was spent in the House; and Giddings and Rhett never served in either the Senate or national executive office. But enough commonalities exist among them to raise serious doubts about whether career and constituency shifts can alone explain their different trajectories.

In order to fully unlock the two major puzzles of Adams's political career, we need to look at the intersection of Adams's views on slavery and Union. We also need to look at those views both across time and in comparison to the views of the other leading figures of his political generation (which may themselves have changed over time).

18.3 Adams in Comparative and Temporal Perspective

In pursuing this comparative-temporal perspective, our first task is to categorize the leading figures of Adams's political generation on two dimensions: the strength of their proslavery or, alternatively, antislavery sentiments, and their conceptions of the Union (Figure 18.1). This comparison draws attention to the distinctiveness of Adams's position on slavery and union. (I include this table only for purposes of illuminating Adams's position. A full exposition of the table would take us too afield.)

Given this array, we can clearly see why various figures would peel off either from the Union (Rhett; Calhoun) or from their proslavery (Clay) or antislavery (Webster) sentiments in contexts where they seemed to conflict. The "tough" middle-row cases went for union (Jackson; Van Buren in the 1830s) or their antislavery sentiments (Van Buren in the 1840s; Giddings) depending on the precise political context (nullification crisis; Texas annexation). The "beauty" of Adams's position was that he did not have to make such choices. For Adams, the political context re-entered the equation only in terms of how it connected slavery to union, not in terms of changing the relative strength of either his unionist or antislavery sentiments.

In a comparative perspective, Adams did not differ from the other leading figures of his political generation in his acceptance of liberal republican principles or in his conviction that the Union embodied those principles. Liberal republican principles were consensual. But that consensus did not preclude serious disagreements from arising between Adams and other political leaders over whether the continued existence of slavery undermined the nation's commitment to liberal republican principles or even

	Strong proslavery	*Weak proslavery*	*Weak antislavery*	*Strong antislavery*
Weak union as a confederation	Robert Barnwell Rhett			William Lloyd Garrison
Strong union as a confederation	John C. Calhoun			
Strong union as a vessel for nationalist sentiments		Andrew Jackson	Martin Van Buren	Joshua R. Giddings
Strong union as a site of state building		Henry Clay	Daniel Webster	
Strong union as a moral entity				John Quincy Adams

Figure 18.1 Dimensions of slavery and union in Adams's political generation.

over whether the institution was itself inconsistent with those principles (Ericson, 1993, 2001).

From a temporal perspective, the key point is, again, that Adams was an apostle of union who over time shifted from believing that the continuing presence of slavery on American soil was not undermining the moral purpose of the Union to believing that it was. The tipping point for Adams and a number of other Northern politicians probably occurred around 1835, with the adoption of the Gag Rule in the House of Representatives and the closing of the United States mails to antislavery literature in the Southern states (Frederick, 1991; John, 1995: 257–280; Ludlum, 1941; Wyly-Jones, 2001). These events may also have constituted a tipping point for Calhoun and a number of other Southern politicians to move in the opposite direction. Yet in thinking of these events as a tipping point, it is important to note that they did not seem to have much of an effect on more moderate politicians such as Clay, Jackson, Van Buren, and Webster, except to reaffirm their strong unionist sentiments. They, however, did not believe, as Adams did, in the Union as a moral entity.

At least for Adams then, changes in the broader political context were the primary factors propelling him to take a more vocal antislavery stance, not changes in his career orientation or political constituency. Prior to the 1830s, Adams could separate his antislavery views from the moral purpose of the Union because he did not believe that the presence of slavery was undermining that purpose. The presence of slavery was rather merely a distraction from the Union's moral purpose, though he certainly recognized its potential to become much more than merely a distraction. Still prior to the 1830s, he felt no powerful urge to attack slavery publicly. Instead, he consigned himself to sniping at slavery and slaveholders in his private diary, while maintaining a studious public silence on the slavery-related issues of the day, such as the First Seminole War and Missouri crisis.[11] On the day after the House of Representatives had passed the "first" Missouri compromise, pairing the admissions of Missouri and Maine into the Union and dividing the rest of the Louisiana Purchase into free and slave territory, Secretary of State Adams discussed the compromise with Secretary of War Calhoun. In his diary, Adams reported that Calhoun had taken the occasion to defend slavery as "the best guarantee to equality among the whites" because "domestic labor was confined to the blacks." Adams's gloss was that:

> The discussion of this Missouri question has betrayed the secret of their [Southern slaveholders'] souls. In the abstract they admit that slavery is an evil, they disclaim all participation in the introduction of it, and cast it all upon the shoulders of our old Grandam Britain. But when probed to the quick upon it, they show at the bottom of their souls pride and vainglory in this condition of masterdom. They fancy themselves more generous and

> noble-hearted than the plain freemen who labor for subsistence. They look down upon the simplicity of a Yankee's manners because he has no habits of overbearing like theirs and cannot treat negroes like dogs. It is among the evils of slavery that it taints the very sources of moral principles. (C.F. Adams, 1874–1877: 5.10, Mar. 3, 1820)

Despite such strong antislavery sentiments, the first-career Adams seemed to believe that publicly attacking slavery would be counterproductive to the moral purpose of the Union by undermining the national unity upon which it rested. On the day after the House of Representatives had passed the "second" Missouri compromise requiring Missouri to exempt the (black) citizens of other states from the black-exclusion clause in its proposed state constitution, Adams commented in his diary:

> They [Southern slaveholders] have threatened and entreated, bullied and wheedled, until their more simple adversaries have been half coaxed, half frightened into a surrender of their principles for a bauble of insignificant promises. The champions of the North did not, however, judiciously select their position for this conflict. There must be at some time a conflict upon this very question between slave and free representation but this is not the time, nor was this the proper occasion for contesting it. (C.F. Adams, 1874–1877: 5.308, Feb. 28, 1821)

With such a mindset, Adams actually favored the Missouri compromise, at least the first one, as promoting a stronger union (C.F. Adams, 1874–1877: 5.12, Mar. 3, 1820).[12] He could even directly serve the interests of Southern slaveholders on such ancillary issues as ensuring that they were compensated by Great Britain for the slaves they "lost" during the War of 1812 and acquiring Florida from Spain, believing that those actions would also function to strengthen the Union. Adams, nonetheless, gave notice, at least to himself, that the occasion might well arise in the future when he would have to take a strong public stance against slave interests because of the potential threat they posed to the moral purpose of the Union and, perhaps, to the Union itself.

In projecting the moral purpose of the Union across time, Adams even contemplated a point at which he might favor disunion and civil war if the result was the abolition of slavery and the reconstitution of a "purer" union. After recording a conversation that he had with Pennsylvania senator Henry Baldwin in November 1820 about the first and (impending) second Missouri compromises, Adams offered the following prophecy:

> If slavery be the destined sword in the hand of the destroying angel which is to sever the ties of this union, the same sword will cut in sunder the bonds of slavery itself. A dissolution of the Union for the cause of slavery would be followed by a servile war in the slave-holding States, combined with a war

> between the two severed portions of the Union. It seems to me that its result must be the extirpation of slavery from this whole continent; and, calamitous and desolating as this course of events in its progress must be, so glorious would be its final issue, that god shall judge me, I dare not say that it is not to be desired.[13]

Yet, prophecy is not advocacy. Even during his second career, Adams continued to believe that the abolitionists' advocacy of immediate emancipation was counterproductive. After writing a letter refusing John G. Whittier's invitation to attend the 1837 annual meeting of the New England Anti-Slavery Society in Boston, Adams remarked in his diary:

> Upon this subject of antislavery my principles and my position make it necessary for me to be more circumspect in my conduct than belongs to my nature. … It is also to be considered that at this time the most dangerous of all the subjects for public contention is the slavery question. In the South, it is a perpetual agony of conscious guilt and terror attempting to disguise itself under sophistical argumentation and braggart menaces. In the North, the people favor the whites and fear the blacks of the South. … The abolitionists are gathering themselves into societies, increasing their numbers, and in zeal they kindle the opposition against themselves into a flame; and the passions of the populace are all engaged against them (C.F. Adams, 1874–1877: 9.349–350, Apr. 19, 1837).[14]

At that point, Adams added another admonition to himself, now that he had taken a more vocal stance against slave interests. He recalled that "[t]he exposure through which I passed in the late session of Congress was greater than I could have imagined possible; and, having escaped from that fiery furnace, it behooves me well to consider my ways before I put myself in the way of being cast into it again" (C.F. Adams, 1874–1877: 9.350, Apr. 19, 1837). Adams had, however, spent the session attacking the Gag Rule and attempting to deflate the trial balloons floated by various Southern and Northern members of Congress to annex Texas to the United States. He had not advocated the dissolution of the Union, a servile war, or the extirpation of slavery. It was the abolitionists who publicly advocated such things, and Adams was, again, admonishing himself to keep his distance from them.

Nevertheless, Adams continued to throw his political weight against a slave-power conspiracy, which, he believed, tightly controlled not only Southern politics but increasingly national politics with the assistance of its Northern "doughface" allies.[15] In his view, this conspiracy was jeopardizing both the Union and its moral purpose by supporting the Gag Rule and the annexation of Texas. In extended remarks on the occasion of presenting a series of antislavery petitions against the annexation of Texas in June 1838, Adams made clear that he supported the purpose of the petitions as he read them, one by one over a three-week period, despite the fact that they were formally "gagged" as soon as he presented them. After South Carolina congressman John Campbell claimed that abolitionist agitation had, in fact, been counterproductive to the antislavery cause because it "had resulted in the almost universal conviction at the South, that slavery, as it existed there, was neither a moral nor a political evil," Adams retorted:

> I am well aware of the change which is taking place in the moral and political philosophy of the South. I know well that the doctrine of the Declaration of Independence, that "all men are born free and equal," is there held as incendiary doctrine, and deserves Lynching; that the Declaration itself is a farrago of abstractions ... and that is the very reason that I want to put my foot on such doctrine ... and pursue it till it is made to disappear from this land ... Sir, this philosophy of the South has done more to blacken the character of this country in Europe than all other causes put together. They point to us as a nation of liars and hypocrites, who publish to the world that all men are born free and equal, and then hold a large portion of our own population in bondage.[16]

The difference between the first- and second-career Adams was therefore not that his views on slavery and union had changed but that the political context had. Not only had the nation witnessed more radical attacks on slavery, it had also witnessed more rabid defenses of the institution. Adams was certainly impressed. Both sides of this debate called into question the practical coexistence of slavery and union, especially as both sides became more disunionist in their own rhetoric. Ironically, the House of Representatives nearly censured Adams in February 1842 for presenting a petition from 46 residents of Haverhill, Massachusetts, which advocated disunion "because a vast proportion of the resources of one section of the Union [the North] is annually drained to sustain the views and course of another section [the South] without any adequate return."[17] Even though the petition was, once more, immediately gagged, Virginia congressman Henry Wise moved to censure Adams for presenting such a "disloyalist" petition. The House initially approved Wise's motion but eventually voted to table it, after Adams had transformed the censure attempt into his own *cause celebre*. The irony is that when he presented the Haverhill petition Adams had himself moved that it should be referred to a select committee with explicit instructions to write a report repudiating its disunionist logic.[18]

Again, the Giddings comparison is instructive. After the successful slave revolt abroad the *Creole* in 1841, Giddings introduced a series of resolutions urging the Tyler administration not to pursue the case, as by demanding that British authorities on Nassau, where the Africans aboard the ship had sought asylum, extradite them to the United States to face murder charges. (During the revolt, the leaders of the rebellion had killed John Hewell, the slave dealer who was transporting them from Hampton Roads, VA, to New Orleans.) Giddings addressed the personal fate of the *Creole* Africanswith a resolution declaring "that the persons on board the said ship, in resuming their natural rights of personal liberty, violated no law of the United States, incurred no legal responsibility, and are justly liable to no punishment." His last resolution drew a connection between the case and Congress's failure to regulate the interstate slave trade, asserting "that all attempts to exert our national influence in favor of the coastwise slave trade, or to place this nation in the attitude of maintaining a 'commerce in human beings,' are subversive of the rights and injurious to the feelings of the free states, are unauthorized by the Constitution, and prejudicial to our national character."[19] In relatively quick succession, Giddings was officially censured by the House of Representatives, resigned his seat, was overwhelmingly re-elected in a special election, and returned to the House to deliver a triumphant speech which applauded the heroism of the *Creole* rebels for slaying "the slave-dealer [who] thrust himself between them and their freedom, and attempted to disrobe them of the liberty which God had given them" (Giddings, 1853: 30, "Reduction of the Army," June 4, 1842; W.L. Miller, 1996, 444–454).[20]

Adams, in contrast, never publicly spoke of the justice or injustice of the *Creole* case, only noting in his diary how Calhoun was likely to suffer "heart-burnings" over the fact that it was not among the Anglo-American disputes addressed by the Webster–Ashburton Treaty (C.F. Adams, 1874–1877: 11.219, July 24, 1842).[21] Two months earlier, Adams had personally counseled Giddings against presenting a congressional resolution to cut off funding for the prosecution of the Second Seminole War – which both believed was a war of slavery expansion (C.F. Adams, 1969: 10.256. Apr. 7, 1840; Giddings, 1858) – because he doubted "the expediency of agitating it" (C.F. Adams, 1874–1877: 11.153, May 11, 1842). To Adams, Giddings betrayed a distressing insensitivity to the potential disunionist effects of his antislavery agitation. Even as Adams engaged in some of that agitation himself, he tempered it with a strong commitment to the cause of union, which, unlike Giddings, he continued to believe was a moral cause.

In understanding Adams's second-career position on slavery and union, it is important to recognize that he could well have (still) believed that protecting the moral purpose of the Union might require a *temporary* disunion at some future point in time in order to abolish slavery. He also could well have (still) believed that it did not require the immediate abolition of slavery or even the advocacy of such a policy at the present time. What had changed was that he now believed it was essential to publicly attack both slavery and the Southern congressmen who were now more vocally defending the institution in order to reassert the moral purpose of the Union, especially in cases where those congressmen were directly undermining that purpose, such as in supporting the Gag Rule and the annexation of Texas. In this respect, Adams's position strongly anticipated the position that Lincoln and the other leading members of the Republican party would take in the next political generation's disputes over slavery. Both Bemis and Greenstone recognize this continuity,

Bemis more so than Greenstone, but neither sufficiently (Bemis, 1956: 545–546; Greenstone, 1993: 214, 231, 277). For instance, Lincoln's language in his 1854 "Peoria Speech" opposing the Kansas–Nebraska Act because it reopened free territory to slavery closely mirrored Adams's language in his 1838 remarks opposing the annexation of Texas because it would add new slave territory to the United States. To quote Lincoln:

> Our republican robe is soiled, and trailed in the dust. Let us re-purify it. Let us turn and wash it white, in the spirit, if not the blood of the Revolution. Let us turn slavery from its claim of 'moral right,' back upon its existing legal rights, and its argument of "necessity." Let us return to the position our fathers gave it; and there let it rest in peace. Let us re-adopt the Declaration of Independence, and with it, the practices, and policy, which harmonize with it. … If we do this, we shall not only have saved the Union; but we shall have so saved it, as to make, and to keep it, forever worthy of saving. (Basler, 1953: 2.276, "Speech at Peoria, Illinois," Oct. 16, 1854)

18.4 Conclusion

We do not need to see Adams as having changed his views about either the intrinsic evils of slavery or the moral purpose of the Union to explain the differences between his first- and second-career positions on slavery. Nor does his career shift itself or the dynamics of sectional polarization adequately explain those differences. Role and constituency effects were important but the pivotal factor was the change from believing that the continuing presence of slavery on American soil was not directly threatening the moral purpose of the Union to believing that it was. Lincoln shared the latter belief, though his epiphany apparently occurred much later than Adams's did. He also shared Adams's belief that the advocacy of the immediate abolition of slavery would not promote but, instead, undercut the task of rededicating the Union to the cause of freedom and the abolition of slavery at some future point in time. What was necessary in the present time was, in Lincoln's words, that the "public mind shall rest in the belief that it [slavery] was in the course of ultimate extinction" (Basler, 1953: 3.18, "First Debate with Stephen A. Douglas at Ottawa, Illinois," Aug. 21, 1858).

For Lincoln, of course, the future became the present as he personally played out Adams's emancipation-through-war scenario. It is hard to imagine Adams himself playing that role, which suggests that the major differences between the two lay more in matters of statesmanship than in their views on slavery and union. Lincoln was, unapologetically, a democratic statesman who was willing and able to mobilize public support for his policies in a way Adams never did. Whether Adams could have under the same wrenching circumstances faced by Lincoln is highly debatable.

Notes

1 Given the extraordinary length of Adams's political career – which stretched from 1794, when President George Washington appointed him minister to the Netherlands, to 1848, when he died while a member of Congress – his political generation would include three age cohorts.

2 Adams's diplomatic career was interrupted by an abbreviated United States senate term (1803–1808). Bemis (1956: 55–151) treats Adams's presidency (1825–1829) in his second volume as a "transitional" career. A better tactic would be to divide Adams's political career into executive and congressional careers.

3 For a similar lack of resolution, see D.W. Howe (1979: 43–44, 63–68); M.J. Wilson (1974: 5, 36, 48, 102–107, 135). Lynn Parsons (1973) faced a comparable quandary in attempting to explain Adams's apparent shift on the issue of Native American removals.

4 On these two senses of mission, see Merk (1963: 264–266). With respect to Canada, Adams was, nonetheless, a powerful proponent of all-Oregon (C.F. Adams, 1874–1877: 12.220–21, Dec. 14, 1844; 12.243–244, Feb. 9, 1845; 2.254–555, Mar. 25, 1846; 12.257, Apr. 13, 1846).

5 Adams went on to commend a variety of such "seminaries of learning," including the already established West Point, a long-discussed national university, trans-continental and trans-oceanic scientific expeditions, and a new, proposed national observatory (*Register of Debates*, 19th Cong., 1st Sess., 1825, 6–7, Appendix). Later, he sought to have the Smithsonian bequest allocated to establish such an observatory (C.F. Adams, 1874–1877: 10.25, June 23, 1838; 10.44, Nov. 29, 1838; 10.57, Dec. 8, 1838; 11.112, Mar. 19, 1842; 11.336, Mar. 10, 1843). On the distinction between quantitative and qualitative development, see M. J. Wilson (1974: 4–7).

6 C. F. Adams, 1874–1877: 3.234, June 28, 1815; 3.255–259, Aug. 16, 1815; 4.26–278, Dec. 1, 1818–Feb. 25, 1819; 5.161, June 28, 1820; 6.45, July 13, 1822; 7.213, Dec. 16, 1826; 7.240, Mar. 15, 1827. Matthew Mason (2002: 675–676) asserts that Adams was a "bulldog" in pursuing the War of 1812 slave claims. Adams had also sought to acquire as much of Texas as possible in the Adams–Onís Treaty negotiations (C.F. Adams, 1874–1877: 4.26–278, Dec. 1, 1818–Feb. 25, 1819).

7 C.F. Adams, 1874–1877: 11.218–219, July 24, 1842; 11.342, Mar. 22, 1843; 12.162, Feb. 6, 1843; 12.163, Feb. 8, 1843; 12.272–273, Sept. 14, 1846; 12.273–275, Sept. 23–24, 1846; J.Q. Adams, 1838; J.Q. Adams, 1841. Adams later observed, somewhat counterfactually, that he had supported the acquisition of Texas before it became slave territory (J.Q. Adams, 1838: 108).

8 C.F. Adams, 1874–1877: 9.349–350, Apr. 19, 1837; 9.365. Sept. 1, 1837; 9.544, May 27, 1838; 10.39, Nov. 10, 1838; 10.43, Nov. 24, 1838; 10.132, Sept. 28, 1839; 10.450, Mar. 22, 1841; 11.23, Sept. 22, 184; 11.374, May 8, 1843; 11.379, May 31, 1843. Tappan and Theodore Weld also assisted Adams in his censure battle (C.F. Adams, 1874–1877: 11.75–76, Jan. 27–28, 1842; 11.79, Jan. 31, 1842).

9 One other explanation is noteworthy. Both Robert Remini (2002: 138–139) and Leonard Richards (1986: 9, 15) claim that Adams's congressional career

was, in part, motivated by a desire to seek revenge for the strong Southern opposition to his presidency and re-election bid. Yet, as Richards acknowledges, this explanation is speculative, not based on any autobiographical evidence.

10 These antislavery petitions also typically prayed for the abolition of the slave trade in the District of Columbia,which Adams did support (C.F. Adams, 1874–1877: 9.418, Oct. 23, 1837).

11 Following the First Seminole War, secretary of state Adams was the cabinet member who most strongly opposed censuring General Andrew Jackson for his filibustering in Florida during the war, when Jackson's invading force seemed to indiscriminately target Seminoles, black maroons, British adventurers, and Spanish colonists (C.F. Adams, 1874–1877: 4: 248, Feb. 9, 1819).

12 Adams was less willing to support the "second" Missouri compromise because he felt that Congress should have required Missouri to delete the black-exclusion clause from its proposed state constitution (C.F. Adams, 1874–1877: 5.205, Nov. 24, 1820; 5.208–210, Nov. 29, 1820; 6.342–343, May 20, 1824; 6.353–354, May 24, 1824).

13 C.F. Adams, 1874–1877: 5.210, Nov. 29, 1820. Adams believed that such a war offered the only constitutional means by which the federal government could abolish slavery (C. F. Adams 1969: 4:530, Feb. 23, 1830; 4:531, Feb. 24, 1820). Baldwin was a strong supporter of both Missouri compromises and later became the only Supreme Court justice to dissent from the *Amistad* decision (C.F. Adams, 1874–1877: 5:208, 210–11; *United States v. Amistad* 40 US, 1841: 518).

14 Whittier was a founding member of the American Anti-Slavery Society as well as a New England Anti-Slavery Society board member. On the "passionate" Northern opposition to the abolitionists, see L.L. Richards (1970).

15 C.F. Adams, 1874–1877: 9.255, Aug. 18, 1835; 10.41, Nov. 10, 1838; 10.463, Apr. 15, 1841; 11.519, Feb. 24, 1844. Later, Adams targeted the three-fifths rule, which would obviously boost the power of any such conspiracy, when he presented a Massachusetts state resolution, drafted by his son (Charles Francis), supporting a constitutional amendment to delete the rule (C.F. Adams, 1874–1877: 11.455, Dec. 21, 1843; 11.472–473 (Jan. 1, 1844).

16 Adams, John Quincy, *Speech of John Quincy Adams, of Massachusetts, Upon the Right of the People, Men and Women, to Petition; on the Freedom of Speech and of Debate in the House of Representatives of the United States; on the Resolutions of Seven State Legislatures, and the Petitions of More Than One Hundred Thousand Petitioners, Relating to the Annexation of Texas to the Union*: 82–83 (Washington, DC, 1838). Mason (2002, 2009) shows how British propagandists used the hypocrisy charge to great effect against the United States in international contexts.

17 *Congressional Globe*, 27th Cong., 2nd Sess., 1842: 168.

18 Bemis, 1956: 427–436; *Congressional Globe*, 27th Cong., 2nd Sess., 1842: 168; Frederick, 1991: 138, 154n115; W.L. Miller, 1996: 225–273. Five years earlier, Adams had drawn the ire of Southern congressmen for presenting two "frivolous" petitions, one from a group of Fredericksburg, VA, "ladies" calling for the prohibition of the slave trade in the District of Columbia and one (probably apocryphal) from a group of slaves claiming to prefer slavery to freedom. An attempt to at least rebuke Adams for "casting disrespect" on the

House failed, though a sizable majority voted for a resolution affirming that slaves had no constitutionally protected right to petition Congress (Bemis, 1956: 343–347; *Congressional Globe*, 24th Cong., 2nd Sess., 1837: 162–175; Frederick, 1991: 134–137; W.L. Miller, 1996: 429–444).

19 *House Journal*, 27th Cong., 2nd Sess., March 21, 1842, 567.

20 Unlike Adams, Giddings was not even afforded an opportunity to defend himself, probably a testament both to the less restrained nature of his congressional behavior and to the fact that he was not a former president (*House Journal*, 27th Cong., 2nd Sess., Mar. 21–23, 1842, 570–586; W.L. Miller, 1996: 449–453).

21 Eventually, Great Britain paid compensation of $110 330 to the insurers in the *Creole* case (Moore, 1898: 1.417). Adams's initial reaction to the *Amistad* case was also relatively muted (C.F. Adams, 1874–1877: 131–132, Sept. 23, 1829; 133–135, Oct. 1–2, 1839). For his part, Giddings took the lead in ensuring that the federal government did not reimburse the Spanish claimants in the case for their losses (Giddings, 1853: 73–96, "The Amistad Negroes," Apr. 18, 1844; *Congressional Globe*, 33rd Cong., 1st sess., 1853: 52–54, Appendix).

Further Reading

Hargreaves, M.W.M. (1985). *The Presidency of John Quincy Adams.* Lawrence, KS.

Mason, M.E. (2006), *Slavery and Politics in the Early American Republic.* Chapel Hill, NC.

Nagel, P.C. (1964). *One Nation Indivisible: The Union in American Thought.* New York.

Nagel, P. C. (1998). *John Quincy Adams: A Public Life, A Private Life.* New York.

Parsons, L.H. (2009). *The Birth of Modern Politics: Andrew Jackson, John Quincy Adams, and the Election of 1828.* New York.

Chapter Nineteen

John Quincy Adams, Cosmopolitan

Bethel Saler

President John Quincy Adams declared in his First Annual Message to Congress of 1825 that the legislature needed to encourage national improvement in the very broadest sense, not just through laws that promoted agriculture, commerce, domestic manufactures and mechanics, but also those that nurtured "the elegant arts, the advancement of … literature, and the progress of the sciences, ornamental and profound." Probably the most famous of his many bold proposals called for a national university and a national astronomical observatory with an astronomer in constant attendance. With 130 of these "lighthouses of the skies" in the "comparatively small territorial surface of Europe," and not one in "the whole of the American hemisphere," Adams concluded that this "darkness" was one of the many ways that the United States remained intellectually dependent on and inferior to Europe (Adams, 1825b). Adams's "ambitious schemes" in his 1825 message – integrating the arts and sciences (including discovery of the continental West along with the wide skies above) with the more conventional formal politics of internal improvements, patent laws and foreign trade policies – encapsulated, as Daniel Walker Howe noted, "his own daily program for self-development writ large" (D.W. Howe, 1979: 45; for an example of Adams's demanding daily schedule for a full day of intellectual pursuits and public work, see C.F. Adams, 1874–1877: 1.379).

Adams's measurements of the United States against Europe, however, also drew upon personal experience and observation, during his European education, and from his extensive diplomatic relations with European states. Most of all, his comprehensive perspective of the United States in a

A Companion to John Adams and John Quincy Adams, First Edition.
Edited by David Waldstreicher.

wider world, a perspective that valued cultural and scientific achievement as integral features of national, sovereign authority, expressed John Quincy Adams's cosmopolitanism.

Historians have puzzled over how best to characterize the second President Adams. His astonishing scholarly breadth across mathematical, scientific, historical and literary fields, versatility in seven languages, avid absorption of European customs and arts, and service to a vast array of social and academic associations and institutions testify to his rich cultural life (Howe, 1979: 44). Pursuits of intellect and sensibility intertwined with Adams's long life in government as his diaries minutely recount; he discerned political lessons in poetry and plays, and he littered his official correspondence and public addresses with references to ancient and modern European histories, political theories, and literature. Given Adams's immersion in Enlightenment history, classical studies, and European philosophies, it is unsurprising that scholars have variously identified his ideas with Ciceronian "civic humanism," the classical republicanism of his father's Revolutionary generation or the English "Country Party" (D.W. Howe, 1979: 44–52; Lewis, 2001: xii–xvi, 1; R.R. Thompson, 1991: 162–167). At the same time, institutional historians have exposed the popularity of Adams's vision of internal improvements and the crucial role played by the national government over the antebellum period in the emergence of a nationally networked economy (S.P. Adams, 2008; Larson, 2001).

Rather than a study in contrasts and contradictions, though – of Enlightenment humanism and ambitious, antebellum institutionalism – John Quincy Adams's many angles spoke of the pluralism and historical dynamism of the cosmopolitan ideal and of his version of that ideal. Indeed, this European-originated, abstract notion took on new tones when applied to the New World early republic. Adams's cosmopolitan sensibilities generated a credo of federal union, of cultural and political autonomy and of commercial reciprocity rooted in his own explorations –via his scholarship and public service – of the commonalities *and* incommensurable differences among nations of the world.

The term cosmopolitanism refers to an ideal most commonly associated with the European Enlightenment of the long eighteenth century, but which boasts a history stretching back to antiquity and a plurality of meanings, none of which "existed in doctrinal purity" (Schlereth, 1977: xi). Historians focusing just on the multi-pronged cosmopolitanism of the eighteenth-century Enlightenment are nonetheless careful to note that, apart from the simple definition of someone who identified beyond the nation, this abstract notion had a variety of interpretative twists between 1600 and 1800 (Jacob, 2006: 2). French *philosopher* Denis Diderot defined cosmopolitans in his Encyclopedia of 1751 as "strangers nowhere in the world," and citizens "of the cosmopolis, the world city." The chimerical, yet familiar Enlightenment concept grew to encompass Christian (largely Protestant)-inflected morality, social reformism, and political and economic internationalism (Schlereth, 1977: xi–xii, 1; Jacob, 2006: 126). Diderot, along with other Enlightenment thinkers, viewed *cosmopolite* and *philosophe* as interchangeable terms, part of an informal, transnational body of intellectuals dedicated to increasing the universal wealth of human knowledge and civilization (Schlereth, 1977: 1–2; O'Brien, 1997: 1–3). Although often put in terms "more symbolic and theoretical than actual and practical," aspiring cosmopolitans challenged the provincial narrowness, parochial prejudices and aristocratic pretensions of their societies in favor of a basic unity of mankind. In such a spirit, *philosophe* David Hume argued that the advancement of "the refined arts" rather than "politeness and breeding" fostered civilization and a more connected humanity; by the same logic, intellectual pursuits were not the exclusive domain of the noble classes but open to all with the necessary industry and capacity (Schlereth, 1977: xii–xiii, 2–3).

Despite the definitional elusiveness of the cosmopolitan ideal, by the second half of the eighteenth century a distinct set of characteristics and activities identified a population of peripatetic intellectuals from Europe and the United States who promoted a cosmopolitan ethos of intellectual solidarity in coffee houses, salons, libraries, circulating print journals, personal correspondence, clubs, and academies. Women intellectuals moved in these heady cosmopolitan circles, often as the brilliant hostesses of salons, yet men still composed the majority of the cosmopolitan elite. All such seekers of knowledge traveled frequently to gather in each other's company in the major urban centers in Europe. While Paris remained "Europe's coffee house" and modern French along with classical Greek and Latin the lingua franca among such intellectuals, an emerging intellectual elite also gathered in informal groups and formal academies in other major European cities including London, Amsterdam, Berlin, and The Hague. Most of these "citizens of the world" either read or spoke numerous languages. By the late eighteenth century, Edmund Burke observed that, "Europe possessed 'a system of manners and education that was nearly similar to all in this quarter of the globe' such that 'no citizen of Europe could be altogether an exile in any part of it.'" (Schlereth, 1977: 2). The expected bill of fare among this transnational elite stretched across a dazzling range of fields; they delved deeply into comparative philosophy, natural and experimental sciences, archaeology, economy, poetry, literature, music and other fine arts, political theory and history – of both the ancient and modern worlds. Moreover, formal agencies and institutions such as national academies, salons, and associations governed by this same intellectual class promoted professional recognition, standards, and canonization of texts as well as public discussion and critique (Schlereth, 1977: 1–12).

A moral as well as intellectual imperative drove cosmopolitan thinkers to advance pluralistic understandings of western civilization and of a broader humanity. Cicero's ideal of *humanitas* inspired many worldly thinkers (including John Quincy Adams) to pursue both an individual and universal standard of virtue achieved through contributing to the knowledge of their countries and toward the progress of humanity (Schlereth, 1977: xix–xx). Yet Enlightenment writers disagreed profoundly over how to conceive of humanity itself. Probably the most basic opposition pitted Jean Jacques Rousseau's "natural man" model, which celebrated an original human society based in the natural world and uncorrupted by social artifice, against a different perspective that saw cultural agency as the single most defining feature of humanity. As Edmund Burke succinctly put it, "art is Man's nature"; or in other words, and in sharp contrast to animals, humans possessed "rational, emotive, aesthetic, and imaginative" abilities to apprehend, invent, inscribe, and shape their social worlds. Social artifice and cultural production set humans apart from all other creatures.

Political theorist Sankar Muthu identifies this construction of a constitutively pluralistic humanity as definitive of an Enlightenment anti-imperialist tradition, and he locates it more specifically in the works of Denis Diderot (1713–1784), Immanuel Kant (1724–1804) and Johann Gottfried Herder (1744–1803). Not only did these *philosophes* argue for a culturally active humanity, but because each community or society's cultural agency necessarily took place within specific social, physical, and historical contexts, this cultural diversity also reflected "incommensurable differences" (Muthu, 2003: 1–10). Called "the father of German studies" in America, John Quincy Adams translated Kantian philosophy for his father, owned the works of Herder, and quoted Diderot as well (W.J. Morris, 1990: 28; C.F. Adams, 1874–1877: 2.69). More importantly though, these *philosophes*' idea of a culturally diverse humanity paralleled Adams's own perceptions of the peculiarities and incommensurable differences between the American republic and European states, and his attention to detecting such cultural distinctions in art as well as in political institutions and ideologies.

John Quincy Adams's education and early diplomatic assignments in Europe formed a set of experiences, literary and linguistic fluencies, and moral, aesthetic and political beliefs reflective of the Enlightenment, cosmopolitan ideal. His earliest diaries covering the time he spent in Europe from late 1778 through 1785 relate his intensive readings and studies in the classics, literature, poetry, natural history, philosophy, languages, and history. Both his parents supervised John Quincy's education over the first two decades of his life: his mother Abigail while he was a young boy in Braintree and his father, John, during the seven years of his adolescence spent in Europe. Along with a reverence for "Religion, Morality and Liberty," his parents encouraged him to master an Enlightenment bill of fare that stressed "a Taste for Literature, includ[ing] the Love of Science and the fine Arts," in combination with the genteel refinements such as handwriting, social etiquette, dancing, fencing, horseback riding, and skating – these last three, John Adams explained, would provide him an "Elegance of

Motion, which is charming to the sight" (Lewis, 2001: 2, 4). Still, the senior Adams firmly prioritized oral and written expression, classical languages and history – all useful to their current revolution–above mathematics, science and geography, and he deemed "genteel refinements" such as dancing, painting and fencing a luxury (Parsons, 1998: 11–13, 20).

Indeed, both Abigail and John Adams took a very pragmatic view of intellectual pursuits; these did not constitute an end in themselves. In a 1780 letter to Abigail, John Adams sketched a long generational evolution before his descendants fully enjoyed the safety and security necessary to practice the (non-essential) fine arts: "I must study Politicks and War that my sons may have liberty to study Mathematics and Philosophy. My sons ought to study Mathematics and Philosophy, Geography, natural History, Naval Architecture, Commerce and Agriculture, in order to give their Children a right to study Painting, Poetry, Musick, Architecture, Statuary, Tapestry and Porcelaine" (Parsons, 1998: 20). John Adams, therefore, guided his son John Quincy's studies with very explicit, immediate aims. For instance, he suggested that John Quincy "read Thucydides history of the Peloponnesian War" since "the future circumstances of your Country, may require other Wars, as well as Councils and Negotiations" (Parsons, 1998: 12).

An obedient son who strove to fulfill his parents' admonitions, John Quincy Adams, in fact, far exceeded his parents' suggested curriculum. His avid intellectual curiosity and self-discipline propelled his studies, along with a natural facility for languages, and his insistence on blending "Politicks and War" with poetry and literature. Adams's early diaries chronicle his mental journeys through classical Greek and Latin literature, rhetoric, history, and the philosophy of canonical writers like Thucydides, Plato, Horace, Virgil, Caesar, and Cicero. Reading classical texts in their original languages provided common referents and refined languages unifying an international Republic of Letters (Schlereth, 1997: 9–10). He also closely followed the footsteps of earlier eighteenth-century cosmopolitans by taking full advantage of the array of intellectual hotspots and cultural wealth in the urban centers of Europe. While living in or touring Paris, Leyden, St Petersburg, The Hague, London, Berlin, Stockholm, and Copenhagen, John Quincy Adams eagerly patronized the coffee houses and social clubs, the theaters, operas, curiosity cabinets, museums and private painting collections, the booksellers, subscription libraries and academies. Especially as regards entrée into the more exclusive exhibits, Adams benefited from his father's eminent and international network of political dignitaries and "gentlemen of letters."

John Quincy Adams's first tour of London at age 17 already exemplified his energetic attention to the arts, sciences, and erudite circles thriving in the urban centers of Europe. Along with the main tourist attractions such as Westminster Abbey, St Paul's Cathedral, the courts of law, and parliament, Adams sought out the major art and artists of London. He viewed the paintings of Robert Pine, Joshua Reynolds, and John Singleton Copley and visited the American spy and wax modeler, Mrs Patience Wright's Waxworks (Allen et al., 1981: 1.198). A week later, he saw Irishman James Barry's "The Progress of Society," a much celebrated six-painting series depicting "the cultivation of 'human faculties' in the civilization of mankind hanging in the Great Room of the Society for the Encouragement of Arts, Manufactures and Commerce." (Allen et al., 1981: 1.201). He dined too with fellow Americans John Singleton Copley and Benjamin West, and West took John Quincy on a private viewing of the art at Buckingham Palace where he reveled in the southern and northern Renaissance art of Raphael, Van Dyke, and Rueben. From Renaissance art, they ended their palace tour with West's own Enlightenment cluster of heroic depictions of "the death of General Wolfe, of the Chevalier Bayard; and of Epaminondas, Regulus coming out of the Senate, and Hannibal, swearing eternal enmity to the Romans." A little over two weeks later, West escorted John Quincy on a tour of the sculpture housed in the Royal Academy of the Arts (Allen et al., 1981: 1: 205).

While in London and in Europe more generally, John Quincy also relished the latest scientific discoveries. Over two centuries of European exploration in Asia and the Americas had provided both sources and momentum to the question of human universality and incommensurable differences. During his visit to the Holuphusicon, Sir Ashton Lever's museum of natural history in London, Adams leaned toward a culturally pluralistic view when he readily acknowledged the innovation and artistry of the native artifacts collected on the last voyage of Captain Cook. From the sacred idols of wood and feathers and intricate feathered robes to the quotidian fish hooks and ropes, he declared all, for the most part, "very ingeniously done," and "show [that] those People had arrived at a certain degree of Civilization" (Allen et al., 1981: 1.200).

From these ethnographic distinctions of natural *history*, Adams easily switched to the more universal, objective value of natural *science*. To his disappointment, he caught the transactions of the Royal Society "on a barren night," and had to listen to a disappointing paper about the recent earthquake in Calabria. The night was redeemed, however, when he supped at the London Coffee House with the Club of Honest Whigs, an intellectual association initiated by Benjamin Franklin and composed mostly of dissenting clergymen and men with scientific interests (Allen et al., 1981: 1.203). Although the Royal Society had proved a disappointment, a couple months previously in Paris, John Quincy had witnessed one of the first hot air balloons. He judged the significance of this "experiment of the flying globe," to be "a very important one," given its potential for the good of all mankind (Allen et al., 1981: 1.187–188). Not all scientific claims reached the progressive heights of the "flying globe," though. John Quincy deemed Franz Mesmer's then very popular theory of animal magnetism, for example, full of pretense.

Pretense and artifice also had its charms. Of all the captivating arts and sciences in Europe, none delighted the young John Quincy Adams more than the theater. During his first trip to Paris in 1778, he wrote to his sister Abigail of his great delight in all the "Spectacles." Their father preferred him to attend tragedies by Racine or Voltaire, and the 12-year-old Adams already had enjoyed the opera numerous times. Still, while these other amusements were agreeable, he declared that "the wit the passions the sentiments the oratory the poetry the manners and morals are at the French Comedy."[1] Because different national touring companies criss-crossed Europe, John Quincy not only enjoyed a range of different kinds of spectacles – whether opera, ballet, dance, varieties, tragedies, or his favorite comedies – in all the major European cities, but he also gained a comparative sampling of distinct national interpretations of each form.

The immediate and public nature of theater also gave John Quincy Adams insight into national sensibilities and political disputes. While accompanying his father to Paris, serving as a French translator to US envoy Francis Dana in Russia or as a diplomat in his own right, John Quincy Adams already had a close-up view of the political maelstroms in Europe but from the perspective of an American outsider. From the different national plays and performances, he could partake vicariously in the internal political divides and sometimes implicit grudges stretching back across history among the different European powers. Indeed, interesting political content might redeem an otherwise mediocre performance. Such was John Quincy Adams's verdict on the rewrite of Othello by Ducis entitled *Othello, ou le More de Venise*. He observed in his diary that it was a "wretched travestie"; however, it at least had "the merit ... of containing sarcasms upon aristocracy, and abuse upon the government of Venice." (C.F. Adams, 1874–1877: 1.180).

Late eighteenth-century European performers, writers, and viewers alike were acutely aware of the political power of theatrical spectacles to convey moral lessons and to influence public debate. John Quincy recorded in his diary the imprisonment of French publisher, diplomat, and playwright Pierre Beaumarchais in 1785 for criticism of the French court and king in his famous comedy, *Le Marriage de Figaro* and subsequent public writings (Williamson, 2000: 897–898). State oppression and regulation of theatrical performances only underscored a common assumption within most European states that theater had a public responsibility to offer moral instruction and to give shape to civic society. In the Paris of 1783, for instance, John Quincy Adams was enjoying a popular new tragic form, the *tragedie bourgeoise* that countered the libertinage of ancien-regime aristocrats with an emphasis on moderation, chastity, and sexual honor (Allen et al., 1981: 183–184, 233–234; Williamson, 2000: 897).

The political power of theater as a public institution would have been familiar to John Adams, John Quincy Adams and other Americans living abroad in Europe in the 1780s. From the American Revolution onward, republicans seized on the public and political power of theater – in street performances, public toasts, parades and staged plays – to fight for their opposing visions of the contours of their republican confederation, the civic values to promote among their citizens, and which economic actors should be favored as the citizen subjects and social models of their new nation (Waldstreicher, 1997; S.P. Newman, 1997; Withington, 1991). At the same time, Americans clashed – sometimes violently – over their ideas about theater itself. The Continental Congress proclaimed in 1774: "We will discountenance every species of extravagance and dissipation, especially all horse-racing, and all kinds of gaming, cock-fighting, exhibition of shews, plays, and other expensive diversions and entertainments." The primarily British productions during the Revolution pitted anti-theater-identified "patriots" against pro-theater supporters, castigated as "Tories." Over the next two decades, pro- and anti-theater antagonists divided again along the new political battle lines of federal constitutionalists versus anti-federalists, who wished that majority power remain with the states (J. Brown, 1995: 6; Nathans, 2003: 37–70; J. Shaffer, 2007; Withington, 1991). John Quincy Adams took a third approach that harkened back to the Revolution and resistance to tyrannical laws when he weighed in against the Massachusetts anti-theater prohibition in 1792 under the pseudonym Menander. He argued for the unconstitutionality of Massachusetts' prohibition and the right of the people to contravene a legislative act judged so (W.C. Ford, 1913–1917: 1.127–130).

The power and potential danger of theater, similar to other forms of art, lay not just in explicit political arguments but also in meanings charged in sentiment and evoking specific sensibilities. Tragedies especially played upon peoples' emotions, and more particularly on the innate human ability to sympathize, a power beyond reason, and what moral sense philosophers like John Locke and Adam Smith considered the foundation of human morality (McConachie, 1998: 138–139; for JQA's discussion of reading Locke's *Essay on Understanding*, see Allen et al. 1981: 1.394–395). In his diaries, John Quincy Adams mused over what was revealed by the different plays and national theaters he attended about contrasting national sensibilities. In these meditations, he joined other cosmopolitans in thinking about diverse cultures and romantic characterizations of nation states. John Quincy, for example, described the "American Union as a moral Person in the family of Nations" (Lang and Russell, 1990: 11–12; Tatum, 1941: 383). Although individual European nations had long tried to differentiate themselves from their near neighbors, the emerging romance of the nation was something new (Anderson, 1983; Colley, 1992; Hunt, 1992). After attending Prosper Crébillon's tragedy *Rhadamisteet Zenobie*, Adams observed that while the author "is regarded as one of the best dramatick poets of France," his tragedies are so deep that several "miscarried" on their first showing. The trouble, Adams speculated, stemmed from the French difficulty of bearing tragedy and especially when the story ended with "the Death of the Hero." By contrast, during the performance of an English tragedy at the Drury Lane Theatre, London, with the great tragedian Mrs Siddons in the lead, a young woman was so overcome as to nearly faint, and had to be carried out. Adams pondered over the incident: "I am told that every Night Mrs. Siddons performs; this happens, to some persons. I never heard of anything like it, in France: Whether this proves there is more Sensibility here, that the Tragedies are deeper, or that they are better performed, is a problem. Perhaps all those Reason's may be given" (Allen et al., 1981: 1.184–85, 198).

Heightened sensitivity to cultural particularities, emotional intelligence, wit, reason, and a wide erudition all proved advantageous to John Quincy Adams's formal and informal exchanges while serving in various diplomatic posts in Europe. In a sense, diplomacy offered the perfect pragmatic application of cosmopolitan ideals. To further a connected humanity, to foster progress and self-definition of one's own nation state within a wider world, and to discern cultural distinctions and shared values among the different states – all these fell within the purview of the diplomat. In the spirit of Hume, John Quincy Adams much preferred his frequent intellectual exchanges with like-minded, worldly ministers to the mannered pretensions of the diplomatic rituals and high-society events that composed such a large part of European diplomacy. His diaries recount his continual frustration with the "tedious" dinners, balls, and tea and card parties he endured during his different sojourns as US diplomatic representative to The Hague, Great Britain, the Kingdom of Prussia, and Tsarist Russia. After the second ball in two evenings with the same set of Prussian royalty and court society, he observed that "[t]here is stiffness, coldness, formality, politeness, labored affability, studied attention, and every thing except that mutual *abandon* (to use the French phrase) which constitutes the charm of conviviality." He also suffered the officious run-arounds and hidebound diplomatic rituals of these Old World monarchies and republics, what he referred to as the "forms and precedences and titles, and all the trash of diplomatic ceremony" (C.F. Adams, 1874–1877: 1.215, 207).

Against such tedium and affectation born of Old World aristocratic pretensions, John Quincy Adams lauded the informed conversation and diplomatic salons of other ambassadorial "gentlemen of letters" as they attended plays, operas, and other spectacles or discussed literature, philosophy, and science as part of their consular interactions. While stationed at The Hague in 1795, for instance, Adams remarked on a dinner at "Count Lowenhielm's with a company principally diplomatic," during which the Portuguese minister Mr Araujo "had much to say of Rousseau." On a walk with the Prussian minister Baron Bielfield ten days later, John Quincy recounted that "[o]ur conversation was political, literary, and critical, without sliding, as it often does, into the bottomless pit of metaphysics." At another dinner, this time in London while on a temporary mission, Adams supped with an assortment of distinguished and scientific gentlemen and recalled that "conversation was miscellaneous: philosophical, political and literary" (C.F. Adams, 1874–1877: 1.110, 111, 136).

Supplementing these cerebral exchanges with other diplomats, John Quincy relied on European history to better understand the comparative pasts, passions, and characters of the nations where he served. As his diaries make clear, Adams read (and re-read) all the major Enlightenment historians; and most of them – such as David Hume, William Robertson, David Ramsay, and Edward Gibbon – wrote from a cosmopolitan perspective. As Historian Karen O'Brien has shown (1997), these cosmopolitan historians constructed narratives of "national self-invention," stories that mapped out distinct histories and identities from "the interplay of likeness and difference within the family of Christian churches and nations" (K. O'Brien, 1997: 1, 4). In combination with national histories, Adams also turned to the memoirs of prior diplomats and politicians to get a better feel for the peculiarities and details of a specific nation state. While a diplomat to The Hague in the midst of the negotiations between the French republic and the new Batavian republic in 1795, for instance, John Quincy Adams read in succession the memoirs of Count D'Estrades, Count d'Avaux, and the marquis de Torcy, all leading seventeenth-century French ambassadors who had dealings with the Netherlands. As US minister plenipotentiary to Prussia, moreover, he gauged where Count Mirabeau's *The Secret History of the Court of Berlin*, proved accurate or not for the current Prussian royals and their administration (C.F. Adams, 1874–1877: 1.110; 1.111; 1.75–76; 1.211).

Count Mirabeau's sensational *Secret History*, however, proved the exception to the way John Quincy employed history to understand the different European nations. Adams was well aware that in the midst of the revolutionary turbulence of the 1790s and the unnerving sense of the birth of a new age, the past seemed inapplicable to many Europeans. Portuguese diplomat and intellectual Antonio de Araujo, a favorite colleague at The Hague, urged John Quincy not to look to history for models, for "[t]here is not, indeed the same advantage in possessing the principles and experience of able negotiations, because the present state of opinions and of practice requires a different theory."Araujo's advice in 1795 stood in polar opposition to John Adams's suggestion in 1777 that his son read the ancient history of Thucydides for resemblances to and guidance for their current Revolution.[2] John Quincy Adams's own conviction that nations were unpredictable bodies that typically acted against their real interests made him skeptical of universal historical models or the idea that one could project a nation's future from its past. Nonetheless, he defended the value of reading history. "At least it increases the knowledge of history," Adams maintained. And by thus supplying comparative, historical context, he further reasoned, it "gives lessons of *analogy* which have some use for application to every position of affairs among men" (C.F. Adams, 1874–1877: 1.111–112; 1.110; W.C. Ford, 1913–1917: 3.279).

Seeing history as analogy spoke to the subtleties of discerning likeness and difference in individual nations over time and to the sometimes intangible national variations – particular sensibilities – distinguishing one European nation from another. Evaluating translations of western literature, another of John Quincy Adams's intellectual employments, similarly offered a rich source for the cosmopolitan inquiry into comparative national opacities and resemblances. Adams described, for example, what appeared to be a heady dinner party in June 1796 in which the company dined on energetic critiques of specific translations. The guests included Mr Araujo;[3] Prussian minister Baron Bielfeld; Mr Franciso Manoel, considered the most eminent Portuguese poet of his day; and John Quincy's younger brother, Thomas Boylston Adams. The party spent most of the evening swapping opinions on a wide variety of translations of major texts. Araujo, for example, proclaimed Jacques Delille's translation of the Georgics the "only good French poetical translation extant." The Italian translation of Virgil by Hannibal Caro was deemed undeserving of its reputation, "and not equal to Dryden's." After dinner, they compared President (Charles-Jean-François) Henault's translation of Lucretius with the original Latin epic poem, concluding that, "it has merit, but very weak lines." Their critiques of these various translations epitomized yet another kind of circulation of the creative energies of the different European nations. As transformed literary products standing alongside the original texts, translations revealed to cosmopolitan readers cultural differences in language, aesthetics, and metaphor. Equally intriguing, the work of translation, like other forms of cultural activity, also had political import and cost. Mr Manoel, John Quincy related in his dairy, "was compelled to flee the fangs of the Inquisition [in Portugal] for having translated Voltaire's Pucelle d'Orleans" (C.F. Adams, 1874–1877: 1.168–169).

From this extended exposure to the arts and diplomacy in different European cities, John Quincy Adams delineated the differences and peculiarities of his own New World republic. He hardly could avoid such comparisons given that at each of his diplomatic postings, the local dignitaries pressed him with questions and opinions about America. After some discussion on American neutrality, for instance, French minister plenipotentiary François Noel remarked that, "America was becoming every day more interesting as an object of observation." Noel had a great desire to visit the continent himself, and he had heard that the orientalist, the comte de Volney, famous for his observations of Egypt and Syria, now was touring America. Noel hoped that Volney's explorations "would produce general and useful information." The loose association of the United States with non-western places came up again for Adams in a conversation with the

Prussian princess Louise, sister to the queen. The princess spoke of America and of having read M. Valliant's travels, exposing that she had confused America with Africa, the subject of François le Valliant's recently published narrative (C.F. Adams, 1874–1877: 1.125–126, 214).

In one sense, Europeans' perception of America as distant and having a certain novelty well suited Adams's own steadfast desire that the American republic maintain a strict policy of neutrality in all European conflicts. He had first articulated his views on neutrality in political essays under the pseudonyms "Marcellus" and "Columbus" in 1793 while Citizen Genet promoted the French revolutionary cause in the United States, and he persisted in his advocacy through letters and reports to the State Department while stationed at The Hague and in Prussia.[4] His conviction that America should avoid all entanglements with foreign powers, in fact, received its widest circulation in President Washington's Farewell Address of 1796, the president having been influenced by Adams's essays and reports (Lewis, 2001: 10).

John Quincy Adams championed a policy of neutrality to secure and protect the federal union, the core feature of the American republic distinguishing it from European states and all the troubles they endured. Starting with his "Marcellus" and "Columbus" essays, Adams continuously warned in his public writings that the greatest danger to the Union lay in internal conflicts, whether prompted by domestic issues such as slavery or from warring sympathies with foreign powers. Contemplating the political fights in the US republic over support for the French revolutionaries, John Quincy remarked to his father in 1794 that though the "external enemies ... may distress us, ... we can be ruined only by ourselves." For, to heal their divides and unite remained "the duty of every American" (W.C. Ford, 1913–1917: 1.178). Europeans too recognized and echoed back to Adams his concerns about the vulnerability of the voluntary American union. Prussian Prince Henry, for example, inquired about whether "the centre of union" was "sufficiently strong enough to keep us together, and to stand the trials of inconveniences incident to republican and especially federative Governments" (C.F. Adams, 1874–1877: 1.210). The very composition of the American union – the collective self-governance as one nation out of many disparate parts and interests – also made it especially vulnerable to internal divides. John Quincy commented with resignation to his father that as "you well know ... in our country the passions, always at work, will never suffer opinions for any length of time to harmonize..." (W.C. Ford, 1913–1917: 6.209).

Despite his worries about disunion, Adams took pride in the notable contrasts between the federal union and European states – especially the greater freedom of opinion and energies enjoyed by American citizens. In a discussion about Jay's Treaty in 1795, British Undersecretary of State George Hammond tried to goad Adams into anger regarding the Republican opposition to the treaty in the United States. "He [Hammond] talked about the Virginians, the Southern People, the democrats." John Quincy promptly informed the Undersecretary that he considered them "all in no other light than as Americans." He added in his diary that certainly with foreigners he would speak of the Republicans in no other way. Yet Adams also stressed that the very visibility of the "anti-federalist" critique reflected a particular strength of the American republican system. Although all governments provoked opposition, in America, Adams told Hammond, "opposition speaks in a louder voice than anywhere else. Everything comes out. We have no lurking disaffection that works in secret and is not seen." That is, rather than the intrigue and repression so common to European states, Americans enjoyed freedom of thought and government transparency (C.F. Adams, 1874–1877: 1.143).

Liberty of opinion proved one of the several peculiarities of the US federal system that John Quincy had to explain to Europeans. In these details lay more profound differences of principle and the starting premises that separated the New World republic from Old World regimes. When he arrived in London as temporary agent in 1795, for example, he faced pressure from the British administration to act in the full capacities of a minister plenipotentiary of the United States. Adams stressed that his credential letter designated clearly his specific and limited orders, and that no subjective leeway existed; he was bound by an articulated, legal framework (C.F. Adams, 1874–1877: 1.162–164). "[T]he thing with us is *Constitutional*; and were I to assume the character of a Minister at this Court, and act under it, I should not only be impeachable for it, but it would be deceiving you not to tell you that the United States would be bound by none of my acts" (C.F. Adams, 1874–1877: 1.164). Adams thus relied upon the abstract nature of political power in a representative government. Authority resided in the objective structures of the US Constitution and not in individual persons (and their characters and reputations).

John Quincy Adams confronted the dissonance of this new, impersonal vision of the diplomat more starkly when he faced the European custom of diplomatic gift-giving. Upon leaving his post at The Hague to become US minister to Prussia in 1797, Adams contended with Mr Van Leyden, the secretary to the Committee on Foreign Affairs for the Dutch republic, over the longstanding custom of leave-taking presents to foreign ministers. Adams insisted that an article in the constitution prohibited his acceptance of any gift from a foreign government. But as M. Van Leyden pointed out, he would insult the Dutch government by refusing. They finally agreed that, "it might be left for future arrangement," so that Adams could solicit the consent of Congress to accept the presents (C.F. Adams, 1874–1877: 1.191). In this political impasse, Adams spoke as an impersonal representative of the national government whereas Mr Van Leyden wanted to recognize the individual service and personhood of Adams, the man who carried out the work and whose character did honor to his nation. Though a subtle distinction in emphasis, it told of very different political assumptions.

While John Quincy Adams was highlighting the core distinctions of the American republic to Europeans during his different diplomatic postings from 1794 through 1801, Republicans and Federalists in the domestic realm battled over conflicting interpretations of their federal system. During this time, John Quincy complained to his family about the dearth of news about the United States and the inattention to his diplomatic reports from the Department of State. In fact, he felt doubly frustrated. In a letter to his father from The Hague in 1797, he warned, "all my American correspondents, public and private, as they appear to care nothing about the affairs of Europe, seem alike to think us indifferent to those of America. This inattention will eventually produce consequences very serious to our country and its government" (W.C. Ford, 1913–1917: 2.78–79).

Through his diplomatic exchanges and from living in Europe, Adams had come to appreciate fully the singularity of the American union. He thought it all the more imperative, therefore, to increase Americans' awareness of the unattractive alternative embodied by the European states. In published essays and private letters from abroad, Adams tried to redress Americans' inattention to the ongoing warfare and oppression constitutive of the European system of states. "The European *condition of society*," he explained in a letter to his brother Thomas, stood as a portent of the miseries incumbent in a land divided into wholly independent, territorially competitive states. In the ruthless struggles for territory, he exclaimed, "[w]hat a number of sovereign states have been swallowed up in the vortex of the last ten years, for the crime of being weak and unable to resist an invading army! What a number more are upon the point of suffering the same fate!" Sovereign survival required each European state to maintain a permanent army, and the people suffered the heavy costs in loss of civic rights and income. He concluded with the dark forecast that "standing armies, intolerable taxes, forced levies, contributions, conscriptions, and requisitions, … [were] the unavoidable and fatal chain of which disunion is but the first link" (W.C. Ford, 1913–1917: 2.500–502).

Returning to the United States from his posting in Berlin in the fall of 1801, John Quincy spent little time practicing law before the Massachusetts Federalists conscripted him for public office. While serving as a state senator from Suffolk county in 1802, Adams made an unsuccessful bid for a seat in the US House of Representatives. The following year, the Federalist-dominated Massachusetts state legislature elected him as one of their two representatives to the US Senate. With only a couple years of legislative experience preparing him for the Senate, John Quincy Adams nonetheless had confirmed the political *credos* that would guide his decisions for at least the next two decades. These pivotal commitments developed out of his many prior years of comparative thinking about the American republic in relation to Europe. In an autobiographical sketch in 1809, Adams succinctly outlined "two political principles that form the basis of the system of policy best suited to the interests and the duties of this country. One in relation to its internal concerns, UNION, the other in respect to its intercourse with foreign nations, INDEPENDENCE" (W.C. Ford, 1913–1917: 3.300; Lewis, 2001: 22). He had publicly advocated these interdependent principles in one form or another since his "Marcellus" and "Columbus" essays on US neutrality in 1793.

Moreover, soon after his return to the United States and with his sights set on national office, Adams declared his resolution to abjure from all party-led decisions, famously pronouncing that though "a politician in this country must be the man of a party. I would fain be the man of my whole country" (C.F. Adams, 1874–1877: 1.249: Lewis, 2001: 12). When viewing the events of America from a distance, John Quincy more readily could see the American republic as a whole, rather than being drawn into sectional, social and ideologically driven perspectives. A biographer of Josiah Quincy noted that unlike Quincy or other New England Federalists who "lacked that wider perspective, that willingness to identify with all Americans rather than with just those of his section and class," Adams's "many years in Europe ... made him an implacable American." James E. Lewis, Jr., points out that by 1801, John Quincy "appears to have already developed in full his notoriously difficult personality." Thus, Adams's emphatic insistence on his independence and nonpartisanship appeared to be as much a personal as political matter to family and colleagues – reflective of a fundamental contrariness and a rigid tendency to paint his opposition as morally corrupt and generally self-serving (R.R. Thompson, 1991: 183; Lewis, 2001: 12).

Adams's insistence on staying politically independent of party machinations resulted in his frequent opposition and eventual alienation from his political patrons, the New England Federalists. Many historians have chronicled the Federalists' escalation of frustration and fury over John Quincy's dissenting votes in the Senate. As Adams admitted in 1804, "my opinions and votes have been much oftener in unison with the [Jefferson] administration than with their opponents" (R.R. Thompson, 1991: 183, 177). The final straw appeared to come when Adams helped write draft resolutions at a Republican meeting in Boston pledging support for all necessary actions taken by the Jeffersonian administration against Great Britain. The following day, one Federalist told Adams, that he should "*have ... [his] head taken off* by the Federalists for apostasy." Rather than he having abandoned the Federalist party, Adams judged that the Federalists had "deserted their country" (H. Adams, 1877: 183; R.R. Thompson, 1991: 177; Lewis, 2001: 23; C.F. Adams, 1874–1877: 1.469).

In his review of the posthumous writings of Federalist Fisher Ames in 1809, John Quincy Adams had the leisure to respond fully to the fierce opposition waged by the Federalists against the policies of the Jefferson administration and his own apostate positions. Throughout his review, John Quincy invoked a disembodied, collectively shared "American patriotism" as antidote to the jealous accusations made by Ames and the Federalists against various sectional interests allegedly threatening the Union. As Adams observed, "the most pernicious and fatal errors [are] for the people of any one part of this union to admit into their minds such sentiments against the rest." He called on legislators at all levels of government to make it their "first study" to "promote a spirit of conciliation" and to bind those too loosely attached through "an accommodating disposition toward their interests" (J.Q. Adams, 1809: 43, 37). Adams elaborated further on these emotional, internalized sources of patriotism and so, cords of union:

> The sense of common rights, of common enjoyments, of common moral and political principles, of congenial habits, manners, sentiments and even prejudices, the instincts of attachment to our native land, the love of fame, which, though an individual passion, identifies itself so naturally with the love of our country, ambition, which an accurate and close observer will find burning in the American breast more fiercely than that avarice, which strikes the superficial eye; the obligation of social duty. (J.Q. Adams, 1809: 54)

In other writings and legislative work, he provided more concrete means with which most of these affective national ties – of rights, enjoyments, morality, ambition, and so on – could be forged. For instance, he judged the Louisiana Purchase to be "of the highest advantage to us." Kentucky senator John Breckenridge's speech on the Senate floor proved especially persuasive to John Quincy of the Purchase's tremendous worth in lands, river commerce, and a major port city – all of which would better attach Westerners to the rest of the Union.[5] Six years after the Purchase, Adams answered Ames's scurrilous charge that Westerners had sunk into barbarism with the opposite depiction, and one that detailed his aspirations for Americans more generally: "American patriotism contemplates with very different sensations the rapid progress of these [western] settlements. The active enterprise and hardihood of character which distinguishes many of the setters; the rapidity with which population, cultivation, social enjoyments are constantly multiplying, with wealth and art, and science in their train" (J.Q. Adams, 1809: 43). The American genius for rapid territorial expansion also secured a portion of the Republic's "proper dominion" over "the [entire] continent of North America," simultaneously securing their expansive union from *foreign* colonization and fulfilling what John Quincy perceived as the United States' continental destiny (LaFeber, 1965: 36; W.C. Ford, 1913–1917: 4.128).

Along with territorial expansion, John Quincy envisioned building emotional ties and social networks of union through a thriving, commerce of domestic manufactures and via a cultural nationalism – distinctively original American literature, plays, fine arts, as well as scientific discoveries. Adam Smith called the eighteenth century an age of commerce and prose

(K. O'Brien, 1997: 7). In the early nineteenth century, John Quincy wanted the young American republic to lay claim to her full share of all forms of those carrying trades. To this end, he, his brother Thomas Boylston (who served as manager of the journal) and his father assisted Federalist editor Joseph Dennie to launch a weekly journal of "politics and literature," entitled *Port Folio*. John Quincy proved the most prolific contributor, and his submissions ranged from translations to travel accounts, poetry, and political commentary. He hoped the journal "would help remove 'that foul stain of literary barbarism, which has so long exposed our country to the reproach of strangers, and to the derision of her enemies." In a more modest vein, he wished "to excite a taste for poetry" among his countrymen. Lastly, John Quincy vowed to his brother Thomas upon finding out that "the English nation still possess[es] exclusively the carrying trade of all our literature and science; and that we can know nothing of foreign letters but through the medium of translations made in England. This evil I can but very partially contribute to remove. But what I can do, shall be done" (Kerber and Morris, 1965: 451–452, 454).

In the turbulent period after the War of 1812, Adams was all the more convinced of the vital necessity for the United States to achieve independence on all fronts – cultural, economic, and political. Neither the peace treaty of Ghent that the Adams-led delegation negotiated with Britain in 1814 nor the Congress of Vienna in 1815 filled John Quincy with much confidence in the future stability of the European state system. Moreover, the war with Britain had revealed all the deficiencies still preventing the American union from gaining full independence and thus, a shield from the political turmoil and threats of European states. Adams, for instance, called for "a more vigorous and independent system of finance," as well the growth of their domestic manufactures, and a "respectable navy" (W.C. Ford, 1913–1917: 5. 314). Yet he could also see ways in which Americans had gained renewed energies from the War of 1812, not least their creative and cultural agency. John Quincy Adams took delight from the "new literary and philosophical societies forming in various parts of our country, and there is every possible demonstration of the increased and increasing interest in the pursuits of literature and science taken by the people of the United States." The late war, he was convinced, had "not a little contributed to give this new impulse, and it is one of the benefits which we have derived from it" (W.C. Ford, 1913–1917: 5.402).

Adams's much-desired trifecta of American cultural, economic, and political self-sufficiency, however, in no way implied national isolation. Rather, his defining creed of "union" and "independence" espoused a cosmopolitan ideal for the relations of nations, equal and independent members in a global network of mutual commercial and intellectual benefit. Thus, after the War of 1812, in his positions as first US minister to Britain and then secretary of state, Adams sought non-discriminatory treatment in

American maritime and other kinds of commercial trade with other nations, including open access to each other's colonial ports. Commercial reciprocity stood in Adams's mind as one of "the ingredients of our national independence," encompassed in the American Revolution's declared inalienable right to the pursuit of happiness and also justified by "the Christian precept to love your neighbor as yourself" (C.F. Adams, 1874–1877: 5.427; LaFeber, 1965: 48–49; Lewis, 2001: 78).

With this same broad Christian invocation for a reciprocal public good and equality of fellowship, John Quincy Adams addressed Congress in 1825. "The spirit of improvement is abroad upon the earth," he announced. "It stimulates the hearts and sharpens the faculties not of our fellow citizens alone, but of the nations of Europe and of their rulers" (J.Q. Adams, 1825b). Further, as compared to Europe, the American republic enjoyed unparalleled political freedoms made possible by its distinctive federal union. In his review of Federalist Fisher Ames' writings in 1809, Adams had set forth the simple syllogism that "[u]nion is peace; and peace is liberty" (J.Q. Adams, 1809: 38). Sixteen years later in his first address to Congress, he added the third line "liberty is power," and because of its exceptionally large portion of liberty, the United States constituted a very powerful nation indeed. Such powers, Adams preached, must be tied to the public improvement of one's society and to wider humanity – the fundamental tenets of Ciceronian cosmopolitanism. He therefore exhorted his fellow representatives not to hide behind the excuse that "we are palsied by the will of our constituents," but to join in this international spirit of improvement (J.Q. Adams, 1825b).

For many historians, President Adams's unfortunate phrase, "palsied by the will of our constituents" symbolized his tone-deafness to current political trends and, more particularly, to the growing importance of universal male suffrage. While he engaged fully in domestic debates, John Quincy weighed popular politics with national interests and the latter with international concerns. That is, Adams thought about American politics in terms of three interconnected planes: (1) the diversity of individual interests, parties, states and sections, all these protected, limited and balanced by the US Constitution; (2) the collective interest of the federal union embodied in the activities and policies of the national government; and (3) the American nation-state participating in a pluralized cultural and political world of sovereign nations. The unpredictability and turbulence of this latter international network of nation states – stretching at least as far back as the Treaty of Westphalia – made the acquisition of national self-sufficiency, in realms of culture, science, and economy, so critical to the survival of the New World American republic. Further, the fact that John Quincy Adams comprehended the United States – its goals, strengths, and weaknesses – in relation to other nations and from a more culturally cosmopolitan perspective pushed him to champion grander national initiatives than those pursued by his successors. It is clear from his support for the Louisiana Purchase and his numerous negotiations with Spain, Russia, and Britain over acquiring their remaining North American lands and/or gaining fishing and trading rights that John Quincy Adams advocated western territorial expansion. He did so though as part of a more ambitious, global vision for American commercial expansion and intellectual achievement.

When he discovered in 1836 that a Frenchman had recently translated and published both his inaugural speech and first address to Congress under the title of "expositions of the American system of governance," John Quincy retorted that, "it was only *my* system" (Lewis, 2001: 143). Perhaps the Frenchman heard familiar notions in President Adams's addresses, such as an awareness and sense of moral responsibility for living in a wider world or competitive cultural nationalism distinguishing one state within a constellation of nation states. John Quincy Adams, on the other hand, heard only failure in the Frenchman's mistitle, the failure to convince Americans of his ambitious vision to make the federal union a fully independent, New World power against Old World threats. Instead of his plans for the US republic's eventual greatness, he lamented that "[t]he American Union as a moral Person in the family of Nations, is to live from hand to mouth" (Tatum, 1941: 383).

Notes

1 John Quincy Adams to Abigail Adams, II, Sept. 27, 1778, *Adams Family Papers.*
2 John Adams to John Quincy Adams, July 27, 1777, and Aug. 11, 1777, *Adams Family Papers.*
3 See "Araujo," *The Biographical Dictionary of the Society for the Diffusion of Useful Knowledge*, vol. III: 242 (London, 1843).
4 *Columbian Centinel*, Apr. 24, May 4, May 11, Dec. 4, 1793.
5 Annals of Congress, Senate, 8th Congress, 1st Session. In *American Memory: A Century of Lawmaking for a New Nation: U.S. Congressional Documents and Debates*, 1774–1875: 65, 68. At http://memory.loc.gov/ammem/amlaw/, accessed Nov. 20, 2012.

Further Reading

Bemis, Samuel Flagg (1949). *John Quincy Adams and the Foundations of American Foreign Policy.* New York.

Howe, Daniel Walker (1979). *The Political Culture of the American Whigs.* Chicago.

Thompson, Robert R. (1991). John Quincy Adams, Apostate: From "Outrageous Federalist" to "Republican Exile," 1801–1809. *Journal of the Early Republic* 11: 161–183.

Lewis, James E., Jr. (2001). *John Quincy Adams: Policy Maker for the Union.* Wilmington, DE.

Chapter Twenty

John Quincy Adams and the Tangled Politics of Slavery

Matthew Mason

For most of his post-presidential Congressional career, John Quincy Adams was an antislavery dynamo. Seeing the blighting political effects of the power of slaveholders behind all of the policies and proclivities of his partisan and sectional opponents, he sought to call "the whole freedom of this Union" forth "in its own defence" against "the hideous reality of the slave ascendancy in the Government of this Union" (C.F. Adams, 1874–1877: 11.381, 408). So he fought for years against the annexation of Texas as a slave state into the Union, seeing "the freedom of the human race" as the stakes of this struggle (C.F. Adams, 1874–1877: 12.13–14, 22, 25, 49, 57, 60, 68). He touched off violent debates in the House of Representatives by introducing Massachusetts' legislature's resolutions calling for the repeal of the three-fifths clause of the Constitution and even a petition from constituents to dissolve the Union, pleading "the feelings of my constituents, under their sense of the wrongs endured by them, resulting from the slave representation in Congress" (C.F. Adams, 1874–1877: 11.472–473; Mason, 2006: 214–219). And most famously, he warred from 1836 through 1844 against the infamous Gag Rule, which suppressed just such antislavery petitions – requesting Congress to abolish slavery and/or the slave trade in the District of Columbia, for instance[1] – as Adams had introduced from his first moments in the House.

In the process, Adams piled up a list of allies and enemies that rendered his antislavery credentials impeccable. He joined the abolitionist legal team pleading before the Supreme Court for the liberty of the mutinous slaves of the slave ship *Amistad*, and somewhat less famously gave legal counsel

A Companion to John Adams and John Quincy Adams, First Edition.
Edited by David Waldstreicher.

to the defense of Rev. Charles T. Torrey against charges of aiding runaway slaves (H. Jones, 1987; C.F. Adams, 1874–1877: 12.68–69). Both in private and in public, he manifested ever-increasing irritation with acquaintances who remained indifferent to the issues surrounding slavery, especially "the Northern political sopranos, who abhor slavery and help to forge fetters for the slave" (C.F. Adams, 1874–1877: 11.29, 65, 202, 284–85). Routinely branding Southern politicians – up to and including President John Tyler – as "slave-breeders," at least after 1842 he refused "party communion with the Whigs of the slave representation" (C.F. Adams, 1874–1877: 11.116, 382–384). Especially after Adams argued that the federal government would have authority to abolish slavery when intervening in a slave rebellion, white Southerners in and out of Congress returned his hostility with interest. One portrayed Adams as the equivalent of the instigators of the Haitian Revolution, "who shed the blood of a sleeping infant and stuck a pole through its warm and quivering body, and under that standard marched with torch in one hand and sword in another." Others spoke only slightly less colorfully of Adams having joined in waging "war" on the South, and Southern death threats became routine in the Congressman's mail (C.F. Adams, 1874–1877: 11.103, 159; Mason, 2006: 218).

This undeniably attractive antislavery crusade of the best ex-president in American history has long captured the imagination of historians, but its heroic qualities have tended to divert scholars from fully explaining this phase of his career. His contemporary and first full-scale biographer Josiah Quincy set the tone, portraying Adams as consistently antislavery, ever and always the target of the machinations of the "slave-power" (Quincy, 1859). For Bennett Champ Clark, "Adams's position on slavery from first to last was singularly consistent" and as such required no explanation (Clark 1932: 292, 351–407). Mid-twentieth-century biographers, agreeing that Adams always opposed slavery – for Samuel Flagg Bemis his great Gag Rule fight was "abolitionist at heart" – lavished very little mental energy on explaining his open embrace of antislavery politics after 1836 (Lipsky, 1950: 41–42, 121–127; Bemis, 1956). For more recent biographer Paul Nagel, Adams's antislavery was so thoroughgoing that he could never join a full political alliance with such "a compromiser" as Massachusetts Whig and staunch Unionist Edward Everett (Nagel 1997: 332). More than Adams biographers stand in the glare of the antislavery jouster's armor. Tellers of the Gag Rule story, and of the legal tale of the *Amistad*, both in print and on film, cast him in a heroic role (H. Jones, 1987; Dreamworks, 1997; Miller, 1996; Freehling, 1990: 337–52). It is unsurprising that Daniel Walker Howe (2007), who dedicated his prize-winning synthesis of antebellum America to Adams's memory, would follow suit. But even Sean Wilentz's massive (2005) political survey of the early republic, which votes for Andrew Jackson on every page, offers grudging admiration to Adams's Gag Rule combat (D.W. Howe, 2007: 514–515, 522–524, 585, 609–611; Wilentz, 2005: 471–472, 521, 554). Biographer Robert Remini has likewise reviewed in detail this glorious epoch in Adams's life, but offers at least a hesitant explanation. Noting that "John Quincy Adams had shown little concern about slavery during his early career," Remini attributes the change to "his desire to punish" the South and Democrats "for having wrecked his administration," along with the growth of slavery as a political issue in the 1830s (2002: 137–155).[2] Leonard Richards (1986), who has offered the fullest analysis of Adams's shift into an open antislavery career, also begins with his "need for revenge, or something closely akin to it," on the South. Adams cared deeply about slavery's impact on the nation, but in Richards's final analysis the acclaim and policy victories he achieved meant his antislavery phase constituted sweet victory over his political enemies in the South and the Democracy (L.L. Richards, 1986: 3–26, 113–203).

Not only do these interpretations offer only first steps in explaining the change in Adams's approach to slavery over time, but they also overstate the single-mindedness of his antislavery focus during his heroic phase. Richards, for instance, may have been confused over whether to depict Adams as consistently or increasingly antislavery, but he had no doubt that as congressman he was "constantly stressing" the need to resist the Jacksonians' proslavery agenda (L.L. Richards, 1986: 57). And Richards follows other biographers in setting up a neat divide: before 1836 Adams was dealing with all kinds of different issues, but after 1836 it was antislavery nearly all the time (L.L. Richards 1986: 30, 32, 37, 54, 75, 89–112; comparing Richards, 1986: 1–88 with 89–203 gives the impression of the clean break in 1836 to a tunnel-visioned antislavery career). Attending to Adams's public shifts on slavery from 1814 to 1848 reveals instead a story of shifting and continually overlapping personal, policy, and ideological priorities. This is less a tale of growing antislavery in Adams's heart than it is an explanation of how slavery rose to the foreground of his competing priorities.[3] Such an account is best pursued chronologically, with attention to the degree to which antislavery aligned with his numerous other commitments during his diplomatic, presidential, and congressional careers.

As an American negotiator of the Treaty of Ghent at the end of the War of 1812 and as a two-term secretary of state under President James Monroe, Adams expressed his hatred of slavery and of the power of slaveholders in private, but pursued policies that contradicted this stance. While this was surely in part the result of following the orders of the Virginian presidents he served, it also stemmed from deep anglophobia, a powerful commitment to the constitution and the Union, and ambition for the presidency. None of these priorities encouraged a public stance against slavery or the South.

Both in the negotiations at Ghent and as secretary of state, Adams pushed hard and long for the British to pay reparations to American slaveholders for the slaves their armed forces had liberated during the War of 1812. In this he followed the instructions of his superiors, but did so with a bulldog's determination rather than perfunctorily. Notwithstanding any antislavery feelings he had at this time, he lectured his British counterparts that "by the usages of war among civilized nations" slaves constituted "private property" that "ought not to have been taken" (W.C. Ford, 1913–1917: 5.349). Furthermore, Adams bought fully into the American government's line that British troops sold many of the slaves so taken into bondage in the West Indies, contradicting the British claim to be liberators.[4] In a June 1822 installment in his long-running series of debates with British ambassador Stratford Canning on slaves taken in the war, Adams recorded having "told him they had no right to carry away private property or to emancipate slaves. He said, banteringly, that if he were at war he would emancipate every slave he could find. 'Then,' said I, 'I would never make peace with you till you paid for them'" (C.F. Adams, 1874–1877: 6.39).

He likewise resisted, in both offices and with full vigor, persistent British proposals for cooperation in suppressing the Atlantic slave trade. The British proposals involved a right to search American vessels for slaves, a hot-button issue for nationalist Americans in the era of the War of 1812. He showed no interest in cooperating with the British until their proposal involved a carefully restricted, mutual right of search.[5] In all of this Adams's distrust of Great Britain trumped whatever antislavery sentiment he shared with her officials. By refusing to foreswear impressing American seamen, he groused, British officials proved that "their humanity for white freemen stops short of" their drive "to unman our independence" in the name of searching "our ships for black slaves to emancipate" (W.C. Ford 1913–1917: 6.550; Mason, 2009: 821–822; Mason, 2002: 668–671).

As this solicitude for American independence suggests, concerns for the international as well as the domestic fragility of the American union helped drive Adams's approach to slavery-related issues. As historian James Lewis has demonstrated,

> through most of his career as a diplomat and statesman, Adams's understanding of the nature and function of the federal union shaped his ideas and policies.…Upon this union depended the successful achievement of the principal goals of the American Revolution,… [and] the greatest evil – that disunion would force the American states to treat each other as hostile nations – involved dangers that were simultaneously internal and external. (Lewis, 2001: xiv, xv)

As a result, when zealous supporters of the American Colonization Society pressed Secretary Adams for federal support for their project of colonizing free black Americans in Africa, he joined the likes of John C. Calhoun in taking a dim view of the constitutionality as well as the advisability of setting up an American colonial establishment in Africa. "Under the color of colonizing black people," he told one Virginian, "I was afraid they would smuggle in upon us a system of establishing Colonies beyond sea, of the consequence of which the people of this country were little aware," much like Britons who sought "under the mask of abolishing the slave-trade" to introduce "a new principle of the law of nations more formidable to human liberty than the slave-trade itself" in the right of search (C.F. Adams, 1874–1877: 4.353–357; see also 4.292–494, 298–99, 436, 444–445, 475–479). He likewise had a conservative's reaction to one Mr. Irvine, "one of the men with whom this age abounds – a fanatic of liberty for the whole human race" who did not understand the American view of liberty "as a blessing to be enjoyed" rather than "as a blessing to be acquired" (C.F. Adams, 1874–1877: 4.444–445). Whatever his private antislavery convictions, Adams could have no truck with the fanatical spirit of the age which threatened the constitutional union.

That he harbored such antislavery convictions, and that they contended with his simultaneous commitment to the constitutional union, becomes apparent when perusing his diary meditations on the Missouri crisis of 1819–1821. Although obviously itching for a fight with Southerners, he also made clear that such a stand would have to be on firm constitutional ground for him to join it. In July 1819, in his first reflections on the proposed Tallmadge Amendment restricting slavery in Missouri, he groused at seeing the aroused "slave-drivers" "bluster and bully" the submissive Northern representatives, but concluded that he could not support the restriction, "because I believe it not compatible either with the Constitution of the United States or with the Louisiana Treaty" (C.F. Adams, 1874–1877: 4.398). Such oscillations between priorities continued: on December 27, 1819, he looked forward to the day when the "seeds of the Declaration of Independence" would mature and slavery would meet its "terrible sublime" ending; yet on January 2, 1820, he recorded his grave fears "for the continuance of this Union" (4.492–93, 495). He cheered on Northern champions like Rufus King, hoping they would find a way "to lay bare in all its nakedness that outrage upon the goodness of God, human slavery" (4.524). But he had also come to see that "no man ought to take an active part" on the restrictionist side without being reconciled to "the separation of the Union," "because it must end in that" (4.517). "This is a question between the rights of human nature and the Constitution of the United States," he aptly summarized (4.528), and as a result of that swirl of competing imperatives, the Missouri question long remained "in a state of chaos in my mind" (4.496).

Adams had the luxury of private perplexity because he was not in Congress debating the issue, but when Congress sent a compromise bill to the president, Adams entered into the cabinet's debate over its constitutionality. In this setting he avowed an antislavery position grounded in the doctrines of the Declaration of Independence, and reversed his earlier position by positing that "I had no doubt of the right of Congress to interdict slavery in the Territories." He repeated the latter argument in a private memorandum to President Monroe dated March 4, 1820 (C.F. Adams, 1874–1877: 5.5–6; W.C. Ford, 1913–1917: 7.1). He did regret bitterly that Congress had not exerted that power in Missouri itself, to the point of lamenting the three-fifths compromise as "a dishonorable compromise with slavery" that had bolstered Southern power, and even fantasizing about "a new Union of 13 or 14 States unpolluted with slavery" (C.F. Adams, 1874–1877: 5.4, 11–14; see also 5.208–211). But while he saw that "there must be at some time a conflict upon this very question between slave and free representation," he concluded that "this is not the time, nor was this the proper occasion, for contesting it." So he finally "favored this Missouri compromise, believing it to be all that could be effected under the present Constitution, and from extreme unwillingness to put the Union at hazard" (C.F. Adams, 1874–1877: 5.12). "If the Union must be dissolved," he added, "slavery is precisely the question upon which it ought to break. For the present, however, this contest is laid asleep" (C.F. Adams, 1874–1877: 5.308).

And unlike hard-core restrictionists, he was content to let it sleep, in part because he had noted that English and other European ambassadors had watched the Missouri debates closely. Seeing evidence of a divided United States, they had concluded that they had no reason to give in to American demands. As Adams pushed those diplomats on such matters as US trade to the British West Indies, this weakness was obviously disastrous from his point of view. For international as well as domestic reasons, then, as Lewis has put it, Adams emerged from the Missouri crisis "as convinced as ever of the importance of shaping policy with an eye on the stability of the union" (C.F. Adams, 1874–1877: 5.40; Lewis, 2001: 67).

Although Adams had a hard time admitting it to himself, another reason he was disposed to let slavery sleep was that he was but one step away from the presidency. Adams was of course but one of several contestants for the presidency looking as secretly as possible towards 1824, but his drive was especially strong and of long standing. Both of his parents had constantly harped on their high hopes for this talented child, whom they treated as "a project almost as much as a person." "You come into life with advantages which will disgrace you if your success is mediocre," exhorted John Adams. "And if you do not rise to the head of ... your country, it will be owing to your own Lasiness, Slovenliness, and Obstinacy." (J.J. Ellis, 2010: 92). Although "every American boy is encouraged to dream that he might one day grow up to become president," historian Joseph J. Ellis has pointed out, "John Quincy spent his entire childhood hearing that anything less than the highest office in the land would be regarded as failure" (J.J. Ellis, 2010: 44, 92–93, 129, 242; Remini, 2002: 1–18).

Faced with such pressures as well as the high hopes that secretaries of state traditionally carried into presidential elections, Adams was also keenly aware that slavery as an element in national politics was always unpredictable and rarely beneficial for politicians. In May 1820, already pondering the 1824 presidential election in his diary, Adams aptly noted that "the Missouri question is indeed a flaming sword that waves round on all sides and cuts in every direction" (C.F. Adams, 1874–1877: 5.54). Six months later, he noted an instructive interview with Rufus King, who told him "that, as a statesman of the Union, he has lost rather than gained ground by his ardent pursuit of this slavery question" during the Missouri debates, "and seems now disposed to say little more about it" (5.206). For all his antislavery ardor during the Missouri crisis, Adams did not reproach King for this retreat. In fact, Adams never left any potential supporter in doubt that he like King hoped to serve as just such a "statesman of the Union." In March 1820, he told Ninian Edwards of Illinois in a conversation relative to the acquisition of Florida that if he were in Congress, "as an Eastern man, I should be disinclined to have either Texas or Florida without a restriction excluding slavery from them." But in a crucial statement of how his office – and hoped-for office – helped order his priorities, Adams affirmed that "as a servant of the whole Union, the interests of every part of the Union were equally dear to me – that there was neither East, West, North, or South to my duty or my feelings" (C.F. Adams, 1874–1877: 5.91). Both Adams's conception of executive offices and his desire to continue and ascend within that branch, then, discouraged any public agitation of the explosive issue of slavery coming out of the Missouri crisis.

With Adams the only Northern candidate in the crowded 1824 election – an election which Americans in all sections carried on very much in the shadow of the bitter Missouri controversy – much of his support and the rhetoric of his supporters was bound to be sectional, but as candidate he only rarely embraced Northern sectionalism. He did remind New Englanders that if Jackson or Calhoun were elected they would be sure to proscribe Yankees from the patronage. But his dominant theme, whether during the popular election or after it moved to the House of Representatives, was his pledge to "be the President not of a section, or of a faction, but of the whole Union" (C.F. Adams, 1874–1877: 6.313, 500; Nagel, 1997: 291–293; Ratcliffe, 2000: 80–97).

To that end, he finessed his story when confronted by opponents and supporters with the question of what his stance on the Tallmadge Amendment had been. Some political allies had made it known in 1820 that Adams had favored the restriction, whereas now both Northern opponents and Southern allies were reporting that he had opposed it. Although Adams knew very well that his enemies were fishing for "an electioneering weapon against me," he rose to the bait. He grasped for the ever-elusive middle ground by spreading one account wherein he had opposed restricting slavery in Missouri but had firmly supported restricting it in Illinois. But his Southern support was much shakier than the Northern, so in election mode Adams generally composed a tale meant to please Southern ears. In May 1824, for instance, when congressman George McDuffie came to Adams to take his leave before going home to South Carolina to electioneer, Adams complained to him that "my opinions had been greatly misrepresented in the Southern country, with a view to excite local prejudices against me," on the all-important historical question of Missouri. He assured McDuffie that he had opposed the Tallmadge Amendment "as contravening both the Constitution and the Louisiana Treaty" (C.F. Adams, 1874–1877: 6.342–343, 353–54; 8.174). He repeated this usefully selective story when eyeing re-election. In spring 1827, staunch supporter Everett requested Adams to clarify what his stance on Missouri had truly been. Adams replied that "when the first Missouri question was before Congress, my opinion was that the restriction proposed upon the State was not compatible either with the Constitution or with the Louisiana Convention." While he claimed not to "disguise, or dissemble it to any one, who desired to know what my opinion was," he professed to have been reluctant to use this no-win electioneering tool in 1824. Reluctant or not, he sighed, clarifying his stance had done no good, for "during the late Presidential canvas, I was represented, at the South as a restrictionist, and in the northwest as a Slave-holder." Yet he failed to instruct Everett not to make electioneering use of this latest Southern-friendly telling (Everett, 1875–1910: J.Q. Adams to Everett, Apr. 11, 1827).

It should be no surprise, then, that upon taking office President Adams continued to preach Unionist pieties. In his inaugural address, he warned vehemently against party spirit in general, and against sectional parties in particular, which "threaten the dissolution of the Union, and with it the overthrow of all the enjoyments of our present lot and all our earthly hopes for the future." He also announced an ambitious agenda of internal and other improvements meant to cement the Union and work in tandem with a foreign policy aimed at minimizing baneful European influence in the western hemisphere (Lewis, 2001: 99–118). Despite the boldness of his improvement agenda, he was painfully aware that he had been elected president "not by the unequivocal suffrages of a majority of the people," and he bent over backwards to assuage especially Southern fears. In November 1825 he was favorable to the idea, raised by a Presbyterian clergyman, of a presidential proclamation of a Thanksgiving for the District of Columbia. But his cabinet opposed it "as a novelty – as liable to imputations of political purposes, of introducing New England manners," and so forth. Adams "acquiesced in these opinions" (C.F. Adams, 1874–1877: 7.53–54, 98).

That same solicitude to avoid needless collisions with Southerners extended to Adams's presidential actions relative to slavery. In September 1826, during a visit from a "female Quaker preacher" who descanted on "the condition of the poor oppressed colored people in this country," he listened to her respectively but gave an evasive answer as to any action he might take. The unlikelihood of his taking antislavery action from the White House came into clearer focus three months later, when he refused a plea for a stay of execution for a slave who had "mutinied" on a slave ship. He protested that "it was very painful to me to refuse an application for a reprieve for a man under sentence of death," but argued that the atrocity of the murder and the danger of opening wide the door to pardons stayed his hand. He did challenge the congressmen from New York urging this matter to "write me a letter requesting" the reprieve, although they – in no more haste to pose as abolitionists than he was – left saying they would probably not dare to write such a letter (C.F. Adams, 1874–1877: 7.148–149, 202, 204). In 1828, when a House of Representatives resolution requested the administration to negotiate with Britain for the return from Canada of American fugitive slaves, the administration complied by proposing a convention. The British government refused to negotiate such a convention, whereupon it died (Clark, 1932: 264–265). This was of course a very far cry from Adams's later approach to the fugitive slave issue when he played the hero in the *Amistad* case.

There were limits to his willingness to accommodate Southern cranks, to be sure. When he was preparing his first message to Congress, secretary of war James Barbour quoted a South Carolinian congressman as wishing "that something conciliatory to the South might be said in the message, to calm their inquietudes concerning their slaves." South Carolinians' "inquietudes" with Adams at this point stemmed in large part from his continuation of the Monroe administration's opposition to their state's infamous Negro Seamen Act. Passed in the panicky aftermath of Denmark Vesey's failed insurrection plot, this law decreed the detainment of all black sailors while their ships were in Palmetto state docks. Adams told Barbour that South Carolina's persistence in enforcing this act despite a Supreme Court justice from South Carolina ruling it unconstitutional "had put it out of my power to say anything soothing to the South on that subject." "In this state of things," he repeated, "for me to say anything gratifying to the feelings of the South Carolinians on this subject would be to abandon the ground taken by" Monroe's administration. Still, he had no desire to needlessly strengthen Calhoun's influence within the opposition, so he decided to say nothing on the Negro Seamen Act. "To be silent," he reminded Barbour, "is not to interfere with any State rights" (C.F. Adams, 1874–1877: 7.56–57).

Such caution failed to soothe his vociferous Southern critics. In January 1826, Speaker of the House John Taylor (a strong restrictionist during the Missouri debates and current Adams supporter) visited the president and reported South Carolinian members' rage at Taylor "for presenting to the House a memorial from a crazy man in France, who invited Congress to destroy all the States which should refuse the emancipation of slaves." In a preview of the Gag Rule fight a decade later, South Carolina's representatives cared little that the administration did not support the petition's plea, portraying its very reading "as proof of a fixed determination of the present Administration to emancipate the Southern slaves." Fire-eating South Carolinians of this sort, aggravated above all by his support of a protective tariff, would continue to bedevil Adams throughout his presidency, to the point of threatening to secede from the Union if he were re-elected in 1828 (C.F. Adams, 1874–1877: 7.103–104; 8.55–56). A much more formidable opposition to Adams surrounding slavery also arose that same year, when the Senate debated the administration's proposal to send a delegate to a conference in Panama of all the newly independent nations in the western hemisphere. The politicians coalescing around Jackson and against Adams sought to make opposition to the Panama gathering a key ingredient in the glue for their nascent party. The Senate conducted a secret debate in which Southerners' solicitude to protect slavery overtly mixed with concerns about national neutrality and sovereignty.[6] Later in his presidency he found himself faced with another truculent Southern state, in the form of Georgia's determination to push through his vacillating responses to its policy of removing Indians from its borders in violation of treaties the tribes had signed with the United States. While he would become a much more certain opponent of Indian Removal in his congressional career, this added to his cumulative bad experience with Southern opponents as president (Remini, 2002: 88–100).

That bad experience continued with Adams's resounding defeat at the hands of Jackson in 1828, but despite overwhelming Southern support for Jackson, Adams did not immediately diagnose his enemies as specifically sectional. Just days before leaving office, Adams reflected in his diary that he had devoted his presidency "to the Union, and to the improvement, physical, moral, and intellectual, of my country." His Northern opponents, he complained, attacked him "for my fidelity to the Union," while Southerners assailed him "for my ardent aspirations of improvement." Still-bitter Northern sectionalists branding him soft on slavery, this gripe suggests, stood with Southern naysayers before his angry verdict. It was not until much later that he ascribed his defeat to slaveholders' ascendancy (C.F. Adams, 1874–1877: 8.100–101; 10.182).[7] Moreover, Adams remained sanguine that "the cause of Union and of improvement will remain" (C.F. Adams, 1874–1877: 8.101). Accordingly, when he entered the House of Representatives just months after losing the presidency, he remained devoted not to an antislavery agenda so much as to his traditional priorities of union and improvement. Even in 1842, he recalled in a speech to his constituents that when he took congressional office in 1831, he had long served and felt a "duty of fidelity, of affection, and of gratitude, to the whole" union, not just to his Massachusetts constituents. He had not yet discerned the Jacksonians' designs to expand the territory and influence of slavery, so "I entered Congress without one sentiment of discrimination between the interests of the North and the South" (Quincy, 1859: 182–183). On the one hand, James Lewis' declaration that Adams's "election as a congressman represented something of a liberation for Adams … from his constant striving to behave as a 'man of the whole union'" is supported not only by his antislavery career after 1836, but also by his March 1820 conversation with Ninian Edwards (Lewis, 2001: 119–140).[8] But on the other hand, such an interpretation of Adams's congressional career not only reads his post-1836 antislavery phase backwards to 1831, but also unduly downplays the continual interplay of past priorities – including deep devotion to the Union – with his ascendant antislavery priority. Far from flipping an antislavery switch the minute he entered Congress, Adams came gradually to the position he occupied on the spectrum of antislavery politics from the Gag Rule fight forwards. Furthermore, far from abandoning past personal and policy priorities, Adams found by 1836 that those same priorities encouraged rather than discouraged an open antislavery stand.

The burning national issue when Adams secured his election to Congress in 1830 and entered the House in 1831 was South Carolina's threat to nullify the federal tariff, and Adams entered this fray firmly on the side of compromise. He did grouse privately that South Carolinians' "domineering spirit" – a spirit he had encountered painfully as president – "naturally springs from the institution of slavery," and that "South Carolinians are attempting to govern the Union as they govern their slaves." And he worried that Jackson, avatar of "the overseer ascendancy," would give in to South Carolina as he had to Georgia on Indian Removal (C.F. Adams, 1874–1877: 8.229–232). But in public, he worked hard to cultivate his image of seeking neither a Southern nor a Northern solution to the impasse; he was for true "compromise – something must be given up on both sides." Indeed, at one strategy session of National Republican leaders in December 1831, Everett raised the question of whether persisting in a protective rather than a revenue-oriented tariff "was not setting the South at defiance." Adams concurred that it would be futile to defy both the South and the Jackson administration, whereas Henry Clay preferred to "defy the South, the President, and the devil" if that was what it would take to get his American System passed complete with a protective tariff (C.F. Adams, 1874–1877: 8.444–848, 459–460).

Adams found himself in a position to advocate compromise from his seat as chair of the important committee on manufactures, which appointment was in fact a signal of the perhaps surprising level of bipartisan respect he received when first entering the House. Indeed, when Adams asked to be relieved of this heavy committee burden in March 1832, it gave rise to a remarkable debate. Both Northerners and Southerners, Democrats and

National Republicans, argued that Adams must keep his chairmanship because he "had it eminently in his power, by his peculiar" position as a revered statesman, "to give repose to those angry passions which now shake the public mind." He was, they gushed, "the only man in the Union capable of taking the high stand of umpire" (*Register*, 22nd Cong., 1st Sess., 2175–2182).[9] The idea of John Quincy Adams as glue for the Union was far from his image after 1836, and must have come as a surprise to him after the tumult of his presidency. But it would have been a pleasant surprise to someone who nurtured not only a love for the Union but also a healthy ego.

As they had during his presidency, however, Southern representatives then proceeded to menace the twin causes of Union and improvement and to bruise his ego, in the process helping to raise up one of their most effective congressional opponents. South Carolinians and Georgians continued at the head of this band of culprits. In January 1831, responding to Georgia's successful defiance of the Supreme Court's rulings against Indian Removal, Adams recorded privately his fear that "the Union is in the most imminent danger of dissolution from the old inherent vice of confederacies, anarchy in the members" (C.F. Adams, 1874–1877: 8.262–263). The very rule of law as well as the Union seemed in mortal peril. Meanwhile, Carolinians' determination to nullify the protective tariff put in jeopardy both the Union and to the National Republican program of economic improvement. "The real question" nullification raised, he told a New York Democrat on Christmas Eve in 1832, "was, whether a population spread over an immense territory, consisting of one great division all freemen, and another of masters and slaves, could exist permanently together as members of one community or not; that, to go a step further back, the question at issue was slavery" (C.F. Adams, 1874–1877: 8.510). That the threats to constitutional union and improvement in the early 1830s emanated from the Lower South suggested to Adams that defending these beloved causes was now consistent with at least a hesitantly antislavery line of diagnosis and argument.

It was also Southern representatives who abruptly ended the brief honeymoon period of personal respect for Adams in the House. In another preview of the Gag Rule controversy in March 1832, Adams presented a memorial from citizens of New York protesting Indian Removal, disclaiming that he was just doing his duty, not eager to reopen that bruising debate. Augustin Smith Clayton of Georgia sprang to his feet to complain that the memorialists "were meddling with what did not concern them," moved by their "fanatical pretensions to superior benevolence, humanity, piety, love to the Indians, and all that." If the House of Representatives "had any respect for a sister State, a sovereign State, they would repel such memorialists as these, they would throw such a memorial under the table, and not aggravate to yet higher degree the feelings of" much-maligned Georgians. "Would that House," he pled, "consent to make itself the instrument of adding excitement to excitement, till they should rend the Union to pieces?" (*Register*, 22nd Cong., 1st Sess., 2013–2014). Northern representatives recoiled at this threat of disunion and attack on the right of petition, and the House refused to table the memorial by a vote of 92 to 91. Clayton was unchastened, insisting that Georgians would "rather give up your Union" than "submit to have these laws annulled," and Clement Comer Clay of Alabama added that the memorial Adams had presented in fact "called upon Congress to wage war on all the Southern States" (*Register*, 22nd Cong., 1st Sess., 2028–2029). Adams seemed genuinely incredulous when he ended that day's debate by disclaiming any warlike intentions towards the South (*Register*, 22nd Cong., 1st Sess.: 2010–2136). In July 1832, in the aftermath of a long tariff debate in the House, Adams was present but did not vote on a charge against a member of contempt of the Speaker. William Drayton of South Carolina pounced, resolving that Adams had "committed a breach of one of the rules of the House," and that a committee be appointed to investigate "a case so novel and so important." A debate ensued the next day, during which Everett cried that Drayton had singled out Adams for "a species of censure which never had been inflicted on any man since the foundation of the Government." The House tabled Drayton's resolutions by a margin of 89 to 63 (*Register*, 22nd Cong., 1st Sess., 3906–312). But this bizarre censure movement, another preview of coming attractions for Adams, confirmed that Southern Democrats were ready to take off their gloves in handling Adams.

This Southern constellation of personal slights and hostility to the Union and improvement came together in early February 1833 to encourage Adams to experiment with antislavery expression in the House. On February 1, Adams took umbrage at Georgian representative Richard Henry Wilde's motion not to receive resolutions on the tariff from the Massachusetts legislature. Adams branded this latest motion to table rather than hear Northern expressions of opinion – from a state legislature, no less – "an insult to the State of Massachusetts" that if passed would divide states "into two classes." If South Carolina's nullification ordinance stood it would stand at the head of one class, "which was at liberty to insult with impunity, not merely an individual, but the whole Government." If Wilde got his way, Massachusetts would belong to the other class, which "might not utter the least reflection" on the issues involved. Here was yet another attempt by a Southerner to silence Northerners' free speech on a vital issue, consistent with a growing picture of domineering behavior from Carolinians and Georgians. The business on February 4 began with a small skirmish that would only confirm Adams in this opinion, as Southerners moved to table rather than hear petitions for the abolition of slavery in the District of Columbia. Adams, though "not in favor of the sentiments expressed in the memorial, was opposed to laying it on the table, as being disrespectful to the petitioners" and hostile to a right "guarantied by the constitution."

Unlike in the more famous 1836 exchange on this issue, the motion lost by a healthy margin, 98 to 75 (*Register*, 22nd Cong., 2nd Sess.: 1564–1565, 1584–1585). But the reader of the congressional record can sense that Adams was ready to explode had the gag on these petitions passed, and to explode in an antislavery direction given that his personal opposition to slavery and hostility to slaveholders' power was aligning more and more with his solicitude for the constitutional union.

As much of a combustion as Adams was capable of on February 4, 1833, came during a speech on the tariff. Clayton had referred in an earlier speech to Southern slaves as not only "capital" but also the South's "machinery," and insisted that white Southerners "had as good a right to profit by them as Northern men had by the machinery they employed" and for which they wanted protection with the tariff. Adams responded not with a humanitarian objection to declaring people machines, but rather by cataloging the sectionally specific "protection" the slavery interest enjoyed under the constitution, starting with slave representation. He jabbed in response to Clayton that the South's so-called "machinery had twenty odd representatives in that hall; representatives elected, not by the machinery, but by those who owned it," whereas Northerners' "looms and factories had no vote in Congress." Given that the slave representation "had ever been, in fact, the ruling power of this Government," then did this not constitute protection of one section "at the expense of another portion of the community?" The constitutionalist Adams would not complain about this bargain made by the Founders, but he did declare that he would not "agree to it if the bargain were now to be made over again." He continued his catalog with the constitution's fugitive-slave clause and federal guarantee of armed support to put down rebellions, all of which made it inconsistent in Southerners to complain of special sectional economic protections. He ended by reiterating his support for compromise on the tariff, but this was a remarkable departure for the cautious politician who had heretofore groused only privately about the undue and deleterious power of slaveholders in the federal government (*Register*, 22nd Cong., 2nd Sess.: 1582–1583, 1612–1616).[10] Southern reaction to the speech was also significant, continuing Adams's instruction in the truth that to address slaveholders' power in the federal government was to touch an extremely sore spot. Drayton rose on February 4 to charge Adams with "having introduced topics that must inevitably excite the most hostile and even furious passions." John Mercer Patton of Virginia joined in the next day by alleging that Adams's words were "as well calculated as any that could have been uttered, to throw a firebrand into our councils" at that dangerous hour. He argued that if Adams's unwillingness to accept slave representation had prevailed in the Constitutional Convention of 1787, "we should never have had this glorious Union, which he now professes so much anxiety to preserve." He addressed all of Adams's arguments for unfair sectional protection, but most pointedly hammered him repeatedly for lacking the Founders' "spirit of mutual forbearance and conciliation," so necessary in 1833. Adams responded with somewhat less surprise than the last time he had been charged with waging war on the South, but insisted that South Carolina's nullification ordinance, not his speech, was responsible for the polarized atmosphere in the House (*Register*, 22nd Cong., 2nd Sess.: 1616–1634, 1640–1651). The fact that Southern representatives had responded most vehemently not to his allusion to slave insurrection but to his sally against the three-fifths clause showed Adams where his policy-cum-personal enemies were most tender, so it is no wonder that he led the fight in Congress nearly a decade later to debate repealing slave representation. And that reaction to Adams's speech, which was no abolitionist rant, confirmed that, as David Waldstreicher has written, the Founders' "federal ratio made it impossible for statesmen … to think of slavery without thinking about property and power." That fact heightened rather than tempered the stakes surrounding it for the South (Waldstreicher, 2009: 78).

Adams remained something of a sleeping giant between this brief foray and his awakening to his antislavery role in January 1836, when the institution of the Gag Rule marked the decisive intersection of personal slights and an attack on Northerners' constitutional rights. In the intervening years, while continuing "grave meditation" over the issue of slavery and its insalubrious impact on the Union and the policies of the federal government, he continued to present abolitionist petitions. Since these met the standard fate of being referred to and dying in committee, if he was itching for another fight with Southerners these occasions presented no such opportunity (C.F. Adams, 1874–1877: 9.23, 206, 235, 247, 252–256, 259). On January 4, 1836, the fight came. In the course of presenting abolitionist petitions on the floor of the House, he recorded indignantly in his diary, "I was instantly interrupted by my next neighbor, John M. Patton, who enquired whether the petition had been received; to which the Speaker answered that it had not; whereupon Thomas Glascock, a new member from Georgia, moved that it be not received, and was proceeding to make a speech, when I called him to order." The Speaker, Tennessee Democrat James K. Polk, ruled against Adams, Adams appealed this decision, and the debate over his appeal consumed the rest of the day and continued into the next. Maneuvers by Southerners and their Northern allies to squash abolitionist petitions continued on through January, and on January 18 another Southerner offered Adams yet another affront. James Henry Hammond of South Carolina, a key mover in the formation of the Gag Rule, interrupted Adams while he was presenting a petition, "and moved that the petition be not received. He had no right to interrupt me," Adams assured his diary, and while Polk "said I was entitled to the floor," Adams's dander was up – permanently (C.F. Adams, 1874–1877: 9.266–276). On June 10, 1836, Adams offered an amendment to a statehood bill for Arkansas, which "kindled a fiery debate of three hours, in which" two Southerners "used insulting language, which I demanded should be taken down by the Clerk, but which [Jesse] Speight [of North Carolina], the Chairman, would not notice." A little over a week after this continued disrespect from Southerners, he recorded in his journal his irrevocable commitment to the "good and great" cause of fighting slavery, specifically of exposing "the fraudulent pretences of slave-holding democracy" so perfectly exemplified by the Gag Rule (C.F. Adams, 1874–1877: 9.294, 298, 310, 333, 454, 497, 508).

He carried into this new cause his old priorities of personal vindication, constitutional union, and improvement. The intersection of those issues had pushed him into "the cause," so there was no reason to abandon them in some single-minded pursuit of abolition at any cost. Significantly, just weeks after recording his entrance into the cause, he accepted the thanks of several abolitionists in Philadelphia, but "gave them a full and candid exposition of my own principles and views" on slavery, "differing from theirs under a sense of the compact and compromise in the Constitution" (C.F. Adams, 1874–1877: 9.301–303). This was but the beginnings of a tense and complicated relationship between the antislavery whirlwind Adams and all varieties of abolitionists. They always conversed with each other respectfully, but more often than not differed on matters of policy as well as of tactics. The old conservative, even in this provocative phase of his career, could not help but consider the abolitionists dangerous and politically inept zealots. Abolitionists' impatience with Adams was similarly pervasive, encapsulated well when the Liberty party ran candidates against him for his House seat.[11]

Also unlike American abolitionists, Adams remained deeply leery of Great Britain's announced antislavery policies. In an August 1839 conversation with a British abolitionist about the impact of Britain's 1833 emancipation of slaves throughout its empire, the constitutionalist Adams protested against "the despotic measures of the English Ministry, suppressing the Legislature of the island of Jamaica to carry through the emancipation laws" (C.F. Adams, 1874–1877: 10.129–30). In May 1843, Adams frankly told American abolitionist Joshua Leavitt that he still "distrusted them [the British] altogether; I believed their real policy far from desiring to favor the abolition of slavery" in Texas or elsewhere, being instead "to weaken" the United States at any cost (C.F. Adams, 1874–1877: 11.374–375, 380, 405–408). His heightened antislavery agenda, however, at times tempered his persistent anglophobia. In June 1843, he used a reply to a Maine meeting commemorating British emancipation as a chance "to bear my testimony, once more, before I go hence, against slavery." And in July 1844 he visited with a British minister and told him how glad he was to see "in the Parliamentary papers of 1839 and '40" Lord Palmerston's declaration "that to promote the abolition of slavery throughout the world was a fixed and settled system of the British Government." Adams genuinely hoped British leaders would not "sacrifice their principles to their policy" and go back on this cheering pronouncement (C.F. Adams, 1874–1877: 11.387, 406; 12.66). As usual, Adams in his journal found just the words to aptly assess his relationship with Antislavery International. "There was considerable diversity," he noted in 1844, "among those generally opposed to slavery" (C.F. Adams, 1874–1877: 12.79–80). That was true both nationally and internationally.

That he fell at a different spot along the antislavery spectrum than did the range of abolitionists was due in large part to his continued commitment to a host of overlapping priorities even after 1836. In November 1840, he lauded the career of Charles Fenton Mercer of Virginia, who had sought through a variety of policy initiatives to advance "the internal improvement of the country" but who had been limited and stifled by "the savage and barbarous genius of slavery." In April 1842, he prayed in his journal that his efforts in Congress would prove "auspicious to the peace of my country and to human freedom!" In November of that year he identified his cause as "the cause of my country and of human liberty. It is the cause of Christian improvement." In his entry for April 22, 1844, he lamented twin blows dealt by Congress to that cause. "This was a memorable day in the annals of the world," he groaned. "The treaty for the annexation of Texas to this Union was this day sent in to the Senate; and with it went the freedom of the human race. In the House it was a no less disastrous day," featuring defeats for a protective tariff and internal improvements.[12] To be sure, he offered a clear statement of his priorities during his post-1836 stage when he confided to his diary that "the deepest of my afflictions is the degeneracy of my country from the principles which gave her existence, … under the transcendent power of slavery and the slave-representation" (C.F. Adams, 1874–1877: 12.37). But the aging statesman would never embrace only one policy priority or identity, and the interrelated causes he fought for included many that he had advocated as president and before.

On December 12, 1831, when Adams inaugurated his career in the House of Representatives by introducing abolitionist petitions, he offered the caveat that he did not "countenance and support" those calling for the abolition of slavery (as opposed to the slave trade) in the District of Columbia. "Whatever might be his opinion of slavery in the abstract," the record states, this was an explosive subject "which he hoped would not be discussed in that House" (*Register*, 22nd Cong., 1st Sess.: 1425–1426).[13] Much as modern students of the antebellum debates over slavery cheer for those who did attack slavery "in the abstract," few in that generation – least of all Adams, whether as diplomat, president, or congressman – could think or talk of slavery only on that plane, bound up as it was with so many practical, policy, and ideological considerations. Thus it took years of prodding to make Adams willing to talk vigorously about slavery, even when representing a Massachusetts congressional district rather than the whole Union in the executive branch. When he told his constituents in 1842 that when he entered Congress "I was not then a sectional partisan, and I never have been," that was in part convenient electoral posturing (Quincy, 1859: 183). But it also captured his self-image in 1842 just as readily as did his private self-description as "the head of the antislavery movement in this country, disavowed by the whole body of abolitionists" as well as slaveholders and "the mongrel Democracy of the North and West" (C.F. Adams, 1874–1877: 12.135–136). That self-image combined his solicitude for the constitutional union – taking pride in the opposition of the lawless abolitionists and in the bisectional nature of his opposition – and his need for personal vindication against the enemies he had always perceived on his every side. Indeed, setting himself up as a sort of American Wilberforce working through the Whig rather than abolitionist instrumentality suited not only his overlapping loyalties, but also his deep "aspirations to live in the memory of after-ages as a benefactor of my country and of mankind" (C.F. Adams, 1874–1877: 12.271).

When Adams died in April 1848, his native state's legislature voted unanimously that Edward Everett offer the first shaping of that memory, in a state-sponsored eulogy. Everett was determined to preserve the consensus nature of the occasion, so he tried his best to downplay "present or past controversies" in his laudatory life sketch (Everett, 1878: 556–596). Abolitionists and radical antislavery politicians assailed Everett's eulogy as failing to do full justice to Adams's antislavery career, and that stung Everett. He complained to Charles Sumner that he had stepped "to the very verge of propriety in the Anti Slavery direction" despite his vow to remember Adams as all things to all people, and that had not been enough for Sumner's "abolition friends." Sumner responded by assuring Everett that "I thought that Mr. Adams's Anti-Slavery character stood forth" in Everett's eulogy "in its proper relief."[14] Unlike his tunnel-visioned "abolition friends," Sumner could perceive no incongruity in the state legislature nominating Everett, the Whig luminary whose career was one long attempt to find middle ground on slavery, to eulogize the fallen Adams. For Everett and Sumner both understood, better than those abolitionists and many modern historians, the need to place Adams's own complex and dynamic career in the tortured politics of slavery "in its proper relief."

NOTES

1 Measured by the number of signatures, the abolition of slavery in the District of Columbia was the leading demand of these petitions, followed by the abolition of the domestic slave trade and the restriction of slavery in the territories; see W.L. Miller, 1996: 306, 311.

2 For a similarly vague argument leaning on the notion of slavery ascending in importance on the national agenda, see Lewis, 2001: 119–140. For a bracing and persuasive argument that the 1820s, not the early 1830s, marked a high point in antislavery politics, see Ratcliffe, 2011.

3 This conceptualization of the issue of slavery follows David M. Potter's insightful analysis, wherein the issue for Americans of the early republic was "not a choice of alternatives – antislavery or proslavery – but a ranking of values. ... The difference between 'antislavery men' and 'conciliationists' in the North was not a question of what they thought about slavery alone, but of how they ranked these priorities." See Potter, 1976: 43–45.
4 W.C. Ford,1913–1917: 5.113–114, 287–288, 334–337, 347–353, 367–369, 406–407, 506–509, 533–537, 554–555; 6.1–2, 26–36, 85–86, 319–320, 334–335; 7.37–39, 82–83; see also Mason, 2002: 671–677.
5 W.C. Ford 1913–1917: vol. 6: 26, 469–72; vol. 7:84–88, 92–94, 164–165, 171–176, 489–516.
6 *Register of the Debates of Congress* (hereafter *Register*), 19th Cong., 1st Sess.: 112–343. For especially good examples of how Southerners injected slavery into this debate and the alarm that caused moderates, see *Register*, 19th Cong., 1st Sess.: 112–132, 207–208, 284–286, 289–291, 329–332. For more on this conference, its context, and the opposition to it, see Lewis, 1998: 190–214; Forbes, 2007: 203–209.
7 This reflection casts doubt on assertions that Adams immediately read his defeat in sectional terms; see e.g. Bemis, 1956: 150–151.
8 My interpretation accords better with Nagel, who accounts for the changes in Adams by his experiences in Congress at least as much as by his defeat in 1828; Nagel, 1997: 296–419.
9 For more on Adams as tariff compromiser, see Clark ,1932: 291; Bemis, 1956: 240–258.
10 While significant, the text of the speech does not sustain Bemis's rather melodramatic account of how in it "for the first time real eloquence poured forth from his heart," unloosing his antislavery soul and turning him against tariff compromise; see Bemis, 1956: 259–272.
11 C.F. Adams, 1874–1877: 9. 268, 349–350, 365, 417–418, 451; 10.39–44, 79–80, 92, 97, 125–126, 128–129, 413; 11.491; 12.67. For a good secondary account of this relationship, see Bemis, 1956: 382–415.
12 C.F. Adams, 1874–1877, vol. 10: 360–361, 457, 459; vol. 11: 137, 267–268, 359, 363, 409; vol. 12: 13–14, 22, 25, 49, 57, 60, 68.
13 For more on his reluctance to discuss the issue in the House in these years, see C.F. Adams, 1874–1877: 8.454–455.
14 Everett to Sumner, May 5, 1848; Sumner to Everett, May 5, 1848 (*Papers of Charles Sumner*, microfilm edition. Houghton Library, Harvard University.).

Further Reading

Adams, C.F., ed. (1874–1877). *Memoirs of John Quincy Adams, Comprising Portions of His Diary from 1795 to 1848*, 12 vols. Philadelphia.
Bemis, S.F. (1956). *John Quincy Adams and the Union*. New York.
Forbes, R.P. (2007). *The Missouri Compromise and Its Aftermath: Slavery and the Meaning of America*. Chapel Hill, NC.
Ford, W. C., ed. (1913–1917). *Writings of John Quincy Adams*, 7 vols. New York.
Freehling, W.W. (1990). *The Road to Disunion*, vol. 1: *Secessionists at Bay, 1776–1854*. Oxford.

Hammond, J.C., and Mason, M., eds. (2011). *Contesting Slavery: The Politics of Bondage and Freedom in the New American Nation*. Charlottesville.
Howe, D. (2007). *What God Hath Wrought: The Transformation of America, 1815–1848*. Oxford.
Jones, H. (1987). *Mutiny on the Amistad: The Saga of a Slave Revolt and Its Impact on American Abolition, Law, and Diplomacy*. Oxford.
Lewis, J.E., Jr. (2001). *John Quincy Adams: Policymaker for the Union*. Wilmington, DE.
Lipsky, G.A. (1950). *John Quincy Adams: His Theory and Ideas*. New York.
Mason, M. (2002). The Battle of the Slaveholding Liberators: Great Britain, the United States, and Slavery in the Early Nineteenth Century. *William and Mary Quarterly*, 59: 665–696.
Mason, M. (2006). *Slavery and Politics in the Early American Republic*. Chapel Hill, NC.
Mason, M. (2009). Keeping Up Appearances: The International Politics of Slave Trade Abolition in the Nineteenth-Century Atlantic World. *William and Mary Quarterly*, 3rd ser. 66: 809–832.
Miller, W.L. (1996). *Arguing about Slavery: The Great Battle in the United States Congress*. New York.
Nagel, P. (1997). *John Quincy Adams: A Public Life, a Private Life*. New York.
Richards, L.L. (1986). *The Life and Times of Congressman John Quincy Adams*. Oxford.
Waldstreicher, D. (2009). *Slavery's Constitution: From Revolution to Ratification*. New York.
Wilentz, S. (2005). *The Rise of American Democracy: Jefferson to Lincoln*. New York.

Chapter Twenty-One

John Quincy Adams's Higher Learnings: Rhetoric, Science, and Intellectual History

Marlana Portolano

John Quincy Adams, perhaps even more than his studious father, was a scholarly patriot. John and Abigail Adams formed their son's habits of thought early, and his intellectual virtues and a lifelong habit of self-education had the double effect of steeping him in the classics and keeping him aware of the growing potential of empirical science to enhance America's development as a modern, democratic nation. Apart from his many legislative and diplomatic roles – ambassador, senator, secretary of state, president, and member of the House of Representatives for nine consecutive terms – John Quincy Adams made contributions to intellectual history that are notable in their own right. These contributions are largely in the promotion of science and letters rather than the theoretical advancement of those subjects, and they are most easily understood in two related categories. First, Adams was a teacher and practitioner of rhetoric and *belles lettres* (the eighteenth-century term for all exemplary written composition, whether oratorical, literary, or historical). He was briefly the first Boylston Professor of Rhetoric and Oratory at Harvard, a position he took as seriously as any scholar who hoped to secure a lifelong career in higher education. In his letters and diary he was a persistent practitioner of rhetorical criticism, a habit that contributed to and informed his participation in government. The second area of Adams's intellectual contribution applies the first: Adams practiced his own theory of rhetoric by taking every opportunity to persuade public and legislative audiences of the importance of learning and research to America's development as a leader among her peer nations.

A Companion to John Adams and John Quincy Adams, First Edition.
Edited by David Waldstreicher.

Some readers may question the importance of Adams's contributions to America's intellectual life because their effects were diffuse or delayed, but such an interpretation of history depends on immediate, pragmatic effects of legislation and neglects the ways in which reputable public speakers can loosen cultural ground for future cultivation. It is true that Adams's writings and teachings on the art of rhetoric made little lasting impression on the way successive professors at Harvard taught the subject, but the very fact that the sixth president of the United States was a scholar of rhetoric is hard to ignore in the context of his political work as a whole. Moreover, the direct effect of rhetorical art on his statecraft cannot be disproved. In Adams's orations in each public office he held, his careful use of classical rhetoric to develop arguments and influence audiences is evident both in his diary entries reflecting on oratorical events and on his writing's structure itself. He used this classical style of discourse because it was recognizable and esteemed by his audience. At the turn of the nineteenth century, classical learning was still the norm in education and cultural life, so Adams used a traditional style of rhetoric even when it seemed stylistically at odds with his promotion of empirical science. As a politician, Adams had a vision of government that included the development of scientific knowledge for the enlightenment of a democratic citizenry. He imagined a role for science in nation building that transcended the government's established need for practical problem-solving and prepared the way for later generations to value science as a high authority for decision-making. During his presidency (1825–1829), Adams's plans to advance science and found a national university seemed overblown because they went beyond his country's immediate needs for practical technology to strengthen agriculture, build new cities, and establish an infrastructure in the frontier. His words did not, however, fall on deaf ears. Before there were professional scientists at all, there had to be a myriad of persuasive acts that would prime the culture for acceptance of government-funded, basic scientific research. Adams's rhetoric in the promotion of science – his State of the Union statements, his report on weights and measures, his efforts during the founding of the Smithsonian, his attempts to win support for a national observatory– contributed cumulatively to changing attitudes in America in favor of government-supported scientific research.

Recent developments in both the history of science and the history of rhetoric have expanded perspectives in these fields to include broader cultural underpinnings of events and their effects. From this point of view, it is not immediate triumph in a single struggle or debate that marks a successful contribution. This is consonant with Adams's own practical philosophy of rhetoric, which accepted Aristotle's injunction that it is not winning a debate that is important, but finding and communicating all the possible means of persuasion for a particular issue and a particular audience. Similarly, many scholars in both the history of science and the history of rhetoric remain interested in the way Adams held his course, never giving up on the inclusion of higher learning and research in American democratic nationhood even when he seemed personally defeated. It was by never relinquishing intellectual virtue, and never losing his faith that America could value higher learning in the long run, that Adams made his contributions for posterity.

In the following sections, I will first briefly recall Adams's upbringing and education at the hands of Revolutionary patriot-scholars such as his father and Thomas Jefferson, and how he learned from this generation through exposure to scientific clubs, travel to Europe, constant reading of the classics, and deep commitment to a vision of the "American experiment." Next I describe John Quincy Adams's scholarship in rhetoric, including the publication of his *Lectures on Rhetoric and Oratory* and a lifelong practice of rhetorical principles as both an orator and a rhetorical critic. My particular emphasis is on Adams's imitation of Cicero, a mental model he valued even more than his father did, and whom he read for inspiration and courage with almost religious devotion. Although it may seem an unusual transition to modern readers, I will then discuss the role that Ciceronian rhetoric – in the mouth of John Quincy Adams – played in advancing astronomy and other fields of basic scientific research during the early years of the nineteenth century, in particular through his oratorical campaigns to found the Smithsonian Institution and a national observatory. Finally, I will reassess Adams's contributions to the field of rhetoric, both in theory and in practice, and assert his importance to American intellectual history.

21.1 Intellectual Virtue and the Adams Family

By contemporary measurements, John Quincy Adams was America's smartest president to date. A study by University of California psychologist Dean Simonton has estimated Adams's IQ at approximately 170 (Simonton, 2006: 419). While native intelligence may partially account for this, the expectations placed upon John Quincy Adams by his parents' Revolutionary generation undoubtedly contributed to his voracious drive for knowledge. As David McCullough (2010) has said of his father John Adams, it "is not possible to understand [the Adamses] without understanding that politics and life, diplomacy and life, the presidency and life are always intertwined. If you don't understand the nature of the human beings caught up in the events of times past, you don't understand what has happened" (McCullough, 2010: 11). By nature, the generation that influenced John Quincy Adams in his formative years was essentially concerned with the good life of the mind. By "the pursuit of happiness," as a right claimed for Americans in the Declaration of Independence, the founding generation did not mean material wealth or a relaxed lifestyle;

they meant that citizens should have the ability to exercise their intellectual (and spiritual) faculties for their own improvement and fulfillment as human beings. John Quincy Adams was trained from boyhood to embrace these values, and his prominent family expected that he would create institutional structures that would ensure the prominence of these values in the business of nation building. He was also expected to follow in the footsteps of his father's promotion of empirical science, which the elder Adams had enthusiastically pursued by founding the American Academy of Arts and Sciences.

In a sense, John Quincy Adams was a man with one foot in the eighteenth century and one foot in the nineteenth. America in this transitional period was, to use the term of Gregory Clark and S. Michael Halloran (1993), an oratorical culture. While the Enlightenment had ushered in a new source of authoritative knowledge in Europe, namely empirical science, America did not have the financial resources required to develop and maintain research institutions like the British Royal Society. Ironically, the Old World had shifted to modernity first because of access to aristocratically entrenched sources of funding. America, in contrast, still retained the classical system of knowledge which valorized the examples of Greece and Rome and saw knowledge as a holistic repository of established authorities accepted by consensus. The leaders of the new nation, in the revolutionary generation and in John Quincy Adams's era of expansion and national identity formation, saw the statesmen orators of democratic Greece and the Roman republic as a golden age of civilizing icons.

This kind of leader, the statesman orator, was largely a Ciceronian tradition that was taught in America's new colleges and embraced by Adams and most of his peers. Such a leader, the tradition taught, should be conversant in all areas of arts and sciences, a kind of Renaissance man. At the same time, he should be committed to civic virtue and the common good, and he should act decisively as a forerunner by making laws, founding institutions, and investing his nation with shared principles. The statesman orator saw himself as an architect of society, an idea reflected in classical works they considered authoritative, such as Cicero's *De Inventione*:

> There was a time when men wandered at large in the fields like animals and lived on wild fare; they did nothing by the guidance of reason, but relied chiefly on physical strength; there was as yet no ordered system of religious worship nor of social duties … nor had they learned the advantage of an equitable code of law. … At this juncture a man – great and wise I am sure – became aware of the power offered by his mind for great achievements if one could develop and improve it by instruction … he assembled and gathered them in accordance with a plan…and then when through reason and eloquence they had listened with greater attention, he transformed them from wild savages into a kind and gentle folk. (Cicero, 1949: 5–7)

John Adams modeled himself after this vision of the statesman orator, but JQA (as he often referred to himself) surpassed his father's general esteem for Cicero, seeing the master orator as a personal totem for his life and his works. Venerating and emulating Cicero furnished JQA with a lifelong paradigm for character development and dutiful, paternalistic leadership. His reverence of Cicero resulted in his owning fourteen editions of the orator's works (W.C. Ford, 1938: 25). He took a volume with him wherever he went. While serving as Secretary of State under President Monroe, he wrote that "living without Cicero at hand would be as a privation of one of my limbs." And as his biographer Samuel Flagg Bemis writes: "The old Roman's stamp of style and feeling shows through many a passage of Adams's letters and Diary and throughout his controversial writings" (Bemis, 1949: 204).

Adams's devotion to Cicero as an ancient icon of civic virtue did not preclude his embrace of empirical science. His interest in the two areas developed simultaneously, which was not, at the time, unusual. Before specialization and professionalization entered the American understanding of science, all knowledge was seen as a holistic human enterprise, progressing from its ancient roots to fuller understanding in the contemporary world. Science was not partitioned from philosophy, mechanics, literature, or the arts. In fact, both John Quincy Adams and his father were invited to be members of Benjamin Franklin's broadly nonspecialist American Philosophical Society, not on the basis of scientific experimentation, but because of their involvement in public life and the resulting opportunities to legislate, encourage, and promote learning broadly, among American citizens and (they believed) humankind. In the early years of America's scientific societies, it was the well-rounded statesman who was able to bring science into consideration at all levels of government.

John Quincy Adams first began to appreciate learning's importance to nationhood at the age of 11, when he accompanied his father on a trip to help Benjamin Franklin and Arthur Lee promote America's cause for nationhood in Paris. On board the ship, JQA read Cicero for the first time and learned French from a surgeon in the French Army. On other trips during his teen years, he observed amnesty negotiations and diplomacy and spent many hours in Europe's great scientific and artistic institutions and exhibitions. In this way, he gained a firsthand understanding of America's lack of development in comparison with older, more aristocratic nations. During his early education, JQA took on the responsibilities outlined by his father in the Massachusetts constitution, which boldly proclaims the state's duty to promote literature, science, and civic virtue – all three of which are grouped together as the good life of the mind:

> Wisdom and knowledge, as well as virtue, diffused generally among the body of the people being necessary for the preservation of their rights and liberties

> ... it shall be the duty of legislators ... to cherish the interests of literature and the sciences .... to encourage private societies and public institutions, rewards and immunities, for [their] promotion ... to inculcate the principles of humanity and general benevolence, public and private charity, industry and frugality, honesty and punctuality in all dealings, sincerity, good humor, and all social affections, and generous sentiments among the people. (Quoted in McCullough, 2001: 223)

As John Quincy Adams set out in public life, especially as he reached the presidency and in his nine terms in the House of Representatives, he kept in mind this paternalistic drive to inculcate the American people with principles of honor and intellectual virtue. Through his association with the founding generation and the Federalists, and in his continuation of their vision of American nationhood, John Quincy Adams took on a special ethos as a leader and a public speaker: it was almost an aura of America's national identity and patriotism. This direct connection with America's origins, combined with his vigorous practice of the Ciceronian discipline of being a statesman orator, made him a notable and popular speaker even when his message was not cause for immediate action.

21.2 The Lectures on Rhetoric and Oratory

It was both John Quincy Adams's scholarly expertise and his privileged social standing that led to his being appointed Harvard's first Boylston Chair of Rhetoric and Oratory in 1806. His friend and distant kinsman, the wealthy Boston merchant Nicholas Boylston, had requested that he be named the first professor when the chair was established. At the time, Adams was a senator in Massachusetts, but because of his deep-seated desire to make a contribution to the formation of young citizen-leaders, he accepted the position part time and began a long process of specialized preparation. On June 26, 1805, his diary notes that he first checked out Leland's *Demosthenes* and Guthrie's *Quintilian* from Harvard's library. He knew that Greek and Roman rhetoric were subjects that he "must for years to come (if my life be spared) explore and cultivate with unabating industry" (Auer and Banninga, 1963 119). Adams's diary provides a record of his extensive readings on the subject of rhetoric in the four years following his appointment at age 39. He made original translations from Greek and Latin, including his own translation of Aristotle's *Rhetoric*; he read scores of classical works in rhetorical theory, literary criticism, and oratory in the context of statecraft; and he read all the orations he could find by masters such as Demosthenes, Aeschines, Isocrates, and Lysias. In English, he paid particular attention to Hugh Blair's *Lectures on Rhetoric and Oratory*, the most popular textbook used in colleges on both sides of the Atlantic, but he also read John Lawson's *Lectures Concerning Oratory*, Bacon's *On Evidence*, George Campbell's *Philosophy of Rhetoric*, Thomas Gibbon's *Rhetoric*, John Walker's *Elements of Elocution*, Thomas Sherridan's *Lectures on Elocution*, Lord Kames's *Elements of Criticism*, Isaac Watts's *Logic*, and a host of English sermons as examples of great oratory. Because Adams was fluent in French, he was also able to read works in that language, including Bridel Arleville's *Abrege de la Rhétorique Francoise*, Rene Rapin's *Réflectionssurl'éloquence*, Jean-Francois de La Harpe's *Lycéeou*, *Cours de littératureancienne et modern*, and Cesar Chesneau Demarsais' *Traite del le construction oratoire* (Auer and Banninga, 1963 123–24).

The three primary sources for his lectures, however, were Aristotle, Cicero, and Quintilian, about whom he wrote: "A subject which has exhausted [their] genius can neither require nor admit much additional illustration. To select, combine, and apply their precepts, is the only duty left for their followers of all succeeding times, and to obtain perfect familiarity with their instructions is to arrive at mastery of the art" (J.Q. Adams, 1810: 28–29). References to Cicero outnumber all other sources combined. The lectures themselves, however, prove that Adams did augment and expand the traditional theory, primarily in the application of classical principles to American government. While Adams taught classical rhetoric in a purist form, in Europe the Enlightenment had transformed the discipline during the eighteenth century. In European scientific societies and in the new research-based universities, the philosophies of René Descartes and John Locke had already elevated empiricism and mathematical logic to the status of absolute truth. This new location of authority affected teachings even in what we now think of as humanities subjects, such as rhetoric – the art of persuasion. European teachers of rhetoric tended to combine Aristotelian and Ciceronian approaches to rhetoric with new approaches to faculty psychology and logic. Invention of written material was no longer the province of rhetorical reasoning, but was left instead to the knowledge-generating disciplines, which were deemed more advanced, and certainly truer than deductive lines of reason based on traditional premises. Blair's *Lectures*, for example, are primarily concerned with guidelines for taste and style, which he believed could be derived by empirical observation of human nature. Campbell's *Philosophy of Rhetoric* exemplifies the Enlightenment by explaining discourse in terms of Francis Bacon's inductive methodology and appeals to evidence. Of course Adams, who was much traveled and partly educated in Europe, was well aware of this context, but he also knew that America had yet to catch up with this world view.

As he introduced the subject of rhetoric at Harvard, Adams emulated Cicero, but combined this approach with the Christian ethical character of nineteenth-century America. In his first oration at Harvard, Adams explained that political power resulted from mastery of the rhetorical arts in ancient times, and that the same holds true for his own students. This is especially true because of the nature of American state and federal governments: "From the preponderancy of democracy in the political constitutions of our country, deliberative assemblies are more numerous, and the objects of their consideration more diversified, than they ever have been in any other age or nation"(J.Q. Adams, 1810: 256–257). However, duty and moral vision must always guide leaders in both republican and democratic government (he distinguishes between the two very little in the *Lectures*):

> In the flourishing periods of Athens and Rome, eloquence was power. Oratory was taught, as an occupation of a life . ...[Our] own nation is at this time precisely under the same circumstances, which were so propitious to the advancement of rhetoric and oratory among the Greeks... Persuasion, or the influence of reason and of feeling, is the great if not the only instrument, whose operation can affect the arts of all our corporate bodies ...[R]eceive the injunction of your duty ... Under governments purely republican, where every citizen has a deep interest in the affairs of the nation, and, in some form of public assembly or other, has the means and opportunity of delivering his opinions, and of communicating his sentiments by speech; where government itself has no arms but persuasion ... the voice of eloquence will not be heard in vain. Gather fragrance from the whole paradise of science, and learn to distill from your lips the honeys of persuasion. (J.Q. Adams, 1810: 29–31, 70)

Similarities with Cicero's ideal orator are immediately apparent, but they are intertwined with hints of Enlightenment language and, especially, a Christianized American character. Before offering a series of reasons for studying the art of rhetoric in contemporary American leadership, Professor Adams invokes a "testimonial of Omnipotence" as the ultimate authoritative proof for his neo-Ciceronian ethical approach to the orator's role. This direct application of classical rhetorical theory to the practice of statecraft in America is one of Adams's most important original contributions to the teaching of rhetoric. As Sandra Gustafson has written (2011: 74), "Like his father, JQA was an important force for promoting Ciceronian values and practices," especially in his rhetorical theory and oratory, and this influence was enhanced by his political prominence. JQA figures prominently in Gustafson's (2000) book about power and oratory as the first major form of verbal art in British North America – *Eloquence is Power: Oratory and Performance in Early America*.

Adams lectured on rhetoric to students and the general public for four years. When he published the *Lectures on Rhetoric and Oratory*, the book comprised two volumes and thirty-two lectures. It is the first complete rhetoric published in America, by which I mean that it treats all five areas of the discipline of rhetoric: invention of arguments, arrangement of material, writing style, oral delivery, and techniques of memory. As I will be demonstrating in the next section how Adams used his rhetorical theory to promote scientific research in early nineteenth-century America, it is worth outlining the contents of his book here.

The first six lectures introduce the history of rhetoric and oratory, including lectures on Cicero and Quintilian. The rest of the first volume and part of the second teach the invention of deductive arguments, precisely the area of rhetoric discarded by most Enlightenment scholars. He categorizes inventive strategies for argument according to each of the three genres of classical speech making: political, judicial, and ceremonial. These genres are defined by their respective purpose and audience. Political oratory, also called deliberative oratory, is addressed to legislative bodies such as the American Congress, and it invents persuasive reasoning for a course of action by making use of practical topics such as means and ends, legality, and possibility. Judicial oratory judges a past action, and its aim is justice. Ceremonial or "epideictic" oratory is closest to education in its purpose: it aims to influence the underlying attitudes of the audience through praise and blame so that gradual cultural change may result. Like many European Enlightenment rhetoricians, Adams adds pulpit oratory to the three traditional genres, including a chapter specifically for future clergy and their critics. Regardless of a student's primary genre, however, the good American orator must acquire a lifelong habit of learning, including a broad introduction through liberal education to the foundations of history, moral philosophy, languages, and literature, followed by specialized education in the student's particular profession.

The constant guidepost of rhetorical invention in Adams's *Lectures* is the orator's intellectual virtue: that is, the mental and moral qualities necessary for persuasion in effective statecraft. Because great power is imparted to skillful orators in a democracy, responsibility and moral vision are paramount. In Lecture 15, Adams writes, "We cannot separate the moral character of the orator from the oratorical power. If we assume a given point, that a man is deficient in the score of integrity, we discard all confidence in his disclosure, and all benevolence to his person. We contemn[sic] his argument as sophistry"(J.Q. Adams, 1810: 345).As a result of this moral imperative, the concept of the *orator perfectus*, an ideal of the orator described by Cicero and Quintilian, is the guiding concept of the *Lectures.* To Adams, Cicero himself was the embodiment of this ideal. In his lecture on the Roman statesman, Adams tells his students:

> I cannot conclude this account of the rhetorical writings of Cicero, without once more urging upon your attention all the works, as well as the life and character of this extraordinary man … . As a rhetorician, we have seen, that he is unrivaled by the union of profound science with elegant taste… . But to the modern detractors of his fame it may be justly replied, that his failings leaned to virtue's side; that his heaviest vices might put the blush to their choicest virtues… . Let us make this the standard of moral and intellectual

> worth, for all human kind; and in reply to all the severities of satire, and all the bitterness of misanthropy, repeat with conscious exultation, "we are the same species of beings, as Cicero." (J.Q. Adams, 1810: 132–138)

The state of perfection implied by this artfully elevated example of Cicero was strictly an ideal: a practicing orator could never actually meet it, but should spend his life trying to attain it. The *Lectures* include this personified moral model as the measure of rhetorical invention at every opportunity.

In his chapters on deliberative and forensic rhetoric, Adams adapts the ideal of the *orator perfectus* to the needs of Christian republican leadership as he conceived of it in the first decade of nineteenth-century America. He counsels students to imagine what Truth, Honor, and Virtue would say if they could speak with a human voice, and to incorporate this language while inventing arguments for particular occasions. The orator must have "formed a correct estimate of good and evil" (J.Q. Adams, 1810: 356) and the ability to overcome obstacles, because a reputation for integrity and judicious problem-solving are required in Congress, in legal practice, and in the pulpit. In Adams's political oratory promoting basic science later in his career, he adopted an ethos that amounted to being the moral guardian of James Smithson's famous financial gift to the United States. As he explained to his Harvard students, the ethos of a well-established civic leader often has to do with values associated with him personally. For an older, respected orator, a paternalistic style and persona is an appropriate strategy in certain circumstances.

In connection with Adams's practice of classical rhetorical principles in Congress, the most relevant advice in the *Lectures* occurs in the sections on deliberative oratory. Again, Adams's notion of deliberative argument emphasizes the importance of the speaker and his character as it is perceived by the audience. The goodwill of the hearers, always sought by an orator, depends on the speaker's ability to project his character and adapt his subject and style to the occasion: " … the particular province of the deliberative speaker is to advise; and what possible effect can be expected from advice, where there is no confidence in the adviser" (J.Q. Adams, 1810: 268). This is the concept of *prepon* or appropriateness in rhetorical invention, which is stressed consistently by classical theorists. Adams also dwells on the use of examples, but adapts the Ciceronian approach by especially urging examples from the Christian gospel, whose founder "delivered his incomparable system of morality altogether through the medium of fables and parables" (J.Q. Adams, 1810: 272). In what might be considered quintessentially whiggish language, Adams pays particular attention to American deliberative assemblies, making original modifications to classical theory in order to fit these legislative bodies:

> From the formation of a national constitution to the management of a turnpike, every object of concern to more than one individual [in the USA] is

> transacted by deliberative bodies. National and state conventions for the purpose of forming constitutions, the Congress of the United States, the legislatures of the several states, are all deliberative assemblies. Besides which, in our part of the country, every town, every parish or religious society, every association of individuals, incorporated for the purposes of interest, of education, of charity, or of science, forms a deliberative assembly, and presents opportunities for the exhibition of deliberative eloquence. (J.Q. Adams, 1810: 256–257)

As he continues his lesson, Adams keeps a persistent eye on Congress and state legislatures as the ultimate settings for deliberative rhetoric in America, thus linking the politician's vocation (and Adams's own public career) with that of the statesman orator:

> The most important scenes of deliberative oratory however in these states are the congress of the union, and the state legislatures. The objects of their deliberation affect the interests of individuals and of the nation, in the highest degree. In seeking the sources of deliberative argument I shall therefore so modify the rules … as to bear constant reference to them. (J.Q. Adams, 1810: 258–259)

The remainder of Adams's chapter on deliberative rhetoric describes three areas from which an orator may draw his lines of reasoning: the subject under consideration, the groups of people deliberating, and the speaker himself. In this way, Adams introduces logos, pathos, and ethos, which Aristotle and later Cicero saw as the three proofs of rhetoric requiring artistic invention of arguments. Logos allowed reasoning about the subject matter, while ethos and pathos dealt respectively with the virtues of the speaker and emotions felt by the audience in a particular circumstance. For occasions requiring deliberative judgments and leading to political action, the "master passion" is jealousy, which often evlolves from a spirit of party. However, according to Adams, the overuse of strong emotions which could prejudice the audience is morally questionable. Evoking jealousy by means of artistic persuasion should be the last resort in an argument plagued by faction, when the speaker is unable to support his arguments by reason; it is effective only if the audience is already prejudiced and ignorant of the subject.

Like his classical models, Cicero and Quintilian, Adams approaches various structures of logical argumentation as another means of rhetorical invention. He includes separate lectures on each of four species of logical argument: confirmation, confutation, ratiocination, and induction. The "enthymeme" or rhetorical syllogism is the most common form of ratiocination – or deductive argument – used in classical rhetoric. As in an ordinary syllogism, the chain of reasoning consists of two general premises that, combined, lead to a more particular conclusion ($x=y$; and $y=z$; therefore $x=z$). In an enthymeme, however, Adams notes that one or sometimes both of the premises are unstated in the discourse of an oration, and the context of running speech may be laced with other stylistic or emotional appeals that are not present in formal logic. An unstated premise is psychologically significant when an orator has correctly appraised the audience, because it assumes that the audience already believes the premise taken as an assumption.

Adams describes the other primary mode of reasoning, induction, as making abroad conclusion from a number of particular instances, or at least a particular experience which may stand symbolically for many experiences. Of the forms of induction Adams describes in the *Lectures*, one is particularly interesting and often used by Adams in his political speeches. This is a method of ensnaring the adversary in a trap of his own faulty arguments. Socrates, Adams points out, sometimes uses this form of reasoning in Plato's dialogues: "You must lead him blind folded from his concessions to his strong hold, and eventually reduce him to silence, to full concession, or precise denial... His concession is your victory, and puts an end to the argument" (J.Q. Adams, 1810: 65–66). This method of arguing through similitude was a favorite of Adams, one he used often and with fruitful results in his political speeches, as I will soon demonstrate.

In his final chapters, Adams's treatment of elocution (the eighteenth-century word for "style") addresses the concepts of purity and clarity, known collectively as "perspicuity," in written composition. This was an Enlightenment ideal in rhetorical education which had been taught by Blair, Campbell, and other belletrists in Europe, and which would soon take a strong hold in American discourse. Simplicity and directness of language, without a cloud of figurative verbiage, was believed to reflect a more truthful, empirical attitude than foregrounding traditional but unexamined beliefs. Here Adams demonstrates again that he is not simply recounting the theories of the ancient rhetoricians, but adapting classical inventive strategies for use in contemporary speaking. In his own speech making, however, Adams would prove to be more a follower of Ciceronian style than of Lockean certitude, even when he held up empirical science as a desirable authority. This is because he embraced fully the classical methods of rhetorical invention described in his book. Adams took for granted that rhetoric was its own discipline, an art worthy of mastering and practicing diligently, especially for the career politician.

Adams's students praised the *Lectures on Rhetoric and Oratory* and petitioned him to publish the book before he left Harvard for his appointment as the first United States minister to Russia. Public attendance of the lectures also attested to his popularity as a speaker and expert on the subject, but audience members from Boston were more critical of Adams's current political performance. As Ralph Waldo Emerson described it,

> When he read his first lectures in 1806, not only the students heard him with delight, but the hall was crowded by the Professors and by unusual visitors… On his return in the winter to the Senate in Washington, he… lost the sympathy of many of his constituents in Boston. When, on his return from Washington, he resumed his lectures in Cambridge, his class attended but the coaches from Boston did not come, and indeed many of his political friends deserted him. (*Letters and Social Aims*, quoted in Goodfellow, 1946).

The contemporary lack of interest in Adams's *Lectures* was no doubt often prompted by political bias. Later criticism was often as cursory: in 1946, before a resurgence of interest in the history of classical rhetoric and its influence, Donald Goodfellow remarked (1946: 389), "Unappealing though we may find these lectures today, they represent his best efforts as the first incumbent of America's first chair of rhetoric and oratory."

The *Lectures on Rhetoric and Oratory* were indeed Adams's best effort. After staying up one night until dawn to read the first published volume, Adams wrote to his mother that he wished just one other person could be moved to do the same someday. Readers in the latter half of the twentieth century began to look deeper and appreciate this work in the context in which it was produced. In 1962, a new edition was edited and published by Jeffrey Auer and Gerald Benninga, who also spent considerable time researching the genesis and composition of the lectures. The text of the *Lectures* began to appear in anthologies and histories of American rhetoric with regularity. As one scholar notes, "Adams, in America's first comprehensive set of lectures on rhetoric as a civic art, would show both that the ideal oratory that calls political community into being had been reborn in America, and that … this oratory has scriptural as well as pagan roots" (Potkay, 1999: 147). Adams's neoclassical ideals were one of the main reasons he had been chosen as the first Boylston Professor, a position whose statutes required the teaching of Aristotle, Cicero, and the classical theory of rhetoric; therefore, criticism of his close adherence to these subjects is beside the point. He does not often refer to contemporary rhetoricians in the *Lectures*, but as we have seen, this does not mean he was ignorant of belletristic and psychological-epistemological approaches to the subject. Rather, his aim was to preserve classical knowledge of rhetorical theory, which he believed to be largely complete, and to introduce its usefulness in the new context of early American democracy. The next holder of the Boylston chair, Rev. Joseph McKean, would begin a trend of introducing more Enlightenment theories and belletristic pedagogy into the role of the professorship, a trend that would ultimately enable creative writers and poets (such as Archibald MacLeish and Seamus Heaney) to hold the position in the twentieth century. But as for John Quincy Adams's initiation of rhetorical studies at Harvard, it was the neoclassical foundation he was most concerned with imparting to students, just as it was neoclassical theory that informed and shaped his practice of political rhetoric. His influence in this should not be underestimated. As Carolyn Eastman has written (2009: 44): "Judging by the frequency with which his [Harvard inauguration] speech was reprinted and excerpted in schoolbooks, magazines, or other collections, Adams clearly did more than inspire a new generation of orators; he established himself as the kind of civic leader he claimed was necessary to the republic's survival."

21.3 John Quincy Adams's Campaigns for Basic Scientific Research

After his professorship at Harvard and for the rest of his career, John Quincy Adams formed a lifelong habit of practicing traditional techniques of invention, composition, and delivery in the pursuit of political eloquence. While his presidency is not remembered for any immediate improvements to the state of learning and science in the nation, his nine terms in the House of Representatives later in life demonstrate his unflagging persistence in the rhetorical promotion of government-supported scientific research. So notable was his oratorical style that the press began to call him Milton's name for Isocrates, "Old Man Eloquence." His devotion to eloquence in the service of science is no more apparent than in his longest-sustained efforts to promote learning in the new democratic nation: that is, his role in the founding of the Smithsonian and in his early publicizing of astronomy.[1]

America's relationship with the science of astronomy is an historically ambiguous one, dependent from its beginnings on the support of a public wary of the impracticalities of star-gazing. Classified as a subfield of geography, astronomy was particularly relevant to the ongoing development of navigation and therefore for increasing trade. Before 1830, America lacked a permanent observatory. There was little knowledge of new scientific developments in Europe and virtually no public patronage. Adams's father had encouraged some research in astronomy in the American Academy of Arts and Sciences, such as the work of Nathaniel Bowditch, and the results appeared in the Academy's *Memoirs.* Franklin's American Philosophical Society also published astronomical observations in its *Transactions*, most notably the contributions of David Rittenhouse and Andrew Ellicott. For the most part, however, these observations were conducted not in observatories but by individuals using their own small telescopes (Warner, 1979: 55–76).

The first American observatory, built by astronomer David Rittenhouse in Philadelphia in 1781 and given to the American Philosophical Society in 1796, was returned to the Rittenhouse family in 1810 for lack of use. After this, attempts by the American Philosophical Society and Harvard College failed to secure enough funding to construct a building or purchase instruments

(Musto, 1967: 87–88). Adams had wanted Harvard to have the first permanent observatory in the United States, and had even pledged $1000 for the purpose in 1823, but Harvard never collected the money because other donations could not be secured (B.Z. Jones and Boyd, 1971: 32).

During his presidency (1824–1828), Adams had unsuccessfully attempted to secure public funding for an observatory, along with several other projects for "internal improvements," including a national university. In 1825, in his first annual report to Congress as president, he had sought to arouse interest in a national observatory by appealing to American patriotism – as well as to the passion of jealousy:

> On the comparatively small territorial surface of Europe, there are existing upward of one hundred and thirty of these light-houses of the skies; while throughout the whole American hemisphere there is not one ... And while scarcely a year passes over our heads without bringing some new astronomical discovery to light, which we must fain receive at second-hand from Europe, are we not cutting ourselves off from the means of returning light for light, while we have neither observatory nor observer upon our half of the globe, and the earth revolves in perpetual darkness to our unsearching eyes? (J.Q. Adams, 1825b: 56)

In light of his simultaneous efforts to make other "internal improvements" such as roads and lighthouses, Adams had tailored the phrase "lighthouses of the skies" to the utilitarian mindset of his audience. His political opponents, however, misrepresented the metaphor, misquoting it "lighthouses *in* the skies" and subjecting him to derision about his lack of practicality. There was strong aversion to Adams's attempts to win federal support for an observatory during his presidency. The majority of Congress believed that support for scientific research was a breach of the constitution unless it could produce immediate utilitarian results for the agrarian economy. The memory of this political aversion haunted Adams ten years later, during his continued efforts to benefit American astronomy in the House of Representatives. A modern appreciation of Adams's rhetorical promotion of science, however, is incomplete if it is limited to immediate effects. His rhetorical art itself, and the mindset that produced it, are of equal interest in the cultural environment that eventually enabled American science and government to exist in closer relation to one another. Adams's long, balanced sentences, typical of Ciceronian oratory, combined with his passion for scientific endeavors involving observation and research, are an important illustration of two competing trends in American political language at the time, one stemming from classical democratic models and the other from science and progress.

During the years of Adams's presidency, the majority of American political leaders were not prepared to include astrophysical observation among the expenditures for government money. Public interest in the science, on the other hand, had begun to show signs of life. A brief list of observatories founded between 1830 and 1840 confirms that Adams's rhetoric was part of a trend toward general curiosity about this science, which he had helped to nourish with his public speaking. The University of North Carolina built the first college observatory in 1831. The oldest observatory in the United States today, the Hopkins Observatory at Williams College, was finished in 1836. Shortly after construction of this observatory, permanent mounted telescopes in dome structures were erected at Western Reserve College at Hudson, Ohio (1837); the Military Academy at West Point (1839); and at Central High School in Philadelphia (1840) (Musto, 1967: 89). Important publications such as the "Report on the progress of astronomy in this century" (1832) by Britain's Astronomer Royal George Biddle Airy, and John Herschel's *Treatise on Astronomy* (1833, reprinted in America in 1834) sparked more public interest, as did lecture series by scientists such as Cincinnati's Orms by MacKnight Mitchel (Warner, 1979: 55–65). During the 1840s, the active practice of astronomy came to fruition with several community and college observatories, the most famous of which was the Cincinnati observatory, founded in 1843. Among other observatories founded in the 1840s were ones at Tuscaloosa, Alabama (1843), Georgetown (1843), Amherst (1847), and Shelby College (1847) (B.Z. Jones and Boyd, 1971: 38). As Adams entered the House of Representatives in 1830, the time was ripe to petition Congress for a national observatory.

In congressional committee reports and in his frequent public lectures and private correspondence on the subject, Adams made several proposals to found a national observatory in Washington. Despite political bias against Adams himself, the effect of these proposals was to water the seed of desire, already planted by the unfulfilled efforts of small communities and colleges before 1830, to catch up with Europe in the national pursuit of knowledge. In this way, Adams's contributions to the Smithsonian debate in Congress during the 1830s and 1840s, especially the publication of both his committee reports and his public lectures, played a part in the growing interest in astronomy after 1830.

When Congress accepted British nobleman James Smithson's bequest in 1838 to found an institution "for the increase and diffusion of knowledge," it agreed to preserve the capital sum of $508 318 and reinvest the interest until a decision could be made about how to use the fund. Adams made it his personal mission to guard the Smithson bequest against fraudulent use and to guide the debate through Congress. He proposed that the first seven years' interest be used to build an astronomical observatory and to secure the means to publish navigational and other useful discoveries related to astronomy. An amateur astronomer himself, Adams had visited several observatories in his travels to Russia and Europe. He believed that knowledge of the stars was important to the economic, political, and international development of the nation, and he saw astronomy as the queen of the sciences. It seemed logical to Adams that the first federally funded, basic scientific research would be astrophysical observation. Moreover, demonstrating his adherence to the good-orator maxim he had taught at Harvard, he was determined to use the bequest according to Smithson's intentions. He saw this as a matter of civic duty and a moral imperative to protect the benefactor's good will.

At the beginning of the Twenty-sixth Congress (1839–1841) Adams stood before the House and delivered a speech on the issue. He aimed to refute a popular proposal to use Smithson's money for a national public university and to introduce his proposal for an observatory. This 1840 report on the Smithsonian, and most of his speeches on astronomy in this debate, made use of a broad range of argumentative techniques that demonstrates his systematic art of classical invention. A brief rhetorical analysis of this speech will illustrate the nature of many speeches he made on behalf of science in this debate, and the ways in which his rhetorical theory informed and shaped his practice of political oratory. In chapters on deliberative rhetoric in the Harvard *Lectures on Rhetoric*, Adams had discussed arguments of legality, contingency, necessity, facility, and possibility. He used each of these in the 1840 report and in his other orations in promotion of science during this period. In addition, he drew on the image his audience had of him as a mature and ethical civic leader, following the Ciceronian principles of the ideal orator.

Adams began his speech with a description of Smithson's will and an argument of legality. The benefactor's intent was the primary reason behind Adams's belief that the fund should be used for scientific discovery and not for public education. Since Smithson had stated clearly in his will that the "increase and diffusion of knowledge among men" was his intent, Adams's first task in persuading his audience was to define this phrase in terms of the legal parameters of the will. He elaborated his definition in a careful Ciceronian period:

> The *increase and diffusion of knowledge among men* present neither the idea of knowledge already acquired to be taught, nor of childhood or youth to be instructed; but of *new discovery*; of *progress* in the march of the human mind; of accession to the moral, intellectual, and physical powers of the human race; of dissemination throughout the inhabited globe. (J.Q. Adams, 1840, emphasis in manuscript)

Since American universities were not yet conceived to be institutions dedicated to research and discovery, Adams's argument made this distinction convincing. Using a metaphor at the end of this series of deductions, he also sets up a pattern of rhetorical amplification which he used throughout his Smithsonian orations: he asserted that Smithson's purpose was "entirely different" from that of mere education, that it "assumed …an interest …

[which would] command grateful acclamations of future ages and illuminate the path of man upon earth with rays of knowledge still gathering with the revolving lapse of time." In addition to emphasizing the Enlightenment's endeavor to build up a store of new knowledge for future generations of Americans, these Baconian light metaphors also reflect a strong religious association, since the "illumination" of wisdom would certainly result from close study of the heavens.

The beginning of the speech also dealt with an ethical proof of Smithson's motivation: the American capitol was Smithson's choice because it was the seat of democratic government and could superintend the benefits not only for the United States but also for the whole world. In this his arguments looked to the inventive categories of contingency and possibility. Adams's use of a guardian *ethos* prophetically presented the United States as a guardian of other nations, this time in terms of scientific knowledge.

As he neared the climactic section of his speech, Adams prepared the audience for his arguments for an observatory. Conscious of his listeners' disparaging opinions on the use of the fund, he first established common ground on the general subject of knowledge:

> … no [personal] preference … is indicated by [Mr. Smithson's] will. It is knowledge, the source of all human wisdom and of all beneficent power; knowledge, as far transcending the postulated lever of Archimedes as the universe transcends this speck of earth upon its face; knowledge, the attribute of Omnipotence, of which man alone in the physical and material world is permitted to partake; the increase and diffusion of which among men is the result to which this … fortune is devoted.... Let not, then, any branch or department of human knowledge be excluded from its equitable share. But it is believed that no one science deserves or requires the immediate application of the…accruing income of the fund so urgently as practical astronomy.[2]

A change in voice from the active to a generalized, passive "it is believed" accompanies his turn from a universal treatment of knowledge to the more controversial subject of astronomy. This passage also linked astronomy with an "attribute of Omnipotence" – an identification he used again and again.

As opposed to the national university plan, a national observatory would have a purpose in legal compliance with Smithson's will. With this premise, Adams launched into a deductive proof of the purpose of astronomy, finally amplifying the subject with a chain of examples and a metaphorical crescendo. The purpose of this use of "ratiocination" was to prove that the object of Smithson's will would be expediently fulfilled by an observatory:

> The express object of an observatory is the increase and diffusion of knowledge by new discovery … The influence of the moon, of the planets, our next door neighbors of the solar system, of the fixed stars, scattered over the blue

> expanse in multitudes exceeding the power of human computation, and at distances of which imagination herself can form no distinct conception; the influence of all these upon the globe which we inhabit, and upon the condition of man, its dying and deathless inhabitant, is great and mysterious ...But to the vigilance of a sleepless eye, to the toil of a tireless hand, and to the meditations of a thinking, combining, and analyzing mind, secrets are successively revealed ... which seem to lift him from the earth to the threshold of his eternal abode, to lead him blindfolded up to the council chamber of Omnipotence, and there, stripping the bandage from his eyes, bid him look undazzled at the throne of God.[3]

Not only would an observatory be expedient, but it would also greatly expand the potential of Smithson's gift in the future. By associating the telescope with the author of creation, Adams draws on a traditional viewpoint advanced since antiquity – that astronomy elevates those who study it because its object is divine handiwork. Eighteenth- and nineteenth-century natural theologians, such as the Englishman William Paley and the American Edward Hitchcock, taught that evidence drawn from the mechanisms of the universe could establish the existence of God and allow inference of his characteristics. Framed this way, Adams's identification of the heavens with knowledge of God also reflects Psalm 19: "The heavens are telling the glory of God; and the firmament proclaims his handiwork" – an allusion which added to the authority of Adams's rhetoric for his nineteenth-century audience, many of whom were eager for ways to see science and religion in harmony.

After these appeals to tradition, Adams turned to inductive reasoning to present an example of the potentials of astronomical discovery as it related to research in geography and navigation. Continuing his metaphor of spiritual mysteries to be discovered, he suggested that the study of magnetism promised to be a vast and interesting topic of study for Smithsonian astronomers:

> What an unknown world of mind, for example, is yet teeming in the womb of time, to be revealed in tracing the causes of the sympathy between the magnet and the pole...that unseen, immaterial spirit, which walks with us through the most entangled forests, over the most interminable wilderness, and across every region of the pathless deep, by day, by night, in the calm serene of a cloudless sky, and in the howling of the hurricane or the typhoon.[4]

Evoking the geophysical tradition of Alexander von Humboldt, Adams authors a metaphor that endows the nineteenth-century astronomical study of the Earth and its atmosphere with a certain wonder and grandeur over and above its usefulness for mapmaking and navigation. While his style differed from the simple, direct "perspicuity" already used by some congressmen in the middle of the nineteenth century, Adams's 1810 *Lectures on*

Rhetoric permitted an expansive style on occasion – a style which twentieth-century critic Richard Weaver terms "the spaciousness of the old rhetoric"(Weaver, 1985: 184). When the cause is great, Adams advised, "… the orator may fairly consider himself, as addressing not only his immediate hearers, but the world at large; and for all future times. …He takes the vote of unborn millions upon the debate of a little senate, and incorporates himself and his discourse with the general history of mankind" (J.Q. Adams, 1810: 274). The style of these arguments also calls to mind Adams's comments on the ethos of a mature orator: "If advanced in years, and elevated in reputation and dignity, the gravity of his manner and the weight of his sentiment should justly correspond with the reverence, due to his station" (J.Q. Adams, 1810: 269).

But Adams's arguments for astronomy were not all so lofty. Drawing on his Jacksonian audience's preference for the practical and the useful, Adams dwelled on the history of astronomy and its benefits to the practical arts of timekeeping and navigation. He paid particular attention to authoritative precedent in this section, explaining that "the discoveries of Newton were the results of calculations founded upon the observations … of Copernicus, of Tycho Brahe, of Kepler, of Flamsteed…" He named several successful observatories in Europe and the practical and theoretical fruits of these institutions, playing on the passion of jealousy and the American sense of inferiority to intellectual institutions of the Old World. Using simple quantitative comparison, he informed his hearers that European governments had almost invariably funded observatories, "the number of which in that quarter of the globe is not at this time less than 120, while throughout the whole range of these United States there is not one."[5]

Adams concluded his arguments by contrasting the smallness of the educational proposal to the magnificent expanse of astronomy, given its association with rising technology and advances in science. He explained that "all the benefits [of the university proposal] would necessarily be confined to a very small number of students from the city of Washington … together with those few who were wealthy enough to move from distant parts." As a moral imperative, Adams believed the fund was for all people, not for one location or class or time. He ended by listing the benefits of an observatory – international prestige, navigational improvement, increase in geographical knowledge, and commercial opportunity. His final sentence brought his hearers down from the heights of a sublime vision to the simple, practical means-and-ends rhetorical topics of a governmental committee: "The bequest of James Smithson fortunately furnishes the means, without needing the assistance of any contribution from public funds of the nation."

This 1840 speech was only the first of dozens Adams gave during the ten years that he shepherded the fund through Congress, each speech making careful use of the art of classical rhetorical invention and elevated style. In addition to his congressional speeches, Adams made a series of lecture tours through the Eastern states publicly exhorting citizens to take an interest in the expansion of basic science, especially astronomy. In 1836, his efforts finally came to fruition: the Smithsonian was founded as the first federally funded institution for scientific observation, discovery, and the accumulation of knowledge for national and public advancement. Soon after, in 1842, the Naval Observatory was founded in Washington, DC, fulfilling Adams's prolonged efforts to found a national observatory in the capital city. Today, Adams is acknowledged for his indispensable role in founding the Smithsonian and is widely regarded as the father of the US Naval Observatory.

21.4 John Quincy Adams, Man of Letters

Adams was not the genius of public eloquence that Cicero was, but his self-modeling after the great orator can be taken a step further. For scholars interested in *belles lettres*, especially in the genres of the personal letter and the diary as literature, Adams made an astounding contribution to higher learning. His rarely interrupted daily diary, begun when he was aged 12 and kept for nearly seventy years, is an invaluable artifact of history and literature that brings vividly to life the cultural tenor of the man himself and the times in which he lived. In this, Adams's contribution is undisputed. To suggest otherwise would be the same as to claim that Cicero's contributions to literature, his letters, and his writings on moral philosophy and rhetoric, were unimportant because the Roman republic gave way to empire in spite of his eloquent exhortations.

Like Cicero, Adams's primary contribution to literature, broadly speaking, are his speeches and autobiographical writings themselves. But, also like Cicero, Adams was a literary critic and a dabbler in poetry during the brief times he was required to spend at his estate between political appointments. He wrote rhetorical analyses of the sermons he heard almost every Sunday and made an expert's remarks on the hundreds of political speeches he heard during his long career. He engaged in theater criticism and wrote a life of William Shakespeare, whom he admired almost as much as he did Cicero. Even more interesting to rhetorical scholars today, he also had a habit of describing his own composition and research processes when he wrote for public audiences, giving today's readers an insider's perspective of the early nineteenth-century mind at work. His book of letters to his son on biblical morality have the literary flavor of Cicero's letters to his son Marcus and brother Quintus. His speeches on many topics continue to be of both rhetorical and historical interest, especially his defense in the famous *Amistad* case, speeches against the Gag Rule in Congress, on the annexation of Texas, and other cases contributing to a formidable body of oratory against slavery. His collected correspondence is a veritable compendium of conversations between great minds, including such luminaries as his father John Adams and mother Abigail Adams, Thomas Jefferson, James Madison, and many others. Not only are these works and his other political commentary an invaluable historical source, they are an unparalleled portrait of JQA the thinker and the man. His poetry, including shorter verses on religion and society, a long poem entitled *The Wants of Man*, and even erotica addressed to his wife Louisa, are mere curiosities in comparison with his mastery of oratorical art and reflective memoir, yet they attest to his literary sensibility and his personal desire to be primarily not a man of power, but a public man of letters.

Never at a loss for words, JQA was as much a writer as a statesman, and modern historians of rhetoric as well as his contemporary biographers have begun to reflect on this side of his personality and his legacy. Although his beloved poetry and even the *Lectures on Rhetoric and Oratory* are seldom read today – to the point that Paul Nagel claims (1997: 419) "it was not poetry or science but the gag rule and the *Amistad* case" that brought him lasting recognition, it would be unfair to say that Adams's contributions to American intellectual history were unimportant. His few achievements as a man of letters make an impressive catalog in their own right: JQA was the first to author a complete American rhetorical theory and the only president to do so, the first Boylston Professor at Harvard, the author of several eloquent political speeches (including those on the Gag Rule and the *Amistad*), an inexorable champion of government-supported scientific research, and the most important diarist that America has yet known.

Note

1 This section analyzing JQA's speechmaking in promotion of astronomy is adapted from my article "John Quincy Adams's Rhetorical Crusade for Astronomy," *Isis* 91(3): 480–503, © 2000 by The History of Science Society. All rights reserved.
2 John Quincy Adams, 1840 Manuscript report 181, HC 29, record group 233, series COMPAPERS, House committee records, United States National Archives.
3 Ibid.
4 Ibid.
5 Ibid.

Further Reading

Adams, John Quincy (1810). *Lectures on Rhetoric and Oratory, Delivered to the Classes of Senior and Junior Sophisters in the Harvard University*, Cambridge, MA.
Adams, John Quincy (1840). Manuscript report 181, HC 29, record group 233, series COMPAPERS, House committee records, United States National Archives.

Auer, J. Jeffery and Jerald L. Banninga (1963). The Genesis of John Quincy Adams'sLectures on Rhetoric and Oratory. *Quarterly Journal of Speech* 49: 119–132.

Bemis, Samuel Flagg (1949). *John Quincy Adams and the Union*. New York.

Cicero, Marcus Tullus (1949). *Cicero's De Inventione*, trans. Harry Mortimer Hubbel, Cambridge, MA.

Clark, Gregory, and Halloran, S. Michael, eds. (1993). *Oratorical Culture in Nineteenth-Century America: Transformations in the Theory and Practice of Rhetoric*. Carbondale, IL.

Eastman, Carolyn (2009). *A Nation of Speechifiers: Making an American Public after the Revolution*. Chicago.

Gustafson, Sandra (2000). *Eloquence is Power: Oratory and Performance in Early America*. Chapel Hill, NC.

Gustafson, Sandra (2011). *Imagining Deliberative Democracy in the Early American Republic*. Chicago.

Musto, David F. (1967). A Survey of the American Observatory Movement, 1800–1850. In Arthur Beer, ed. *Vistas in Astronomy*, vol. 9: *New Aspects in the History and Philosophy of Astronomy*. Oxford.

Nagel, Paul C. (1997). *John Quincy Adams: A Private Life, A Public Life*. Boston.

Potkay, Adam S. (1999).Theorizing Civic Eloquence in the Early Republic: The Road from David Hume to John Quincy Adams. *Early American Literature* 34: 147–170.

Portolano, Marlana (2009). *The Passionate Empiricist: The Eloquence of John Quincy Adams in the Service of Science*. New York.

Rhees, William Jones, ed. (1901). *The Smithsonian Institution: Documents Relative to Its Origin and History*, vol. I: *1835–1887*. Washington, DC.

Weaver, Richard (1985). *The Ethics of Rhetoric*. Davis, CA.

Chapter Twenty-Two

A Monarch in a Republic: Louisa Catherine Johnson Adams and Court Culture in Early Washington City

Catherine Allgor and Margery M. Heffron

22.1 A Woman "Who Was"

English-born Louisa Catherine Johnson Adams holds a unique distinction as America's only foreign-born First Lady. For the Americans who even know the name of "Mrs John Quincy Adams," this is all they know. Such a characterization does not acknowledge that, until Eleanor Roosevelt, she was probably the most literate and educated woman to occupy that position. All of her life, including her White House years, Louisa carried on an extensive correspondence with friends and her natal and marital families – her spirited exchanges with her father-in-law, John Adams, were particularly fine – and produced poems, plays, diary entries, and essays. She has left for historians two astonishing autobiographical documents, "Record of My Life," and the evocatively titled "Adventures of a Nobody" along with the thrilling "Narrative of a Journey from Russia to France – 1815." Louisa desperately wanted to be remembered as "one, *who was*"; in this she succeeded, contradicting her own appellation by proving herself to be an irrefutable "somebody" (Challinor, 1982: 519).

The dearth of scholarship on Louisa Adams is due only partly to her gender, which has relegated many female historical subjects to obscurity. In addition to being overshadowed by her famous and public husband, Louisa as a historical subject cannot compete with her celebrated mother-in-law, Abigail Adams. A formidable intellect and talented writer, Abigail has

A Companion to John Adams and John Quincy Adams, First Edition.
Edited by David Waldstreicher.

attracted scholars and popular historians alike, partly because of her obviously loving relationship with her husband, John Adams, one of the most lively and relatable of the Founders. Louisa and John Quincy Adams loved each other passionately but their marital path was not always smooth. The rather cold and forbidding public face of John Quincy, moreover, has deflected interest from Louisa. As biographers are less attracted to her husband, so they are unlikely to encounter Louisa.

Indeed, most scholars who have taken Louisa as a topic have discovered her while researching or documenting more conventional studies of the male Adamses, beginning with the first and founding editor of the *Adams Papers*, Lyman H. Butterfield. He immediately apprehended Louisa's historical potential, which he sketched out in "Tending a Dragon-Killer: Notes for the Biographer of Mrs John Quincy Adams." Jack Shepherd became interested in Louisa Adams when he wrote the companion book for the PBS series *The Adams Chronicles: Four Generations of Greatness* (1975), going on to write a joint biography, *Cannibals of the Heart: A Personal Biography of Louisa Catherine and John Quincy Adams* (1980). Likewise, Paul C. Nagel was so captivated by the Adams women, including Louisa, that he came across while writing *Descent from Glory: Four Generations of the John Adams Family* (1983) that he devoted a whole volume to *The Adams Women: Abigail and Louisa Adams, Their Sisters and Daughters* (1987).

Still, very few have considered Louisa Adams's political work and significance. This neglect can be attributed to the larger convention of seeing female subjects, especially in an era before suffrage, only in personal ways. In addition, the men who wrote of her worked within biographic conventions that did not consider women, except for the redoubtable Abigail, in political terms. Even after writing at length about Louisa, when it came to his later full-length biography, *John Quincy Adams: A Public Life, a Private Life* (1997), Nagel could not break away from the tradition of sidelining wives in biographies of Great Men. Even as Shepherd framed his as a "dual biography," because it focused mostly on Louisa, he felt the need to focus on the "personal."

But again, adding to historical conventions that ignore women in political histories are circumstances peculiar to Louisa. Louisa's expression of her emotional and psychological life is almost unparalleled for a nineteenth-century woman, as are her extended autobiographical treatments. They were penned, however, not only through the lens of memory, but also during periods of Louisa's depression. Historians cannot resist the temptations of these rich sources and have privileged the memoirs over the letters, which, while seemingly more prosaic, give, for instance, a more balanced view of her relationship with John Quincy. Until the publication of Heffron's forthcoming biography, Joan R. Challinor, in her (1982) dissertation, "Louisa Catherine Johnson Adams: The Price of Ambition," and two articles, has provided the fullest treatment of her life. Tracing Louisa's journey from birth to just before the Washington years, Challinor focused on her subject's psyche and how her personality developed *vis-à-vis* relationships with her natal and marital families. Louisa's deep emotionality, expressed in often anguished prose, is so arresting that she often seems to have seduced her male historical admirers into taking her depictions of John Quincy and her marriage as fact.

Louisa's literary bents, too, have influenced the analytic tools scholars have brought to bear. Katharine T. Corbett's "Louisa Catherine Adams: The Anguished 'Adventures of a Nobody'" (1979) was a literary analysis of Louisa's major work. The latest treatment of Louisa's life, Michael O'Brien's *Mrs Adams in Winter: A Journey in the Last Days of Napoleon* (2010), an amazing feat of historical detection (O'Brien painstakingly recreates the historical journey taken by Louisa from St Petersburg to France), treats Louisa's story almost as a literary device, an extended metaphor on a historical meditation, an impression reinforced by his own considerable writing talents.

Recently, as the historical discipline has begun to examine the political roles of "others," including white women before suffrage, Louisa-as-political-force has emerged. Catherine Allgor evaluated Louisa's political work in two very specific settings: at the Russian Court in "'A Republican in a Monarchy': Louisa Catherine Adams in Russia" (1987) and as the wife of the secretary of state and presidential candidate John Quincy Adams in *Parlor Politics: In Which the Ladies of Washington Help Build a City and a Government* (2000). Louisa has made her appearance as one of Cokie Roberts's *Ladies of Liberty: The Women Who Shaped Our Nation* (2008), which argues for both the historical and political significance of the "Founding Mothers." Heffron's (2010) article, "A Fine Romance: The Courtship Correspondence of Louisa Catherine Johnson and John Quincy Adams" provides a provocative preview for her as-yet-unpublished monograph, "The Other Mrs Adams: A Life of Louisa Catherine Adams." This first, full-scale scholarly biography of Louisa Adams examines Louisa's life in its entirety, including her political participation. This new treatment, along with the volumes of Louisa's writing coming from the *Adams Papers* at the Massachusetts Historical Society, will doubtless spur increased interest, both academic and popular, in Louisa Adams.

This chapter continues the quest for understanding not only what Louisa's political work tells us about her, but how a close look at her life illumines the role of political women in the early republic, as well as the development of the nation. Ironically, it is her "foreign-born" designation that provides the clue to what Louisa brought to her roles as political wife and partner. It was precisely her status as an Englishwoman that framed her contribution to the United States political system. Why Louisa's "foreign" upbringing mattered to her work as a political wife, and to the nation, is part of a larger picture that is only visible when the stories offered by women became part of the mainstream political narrative. The traditional narrative presented the New World as different from the Old, especially in its system of government, as one ruled by exceptional individualist Founding Fathers who threw off the shackles of kings and courts. Studying elite women of the founding era, however, has demonstrated that the early government was more dependent on royal court forms than previously thought. The new and aspiring ruling classes adopted and adapted court practices in order to garner legitimacy from the populace, amass personal power, and facilitate the business of politics.

No matter that the new Americans had fought a war against a monarch and that their ruling philosophy of republicanism shunned all things aristocratic. Ideals of royalty and aristocracy still remained their only available vocabulary of power in the quest to legitimize the republican experiment to the outside world and to themselves. "Authority" – who ruled whom – was the central issue of the American Revolution; the successful rebellion only partly resolved the dilemma. Who was to rule over a country where political sovereignty was vested in "the people" and the nation's survival depended on the civic virtues of said people? The elite men of the founding generation saw themselves as the right and proper rulers. But how were they to convince those of the "lower sort" that their "betters" were really better?

This ironic development had ironic results. In the first years after the Revolution, the new American elites went back to the unrepublican courts for ways to demonstrate their authority. For instance, the formerly rabid anti-monarchical John Adams suddenly started arguing for bestowing titles on lawmakers, following the example of the British House of Lords. He even wanted to call the president "His Majesty" or "His High Mightiness." But, unsurprisingly, the use of Old World forms and ideas rested uneasily within the new republicanism, and even the elite-minded Federalists could only go so far.

In early republican politics, elite white women were often used to cover power in the sense that they eased the tension between political need and ideological purity by taking on the task of conveying aristocratic messages to the masses. Ironically, because they were private citizens, and not elected officials, women had more latitude than did men. So while officials rejected titles as too monarchical and George Washington became "Mr President," his wife Martha became "Lady Washington." James Madison might embody republican simplicity so thoroughly at his wife's soirees that, clad in simple broadcloth, his own guests overlooked him, but his wife could be "Queen Dolley," sweeping through the rooms in pink satin and ermine. A charismatic male leader was a danger in a republic, lest he bewitch the masses into making him a Napoleon. Women had no official power, so the new Americans could project their longings for an aristocratic ruler onto them.

The political work of Louisa Catherine Johnson Adams took this dynamic to a new level. Not only was she superbly equipped to adapt aristocratic practices as her husband's campaign manager, coopting the superiority they conferred to his political ends, she did so at a critical time in the development of the nation and the capital city. When Louisa and John Quincy came to Washington in 1818, determined to get him the presidency, they entered a government that was poised to develop into a democracy ruled by a two-party system. During this time of great growth, the government needed to accommodate power both at the top – in the increasingly powerful branches of government, especially the executive – and at the bottom – from the common man. The Adamses' court-influenced political work, drawing ever-larger groups of people together while accommodating the influence of Congress over the electoral process, played its part in this power struggle.

22.2 "Miss Proud"

Louisa Catherine Johnson was born on February 12, 1775, to an American father, the prosperous merchant Joshua Johnson, and a woman of rather uncertain origins, Catherine Nuth. Louisa's own origins – at least her national ones – were also somewhat uncertain. Her father, who hailed from Annapolis, Maryland, always staunchly proclaimed his "Americanness," although when he left to come to England in 1771, he was still a British colonist. The United States was formed and declared independent while Joshua was working and living in London. Although Louisa would follow her father's lead in asserting her own loyalty to a country she would not see until she was a grown woman – as though nationality were conferred by blood – for all intents and purposes, she was raised to be an upper-class Englishwoman. The infant Louisa joined an older sister, Nancy; in the years to come, five sisters and one brother joined the brood. Though Louisa was baptized as legitimate, her parents probably were not married and would not be until 1785, ten years after her birth. Catherine Nuth herself may have been illegitimate; in any case, she became involved with Joshua as a very young girl (Heffron, forthcoming).

Born on the eve of the American Revolution, Louisa's life was shaped from the start by her family's relationship to America. Her uncle, Thomas Johnson, was one of the fifty-five delegates who attended the First Continental Congress and would later become governor of Maryland. Joshua Johnson wanted to join the fight back in America. "Your cause is noble; it's for liberty you struggle," he declared to his brother, but he did not return home, no doubt because of his growing family (Joshua Johnson to Thomas Johnson, Aug. 4, 1774, cited in Price, 1979). A vocal supporter of the American cause, Joshua found himself under surveillance; later he would return the favor by providing post-Revolutionary intelligence in his position as US consul for London, under President Thomas Jefferson.

With a treaty of commerce and unity between the new United States and France signed in 1778, Joshua transplanted his ever-increasing brood to Nantes, France. There, the Johnsons lived in splendor in a mansion dubbed by neighbors "Le Temple du Gout" (The Temple of Taste). Louisa's mother presided over a large household, entertaining numerous international visitors attracted by the lively hostess's intelligence and wit (Heffron, 2011).

At age 3, Louisa, along with her sister Nancy, was sent to a convent-run boarding school, where she began her education in the accomplishments seen as necessary for upper-class daughters – singing, dancing, needlework, and the social graces, along with basic reading and writing skills. The Johnsons did not return to England until 1783, when Louisa was just eight years old. Though in her memoirs Louisa was probably exaggerating when she wrote that as they left France, she could not remember a word of English, except "yes" and "no," she had undoubtedly absorbed the French language as only the young can do. Her perfect command of what was the official language of courts and diplomacy would stand her in good stead in her future career (Heffron, 2011).

As soon as the Johnsons settled in a house in Tower Hill, London, the three oldest Johnson girls were sent to a boarding school, run by a Mrs Carter, in the nearby borough of Hackney. Sending young children away to board was in keeping with middle-class family practices, but socially, Louisa suffered. By nature shy, she kept herself aloof from the other students; correcting her French teacher's pronunciation only brought her opprobrium from that teacher and teasing from students. Consequently, Louisa remembered: "I became seriously melancholy and almost gloomy, which caused me to be called Miss Proud by my school fellows and placed me in a more painful situation than ever" (Graham et al., forthcoming: 6–7).

At Mrs Carter's school, Louisa began to uncover her intellectual gifts. Because Louisa was taken up by a perceptive teacher, she was saved from the vacuous learning more characteristic of schools for young ladies and learned to appreciate, particularly, the great works of English literature. Louisa also excelled at the usual accomplishments, especially music, for which she showed remarkable aptitude. She stayed at the school until age 13. Thereafter, the Johnson girls continued their education at home, with live-in governesses and visiting instructors who furthered their studies in music, drawing, and dancing. The older Johnson daughters took turns running the household for a week at a time, training to be mistresses of complex domestic households like their own (Heffron, 2011).

Much as she did with "The Temple of Taste," Catherine Nuth made the Tower Hill house into a center of pleasure and entertainment. The family lived extravagantly; where households of similar standing had seven servants, the Johnsons had eleven. Because of Joshua's American connections, every American of note found his or her way to the Johnson table, including

John and Abigail Adams, when John was minister to the Court of St James. They joined artists, merchants, and young men from all corners of the world sent to London to study. Catherine entertained them all, and as the Johnson girls grew into womanhood, they joined in, singing and playing the harp and piano. Shy Louisa soon found herself the center of attention. No wonder, playing "dress up" in her mother's old gowns, she dreamed that a larger world stage was in her future: "I never would be anything but a *Dutchess*, and never answered to any title but that of her grace" (Graham et al., forthcoming: 12).

With all this education, both formal and informal, as well as the investment in clothes and personal adornment, it would seem that the Johnsons were appropriately grooming their daughters for middle- and upper-class English marriages. The quality of their education was what girls of their class enjoyed and was certainly beyond the experience of even elite American girls. Emerging educational theories in America fit uneasily with the acquisition of accomplishments; fancy sewing and dancing did not accord with the pure republicanism of the early American republic. The household-management style modeled by Catherine was geared to large staffs in urban establishments; in America, a land of few big cities and generally rougher conditions, women presided over smaller staffs and took on much of the labor of housekeeping themselves.

The Johnson girls, with gifts both cultivated and natural, could have aspired to marriages to middle-class London merchants or even minor members of the gentry and aristocracy classes (Heffron, 2011). Instead, they were intentionally raised to be American wives. Perhaps Catherine and Joshua realized that with their own sketchy backgrounds, they would not pass muster within an English culture punctilious about family. More seriously, notwithstanding the Johnsons' grand shows and extravagant entertaining, their financial situation was always perilous, with some of Joshua's business practices bordering on the illegal. With no guaranteed dowry, the Johnson girls, no matter how pretty and accomplished, could not expect to make good English marriages. Whatever secret thoughts Joshua and Catherine may have harbored, Joshua outwardly made his choice of American husbands for his girls a matter of patriotism. According to Louisa, in this he was influenced by his brother Thomas, from 1791 to 1793 a Supreme Court justice. Thomas warned him "to be careful that [his daughters] should form connections with none but *men of note* and distinction in his own Country." This letter "induced him to limit as much as possible our acquaintance among the English." Further, Joshua was clear that these "men of note" should be men of the American South (Graham et al., forthcoming: 21–22).

Joshua's preference for Southern men notwithstanding, when young John Quincy Adams showed up on the Tower Hill doorstep on November 11, 1795, he was considered a good catch. He might hail from dour

New England folk, but he was a young man of great accomplishment. As other chapters in this *Companion* have described more fully, John Quincy had spent more time in court circles than any American of his generation (Heffron, 2011). After going home for a Harvard education, John Quincy found himself, at age 27, appointed as the American minister to Holland by President George Washington. A year into the young man's assignment, President Washington asked him to join the American delegation in London for the final ratification of the Jay Treaty. Adding to John Quincy's luster was his father's position as President Washington's vice president; during the son's time in London, the elder Adams would be elected president of the United States.

When John Quincy became a frequent visitor to the Johnson household, the family assumed he was paying court to the eldest girl, Nancy. Louisa joined in this assumption, which allowed her to be freer and easier in her manner than had he revealed his true target. On January 27, 1796, at a ball honoring Louisa's upcoming 21st birthday, he made his intentions towards her "decidedly publick, which brought much trouble on my head," from the jealous Nancy (Graham et al., forthcoming: 41). A tumultuous courtship followed, documented in letters between the two lovers that confirmed that, unfortunately, both were sensitive and quick to wound and be wounded. Both struggled with hiding their personal ambitions; both could be plagued by depression and self-doubt. But they were also intellectually compatible and passionate about each other (Heffron, 2011). John Quincy was the first American whom Louisa came to know intimately, but they shared an odd commonality. They both were more American in name than in experience. Not only had Louisa never been to her father's homeland but John Quincy had basically grown up in European contexts and had suffered severe culture shock when he had gone home to attend Harvard.

After a rocky engagement, the pair married on July 26, 1797, in the Church of All Hallows Barking, west of the Tower of London. A month of bridal festivities ensued, and then as the newlyweds readied themselves for John Quincy's new diplomatic post as minister to the Prussian court, appointed by President John Adams, something occurred that, from Louisa's point of view, blighted her marriage from the start. The last wedding celebratory party had barely ended when Joshua Johnson went bankrupt in late August. Louisa felt this keenly, knowing that it appeared to the world and perhaps to her new husband and his family that she had been foisted onto John Quincy under false pretenses. The expected dowry was not forthcoming, robbing Louisa of any sense of equality or worth in the marriage. She mourned with "the bitter conviction that he might have formed a connection more suitable to the Station that he filled; and with more adequate means to support its consequence" (Graham et al., forthcoming: 99).

22.3 "A Fine Lady"

But Louisa was wrong. Even as she felt that they set out for Berlin under a cloud, she was more than a "suitable" companion for John Quincy. Trained to be an upper-class Englishwoman, skilled in the art of conversation, the deployment of wit, and superbly equipped with excellent French, Louisa was a perfect wife for a diplomat. The United States had never had a minister to Prussia, one of the two great German states, and from 1797 to 1801, John Quincy and Louisa worked hard to establish relations between this great power and the struggling republic. During this time, Louisa suffered several painful and devastating miscarriages, but in April 1801 she finally gave birth to her first son, George Washington Adams.

From the start, Louisa found herself "the object of general attention" at the court of King Frederick William III and Queen Louise. Her court presentation was the first hurdle and, "knees knock[ing]" and full of trepidation, Louisa "felt ready to sink into the floor," but she made such a successful impression that Queen Louise not only spoke with her during the presentation, but also invited her to supper, and "treated [her] with the kindest attention." The various princes and princesses also welcomed her with attention "both flattering, and agreeable." Queen Louise was just a year younger than Louisa herself, and the two bonded. Louisa "dearly loved" Queen Louise, and the queen responded with kindness, especially during Louisa's pregnancies, always ready to rescue her from the uncomfortable schemes of couriers who lived to gossip and connive for precedence (Graham et al., forthcoming: 57, 68–69, 386). That Louisa became such a target early on demonstrates her quick rise in royal favor (Heffron, 2011).

Following her debut, Louisa, alone or with John Quincy, was summoned to court on a regular basis, an honor she characteristically attributed to her position as "the Wife of a Foreign Minister, and daughter in law to the President of the United States" (Graham et al., forthcoming: 82). But it was clear she was valued in her own right. John Quincy's mother, the formidable Abigail, had expressed reservations about Louisa's ability to function as an innocent young woman in an urbane court; never one to boost his wife's self esteem, John Quincy may have had his doubts as well. As Louisa recalled his "very anxiety for my success, rendered him uneasy lest by some gaucherie I should fail" (Graham et al., forthcoming: 74–75). But not only did Louisa not commit social gaffes (an amazing accomplishment given the intricate and particular etiquette of this court), but she doubtless opened doors for her husband that would have been otherwise closed to him. Louisa's special relationship with the royal family provided the all-important access craved by diplomats. Moreover, the business of diplomacy is done at social events, and there, Louisa's beauty, charm, and fluency in French made her an indisputable asset. On more than one occasion, Louisa found herself "the only foreign Lady so distinguished" with some singular honor (Graham et al., forthcoming: 106).

Louisa also brought to her new milieu her formidable intellect and observing eye. From her first days at English schools, where her "foreignness" made her an outsider, Louisa had been assessing her environment and the behaviors of others. Perhaps it was this pose of cool observer that gave her the nickname "Miss Proud." In her memoirs, and letters from this period, Louisa describes the settings and events with relish and dash. Nothing escaped her eyes, from the jewels and gowns to the table settings and liveries, not to mention the intricacy of personal relations. She also had an appreciation for the characters she encountered and a knack for rendering an apt verdict in a few lines, describing a Saxony count and countess as follows: "an excellent couple of the old School, stiff and formal as old Portraits; and with faces exhibiting about as much variety of expression"; she dismissed the Duke of Darmstadt as "a German Lump of obesity" (Graham et al., forthcoming: 73, 152).

Though still an optimistic young woman, Louisa had a knowingness that would mature into a kind of cynicism about people's character and political motives. She might seem dazzled by the material culture of court life, but she never saw anyone but the queen as anything other than a human being engaged in the business of life. No larger-than-life hero worship for her, as evidenced by her trenchant observations about a Count Haugwitz, the head of the Foreign Department: "This man Haugwitz is one of your Arch political deceivers, fully exemplifying the Jesuit and Machevelian doctrines, that *truth* is not needful, when *falsehood* will suffice." Still, Louisa assessed: "The old Count is worthy of all respect – His little peculiarities being only *tedious*, but not vicious " (Graham et al., forthcoming: 89).

Louisa was also surrounded by examples of the role that female political partners could play in a court setting. The Marchessa Luccassini, Louisa wrote, "knew well how to play a political game;" Lady Elizabeth Carysfort "did most of the diplomacy" for Great Britain (Graham et al., forthcoming: 128, 139–140). As befit her station, Louisa's adored Queen Louise actively engaged in diplomatic business. But even though John Quincy found the requisite social situations dull and uninspiring, always longing to return to his books and his study, he did not encourage Louisa's political potential. He wrote of political and military developments to his mother but did not discuss them with his wife. Louisa recalled: "Mr. Adams had always accustomed me to believe that Women had nothing to do with politics, and as he was the glass from which my opinions were reflected, I was convinced of its truth, and sought no further" (Graham et al., forthcoming: 108). Her upbringing stood her in good stead, but nothing could have prepared her for the intricacies of royal life. That she succeeded so brilliantly must be attributed to her intelligence and adaptability to circumstance, enabling her to establish close relationships with the royal family that many other diplomats' wives, who possessed both rank and wealth, could not (Heffron, 2011).

In the end, the mission to Prussia was a success. At a time when Prussia's relations with France, Great Britain, and Russia were delicate, John Quincy obtained the renewal of the Prussian-American Treaty of Amity and Commerce. Dispatched from a country that the larger world assumed was full of savages and rebels, the intellectual John Quincy and cultivated and refined Louisa represented the United States most favorably, leaving impressions that would be critical to the international standing of the new nation for years to come.

When the Adamses were recalled back to the United States, Louisa, with her young son in her arms, set foot in her official homeland for the first time, on September 4, 1801. It would be eight years before the Adamses saw another court. In the meantime, Louisa got her first taste of the "real" America, as represented by the Adams family's home town, Quincy, Massachusetts: "Quincy! What shall I say of my impressions of Quincy! Had I stepped into Noah's Ark, I do not think I could have been more utterly astonished. ... Even the Church, its forms, the snuffling through the nose, the Singers, the dressing and the dinner hour, were all novelties to me." The two elder Adamses also got a look at their son's new bride. Louisa, always sensitive, was still probably correct in concluding that although old John Adams "took a fancy to *me*, and he was the only one," Abigail thought "that I was literally and without knowing it a *fine* Lady ... [who] could not *suit*, however well inclined" (Graham et al., forthcoming: 164–165).

In the years 1801–1809, the young couple began building an American life, divided among Boston, Quincy, and Washington. Again in Boston, Louisa was a presence, securing a place for the young couple among the city's elite, as John Quincy's two brothers and their wives could not (Heffron, 2011). John Quincy half-heartedly practiced law, served a term as US senator, and was appointed the first Boylston Professor of Rhetoric and Oratory at Harvard. Louisa suffered the loss of one stillborn child and rejoiced at the birth of two sons, John and Charles Francis. Busy as she was with her family and her friends, her discerning mind found much fodder in her privileged view of the growing republic. She correctly targeted the new nation's struggle to define class. In traditional European societies, she wrote, one's place in society was fixed by custom and understood by everyone. In democratic America, where everyone was nominally equal, class distinctions still existed, but now they were repressed and resented. She understood, as she later expressed it, that "A Republick of *Equality*, is a sort of *non descript* only to be realized in musty tomes generated in the unpractised and unsocial brains of needy Book-Worms" (Graham et al., forthcoming: 199). She did not realize that in the future she would be called upon, as one with a "social brain," to translate the theories of bookworms into reality.

In 1809, President James Madison appointed John Quincy as plenipotentiary to Russia, a key posting as both countries saw a mutually beneficial trading relationship as a way to sidestep both Great Britain and France, who were using so-called neutral shipping as a weapon in their escalating hostilities. Louisa was devastated at having to go so far away, especially when it was decided, not by her but by her husband and the elder Adamses, that her two oldest children were to be left behind and only two-year-old Charles Francis would accompany his parents, along with Louisa's sister, Catherine. On the eighty-day voyage to what must have seemed like a frozen wasteland, Louisa was "Broken hearted miserable, *alone* in every feeling: my boy was my only comfort" (Graham et al., forthcoming: 284–285).

22.4 A Republican in A Monarchy

The Adams served in Russia from 1809 to 1815. The aim of securing trade agreements with Russia would become even more important after the United States involved itself in the Napoleonic wars by declaring war against Great Britain in 1812. During this time, John Quincy and Louisa suffered their own losses. John Quincy's beloved aunt and sister died; Louisa not only lost her sister Nancy and their mother but she gave birth to and buried an only daughter.

As in Prussia, she would delightedly describe the beautiful walks of the city, the theater, the art in the Hermitage, as well as all the glitter of court life, at the same time learning how society could shape politics. Compared to Berlin, St Petersburg was far more glamorous and the court life correspondingly intricate. In many ways, Louisa replicated her success in Berlin, cultivating a personal relationship with the tsar, as did John Quincy. But if anything, the court at St Petersburg demonstrated even more obviously the importance of the unofficial sphere of social events. Of course, this unofficial sphere had always been a part of political systems, and Louisa did not need to be at one of the most elaborate courts in the world to see that. Back in America, women such as Dolley Madison and many less-famous hostesses who had never been out of the country knew that social events were the place to make connections and agreements, to propose, negotiate, and conduct political business of all kinds, out of the official spotlight (Allgor, 2000: 86–88).

But in St Petersburg, there was no official venue reserved for diplomats. Diplomats traditionally do a great deal of business in homes and at social events; at the Russian court, *all* diplomatic business happened at social events. With no official source of information in place, balls and parties, even those for children, became crucial places to secure and sometimes disseminate intelligence. Louisa observed with wonder the open acknowledgement among the diplomatic corps of the centrality of the social sphere. She reported that the wily Sardinian minister, Joseph de Maistre, requested his sovereign, Victor Emmanuel, to send him a young man to fill a secretarial post who not only would shine as a good dancer, fine conversationalist, and musician, but also one who would be savvy enough to "serve me as an informer with the women to learn the secrets of their husbands." Maistre was not the only one who employed such young men. Louisa called these aides waltzing machines (Shepherd, 1980: 143).

As he had in Berlin, John Quincy despised the "trifling and insignificance" of the constant social obligations, but understood that it would not be "safe or prudent to despise them." Still, one of his aides described him as listless at parties, and "an unfortunate appointment for this Court ... no manners, ... gauche, never was intended for a foreign Minister, and is only fit to turn over musty law authorities." His nickname among his young staff was "the mute of Siberia." John Spear Smith, a nephew of the secretary of state and son of a senator from Maryland, concluded, "Dry sense alone does not do at European Courts. Something more is necessary, which something Mr. A. does not possess" (Allgor, 1997: 38).

But of course, Louisa possessed that "something more" in abundance – charm, charisma, and a genuine interest in other people. While John Quincy embarked on a massive project on weights and measures in his study, Louisa went without her husband to the all-important social events. Often the only diplomatic spouse in court, she gathered the data so vital to diplomacy. Highly intelligent and attuned to nuances in human behavior, Louisa could discern the information presented by a glance or a word. Her perfect French, dancing and musical abilities, and intellectual and Continental sophistication were assets to the American team. Honed in Berlin, her skills in coping with court etiquette and social situations with political implications were polished in St Petersburg. Many times she could divert or subvert tricky situations by playing herself as a simple American, a "republican" in a monarchy. As she did in Berlin, Louisa sent her own signals to the court as the tsar distinguished her in a variety of ways, such as choosing her for an occasion's first dance (Heffron, 2011).

And as with the Berlin posting, the Russian mission was a great success. John Quincy was an able, analytic, and astute diplomat, recognized as such by his peers. The French ambassador to Russia, for example, commented to him, "It seems you are a great favorite here. You have found powerful protection" (Allgor, 1997). But the achievement of the American mission was also because of Louisa's command of the unofficial sphere. The American delegation was held in such high regard by the tsar that in 1814 he offered to broker a peace between the United States and Great Britain. Nothing would come of this effort, but the same year, President Madison sent John Quincy to Ghent to work on the peace treaty that would resolve, however unsatisfactorily, the War of 1812. While in Ghent, he heard the news that he was to be appointed American minister to Great Britain. In late December, he sent word to Louisa, still in St Petersburg, that she was to close up the diplomatic establishment, sell what she could, and join him in Paris. She did all of that with amazing efficiency, transporting herself and her seven-year-old son and servants across the frozen battlefields of war-torn Europe, dodging bullets, bandits, and armies from all sides. She joined John Quincy in Paris and they traveled together to London, where they reunited with their two older sons. The Adamses served in at the British court until 1817, when President James Monroe appointed John Quincy as secretary of state.

22.5 "Affairs of High Importance"

The Washington that welcomed the Adamses back was not the same town they had last seen, nor was the United States the same nation. When they had left for Russia in 1809, the capital city was struggling in its efforts to be a capital of "pure republicanism," eschewing all the corruptions of court life. No extraofficial events or spaces existed – save one – where people could do the unofficial politicking necessary to get things done. A diplomat himself, Jefferson knew the power of social events for political needs and for building political unity. But he deliberately truncated society in order to shore up his own Republican party and vanquish the Federalists (Allgor, 2000: 24–27).

During the Jefferson administration, the only social/political space in town was in secretary of state James Madison's house on "F" Street. Like the Adamses, the Madisons were another pairing of a reserved, intellectual man and gregarious, empathic woman; unlike John Quincy, however, James understood and valued Dolley's work in the unofficial sphere and gave her free rein. From 1801–1809, it was in the house on "F" Street, not the executive mansion, where tasks of political cohesion took place (Allgor, 2000: 76–77, 99–101). While the Adamses were in Russia, James and Dolley took the networks and connections they had made into what would become known during their tenure as the White House. Dolley would continue to provide a governmental system lamentably light on structures with a rudimentary machine within which officials and their families could perform the tasks done by later professionalized party machines. She constructed a space in the White House, the only one in town, that could hold locals, officials and their families, the *corps diplomatique*, and travelers and gave them a regular night to meet – Wednesdays were "Mrs Madison's drawing rooms."

Though no one at the time could exactly apprehend what was happening during the Madison administration, the nation, and thus the capital, was becoming modern, heading for its destiny as a strong nation state, a democracy ruled by two parties. Both James's "hands off" presidential style and Dolley's active implementation of court practices such as social events, material displays, and patronage, unwittingly aided in these developments. For the nation to thrive and grow, it needed a strong sense of nationalism and a federal government that could accommodate power, from the presidential level on down. The burning of the capital in 1814 and the conclusion of the War of 1812 the next year accomplished the first task; the court-like venues and milieus that Dolley created satisfied the second.

So John Quincy and Louisa arrived in a town ripe for some courtly innovation, befitting a nation that had begun to regard itself as major player in the world. James Monroe had already set his administration on a "European … footing of form and ceremony"; he even contemplated "uniform dress" for cabinet members. However, the royal manner of his wife, Elizabeth Kortright Monroe, who had lived in France, only seemed cold and distant to the Washington community. This turn toward monarchical practices did not go unnoticed, and some worried that the emerging "etiquette" signaled that the US government was heading for the kind of courtly corruption that felled Rome (Allgor, 2000: 147–48, 212–13).

It is important to realize, too, that as soon as they set foot on American soil, both John Quincy and Louisa had their eyes on the presidency. It is inconceivable that these two ambitious people could have thought otherwise. As the son of a former president, John Quincy had deeply personal reasons for achieving this highest of offices. As the office of secretary of state was regarded as the stepping stone to the presidency, John Quincy could reasonably expect to be a contender in the election of 1824. The Adamses were not wrong in beginning their campaign as soon as they arrived. Assuming James Monroe would serve two terms, everyone was thinking about his successor years before the election of 1824 (Allgor, 2000: 153–154).

Though the Republican party was in the ascendant, it was splintering, and early on it was assumed that there would be many Republican candidates in 1824. In this era, men did not run for political office. Like a modern-day Cinncinatus at the plow, a candidate's seeming reluctance to take on the public service a public demanded of him proved his republican virtue. Before the family was unpacked, Louisa, then, began working as her husband's campaign manager. Her systematic approach presaged the techniques of later political machines. Her focus was on Congress; not only were presidential candidates nominated by congressional caucus, but the expected crowding of the electoral slate almost guaranteed that the election of 1824 would end up being decided in the House. John Quincy acknowledged the family strategy when he remarked: "The only possible chance for a head of department to attain the presidency is by ingratiating himself personally with the members of Congress." House elections, then, led "to a thousand corrupt cabals between the members of Congress and the heads of the Departments, who are thus almost necessarily made rival pretenders in the succession." John Quincy could afford to present himself as a paragon of incorruptibility, above the fray; Louisa did his campaigning for him (Allgor, 2000: 153–56, 165, 183).

The Adamses began their stay in Washington at a disadvantage; having been gone for eight years, they did not enjoy existing social relationships with congressional families. In this era, people got to know each other through "calling," short ritualized visits that officially opened doors between families. Social inferiors called on those above them; if they were "received," the two families were then free to issue mutual invitations. Washington families, both local and official, had already established connections through previous years of calls; including those of the other "pretenders to the throne," including Henry Clay, John C. Calhoun, and William Crawford. If the Adamses followed the rules for calling, Louisa would have to call on every family one by one, just to catch up (Allgor, 2000: 120–121, 164).

At least, they assumed, as a cabinet family, they could expect members of Congress to pay the first call on them, as a show of respect. But when the president of the Senate *pro tempore*, John Gaillard, and a colleague visited John Quincy in his office on January 5, 1818, they informed him that the Senate's unspoken rule was that senators would pay the "first call" only upon the president and not to cabinet members such as himself. John Quincy expressed surprise at this innovation, but hastened to say that although he had no wish to infringe on this right senators had taken on for themselves, he hoped that the delegation understood that their stand did not obligate him in any way to visit them. John Quincy's impression was that the delegation agreed and all departed "in perfect good humor on the subject" (Allgor, 2000: 149).

Louisa then made her move, allying herself with Elizabeth Kortright Monroe, who had declared that though she would return all calls paid to her, as the president's wife, she would not initiate any. These policies of the two households caused many "heartburnings," and people reacted to Elizabeth's too-royal prerogative with boycott. The first drawing room of the 1819–1820 season opened to a "beggarly-row of empty chairs." This would not do in a town where social structures took the place of political ones. Resolving this situation, establishing who was supreme in the pecking order, prompted a cabinet meeting to discuss the situation (Allgor, 2000: 149–52).

As is typical in such etiquette affairs, denial abounded. Part of the unofficial sphere's power is that it is hidden; when the hidden comes to light, people are uneasy about acknowledging the unofficial sphere's importance. John Quincy noted a visit by Louisa to Elizabeth to discuss "affairs of etiquette in visiting, which, it appears, are affairs of high importance here." Louisa wrote to her father-in-law sarcastically "You will at least have the happiness of living to see the day when the prosperity of the country has arrived at such a pitch of greatness, that the Congress can find no better subjects to regulate than the common and social intercourse of general society." But both, as seasoned diplomats, were posing; they knew that this was a power struggle with high stakes, as did John Adams when he replied seriously to Louisa's feigned exasperation, advising her "as discreetly as possible" to follow Elizabeth Monroe's lead (Allgor, 2000: 152–53).

Savvy politicians that they were, the Adamses would not have risked alienating the political community that they were courting without a significant payoff. Asserting themselves as social leaders was crucial in a town so dependent on society for its politics. Requiring that official families call upon them would most efficiently open up relations to multiple households, thus depriving their rivals of the home turf advantage. Their stand in the "etiquette wars" allied them with the highest family in the land, checking the growing power of a Congress who thought it could dictate policy to a cabinet member. The principle was important, but the Adamses did not let principle trump practicality. As a matter of fact, John Quincy did initiate calls, and as the quest for the presidency accelerated, Louisa would not miss a house in her calling campaign (Allgor, 2000: 162–163).

But they went even further. In his final letter to Congress on the affair, John Quincy stated that though he would not pay visits of form, he was happy to return visits and would be "happy to invite to my house every member of the Senate, whether he had or had not paid me a visit." This statement was a radical innovation, meaning that Louisa and John Quincy could invite any man or family they found useful without any preliminaries (Allgor, 2000: 164–165). Any resentment felt by the official families at being put in their place was soon mitigated by the gracious welcome provided by their hostess (in contrast to the cold Elizabeth Monroe) and the exciting developments at the Adamses' house.

In a culture where elections were run in the unofficial sphere, of course, Louisa was not the only canny wife of a canny man. As the election of 1824 neared, cabinet families spent vast resources of time and money on social events. Cabinet members were expected to socialize as often as they worked, and they visited members of Congress "very freely." Louisa's deprecations and sarcasms, like John Quincy's, often reveal more than they intended. She wryly remarked to old John Adams that "it is understood that a man who is ambitious to become president of the United States, must make his wife visit the Ladies of the members of Congress first," adding "otherwise, he is totally inefficient to fill so high an office." She gleefully reported: "You would laugh could you see Mr. A. every morning prepare a set of [calling] cards with as much formality as if he was drawing up some very important article to negotiate in a commercial treaty" (Allgor, 2000: 157, 167–168).

Their primary strategy lay in home entertaining. In a portentous move, the Adamses bought the former Madison "F" Street home, which had been the social center of the city for many years. As the election neared, they readied the house for the final push of entertaining and campaigning.

In 1823, they built an addition, consisting of spaces that would be used for events, including two large reception rooms, two back rooms, and five or six smaller rooms. Louisa's most far-reaching innovation was borrowed partly from the woman Louisa called "dear Dolley." A great strength of Dolley Madison's drawing room lay in its regularity; every Wednesday, everyone had a place to "see and be seen," as one guest opined. Instead of merely giving a lot of parties like the other cabinet wives, Louisa instituted "Mrs Adams's Tuesday nights." Rather than randomly inviting guests for a single occasion, she introduced a subscription system, issuing invitations for the whole congressional season, which lasted from late fall until Congress adjourned in the spring (Allgor, 2000: 168–170).

In December 1819, Louisa announced that she had "open[ed] my campaign, having given a general invitation for every Tuesday during the winter." The innovation apparently caused "some noise and jealousy," but once again, the Adamses stole the spotlight and other so-called subscription events followed. As rival wives imitated the practice, it became understood that no matter how many invitations a family or candidate received, they would go only to a single candidate's parties during a season. New York congressman Thomas Hubbard's joke that Mrs Adams had given him "*fair* and what Mr. Storrs would call *legal* notice of her tea party," conveyed both the institutional nature of the practice and the level of commitment. In a town where social allegiance signaled political alliance, John Quincy's crowded drawing room sent a message of political popularity and solidarity (Allgor, 2000: 169–170, 175).

"Mrs Adams's Tuesdays" were crowded, not merely because she was the first to issue subscriptions. They were popular from the start because of the quality of the food and entertainment and because of Louisa herself. At presidential drawing rooms and the homes of other cabinet wives, conversation was the primary amusement. In contrast, Louisa drew on her English home training and court experience to provide entertainments that were performance-oriented and showy, featuring music and dancing. When no music was to be had, Louisa herself would perform, as she had many times at Tower Hill. The sight of this cultured lady, perhaps at the most refined of instruments, the harp, signaled to all that she and her family were indubitably of the "better sort" and worthy to lead the nation. In the mind of these former colonists, superior people were visibly superior by the possession and use of material culture (Allgor, 2000: 170–172).

When Louisa wrote, "The eye of the public is already on me," she was acknowledging the importance of this evaluative capacity. Her rivals could not compete. One congressman thought the wife of William Crawford was a kind woman and an affectionate wife and mother, but "she is plain, almost to coarseness and is without any of the airs and graces, which seem appropriate to the wife of a president." John Adams had correctly predicted to Louisa "your experience in Berlin, St. Petersburg, and St. James's, your sense, wit, and perfect fluency and purity in the French language will hold you constantly besieged." No wonder at the first presidential drawing room of 1820, Louisa noted with mortification that people "teased" her, asking her how she would "behave in this same situation, as it was likely I should be tried in four years from this time" (Allgor, 2000: 173, 172, 171, 154).

22.6 "All are Gone to Mrs. Adams'"

As the election neared, the stakes rose. On December 20, 1823, Louisa and John Quincy, swayed by their son John's enthusiasm for the idea, decided to give a ball in honor of Andrew Jackson. Invitations were rushed out, as there was a question of timing. If the ball were to have maximum impact, it had to be held before the congressional caucus was held in late January or early February. Also, in a political and family culture that demanded republican simplicity, one could not merely give a ball for entertainment's sake. Lavish expenditures must be justified; the traditional time for a ball was George Washington's birthday on February 22, but that date fell too late for the caucuses. The only suitable date was January 8, the anniversary of General Jackson's victory in New Orleans in 1815 (Allgor, 2000: 176–177).

What might have given the Adamses pause is that Andrew Jackson himself had emerged as a presidential contender, albeit a dark horse. But the anniversary of the battle of New Orleans had become a traditional time to host a ball in cities across the United States. Perhaps the Adamses had hopes that this influential candidate might decide to join their camp, bringing votes from the West and South with him. No doubt celebrating a rival must have pleased John Quincy's sense of incorruptibility. Having the enormously popular general at his house would allow John Quincy to bask in the hero's popularity, and, if done well enough, it would be the Adamses, rather than Jackson, who would occupy the spotlight. In the event, that is just what happened. Once Washington City got wind of what was happening at "F" Street, the ball was anticipated to be the event of all events. Louisa and John Quincy issued over five hundred invitations, many of them hand-delivered by Louisa. Others begged for an invitation, and Louisa marveled that the "number of persons who come to be invited on this occasion exceed belief" (Allgor, 2000: 177–178).

It is not overstating the case to say that this was a performance on a massive scale. Like a good director, Louisa had "a beautiful plan in my head which I shall endeavor to have executed." She even had scripts for the event, in the form of etiquette manuals, guides on ballroom organization and behavior, including dancing. With little choice of music, Louisa hired the Marine band, but she explicitly chose certain dances and excluded others. Though John Quincy and Louisa both waltzed beautifully, the "valse" was considered racy in the provincial capital, as well as some of the trendier Spanish dances. Louisa chose cotillions and reels, dances that required group participation and cooperation (Allgor, 2000: 178–179).

After clearing out rooms to hold the guests, taking off doors to allow movement between rooms, and transferring John Quincy's study to a backroom, Louisa installed pillars to prop up the second story where the guests would have supper. When it came to decor, she drew on her experiences of European and British gentry style, seen both at home and abroad. The whole Adams family spent from December 22 to the day of the ball decorating the spaces with laurel, wintergreen, evergreens, and roses, woven into garlands and wreaths. At a ball given by the British minister the year before, a man from Baltimore had chalked beautiful designs on the floor. Louisa hired him to do the same, following her own designs. The chalking took a full day to complete – an extravagant elegance, as it would be swept away in the first dance (Allgor, 2000: 179, 178, 180).

As January 8 neared, the capital was dizzy with anticipation. The press, which did not normally report on women or on social events, seized on the occasion, squibbing the story with both prose and poetry. One published poem began: "Wend you with the world tonight?," concluding with "Belles and matron, maids and madams/All are gone to Mrs. Adams." Finally the day was at hand. The guests began arriving at 7.30 p.m., guided by bonfires lit two blocks away. Within the hour, according to Charles Francis, "even the staircase up to Mary's chamber [possibly the third floor] began to be thronged" (Allgor, 2000: 179–80).

Upon entering the home, guests were greeted by Louisa and John Quincy, and then moved to the impressive entertainment rooms, festooned with greenery, flowers, and "small illumination lamps." The chalked floors were a rich carpet of color, with spread eagles, flags, and the motto, "Welcome to the Hero of New Orleans." The hero himself appeared at 9 o'clock; everyone crowded in to speak to him. Charles Francis reported, "The ladies climbed the chairs and benches to see General Jackson." Louisa "gratified the general curiosity," by "gracefully" taking Jackson's arm and leading him through the crowd. In so doing, she captured the spotlight, representing her husband, her family, and all the political freight associated with the event. She prepared her dress accordingly. Rather than asserting any aristocratic claim with a display of gold and diamonds, Louisa chose an ensemble that commanded authority and power but also maintained a republican simplicity. She moved through the crowd in a "suit of steel" – a steel lamé – with "ornaments for head, throat, and arms" of "cut-steel," all producing a "dazzling effect." Ever the sober republican, John Quincy appeared in a simple suit, the only male there not in formal wear (Allgor, 2000: 180–181).

When supper was announced, Louisa led the general to the head of the table, which was laid out in luxurious food, presented in the sumptuous style she had observed in St Petersburg and London. Elaborate sculpted suppers were the rage in Europe and her table featured "natural and candied fruits, pies, sweetmeats, tongues, games ... prepared in the French style and arranged in the most exquisite taste." General Jackson left shortly after supper to attend another, public ball, "where he expected to be greeted by the people with great joy," but where, in fact, there were only a few attendees. Everyone, as the newspaper had predicted, had "gone to Mrs. Adams." Jackson's early exit seemed almost incidental to the event; the night belonged to Louisa (Allgor, 2000: 181).

In the years to come, there would be other "Jackson balls," but the "Adams ball," as this was known, remained unsurpassed in the annals of Washington history, as both a social and political event. It represented the apogee of the Adamses' campaign efforts and a culmination of the court ways that Louisa had learned over so many years. Social events were for cohesion and persuasion, and on one grand night, Louisa and John Quincy brought everyone of importance into their home, reconciling their enemies, introducing new supporters, and weaving everyone more tightly into their circle. The company shared food together, danced in the collaborative dances Louisa chose, and felt happy and grateful to the family who made this occasion possible. The event increased John Quincy's popularity and made him the frontrunner in the election. It is too much to say that those who supped at his table and danced through the night "owed" him a vote. Rather, the effect was more subtle and psychological. The magnificence of the event had taken electioneering to a new plane, one occupied solely by the Adamses (Allgor, 2000: 181–182).

While the ball did not have an effect on the congressional caucus – it chose William Crawford – the poor congressional showing at the caucus of 66 members out of 291 indicated the growing irrelevance of the caucus within the splintering Republican party. The election of 1824 played out exactly in the way many had predicted. Andrew Jackson won the most votes, with a total of 152901; John Quincy Adams won 114023; Henry Clay received 47217; and William Crawford garnered 46979. Even after the electoral college weighed in, no candidate had a clear majority, and the election went into the House. There, the representatives of each state voted among themselves, and the majority position counted as that single state's vote. Only the top three candidates were considered (the electoral college's votes had given the No. 3 spot to Crawford), but while the fourth, Clay, might be out of the running for president, he wielded great power. As Speaker of the House, Clay commanded congressional support that he could swing toward a candidate of his choosing (Allgor, 2000: 183–184).

It was at this fraught moment that an event that has long puzzled historians took place. From the evidence of John Quincy's own diaries, it seems that he entered into what enemies would later call the "corrupt bargain," promising Henry Clay the coveted post of secretary of state (and thus a solid hope of the next presidency) in return for his support. Historians who paid attention to John Quincy's many protestations against ambition and his own vaunted political virtue have argued against this obvious interpretation, making their case, on the basis of his character, that he could not have been guilty of such base political behavior. So upright and uptight a man could not be seduced into corruption in a few days, whatever the pressure. But, of course, had historians paid attention to what Louisa had been doing, since 1817, they would have realized that John Quincy was as ambitious as any man, and the deal with Clay, far from being an anomaly, was the end result of years of campaigning (Allgor, 2000: 185–186).

The men who had attended dinners, parties, and Tuesday nights under the Adamses' roof gathered on February 9, 1825, to elect a president. In theory, the House would vote until it had a majority; in practice, getting a clear first vote was crucial, as subsequent voting would cause fragile alliances and promises to crumble. Even with Clay's help, John Quincy needed New York's vote. The New York coalition was split, with 17 for Adams and 17 for Crawford; elderly Stephen Van Rensselaer was the holdout. Divided in his own mind, and harassed from all sides, Van Rensselaer, according to the story, bowed his head for divine guidance. Spying a ballot ticket with John Quincy's name on it, he went for Adams over Crawford. His fellow delegates did not take this betrayal, as they saw it, lightly. Delaware representative Louis McLane commented: "He has betrayed those with whom he broke bread." Surely, however, it is also significant that long before the presidential election, Van Rensselaer "voted" for John Quincy by breaking bread in the Adams house (Allgor, 2000: 184–185).

As we know, like his father, John Quincy endured a one-term, doomed presidency. On one hand, his view of government was too modern, including federal internal improvements and "lighthouses in the sky." On the other, during his re-election campaign, his enemies painted him as an old-fashioned aristocrat, who used public funds to buy "gambling furniture" (a billiard table in fact not bought with public funds). In a dynamic that other First Ladies would experience, Louisa found herself sidelined once the great object was achieved. Though she performed her duties well, Louisa spent her White House years depressed and withdrawn (Allgor, 2000: 191–193).

The way to evaluate the Adamses' work is not to look to what happened to them, but at what happened to the system. In the next decade, executive power grew significantly. Political parties became institutionalized, performing the necessary tasks of party cohesion, including patronage, that women such as Louisa had executed. Party machines also took over political campaigns, using techniques with which Louisa would have been familiar. European governments, such as Great Britain, struggled toward modernity by bureaucratizing and systematizing their monarchy; the United States found it useful to accompany their modernizing process by using courtly techniques and structures in order to become the most powerful nation state in the modern world.

Further Reading

Allgor, C. A. (1997). "A Republican in A Monarchy": Louisa Catherine Adams in Russia. *Diplomatic History.*

Allgor, C. A. (2000). *Parlor Politics: In Which the Ladies of Washington Help Build a City and a Government.* Charlottesville, VA.

Butterfield, L. H. (1974). Tending a Dragon-Killer: Notes for the Biographer of Mrs. *John Quincy Adams. Proceedings of the American Philosophical Society* 118: 165–178.

Challinor, J. R. (1985). "A Quarter-Taint of Maryland Blood": An Inquiry into the Anglo/Maryland Background of Mrs. John Quincy Adams. *Maryland Historical Magazine.*

Challinor, J. R. (1987). The Mis-Education of Louisa Catherine Johnson Adams." *Proceedings of the Massachusetts Historical Society.*

Corbett, K. T. (1979). Louisa Catherine Adams: The Anguished "Adventures of a Nobody." In Kelley (1979).

Graham, Judith S. Luey, Beth, Hogan, Margaret A. and Taylor, C. James, eds. (forthcoming). *Diary and Autobiographical Writings of Louisa Catherine Adams,* 2 vols. Cambridge, MA.

Heffron, M. M. "A Fine Romance": The Courtship Correspondence of Louisa Catherine Johnson and John Quincy Adams. *New England Quarterly* 83: 200–218.

Heffron, M. M. (2011). *The Other Mrs. Adams: A Life of Louisa Catherine Adams.* Unpublished MS.

Kelley, M. (1979). *Woman's Being, Woman's Place: Female Identity and Vocation in American History.* Boston.

O'Brien, M. (2010). *Mrs. Adams in Winter: A Journey in the Last Days of Napoleon.* New York.

Nagel, P. C. (1983). *Descent from Glory: Four Generations of the John Adams Family.* New York.

Nagel, P. C. (1987). *The Adams Women: Abigail and Louisa Adams, Their Sisters and Daughters.* New York.

Nagel, P. C. (1999). *John Quincy Adams: A Public Life, a Private Life.* Boston.

Price, J. M., ed. *Joshua Johnson's Letterbook, 1771–1774.* At www.british-history.ac.uk, accessed Nov. 7, 2012.

Roberts. C. (2008). *Ladies of Liberty: The Women Who Shaped Our Nation.* New York.

Shepherd, J. (1975). *The Adams Chronicles: Four Generations of Greatness.* Boston.

Shepherd, J. (1980). *Cannibals of the Heart: A Personal Biography of Louisa Catherine and John Quincy Adams.* New York.

Part III

Images and Legacies

Chapter Twenty-Three

Thomas Jefferson and the John Adams Family

Herbert E. Sloan

For half a century, from 1775 to 1826, the first two generations of the Adams family were entwined with Thomas Jefferson. As with all relationships, this one varied over time. It began on a strong note in the 1770s and 1780s, then cooled and virtually disappeared in the last decade of the eighteenth century and first decade of the nineteenth, only to be resurrected – miraculously, one might say – a few years after Jefferson left the White House. Throughout, Jefferson was of more concern to the Adamses than they were to him. That pattern would be continued after the deaths of the two statesmen in 1826, with John Quincy Adams reacting strongly (and not favorably) to the first edition of Jefferson's writings and his grandson Henry Adams carrying on the family's efforts to come to an understanding with the third president in his *History*. The essay will focus on Jefferson and the first two generations of the Adams family.

American historians – Americans more generally, in fact – have long been in the habit of using the Adams–Jefferson relationship as a way of taking the measure of the Revolution and the early republic, indeed of the United States more generally. The contrasts between Jefferson and the Adamses make this a virtually irresistible move. On the one hand, there is tart, no-nonsense Abigail Adams, the greatest wife in American political history, and her husband, short, rotund John Adams, son of a modest Massachusetts family, seemingly fond of aristocracy if not an outright monarchist, conservative, skeptical, "sometimes absolutely mad" (if you follow Benjamin Franklin), unable to grasp America's exceptional destiny (Boyd et al., 1950: 15: 316, Jefferson to James Madison, July 29, 1789,). And on the other

A Companion to John Adams and John Quincy Adams, First Edition.
Edited by David Waldstreicher.

hand, there is Thomas Jefferson, born on a Virginia plantation with a silver spoon in his mouth, tall, slender, a democrat when it was not yet fashionable to be one, at the same time something of a snob and an epicure whose tastes were anything but plebian, a confident believer in the ultimate wisdom of the people, author of the Declaration of Independence (none of John Adams's writings came close to achieving even a fraction of the fame that accrued to Jefferson on the basis of that one composition), eternal optimist, slaveholder. If historians are in the habit of stressing the differences between Jefferson and the Adamses, they also think it important to find room for both the Adamses and Jefferson in the American story. Unlike the other overarching contrast dominating the early republic, that between Thomas Jefferson and Alexander Hamilton, this one apparently does not require us to choose one side over the other. Jefferson and the Adamses would end by agreeing to disagree, in effect, where Jefferson and Hamilton were always at loggerheads and in the minds of interpreters down to the day have continued to offer opposing views of the American prospect.

In recent decades, the story of Jefferson and the Adamses has gained in nuance and complexity, in part thanks to the integration of additional players. We no longer think of it exclusively in terms of John and Thomas; these days, Abigail rarely fails to find her place, though usually as a slightly secondary figure. As for the children she and John raised, they still do not appear as frequently as they might. When it comes to the two youngest, Charles and Thomas Boylston, this probably does no real damage. Their older sister Abigail ("Nabby") had more contact with Jefferson; she, too, was a part of the family he got to know during his European years, when he also became acquainted with her future husband, the feckless William Stephens Smith, who moved in and out of Jefferson's life for the next quarter-century. But it was John Quincy among the second generation who had the most important role to play in the Adams–Jefferson relationship. Reminiscing about the 1780s from the vantage point of 1825, John Adams reminded Jefferson that when they were in Paris John Quincy had been "almost as much your boy as mine" (John Adams to Thomas Jefferson, Jan. 22, 1825, in Cappon, 1959: 606–607). Yet by the early 1790s a considerable distance had opened up between Jefferson and John Quincy, nor would that change later on, even after John Quincy switched his allegiance from the Federalists to the Democratic Republicans, Jefferson's party.

Looked at over the long term, we can discern four main stages in the relationship between Jefferson and the Adamses. The first starts with the initial moment of contact in 1775, flowers in the 1780s, and comes to an end with the 1791 break between John Adams and Thomas Jefferson over Jefferson's endorsement of Thomas Paine's *Rights of Man*. The second, a period of distant and gradually deteriorating relations, lasts from 1792 through the beginning of 1801. The third, when contact between Jefferson and the senior Adamses all but ceased, covers the years 1801 through1811.

This is the absolute nadir of the relationship. The fourth and final stage begins with the resumption of correspondence between John Adams and Thomas Jefferson at the beginning of 1812 and lasts until their deaths on the Fourth of July in 1826. And after 1826, there is a coda, as John Quincy Adams continues to ruminate on Thomas Jefferson.

John Adams and Thomas Jefferson met for the first time in the summer of 1775 (Peterson, 1976: 1). Both were delegates to the Second Continental Congress, then assembled in Philadelphia. Older than Jefferson by eight years, Adams was a seasoned veteran of resistance politics, with a reputation throughout the colonies as one of those Massachusetts firebrands, the "brace of Adamses," the other half of which was his cousin Sam Adams. In contrast, Jefferson had only recently acquired fame beyond Virginia, thanks to his authorship of *The Summary View of the Rights of British America*. Each gained an initial impression of the other that was quite favorable (Butterfield et al., 1961: 2.218; Boyd 1950–: 11.94, Thomas Jefferson to James Madison, Jan. 30, 1787). In the spring of the following year, Congress moved closer to a formal break with the mother country, and both Adams and Jefferson were named to a committee charged with preparation of a declaration of independence. In hindsight, this would be a crucial moment in the relationship. Hitherto Adams had been the dominant figure, certainly so in the eyes of the public. No one could have predicted, in 1776, that Jefferson, the Declaration, and the Fourth would become inseparably linked in the minds of generations of Americans, or that it would be Jefferson, not Adams, who received a memorial in the nation's capital.[1] But from now on, John Adams would repeatedly find himself receiving second billing, and it would rankle.[2]

Adams at first imagined that July 2, the day he had helped to carry the motion for American independence, would be the date his countrymen remembered. He wrote to Abigail Adams that "The Second Day of July, 1776, will be the most memorable Epocha in the History of America. I am apt to believe, that it will be celebrated, by succeeding Generations as the great anniversary Festival ... from one End of this Continent to the other, from this Time forward forever more" (John Adams to Abigail Adams, July 3, 1776, Butterfield et al., 1963–: 2:30). It was not to be, and three decades later Adams would be asking his friend Benjamin Rush, "Was there ever a *coup de théâtre* that had so great effect as Jefferson's penmanship of the Declaration of Independence?" (Schutz and Adair, 1966: 44) In the last years of his life, as the fiftieth anniversary of the Declaration approached, John Adams found himself involved in controversies over what exactly had happened in Congress, the Declaration's originality or lack thereof, and other issues. Even if no one was prepared to shower John Adams with glory, at points it seemed as though he was doing his best to see that others (Thomas Jefferson included) were cut down to proper size (Peterson, 1976: 120–121; Maier, 1997: 180–184). While it took time before it became clear to Adams's and Jefferson's fellow Americans how important the Declaration would be for later generations, it was Jefferson the drafter to whom they would give the credit, not Adams the committee member. In 1776, of course, John Adams could not know this, but it was a portent of things to come in terms of their relationship and of their enduring reputations.

Jefferson returned to Virginia in the fall of 1776, and although they corresponded occasionally, the two men would not see each other again until Jefferson and his daughter Martha arrived in France in 1784. Yet even before they re-established direct contact, Jefferson had begun to form an image of John Adams that was, one might say, mixed. Adams's dispatches from Europe struck many members of Congress as vain and boastful, and the notion that Adams lacked balance was widespread. Jefferson said as much in 1783, and that sense of the Massachusetts statesman was reinforced on more than one occasion by James Madison, whose views of Adams were extremely critical. In many ways, this understanding of Adams remained with Jefferson for the rest of his life.[3]

Once in Paris, Jefferson encountered not only John Adams but also Abigail, and Nabby and John Quincy Adams. The two families were in frequent, even constant touch until the Adamses left Paris in May of 1785 for London, where John Adams was to be the American minister to the Court of St James's. With Franklin's departure for America, Jefferson now became the sole American envoy in France. Adams's appointment in London, important though it might seem, in fact meant relatively little; Jefferson, as minister to France, was at the center of things, so far as America's foreign relations were concerned. France, after all, was America's great ally, whereas Britain was the former colonial master and still in many ways the enemy (Marshall, 2012; Malone, 1951).

It was during the European sojourn that Jefferson got to know and appreciate Abigail Adams, and also then that the Virginian took John Quincy Adams under his wing. These were the best, or at least the easiest, years in the Jefferson–Adams relationship, ones that both sides would look back on with fondness after the storms of the 1790s and early 1800s. Jefferson figured frequently in John Quincy Adams's diary; he was, the adolescent wrote, a "man of universal learning and very pleasing manners" (Allen et al., 1981: 1.224). Even after the Adamses decamped for England, Jefferson stayed in close touch by letter. He shopped for Abigail Adams in Paris, and she returned the favor by executing his commissions in the British capital (Cappon, 1959: 185–187, 192–194). And when Jefferson's younger daughter Polly arrived in England from Virginia in 1787, accompanied only by her slightly older companion Sally Hemings, it was Abigail Adams who took charge of the pair until they could be delivered to Sally's master and Polly's father (Cappon, 1959: 178–180, 183–188). Diplomatic business brought Jefferson to London in the spring of 1786, and he and John Adams then took a tour of the English countryside (Jefferson wanted to sample the wonders of English landscape gardening; John Adams had less-focused goals). They met again in March, 1788 when a financial crisis forced the two American envoys to make an emergency trip to Amsterdam, where they managed to rescue American credit with the Dutch bankers at virtually the last possible moment. And then the Adamses returned to America in the spring of 1788.

Jefferson stayed on in Europe for the next year and a half. It was an important period in his life. He found himself caught up in the early stages of the French Revolution, and he was more than simply an observer. Had John and Abigail Adams known what he was up to, one suspects they would have been horrified. But his letters to the Adamses contained relatively bland accounts of the events he was witnessing, and nothing about his role in them. Still, they may not have needed direct information to sense the direction he was taking. Already in 1787, commenting on Shays' Rebellion, he had written to Nabby's husband, William Stephens Smith, that "the tree of liberty must be refreshed from time to time with the blood of patriots & tyrants. it is it's natural manure" (Boyd et al., 1950–:13:356, Thomas Jefferson to W.S. Smith, Nov. 13, 1787). And his comments to John Adams on the new American constitution were fairly critical. Adams was enthusiastic about the document; Jefferson, however, told him that "I confess there are things in it which stagger all my dispositions to subscribe to what such an assembly has proposed," adding that "all the good of this new constitution might have been couched in three or four new articles to be added to the good, old, and venerable fabric, which should have been preserved even as a religious relick" (Cappon, 1959: 210, 212).

Jefferson was beginning to articulate an attitude toward political developments in France and America that would ultimately drive him apart from the Adamses. He was also beginning to learn more about John Adams's political opinions. John Adams would later insist that he and Jefferson had never explained their views to each other during the time they spent together, and it is clear that Adams was right about this. Then, In 1787, Jefferson read the first volume of Adams's lengthy (and cranky) *Defence of the Constitutions of the United States*, a work that may seem virtually unreadable today but that created something of a scandal at the time. Jefferson actually succeeded in preventing its translation into French (Cappon, 1959: 174–175; Appleby, 1968: 1084–1091). Was John Adams a not-so-closet monarchist? There were those who read *The Defence* that way. Jefferson certainly had his doubts about it, as did Jefferson's confidant Madison, whose negative views of John Adams were increasingly helping to color Jefferson's doubts about his friend's political wisdom.

In September of 1789 Jefferson, too, left Europe, going home to deal with his debts and other matters that required his attention. He landed in Virginia to find that President Washington wanted him to serve as secretary of state. With some reluctance, he accepted the offer. In April of 1790, he arrived in New York City, then the capital. John and Abigail Adams were there as well, John serving as vice president and Abigail playing a social role in the administration. But the Adams family was now scattering: John Quincy (Harvard class of 1787) was preparing for a legal career in Massachusetts, and Charles (Harvard 1789) was studying in a New York law office; Nabby, the wife of William Stephens Smith, was pregnant with her third child; and Thomas was finishing his degree at Harvard.

With little to occupy him as vice president, and having finished the third and final volume of *The Defence* in 1788, John Adams began to write for the American press, creating a series of thirty-two essays that, while posing as commentaries on the works of a Renaissance-era French historian, were actually a set of reflections on contemporary political problems. These were *The Discourses on Davila*, another production that did little to shore up Adams's reputation for sound political judgment. Jefferson found them disturbing, more evidence, perhaps, that John Adams was unreliable when it came to the republican verities. Despite his closeness to the Adams family during the years in Europe, his contact with them in New York (and then in Philadelphia where the capital moved in the fall of 1790) seems not to have left many substantial traces in the surviving letters (though Abigail Adams did note that he enlivened "the social circle" in the spring of 1790; see Butterfield, et al. 1963–:9:40). Jefferson was now in the thick of things, politically speaking, facing off in Washington's cabinet against Alexander Hamilton, the secretary of the treasury. John Adams, whatever his formal rank as vice president, was decidedly not a player at this stage; again, as with the Declaration, as with the European missions, the Virginian was apparently at center stage, the older New Englander filling a mere supporting role.

Perhaps the break between Jefferson and the Adamses was inevitable, but when it came its proximate cause was Jefferson's carelessness. He was one of the first in America to receive a copy of *Rights of Man*, Thomas Paine's incendiary 1790 response to Edmund Burke, a ringing endorsement of the proceedings in France to whose early stages Jefferson had been a party. When he sent his copy to the printer who was going to publish the American edition of *Rights of Man*, Jefferson enclosed a note of endorsement that denounced those responsible for "the political heresies which have sprung up amongst us." John Adams was not mentioned by name, of course, but it took very little imagination to guess that Jefferson intended his comments to apply to Adams. The printer included the note in his edition, and John Adams was properly outraged. What was Jefferson saying, he asked his old friend – that he, Adams, was a monarchist? Jefferson did his best to weasel out of his remarks, which, after all, he had never intended should be public. Still, Jefferson told the president that for Adams he had "a cordial esteem, increased by long habits of concurrence of opinion in the days of his republicanism; and even since his apostacy to hereditary monarchy & nobility, tho' we differ, we differ as friends should do" (Boyd et al., 1950–: 20.291, Thomas Jefferson to George Washington, May 8, 1791).

Then a new series of newspaper essays began to appear, under the *nom de guerre* of "Publicola." They denounced Paine and praised Burke, and Jefferson was quite sure they were at least in part aimed at him. He also had the strongest of suspicions that a certain senior statesman given to scribbling for the public papers was responsible for the pieces. John Adams, however, denied authorship. Jefferson was not convinced. In fact, it was John Quincy Adams who had written as "Publicola"; whatever affection for Jefferson may have remained from their Paris days was now quite clearly gone. John Quincy Adams would continue to regard Jefferson as wrongheaded and untrustworthy, even when he chose to side with the Democratic Republicans a decade and a half later. Far more than his father, he seems to have been unwilling to forgive his sometime mentor. Once Jefferson understood that John Quincy was "Publicola," he added another Adams to his list of apostates from the true republican faith.[4]

Jefferson waited until July 1791 before attempting to explain his gaffe to Adams (the American edition of *Rights of Man* had been published the previous May). The letter betrayed a guilty conscience, as Jefferson insisted he had not intended his comments to become public and then went on to say that, of course, "you and I differ in our ideas of the best form of government," which, he added, "is well known to us both." Adams vehemently denied that the two of them had ever "had a serious conversation together that I can recollect concerning the nature of Government. The very transient hints that have passed between Us have been jocular and superficial, without ever coming to any explanation." Jefferson was "wildly mistaken" if he ever thought that Adams had proposed a hereditary executive or hereditary senate in either the federal or the state constitutions. His views had been misreed, Adams insisted, and "made the pretence for overwhelming me with floods and Whirlwinds of tempestuous Abuse, unexampled in the History of this Country" (Cappon, 1959: 246, 248–249). By the end of 1791, then, the first phase of the Jefferson–Adams relationship was decidedly over.

The second phase of the relationship covers the period from the end of 1791 through the beginning of Jefferson's first term in 1801. "I am really astonished at the blind Spirit of Party which has Seized on the whole soul of this Jefferson," the vice president exclaimed at the end of 1792. "There is not a Jacobin in France more devoted to Faction" (Butterfield et al., 1963–: 9.360) Adams grew increasingly skeptical about his old friend, and so in December 1793, just as Jefferson was about to retire as secretary of state, he would write to Abigail of Jefferson's "want of Candour, his obstinate Prejudices both of Aversion and Attachment, his real Partiality in Spite of all his Pretensions and his low notions about many Things." And to John Quincy he wrote the following month that "I am not sorry for it [Jefferson's resignation] on the whole because his Soul is poisoned with Ambition and his Temper imbittered against that Constitution and Administration" (Boyd et al., 1950–: 9.484–485, John Adams to John Quincy Adams, Jan. 3, 1793 [1794]; Hogan and Taylor, 2007: 345).

There was little written communication between the Adamses and Jefferson in this period, and Jefferson was away in Virginia from the beginning of 1794 until he returned to the capital in 1797, this time as vice president. Jefferson and John Adams were opposing candidates in the election of 1796, but on the surface Jefferson did not express much disappointment when John Adams carried the contest by the slender margin of three votes in the electoral college. Adams had always been his senior, Jefferson remarked, and if Adams had failed this time, his career would have been finished (obviously, Jefferson did not see the vice presidency as the end of his prospects). At first, it seemed as though there might be a reconciliation between the two, but Jefferson's allies, especially James Madison, cautioned him against such a move. When Jefferson walked home with Adams after a farewell dinner for Washington, in March 1797, it was the last occasion for several years in which the two would exchange anything other than purely formal words (Peterson, 1976: 66–72).

Relations with France went from bad to worse during John Adams's presidency, and Jefferson's anglophobia made him unwilling to accept a hostile policy toward America's revolutionary ally that could only benefit the British. He opposed the Quasi-War and the measures that supported it, whether the Direct Tax or the Alien and Sedition Acts. The Adams family had no use for the vice president's stand, or for his supporters' furious attacks on the president. (Abigail Adams was particularly incensed by the activities of Democratic Republican journalists; see Gelles, 2009: 247–248.) John Adams imagined that his moderation and the eventual resolution of issues with France in the Convention of Mortefontaine in 1800 had served his country well; for Jefferson and Co., the Federalists deserved no credit, given that they had created the troubles in the first place.

Thus, foreign policy continued to keep the two apart. So, one suspects, did the presidential couple's lengthy absences from Philadelphia. For months on end, Abigail Adams did not leave her house in Braintree, confined there much of the time by ill health. John Adams thought it his duty to be with her, and Jefferson himself spent as little time in Philadelphia as he could possibly manage. The move to the new capital in Washington, DC, in 1800, brought the Adams couple and Jefferson back into the same physical space, but it did not restore relations. Jefferson called on John Adams when it looked as though the lame-duck Federalist Congress might try to take advantage of the tied election to block his elevation to the presidency; Adams refused to lift a finger on behalf of his onetime friend and colleague (Peterson, 1976: 86–91).

Abigail Adams left the new capital in February 1801; her husband famously followed early on the morning of March 4, and did not attend his successor's inauguration. So began what might be called the third stage and the absolute low point in relations between the Adamses and Jefferson. Following the inauguration, Jefferson and John Adams engaged in a polite exchange, and then there was silence (Cappon, 1959: 164). The year 1804 witnessed Abigail Adams's condolences to Jefferson on the death of his younger daughter, the one she had looked after in London in 1787. But it was an example of the adage that no good deed goes unpunished, for when Jefferson replied, he noted that "one act of Mr. Adams's life, and one only ever gave me a moment's personal displeasure. I did consider his last appointments to office as personally unkind." This led to a long and fierce reply from Abigail Adams (written without her husband's knowledge), denouncing Jefferson for political sins of all sorts, and especially his patronage of James T. Callendar. Jefferson replied, and Abigail Adams issued a rebuttal, adding new matter in the form of a charge that Jefferson was responsible for the dismissal of John Quincy Adams as a commissioner in bankruptcy. Jefferson insisted that this was not the case, and there was another reply from Quincy, this one with a postscript by John Adams, saying that he had known nothing of the correspondence until the previous evening when his wife had shown it to him. He had, he said, "no remarks to make upon it in this time and in this place" (Cappon, 1959: 268–282). And there the correspondence ended. Each side retired to its tent and, as it were, continued to sulk. Jefferson, in any case, had his duties as president, and the Adamses were not high on his list of concerns.

In 1803, the Massachusetts legislature sent John Quincy Adams to the Senate, where he remained until 1808 (Bemis, 1949: 111–155). On at least eight occasions Jefferson entertained John Quincy (who was often accompanied to the White House by his wife, Louisa Catherine Adams), just as he entertained all of the members of Congress (Stanton, 2005; C.F. Adams 1874–1877: 1.272, 281, 316–317, 330–331, 378, 457–458, 472–473, 480–481.) John Quincy's diary suggests that these were not particularly comfortable events, at least not for him. Though, as we have seen, he and Jefferson had known each other in Paris, almost twenty years before, there had been too much water under the bridge since then for them to resume their former footing. John Quincy's political views had not changed since the days when he wrote as "Publicola," and his recent translation of Friedrich von Gentz's comparison of the American and French revolutions, with its suggestion that the New World episode was safely conservative while the Old World one was a disaster, would hardly have been to Jefferson's taste, no matter what he had come to think of Bonaparte (J.Q. Adams, 1800). And there was more to suggest John Quincy's distance from the president. The "Publius Valerius" essays of 1804 attacked the policies of Jefferson's first term in slashing fashion; writing as "Tom Paine," John Quincy also expressed his distaste for Jefferson in anonymously published poetry, indicting the Virginian's relationship with Sally Hemings (W.C. Ford, 1913–1917: 3.46–77; Basker, 2002: 576–578; Kerber and Morris, 1966: 457, 470).

John Quincy Adams's diary records his generally low opinion of Jefferson. The president's table talk John Quincy found ridiculous, and he doubted the veracity of many of the stories Jefferson told his guests (C.F. Adams 1874–1877: 1.330–331, 457–458). And though his parents had ceased to communicate with Jefferson, John Quincy made sure that he told his family about his encounters with the chief executive, whether on business or in social situations. Most of what he had to say was formal and correct, but some of it could sound a poignant note as well. Thus in 1809, while in Washington on legal business, he encountered the newly retired president at one of the inaugural balls. "I had some conversation with [Jefferson]," John Quincy wrote his wife; "he asked me whether I continued as fond of POETRY as I was in my youth. I told him, yes, that I did not perceive I had lost any of my relish for good poetry." To which Jefferson replied that he continued to read Homer with satisfaction, "but did not take much delight in Virgil."[5] There were not many men in Washington with whom Jefferson could have had this conversation.

In 1808, John Quincy Adams found himself compelled to resign his seat in the Senate after supporting Jefferson's policy of commercial retaliation against the British. The following year, Madison, the new president, appointed him minister to Russia. This sign of favor, along with John Adams's support for the administration's foreign policy, seemed to signal the possibility of a reconciliation between the senior Adamses and Jefferson. But it took more than John Quincy Adams's move to the Democratic Republican fold to bring about a renewal of contact. Still corresponding with both Thomas Jefferson and John Adams, convinced that the two men still had something to say to each other, the aging Benjamin Rush made it his task to renew the ties between them. In 1811 he wrote separately to each of them, testing the waters to see whether his goal was possible.[6] It was, and in January 1812 a letter from the Adams home in Quincy arrived at Monticello. It informed Jefferson that arriving under separate cover would be what John Adams called "two Pieces of Homespun," in fact a copy of his son John Quincy's recently published Harvard *Lectures on Rhetoric and Oratory*. Jefferson wrote back, slightly confused by Adams's little joke, but in friendly enough fashion. The ice had been broken (Cappon, 1959: 290–293).

For the next fourteen years, one of the great American correspondences followed. John Adams had far less to occupy him in those years than was the case for Jefferson, and so it is no surprise that the letters reaching Monticello from Quincy outnumbered those flowing in the other direction by a ratio of two to one. Throughout the exchange, John Adams played the role of initiator, gadfly, and spark. Jefferson did not always know quite what to make of the letters he kept receiving (twenty-nine in the peak year of 1813, compared to the six he sent Adams that year). He had no desire, even now, to engage in polemics with Adams – he had always hated face-to-face confrontations, and it was no different in his later years. Adams had little hesitation when it came to that sort of thing, but Jefferson would not be drawn.

One consequence of Adams's leisure in retirement was that he had a great deal more time for reading than Jefferson. Because of the remarkable (for its day) size of Jefferson's library, we are accustomed to think of him as devouring books. And yet of the two men, Adams was probably the better-read. At least that was the verdict of Gilbert Chinard, the biographer of both, who wrote that Adams was "a catholic spirit who loved to play with ideas and paradoxes, a contrary mind, ... more widely read than any of his American contemporaries, not excepting Jefferson" (Chinard, 1929: 323; see also Baron and Wright, 2010). This meant that Adams bombarded Jefferson with book titles, noting this or that remarkable thing he'd learned from the latest volume he'd devoured. Jefferson found it all a bit overwhelming. He had, he confessed to Adams, only managed to read "Half a dozen 8vo.s [octavos]" in a year, and he was amazed by the quantities Adams devoured in the same space of time – "Forty three volumes read in one year, and 12. of them quartos!" If only, Jefferson complained, he could escape the need to spend his daylight hours on his correspondence (Cappon, 1959: 505).

If the letters always had a good deal to say about the shared past, there was also, in the early years, a heavy emphasis on theology and philosophy. Jefferson, for example, had little use for Plato; Adams found him considerably more interesting. Adams's skepticism had not decreased with age. "Where are now in 1813, the Perfection and perfectability of human Nature? Where is now, the progress of the human Mind? Where is now the Amelioration of Society?" (Cappon, 1959: 358). Jefferson did not reply to these questions. But the correspondence went on nonetheless. Jefferson also chose not to follow Adams into some of the theological byways the latter pursued. Nor were Jefferson's tastes in literature as catholic as Adams's, who took a great deal of pleasure in the fiction and poetry of the Romantic authors of the day.[7]

After what had happened in 1804, it comes as no surprise that Abigail Adams initially left the Quincy side of the renewed correspondence to her husband. Later on, and once in a great while, she would send a letter of her own to Jefferson (Cappon, 1959: 366–367, 377–378, 500, 503–504, 511, 514). And from time to time John Adams would mention her doings. But this did not mean that Abigail Adams was relegated to the sidelines. Jefferson's letters were shared with members of the extended Adams family, and it was not long before she was reporting to other family members what Mr Jefferson thought about this or that subject. She knew, as well, what her husband was writing to Jefferson, and at least on one occasion she added a postscript of her own to his missive. "I have been looking for some time for a space," she wrote, "in my good Husband's Letters to add the regards of an old friend, which are still cherished … through all the changes … which have taken place since we first became acquainted" (Abigail Adams to John Quincy Adams, Aug. 27 1816 and May 30, 1818, in Kaminski, 2009: 233, 234). Then, in 1818, Abigail Adams died. Her husband was devastated, and Jefferson sent his condolences (Cappon, 1959: 358, 528–530).

One name that figures only rarely in the correspondence is that of John Quincy Adams. There is, to be sure, John Adams's famous description of his son as "our John," harking back to the 1780s, a description that appears in his letter noting the probable outcome of the election of 1824. One might have thought that congratulations to the proud parent of the new president would have been in order in 1825, but Jefferson's reply has a rather perfunctory character, with a somewhat clotted syntax that might be taken as suggesting mixed feelings on the Virginian's part (Cappon, 1959: 607, 609). In any case, Jefferson, who despised the American System, was, as one scholar has put it, "left … stunned and sputtering with rage" by John Quincy Adams's 1825 message to Congress (McCoy, 1986: 118; Burstein and Isenberg, 2011: 588–593). For John Adams, his son's achievements were a matter of enormous pride. Jefferson had no sons, and by the time John Quincy took office his family was coming apart as he plunged headlong into bankruptcy. Was the contrast too difficult for Jefferson? After all the years in which life had seemingly dealt him the better hand, did it now appear as though the Adamses were in the ascendant?

Inevitably, the two elder statesmen found themselves turning to the State of the Union in the years after the War of 1812. (The war itself had been a delicate subject, given's Adams's remarks on the policies that had led to it, and both men must have been happy to reach less treacherous ground.) All was not well, now that peace had returned, and to a greater degree than one might have expected, the two were in relative agreement about the nature of the problems. This was certainly true when it came to the state of the country's finances. John Adams had never really disagreed with Thomas Jefferson about these matters and certainly not when it came to the shortcomings of Hamiltonian economics. The expansion of banks of issue in the postwar period struck both of them as exceedingly dangerous, and they agreed in prophesying the worst. When the panic of 1819 finally came, they could only shake their heads; they had said this was what would happen, and now disaster had struck. Jefferson did not add that it was also a personal disaster, but it was, and that added to the asperity with which he expressed himself in his letters on the subject (Cappon, 1959: 401–402, 424–425, 532, 546–547, 548).

Then there was slavery and the Missouri crisis. Coming fast on the heels of the panic of 1819, it further strengthened the aging patriots' sense that all was not well. John Adams was not the recipient of some of Jefferson's best-known remarks on the Missouri comprise ("the fire bell in the night";

"the wolf by the ears") but it was clear enough from what he wrote that, like Jefferson, he regarded the division over slavery on geographical lines as a dangerous portent for the future of the nation (Jefferson, 1984; 1424; Cappon, 1959: 548, 548–549, 551, 569–570, 571).

By 1820, the pace of the correspondence had begun to slow down. Five letters were written in 1820, six in 1821, seven in 1822, then a spike to ten in 1823, followed by a dip to three in 1824, followed by eight in 1825, and three in 1826. But if the pace was flagging, the content of the letters of the last years suggested that the two aging statesmen remained alert and interested until the end. Jefferson's life was more complicated (he had both the University of Virginia and his own collapsing fortunes to keep him occupied), while Adams's was one increasingly confined to his house and his books and his family.

If during those years John Adams wrote at length about his reading and his other interests, he had less to say about his brief return to politics in 1820. He had been elected a delegate to the Massachusetts Constitutional Convention, called to consider revisions to the state's constitution of 1780, a constitution of which John Adams was the principal author and of which he was extremely proud. Jefferson firmly believed that the Virginia constitution of 1776 (written while he was serving in the Continental Congress) needed to be replaced with a more satisfactory version. And in fact over the years Jefferson had sent a good many letters to his correspondents discussing his theory of periodical constitutional revision, though not to John Adams, it bears noting (Sloan, 1995). It was clearly one of those subjects Jefferson knew better than to raise with Adams. Adams opposed most of the proposals to alter the Massachusetts charter, especially those that would have removed property qualifications for voters (Peterson, 1961: 3–15, 68–70; Scalia, 1999). To be sure, much earlier in their resumed conversation, Adams, citing the *Defence* and *Davila*, had given Jefferson a taste of some of his thinking on what belonged in a constitution, but on this as on many other subjects, there was nothing like a full dialogue between the two aging sages (Cappon, 1959: 355–358).

In fact, neither now, at the close of their lives, nor earlier had the two of them ever seriously attempted to understand the other. John Adams was absolutely right when he told Jefferson in 1791 that they had never explained themselves to each other. They remained, as they had been from the start, at a distance from each other. Adams always had his doubts about democracy; Jefferson always thought the few, rather than the many, were the problem. And each of them held on to the views of the other they had formed long before. Correspond they might, but neither was about to alter a long-nourished sense of what the other's role in America's history had been.

What was different after 1812 was that they agreed, in effect, to disagree. John Adams, clearly, got far too much pleasure out of the exchange to want to bring it to an end by insisting on points he must have known Jefferson would never accept. As for Jefferson, the Virginian negotiated his way through the thickets, sidestepping the pitfalls, and doing his best to remain as polite as he could. That meant, of course, that he often withheld his opinions and certainly that he deliberately failed to take some of the bait that Adams threw out to him. In short, Jefferson was not candid. John Adams, on the other hand, had far fewer inhibitions, and so in the end his was the livelier side of their remarkable correspondence.

As he lay dying on July 4, 1826, John Adams is said to have uttered the words "Thomas Jefferson survives." Jefferson, however, failed to mention Adams in his last remarks (which may have been "Is it the Fourth?") Jefferson's probable question more than hints at a preoccupation with his place in history, just as John Adams's words suggest that he still hadn't been able to put Jefferson behind him. In that sense, Adams was more prophetic than he could have known.[8]

John Quincy Adams would return to Washington, DC, after he was defeated in his attempt at re-election in 1828. It was there that he read Thomas Jefferson Randolph's four-volume 1829 edition of his grandfather's papers, the *Memoir, Correspondence and Miscellanies.* He was not impressed. Jefferson, in John Quincy Adams's eyes, was a deeply problematic character. If the Virginian had been devoted to liberty, and John Quincy Adams did not deny that, there was also good reason to deplore his behavior. "His treatment of Washington, of Knox, of my father, of Hamilton, of Bayard, who made him President of the United States, and, lastly, of me, is marked with features of perfidy worthy of Tiberius Caesar and Louis the Eleventh of France." Some years later, refreshing his recollection on the point of Jefferson's antislavery views, Adams noted that "His treatment of my father was double-dealing, treacherous, and false beyond all toleration." In short, he concluded, Jefferson's "success through a long life ... seems, to my imperfect vision, a slur upon the moral government of the world" (Nevins, 1928: 409, 468). Clearly John Quincy lacked his father's ability to engage with Jefferson. Equally clearly, the Adams family was not done with the man from Monticello.

There was more to come, and it would be John and Abigail's great-grandson, John Quincy's grandson Henry, who wrote the classic account of Jefferson's presidency in *The History of the United States During the Administration of Thomas Jefferson* (H. Adams, 1984b). But it was not only the Adamses who produced historians. Jefferson's great-great-grandson, Archibald Cary Coolidge, was a member of the Harvard History Department from 1893 until his death in 1928. A student of international relations, Coolidge chose not to devote his scholarly attention to his distinguished progenitor, and so it was the Adamses, in a sense, who had the last word.[9] But what a magnificent last word it was. Jefferson might not have liked everything it had to say, but he would have had to acknowledge that in the end the Adamses paid him due tribute.

Notes

1 On the creation of the Jefferson Memorial – a Democratic riposte to the Republicans' Lincoln Memorial, as it were – see Merrill D. Peterson, 1960: 420–432. Efforts to erect something similar for not merely John Adams, but for all four generations of the historic Adams family, have not gotten beyond the early stages. See http://adamsmemorial.org/ accessed Nov. 8, 2012.

2 As Merrill Peterson put it: "The New Englander was, basically, an insecure person. His yearnings for fame, his notorious vanity and airs of conceit, grew from massive layers of self-doubt" (Peterson, 1976: 8).

3 Boyd et al., 1950–: 6.241, 11.94–95, Thomas Jefferson to James Madison, Feb. 14, 1783, Jan. 30, 1787; Boyd et al., 1950–: 6.265; 14.297–300, Madison to Thomas Jefferson, May 6, 1783; Oct. 7,1788.

4 Julian Boyd's editorial note, "*Rights of Man*: The Contest of Burke and Paine in America" (Boyd et al., 1950–: 20.268–290), tells this story as Jefferson might have.

5 Ford, 1913–1917: 3.77, John Quincy Adams to John Adams, Nov. 3, 1804; W.C. Ford, 1913–1917: 3.288–289, John Quincy Adams to Louisa Catherine Adams, Mar. 3, 1809.

6 The details of how this happened are described in Peterson, 1976: 100–104. For an explanation of the reconciliation that focuses on its sources in domestic events in the Adams household, see Gelles, 2009: 276–277.

7 Adams discussed this aspect of his reading with other correspondents, but not with Jefferson. See, e.g., Schutz and Adair: 187–188 (John Adams to Benjamin Rush, Dec. 27, 1810, praising Jane Porter's 1810 *The Scottish Chiefs* and Sir Walter Scott's poetry).

8 In fact, Jefferson was already dead when Adams uttered his words. See Ferling, 1992: 444. The Monticello website has an excellent discussion of the problems surrounding what Jefferson did or did not say. See www.monticello.org/site/research-and-collections/jeffersons-last-words. For a stimulating look at what it may mean that the two died on the same day, see Battin, 2005: 175–185.

9 Coolidge joined the department in 1893 after receiving his PhD at Freiburg in 1892. Best known for his work on European diplomatic history, he is also remembered as the director of the Harvard libraries from 1910 to his death in 1928 (Coolidge and Lord, 1932; Byrnes, 1982).

Guide to Further Reading

The basic documentary source for Jefferson and the early Adamses remains Lester J. Cappon, ed., *The Adams–Jefferson Letters: The Complete Correspondence between John and Abigail Adams and Thomas Jefferson*, 2 vols. (1959). I have used the 1987 one-volume reprint. The texts in Cappon's collection are gradually being replaced by those in Julian P. Boyd et al., eds., *The Papers of Thomas Jefferson*, 38 vols. to date (1950–) and, for the important later correspondence, J. Jefferson Looney, ed., *The Papers of Thomas Jefferson: Retirement Series*, 8 vols. to date (Princeton, 2004–). While Cappon collected all the letters and provided reliable texts, the annotation in his edition is minimal, and in many cases readers will find much-needed explanatory information in the Princeton editions. For a sampling of the theme of Adams and Jefferson agreeing to disagree, see Merrill D. Peterson, *Adams and Jefferson: A Revolutionary Dialogue* (1976), and Joanne B. Freeman, "Jefferson and Adams: Friendship and the Power of the Letter," in Frank Shuffelton, ed., *The Cambridge Companion to Thomas Jefferson* (2009), 168–178. On the enduring Jefferson–Hamilton conflict, see Stephen Knott, "'Opposed in Death as in Life': Hamilton and Jefferson in American Memory," in Douglas Ambrose and Robert W. Martin, eds., *The Many Faces of Alexander Hamilton: The Life and Legacy of America's Most Elusive Founding Father* (2006), 25–53. The best account of John Adams's later years is to be found in Joseph E. Ellis, *Passionate Sage: The Character and Legacy of John Adams* (1993) Also helpful in placing the later Adams is Peter Shaw, *The Character of John Adams* (1976).

Chapter Twenty-Four

The Adamses on Screen

Nancy Isenberg and Andrew Burstein

Has Abigail or John Adams ever really been forgotten? In the hype surrounding David McCullough's popular 2001 biography *John Adams*, the publisher's pitch (and, later, received wisdom) was that this "magisterial" work had restored the second president to his rightful place in historical memory. The claim was only half-right: historical memory does appear to be getting shorter and shorter; but the notion that Adams had to be "recovered" was little more than a marketing ploy. Like an expensive Hollywood blockbuster (which it would enlarge into later in the decade), *John Adams* was lavished with praise before its release, and the avuncular McCullough was crowned as America's storyteller. He was the "American Homer" and a "national treasure," the latter, of course, a metaphor most commonly applied to the Declaration of Independence and other pieces of precious parchment kept under treated glass at the National Archives. Predictably, McCullough received a Pulitzer Prize (his second), the brass ring of commercial publishing. By 2007, over 3 million copies had been sold, making his single-volume treatment the bestselling literary biography in American history (Gates, 2001; Leopold, 2001; Thomas, 2001; Massachusetts Cultural Council, 1999; Rose, 2008; Billington, 2003; Conn, 2009: 47).

The success of the book quickly leached into politics. It gave momentum to a campaign to erect a monument to "His Rotundity" in the Tidal Basin in Washington, DC. Testifying before Congress that Adams's likeness belonged in the neighborhood of the Jefferson Memorial, historian Joseph Ellis said that Americans needed to remember the forgotten Founder who was, he said, "probably the most under-appreciated great man in American

A Companion to John Adams and John Quincy Adams, First Edition.
Edited by David Waldstreicher.

history" (Parry-Giles, 2008: 92). Citizens also needed to know the great man's wife Abigail, whom Ellis described as his "one woman cabinet." In his words, their dynastic "love story" had produced the "greatest political and intellectual family in American political history" (Lambrose, 2002: 212).

For this historian, putting Adams on par with Jefferson was crucial. The same was true for McCullough, who testified before Congress as well. He had embarked on a dual biography of Adams and Jefferson, but abandoned Jefferson when he discovered that he could not identify with him. Dueling monuments would correct the gross imbalance in their legacies. John would not have to stand up to Jefferson alone. He would be part of a triumvirate that included his wife Abigail and their presidential son John Quincy (Pasley, 2002).

The cultural power brokers in Hollywood took notice, leading to the creation of a big-budget series. With its cinematic fireworks, HBO's 2008 *John Adams* dramatically projected the lives of the historic couple in high definition. The production won more Emmys than any other mini-series to date, thirteen in all, and four Golden Globes. What had begun as McCullough's valentine to John Adams turned into a media orgy over the supposedly forgotten founder and his spunky wife.

The HBO mini-series was not the first on the Adamses. In 1976, for the nation's bicentennial, public television aired an even longer work, *The Adams Chronicles.* This thirteen-part saga devoted most of its time to John and Abigail, though in its effort to create a dynastic family, it covered their heirs as well. John Quincy Adams was featured as diplomat, secretary of state, and president; his son Charles Francis Adams was the family historian; Charles Francis's son Henry Adams was a public intellectual and academic historian whose work continues to receive public notice in the twenty-first century.

The 1976 series won numerous awards. Contemporary critics, enamored with the HBO production, somehow ignored its predecessor. In fact, the HBO *John Adams* borrowed heavily from *The Adams Chronicles* in the way it developed its characters, in selecting which scenes to shoot, and in its portrayal of the couple's marriage. There is rich irony in this: the PBS series, in combination with earlier popular culture and film images of the Adamses, was far more influential in shaping the narrative than its ostensible source, David McCullough's biography.

It is the persistence of the Adamses in popular culture, not their omission, that best explains their popularity in the twenty-first century. Just four years before *The Adams Chronicles* appeared, John and Abigail made their singing debut in the musical production *1776.* Going back another quarter-century to 1952, Abigail (and her idealized marriage) was featured in one of the first shows of the Hallmark Hall of Fame television series; it was entitled, "A Woman of the Ages." In 1964, one of the most heralded actresses of the twentieth century, Helen Hayes, played Abigail in a live stage performance of *The White House* in the real White House. William Gibson, author of *The Miracle Worker*, the famous television play about

Helen Keller, contributed an Abigail and John piece with his 1969 stage play, *American Primitive*. Gibson described the work as "eyewitness history," and deliberately employed a familial metaphor in calling what he had done "self-portraits of two of our parents." Stage and television actor William Daniels, best known for his role in the television series *St. Elsewhere*, first made a career of playing Adamses, father and son. In the 1952 Hallmark drama, he was cast as the young John Quincy Adams; in *1776*, he reprised his stage role as John Adams; in *The Adams Chronicles* he was John Quincy once more (Altschuler, 2007: 7; Dasgupta, 1984: 295).[1]

Actually, the history of the Adamses in film is even older than this. In *The Declaration of Independence* (1911), one of the first movies made by the Edison Company, John and Abigail were the starring attractions. Broadway actress Miriam Nesbitt, who appeared in over 120 silent films, played Mrs John Adams. Harry Linson was John, while Nesbitt's future husband, Marc McDermott, was cast as Thomas Jefferson.

The refrain that the Adamses have languished in obscurity belongs to Founding Father legend rather than to historical truth. It is derived, in part, from John Adams's own complaints that his contributions to America's independence, as well as his presidency, would be erased from history. He intensely disliked the blind idolatry of George Washington and was well aware that any criticism he might make of the "First of Men" would be dismissed as jealous cant. In 1790, then Vice President Adams confessed to a fellow signer of the Declaration, Dr Benjamin Rush (who demonstrably shared his view) that "the History of our Revolution will be one continued Lye [*sic*] from one end to the other. The essence of the whole will be *that Dr. Franklins electrical Rod, smote the Earth and out sprung General Washington. That Franklin electrified him with his rod – and thence forward these two conducted all the Policy, Negotiations, Legislatures and War.*" With irresistible logic, he added: "One nation cannot adore more than one man at a time." Adams recognized that, in the public's opinion, fable would always trump historical accuracy (Butterfield 1951: 1207).

When writing the trusted Rush, Adams did enjoy gossiping about the foibles of Washington and others. His most famous insult, that Alexander Hamilton was the "bastard brat of the Scot peddler," was one of many ribald slurs he forwarded to the Philadelphia physician. He was no less annoyed by the sanctification of the Declaration of Independence, telling Rush in 1811 that it was a "juvenile" production. Jefferson's composition was "all theatrical show," he insisted. Not only did "Jefferson r[u]n away with all the stage effect," but also the "glory of it." If Washington was a man of modest attainments, Jefferson was a publicity hound, stealing the limelight. The Virginian's authorship had diverted the public from honoring what Adams felt was far more momentous: his own July 2nd oration on the floor of the Continental Congress, urging passage of the resolution for independence (P. Shaw, 1976: 100; Bailyn, 1962: 252; Schutz and Adair, 1967: 48).

In declaring that a nation rarely had room for more than one celebrated founder, Adams refused to let the already standard version of history take its course. In retirement, he devoted considerable time to repairing his reputation. In 1809, he wrote a series of letters to a Boston newspaper, defending his presidency against one of its loudest critics – the late Alexander Hamilton. Adams waged a private paper war with Mercy Otis Warren, who claimed in her multi-volume *History of the American Revolution* (1805) that he had a "partiality in favor of monarchic government." She had confined his role in the Revolution to a mere four pages (P. Shaw, 1976: 295; Zagarri, 1995: 150–153).

Warren was not just any woman. She was a member of the prominent Otis family of Massachusetts, a political playwright and poet, and a constitutional essayist. Impressed with her mind, John Adams had earlier encouraged her to write a faithful account of American independence. He projected that she would become the American Catherine Macaulay, referring to the celebrated eighteenth-century English historian. But despite their friendship and his previous regard for her talents, Adams found it impossible to forgive her after reading her epic history. It seems that hell hath no fury like a Founder scorned! (Zagarri, 1995: xv, 7–8, 55, 90, 155, 158–159).

The second president took a radically different approach in repairing the breach with his former vice president, who had wrested the presidency from him in 1801. Jefferson had grown extremely close to both John and Abigail during the years when their respective diplomatic missions in Europe coincided; Abigail had called Jefferson "one of the choice ones of earth." In the 1790s, partisan wrangling, newspaper attacks, and nasty gossip soured the relationship. By 1801, with Jefferson's victory over Adams, all communication, cordial or otherwise, came to an abrupt end. Ten years later, with the healing intervention of Dr Rush, Adams renewed his friendship with Jefferson. While they would never gaze on each other again, the two ex-presidents engaged, for fifteen years, in wide-ranging correspondence on politics, ancient philosophy, celebrity, even sex (Burstein, 1995: 8, 175, 178–179, 185).

The letters were carefully calculated. Without them, modern filmmakers might not have been able to wrap their heads around an Adams who stood toe-to-toe with the eloquent Jefferson. In marrying his fortunes to Jefferson's, Adams seemed intent on proving that the two of them were really not that far apart in their political beliefs – or, more critically, in intellectual and historical stature. The exchange of letters displayed the two men as congenial sparring partners and, more important, equals. Adams relished this image of himself. Indeed, the point is that he has convinced many popular writers and historians that his self-image is the most appealing and most accurate image of him.

Abigail's elevation into a founding icon took a somewhat different path. In 1826, soon after her husband's death, along with Jefferson, on the fiftieth

Fourth of July, she was praised in a Boston newspaper as a "critical instrument," helpmeet, and spiritual counselor, who relieved her husband of "political burdens," which in turn helped him "promote the general welfare." Indeed, her fame and her legacy remained tied to that of her husband; in most depictions, she stands at his side, nurturing and encouraging him, the devoted wife and trusted confidante (Barker-Benfield, 2010: 3).

Minimizing the very real tensions arising from the great amount of time they spent apart, everyone seems to want to tout the Adamses' marital harmony. In his well-received 1962 biography of John, Page Smith called Abigail a loving "gyroscope" for her husband. He expressed admiration for the balance maintained throughout their fifty-four year marriage, seeing theirs as an enduring partnership unmatched in history. The founding editor of the modern edition of the Adams Papers went so far as to claim that their rich and perceptive letters revealed that the pair could "read each other's mind" (Barker-Benfield, 2010: 4; Page Smith, 1962: 1.71; Butterfield, et al., 1975: 8).

But this, too, was derivative. The untarnished legend of the perfect marriage that modern filmmakers have as their source of emotional "truth" really took form in the 1840s, when John and Abigail's grandson Charles Francis Adams first published the couple's personal letters. For the centennial celebration of 1876, he issued a new edition of his *Familiar Letters of John Abigail and his Wife, Abigail Adams, During the Revolution.* In 1975, as the bicentennial approached, three editors of the Adams Papers issued a new edition of letters, *The Book of Abigail and John*, covering the period from 1762 to 1784. The same editors continued what Charles Francis had begun, describing the two as "the prototypical American couple" (C.F. Adams, 1840: 1.xli, ixvii–lxx; Gelles, 1988: 656; Barker-Benfield, 2010: 3; Butterfield et al., 1975: 9).

Between Charles Francis Adams's second edition and the more scholarly version of the couple's letters published in 1975, American readers were entertained by all kinds of pulp fiction and trite nonfiction. Dorothie Bobbé brought silly romantic fluff to her 1929 *Abigail Adams, The Second First Lady*. Janet Whitney followed with the first full-length biography of Abigail in 1947, while violating virtually every canon of serious scholarship. She invented dialogue and imputed inner thoughts to her heroine. For Whitney, romantic clichés defined the couple: John was a "man's man," and Abigail possessed that "ideal combination" of intelligence and "feminine softness," which allowed John, more than the other Founders, to achieve the "perfect mating." As his path was shaped by the forces of history, Abigail "chose it with him," dutifully assisting John as he pursued his higher destiny (J. Whitney, 1947: 9, 29, 76, 130; Gelles, 1988: 661–662).

But the worst romantic drivel came from the imagination of Irving Stone, a highly successful writer of biographical novels. His first successful publication within this genre was *Lust for Life* (1934), based on Vincent

Van Gogh's letters. He again received popular acclaim for *The Agony and the Ecstasy* (1961), recreating the life of Michelangelo. Both books became big-budget Hollywood films. His 1950 novel, *The President's Wife*, was made into a film starring Charlton Heston as the backwoods general Andrew Jackson, with vivacious Susan Hayward as Rachel Jackson, *sans* the corncob pipe. The rough-hewn Jackson is portrayed as a "Father Knows Best" sort of fellow, domestic and loving; in the scripted words of Susan Hayward's Rachel, this was "the side of the man that I see." Rachel's only aim in life was to love her man.

Stone's cloying *Those Who Love* (1965) was his Adams piece. It recast Abigail as a Rachel Jackson type, that is, the perfect 1950s housewife who wouldn't want to "change a thing" about her husband. Abigail's uncontrollable "awe" for John transformed her from a "gay, bright girl" to a complete woman. Marriage was the essence of her being. Stone rhapsodizes: "The fulfillment of their love had been more meaningful than she could have dreamed." In this construction, every little girl should hope to grow up and marry a man like John Adams (Stone, 1965: 53– 57, 80, 129).

24.1 The Plain Dealer: *1776*

The glorious schmaltz of the 1950s and 1960s paved the way for the musical *1776*, which was first staged on Broadway in 1969. Made into a Columbia Pictures film in 1972, it centered on the effort to secure independence in the Second Continental Congress. John Adams is the lead, Franklin, in the words of one commentator, his "sage sidekick," with Jefferson as the silent, lovesick author of the Declaration. Abigail is a principal character, though she is not in Philadelphia; John has imaginary conversations with her, especially when he retreats to the bell tower in disgust over the do-nothing Congress. He sits beside the Liberty Bell, the voice of liberty and political salvation. Abigail is his conscience (Seiler, 2003: 154).

The film is over-the-top camp, silly, comedic, a gleeful romp, punctuated by moments of slapstick. As Thomas Fleming writes in Mark Carnes (ed.) *Past Imperfect* (1996), a collection of essays on history in the movies, the film *1776* reduces the Continental Congress to a forerunner of the fraternity featured in the 1978 film "*Animal House*." Yet in drawing this comparison, Fleming appears unaware of the history of camp, which the play draws upon, and which goes back even earlier than the American Revolution, to English Restoration farces of the seventeenth century. A farce is comic drama that relies on stock characters, outrageous plot twists, sexual innuendo, and large doses of buffoonish behavior. The very idea of the Founders dancing and singing pushes the limits of credulity. It quickly becomes clear in the Warner Brothers film that sex and virility constitute the driving force in this bawdy bicentennial tale (Fleming, 1996: 92).

In the musical, Congress is cast as a menagerie of fools. Stephen Hopkins of Rhode Island is a pious Quaker with a weakness for rum. Samuel Chase of Maryland is a portly man with a preposterous wig. Known among his enemies as "Bacon Face," Chase eats in Congress and is so unwieldy that he becomes stuck in his chair. President John Hancock's major duty is not pounding the gravel but swatting flies. Thomas McKean of Delaware wears plaid and speaks in Scottish brogue. The men rarely debate ideas, preferring instead to trade jokes and insults.

John Adams's principal enemy in the faux-drama is John Dickinson of Pennsylvania, who is caricatured as a smooth-tongued elitist. Adams and Dickinson come to blows – a clashing of canes, not fists – after a fast-paced exchange of absurd taunts. The Pennsylvanian calls Adams "this this *a-gi-ta-tor*, this demagogue, this madman," and Adams, stuttering in anger, bursts out with: "you-you-you-fribble!" ("Fribble" implied effeminacy, the eighteenth-century version of "girly-man.") Next, John calls him a coward. The insults fly:

DICKINSON: "Madman!"
ADAMS: "Landlord!"
DICKINSON: "Lawyer!"

With this final, apparently unforgivable slur, a frenzied melee breaks out among the delegates, with an impulsive bit of swordplay (Stone and Edwards, 1972: 46–47).

Peter Stone, the author of the play, decided to conflate the two Adamses (Samuel and John), which explains why Dickinson calls John an agitator. Apparently, too many Adamses would have confused the presumably history-challenged audience. Indeed, this is a problem for most of the films about the extended Adams family, insofar as Cousin Samuel's very presence cannot but detract from John's role as the singular prophet of American liberty (Stone and Edwards, 1972: 169).

Though there is no evidence that such an event ever occurred, the preceding episode resembled a famous brawl that took place twenty-two years later on the floor of the House of Representatives. In 1798, shortly after Irish-born Vermont representative Mathew Lyon spat in the face of Yale-educated Connecticut congressman Roger Griswold, the offended Griswold advanced on Lyon, with a cane raised in anger. To defend himself, the Irishman desperately grabbed fireplace tongs, and the two had at it. In *1776*, the congressional brawl represents a dramatic inversion of expectations, as the veneer of gentlemanly respectability is shed, revealing the fallible and fractious nature of the men we traditionally imagine as deep thinkers and moral giants (Burstein and Isenberg, 2010: 328).

The plot of *1776* concerns John Adams's inability to persuade his fellow delegates to support independence. He is, in his own words (and this is taken from the real John Adams's writings), "obnoxious and disliked." In the first musical number, John dashes through the large hall while the rest of the congressional chorus sings, "Sit down, John, For God's sake, sit down." The number ends when a voice cries out, "Will someone shut that man up!" "Never, never!" John retorts, fleeing the chamber in disgust (Stone and Edwards, 1972: 4).

He is convinced he is right, and that the do-nothing Congress is to blame. There is one remarkable line – "Consider yourselves fortunate that you have John Adams to abuse, for no sane man would tolerate it!" – that smacks of modern history. Adams sound very much like an embittered Richard Nixon, after the failed presidential candidate of 1960 lost the California governor's race in 1962 and called what he fashioned as his last press conference ever. With that famous Nixon snarl, he harangued the circle of reporters by pronouncing: "You won't have Dick Nixon to kick around anymore." There's a bit of pre-presidential Nixonian frustration in *1776's* John Adams. Lacking in tact, he needs the help of the cannier, calculating Franklin if he is to succeed at all (Stone and Edwards, 1972: 3; Wills, 2002: 412).

The gouty old Doctor F, who exudes confidence and knows the ropes, tells John to step aside and let someone else bring forward the resolution for independence. The scheme is to persuade Richard Henry Lee to ride to his home state of Virginia and get the legislature there to back independence. Though the historical Lee was a classical scholar, this Lee is the most buffoonish of all the characters in the film, a colonial version of Gomer Pyle of the 1960s TV sitcom, wide-eyed, good-natured, but too dense to realize that Franklin and Adams are pulling his strings. He even sounds like the hapless Gomer, whose favorite catch phrase was a sing-songy "G-o-l-l-y." The film *1776* features a tune that is a play on his name: "Here a Lee, There a Lee, Everywhere, a Lee, Lee" (Stone and Edwards, 1972: 15–19).

The delegates need more than the resolution, of course. They must have an official Declaration of Independence. The drafting committee is formed: Franklin, Adams, Jefferson, Robert Livingston, and Roger Sherman. A quill pen is passed among them, and ends up in Jefferson's hands. He is distraught. "Virginia's most famous lover," as John tags him, wants to return to and visit with his young bride (Stone and Edwards, 1972: 67).

Just as important to the film is its sexual humor. Lee talks about stopping at home to "refresh the missus," and sings that all the women of Virginia are "full bosomed." When Jefferson says he must return to his wife, the Quaker Stephen Hopkins tells him, "Give her a good one for me, young feller!" John and Abigail sing about their separation in terms of enforced celibacy, each taking up vows "like a nun in a cloister" and "a monk in an abbey." Thomas Jefferson is only able to finish the hallowed Declaration after John (acting as his pimp) retrieves his wife from Virginia. Martha Jefferson then sings an entire song about how Thomas woos her to bed with his violin – or more accurately, plays her like a violin. Castration jokes, breeding humor, rakish fun, virility contests, and fertility references are the principal forms of comedy in the film (Stone and Edwards, 1972: 14, 18, 30, 67–68, 72, 78–81).

It is remarkable how closely the play and film imitate a Restoration farce. We have the stock characters (the glutton is Chase; the graybeard, Franklin; the rake, Jefferson). Like most Restoration plays, which directed their riotous satire at court politics, this one converts the Continental Congress into a republican court, where most of the film plays out.

The stage play that most resembles *1776* is William Wycherley's *The Plain Dealer* (1676). Its lead character, Manly, is a misanthropic figure like John Adams. Both Manly and John are obsessed with the hypocrisy of others and speak their minds regardless of consequences. They are, above all, men of action rather than wit. Manly's typical form of speech is the outburst, the complaint; he rails against human foibles and mindless ceremony. In like manner, John Adams sings about the curse of being sent to "foul, fetid" Philadelphia, and protests the "piddle, twiddle" actions of the Congress, where "not one damned thing do we solve" (Stone and Edwards, 1972: 5; Berman, 1984: 466–468, 471, 474).

John is like Manly, a plain-dealing man, and the only honest man in the room. He alone tells the truth (as he sees it). Adams and Manly are narcissists, prone to folly, because they cannot quite understand how society works. When Jefferson finishes his draft of the declaration, John says: "It's a masterpiece. I'm to be congratulated." Franklin gently but purposefully mocks him here and throughout the film. Knowing that Adams is oblivious to his self-centered fantasy, both Franklin and Abigail serve as his handlers; they curb his egocentric excesses and make harmless his pessimism. Franklin's outburst as the drama rises perfectly captures Adams's misanthropic tendencies: "Either start learning how to live with them," the old man tells him, "or pack up and go home – but in any case, stop acting like a Boston fishwife!" (Stone and Edwards, 1972: 102, 124).

Adams's adversary in the film, John Dickinson, leader of the conservative faction in Congress, resembles "Lord Plausible" in *The Plain Dealer*. It is he whom Manly castigates as the embodiment of superfluous ceremony. Though centuries separate them, playwrights William Wycherley and Peter Stone both use the metaphor of the dance to describe the stifling ritual of the immovable status quo: Dickinson leads Congress in a minuet of "cool, cool conservative men" and their "neatly ordered lives, with well-endowered wives." It is yet another example of sexual innuendo, for rather than dreaming of "well-*endowed* wives" (the full-bosomed maids of Virginia that Richard Henry Lee praised), they wish for large dowries that will be passed from father-in-law to new husband – property, not feminine beauty, is the physical asset valued by the ruling elite (Stone and Edwards, 1972: 92–94; Berman, 1984: 471).

Abigail herself is a composite of the two major female characters in *The Plain Dealer*. Fidelia (names are transparent) overlooks Manly's flaws because she is in love with him, while Olivia (a name taken from Shakespeare's gender-bending *Twelfth Night*), is equipped with a ready wit and reminds Manly of his shortcomings. Wycherley's Olivia has a masculine wit, military metaphors to describe love quarrels, and refuses to be conquered by Manly (Rogers, 1961: 149, 154–155, 158; Hynes, 1996: 177–178).

In their last dialogue, Abigail reveals to John her double nature. He has humbly retreated to the bell tower and opens his imaginary conversation with her by wondering what has happened to him: "John Adams, the great John Adams, Wise man of the East." He pleads for her help, and she replies by prodding him to admit that he is a desperate man: "You don't usually need my advice." John responds (oblivious to how insulting his words are): "Yes, well, there doesn't appear [to be] anyone else right now."

John then lists his faults:

> "Obnoxious and disliked."
> ABIGAIL: "Nonsense, John."
> JOHN: "That I am unwilling to face reality."
> ABIGAIL: "Foolishness."
> JOHN: "That I am pig-headed."
> ABIGAIL (SMILING): "Ah, well, there you have me, John.
> I'm afraid you *are* pig-headed.
> (Stone and Edwards, 1972: 124–126)

She is the witty Olivia, until she dismisses the notion that he has ever failed her, adding a line that retains the double meaning of pride and exasperation: "After all, I am Mrs. John Adams – that's quite a lot for one lifetime." Quoting back his own words to him, she chastises him for diminishing himself: in doing so, he diminishes her as his wife. The substance of their earlier exchange is a quantity of saltpeter (fertilizer) that he had asked her to collect from the women of their Boston neighborhood. It is delivered to him in Philadelphia, and through her reliability and generosity, she rescues him from his depression (Stone and Edwards, 1972: 126–128).

The film ends with the signing of the Declaration. Adams and Jefferson battle through one more contest of manhood, when Adams insists that the penman change "inalienable" to "unalienable." Jefferson (played by the 6 ft 6 in Ken Howard), towers over Adams (William Daniels is 5 ft 7 in), and Adams backs down. Franklin, the presumptive tutor, says, "Good for you John!" But under his breath, John insists that he will speak to the printer about the "in/un" matter later. So, John Adams is still John Adams, stubborn and demanding, but perhaps a little less aggressively self-righteous. As he signs the Declaration, the liberty bell starts ringing. One by one, the others sign, as a light shines on Adams's face. He is no longer one angry man railing against the world. He stands at a table alongside Franklin and Jefferson, silently frozen in time, the text of Declaration looming over the final scene (Stone and Edwards, 1972: 141–142).

The "First of Men" – George Washington – never makes an appearance. His reputation is safely guarded from the campier moments of the film. He is, however, something of a prophet of doom. His part is restricted to the reading of his dispatches, which are always filled with news of disaster, if not utter despair. His activities remain separated from the circus of politics, but his absence makes him less of an agent of change than the other actors. He is little more here than a frustrated instrument of the Continental Congress.

Though Adams alludes to his future fate as the forgotten Founder, wrongly overshadowed by Franklin's electrical rod that begets the divine Washington, the New Englander's starring role in the play and film suggests that he protests too much. The message of *1776* is that a trio of eccentric men – the obnoxious Adams, the devilish Franklin, and the rakish man of words Jefferson – all need each other if, in Franklin's words, they are to play "midwives to an egg" (Stone and Edwards, 1972: 103).

Abigail is the supportive helpmeet, the caretaker of the family in John's absence. But she is most of all his muse. His imaginary conversations render her an oracle of sorts; she not only reads his mind, but also brings out his best qualities. In the golden age of Hollywood, that's what the spunky female lead did. She stands by her man, while her husband occupies center stage as one of the sacred Trinity in the singular achievement of American independence. This Trinity required earthy qualities: the masterful cunning of Franklin, the virile prose of Jefferson, and the pigheaded determination of the plain dealer from Massachusetts.

24.2 The American Dynasty

The Adams Chronicles aired on PBS in 1976. This ambitious series was the most elaborate televised story to feature the Adamses, and it looked to a British theatrical model for a highbrow style of storytelling. It was a close relative to successful British productions *Upstairs/Downstairs* and *The Six Wives of Henry VIII*, involving nine different playwrights, six directors, historical consultants from the Adams Papers project, over three thousand costumes, and a large cast. George Grizzard played John Adams throughout; two actresses, Kathryn Walker and Leora Dana, were featured as the young and the mature Abigail respectively.[2]

The Adams Chronicles was a pastiche of different genres. It was, first, a dynastic family soap opera, which focused on courtship, marriage, and troubled children, much like a Jane Austen novel. It was also part history textbook, with each of the Adams men donning the robe of schoolmaster, explaining the dynasty's major accomplishments and recognized failures.

Perhaps the best example of this narrative convention occurs when John Quincy Adams, as secretary of state, stands in front of a map of the United States, like a teacher at the head of the class, and lectures President Monroe on the value of the "Monroe" Doctrine.

The PBS Adams saga was, finally, a Greek tragedy. In his introduction to the companion book, former professor Daniel Boorstin, newly appointed Librarian of Congress, emphasized this irony. For Boorstin, family patriarch John Adams was a "self-made aristocrat," beneficiary of the American dream; yet his children suffered under a "heavy burden" as heirs in a country that celebrated democracy and disavowed Old World aristocracies. The Adams curse defined the classic paradox: they were moral paragons and thorough misfits, architects of America's creation who become exiles from Eden once the hurly-burly circus of partisan politics took hold (Shepherd, 1975: xxxi).

In the opening scene, John Adams appears the rustic Everyman, a self-fashioned counterpart to King George III, who rules by way of a formal inheritance. The narrative voiceover notes that the pair are the same age, yet two men could not be more different. The king is a debauched and effeminate royal, surrounded by opulence. In a later episode he is called "madman" (in fact he suffered from dementia, but much later in life); it is the same slur Dickinson uses against Adams in *1776*. But in *The Adams Chronicles*, John is seen as anything but unhinged: pitching hay and splitting rails, he is an iconic rival to Abe Lincoln as the first log-cabin president. A constant refrain for John and Abigail is their shared desire to depart the bustle (and taint) of politics and return to their pastoral homestead. The family hearth is their touchstone, the source of their innately American virtue.

The two actresses who play Abigail illustrate two distinctly different marriages. Kathryn Walker is the younger and more robust, appearing onscreen from the Adamses' courtship through the period of John's post-Revolutionary role as minister to Great Britain. Walker was apparently well-suited to historical drama: the year before, she played Martha Washington in the Hallmark Hall of Fame version of "Valley Forge." A few years later, she would play Anna, granddaughter of Franklin and Eleanor Roosevelt, in another mini-series.

Though she never admitted it, Walker chose as her model for Abigail the actress Katherine Hepburn. Indeed, for a strong female protagonist, many actresses have borrowed from Hepburn, whose feminist credentials dated back to her suffragist mother. The other obvious reason for modeling her character after "the great Kate" is that the witty New Englander was routinely paired with Spencer Tracy, whose gruffness and Everyman qualities matched the screen persona of John Adams. In *State of the Union* (1948), Tracy starred as a presidential candidate whose virtue is threatened by monied interests; Kate, his no-nonsense wife, ultimately saves him. The following year, in *Adam's Rib*, they played husband and wife as dueling attorneys: Hepburn the feminist, Tracy the male chauvinist. Hepburn wins the trial, while Tracy gets in the last word, forcing her to admit he was right all along. To extend the genealogy, in the last of the Tracy–Hepburn films, *Guess Who's Coming to Dinner?* (1967), the couple copes with their only daughter marrying a black man. The daughter is played by Katherine Houghton Grant, Hepburn's niece – and Grant appears in two episodes of *The Adams Chronicles*, as the Adamses' only surviving daughter, Abigail's namesake, who was known as "Nabby" (Dickens, 1971: 139–146, 184–188).

In *The Adams Chronicles*, Walker's Abigail is feisty, ready and able to curb John's vanity. She carries herself with a natural grace that her somewhat naïve but endearing mate is unable to muster. The bedroom is their conference room, where Abigail smoothes John's rough edges and gives him words of encouragement. George Grizzard, as Adams, had earlier made a name for himself in Edward Albee's contentious plays about marital strife; as one critic noted, his distinctive talent for moving quickly from "geniality to intensity" suited him for the emotional swings of Adams (Berkvist, 2007).

The PBS version of the Adamses' marriage is a consummate love match. When John reunites with Abigail in France after years of separation, he remarks the next day of being "twenty years younger than yesterday," implying that they had enjoyed a night-time romp in the hay. Both are obliged to defend their sexual fidelity: when Jefferson alludes to an attractive "wench" (one of John's servants) in France, John states definitively that he "only thinks of Abigail." James Lovell, a Massachusetts member of Congress (who in real life engaged in a racy correspondence with Abigail), dares to make a pass at Walker's Abigail. She sends him away, telling her daughter: "There is nothing on this farm that could satisfy his appetite!" The television series clumsily tries to address an obvious tension: why, if the Adamses were so much in love, did they spend eight years apart? In 1970s America, the assumption is, "If you can't be with the one you love, love the one you're with"; so if absence doesn't make the heart grow fonder anymore, scriptwriters had to manufacture impossible scenes in which the couple confirmed their chaste devotion to each other (Holton, 2009: 136).

Walker's Abigail, like Hepburn, had to bow to male privilege. Though strong, she acknowledged her dependence on John. She can grab a rifle, ready to defend her home when John is away from the farm, but when she realizes the noise is only a bucket hitting the wall of the well, she collapses in fear. Her heroism is circumscribed, her feminism undercut.

She confesses to John that she must be content with the "small part of the world" that is hers, and knows that women must "conceal their passions from the world." This telling line distorts the historical Abigail Adams's more complicated and radical vision for women during the Revolution. She wished for women to have the same educational opportunities as men, and she celebrated women's sacrifices in war. She firmly believed that wives should be able to protect themselves and their property, enjoying economic and political rights. The problem with the televised version of Abigail's mind is that she has women consenting to their subordination; she agrees that women have no place on the public stage, that they cannot demand rights as full citizens, but must accept their domestic roles as wives and mothers in exchange for national independence. As John creates a new social contract for a new nation, Abigail simply reaffirms her marital contract, with her social status remaining unchanged. In the scene where she finally erupts in anger, complaining to John about his absences and her sacrifices, he wins her back, not by giving her flowers, but sewing "pins." She kisses and forgives him, once more casting the couple in an Irving's Stone-like version of marital bliss.

John is less contentious in *The Adams Chronicles* than he appears in *1776*. Samuel Adams is his sometimes rival, but mostly his tutor, taking over the role that Franklin assumed in the musical. It is Sam who lures John into protesting British policies, and at the Continental Congress Sam tells John to listen to the Virginians, for they will be "our best allies." Sam also breaks up a fight between his cousin John and John Dickinson. And, finally, it is Sam who convinces John to stay in Philadelphia and work for independence, when he learns his family has come down with dysentery.

For apparent narrative reasons, Sam must replace Franklin so that the wily Philadelphian can become John's adversary when the two serve as diplomats in France. On arrival in Paris, John is shocked by the Frenchified Franklin, who he declares has been corrupted by the three Vs: "vanity, venery, and Vergennes" (the powerful French minister). Adams is the country bumpkin at Versailles, and so Franklin gladly sends him off to secure a commercial treaty with the Dutch, saying: "You may go to Holland or hell, whichever is closer."

This episode ends with an interesting twist: after he returns with the treaty, Adams proves he has mastered the art of diplomacy, the French language, and proper dress – and Franklin is impressed. Adams, as one critic notes, has learned from "constructive criticism." But the real Adams was nothing like this: he continued to make embarrassing blunders, consistently loathed Franklin, and tried to outmaneuver the latter as a member of the delegation that negotiated the 1783 Treaty of Paris, formally ending the war with Great Britain (Stoddart, 2003: 38; P. Shaw, 1976: 155, 173–189).

Adams's vice presidency and presidency are portrayed as less than heroic. Fellow Federalist Alexander Hamilton, handsome and duplicitous, is the main villain. He is an American Cardinal Richelieu, undermining Adams's presidency by pulling the strings of his cronies who dominate the cabinet. Jeremiah Sullivan, the stage actor who plays Hamilton, steals every scene, which serves to further diminish Adams. Sullivan proved he had a talent for such parts and would subsequently serve as Ian McKellen's understudy in the role of the jealous and conniving Salieri (Mozart's arch enemy), in the original 1980 Broadway production of *Amadeus* (Sullivan Obituary, 1993).

The filmmakers explore Adams's friendship with Jefferson, though the Virginian is a relatively minor character this time around. The oddest rewriting of history that takes place in this regard is that Abigail's famous "Remember the Ladies" debate on women's rights is converted from a 1775 letter to John into a 1785 debate with Jefferson in Paris! She attacks the Declaration of Independence for stating "all men must be created equal," while claiming (quoting from her letter to John) that women were determined to "foment a rebellion," refusing to "bind themselves to laws that deny them representation." John watches silently as she rebukes Jefferson for ignoring women; she then throws a bone to her husband by decreeing that he had relinquished the title of tyrant. In general, Jefferson's relationship to John and Abigail is marginalized because he, like Hamilton, exists primarily as a fanatical partisan.

The John Adams of *The Adams Chronicles* is bewildered by partisanship. In an environment of political combat, he is the nonpartisan dinosaur who loses control of his cabinet. Blindly loyal to Washington (another historic overstatement), he finally stands up to Hamilton in dismissing his cabinet. Even before, he relies on the mature Abigail (now played by Leona Dana), who assists him in making important decisions. It is she who presents the idea of not revealing the names of the French protagonists in the diplomatic scandal known as the XYZ Affair, which leads the United States into a "quasi-war" with France. There is no actual evidence that this happened; but for dramatic value, the First Lady is "wife and conscience," though Dana's Abigail, frail and thin, is a shadow of her former self.

24.3 Old Man Eloquent: John Quincy Adams

The *Adams Chronicles* includes four episodes featuring John Quincy Adams. These cover his diplomatic service under President Madison, secretaryship of state under James Monroe, his one-term presidency, and his seventeen post-presidential years in Congress, leading up to his death in 1848. John Quincy is presented as the lead member of the team which brokers the Treaty of Ghent, ending the War of 1812. A few years later, he directs the acquisition of Florida.

The filmmakers highlight the stark imbalance between his public and private worlds. His family life is far from idyllic. His wife, Louisa Catherine, played by Pamela Payton-Wright, is emotionally unstable, shown making desperate appeals for affection from her aloof husband. Prone to fainting spells and headaches, and having endured several miscarriages, Louisa Catherine is remade as a mad housewife – that is, emotions drawn from genuine history are exaggerated for the small screen.

Louisa Catherine's niece lives with the family, and creates dissension in the Adams clan by flirting with two of the sons: she is engaged to George, but later marries John. George Washington Adams, the eldest, is the most tragic figure of the lot. In an extended scene, his father and brother Charles visit him in his dirty garret in Boston. He confesses to his brother that he has fathered an illegitimate child and regularly hears his father's voice (and censure) in his head. Next, George is reported missing from the steamship *Benjamin Franklin*; his body washes ashore, with all signs pointing to suicide. Louisa Catherine blames her husband for his death.

The John Quincy episodes are bookended in such a way as to reveal his character. In the opening scene, David Birney (who plays him as a young man) heads for England, as his ship is boarded by British officers looking to impress American sailors into the navy. John Quincy uses an obscure British law to undermine this affront, outsmarting his adversaries. A similar storyline closes the John Quincy chapters, in which JQA (played by William Daniels) uses his intellect before the Supreme Court in 1841, to defend several Africans accused of mutiny and murder aboard the Spanish slave ship *Amistad*. In this way, the son of John Adams is an odd blend of the Old and New Worlds, an expert in arcane knowledge and a modern advocate of civil rights.

"Old Man Eloquent," as the ex-president came to be known during his career in Congress, looms even larger in Steven Spielberg's 1997 Dreamworks film, *Amistad*. Historians have recorded that in 1839, from the moment the hijacked schooner entered the port of New London, Connecticut, the story, as they say, had legs. Right away, New Yorkers were entertained by *The Black Schooner*, a play that featured the African mutineers, their leader Cinque, and a fictional female victim, the ship captain's lovely wife. Details of the *Amistad* story filled pamphlets and newspapers, engravings were printed, and the Africans' heads were replicated in a wax museum. Visitors flocked to see the live African prisoners in their Connecticut jail. A group of abolitionists led by Lewis Tappan established a committee to defend them in court, found an interpreter, and tutored the incarcerated men in English, so that they could read the Bible. When Spielberg took on the project, there had already been several well-regarded histories of the case published, as well as novels, television documentaries, and even an opera (Dalzell, 1998: 127–29).

The film covers the journey of Cinque in a quest to tell his story. It is ultimately the humane John Quincy Adams who rises in court as the black victims' most effective interpreter. Spielberg and his creative team direct the African prisoners in speaking their native Mende –sometimes the words are translated, at other times not. The spectator feels the frustration of the prisoners in their struggle to find a voice. In one powerful scene, as Cinque testifies, his translator captures his cadence while speaking in English; the shot of the courtroom dissolves as the words melt into horrific images of the middle passage. Cinque, in a flashback, is seen being kidnapped, imprisoned in a slave fortress on the West African coast, and then herded with others onto the slave ship as its human cargo. He recounts the horror on the high seas, as dozens of men, women and children, chained together, are thrown overboard, weighed down with rocks (Lipkin, 2001: 15, 24–25).

Adams, played by the accomplished Anthony Hopkins, is at first hesitant to become involved in the case. He gives the abolitionist lawyer some advice: "Whoever tells the best story wins." As the film progresses, the story focuses increasingly on the emotional bond forged between Adams and Cinque (played by Djimon Hounsou). The two men meet in Adams's house, accompanied by the translator. They converse in the library, beneath portraits of Abigail and John, and Adams commits to take on the case once the three stroll through the old man's hothouse and the elder statesman observes Cinque tenderly touching an African violet. That gesture of sensibility, his appreciation for beauty, elevates Cinque from an unfeeling savage into Adams's peer, deserving justice. Adding to the symbolism, Cinque tells Adams he will call up his ancestors to assist in obtaining them a victory, and Adams, appearing before the Supreme Court, speaks not only before the justices but also a bust of his own father (Lipkin, 2001: 24, 26).

Hollywood being Hollywood, Spielberg's film veers in the direction of fantasy, making it appear that the Amistad case triggered the downfall of slavery. *The Adams Chronicles* handles the matter imperfectly, if more judiciously: Adams meets the prisoners in jail (he did, in fact), not in his home; and while he is impressed by the Africans, no spiritual bond is forged. Appearing before the Supreme Court, the John Quincy Adams of *The Adams Chronicles* is armed with a pile of books. Rather than reference his blood line, though, he alludes to the first time he spoke before the "illustrious men" of chief justice John Marshall's court. The nostalgia is directed toward his own younger years rather than toward any connection with his late father.

The arguments the historical Adams made were different from those on film and TV. He had pointed to a copy of the Declaration of Independence in the courtroom, the document his father had once mocked as a "juvenile" production. Adams did so knowing that a majority of the justices were Jeffersonians and Jacksonians. He did not stress his growing antislavery credentials, but instead carefully shifted the argument to the independence of the judiciary. He laid out the heavy-handed maneuvers of President Van Buren to interpose his will and circumvent the court ruling on the case. The crux of his argument was that the administration was showing wrongheaded sympathy for the Spanish government. Employing biting satire, he looked at the administration's obstinate empathy for arbitrary power and Old World monarchy, and demonstrated that it had turned its back on the American system of due process.[3]

Adams's peroration extended over eight hours. It was "extraordinary," according to the diary of Justice Joseph Story, but it excluded the pathos conjured by Spielberg's film. What *Amistad* does is to ennoble the Adams line by associating John Quincy's abolitionism with the underlying issues of the Civil War. His father may have presided over a new and independent nation, but it was the son who inaugurated a positive renewal of the covenant, and whose words anticipated a better and freer nation with the end of slavery (Roberts-Miller, 2002: 21).

24.4 The Frog and the Princess: HBO's *John Adams*

When the HBO series *John Adams* was about to air, author David McCullough was engaged to promote it. He claimed that the Tom Hanks production was scrupulously assembled and achieved "in every detail" a sense of "authenticity." It was not a "costume pageant," he assured, but instead captured "the way life was"; the viewer would feel "very much transported into a different world" – the eighteenth century (Steigerwald, 2008).

But the HBO *John Adams* is not any more factual than the campy *1776*. McCullough's assurance of authenticity was what film scholars call the "reality effect," the appearance of truth, or what seems culturally plausible to the audience but has nothing to do with historical veracity. What McCullough admired were the visual props and the atmosphere conveyed: "people with bad teeth and dirt under their fingernails," the "horror of smallpox," a man "having his leg amputated without anesthetics." If the HBO series excelled at anything, it was the dramatization of a number of vignettes that displayed gore and trauma. The tar-and-feathering scene is indeed jarring: a man has his clothes stripped from him, hot tar is poured over his head, he is bathed in feathers, and then carted away amid the jeers of an angry crowd (Steigerwald, 2008; Nichols, 1991: 28; Neale, 2003: 161–162).

If *The Adams Chronicles* had the sterile feel of colonial Williamsburg, the overall atmosphere of the HBO is no closer to reality. The scenes of colonial Boston are hazy, as we first encounter John Adams atop his horse on a dreary, snowy day – the Gothic touches remind one of Tim Burton's set designs in the horror-history film *Sleepy Hollow*. When Adams reaches France it is almost as if he has entered Alice's Wonderland: French aristocrats with rouged and powdered faces are wearing pastel-colored costumes – a nightmarish version of a Rococo painting. Franklin's benefactress, Madame Helvetius, has leathery skin, bringing to mind the dystopian film *Brazil*, in which the face of the protagonist's aging mother looks more like a grotesque mask; her skin is sagging and stretched, the result of numerous face lifts.

As one scholar has observed, historical dramas typically blur the "distinction between fact and metaphor." The HBO series is indiscriminate in the way it dims the line, and the results are confusing. Yet, in relying on the historical Adams's description of himself as "short, thick, and fat," the talented Paul Giamatti arguably comes close to being Adams's double. The same cannot be said for Laura Linney's Abigail Adams. She is not only physically attractive, but utterly captivating on the screen. The glaring contrast between husband and wife reminds one of fairytale characters – *Shrek*, for instance. Giamatti can't help but look like a warty frog next to her. Only in this fairytale, the frog never turns into a prince (Reynaud, 2008: 50; Meschutt, 2001: 77).[4]

Abigail outshines everyone else. At a dinner with Jonathan Sewell, John's college friend who remains loyal to the Crown, Abigail recites a Latin verse, which Sewell must translate for his cloddish wife. (The real Abigail did not know Latin.) She wins the approval of George Washington, who sings her praises (through his wooden teeth), and graciously agrees to carry her letters to her husband. When she arrives in France, Jefferson is giddy in her presence and cannot take her eyes off her. In one scene, he sways back and forth like a love-struck suitor.

Away from the public eye, HBO's Abigail is a domestic superwoman. She is also, not inconsequentially, completely isolated from her extended family and friends. After she has her children inoculated for smallpox, she heroically nurses them back to health entirely on her own. The real Abigail traveled with her sisters and their children to Boston, and stayed at her uncle's mansion during the inoculation crisis (Holton, 2009: 110).

In *The Adams Chronicles*, Abigail voices a deep sense of loss after her mother's death from dysentery. She writes engaging letters to her sisters from France. We even get (if only briefly) a taste of women's political circles, when Federalist socialite Anne Bingham calls on the vice president John Adams's wife. Bingham is dressed in mourning for the French queen, Marie Antoinette, a subtle expression of the ways in which dress symbolized political identity. In the 1790s, Federalists sided with the beleaguered French aristocracy, while some Jeffersonians exchanged their knee breeches for *sans-culottes* to show support for the French Revolution. (Branson, 2001: 63–68).

In the HBO series, however, Abigail is only political in the ways she props up John's career. As in *The Adams Chronicles*, the bedroom is their conference room, but Linney performs as though she were a modern wife and political consultant. In the first episode, which focuses on the highly charged trial of British soldiers accused of committing the "Boston Massacre," Abigail suggests to John how he should fashion his closing arguments in defending British captain Preston and his men. Sitting in bed, reading her husband's oration, she most resembles fictional First Lady Abby Bartlett in TV's *The West Wing*, *circa* 1999. In like manner, she sends John crucial intelligence about the battle of Bunker Hill, which he uses to rally Congress to establish the Continental Army and appoint Washington as its commander. The filmmakers have willfully sacrificed historical accuracy in this, because Bunker Hill actually took place after the appointment of Washington (Stern, 2008).

The HBO series routinely twists the facts and mangles chronology. It is not enough that Abigail and John are historical agents; they must also be eyewitnesses to history. In one scene, Abigail watches from her front yard as the militia retreats from Bunker Hill, with the dead body of Son of Liberty Joseph Warren in tow – never mind that the Harvard-trained physician, Revolutionary orator, and first martyr of the Revolution was unceremoniously buried on the hill by the enemy and only dug up and reinterred many months later. Likewise, General Henry Knox passes through after the capture of Fort Ticonderoga, and Abigail, rifle in hand, converses with him – but neither army took the route past the Adams farm (Fischer, 1994: 285). Even more egregious, John Adams is shown rushing to the scene of the Boston Massacre, then cradling the dying African American "patriot" Crispus Attucks in his arms. In fact, Adams saw nothing at all. He was drawn to the scene but by the time he arrived all was quiet; so he slipped past the soldiers and hurried home to his wife (Zobel, 1970: 204).

The Adams children are inconvenient distractions for the HBO writers. This is especially the case with "Charlie," whose later death as a result of alcoholism must be explained away with *Lifetime* TV pop psychology. Thus, he is typecast as a neglected child, whom John Adams abandons when he heads off to Europe with his first-born John Quincy. But Charles did accompany his father during the latter's second excursion to the Continent. When Abigail travels to France, the HBO writers have her traveling alone, though she was in fact joined by her daughter; next, John Quincy is prematurely dispatched to Harvard. The recurrence to this kind of distortion is done in order to play up the love story. Without children in the way, the writers can treat the audience to a sex scene – alluded to in *The Adams Chronicles*, but here a bodice-ripping reunion. Of course, the foreplay only underscores Giamatti/Adams's frog-like qualities.

Tom Hanks had told his production team: "This is to be David McCullough's John Adams." But the connection to McCullough's glorifying biography is rather tenuous. Historian Jeffrey Pasley has succinctly observed that McCullough's John Adams is "high-spirited, affectionate, loyal to his friends, a kind and dedicated father and husband." Giamatti's Adams has none of these noble qualities. He is troubled by his inner demons, uncomfortable in his own skin, regularly out of sorts, and an angry, demanding father (Steigerwald, 2008; Pasley, 2002). Rather than a true adaptation of McCullough's biography, the HBO remake owes most to *The Adams Chronicles*. When the rivalry between cousins John and Sam Adams is reprised, the later series makes a complete mess of it. Sam comes across as a Union "thug," bringing the mob into the courthouse in order to intimidate John as he tries to defend the redcoats after the Boston Massacre. His hostility toward John is grossly exaggerated, and one is left wondering how Sam could ever have been elected to the Continental Congress. As the cousins head off to Philadelphia, Sam is dressed up, equipped with a fancy carriage, while John wears plain attire. The difference between the two productions lies in the tone used to convey this moment: George Grizzard's

John is amused, whereas Giamatti's is disgusted by his cousin's unrepublican look. By the second HBO episode, Sam, without any explanation, has become John's ally – or, better put, his lapdog. The true historical complexity of the well-respected Samuel Adams is buried (Stern, 2008).

Franklin is still a foe. Grizzard is disturbed by his venery, but the HBO *John Adams* must extravagantly illustrate it. In a completely fictitious scene, John bursts into Franklin's boudoir, where the large man sits in a tub with Madame Helvetius, playing chess. In *The Adams Chronicles* Abigail is shown cleaning the floor of her house with vinegar, which makes sense in the case of dysentery; HBO has her do the same thing for smallpox, which makes no sense.

In Charles's demise, Giamatti's John visits his son's dirty garret in New York. But the scene is actually lifted from the PBS portrayal of George, John Quincy's suicidal son, not Charles, John and Abigail's son. In the HBO version, John disowns Charles, which is true; but Abigail (the good parent) brings him home and nurses him in his final hours – which never happened. The real Charles died without his mother; the real Abigail felt her son's death might be a blessing in disguise (Holton, 2009: 327, 330–331).

Jefferson is a more important figure in HBO's *John Adams* than he is in *The Adams Chronicles*, but only in order to diminish him. The English actor Stephen Dillane does resemble Jefferson: he is tall, thin, and pale, and makes the most of US Senator William Maclay's published diary comment that the Virginian tended to slouch in his chair. In the nuance-resistant HBO production, the gesture becomes a metaphor for Jefferson's duplicity. In the end, *John Adams* rewrites the rekindling of the Adams–Jefferson friendship by having it take place six years later than it did; this is done to have it occur at a dramatic moment, just after Abigail's death, and to suggest that John cannot have a close relationship with anyone else while she is still alive. The parallel deathbed scenes of Adams and Jefferson, who both died on July 4, 1826, are recreated principally in order to condemn Jefferson. Whereas Adams is surrounded by his legitimate heirs, we are meant to believe that Jefferson's only witness was his slave concubine, Sally Hemings (Burstein, 1995: 150–151, 178, 265; Burstein, 2005: 276).

In sum, the highly acclaimed HBO series *John Adams* is not history. It is not even close. It distorts both characters and basic facts. Beyond engaging in dramatic license, it bowdlerizes history, because scriptwriters and producers knew they could get away with it.

The popularizer David McCullough does not have a doctorate in history. He earned a bachelor's degree in English and went on to write for *Sports Illustrated*. Granted, he understands his reader's demand for stories that glamorize hard work and heroic achievement. And so, he blithely dresses up his biographical subjects in the mythic garb of "greatness." If his style borrows heavily from romance, his facts are, for the most part, sound (Waldstreicher, 2002: 190; Stern, 2008).

This cannot be said about American filmmakers. In a perfect world, it would not be the popularizer but the professional historian who refereed Hollywood films. In 1935, after seeing *The Scarlet Pimpernel*, historian Louis Gottschalk insisted to screenwriter Samuel Marx: "No picture of a historical nature ought to be offered to the public until a reputable historian has had a chance to criticize and revise it." Hollywood was not listening to reputable historians then, nor is it now (Smyth, 2006: 14).

Notes

1 Williams Daniels also played Samuel Adams in *The Bastard* (1978), and John Adams in *The Rebels* (1779), both of which belonged to the three-part television mini-series based on John Jakes's novels, billed as the *Kent Family Chronicles.*

2 See press release Aug. 22, 1975, available at http://homepage.mac.com/oldtownman/filmnotes/adamschron2.html, accessed Nov. 9, 2012; also Stoddart, 2003: 31.

3 John Quincy Adams. *Argument of John Quincy Adams, before the Supreme Court of the United States, in the case of the United States, Appellants, vs. Cinque, and Others, Africans, Captured in the Schooner, Amistad, by Lieut. Gedney, Delivered on the 24th of February and 1st of March, 1841, with a Review of the Case of the Antelope, Reported in the 10th, 11th, and 12th Volumes of Wheaton's Reports.* New York: 26, 38, 48, 79–82, 88–89; Roberts-Miller, 2002: 8, 13–14, 19–22; Maltz, 2009: 64–65; Parsons, 1998: 239.

4 Giamatti resembles the portrait of Adams done by Charles Willson Peale around 1794. The portrait that probably most resembles Abigail is by Mather Brown in 1785. Here we see her rather pronounced nose (long, thin, and pointed); the same long nose appears in Gilbert Stuart's 1800 oil painting of Abigail, and the 1804 oil by her relative Lydia Smith Russell (see Oliver, 1967: 51, 71, 138, 228). The less glamorous Allison Janney (press secretary from *The West Wing*) would have been more appropriate casting for Abigail if the filmmakers had wanted a more realistic Abigail.

Further Reading

Burstein, Andrew and Isenberg, Nancy (2010). *Madison and Jefferson.* New York.

Carnes, Mark C., ed. (1996). *Past Imperfect: History According to the Movies.* New York.

Gelles, Edith B. (1988). The Abigail Industry. *William and Mary Quarterly* 45: 656–683.

Holton, Woody (2009). *Abigail Adams.* New York.

McCullough, David (2001). *John Adams.* New York.

Pasley, Jeffrey L. (2002). Federalist Chic. *Common-Place*, Jan. See www.common-place.org.

Rollins, Peter C. and O'Connor, John E. (2003). *Hollywood's White House: The American Presidency in Film and History.* Kentucky.

Rollins, Peter C., ed. (2003). *The Columbia Companion to American History on Film*. New York.
Shaw, Peter (1976). *The Character of John Adams*. Chapel Hill, NC.
Shepherd, Jack (1975). *The Adams Chronicles: Four Generations of Greatness*. Boston.
Smith, Page (1962). *John Adams*, 2 vols. New York.
Smyth, J. E. (2006). *Reconstructing American Historical Cinema: From Cimarron to Citizen Kane*. Lexington, KY.
Stoddart, S. (2003). *The Adams Chronicles*: Domesticating the American Presidency. In Rollins and O'Connor (2003): 30–49.
Stone, I. (1965). *Those Who Love*. New York.
Stone, P. and S. Edwards. (1772). *1776: A Musical Play*. New York.
Thomas, E. (2001). Founder Chic: Live From Philadelphia. *Newsweek*: July 9.
Waldstreicher, D. (2002). Founders Chic as Culture War. *Radical History Review* 84: 185–194.
The Internet Movie Database at www.imdb.com, accessed Nov. 19, 2012.

Chapter Twenty-Five

An American Dynasty

Edith B. Gelles

Absent the Adamses – Abigail and John, Louisa Catherine and John Quincy – from American history and the written chronicle of our country's past would be altered. And poorer. Not just because all of the Adamses were great patriots who sacrificed in order to birth and grow and cultivate the country, but because they were writers. It is fair to say that had there been no Adams record, the history of the Revolution and early republic would be cast and framed differently. In an informal survey of the conventional histories of the era, conducted by myself and therefore admittedly unscientific, none omitted something by an Adams in either the text, footnotes, bibliography, or index. This situation is so extreme – I mean the reliance on our "first dynasty" for direct contemporary evidence – that among women's historians, at least, those who attempt to find someone other than Abigail Adams to quote for the Revolutionary era, tell lackluster stories. No woman, perhaps save her sisters, could write with the elegance and poignancy of Abigail. Nor did anyone write from her unique perspective. So the first point to make about the original Adamses is that they were writers (Gelles, 2002: 3–13).

Among the dynasty's founders, John and John Quincy, father and son, not surprisingly shared many qualities of character, behavior, habits, education, interests, and experience. As befitting a generational gap, they also differed from one another in numerous ways. As its wives and mothers, Abigail and Louisa Catherine, so unlike one another in background and temperament, had a great deal in common, pre-eminently that both carried the burden of being married to Adams men. And together, the first and second generations

A Companion to John Adams and John Quincy Adams, First Edition.
Edited by David Waldstreicher.

of the founding Adamses left a huge legacy as patriots and as literary giants, who sacrificed their families and personal well-being to serve their country.

Together their lives spanned over a century, from the Great Awakening to the eve of the Civil War. They both experienced and shaped the dynamic forces that created, expanded and then established the fault line over which the nation would divide into its greatest civil crisis. When the family patriarch, John Adams, was born in 1735, the population of the British colonies in continental North America has been estimated at about one million (Greene and Harrington, 1933: 5). When the surviving Adams matriarch, Louisa Catherine, died in 1852, more than 23 million people populated thirty-one states (US Census, 1850) that were less than a decade away from imploding.

From their rural New England roots in the early eighteenth century, they became travelers and denizens of half the globe. In Great Britain, they socialized with royalty and aristocracy; in France, they were entertained by marquis and marquionesses; in the Netherlands, bankers, landholders, stadtholders; in Russia and Prussia counts and countesses; in all of them, kings and queens. If, on his first mission abroad, John Adams was unknown and undistinguished from his cousin Sam Adams, the Adamses were in a few short decades renowned as presidents and First Ladies of the new United States. The odyssey of two generations catapulted one family into as unprecedented a change as either would have imagined – or aspired to. Abigail acknowledged the transformation in their lives to her friend Mercy Otis Warren: "If we were to count our years by the revolutions we have witnessed," she wrote in amazement, we could "neither fathom nor comprehend" them (Adams Papers, reel 122, June 26, 1818). Fortunately, all of them –in part to make sense of their lives to themselves, to their family, to their contemporaries and to history – wrote prodigiously.

25.1 A Dynasty of Writers

"We had a severe Shock of an Earthquake," John Adams famously began his first diary entry in 1755. Awakened from his sleep at his parents' home in Braintree, he wrote that "The house seemed to rock and reel and crack as if it would fall in ruins about us" (Butterfield et al., 1961, *Diary*: 1.1). The entries that follow this animated overture hardly predict the life that would take form in the ensuing years. "A very rainy day," or "Fair and fine day," or "A cloudy, dull, day," he assiduously recorded the weather. "Taught school," and "Drank tea at Mr. Swan's with Mr. Thayer," and "Heard Mr. Mccarty." Adams was clearly onto something when he began to write his first diary entries, but it was not about his fascinating existence, for his life in those early years, followed the mundane routine of a youth in search of himself. But on occasion, he gave full tilt to his personality, allowing his natural exuberance and wit to flow onto the page in the unique style that has so captivated historians. Memorably he described his classroom in Worcester: "I sometimes in my sprightly moments, consider my self in my great Chair at School, as some Dictator at the head of a commonwealth," he fantasized. "In this little state I can discover all the Genius's, all the surprising actions and revolutions of the great World in miniature. I have several renowned Generalls but 3 feet high, and several deep-projecting Politicians in petticoats (*Diary*: 1.13–14)." Bernard Bailyn has written that Adams's prose is "the most alive and readable of any written in eighteenth-century America" (Bailyn, 1990: 9).

Years later Adams advised his son John Quincy "never to let a Slovenly Word or Letter go from you. If one begins at your Age, it is easier to learn to write well than ill, both in Characters and Style" (Butterfield et al. 1963–: 5.160). For the purpose of practice, he purchased the 11-year-old a diary. He added, furthermore, that it would be expeditious in the future as an aid to memory (Butterfield et al. 1963–: 1:92). The boy doubted that he had the perseverance or the patience, he complained to his mother in words that would become a repetitious litany for many of the next sixty-eight years during which he assiduously made entries in one of his sixty-plus journal books. He hated the process; it used up valuable time; it physically pained him to write (his right hand was disfigured, due to a childhood accident); it bored him. But he maintained the diary, because his father's admonition stuck. And to his satisfaction in later life, he found cause on numerous occasions to look back at his record to reassure himself of a date, an event, or positions taken by himself or others. The diary was utilitarian, as John Adams maintained, but it also would be a corrective, supplying evidence of lives well lived – or not. John Quincy, especially, was aware of its value to the next generations, be they family or the greater public. Finally, although neither father nor son described it as such, the diary was a friend, a confessor so to speak, an instrumental means, in the Puritan sense, of a place to bare one's soul, to confess faults, hurts, frailties, emotions (Morgan, 1944: 5). Both men used their diaries for their therapeutic effects.

The senior Adams was tough; a diary alone was an insufficient record. A letter book would serve the same purpose of providing evidence of events and documentation for future action. The practice of recording letters, however laborious and onerous, became as obligatory to them, father and son, as religious devotions. Both men struggled under this self-mandated obligation. During his days in the Continental Congress, John had no secretary but himself, and he struggled to copy his letters. Sometimes, when the burden was too great, a family member would serve as clerk. John Quincy often employed his long-suffering wife, but no letter went uncopied.

"A letter book, a Diary, a Book of receipts and expenses–these three Books, kept without intermission should be the rule of duty of every man who can read or write," lamented John Quincy. "But to keep them perseveringly requires a character given to very few of the Sons of men. Above all, it requires a character to which toil is a pleasure, and of which untiring Patience is an essential Element" (C.F. Adams, 1874–1877: 9.159). He observed no irony in this comment.

Whereas his son was his perfect prodigy, John was less scrupulous about his record- keeping until he became a statesman. His early letters were desultorily maintained and copied. And only on occasion did he keep accounts, a task he finally delegated to his competent wife. But late in life, suffering the sting of rejection from office and fearing for his reputation in history, he did make some effort to write an autobiography. In fact, he tried three times and terminated each effort. The autobiography that survives is an assemblage of these three manuscripts, written between 1802 and 1807; none of them is comprehensive, yet some of the most charming anecdotes in history come from this work. For instance, the tale about the journey that he and Benjamin Franklin took in 1776, where the two became roommates in a boarding house and argued about whether to close or leave open the window, comes from the autobiography, as does the description of the perilous sea voyage with his sons in 1779 and the anecdote about his parents' quarrel over a servant. History would indeed be poorer without Adams's recollections, told of himself with such mirth and sparkle (Butterfield et al., 1961: 1.xliv, 65–66; 3.417–18; 2.400–404).

John Quincy's diary contains little mirth and les sparkle. It is so like his "toiling" self, a serious endeavor to do the job well. And that it is. Were there a competition for best record of a public career in American history, John Quincy's sixty-one volumes of diary would unquestionably win. Even during his busiest years as secretary of state and as president, he kept up abbreviated entries in a second diary that he maintained as a jog to his memory until he had the "leisure time" to fill in the full story. The Massachusetts Historical Society now claims these brief entries as history's first "tweets," keeping up a website that follows John Quincy's daily twitters as a public service to fans of both the internet and archival history.[1]

As if the challenge of marrying into the Adams family with its New England-centric ethos of service, probity, erudition, thrift, and sacrifice was an insufficient test of character, Louisa Catherine Johnson Adams, who did not care for writing, found herself surrounded by writers. She was eventually constrained to write her own several charming and vivid memoirs to defend herself and family against political calumny. And, in time, she discovered not only that she liked to write, but that writing provided her with a kind of personal satisfaction that was similar to her fondness for music. Writing calmed her; it gave her a voice, was expressive, allowed her to re-examine her life in a way that strengthened her self-confidence. She began to write poetry and plays; she translated French literature and late in life, to the great delight of her father-in-law, began to send her translations of Plato to him (Butterfield, 1974: 165–178).

Only now, more than a century and a half since her death, will her considerable papers be published alongside those of her famous family members. Until now, Louisa's reputation has been muted. It has been, in fact, greatly underestimated, because the few early references were less focused on her accomplishments than her suffering (Challinor, 1982, 1986; Shepherd, 1980). If John Quincy's historical image has until recently been dour and negative outside of the field of diplomacy, Louisa has been cast as his longsuffering wife. Her grandson Henry Adams bears some blame for this situation, having referred to her as "remote … decorative … a fragile creature" (H. Adams, 1906: 16) descriptions that were repeated by subsequent family biographers. Women's historians have partly rescued Louisa by casting her in the role of an early Washington hostess during her husband's years in the capital (Allgor, 2000: 147–189), until, finally, with the publication of Michael O'Brien's (2010) *Mrs. Adams in Winter*, a window opened on her individual strength of character. The publication of her diary and autobiographical writings (forthcoming from the Adams Papers project in 2013), will doubtlessly put her into her own spotlight.

Not that the previous image of her, that of the longsuffering wife, is entirely misconstrued. Louisa was that, but she was also much more than that. Her early letters, her courtship correspondence with John Quincy, reveal a sometimes defensive, but also sometimes spirited young woman. Her letters home from her various diplomatic postings are poignant and observant. But it was the political slurs that were hurled at her and her background that inspired her first effort at memoir in 1824 during her husband's presidential candidacy. Again in 1835, she wrote for the benefit of her descendants and yet again in 1840. It is this last, bearing the pathetically self-denigrating title of "The Adventures of a Nobody" in her manuscript, that has perhaps most influenced her reputation. Louisa, like her husband, missed the irony of her story (Graham et al., forthcoming). She, too, was a survivor.

For many of her years, Louisa's mother-in-law did not believe that her own prose warranted preservation. "You will burn these letters," she wrote repeatedly to her husband who correctly understood their value. "I really think that your letters are much better worth preserving than mine," he responded (Butterfield et al. 1963–: 2.3). Because of her writing, Abigail Adams has never suffered obscurity. First published in 1840, by her grandson Charles Francis, a selection of her letters went through four editions in their first decade. They thrived through the nineteenth and early twentieth centuries as literary classics, especially among educated women. And then, with the coming of the women's movement in the last quarter of the twentieth century, Abigail Adams's letters became legendary as the best record of the Revolutionary era from a woman's point of view.

Abigail wrote for many of the same reasons that her husband and son did. She wrote to stay in touch, to stay informed, to conduct business and because it was her best means, short of direct conversations with her trusted family and friends, of making sense of her life. By writing them down, the historical cataclysms that she witnessed and experienced became real to her (Gelles, 1992: 161–162). They took the form of a living document of events, of people, and of her consciousness. In her youth, she wrote, "My pen is always freer than my tongue. I have wrote many things to you that I suppose I never could have talk'd" (Butterfield et al. 1963–: 1.310). With time, writing became a habit so ingrained that she gave no thought to performing its rituals. These were not simple. They required paper (often scarce), quills and ink. Much of the time they required silence (the night time), solitude (rare), and candlelight. But when the circumstances of the ritual came together, which most often they did by dint of her efforts, the results soared. Abigail could write like few of her contemporary women and few of her descendants. She wrote as a woman, that is with a woman's sensibility and a woman's outlook. She wrote of women's world and of men's world from her perspective as a woman, a wife, mother, patriot, citizen, and political and social commentator.

If she kept few diaries and wrote no autobiography or memoir, all forms are present in the genre of her letters. She was an original; she was spontaneous, rarely copying as her husband admonished, and she was transparent. She did not hide many of her feelings or her opinions. Thus we have a record of her experiencing labor and giving birth; we know how she felt about Hayden, her farmhand who refused to move out of her house. We get her impressions of Paris before the French Revolution: "I haven't seen it, but I have smelt it" (Butterfield et al. 1963–: 5.436). We know she didn't care for England's Queen Charlotte: "neither attractive or well formed" (Butterfield et al. 1963–: 6.92). We have her take on the White House "built for generations to come" (Mitchell, 1947: 259). And we have an intimate (for the time) record of her long marriage to John Adams in one of the greatest exchanges of correspondence that exist. Like her husband, Abigail could write.

25.2 Dynastic Marriages

As a matter of fact, both the first and second generations of Adamses had long, over a half-century long – and successful – marriages, despite the efforts of chroniclers to find fault (Challinor, 1986: 36–37; Holton, 2009: xx–xxi). Abigail and John are legendary for the fifty-four years of an affectionate and generous relationship that lasted from her youth to her death (John, as was customary, was a decade older than his nineteen-year-old bride, and he outlived her). Louisa Catherine Johnson married John Quincy under circumstances that boded ill, but because of both their characters and their determination, overcame much adversity. If Abigail and John both became nervous as the day of their impending marriage approached, their anxieties were made easy by settling into an anticipated lifestyle that repeated the patterns they saw in their own parents' and neighbors'. In Louisa's case, by contrast, she married a man she little knew, was wrenched from her beloved parents and sisters who soon sailed across the ocean, while she herself began the journey that would be repeated many times, to her husband's remote diplomatic outpost, this time in Prussia. Hers was a hard tempering to a way of life that became permanent (Butterfield, 1974).

Adversity, in fact, became the condition to which all four partners became accustomed. And fortunately, painted portraits survive from all parts of their lives to give visual substance to the portraits they left in letters and diaries. In the early portraits, one sees faces that are bright with anticipation and hope and confidence.

Benjamin Blyth, a Salem limner, painted both Abigail and John, within a few years of their wedding, during a visit that the young couple made to the seaport home of her sister. Blyth, whose only legacy to art history is these "primitive" portraits, was not so successful in the rendering of John. But he painted a charming Abigail (Figure 25.1). She appears to us fresh, calm, intelligent. Her eyes attract immediate attention, the eyes that we will observe again in the much later portrait of her son, John Quincy, painted by the master, John Singleton Copley. Those eyes, dark and penetrating as Blyth saw them, give the impression of high energy, of strong character. Her gaze is direct and uncompromising. Yet, decidedly feminine, dressed in a modest blue dress with a white collar, she wears pearls that she likely didn't own at the time, but in that era, signified a wedding portrait. A pink ribbon holds back her thick dark brown hair. The young Abigail of her portrait matches the lively prose of her early letters (Oliver, 1967: 5–13).

John does not. He hardly appears the successful lawyer that he was or the statesman that he would become, perhaps, because of the blandness of his expression and the poor rendering of his wig that looks almost comical (Figure 25.2). The set of his mouth, however, as well as the full face predicts the more familiar Adams of later portraits. Blyth clearly spent greater talent or time in his depiction of Mrs. Adams. And he was among the earliest of American-born artists, so it is fortunate both that the young, and neither wealthy nor famous couple – the usual profile of people who sat to their portraits in the colonies – chose, perhaps on a whim during a holiday, to sit for theirs. Equally auspicious, the portraits survived (Craven, 1986: 38–39; Lovell, 2005: 7–45).

John Quincy sat for about sixty portraits during his lifetime, the first a late eighteenth- century "primitive," while the last of his portrayals were taken by photographers such as Matthew Brady, spanning the history of early American art (Oliver, 1967: 4). A corpus of portraiture on this dimension hardly suggests a modest personality. Why was it that John Quincy consented to so many exasperating (to him) sittings? Particularly when he

Figure 25.1 *Abigail Adams.* Pastel on paper by Benjamin Blythe, 1766. Courtesy of the Massachusetts Historical Society.

(sometimes rightfully) expressed dissatisfaction with the end product? Was it ego? Or was it his awareness of his place in history that he recorded his image along with his massive diary? It was John Quincy who insisted that his father sit for Gilbert Stuart's last great picture of him. And who pestered Stuart to complete the last portrait of his mother. John Quincy was not without consciousness of the place of the Adamses in early American history. His respect for the record accounted for many of the portraits. He left his letters, his diaries, his accounts, and also he left portraits.

As well, they represent the alternate side of his personality that he tried to suppress, his ambition for office and for fame. In this case he inherited the temperament of his much-tormented father, who struggled from his earliest entries in his diary to harmonize his two natures: his desire to serve and his ambition for fame. Moreover, the recurrent message John Quincy received from both his parents from early youth, related to his exceptionalism both as an Adams and as the successor to the Adams's worldly function: public service (Gelles, 1992: 133–199; Musto, 1969: 269–282). The tension between duty and ambition that so marked the father's character

Figure 25.2 *John Adams.* Pastel on paper by Benjamin Blythe, 1766. Courtesy of the Massachusetts Historical Society.

was present in the nature of the son. The latter, however, for most of his career, coped better with the contradictions in his temperament. He learned to suppress them.

He hoped the portrait of himself would be an "agreeable surprise," John Quincy wrote to his mother of Copley's masterpiece that now hangs in the Boston Museum of Fine Arts (Figure 25.3). "He produced a very excellent picture, as you see," he continued, pleased with the likeness of himself (Oliver, 1967: 40). Abigail was indeed thrilled: "It is allowed to be a favorable a portrait as ever was taken," she responded. "I recognized the striking resemblance of my dear absent son." She sang its praises: "What renders it peculiarly valuable to me is the expression the animation, the true Character which gives it so pleasing a likeness, and I have been not a little flattered by strangers saying, they can trace the resemblance of my features in it" (Oliver, 1967: 38).

The "expression, the animation, the true Character" in this portrait present a handsome young man, a gentleman, a romantic, an esthete. In part it is the background, a landscape, that gives the portrait its sentimental cast, but mostly it is the rendering of light and shadow on the face, the

Figure 25.3 *John Quincy Adams.* Oil on canvas by John Singleton Copley, 1796. Photograph © 2013 Museum of Fine Arts, Boston.

sweetness in the features and visage, the intent gaze that Abigail recognized as so like her own. It was one of the few portraits of himself of which John Quincy approved.

Louisa Catherine Johnson, to whom he became engaged during the same period when he sat for this portrait, also praised its beauty. She, too, thought it captured its subject. She had become reacquainted with John Quincy, then serving as American minister at The Hague, when he was sent to London to take documents to American diplomats. And while the treaty signing had been concluded before his arrival, he did take the opportunity to visit with the Johnsons, a family known to his parents, and indeed to himself as a child when they visited with the then American consul in London. Joshua Johnson, a Marylander, had gone abroad as a commercial agent before the Revolution. During the war, he was unable to take his family home, so they moved to Nantes, where Louisa and her sisters received a rigorous convent education and became fluent in French. Returning to London after the war, Johnson had thrived, producing both more offspring and reasonable wealth. Louisa was the second eldest of seven daughters and one son. Her education continued in one of England's fine educational establishments for wealthy young women (O'Brien, 2010: 84).

Figure 25.4 *Louisa Catherine Adams.* Oil on canvas by Edward Savage, *c.* 1794. Courtesy of the National Park Service, Adams National Historical Park.

A wealthy young woman is who we see in her portrait (Figure 25.4), believed to have been painted by Edward Savage, though the dating is uncertain. For many years it was thought to have been the work of Mather Brown, which would have dated it from the early to mid-1790s. Experts now believe that it was painted later by the American artist Savage. The portrait, like the Blyth portrait of Abigail, shows a lovely young woman, poised and confident, staring directly at the painter, who depicted her with more depth of feeling and sophistication of technique than Blyth was capable of. Like Copley's John Quincy, she is clearly genteel, though not aristocratic. She is dressed in a pale soft fabric and her hair is unadorned. She wears no jewelry but a black band on her wrist that mystifies historians. Was she in mourning or was it an ornament?

Together, the portraits of Louisa Catherine and John Quincy, though not painted as a set like those of Abigail and John Adams, accomplish the same purpose of presenting us the picture of a couple at the outset of their marriages and their maturity, the partnerships that provided the basis for the rest of their lives. At the center of both marriages, indeed foundational to those marriages – what made them work for the more than half-century that each of them lasted – was the quality of trust. While there were many other essential components to their relationships – religion, values, children, physical attraction, and taste – trust was basic.

It need not have been so. Each couple was harshly buffeted by misfortune, both personal and historical, and while they lived in an era that opposed the breakup of marriage, the marriages could have become cold. They could have chosen separate paths from each other; they could have become estranged; or lived hostilely together or apart; but they did not. They chose to remain warm partners, despite the adversity that the times and life itself sent in their directions. In practice, they experienced their marriages differently, not only because of the revolutionary changes in their times, but also because of their personalities and temperaments. They do, in fact, tell us that despite overall legal and social conditions, every marriage is different and differently experienced (Coontz, 2005: 306). And for as much as Abigail and John's marriage has been idealized in history, John Quincy's, less well-studied, has been considered a mismatch and a hardship. In fact, both marriages existed in a patriarchal world that insured separation of work and responsibilities as well as of legal and social rights for men and women (Barker-Benfield, 2010; J.J. Ellis, 2010; Gelles, 2009; Challinor, 1986; Shepherd, 1980). The revolutions they participated in and lived through did not change that.

Both generations of Adamses subscribed to this principle; they could hardly have believed differently in their times. However, within the framework of patriarchy and essentialism – the premise that women and men by nature are differently created – they had leverage. Both the Adams women and men increasingly recognized the space for self-determination in the course of their long marriages and used those spaces to grow as individuals, but always within the confines of their social class and also the condition of being Adamses (Gilligan, 1982; Chodorow, 1978; Elshtain, 1981).

John Quincy never doubted that his primary function in life was service, an ethos inherited from his puritanical parents. He knew it because of his education, his training, his religion and his extraordinary youthful travels. He learned it from his parents' persistent messages to him. He learned it from the expectations of other people who saw his potential, such as President George Washington, whose appointment of him as minister to The Netherlands at age 26 was as much a surprise to his father as to himself. He was already launched on a successful legal career when the call came. It went against his design for his life and his wishes. However, without great hesitation or self-examination, he accepted. His father, by contrast, had moved more cautiously when he first began to serve; he had already a family to support and the risk of participating in the rebellion jeopardized his lucrative legal practice. Once committed, however, he remained steadfast for the remainder of his professional life, and he committed Abigail as well (Gelles, 2009: 44–69).

She had wept, he reported to his diary, when she received the news of the Boston Massacre. Pregnant, at home alone in Boston with her children and servants, she was greatly frightened by the reports of the shootings. Then she stalwartly supported his decision to represent the British soldiers accused of murder, an unpopular risk among the belligerents of Boston. Years later she demonstrated her support by sewing him a new vest for his travels to Philadelphia – neither of them had ventured so far in their young lives – to the Continental Congress, thinking that the separation would not last more than a couple of weeks. When it dragged into months and then years, she protested. Next came the first call for John to go to France, and later the repeated second call to go to Paris; she remonstrated not only to John, but in writing to the committee chair in Congress, James Lovell. As the years went on, and the separations from John Adams lengthened, she learned, unwillingly but dutifully, to live as a single mother – or a "widow" as she sometimes characterized herself. She passed her time running her household and participating in her social world, as she would during ordinary times, but also doing John's tasks; making decisions about her children's education, supervising her farm and farmhands for several years until, worn down by the chore, she rented to tenants. To earn money, she began a small business enterprise of selling items John forwarded to her from Europe and to invest in the currency markets that developed as the new national government experimented with its finances. She purchased land in her husband's name, as women could not legally own property. She wrote all of this in her letters (Gelles, 1992, 2002; Levin, 1987; Withey, 1981).

And she read. During this period, Abigail began reading in John's library, first as tutor to her eldest son John Quincy and then pursuing her own broad interests. As result, she became an erudite woman. While John Adams joined the statesmen and generals who won the war, Abigail at home kept alive their domestic world. Like other women, she maintained the families and communities that became America (Berkin, 2005). At the same time, Abigail grew prodigiously from the young wife who wept at the fearful shootings in Boston into the citizen who served in public roles as a diplomatic wife and First Lady. In the process, she set standards for other women to become educated, to function independently, and to serve in public. She recorded her remarkable odyssey in letter after letter to family members and friends.

And so she empathized with the daughter-in-law whom John Quincy brought home to Quincy in 1801. Historians and biographers have recorded this meeting, based upon Louisa Catherine's incredulous reaction to her first American experience. "What shall I say of my impressions of Quincy! Had I steped into Noah's Ark, I do not think I could have been more utterly astonished – Dr. Tufts! Deacon French! Mr. Cranch! Old Uncle Peter! And Capt Beale!!!" Louisa remembered meeting the Adamses' elderly and, to her, eccentric relatives and friends. "Even the Church, its forms, The sniffling through the nose, the Singers, the dressing and the dinner hour, were all novelties to me; and the ceremonious parties, the manners, and hours of meeting ½ past four were equally astonishing to me." She concluded, "I was literally and without knowing it a *fine* Lady" (Graham et al., forthcoming: 100). Louisa's commentators have further presumed that Abigail disapproved of her son's choice of a non-native-born American, and it is true that she worried about his marriage to a convent-bred English gentlewoman. But Abigail's reaction was immediate and not long-lasting, a typical mother's concern before she had met his fiancée. In fact, very little is made of the circumstances in which the two women met, another moment that Louisa recorded: " Both Mr. & Mrs. Adams received me very kindly," and later, "Mrs. Adams was too kind" (Graham et al., forthcoming: 98, 100).

John Quincy's marriage to Louisa Catherine is often viewed as a rebound romance after an aborted love affair during his early years with 16-year-old Mary Frasier. What is mostly known about that romance is Abigail's cautionary warning to her son that he was too young to take on the responsibilities of a husband. At that time a man had to be prepared immediately to support a family, which John Quincy was not. Like his father, who had very nearly proposed to Hannah Quincy, his first youthful love, but realized in a moment of prudent insight that it would be rash, so it was that a generation later, the parents were alarmed for the prospects of their eldest son. About the Hannah Quincy affair, John had written that an early marriage would have "depressed me to absolute Poverty and obscurity to the End of my Life" (*Diary*: 1.87). Now John Quincy's parents were agreed on this fact; Abigail was the bearer of the message. The Adamses were following the social prescriptions of their time and class. And John Quincy, lovelorn and miserable – as his father had been over the loss of Hannah Quincy – quit the romance and focused on his career. He did what most young men of his sort did, prepared for his future. Unlike many of his friends, however, he apparently did not live a dissolute life, but rather stayed firm in his commitment to work until love again struck, this time when he was safely out of reach of his parents in England (Nagel, 1997: 109–112).

The circumstances of his courtship and marriage to Louisa Catherine Johnson, even though not complicated by parental supervision, had their own troublesome moments. John Quincy may have proposed to Louisa and her parents on impulse during his brief visit to London, an impulse that later caused him reservations. At the same time, Joshua Johnson was experiencing financial reverses that prompted him to uproot his family from their known home in England to return to the Johnson home in Maryland. Before departing, he applied some pressure on John Quincy, who would no longer receive a dowry, to marry hastily. The long-term effect of these events – her father's impoverishment, the loss of her bridal gift, and the swift marriage before the departure of her beloved family – so distressed the young woman that she carried the emotional wounds into her middle age, writing poignant testimonies of those hard circumstances, not her fault, but scarring her psyche into her late-life memoirs. She always worried that John Quincy had been rushed into marriage before he was ready, which may have been the case. But once done, he was a devoted and committed husband – and also in-law. The Adamses – both generations – supported, even rescued the Johnsons many times over the years. It was a deep hurt for Louisa to see her family so reduced in condition.

The Adamses' marriages, then, could hardly have been more differently launched. Abigail and John had courted for at least three years; their families were known to each other; John had a viable law practice. And all of this happened within the scrutiny of their families and communities, among whom the young couple would settle down to create their household and raise a family.

The poignancy with which Louisa Catherine writes of her early marriage reads like the stuff of sentimental fiction, which, it was not. It was her all-too-true experience that she was too quickly wrenched from her family and launched into a world of strangers with a husband who was himself insecure and experimenting with too many new roles.

John Quincy had not chosen to be posted as American minister to Berlin, which is where the young couple found themselves. After The Netherlands, President Washington had assigned John Quincy to Portugal, but his successor decided that it was more urgent to send the young man to renegotiate treaties with both Prussia and Sweden, treaties that he had made during his diplomatic years and that had now lapsed. In the face of the European configurations that had shifted in the wake of the French Revolution, the United States needed allies. So John Adams disrupted his son's plans for the warmer climate, both political and geographic, of Portugal, sending him instead to the stormy cold winters of the North. It wasn't just the climate that upset John Quincy. He regretted the inevitable charges of nepotism that would follow, but after several exchanges with both parents that expressed his dismay, he relented. He and Louisa Catherine headed north in the cold of winter, bringing on her first miscarriage and a terrible illness.

Nevertheless, John Quincy successfully renegotiated the treaties, while Louisa Catherine suffered three more miscarriages and constant illness. Neither of the young marrieds had reason to celebrate those first years; Louisa whose lifelong physical frailty was induced by the loneliness and naïveté of her circumstances and John Quincy, thrust into both marriage and an unwanted diplomatic post. They, nevertheless, survived and having overcome such adverse circumstances had been tempered into the realities they would confront in the years ahead. If Abigail and John had experienced a more benign beginning to their relationship – and it, too, had its trials as John moved his family back and forth twice to Boston during the first decade of their marriage for either professional or health reasons – they, too, then faced major disruption to their plans in the form of the unanticipated war against Britain.

Two sets of portraits, the "primitives" of Benjamin Blyth, depicting a young confident Abigail and John, a couple, embracing their newly established family life, and the lovely paintings, done at the same stage in their lives, though separately, Copley's John Quincy and Savage's Louisa Catherine, bring us into contact with the youthful Adamses before they could have anticipated the amazing developments that shaped their long marriages and careers.

As luck (and history) would have it, many more portraits exist of the male Adamses than the women. For one thing, because artists were eager to enhance their reputations and profits by painting famous politicians, they made copies and engravings that were sold not just to galleries, but to friends and supporters, as well as to ordinary citizens who wished to commemorate their patriotic support by owning replicas of their heroes' images. As result, not only are there original paintings, but numerous copies, some of them very bad, that circulated well into the nineteenth century. After mid-century, photography became popular, making copies even more available.

25.3 Dynastic Statesmanship

By middle age, all of the Adamses' portraits depict figures who have lost their youthful sparkle. They aged, of course, but they also wear expressions that reveal evidence of weighty experiences. Of the many portraits of John that followed his hard-earned success as a diplomat – the initial shunning by both the French and the Dutch; his dogged persistence that finally won support of the bankers in Amsterdam and peace negotiators from England – none surpasses Copley's full-length depiction, taken to celebrate his triumph at the Peace of Paris in 1783. In the course of the years he had suffered the rebuffs not only of Vergennes, the French foreign minister, but his own colleague in Paris, who famously wrote of Adams: "He means well for his country, is always an honest man, often a wise one, but sometimes, and in some things, is absolutely out of his senses" (Franklin, 1987: 1065). The Dutch, originally allies of Britain, had to be won over to invest in the risky chance of American success, and Adams, after exerting both patience and diligence, triumphed with the loans that made it possible for his nation to continue the war effort. The process nearly cost his life, as he contracted a severe case of typhus, which he attributed to the damp climate of The Netherlands. The Copley portrait (Figure 25.5) shows not the misery of his diplomatic years, but the triumphant statesman, rotund and proud (Ferling, 1992: 241–242; Ferling, 2000: 256, 265; Rakove, 2010; 263–67; Page Smith, 1962: 363–733).

Figure 25.5 *John Adams.* Oil on canvas by John Singleton Copley, 1783. Photograph © 2013 Museum of Fine Arts, Boston.

In this life-size portrait, Adams holds a copy of the peace treaty, while before him on a table rests a map of America, and at his feet, the globe. Copley did not restrain his (perhaps hyperbolic) veneration in this clearly heroic pose of the master diplomat. It reveals none of the distresses and torment that Adams went through before this happy conclusion to his embassy in Europe. It was, he later claimed, his finest hour. It was also, as Abigail pointed out to her son, when he stayed abroad as a diplomat for too many years, a formula for obscurity. "Services rendered to a Country in a diplomatic line can be known only to a few" (Adams Papers, reel 398, Sept. 1, 1800).

The sole portrait that exists of Abigail from her middle age (Figure 25.6) may not even be of her (Oliver, 1967: 46–54). At first attributed to the American artist, Mather Brown, its authenticity has been questioned, and for good reason. In part, the facial features appear cartoonish. Nevertheless,

Figure 25.6 *Abigail Adams.* Oil on canvas by an unidentified artist, *c.* 1785. Courtesy of the Fennimore Art Museum, Cooperstown NY. Photograph by Richard Walker.

it bears enough resemblance, I believe, to represent Abigail, albeit a mature, serious, even stern woman who has made some effort in her attire to be elaborately decked out as a diplomat's wife. Her hair is frizzed, and covered by a fancy cap (Abigail always wished her hair to be covered, the artist Gilbert Stuart commented about his sketch of her). The full impression of this portrait looks like Abigail as both her earlier and later portrayals appear, though the eyes and the mouth are rendered as caricatures, by comparison with the rest of the family portraits and that of Thomas Jefferson, painted by Mather Brown in the same period.

Assuming, then, that this portrait presents Abigail as the wife of the American minister in London, a position that exposed her to a lifestyle she could not have imagined at home in Quincy – for instance, the multiplicity of servants she was required to maintain – the severity of the facial expression may suggest many things about her recent history. There were the years that she lived as a single parent and breadwinner, while John served his country at home and abroad. There was her brave decision to travel abroad to be with him, when he chose not to return after the signing of the peace treaty, but hoped for the embassy post in London. There was her natural shyness as a provincial American, learning to function within the protocols of diplomatic society in the Old World, which brought out in her a kind of xenophobic conservatism. So persuaded was she from the start that Europe was corrupt and America pristine that she insisted her eldest son return to New England for his higher education. Decadence was the alternative that she observed among young Americans who stayed abroad too long (Gelles, 2009: 171–173).

Still, she loved the arts and appreciated nature as she saw it differently in her travels. She scrutinized the social and political scene and hoped that Americans would behave differently. Her stern expression of the portrait may express the strength of character that developed in her wartime experiences or it may reveal her disapproval of European culture to which she always felt a stranger – she was "in the midst of the world in solitude," she wrote – her sense of being a misfit (Butterfield et al. 1963–: 5.452). Or it may simply have been the artist's choice to render her serious. Her letters of the time show much more; they have grace and wit, warmth and humor. Abigail grew into herself as a strongly independent individual during her wartime experience, and with her European sojourn, she prepared for her expanded role in the political and social arenas that she would have preferred to avoid in her future as wife of the vice president and then First Lady of her country.

Her European experience allowed her to empathize with her daughter-in-law's plight as a diplomatic wife, though Louisa Catherine's trials were greater. Abigail traveled to Paris and London, but Louisa was posted to Berlin and St Petersburg. While neither city was a hardship posting, getting there was, and living there where few Americans traveled was even more alienating for a young wife who often miscarried and was sick. Furthermore, none of this happened by her choice, something that further connected her to Abigail. It was John Quincy's career that first landed her in Prussia, where at least she had the consolation of the presence of her husband's secretary, who was also her brother-in-law. Thomas Boylston Adams was her frequent companion and nurse as his brother carried out his duties (Paltsits, 1916).

Later, in 1809, when John Quincy was compelled to make a quick decision to accept the post offered him by President Madison to represent his country at the Russian court, he did so without consulting his wife. Adding to her misery, the Adamses – and probably it was John Quincy's decision – left behind their two elder sons in the care of their grandparents, taking with them the infant Charles. Like Abigail, who had gone abroad with only her daughter as a companion, leaving Charles and Thomas in the care of her sisters, Louisa, too, suffered this cruel separation from her children.

Abigail commiserated as well with her daughter-in-law's impecunious circumstances. Foreign ministers were expected to entertain on salaries that were provided by their own governments, but most European diplomats were appointed because of their high-born status. They had private fortunes to supplement the cost of the mansions they resided in, the horses and coaches in which they traveled, the clothing and jewels they displayed at the lavish parties and balls that they gave. "They will starve their diplomats," Abigail wrote in indignation, knowing that Louisa Catherine suffered from her straightened position.

But this was not the worst of her suffering – and John Quincy's. Miraculously and painfully Louisa Catherine had given birth to a baby girl, named Louisa, who for one year gave joy to her parents. Then the child contracted dysentery and despite the desperate care given and enlisted by her parents, she died. Louisa and John Quincy were devastated by the loss. Once more, Abigail understood and sympathized. In the only statement she ever wrote about the death of her own one-year old daughter in 1777, she expressed compassion for her bereaved daughter-in-law: "I have felt the pangs of loosing an infant" (Adams Papers, reel 416, Sept. 7, 1813). She also knew that no amount of commiseration could comfort the grieving parents.

The portraits of the middle aged Louisa were taken after her return from these diplomatic sojourns, including the two happy years that the reunited Adams family spent in London, where John Quincy served, as had his father before him, as the American minister. There are two portraits, one done in 1816 and the next at the start of her years as first lady (Figure 25.7). Neither of them resembles the young woman of the Savage portrait. In part that is the consequence of painting conventions that had developed in America over three decades. In part it has to do with costuming – or rather, the fashions of the time. In either case, the setting and what Louisa Catherine wears overwhelm the portraits. It takes effort to overcome the distraction of velvet, feathers, and a harp to see the serene visage of a woman, who, to read her memoirs and her letters, was hardly serene. The woman in both portraits is a matron; her youthful glow is gone. In fact, one would be hard-pressed to recognize the young Louisa in these later portraits, perhaps because they are so stylized. In neither case is she captured as the animated figure of earlier work, but rather she is staring vacantly off into space. Her social position and not her personality or character is on display.

That position was consort to John Quincy Adams, secretary of state and later to be president of the United States. From his perspective, his star was on the rise. From hers, she had been reunited, if only for a few years, with her older sons and had become a major figure in the social scene at the nation's capital, hosting dinners and parties in her F Street home, one of which, the ball to celebrate Andrew Jackson on the eve of the election of 1824, has become renowned for its impact on Washington's social world (Allgor, 2000: 176–182). So elaborate and so crowded was the Adams home on the night of that event that the second story had to be reinforced by additional beams to support the weight of the company. It, too, was

Figure 25.7 *Louisa Catherine Adams.* Oil on canvas by Charles Bird King, 1824. Courtesy of the Smithsonian American Art Museum, Adams-Clement Collection, gift of Mary Louise Adams Clement in memory of her mother, Louise Catherine Adams Clement.

recorded by several paintings and engravings, to say nothing of letters, diaries and newspaper articles of its day.

Mirroring the full-length Copley portrait of his father at the pinnacle of his diplomatic triumphs, the life-size oil of John Quincy Adams – begun by Gilbert Stuart (the head), who then died, and completed by Thomas Sully – is also a masterpiece that earned his approval (Figure 25.8). Unlike Copley's elaborate setting for John Adams, the dignified republicanism of an American president is exhibited in the figure and the décor. While a periwig hides the famous Adams dome in Copley's portrait, John Quincy's bald pate is on full view (wigs had gone out of fashion in the United States, befitting an egalitarian ethos) (Page Smith, 1962: 825). Short of stature, still appearing fit, his grandeur is the intelligence and the strength of character of the man who has just become president of the United States. And unlike the portraits of his wife from this period, this is a painting of the man not his office. As the times had changed, so had the Adams men.

Figure 25.8 *John Quincy Adams.* Oil on canvas by Gilbert Stuart, 1825, and Thomas Sully, 1829–1830. Courtesy Harvard Art Museums/Fogg Museum, Harvard University Portrait Collection, Bequest of Ward Nicholas Boylston to Harvard College, 1828, H187. Photo: Imaging Department © President and Fellows of Harvard College.

25.4 A Dynasty of Presidents

John Adams had expected to succeed George Washington to the presidency. He wanted to succeed Washington. He sat out his years in the vice presidency – "the most insignificant office that ever the invention of man contrived or imagination conceived" (Butterfield et al. 1963–: 9.477) – as leading to the highest office. Still, he cautiously prepared himself in case he lost: "I can pronounce Thomas Jefferson to be P. of U.S. with Firmness & good grace" (Adams Papers, reel 382, Dec. 7. 1796). But to Abigail he wrote honestly:

"Idon't know how I should live out of it," and continued: "I don't love slight neglect, contempt, disgrace nor insult more than Others. Yet I believe I have firmness of mind enough to bear it like a man, a hero, and a philosopher" (Adams Papers, reel 381, Feb. 10, 1796).

Adams, if he knew himself – and here he did – underestimated the magnitude of the challenges, the strife and the slurs, the capriciousness of politics, and the inconstancy of people. At the age of 62 he took the oath of office, noting to Abigail afterwards that he perceived in Washington's demeanor at the ceremony: "Ay, I am fairly out and you are fairly in. See which of us will be the happiest" (Adams Papers, reel 383, Mar. 9, 1797).

John Quincy's route to the presidency was the more noble office of secretary of state, in common with his two predecessors. he, too, expected to become president and wanted to be president, for different reasons than his father. If John Adams saw himself as "heir apparent" because of his office, John Quincy saw himself simply as "heir apparent." His entire upbringing, education, and career had prepared him for this office. He had ambitions for his administration; he had expectations, ideals, plans. Unlike his father, however, he did not enjoy a period of musing, of excitement, of anticipation. His ascent to the office was vexed by political machinations, to which he became a party, and that damaged his soul and spoiled his triumph.

Neither father nor son would, in his career as politician, acknowledge the legitimacy of political partisanship. In retrospect, it was a naïve posture. To them this position represented integrity in the government they envisioned, one in which men functioned with the best interests of the country in mind and in which those best interests should be collectively agreed upon. They expected to rise above party, to overcome the sordid backroom transactions of men who traded principle for personal profit. Put bluntly, to them their opposition was either misguided in their thinking (Jefferson, for instance) or scoundrels (Jefferson again). However, John Quincy, when the chips were down, that is when he came in second in the popular vote to Jackson, who had not the majority needed to win the election, was willing to bargain for the top office with some backroom politics of his own that to this day has not been proved. It cost him not just his principles, but an effective presidency (Bemis, 1956: 40–41; G.W. Howe, 2007: 204–211; Parsons, 2009: 106).

Both Adamses suffered the disappointment of a single term as president. And for too long historians regarded both men as failed leaders, while lionizing their successors as great democrats and great presidents. While there are many ways to account for this irony, it was their personalities – as well as, perhaps, their background of experience in diplomacy rather than politics – that most accounts for their reputations. John wore his heart on his sleeve, while his son did the opposite, suppressing his emotions.

In fact, only during the last half-century has John's great success as president been properly acknowledged. His boldness in dealing with

France, when his countrymen were clamoring for a war of honor and profit, prevented a catastrophe that might have overwhelmed the fledgling economy and resources of a new nation. His reward was a campaign waged by politicians on both sides of the spectrum to malign both his policy and his person. It was a campaign to which he offered no counter-offensive, but, retiring to his home and his farm, he allowed his contemporaries to malign him. He was labeled a monarchist. He was called insane. He was considered unfit for office. And he was wounded. He retired in ignominy, leaving the capital before the inauguration of his successor, whom Abigail dubbed in contempt: "A man of the people" (Ferling, 1992: 409–410; McCullough, 2001: 262–264).

John Quincy was on a winning streak during his years as secretary of state, the so-called Era of Good Feeling. His great mission was to expand the nation from ocean to ocean, for internal improvements of roads and canals, to provide enlightenment of its citizens in the form of schools and museums, to establish standards of weights and measures, a diverse spectrum of issues to grow America into itself as a great nation, different from the socially stratified and degenerate nations in Europe. As the author of the Monroe Doctrine that would close off the western hemisphere from European interference, he had a modern and progressive program for the expansion of cities, industries, farming, education – all the campaign issues that have become standard political rhetoric for over two centuries. He meant to accomplish a great deal and was forced to settle for little. His enemies wouldn't forgive the "corrupt bargain" of 1824.

His inaugural speech acknowledged as much. "Less possessed of your confidence in advance than any of my predecessors, I am deeply conscious of the prospect that I shall stand more and oftener in need of your indulgence," he told the crowded chamber, promising the "unceasing application of all the faculties allotted" to him in service to his country (Bemis, 1956: 52–53).

Despite his unceasing application of faculties, his political enemies confounded his best efforts to enact his policies, and when the time came for re-election, he was aware of its futility. His presidency had become a stage for political payback, and his enemies rejected his best intentions "for the welfare of the country." The campaign of 1828 was nasty, and when it was over, like his father before him, he shunned his successor's inauguration.

What was it about the two Adamses that has evoked such strong and negative reactions? Why is it that no mythologies have enshrined them as with Washington (Father of his country): Jefferson (synonymous and eponymous for "democracy"): Madison (Father of the Constitution): Monroe (Era of Good Feelings): Jackson (the People's President). No small part of this disregard, both in their times and historically, derives from the same source as their lasting contributions: they were writers. They left some of the best, most useful, most literate prose in early American history. It has been used against them in two ways.

Because their diaries, letters, and memoirs are so often personal, both men are transparent, the father especially. John Adams left a record of events, but he also wrote about his opinions, aspirations, moods, anxieties, antagonisms, hatreds, wounds, feuds, and pomposity in spontaneous language that no other Founder left behind. George Washington had a cool grip on his public persona (J.J. Ellis, 2004: Ferling, 2009). Jefferson remains an enigma to the hordes of biographers who strive to interpret him (Burstein, 2005; J.J. Ellis, 1993). Adams, on the other hand, by writing of himself in language so blunt, insightful, amusing, revealing, and often harsh left a legacy that, when taken at face value, may be used – and generally is – to distract from his image. Furthermore, his spontaneity could erupt in speech and behavior. Adams was a passionate man without guise. His transparency, his volatility, his passion became the bombs that backfired. He could be petty as well as brilliant; he was whiney as well as visionary; he was ordinary as well as great. He knew his faults as well as his contemporaries knew them, but unlike his fellow Founders, he did not destroy his own record of them. "When I look in the Glass," he confessed to his diary, "I am but an ordinary Man … my Eye, my Forehead my Brow, my Cheeks, my Lips, all betray this Relaxation," and, he concluded, "The Times alone have destined me to Fame – and even these have not been able to give me, much" (Butterfield et al., 1961: 2.362–363).

The son, characteristically, was the opposite; composed, careful, meticulous, balanced, so fastidious and sober that his diaries often are as dreary as diplomacy. Except when they are not. For John Quincy, too, used his diary as therapy when his life was most anguished. "I felt a depression of spirits to which I have hitherto been entirely a stranger," he wrote as a young man. He, too, failed to excise his worst demons as expressed on the written page, and those diaries have been combed for evidence of weakness and even psychic disorder. At the least, he is considered cold and unfeeling. At worst, a depressive. One biographer has written that after graduating from Harvard, the young man "lost his struggle against melancholy and sank into full-fledged clinical depression, a condition that recurred occasionally throughout his life." This author suggests that over the years, changes developed in John Quincy's brain chemistry that could have been alleviated had he lived in the age of Prozac" (Nagel, 1997: 60).

The point is that in either respect his written legacy has become material for the most negative of portrayals. Like his father, his transparency in print that he did not censor or burn has been used to malign him personally, and his character demeaned. In demeanor, he was reputedly quite different than his father; a diplomat by background and grooming, and not a lover of social convention. His writing is used to confirm his social traits (Nagel, 1997).

And, secondly, at its worst in both cases, the genius, the brilliance, the erudition, the service and the sacrifices have been subverted, because these qualities contradict the preponderant character of American politics, then and now: populism. When Abigail wrote that John had been defeated by a "man of the people," she referred to the impulse in American political life that rejects the profoundly intellectual person as an elitist, an aristocrat, an outsider to the culture. While wealth is no barrier to high office, the appearance of great erudition is.

This is not to say that the only reasons the Adamses were each limited to one term as president related only to the transparency and erudition of their writings. More was at stake in both elections that had to do with local politics than with the legacy of diaries, letters and books, and reports. But it is to say that in the political climate of their times, and in the personal style that is most appealing to Americans historically, the Adamses were not destined to be popular, and the evidence for their falling short is documented by their own writing.

25.5 The Moral Compass

In the end, however, their written legacy provides the record of their greatest triumphs: their careers as statesmen. John Adams and John Quincy Adams, each in his own style and with the energy and ethical impulses that drove him, dedicated their lives to creating and expanding the ideas and ideals that would propel the nation and its people to become distinct as an experiment with government and modernity. Both sacrificed immediate personal family lives and careers, because, as heirs to their Puritan forebears, they sought to create a world that secularized the moral values of human perfectibility through social connection within the bonds of a good government. Both were steeped in the knowledge of ancient philosophers as well as more recent enlightened thinkers as models to experiment with new world practice (J.R. Howe, 1966; P. Shaw, 1976).

John Adams was moved by his own background, education, and circumstances to theorize about government. As a young man he wrote the *Dissertation upon Canon and Feudal Law* to examine the uniqueness of the colonies as distinct from the Old World. Later in his *Thoughts on Government* he proposed a tripartite division into independent branches in order to balance power, a scheme that he wrote into the constitution of the commonwealth of Massachusetts. That document and his *Defense of the Constitutions* provided a blueprint for the Framers in 1787. He was not only a partisan in the Revolution, he was one of, if not the greatest theoretician of government for the independent nation (G.S. Wood, 1969: 568).

Of the next generation that inherited this experimental government, still fraught by opposition parties, John Quincy Adams was shaped not only by his unprecedented education and diplomatic experience to understand the maneuverings and intrigues of the Old World and to envision his new nation freed of interference from that world and fated to expand its novel destiny. His brilliance as a tactician and negotiator achieved fulfillment with the Transcontinental Treaty that insured the boundaries of the United States from the Atlantic to the Pacific oceans. His firm conviction about America for Americans (in the words of his first great biographer, Samuel Flagg Bemis) excluded Europeans from further colonizing the western hemisphere while supporting Latin Americans in their revolutions. The development of roads and canals, universities and the arts, common currency and weights, all the mechanisms that unite a burgeoning and diverse people into nationhood, these were his aspirations.

They were aspirations with roots deep in the New England past that made Adamses different than the "greats" who surrounded them in office, the Virginia and Tennessee gentry. Its source was Puritanism, the religious outlook that was more a system of rules for behavior than a theological persuasion and had become a way of life by the eighteenth century. With anxiety over salvation at its core and redemption as its promise, its single-minded focus was on sin that could be mitigated through constant self-examination and striving (P. Miller, 1939: 5, 21–34, 286–302; 1956: 1–15). It personified the character of the young John Adams. His preoccupation with internal tensions – ambition, greed, envy, indolence – marked the pages of his early diary, itself a relic of Puritan self-surveillance. How to overcome his sinful nature became his major project. Hard work, self-sacrifice, service to the community – these were the means he knew to solve the dilemma of his selfhood.

Neither teaching, nor the law, nor community service satisfied his ever-driven quest for personal redemption. Only politics, once he discovered that he could play a role, a big role, even a significant role, began to assuage his driven nature. He brought into politics the erudition of a philosopher of human behavior, the thinking and rhetorical skills of a lawyer, a native brilliance of intellect, a raging capacity for hard work, and a personality at once trenchant, forceful, even severe, first to himself, then to others. He was, as well, passionately sensitive, caring, and droll. He was unforgiving of his enemies, of malingerers, of corruption. And he brought all this to bear on his country that he clearly saw in the image of the human predicament, because it was the product of human thought and energy. It, too, was subject to sin and corruption that would be surmounted by good organization and good laws. It was his passionate nature, above all, that found satisfaction in the struggle to create a new nation and government.

Strangely, in old age, after too many political disappointments and setbacks, he mellowed, his passion tamed into resignation with his imperfect self and his imperfect government. He refused to answer the question put to him by Jefferson: Would he, had he the opportunity, do it all over again?

And when his eldest son had entered the political fray at the highest level, he advised him against continuing. The costs were too high. The pain was too great. He could not bear to see his son suffer the agonies that had tormented his own last efforts in office. He had become, if he had not always been, the consummate skeptic, if an ironical one. In old age, his commentary was, if not caustic, then amused. The old Puritan was tamed (J.J. Ellis, 1993).

But the younger one was not. Nor would he ever be. If John Adams inherited the mantle of secular Puritanism, his eldest son was a throwback to the originals. John Quincy Adams more resembled his ancestors than his immediate progenitors. He would have been comfortable among the generation of William Bradford and John Cotton and John Winthrop, the more so as he aged than in his youth. Life experiences registered with John Quincy differently than with his father. Both men were sensitive; both men cared deeply about other people, about how they engaged in life's unforeseen, even astonishing meandering currents.

But the son's style was more deliberate, more controlled. Partly, he was anchored in a different period, one fraught with a new set of uncertainties. The Revolution that he had witnessed as a youth ended, and his era was one of building on the transformations of the earlier period. Moreover his youthful experiences, even, one might say, his lack of a youth, fashioned a unique persona. In one respect, he was his parents' ideal progeny. He was learned, he served, he had ambition, he worked hard, he was religious. It is fair to say that no young man in America had the experiences of a young John Quincy, who with his father's early departure from home, lived with his mother, younger siblings, and servants in a household under military siege for some years; who traveled back and forth to Europe several times before he came of age; who studied in European schools, traveled about Europe, and mixed with heads of state. Like his Puritan forebears, he learned to turn his back on Europe's temptations and spend his adult years as an advocate for American exceptionalism. His own errand into the wilderness, his covenant entailed the enlargement and the improvement of the "city upon a hill." These metaphorical premises were bred into his nature. If he did not love to engage socially, that was of no account; it was his destiny as an Adams to perform his duty, as his parents had modeled it for him. Whereas the child John Adams rebelled against his father's wish to send him to school (he wanted to be a farmer), John Quincy never rebelled. He was formed by his times, his family, and his vocation to do his duty. As a good Puritan, he followed the rules religiously.

Religion played no small part of his personal motivation. As his father embraced a more liberal Congregationalism in belief and practice, John Quincy became more devout as his years passed, reading several chapters of the Bible every morning upon waking, writing long religious sermons to his sons in letters, thanking his God for blessings when good things happened, be they the birth of a child or the passage of a law, regarding adversity as punishment for his own sins. In form, he was a carbon copy of the originals and he was driven by the same zealousness and sense of purpose in life as those earliest adventurers who peopled the coast of Massachusetts. He was as dour, as driven, as purposeful, as obstinate and intractable in his beliefs about the worldly as the spiritual realm. It made him uncomfortable as a social being in the material world. Unlike his father, he never mellowed, he never was tamed, he merely slowed down, but the manner in which he aged brought him his greatest satisfaction and glory.

Freed from political considerations, freed from family obligations, free from everything but himself, he turned his energies to slavery, the scourge that remained unfixed from the days of the Founders until his time in the House of Representatives. For sixteen years, he did what no other past-president up to his time – or after – had done. He accepted the lower status of representative to Congress and continued to wage the battles that offended his basic sense of right and wrong, as it had offended his father before him. Whereas the father thought for much of his career that the vile system of slavery would collapse of its own economic and social futility, but lately had acknowledged that it would require the intervention of a government to end it, the son made it his last great mission. His battle against the spread of slavery, against the Gag Rule, and his defense of the *Amistad* mutineers became his signature crusade at the end of his life. Unlike his father, who mellowed in old age but still groused in his valedictory "Thomas Jefferson survives," John Quincy, when he died in the House where he served his last sixteen years, uttered as his last words: "I am content."

25.6 The Matriarchs

If John and John Quincy were – each of them – guided by a tradition with roots in old New England, tempered by classical learning as well as the enlightened treatises of seventeenth and eighteenth century philosophers, their wives lived in a cultural paradigm that guided their beliefs, behavior, and understanding of their places in the world as women – wives, mothers, caretakers – domestic beings before anything else. Whatever they accomplished, any sense of themselves as individuals apart from socially and religiously regulated positions was tangential. Their roles were prescribed; their lives were intended to repeat those of their mothers and grandmothers before them. They lived in a world that was determined by biology. How and when and whom they married may have fallen somewhat within the orbit of their discretion. How many and how often they reproduced likely was not. If and how they were educated was determined by social class as well as gender. So were their styles and tastes. They were born into a patriarchal world that mandated women's subordinate roles to men and governed by rules – since Blackstone codified into law – that made their bodies their fate (Bell and Offen, 1983: 29–30).

For that reason Abigail and Louisa Catherine are more remote to us in the twenty-first century than their husbands, and when we try to recapture them as historical figures, the challenge to us as historians is greater. While the Revolution changed John and John Quincy's lives, it neither freed their wives from the limitations of the marriage contract, nor gave them greater equality, nor allowed them greater participation in their future lives. It did not permit them to engage in the political process. It did not give them economic independence. Perhaps it slightly opened educational opportunities for their daughters. The process of change that occurred for men through revolution and modernity would become a long and open-ended crusade for women. The last bastions of the patriarchy could not be won on a battlefield, but only by legal transformations over two more centuries and are not yet completed. In the great drama of their time, the American Revolution and the founding and expansion of the new nation, Abigail and Louisa Catherine were complementary to the starring roles played by their husbands (Berkin, 2005; Crane, 1999; Norton, 1980; Hoff-Wilson, 1976; Offen, 1988; Okin, 1989; Pateman, 1988; Shammas et al., 1987; Zagarri, 2007).

Abigail protested the injustice of the situation, writing to her sister: "I will never consent to have our sex considered in an inferior point of light. As each planet shines in their own orbit, God and nature designd it so," she declared. "If man is Lord, woman is *Lordess.*"[2] She meant that woman's domestic role was equal in status to that of men; it was merely spent in a separate sphere, which is how she understood the governance of the natural universe. Louisa's protests were differently carried out. Louisa addressed her *Narrative of a Journey from Russia to France* to anonymous women as inspiration, to "show that many undertakings which appear very difficult and arduous to my Sex, are by no means as trying as imagination forever depicts them," and she added that her example should demonstrate that the "fancied weakness of feminine imbecility" was a myth (*Narrative*, in Graham et al., forthcoming: 1). Abigail and Louisa recorded their woman-centered legacies as daughters, mothers, and political wives by writing their stories in letters and diaries. Both were conscious of the constraints that society had constructed because they were women, and both of them accepted, adapted to, and chafed at the rules. To them, different as they were, writing became a weapon.

Neither woman enjoyed being a First Lady (although the role existed, the office did not acquire this title until the nineteenth century), but both acquiesced and suffered their positions because they deemed it necessary as wives to men they respected, even revered. Abigail, more than her daughter-in-law, participated as consort during John's one term as president (Gelles, 2009: 234–265). Louisa, whose situation was more complex because of her frail health and her husband's mounting reserve, considered the White House her prison.

The role of First Lady was that of wife writ large, and both Adams women stayed the course. They were by this time mothers, grandmothers, matrons, matured in the crucible of marriage to politicians who were first – perhaps foremost – married to their nation. They believed it their duty to support the careers of men who, they knew, were giants in their time. In retrospect, the historical record demonstrates – to paraphrase Abigail – that if John and John Quincy were giants, Abigail and Louisa Catherine were *giantesses*, not the least because they suffered and triumphed as wives with all the honor that Abigail demanded was owed to that calling.

Absent any one of these four great figures from their era, and its history would be differently recorded, and poorer.

Notes

1 See www.masshist.org/adams/jqa.php (accessed Nov. 9, 2012).

2 Shaw Papers, microfilm edn., 4 reels. Library of Congress, Manuscripts Division: July 19, 1799.

Further Reading

Adams Papers, microfilm edition, 608 reels. Massachusetts Historical Society.

Adams, Charles Francis, ed. (1851–1856). *The Works of John Adams, Second President of the United States: With a Life of the Author, Notes and Illustrations, by His Grandson Charles Francis Adams*, 10 volumes. Boston.

Adams, Charles Francis, ed. 1874–1877. *Memoirs of John Quincy Adams, Comprising Portions of His Diary from 1795 to 1848*, 12 vols. Philadelphia.

Adams, Charles Francis, ed. (1848). *The Letters of Mrs. Adams, the Wife of John Adams.* 4th edn. Boston.

Adams, Henry (1961). *The Education of Henry Adams.* Boston.

Adams, John Quincy. *The Diaries of John Quincy Adams: A Digital Collection.* Online at www.masshist.org/jqadiaries/index.cfm, accessed Nov. 19, 2012.

Akers, Charles W. (1980). *Abigail Adams: An American Woman.* Boston.

Anthony, Carl Sferrazza. (1990). *First Ladies, the Saga of the Presidents' Wives and Their Power, 1789–1961.* New York.

Butterfield, Lyman H. (1959), The Papers of the Adams Family: Some Account of Their History. *Massachusetts Historical Society Proceedings* 71: 328–356.

Cappon, Lester, ed. (1959). *The Adams–Jefferson Letters: The Complete Correspondence between Thomas Jefferson and Abigail and John Adams*, 2 vols. Chapel Hill, NC.

Freiberg, Malcolm (1994). "The Adams Manuscript Trust, 1905–1955." *Massachusetts Historical Society Proceedings* 106: 112–127.

Gelles, Edith B. (1992). *Portia: The World of Abigail Adams.* Bloomington, IN.

Gelles, Edith B. (2002). *Abigail Adams: A Writing Life. New York. (Originally pub. as "First Thoughts": Life and Letters of Abigail Adams*, New York, 1998.)

Gelles, Edith B. (2009). *Abigail and John: The Portrait of a Marriage.* New York.

Hogan, Margaret A., and Taylor, C. James, eds. (2007). *My Dearest Friend: Letters of John and Abigail Adams.* Cambridge, MA.
Kaminski, John P. ed (2009). *The Quotable Abigail Adams.* Cambridge, MA.
Kerber, Linda K. (1976). "The Republican Mother: Women and the Enlightenment – An American Perspective." *American Quarterly* 28:, 187–205.
Kerber, Linda K. 1988. "Separate Spheres, Female Worlds, Women's Place: The Rhetoric of Women's History." *Journal of American History* 75: 9–39.
Lomask, Milton (1965). *John Quincy Adams: Son of the American Revolution.* New York.
Mitchell, Stewart, ed. (1947). *New Letters of Abigail Adams, 1788–1801.* Westport, CT.
Nagel, Paul C. (1983). *Descent from Glory: Four Generations of the John Adams Family.* New York.
Nagel, Paul C. (1987). *The Adams Women: Abigail and Louisa Adams, Their Sisters and Daughters.* New York.
Nagel, Paul C. (1997). *John Quincy Adams: A Public Life, A Private Life.* New York.
Oberg, Barbara, and Ben-Atar, Doron, eds. 1998. *Federalists Reconsidered.* Charlottesville, VA.
Shepherd, Jack (1980). *Cannibals of the Heart: A Personal Biography of Louisa Catherine and John Quincy Adams.* New York.
Smith, Page (1962). *John Adams*, 2 vols. New York.
Smith, Page (1970). *Daughters of the Promised Land: Women in American History.* Boston.

References

Adair, Douglass (1974). *Fame and the Founding Fathers: Essays of Douglass Adair*. New York. (Repr. Indianapolis, 1998.)

Adams Family Papers: An Electronic Archive. Massachusetts Historical Society, Boston, MA. At www.masshist.org/digitaladams/, accessed Nov. 20, 2012.

Adams Papers. MHS digital editions, Massachusetts Historical Society, Boston, MA. www.masshist.org/publications/accessed Nov. 20, 2012.

Adams Papers, microfilm edition, 608 reels. Massachusetts Historical Society, Boston, MA.

Adams, Brooks (1919a). Introductory Note. In H. Adams (1919).

Adams, Brooks (1919b). The Heritage of Henry Adams. In H. Adams (1919).

Adams, Charles Francis (1840). *Letters of Mrs. Adams, The Wife of John Adams*. Boston. (4th edn., 1848.)

Adams, Charles Francis, ed. (1850–1856). *The Works of John Adams, Second President of the United States: With a Life of the Author*, 10 vols. Boston.

Adams, Charles Francis, ed. (1874–1877). *Memoirs of John Quincy Adams, Comprising Portions of His Diary from 1795 to 1848*, 12 vols. Philadelphia.

Adams, Charles Francis (1876). *Familiar Letters of John Adams and His Wife Abigail Adams, During the Revolution. With a Memoir of Mrs. Adams*. New York.

Adams, Charles Francis, ed. (1878a). *Correspondence between John Adams and Mercy Warren*. (Repr. New York, 1972.)

Adams, Charles Francis, ed. (1878b). Appendix to Correspondence between John Adams and Mercy Warren, *Collections of the Massachusetts Historical Society*, 5th ser. 4: 493–511.

Adams, Henry (1906). *The Education of Henry Adams: An Autobiography*. Boston. (Repr. 1961.)

A Companion to John Adams and John Quincy Adams, First Edition.
Edited by David Waldstreicher.

Adams, Henry, with Adams, Brooks (1919). *The Degradation of the Democratic Dogma*. New York.

Adams, Henry, ed. (1877). *Documents Relating to New-England Federalism: 1800–1815*. Boston.

Adams, Henry (1984a). *The History of the United States during the Administration of Thomas Jefferson, 1801–1809*, vol. 1. New York.

Adams, Henry (1984b). *The History of the United States during the Administration of James Madison, 1809–1817*, vol. 2. New York.

Adams, James Truslow (1933). *The Adams Family*. Boston.

Adams, John (1776). *Thoughts on Government, Applicable to the Present State of the American Colonies. In a Letter from a Gentleman to His Friend*. Philadelphia.

Adams, John (1797). *A Defence of the Constitutions of Government of the United States of America, Against the Attack of M. Turgot in his Letter to Dr. Price, Dated the Twenty-Second Day of March, 1778*, 3 vols. Philadelphia.

Adams, John (1823). *Correspondence Between the Hon. John Adams, Late President of the United States, and the late Wm. Cunningham, Esq. Beginning in the Year 1803, and Ending in 1812*. Boston.

Adams, John and Tudor, William (1819). Letters From the Hon. John Adams, to the Hon. Wm. Tudor, and Others, on the Events of the American Revolution. In John Adams and W. Tudor, eds., *Novanglus, and Massachusettensis; or, Political Essays, Published in the Years 1774 and 1775*: 229–312. Boston.

Adams, John Quincy, trans. (1800). *The Origins and Principles of the American Revolution, Compared with the Origins and Principles of the French Revolution. Translated from the German of Gentz* Philadelphia.

Adams, John Quincy (1809). *American Principles: A Review of Works of Fisher Ames*. Boston.

Adams, John Quincy (1810). *Lectures on Rhetoric and Oratory, Delivered to the Classes of Senior and Junior Sophisters in the Harvard University*, Cambridge, MA.

Adams, John Quincy (1821). *An Address Celebrating the Anniversary of Independence, at the City of Washington on the Fourth of July 1821*. Washington.

Adams, John Quincy (1825a). Inaugural Address of John Quincy Adams, President of the United States (March 4, 1825). *American State Papers: Foreign Relations*: 5: 753–755.

Adams, John Quincy (1825b). First Annual Message (Dec. 6, 1825), *Register of Debates*, 19th Cong., 1st Sess., 2–8 (Appendix).

Adams, Sean Patrick (2004). *Old Dominion, Industrial Commonwealth: Coal, Politics, and Economy in Antebellum America*. Baltimore.

Adams, Sean Patrick (2008). The Tao of John Quincy Adams, Common-Place 9: 1 (Oct. 2008). At www.common-place.org/vol-09/no-01/adams, accessed Nov. 19, 2012.

Akers, Charles W. (1980). *Abigail Adams: An American Woman*. Boston. (Repr. New York, 2000.)

Aldrich, John H. (2005). The Election of 1800: The Consequences of the First Change in Party Control. In Bowling, Kenneth. R. and Donald R. Kennon, 2005. *Establishing Congress: The Removal to Washington, DC, and the Election of 1800*: 23–38. Athens, OH.

Allen, David Grayson, Robert J. Taylor, Marc Friedlaender, and Celeste Walker (1981). *The Diary of John Quincy Adams*, 2 vols. Cambridge, MA.

Allgor, Catherine A. (1997). "A Republican in A Monarchy": Louisa Catherine Adams in Russia. *Diplomatic History*: 15–43.

Allgor, Catherine A. (2000). *Parlor Politics: In Which the Ladies of Washington Help Build a City and a Government.* Charlottesville, VA.

Allison, John Murray (1966). *Adams and Jefferson: The Story of a Friendship.* Norman, OK.

Altschuler, Bruce (2007). A Century of Presidential Plays. *PRG Report* 29: 3–8.

Ammon, H. 1971. *James Monroe and the Quest for National Identity.* McGraw-Hill.

Anderson, Benedict (1983). *Imagined Communities: Reflections on the Origin and Spread of Nationalism.* London.

Anderson, Fred (2000). *Crucible of War: The Seven Years War and the Fate of Empire in British North America, 1754–1766.* New York.

Appleby, Joyce (1968). The Jefferson-Adams Rupture and the First French Translation of John Adams' *Defense. American Historical Review* 73: 1084–1091.

Appleby, Joyce (1973). The New Republican Synthesis and the Changing Political Ideas of John Adams. *American Quarterly* 25: 578–595.

Archer, Richard (2010). *As If In an Enemy's Country: The British Occupation of Boston and the Origins of the American Revolution.* New York.

Auer, J. Jeffery, and Banninga, Jerald L. (1963), The Genesis of John Quincy Adams's Lectures on Rhetoric and Oratory, *Quarterly Journal of Speech* 49: 119–32.

Austin, James T. (1828). *The Life of Elbridge Gerry*, 2 vols. Boston.

Axtell, James (1985). *The Invasion Within: The Contest of Cultures in Colonial North America.* New York.

Bailyn, Bernard (1962). Butterfield's Adams: Notes for a Sketch. *The William and Mary Quarterly* 19: 238–256.

Bailyn, Bernard (1967). *The Ideological Origins of the American Revolution.* Cambridge, MA.

Bailyn, Bernard (1990). *Faces of Revolution: Personalities and Themes in the Struggle for American Independence.* New York.

Bailyn, Bernard (1992). John Adams. In *Faces of Revolution: Personalities and Themes in the Struggle for American Independence*: 3–21. New York.

Baker, Pamela (2002). The Washington National Road Bill and the Struggle to Adopt a Federal System of Internal Improvement, *Journal of the Early Republic* 22: 437–464.

Banning, Lance (1978). *The Jeffersonian Persuasion: Evolution of a Party Ideology.* Ithaca, NY.

Barker-Benfield, G. J. (2010). *Abigail and John Adams: The Americanization of Sensibility.* Chicago.

Baron, Robert C., and Wright, Conrad Edick eds. (2010). *The Libraries, Leadership, and Legacies of John Adams and Thomas Jefferson.* Boston, MA.

Basker, James G. ed. (2002). *Amazing Grace: An Anthology of Poems about Slavery, 1660-1810.* New Haven and London.

Basler, Roy P., ed. (1953). *The Collected Works of Abraham Lincoln.* New Brunswick.

Battin, Margaret P. (2005). *Ending Life: Ethics and the Way We Die*. New York.
Beer, Arthur, ed. (1967). *Vistas in Astronomy: New Aspects in the History and Philosophy of Astronomy*, vol. 9. Oxford.
Bell, Susan, and Offen, Karen M. 1983. *Women, the Family, and Freedom: The Debate In Documents. Volume I, 1750–1880*. Stanford, CA.
Bemis, Samuel Flagg (1949), *John Quincy Adams and the Foundations of American Foreign Policy*. New York.
Bemis, Samuel Flagg (1956), *John Quincy Adams and the Union*. New York. (Reprint, 1984.)
Berkin, Carol 2005. *Revolutionary Mothers: Women in the Struggle for America's Independence*. New York.
Berkvist, R. 2007. George Grizzard, Actor noted for Albee Roles, dies at 79. *New York Times*, A23.
Berman, Ronald (1984). Wycherley's Unheroic Society. *English Literary History* 51: 465–478.
Bernstein, Peter (2005), *Wedding of the Waters: The Erie Canal and the Making of a Great Nation*. New York.
Biddle, Alexander (1892). *Old Family Letters: Copied from the Originals for Alexander Biddle. Series A*. Philadelphia.
Billington, James (2003). David McCullough, Chronicler of America: An Appreciation. *Humanities* 24, May–June.
Black, Jeremy (2010). *A History of Diplomacy*. London.
Bobbé, Dorothie (1929). *Abigail Adams: The Second First Lady*. New York.
Bobbé, Dorothie (1930). *Mrs and Mrs. John Quincy Adams: An Adventure in Patriotism*. New York.
Bolkhovitinov, Nikolai (1975). *The Beginnings of Russian-American Relations, 1775–1815*. Cambridge, MA.
Bonney, Richard (1995). *Economy Systems and State Finance*. Oxford.
Bowen, Catherine Drinker (1950). *John Adams and the American Revolution*. Boston.
Bowling, Kenneth R., and Veit, Helen E. 1989. *The Diary of William Maclay and Other Notes on Senate Debates, March 4, 1789-March 3, 1791*. Baltimore, MD.
Boyd, Julian P. et al., eds. (1950–), *The Papers of Thomas Jefferson*, 38 vols. to date. Princeton.
Bradburn, Douglas (2008). A Clamor in the Public Mind: Opposition to the Alien and Sedition Acts. *William and Mary Quarterly* 55: 565–600.
Bradburn, Douglas (2009). *The Citizenship Revolution: Politics and the Creation of the American Union, 1774–1804*. Charlottesville, VA.
Branson, Susan (2001). *These Fiery Frenchified Dames: Women and Political Culture in Early National Philadelphia*. Philadelphia.
Breen, Timothy H. (1967). John Adams' Fight against Innovation in the New England Constitution: 1776. *New England Quarterly* 40: 501–520.
Brooke, John (2010). *Columbia Rising: Civil Life on the Upper Hudson from the Revolution to the Age of Jackson*. Chapel Hill, NC
Brown, Gordon S. (2005). *Toussaint's Clause: The Founding Fathers and the Haitian Revolution*. Jackson, MI.
Brown, Jared (1995). *The Theatre in America During the Revolution*. Cambridge.

Brown, Ralph Adams (1975). *The Presidency of John Adams.* Lawrence, KS.

Brown, Richard D. (1966). The Missouri Crisis, Slavery, and the Politics of Jacksonianism. *South Atlantic Quarterly* 61: 55–72.

Brown, Richard D. (1989). *Knowledge is Power: The Diffusion of Information in Early America, 1700–1865.* New York.

Brown, Richard D. (2001), The Disenchantment of a Radical Whig: John Adams Reckons with Free Speech. *In Ryerson* (2001): 171–185.

Brown, Walt, Jr. (1995). *John Adams and the American Press: Politics and Journalism at the Birth of the Republic.* Jefferson, NC.

Buel, Richard (2005). *American on the Brink: How the Political Struggle over the War of 1812 Almost Destroyed the Republic.* New York.

Burstein, Andrew (1995). *The Inner Jefferson: Portrait of a Grieving Optimist.* Charlottesville, VA.

Burstein, Andrew (2005). *Jefferson's Secrets: Death and Desire at Monticello.* New York.

Burstein, Andrew, and Isenberg, Nancy (2010). *Madison and Jefferson.* New York.

Butterfield, Lyman H., ed. (1951). *Letters of Benjamin Rush.* Princeton.

Butterfield, Lyman H. (ed. (1966). *The Earliest Diary of John Adams: June 1753–April 1754, September 1758–January 1759.* Cambridge, MA.

Butterfield, Lyman H. (1974). Tending A Dragon-Killer: Notes for the Biographer of Mrs. *John Quincy Adams. American Philosophical Society Proceedings* 118: 165–178.

Butterfield, Lyman H., Faber, Leonard C., and Garrett, Wendell D., eds. (1961). *The Adams Papers: Diary and Autobiography of John Adams,* 4 vols. Cambridge, MA.

Butterfield, Lyman H. et al. (eds.) (1963–). *Adams Family Correspondence,* 10 vols. to date. Cambridge, MA.

Butterfield, Lyman H., Friedlaender, M., and Kline, M. (1975). *The Book of Abigail and John: Selected Letters of the Adams Family, 1762-1784.* Boston. (2nd edn. 2000.)

Byrnes, Robert F. (1982). *Awakening American Education to the World: The Role of Archibald Cary Coolidge, 1966–1928.* South Bend, IN.

Calhoon, R.M. (1973). *The Loyalists of Revolutionary America, 1760–1781.* New York.

Callender, Guy Stevens (1902). The Early Transportation and Banking Enterprises of the States in Relation to the Growth of Corporations.*Quarterly Journal of Economics* 17: 111–162.

Cappon, Lester J., ed. (1959). *The Adams–Jefferson Letters: The Complete Correspondence Between Thomas Jefferson and Abigail and John Adams.* Chapel Hill, NC. (Repr. 1987.)

Carey, George W. ed. (2000). *The Political Writings of John Adams.* Chicago.

Carnes, Mark C., ed. (1996). *Past Imperfect: History According to the Movies.* New York.

Carroll, Warren Hasty (1959). John Adams, Puritan Revolutionist: A Study of His Part in the Making of the American Revolution, 1764–1776. PhD diss., Columbia University.

Carp, Benjamin L. (2010). *Defiance of the Patriots: The Boston Tea Party and the Making of America.* New Haven.

Cave, Alfred A. (1964). *Jacksonian Democracy and the Historians.* Gainesville, FL.

Challinor, Joan Ridder (1982). Louisa Catherine Johnson Adams: The Price of Ambition. PhD diss., American University.
Challinor, Joan Ridder (1986). The Mis-Education of Louisa Catherine Adams. *Massachusetts Historical Society Proceedings*, 98, 21–48.
Chamberlain, Mellen (1898). *John Adams, Statesman of the American Revolution, with Other Essays and Addresses Historical and Literary*. Boston, MA.
Charles, Joseph (1956). *Origins of the American Party System: Three Essays*. Williamsburg, VA. (Repr. New York, 1961.)
Chinard, Gilbert (1929). *Thomas Jefferson: The Apostle of Americanism*. Boston.
Chinard, Gilbert (1933). *Honest John Adams*. New York.
Chodorow, Nancy (1978). *The Reproduction of Mothering*. Berkeley.
Cicero, Marcus Tullus (1949). *Cicero's De Inventione*, trans. Harry Mortimer Hubbel, Cambridge, MA.
Clarfield, Gerard (1979). John Adams, the Market, and American Foreign Policy. *New England Quarterly* 52: 345–357.
Clark, Bennett Champ (1932). *John Quincy Adams: Old Man Eloquent*. Boston.
Clark, Gregory, and Halloran, S. Michael (1993), *Oratorical Culture in Nineteenth-Century America: Transformations in the Theory and Practice of Rhetoric*. Carbondale, IL.
Clarke, Fred G. (1964). *John Quincy Adams*. New York.
Cleves, Rachel Hope (2009). *The Reign of Terror in America: Visions of Violence from Anti-Jacobinism to Antislavery*. New York.
Colbourn, H. Trevor (1965). *The Lamp of Experience: Whig History and the Intellectual Origins of the American Revolution*. Chapel Hill, NC. (Repr. Indianapolis 1998).
Cole, Donald B. (2009). *Vindicating Andrew Jackson: The Election of 1828 and the Rise of the Two-Party System*. Lawrence, KS.
Colley, Linda (1992). *Britons: Forging the Nation, 1707–1837*. New Haven.
Condillac (1930). *Condillac's Treatise on the Sensations*, trans. Geraldine Carr. London.
Condorcet, M. (1795). *Outlines of an Historical View of the Progress of the Human Mind*. London.
Conn, Peter J. (2009). John Adams. *Great American Bestsellers: The Books That Shaped America*. The Teaching Company.
Cook, Harold J. (1999). Bernard Mandeville and the Therapy of the Clever Politician. *Journal of the History of Ideas* 60: 101–124.
Coolidge, Harold Jefferson, and Lord, Robert Howard (1932). *Archibald Cary Coolidge: Life and Letters*. Boston.
Coontz, Stephanie (2005). *Marriage, a History: From Obedience to Intimacy or How Love Conquered Marriage*. New York.
Coquillette, Daniel R. (1984). Justinian in Braintree: John Adams, Civilian Learning, and Legal Elitism, 1758–1775. In Daniel R.Coquillette, ed. *Law in Colonial Massachusetts, 1630–1800*: 359–418. Boston.
Corbett, Katherine T. (1979). Louisa Catherine Adams: The Anguished Adventures of a Nobody. In Mary Kelley, *Woman's Being, Woman's Place: Female Identity and Vocation in American History*. Boston.
Corner, George W., ed. (1948). *The Autobiography of Benjamin Rush: His Travels Through Life Together with His Commonplace Book for 1789–1813*. Princeton.

Cott, Nancy F. (1977). *The Bonds of Womanhood: Woman's Sphere in New England, 1780–1835.* New Haven.

Crackel, Theodore, ed. (2008). *The Papers of George Washington Digital Edition.* Charlottesville,VA.

Crane, Elaine Forman (1999). Political Dialogue and the Spring of Abigail's Discontent. *William and Mary Quarterly* 56: 745–774.

Craven, Wayne (1986). *Colonial American Portraiture: The Economic, Religious, Social, Cultural, Philosophical, Scientific, and Aesthetic Foundations.* Cambridge.

Crosby, Alfred W. (1965). *America, Russia, Hemp, and Napoleon: American Trade with Russia and the Baltic, 1783–1812.* Columbus, OH.

Cunningham, Noble E. (1957). *The Jeffersonian Republicans: The Formation of Party Organizations, 1789-1801.* Chapel Hill, NC.

Cunningham, Noble E. (1985). Election of 1800. In Schlesinger (1985): 101–156.

Cunningham, Noble E. (1996). *The Presidency of James Monroe.* Lawrence, KS.

Dalzell, Frederick (1998). Review: Dreamworking Amistad: Representing Slavery, Revolt, and Freedom in America, 1839 and 1997. *New England Quarterly* 71: 127–133.

Dangerfield, George (1965). *The Awakening of American Nationalism, 1815–1828.* New York.

Daniel, Marcus (2009). *Scandal and Civility: Journalism and the Birth of American Democracy.* New York.

Dasgupta, G. (1984). William Gibson (1914–). In Stanley Hochman, ed., *McGraw-Hill Encyclopedia of World Drama: An International Reference Work in Five Volumes*: 294–295. New York.

Dauer, Manning. J. (1953). *The Adams Federalists.* Baltimore. (Rev. edn. 1968.)

Davis, David Brion (1990). *Revolutions: Reflections on American Equality and Foreign Liberations.* Cambridge, MA.

Davis, David Brion (1999). *The Problem of Slavery in the Age of Revolution, 1770–1823*, 2nd edn. New York.

DeConde, Alexander (1957). Washington's Farewell, the French Alliance, and the Election of 1796. *Mississippi Valley Historical Review* 43: 641–658.

DeConde, Alexander (1959). *Entangling Alliance: Politics and Diplomacy under George Washington.* Durham, NC.

DeConde, Alexander (1966). *The Quasi-War: The Politics and Diplomacy of the Undeclared War with France, 1797–1801.* New York.

Dickens, Homer (1971). *The Films of Katharine Hepburn.* New York.

Dickson, Charles Ellis (1987). Jeremiads in the New American Republic: The Case of National Fasts in the John Adams Administration, *New England Quarterly* 60: 187–207.

Diggins, John Patrick (2003). *John Adams.* New York.

Diggins, John Patrick, ed. (2004). *The Portable John Adams.* New York.

Dilts, James (1996). *The Great Road: The Building of the Baltimore and Ohio, the Nation's First Railroad, 1828–1853.* Stanford, CA.

Dorfman, Joseph (1946). *The Economic Mind in American Civilization, 1606–1865*, 2 vols. New York.

Dreamworks (1997). *Amistad*, dir. Steven Spielberg.

Dunaway, Wayland Fuller (1922), *History of the James River and Kanawha Company*. Columbia.

Dunlavy, Colleen (1994), *Politics and Industrialization: Early Railroads in the United States and Prussia*. Princeton.

Dunn, Susan (2004). *Jefferson's Second Revolution: The Election Crisis of 1800 and the Triumph of Republicanism*. Boston.

East, Robert A. (1962). *John Quincy Adams: The Critical Years, 1785–1794*. New York.

Eastman, Carolyn (2009). *A Nation of Speechifiers: Making an American Public after the Revolution*. Chicago.

Egerton, Douglas R. (2002). The Empire of Liberty Reconsidered. In Horn et al.(2002): 309–330.

Elkins, Stanley and Eric McKitrick (1993). *The Age of Federalism: The Early American Republic, 1788–1800*. New York.

Ellis, Joseph J. (1993). *Passionate Sage: The Character and Legacy of John Adams*. New York. (Repr. 2001.)

Ellis, Joseph J.(2004). *His Excellency: George Washington*. New York.

Ellis, Joseph J. (2010). *First Family: Abigail and John Adams*. New York.

Ellis, Richard E. (2007). *Aggressive Nationalism: McCulloch v. Maryland and the Foundation of Federal Authority in the Young Republic*. New York.

Elshtain, Jean Bethke (1981). *Public Man, Private Woman: Women in Social and Political Thought*. Princeton.

Ericson, David F. (1993). *The Shaping of American Liberalism: The Debates over Ratification, Nullification, and Slavery*. Chicago.

Ericson, David F. (2001). *The Debate over Slavery: Antislavery and Proslavery Liberalism in Antebellum America*. New York.

Eustace, Nicole (2008). *Passion is the Gale: Emotion, Power, and the Coming of the American Revolution*. Chapel Hill, NC.

Evans, John Charles (2006). The Relevance of John Adams: Combining Liberal, Republican and Christian Ideals in Early American Political Thought. PhD diss., University of Wisconsin-Madison.

Everett, Edward (1675–1910). *Papers*. Microfilm edition, Masachusetts Historical Society.

Everett, Edward (1878). *Orations and Speeches on Various Occasions*, vol. 2, 9th edn. Boston.

Farrell, James M. (1989). John Adams's *Autobiography*: The Ciceronian Paradigm and the Quest for Fame. *New England Quarterly* 62: 505–528.

Farrell, James M. (1991). *Pro Militibus Oratio*: John Adams's Imitation of Cicero in the Boston Massacre Trial. *Rhetorica* 9: 233–249.

Farrell, James M. (1992a). "Syren Tully" and the Young John Adams. *Classical Journal* 87: 373–390.

Farrell, James M. (1992b). New England's Cicero: John Adams and the Rhetoric of Conspiracy. *Proceedings of the Massachusetts Historical Society*, 3rd ser. 104: 55–72.

Farrell, James M. (1994). Letters and Political Judgment: John Adams and Cicero's Style. *Studies in Eighteenth-Century Culture* 24: 137–153.

Farrell, James M. (2002). Classical Virtue and Presidential Fame: John Adams, Leadership, and the Franco-American Crisis. In Leroy G. Dorsey, ed., *The Presidency and Rhetorical Leadership*: 73–94. College Station, TX.

Farrell, James M. (2006). Writs of Assistance and Public Memory: John Adams and the Legacy of James Otis. *New England Quarterly* 89: 533–556.

Fea, John (2011). *Was America Founded as a Christian Nation?: A Historical Introduction.* Louisville, KY.

Fehrenbacher, Don (2001), *The Slaveholding Republic: An Account of the United States Government's Relations to Slavery.* New York.

Fenton, Elizabeth (2011). *Religious Liberties: Anti-Catholicism and Liberal Democracy in Nineteenth-Century US Literature and Culture.* New York.

Ferguson, E. James (1967). *Selected Writings of Albert Gallatin.* Indianapolis.

Ferling, John E. (1992). *John Adams: A Life.* Knoxville, TN.

Ferling, John E. (1994a). John Adams, Diplomat. *William and Mary Quarterly*, 3rd seri. 51(2), April: 227–252.

Ferling, John E. (1994b). *John Adams: A Bibliography.* Westport, CT.

Ferling, John E. (2000). *Setting the World Ablaze: Washington, Adams, Jefferson, and the American Revolution.* New York.

Ferling, John E. (2004). *Adams vs. Jefferson: The Tumultuous Election of 1800.* New York.

Ferling, John E. (2009). *The Ascent of George Washington.* New York.

Fischer, David Hackett (1994). *Paul Revere's Ride.* Oxford.

Fleming, Thomas (1996). 1776. In Carnes (1996): 90–93.

Forbes, Robert Pierce (2007). *The Missouri Compromise and Its Aftermath: Slavery and the Meaning of America.* Chapel Hill, NC.

Ford, Lacy K. (2009). *Deliver Us from Evil: The Slavery Question in the Old South.* New York.

Ford, Worthington C. et al., eds. (1904–1937), *Journals of the Continental Congress, 1774–1789*, 34 vols. Washington.

Ford, Worthington C., ed. (1913–1917). *Writings of John Quincy Adams*, 7 vols. New York.

Ford, Worthington C., ed. (1938). *Letters of Henry Adams (1892–1918).* Boston and New York.

Frazer, Gregg L. (2012). *The Religious Beliefs of America's Founders: Reason, Revelation, and Revolution.* Lawrence, KS.

Frederick, David C. (1991). John Quincy Adams, Slavery, and the Disappearance of the Right of Petition. *Law and History Review* 9: 113–155.

Freehling, William (1990). *The Road to Disunion: Secessionists at Bay, 1776–1854.* New York.

Freeman, Joanne B. (1999). The Election of 1800: A Study in the Logic of Political Change. *Yale Law Journal* 108(8), June: 1959–1994.

Freeman, Joanne B. (2001a). *Affairs of Honor: National Politics in the New Republic.* New Haven.

Freeman, Joanne B. (2001b). The Presidential Election of 1796. In Ryerson (2001): 142–167.

Freeman, Joanne B. (2003). Explaining the Unexplainable: The Cultural Logic of the Sedition Act. In Jacobs et al. (2003): 20–49.

Garraty, John A. (1963). Review of Page Smith. *John Adams. William and Mary Quarterly*, 3rd Ser. 20: 454–458.

Gates, David (2001). Founding Fathers: John Adams is in The House. *Newsweek*, May 21.

Gaustad, Edwin S. (1987). *Faith of Our Fathers: Religion and the New Nation*. San Francicso.

Gelles, Edith B. (1988). The Abigail Industry. *William and Mary Quarterly* 45: 656–683.

Gelles, Edith B. (1992). *Portia: The World of Abigail Adams*. Bloomington, IN.

Gelles, Edith B. (1998). *First Thoughts: Life and Letters of Abigail Adams*. New York.

Gelles, Edith (2001). "Splendid Misery": Abigail Adams as First Lady. In Ryerson (2001): 186–235.

Gelles, Edith B. (2002). *Abigail Adams: A Writing Life*. London. (2nd edition of Gelles, 1998).rling

Gelles, E. (2009). *Abigail and John: Portrait of a Marriage*. New York.

Gibbon, Edward (1994). *The History of the Decline and Fall of the Roman Empire*, ed. David Womersley, 3 vols. London.

Giddings, Joshua R. (1853). *Speeches in Congress*. Boston.

Giddings, Joshua R. (1858). *The Exiles of Florida: The Crimes Committed By Our Government against the Maroons Who Fled from South Carolina and Other Slave States*. Baltimore. (Repr. 1997.)

Gilbert, Felix (1961). *To The Farewell Address: Ideas of Early American Foreign Policy*. Princeton.

Gilligan, Carol (1982). *In a Different Voice: Psychological Theory and Women's Development*. Cambridge, MA.

Goff, Philip Kevin (1993). The Religious World of the Revolutionary John Adams. PhD diss.,University of North Carolina.

Goodfellow, Donald M. (1946). The First Boylson Professor of Rhetoric and Oratory. *New England Quarterly*, 19: 372–389.

Goodman, Paul (1967). The First American Party System. In W.N. Chambers, *The First Party System*: 56–89. New York. (2nd edn., 1972.)

Goodrich, Carter (1968), State In, State Out: A Pattern of Development Policy. *Journal of Economic Issues* 2: 365–383.

Graham, Judith S., Luey, Beth, Hogan, Margaret A., and Taylor, C. James, eds. (forthcoming). *Diary and Autobiographical Writings of Louisa Catherine Adams*, vols. 1 and 2: 1778–1849. Cambridge, MA.

Grant, James (2005). *John Adams, Party of One*. New York.

Green, Michael (1982). *The Politics of Indian Removal: Creek Government and Society in Crisis*. Lincoln, NE.

Greenberg, Kenneth (1996). *Honor and Slavery*. Princeton.

Greene, Evarts Boutell and Harrington,Virginia D. (1933). *American Population Before the Federal Census of 1790*. New York.

Greenstone, J. David (1993). *The Lincoln Persuasion: Remaking American Liberalism*. Princeton.

Gross, Robert A. (ed.) (1993). *In Debt to Shays: The Bicentennial of an Agrarian Rebellion*. Charlottesville, VA.

Guerrero, Linda Dudik (1982). *John Adams' Vice Presidency, 1789–1797: The Neglected Man in the Forgotten Office*. New York.

Gustafson, Sandra (2000). *Eloquence is Power: Oratory and Performance in Early America*. Chapel Hill, NC.

Gustafson, Sandra (2011). *Imagining Deliberative Democracy in the Early American Republic*. Chicago.

Hamer, Philp (1935), Great Britain, The United States, and the Negro Seamen Acts, 1822–1848. *Journal of Southern History* 1: 3–28.

Hamilton, Alexander (1800). *Letter from Alexander Hamilton, Concerning the Public Conduct and Character of John Adams, Esq., President of the United States*. New York.

Hammond, Bray (1957). *Banks and Politics in America from the Revolution to the Civil War*. Princeton.

Hammond, John Craig (2007). *Slavery, Freedom, and Expansion in the Early American West*. Charlottesville, VA.

Hammond, John Craig, and Mason, Matthew, eds.(2011). *Contesting Slavery: The Politics of Bondage and Freedom in the New American Nation*. Charlottesville, VA.

Handler, Edward (1964). *America and Europe in the Political Thought of John Adams*. Cambridge, MA.

Haraszti, Zoltan (1952). *John Adams and the Prophets of Progress*. Cambridge, MA.

Hargreaves, Mary W.M. (1985). *The Presidency of John Quincy Adams*. Lawrence, KS.

Hartz, Louis W. (1948), *Economic Policy and Democratic Thought: Pennsylvania, 1776–1860*. Cambridge, MA.

Hartz, Louis W. (1955). *The Liberal Tradition in America*. New York.

Haynes, Sam (2010). *Unfinished Revolution: The Early American Republic in a British World*. Charlottesville, VA.

HBO (2008). *John Adams* (HBO mini-series).

Heale, M.J. (1982). *The Presidential Quest: Candidates and Images in American Political Culture, 1787–1852*. New York.

Hecht, Marie B. (1972). *John Quincy Adams: A Personal History of an Independent Man*. New York.

Heffron, M. M. (2010). "A Fine Romance": The Courtship Correspondence between Louisa Catherine Johnson and John Quincy Adams. *New England Quarterly* 83: 200–218.

Heffron, M. M. (2011). The Other Mrs. Adams: A Life of Louisa Catherine Adams. Unpublished MS.

Hendrickson, David C. (2003). *Peace Pact: The Lost World of the American Founding*. Lawrence, KS.

Hicks, Philip (2005) Portia and Marcia: Female Political Identity and the Historical Imagination, 1770–1800. *William and Mary Quarterly* 62: 265–294.

Hill, Peter P. (2003). The Early National Period, 1775–1815. In Robert D. Schulzinger, *A Companion to American Foreign Relations*: 48–63. Oxford.

Hoff-Wilson, Joan (1976). The Illusion of Change: Women and the American Revolution. In Alfred F. Young, ed., *The American Revolution: Explorations in the History of American Radicalism*: 383–445. DeKalb, IL.

Hofstadter, Richard (1968). *The Progressive Historians*. Chicago. (Repr. 1979.)

Hofstadter, Richard (1969). *The Idea of a Party System: The Rise of Legitimate Opposition in the United States, 1780–1840*. Berkeley.

Hogan, Margaret A., and Taylor, C. James, eds. (2007). *My Dearest Friend: Letters of Abigail and John Adams*. Cambridge, MA.

Holmes, David L. (2006). *The Faiths of the Founding Fathers*. New York.

Holton, Woody (2009). *Abigail Adams: A Life*. New York.

Hopkins, James F., ed. (1959). *The Papers of Henry Clay*, vol. 1: *The Rising Statesman, 1797–1814*. Lexington, KY.

Hopkins, James F. and Hargreaves, Mary W.M., eds. (1963). *The Papers of Henry Clay*, vol. 3: *The Presidential Candidate 1821–1824*. Lexington, KY.

Horn, James, Lewis, Jan Ellen, and Onuf, Peter S. eds. (2002). *The Revolution of 1800: Democracy, Race, and the New Republic*. Charlottesville, VA.

Howe, Daniel Walker (1979). *The Political Culture of the American Whigs*. Chicago.

Howe, Daniel Walker (2007). *What Hath God Wrought: The Transformation of America, 1815–1848*. New York.

Howe, John R., Jr. (1966). *The Changing Political Thought of John Adams*. Princeton.

Hume, David (1778). *The History of England*. London. (Repr. Indianapolis 1983).

Hunt, Lynn (1992). *The Family Romance of the French Revolution*. Berkeley.

Hutchinson, Peter Orlando, ed. (1884–1886). *The Diary and Letters of His Excellency Thomas Hutchinson*, Boston.

Hutson, James H. (1980). *John Adams and the Diplomacy of the American Revolution*. Lexington, KY.

Hutson, James H., ed. (2005). *Founders on Religion*. Princeton.

Hynes, Peter (1996). Against Theory? Knowledge and Action in Wycherley's Plays. *Modern Philology* 94: 163–189.

Iacuzzi, Alfred (1952). *John Adams, Scholar*. New York.

Immerman, Richard H. (2004). Psychology. In Michael J. Hogan and Thomas Paterson, *Explaining the History of American Foreign Relations*, 2nd edn: 103–122. New York..

Immerman, Richard H. (2009). *Empire of Liberty*. Princeton.

Innes, Stephen (1983). *Labor in a New Land: Economy and Society in Seventeenth Century Springfield*. Princeton.

Innes, Stephen (1995). *Creating the Commonwealth: Economic Culture in Early New England*. New York.

Irelan, John Robert (1886). *History of the Life, Administration, and Times of John Adams, Second President of the United States. The Revolution and the Establishment of the American Union*. Chicago.

Irvin, Benjamin C. (2002). *Samuel Adams: Son of Liberty, Father of Revolution*. New York.

Israel, Jonathan I. (2011). *Democratic Enlightenment: Philosophy, Revolution, and Human Rights 1750–1790*. Oxford.

Jacob, Margaret C. (2006). *Strangers Nowhere in the World: The Rise of Cosmopolitanism in Early Modern Europe*. Philadelphia.

Jacobs, Meg, Novak, William J., and Zelizer, Julian, eds. (2003). *The Democratic Experiment: New Directions in American Political History*. Princeton.

Jefferson, Thomas (1984). *Writings*, ed. Merrill Peterson. New York.

John, Richard R. (1995). *Spreading the News: The American Postal System from Franklin to Morse*. Cambridge, MA.

John, Richard R. (2010), *Network Nation: Inventing American Telecommunications*. Cambridge, MA.

Johnson, Paul (1978), *A Shopkeeper's Millennium: Society and Revivals in Rochester, New York, 1815–1837.* New York.
Johnson, Ronald A. (2011). A Revolutionary Dinner: US Diplomacy toward Saint-Domingue, 1798–1801. *Early American Studies* 9: 114–141.
Jones, Bessie Zaban, and Boyd, Lyle Gifford (1971). *The Harvard College Observatory: The First Four Directorships, 1839–1919.* Cambridge, MA.
Jones, Howard H. (1987). *Mutiny on the* Amistad: *The Saga of a Slave Revolt and Its Impact on American Abolition, Law, and Diplomacy.* New York.
Kaminski, John P., ed. (2009). *The Quotable Abigail Adams.* Cambridge, MA.
Keller, Rosemary (1994). *Patriotism and the Female Sex: Abigail Adams and the American Revolution.* Brooklyn, NY.
Kennedy, Emmet (1978). *A Philosophe in the Age of Revolution: Destutt de Tracy and the Origins of Ideology.* Philadelphia.
Kennedy, John F. (1956). *Profiles in Courage.* New York.
Kennedy, John F. (1963). Review of *The Adams Papers, Series I: Diary and Autobiography of John Adams. American Historical Review* 68(2), Jan: 478–480.
Kennedy, Roger (2003). *Mr. Jefferson's Lost Cause: Land, Farmers, Slavery, and the Louisiana Purchase.* Oxford.
Kerber, Linda K., and Morris, Walter John (1966). Notes and Documents: Politics and Literature: The Adams Family and the Port Folio. *William and Mary Quarterly* 23: 450–476.
Ketcham, Ralph (1984). *Presidents Above Party: The First American Presidency, 1789–1829.* Chapel Hill, NC.
Klepp, S. (2009). *Revolutionary Conceptions: Women, Fertility, and Family Limitation in America, 1760–1820.* Chapel Hill, NC.
Knollenberg, Bernhard (1963). John Dickinson vs. John Adams: 1774–1776. *Proceedings of the American Philosophical Society* 107: 138–144.
Koch, Adrienne (1963). *Adams and Jefferson: Posterity Must Judge.* Chicago.
Koch, Adrienne, and Peden, William, eds. (1946). *Selected Writings of John & John Quincy Adams.* New York.
Kuroda, Tadahisa (1994). *The Origins of the Twelfth Amendment: The Electoral College in the Early Republic, 1787–1804.* Westport, CT.
Kurtz, Stephen G. (1957). *The Presidency of John Adams: The Collapse of Federalism, 1795–1800.* Philadelphia.
Kurtz, Stephen G. (1968). Notes and Documents: The Political Science of John Adams: A Guide to His Statecraft. *William and Mary Quarterly*, 3rd ser. 25(4), Oct.: 605–613.
Labaree, Benjamin Woods (1964). *The Boston Tea Party.* New York.
Lafeber, Walter, ed. (1965). *John Quincy Adams and American Continental Empire: Letters, Speeches & Papers.* Chicago.
LaFontaine, Charles V. (1976). God and Nation in Selected US Presidential Inaugural Address, 1789–1945: Part One. *Journal of Church and State* 18: 39–60.
Lambert, Frank (2003). *The Founding Fathers and the Place of Religion in America.* Princeton.
Lambrose, R.J. (2002). The Abusable Past. *Radical History Review* 83: 211–214.
Lang, Daniel G., and Russell, Greg (1990). The Ethics of Power in American Diplomacy: The Statecraft of John Quincy Adams. *Review of Politics* 52: 11–12.

Larson, Edward J. (2007). *A Magnificent Catastrophe; The Tumultuous Election of 1800, America's First Presidential Campaign*. New York.

Larson, John Lauritz (2001). *Internal Improvement: National Public Works and the Promise of Popular Government in the Early United States*. Chapel Hill, NC.

Latner, Richard (1993). Preserving the Natural Equality of Rank and Influence: Liberalism, Republicanism, and Equality of Condition in Jacksonian Politics. In Thomas Haskell and Richard Teichgraeber, eds., *The Culture of the Market: Historical Essays*: 189–230. Cambridge.

Leopold, T. (2001). David McCullough brings John Adams to Life. *CNN Entertainment*, July 7.

Lepore, Jill (2008). The Divider: In HBO Miniseries, John Adams Is the Indispensable Man. *New Yorker*, Mar. 17.

Levin, Phyllis Lee (1987). *Abigail Adams: A Biography*. New York.

Lewis, James. E., Jr. (1998). *The American Union and the Problem of Neighborhood: The United States and the Collapse of the Spanish Empire, 1783–1829*. Chapel Hill, NC.

Lewis, James E., Jr. (2001). *John Quincy Adams: Policymaker for the Union*. Wilmington, DE.

Lint, Greg L. (1978). John Adams on the Drafting of the Treaty Plan of 1776. *Diplomatic History* 2: 212–320

Lint, Greg L. (2001). John Adams and "The Bolder Plan." In Ryerson (2001): 105–114.

Lipkin, Steve (2001). When Victims Speak (or, What Happened When Spielberg Added Amistad to his List?) *Journal of Film and Video* 52: 15–32.

Lipsky, George A. (1950). *John Quincy Adams: His Theory and Ideas*. New York. (Repr. 1965.)

Livermore, Shaw Jr. (1962). *The Twilight of Federalism: The Disintegration of the Federalist Party, 1815–1830*. New York. (Repr., 1972.).

Locke, John (1975). *An Essay Concerning Human Understanding*, ed. Peter H. Nidditch. Oxford.

Lord, Donald C., and Robert M. Calhoon (1969). The Removal of the Massachusetts General Court from Boston, 1769–1772. *Journal of American History* 55: 735–755.

Lovell, Margaretta M. (2005). *Art in a Season of Revolution. Painters, Artisans, and Patrons in Early America*. Philadelphia.

Ludlum, Robert P. (1941), The Antislavery "Gag Rule": History and Argument. *Journal of Negro History* 26: 203–243.

Lynd, Staughton (1967). *Class Conflict, Slavery and the US Constitution: Ten Essays*. Indianapolis. (Repr. New York 2009.)

Maier, Pauline (1972). *From Resistance to Revolution: Colonial Radicals and the Development of Opposition to Britain, 1765 to 1776*. New York.

Maier, Pauline (1980). *The Old Revolutionaries: Political Lives in the Age of Samuel Adams*. New York.

Maier, Pauline. (1997). *American Scripture: Making the Declaration of Independence*. New York.

Majewski, John (2000). *A House Dividing: Economic Development in Pennsylvania and Virginia Before the Civil War*. Cambridge.

Malone, Dumas (1951). *Jefferson and the Rights of Man*. Boston.

Maltz, Earl (2009). *Slavery and the Supreme Court, 1825–1861*. Lawrence, KS.

Marshall, Peter James (2012). *Remaking the British Atlantic: The United States and the British Empire after American Independence*. Oxford.

Mason, Matthew (2002). The Battle of the Slaveholding Liberators: Great Britain, the United States, and Slavery in the Early Nineteenth Century. *William and Mary Quarterly*, 3rd ser. 59: 665–696.

Mason, Matthew (2006). *Slavery and Politics in the Early American Republic*. Chapel Hill, NC.

Mason, Matthew (2009). "Keeping Up Appearances": The International Politics of Slave Trade Abolition in the Nineteenth-Century Atlantic World. *William and Mary Quarterly* 66: 809–32.

Massa, Mark (2005). *Anti-Catholicism in America*, 2nd edn. New York.

Massachusetts Cultural Council (1999). Humanist David McCullough. Commonwealth Awards: 1999 Recipients. At www.massculturalcouncil.org/conference/bios_99.asp, accessed Nov. 9, 2012.

Matthewson, Tim (2003). *A Pro-Slavery Foreign Policy: Haitian-American Relations during the Early Republic*. New York.

May, Ernest R. (1975). *The Making of the Monroe Doctrine*. Cambridge, MA.

May, Henry (1976). *The Enlightenment in America*. New York.

McConachie, Bruce (1998). American Theatre in Context, from the Beginnings to 1870. In Don B. Wilmeth and Christopher Bigsby, eds., *The Cambridge History of American Theatre*, vol. 1: *Beginnings to 1870*. Cambridge.

McCormick, Richard P. (1982). *The Presidential Game: The Origins of American Presidential Politics*. New York.

McCoy, Drew (1980). *The Elusive Republic: Political Economy in Jeffersonian America*. Chapel Hill, NC.

McCoy, Drew (1986) Political Economy. In Peterson, M., ed. *Thomas Jefferson: A Reference Biography*:100–118. New York.

McCoy, Drew (1987). An Unfinished Revolution: The Quest for Economic Independence in the Early Republic. In Jack P. Greene (ed.), *The American Revolution its Character and Limits*: 131–148.

McCoy, Drew (1989). *The Last of the Fathers: James Madison and the Republican Legacy*. New York.

McCullough, David (2001). *John Adams*. New York.

McCullough, David (2010). John Adams and the Good Life of the Mind. *Records of the American Academy of Arts and Sciences*: 10–16.

McGlone, Robert E. (1998). Deciphering Memory: John Adams and the Authorship of the Declaration of Independence. *Journal of American History* 85: 411–438.

McKeon, Michael (2005). *The Secret History of Domesticity: Public, Private, and the Division of Knowledge*. Baltimore.

Merk, Frederick. (1963). *Manifest Destiny and Mission in American History: A Reinterpretation*. New York.

Meschutt, David (2001). A Long-Lost Portrait of John Adams and an Unknown Portrait of Abigail Adams by James Sharpless. *American Art Journal* 32: 76–93.

Middlekauff, Robert (1996). *Benjamin Franklin and His Enemies*. Berkeley, CA.

Mihm Stephen (2007). *A Nation of Counterfeiters: Capitalists, Con Men, and the Making of the United States.* Cambridge, MA.
Miller, John C. (1960). *The Federalist Era, 1789–1801.* New York.
Miller, Perry (1939). *The New England Mind: The Seventeenth Century.* Boston.
Miller, Perry (1956). *Errand Into the Wilderness.* New York.
Miller, William Lee (1996). *Arguing About Slavery: The Great Battle in the United States Congress.* New York.
Mitchell, Stewart, ed. (1947). *New Letters of Abigail Adams 1788–1801.* Boston.
Moore, John Bassett (1898). *History and Digest of the International Arbitrations to which the United States Has Been a Party.* Washington, DC.
Morgan, Edmund S. (1944). *The Puritan Family: Religion and Domestic Relations in Seventeenth-Century New England.* New York.
Morgan, Edmund S. (1976). *The Meaning of Independence: John Adams, George Washington, Thomas Jefferson.* Charlottesville, VA. (Repr. 2004.)
Morris, Richard B. (1967). *The American Revolution Reconsidered.* New York.
Morris, Richard B. (1973). *Seven Who Shaped Our Destiny: The Founding Fathers as Revolutionaries.* New York.
Morris, Walter J. (1990). John Quincy Adams and Alexander Hill Everett: Pathfinders of Herman Studies. In Arthur O. Lewis, W. LaMarr Kop, and Edward J. Danis, eds., *America, Anglo-German and American-German Crosscurrents*, vol. 4. Lanham, MD.
Morse, Anson D. (1899). The Politics of John Adams. *American Historical Review* 4: 292–312.
Morse, John T. (1882). *John Adams.* Boston. (Repr. 1898.)
Murphy, Gretchen (2005). *Hemispheric Imaginings: The Monroe Doctrine and Narratives of US Empire.* Durham, NC.
Musto, David F. (1967). A Survey of the American Observatory Movement, 1800–1850. In Beer (1967): 87–92.
Musto, David F. (1969). The Youth of John Quincy Adams. *American Philosophical Society Proceedings*, 113, 269–282.
Muthu, Sankar (2003). *Enlightenment Against Empire.* Princeton.
Nagel, Paul C. (1964). *One Nation Indivisible: The Union in American Thought.* New York.
Nagel, Paul C. (1983). *Descent from Glory: Four Generations of the John Adams Family.* New York.
Nagel, Paul C. (1987). *The Adams Women: Abigail and Louisa Adams, Their Sisters and Daughters.* New York.
Nagel, Paul C. (1997). *John Quincy Adams: A Public Life, A Private Life.* New York. (Repr. Cambridge, MA, 2000.)
Namerode, E. (2011). Abigail Adams: The Last Will. Masters thesis, Fordham University.
Nathans, Heather S. (2003). *Early American Theatre from the Revolution to Thomas Jefferson: Into the Hands of the People.* Cambridge.
Neale, S. (2003). Questions of Genre. In B.K. Grant, *Film Genre Reader III*: 160–184. Austin, TX.
Nelson, W.H. 1961. *The American Tory.* Oxford.
Neustadt, Richard E. (1990). *Presidential Power and the Modern Presidents: The Politics of Leadership from Roosevelt to Reagan.* New York.

Nevins, Allan, ed. (1928). *The Diary of John Quincy Adams, 1794–1845*. New York. (Repr. 1951.)
Newman, Paul Douglas (2004). *Fries's Rebellion: The Enduring Struggle for the American Revolution*. Philadelphia.
Newman, Simon P. (1997). *Parades, and the Politics of the Street: Festive Culture in the Early Republic*. Philadelphia.
Nichols, Bill (1991). *Representing Reality*. Bloomington, IN.
Nicolson, Colin (2001). *The "Infamas Govener": Francis Bernard and the Origins of the American Revolution*. Boston.
Norton, Mary Beth (1980). *Liberty's Daughters: The Revolutionary Experience of American Women, 1750–1800*. Boston.
O'Brien, Karen (1997). *Narratives of Enlightenment: Cosmopolitan History from Voltaire to Gibbon*. Cambridge.
O'Brien, Michael (2005). *Henry Adams and the Southern Question*. Athens, GA.
O'Brien, Michael (2010). *Mrs. Adams in Winter: A Journey in the Last Days of Napoleon*. New York.
Offen, Karen (1988). Defining Feminism: A Comparative Historical Perspective. *Signs: Journal of Women in Culture and Society*, 14, 119–157.
Okin, Susan (1989). *Justice, Gender and the Family*. New York.
Oliver, Andrew (1967). *The Adams Papers, Series IV: Portraits of John and Abigail Adams*. Cambridge, MA.
Onuf, Peter S. (1998). A Declaration of Independence for Diplomatic Historians. *Diplomatic History* 22: 71–83.
Onuf, Peter S., and Onuf, Nicholas (1993). *Federal Union, Modern World: The Law of Nations in an Age of Revolution, 1776–1814*. Madison.
Osler, Margaret J. (1970). John Locke and the Changing Ideal of Scientific Knowledge. *Journal of the History of Ideas* 31: 3–16.
Paltsits, Victor Hugo, ed. (1916). *Berlin and the Prussian Court in 1798: The Journal of Thomas Boylston Adams, Secretary to the United States Legation at Berlin*. New York.
Parker, Theodore (1870). *Historic Americans*. Boston. (Ed. with notes by Samuel A. Eliot, 1908).
Parry-Giles, Trevor (2008). Fame, Celebrity, and the Legacy of John Adams. *Western Law Journal* 72: 83–101.
Parsons, Lynn Hudson (1973). "A Perpetual Harrow upon My Feelings": John Quincy Adams and the American Indians. *New England Quarterly* 46: 339–379.
Parsons, Lynn Hudson (1998). *John Quincy Adams*. Madison, WI.
Parsons, Lynn Hudson (2009). *The Birth of Modern Politics: Andrew Jackson, John Quincy Adams, and the Election of 1828*. New York.
Pasley, Jeffrey L. (2001). *The Tyranny of Printers: Newspaper Politics in the Early American Republic*. Charlottesville, VA.
Pasley, Jeffrey L. (2002). Federalist Chic. *Common-Place*, Jan. At www.common-place.org/publick/200202.shtml, accessed Nov. 19, 2012.
Pasley, Jeffrey L.(2003). The Election of 1796. In Shade et al. (2003): 96–109.
Pateman, Carole. 1988. *The Sexual Contract*. Stanford, CA.
Paynter, John E. (1996). The Rhetorical Design of John Adams's *Defence of the Constitutions of… America*. *Review of Politics* 58(3): 535–560.

Peek, George A. ed. (1954). *The Political Writings of John Adams.* Indianapolis.

Pencak, W. (2001). John Adams and the Massachusetts Provincial Elite. In Ryerson (2001): 43–71.

Pennsylvania Society for the Promotion of Internal Improvements (1826). *To the Citizens of the Commonwealth of Pennsylvania.* Philadelphia.

Perkins, Bradford (1964). *Castlereagh and Adams: England and the United States, 1812–1823.* Berkeley.

Perl-Rosenthal, Nathan (2011). Private Letters, Public Diplomacy: The Adams Network and the Quasi-War, 1797–1798. *Journal of the Early Republic* 31: 283–311.

Peterson, Merrill D. (1960). *The Jefferson Image in the American Mind.* Charlottesville, VA. (Repr. 1998.)

Peterson, Merrill D., ed. (1961). *Democracy, Liberty, and Property: The State Constitutional Conventions of the 1820s.* Indianapolis.

Peterson, Merrill D. (1976). *Adams and Jefferson: A Revolutionary Dialogue.* New York. (Repr. 1978.)

Peterson, Merrill (1988). *The Great Triumvirate: Webster, Clay, and Calhoun.* Oxford.

Phillips, Kim (1989). *William Duane, Radical Journalist in the Age of Jefferson.* New York.

Potkay, Adam S. (1999). Theorizing Civic Eloquence in the Early Republic: The Road from David Hume to John Quincy Adams. *Early American Literature* 34: 147–170.

Potter, David M. (1976). *The Impending Crisis, 1848–1861.* New York.

Potter, Janice (1983). *The Liberty We Seek: Loyalist Ideology in Colonial New York and Massachusetts.* Cambridge, MA.

Preyer, Kathryn T. (2009). *Blackstone in America: Selected Essays of Kathryn Preyer.* Cambridge.

Price, Jacob M., ed. (1979). *Joshua Johnson's Letterbook*, 1771–1774. At www.british-history.ac.uk, accessed Nov. 7, 2012.

Quincy, Josiah (1859). *Memoir of the Life of John Quincy Adams.* Boston. (Repr. 1860.)

Rakove, Jack (2010). *Revolutionaries.* New York.

Ratcliffe, Donald J. (2000). *The Politics of Long Division: The Birth of the Second Party System in Ohio, 1818–1828.* Columbus, OH.

Ratcliffe, Donald J. (2011).The Decline of Antislavery Politics, 1815–1840. In J.C. Hammond and Mason (2011): 267–290.

Read, James H. (2000). *Power versus Liberty: Madison, Hamilton, Wilson, and Jefferson.* Charlottesville, VA.

Reid, John Phillip (1974). A Lawyer Acquitted: John Adams and the Boston Massacre Trials. *American Journal of Legal History* 18 (1974): 189–207.

Reid, John Phillip (1977). *In a Defiant Stance: The Conditions of Law in Massachusetts Bay, the Irish Comparison, and the Coming of the American Revolution.* University Park, PA.

Reid, John Phillip (1980). In the Taught Tradition: The Meaning of Law in Massachusetts-Bay Two Hundred Years Ago. *Suffolk University Law Review* 14: 931–974.

Reid, John Phillip, ed. (1981). *The Briefs of the American Revolution: Constitutional Arguments between Thomas Hutchinson, Governor of Massachusetts Bay, and James Bowdoin for the Council and John Adams for the House of Representatives.* New York.

Reid, John Phillip (1993). *Constitutional History of the American Revolution: The Authority of Law.* Madison, WI.

Remini, Robert (1959). *Martin Van Buren and the Making of the Democratic Party.* New York.

Remini, Robert (2002). *John Quincy Adams.* New York.

Reynaud, D. (2008.) Dealing with Historical Movies in the History and English Classroom. *Teach Journal of Christian Education* 2(2): 48–52. Online at http://research.avondale.edu.au/arts_papers/2, accessed Nov.19, 2012.

Rhett, Robert Barnwell (1838), *Address to the People of Beaufort and Colleton Districts upon the Subject of Abolition.* Washington, DC.

Richards, Laura E. (1917). *Abigail Adams and Her Times.* New York: D. Appleton.

Richards, Leonard L. (1970). *"Gentlemen of Property and Standing": Anti-Abolition Mobs in Jacksonian America.* New York.

Richards, Leonard L. (1986). *The Life and Times of Congressman John Quincy Adams.* New York.

Richards, Leonard L. (2001). *The Slave Power: The Free North and Southern Domination, 1780–1860.* Baton Rouge.

Richardson, James Daniel (1897). *A Compilation of the Messages and Papers of the Presidents, 1789–1908.* New York: Bureau of National Literature and Art.

Roberts. Cokie (2008). *Ladies of Liberty: The Women Who Shaped Our Nation.* New York.

Roberts-Miller, Patricia (2002). John Quincy Adams's Amistad Argument: the Problem of Outrage; or, the Constraints of Decorum. *Rhetorical Society Quarterly* 32: 5–25.

Robertson, Andrew W. (2003). The Election of 1800. In Shade et al. (2003): 113–127.

Robertson, William (1827). *The Works of William Robertson, DD*, 8 vols, ed. Dugald Stewart. London.

Rogers, Katharine M. (1961). Fatal Inconsistency: Wycherley and the Plain-Dealer. *English Literary History* 28: 148–162.

Rojas, Martha Elena (2003). Diplomatic Letters: the Conduct and Culture of US Foreign Affairs in the Early Republic. Unpublished PhD diss., Stanford University.

Rose, Charlie (2008). A Conversation with David McCullough. Charlie Rose Show, July 8. At www.charlierose.com/view/interview/9000, accessed Nov. 9, 2012.

Rossignol, Marie-Jeanne (2004). *The Nationalist Ferment: The Origins of US Foreign Policy, 1789–1812*, trans. Lillian A. Parrott. Athens, OH.

Rothbard, Murray (1962). *The Panic of 1819: Reaction and Policies.* New York.

Rothman, Adam (2005). *Slave Country: American Expansion and the Origins of the Deep South.* Cambridge, MA.

Rowe, Gail Stuart (1978). Thomas McKean: The Shaping of American Republicanism. Boulder.

Russell, Greg (1995). *John Quincy Adams and the Public Virtues of Diplomacy.* Columbia.

Ryerson, Richard Alan, ed. (2001). *John Adams and the Founding of the Republic.* Boston.

Ryerson, Richard Alan (2004). Adams, John (1735–1826). In H.C. Matthew et al., eds., *Oxford Dictionary of National Biography Online.* At www.oxforddnb.com/view/article/68575. Accessed Nov.10, 2011.

Sadosky, Leonard, (2009). *Revolutionary Negotiations: Indians, Empires, and Diplomats in the Founding of America.* Charlottesville, VA.

Saltman, Helen Saltzburg (1980). John Adams's Earliest Essays: The Humphrey Ploughjogger Letters. *William and Mary Quarterly* 37: 125–135.

Saul, Norman E. (1991). *Distant Friends: The United States and Russia, 1763-1867.* Lawrence. KS.

Saxton, Alexander (1990). *The Rise and Fall of the White Republic: Class, Politics, and Mass Culture in Nineteenth-Century America.* New York.

Scalia, Laura J. (1999). *America's Jeffersonian Experiment: Remaking State Constitutions, 1820–1850.* DeKalb, IL.

Schaffel, Kenneth (1986). The American Board of War, 1776–1781. *Military Affairs* 50: 185–189.

Scheiber, Harry (1969). *Ohio Canal Era: A Case Study of Government and the Economy, 1820–1861.* Athens, OH.

Scherr, Arthur (1991). John Adams, Providential Rhetoric and Party Warfare: A Note on Massachusetts Politics in the Late 1790s, *Mid-America* 73: 7–27.

Schlereth, Thomas J. (1977). *The Cosmopolitan Ideal in Enlightenment Thought: Its Form and Function in the Ideas of Franklin, Hume, and Voltaire, 1694–1790.* South Bend, IN.

Schlesinger, Arthur M. (1945). *The Age of Jackson.* Boston.

Schlesinger, Arthur M., ed. (1985). *History of American Presidential Elections, 1789–1968.* Chelsea House.

Schlesinger, Arthur M. (1989). The Ages of Jackson. *New York Review of Books, Dec. 7*: 48–51.

Schlesinger, Arthur M. (1997). Rating the Presidents: Washington to Clinton. *Political Science Quarterly* 112: 179–190.

Schlesinger, Arthur M. (2000). *A Life in the Twentieth Century.* Boston,.

Schocket, Andrew (2007). *Founding Corporate Power in Early National Philadelphia.* DeKalb, IL.

Schulte Nordholdt, J. W. (1981). *Till I Knew John Adams.* Amsterdam.

Schulte Nordholdt, J. W. (1982). *The Dutch Republic and American Independence.* Chapel Hill, NC.

Schutz, John A., and Adair, Douglass, eds. (1966). *The Spur of Fame: Dialogues of John Adams and Benjamin Rush, 1805–1813.* San Marino, CA. (Repr. Indianapolis, 1998.)

Seavey, Ormond (1988). *Becoming Benjamin Franklin: The Autobiography and the Life.* Philadelphia.

Seiler, C. (2003). The Founding Fathers. In Peter C. Rollins, ed., *The Columbia Companion to American History on Film*: 154–155. New York.

Selby, John (1976). Richard Henry Lee, John Adams, and the Virginia Constitution of 1776. *Virginia Magazine of History and Biography* 84: 387–400.

Sellers, Charles (1991). *The Market Revolution: Jacksonian America, 1815–1846.* New York.

Seward, William Henry (1855). *The Life and Public Services of John Quincy Adams, Sixth President of the United States. With the Eulogy Delivered Before the Legislature of New York.* New York.

Sexton, Jay (2011). *The Monroe Doctrine: Empire and Nation in Nineteenth Century America.* New York.

Shade, William G., Campbell, Barrard C., and Coenen, Craig R. (2003). *American Presidential Campaigns and Elections.* Armonk, NY.

Shaffer, Jason (2007). *Performing Patriotism: National Identity in the Colonial and Revolutionary American Theater.* Philadelphia.

Shammas, Carole, Salmon, Marylynn, and Dahlin, Michael (1987). *Inheritance in America: From Colonial Times to the Present.* New Brunswick.

Shankman, Andrew (2003). A New Thing on Earth: Alexander Hamilton, Pro-Manufacturing Republicans, and the Democratization of American Political Economy. *Journal of the Early Republic* 23: 323–352.

Shankman, Andrew (2008). Were Jeffersonian Charges of Monarchism Really Just Sleazy Hysterical Smears? *Common Place* 9. At www.common-place.org/pasley/?m=20081022, accessed Nov. 10, 2012.

Shankman, Andrew (2011). Neither Infinite Wretchedness nor Positive Good: Mathew Carey and Henry Clay on Political Economy and Slavery During the Long 1820s. In J.C. Hammond and Mason (2011): 247–266.

Sharp, James Roger (1993). *American Politics in the Early Republic: The New Nation in Crisis.* New Haven.

Sharp, James Roger (2010). *The Deadlocked Election of 1800: Jefferson, Burr, and the Union in the Balance.* Lawrence, KS.

Shaw, Peter (1976). *The Character of John Adams.* Chapel Hill, NC.

Shaw, Ronald (1966), *Erie Water West: A History of the Erie Canal, 1792–1854.* Lexington, KY.

Shepherd, Jack (1975). *The Adams Chronicles: Four Generations of Greatness.* Boston.

Shepherd, Jack (1980). *Cannibals of the Heart: A Personal Biography of Louisa Catherine and John Quincy Adams.* New York.

Sheriff, Carol (1996). *The Artificial River: The Erie Canal and the Paradox of Progress, 1817–1862.* New York.

Shields, David (1997). *Civil Tongues and Polite Letters in British America.* Chapel Hill, NC.

Shuffelton, Frank, ed. (2004). *The Letters of John and Abigail Adams.* New York.

Siemers, David J. (2009). *Presidents and Political Thought.* Columbia.

Simonton, D. K. (2006). Presidential IQ, Openness, Intellectual Brilliance, and Leadership: Estimates and Correlations for 42 US Chief Executives. *Political Psychology* 27: 511–639.

Sisson, Daniel (1974). *The American Revolution of 1800.* New York.

Skowronek, Stephen (1993). *The Politics Presidents Make: Leadership from John Adams to George Bush.* Cambridge, MA. (2nd edn. 1997.)

Sloan, Herbert E. (1995). *Principle and Interest: Thomas Jefferson and the Problem of Debt.* New York.

Smith, James Morton (1956). *Freedom's Fetters: The Alien and Sedition Laws and American Civil Liberties.* Ithaca, NY.

Smith, Margaret Bayard (1906). *First Forty Years of Washington Society.* New York. (Repr. 1969.)

Smith, Maurice H. (1978). *The Writs of Assistance Case.* Berkeley.
Smith, Page (1962). *John Adams*, 2 vols. Garden City, NY.
Smith, Page (1984). *Dissenting Opinions.* San Francisco.
Smith, Page (1985). Election of 1796. In Schlesinger (1985): 59–98.
Smith, Paul H. et al., eds. (1977–2000), *Letters of Delegates to Congress, 1774-1789*, 26 vols. Washington, DC.
Smitten, Jeffrey (1985). Impartiality in Robertson's History of America. *Eighteenth Century Studies* 19: 56–67.
Smyth, J. E. (2006). *Reconstructing American Historical Cinema: From Cimarron to Citizen Kane.* Lexington, KY.
Spann, Edward K. (1957), John W. Taylor, The Reluctant Partisan, 1784–1854. PhD diss., New York.
Stagg, John C.A. (1983). *Mr. Madison's War: Politics, Diplomacy and Warfare in the Early American Republic.* Princeton.
Stagg, John C.A. (2009). *Borderlines in Borderlands: James Madison and the Spanish–American Frontier, 1776–1821.* New Haven.
Staloff, Darren (2005). *Hamilton, Adams, Jefferson: The Politics of Enlightenment and the American Founding.* New York.
Stanton, Lucia (2005). Nourishing the Congress: Hospitality at the President's House. In Damon Lee Fowler, ed., *Dining at Monticello: In Good Taste and Abundance.* Chapel Hill, NC.
Staum, Martin (1980). *Cabanis: Enlightenment Medical Philosophy in the French Revolution.* Princeton.
Steigerwald, Bill (2008). Interview with David McCullough. Campaign.com, at http://www.thedocisin.net/?tag=steigerwald&paged=6, accessed Nov. 19, 2012.
Stern, Jeremy A. (2008). What's Wrong with HBO's Dramatization of John Adams's Story. *History News Network*, Oct. 27. At http://hnn.us/articles/56155.html, accessed Nov. 20, 2012.
Stinchcombe, William C. (1969). *The American Revolution and the French Alliance.* Syracuse, NY.
Stinchcombe, William C. (1977). John Adams and the Model Treaty. In Lawrence S. Kaplan, ed., *The American Revolution and A Candid World*: 69–84. Kent, OH.
Stinchcombe, William C. (1980). *The XYZ Affair.* Westport, CT.
Stockton, Constant Noble (1971). Hume – Historian of the English Constitutions. *Eighteenth Century Studies* 4: 277–293.
Stoddart, S. (2003). *The Adams Chronicles*: Domesticating the American Presidency. In Peter C. Rollins and J.E. O'Connor, *Hollywood's White House: The American Presidency in Film and History*: 30–49. Lexington, KY.
Stone, I. 1965. *Those Who Love.* New York.
Stone, Peter and Edwards, Sherman (1972). *1776: A Musical Play.* New York.
Stout, Harry S. (1986). *The New England Soul: Preaching and Religious Culture in Colonial New England.* New York.
Sullivan Obituary (1993). Jeremiah Sullivan, 58, Actor and Astrologer. *New York Times*, Dec. 15.
Szatmary, David P. (1980). *Shays' Rebellion: The Making of an Agrarian Insurrection.* Amherst, MA.

Tatum, Edward H., Jr. (1941). Ten Unpublished Letters of John Quincy Adams, 1796–1837. *Huntington Library Quarterly* 4: 371–373.

Taylor, Alan (2011). *The Civil War of 1812: American Citizens, British Subjects, and Indian Allies.* New York.

Taylor, George Rogers (1951). *The Transportation Revolution, 1815–1860.* New York.

Taylor, Robert J. (1977). John Adams: Legalist as Revolutionist. *Proceedings of the Massachusetts Historical Society, 3rd ser.* 89: 55–71.

Taylor, Robert J. (1980). Construction of the Massachusetts Constitution. *Proceedings of the American Antiquarian Society* 90: 317–346.

Taylor, Robert J. et al. (eds.) (1977–). *The Adams Papers, Series III: The Papers of John Adams,* 15 vols to date. Cambridge, MA.

Thomas, Evan (2001). Founder Chic: Live From Philadelphia. *Newsweek.*: July 9.

Thompson, C. Bradley (1996). John Adams and the Coming of the French Revolution. *Journal of the Early Republic* 16: 361–387.

Thompson, C. Bradley (1998). *John Adams and the Spirit of Liberty.* Lawrence, KS. (Repr. 2002.)

Thompson, C. Bradley, ed. (2000). *The Revolutionary Writings of John Adams.* Indianapolis, 2nd edn. (First pub. 1998.)

Thompson, Robert R. (1991). John Quincy Adams, Apostate: From "Outrageous Federalist" to "Republican Exile," 1801–1809. *Journal of the Early Republic* 11: 161–183.

Tinckom, Harry M. (1950). *The Republicans and Federalists in Pennsylvania, 1790–1801: A Study in National Stimulus and Local Response.* Harrisburg, PA.

Townsend, Camilla (2004). *Pocahontas and the Powhatan Dilemma.* New York.

Tracy, Antoine Louis Claude Destutt, comte de (1811). *A Commentary and Review of Montesquieu's Spirit of Laws,* trans. Thomas Jefferson. Philadelphia. (Repr. New York, 1969.)

Tracy, Antoine Louis Claude Destutt, comte de (1817). *A Treatise on Political Economy.* In John Morris Dorsey, *Psychology of Political Science, with Special Consideration for the Political Acumen of Destutt de Tracy.* Detroit.

Trees, Andrew S. (2001). John Adams and the Problem of Virtue. *Journal of the Early Republic* 21: 393–412.

Trees, Andrew S. (2004). *The Founding Fathers and the Politics of Character.* Princeton.

Trouillot, Michel-Rolph (1995). *Silencing the Past: Power and the Production of History.* Boston.

Turgot, Anne-Robert-Jacques (1895). The Life and Writings of Turgot, Comptroller of France, 1774–1776, ed. W. Walker Stephens. London.

Turner, Kathryn (1960). The Appointment of Chief Justice Marshall. *William and Mary Quarterly* 17: 143–163.

Upton, Leslie F.S. (1977). The Dilemma of the Loyalist Pamphleteers. *Studies in Burke and His Time* 18: 71–84.

Usselman, Steven (2002). *Regulating Railroad Innovation: Business, Technology, and Politics in America, 1840–1920.* Cambridge.

Van Atta, John (2001). Western Lands and the Political Economy of Henry Clay's American System. *Journal of the Early Republic* 21: 633–665.

Varg, Paul A. (1963). *The Foreign Policy of the Founding Fathers.* East Lansing, MI.
Waldman, Steven (2008). *Founding Faith: Providence, Politics, and the Birth of Religious Freedom in America.* New York.
Waldstreicher, David (1997). *In the Midst of Perpetual Fetes: The Making of American Nationalism, 1776–1823.* Chapel Hill, NC.
Waldstreicher, David (2002). Founders Chic as Culture War. *Radical History Review* 84: 185–194.
Waldstreicher, David (2004). *Runaway America: Benjamin Franklin, Slavery and the American Revolution.* New York.
Waldstreicher, David (2009). *Slavery's Constitution: From Revolution to Ratification.* New York.
Wallace, Anthony F.C. (1993). *The Long and Bitter Trail: Andrew Jackson and the Indians.* New York.
Walsh, Correa M. (1915). *The Political Science of John Adams.* New York.
Warner, Michael (1990). *The Letters of the Republic: Publication and the Public Sphere in 18th-Century America.* Cambridge, MA.
Warren, Jack D. (2001). In the Shadow of Washington: John Adams as Vice President. In Ryerson (2001): 117–141.
Warren, Mercy Otis (1988). *History of the Rise, Progress, and Termination of the American Revolution: Interspersed with Biographical, Political, and Moral Observations*, ed. Lester S. Cohen, 2 vols. Indianapolis.
Warner, Deborah Jean (1979). Astronomy in Antebellum America. In Nathan Reingold, ed., *The Sciences in the American Context: New Perspectives.* Washington, DC.
Watson, Harry (1990). *Liberty and Power: The Politics of Jacksonian America.* New York.
Way, Peter (1993). *Common Labour: Workers and the Digging of North American Canals, 1780–1860.* Cambridge.
Weaver, Richard (1985). *The Ethics of Rhetoric.* Davis, CA.
Weeks, William Earl (1992). *John Quincy Adams and American Global Empire.* Lexington, KY.
Weisberger, Bernard A. (2000). *America Afire: Jefferson, Adams, and the Revolutionary Election of 1800.* New York.
Wexler, Victor G. (1976–1977). David Hume's Discovery of a New Scene of Historical Thought. *Eighteenth Century Studies* 10: 185–202.
Wheelan, Joseph (2009). *Mr. Adams's Last Crusade: John Quincy Adams's Extraordinary Post-Presidential Life in Congress.* New York.
White, Ashli (2010). *Encountering Revolution: Haiti and the Making of the Early Republic.* Baltimore.
White, Richard (1991). *The Middle Ground: Indians, Empires, and Republics in the Great Lakes Region, 1650–1815.* New York.
Whitford, Noble (1906). *History of the Canal System of the State of New York.* Albany, NY.
Whitney, Janet (1947). *Abigail Adams.* Boston.
Whitney, Peter (1819). *A Sermon Delivered on the Lord's Day Succeeding the Interment of Madam Abigail Adams.* Boston.
Wilentz, Sean (2005). *The Rise of American Democracy: Jefferson to Lincoln.* New York.

Wilentz, Sean (2007). *Andrew Jackson.* New York.
Williams, William Appleman (1959). *The Tragedy of American Diplomacy.* New York.
Williamson, George S. (2000). What Killed August von Kotzebue? The Temptations of Virtue and the Political Theology of German Nationalism, 1789–1819. *Journal of Modern History* 72: 890–943.
Wills, Garry (2002). *Nixon Agonistes: The Crisis of the Self-Made Man.* Boston.
Wills, Garry (2003). *Negro President: Jefferson and the Slave Power.* New York.
Wills, Garry (2005). *Henry Adams and the Making of America.* Boston.
Wilson, Clyde N., et. al., eds. (1959–2003), The Papers of John C. Calhoun. Columbia.
Wilson, Major J. (1974). *Space, Time, and Freedom: The Quest for Nationality and the Irrepressible Conflict, 1815–1861.* Westport.
Wiltse, Charles M., ed. (1974–1989). *The Papers of Daniel Webster: Speeches and Formal Writings.* Hanover, NH.
Wirls, Daniel, and Wirls, Stephen (2004). *The Invention of the United States Senate.* Baltimore.
Withey, Lynne (1981). *Dearest Friend: A Life of Abigail Adams.* New York.
Witte, John Jr. (1999). "A Most Mild and Equitable Establishment of Religion": John Adams and the Massachusetts Experiment. *Journal of Church and State* 41: 213–252.
Withington, Ann Fairfax (1991). *Toward a More Perfect Union: Virtue and the Formation of American Republics.* New York.
Wood, Gordon S. (1966). Rhetoric and Reality in the American Revolution. *William and Mary Quarterly* 23: 4–32.
Wood, Gordon S. (1969). *The Creation of the American Republic, 1776–1787.* Chapel Hill, NC.
Wood, Gordon S. (1998). *The Creation of the American Republic, 1776–1787*, 2nd edn. New York.
Wood, Gordon S. (2004). *Revolutionary Characters: What Made the Founders Different.* New York.
Wood, Gordon S., ed. (2011a). *John Adams: Revolutionary Writings: 1755-1775.* New York.
Wood, Gordon S., ed. (2011b). *John Adams: Revolutionary Writings: 1775-1783.* New York.
Wood, Joseph (1996). The Idea of a National Road. In Karl Raitz, ed., *The National Road.* Baltimore.
Wright, John F. (1995). British Government Borrowing in Wartime, 1750–1815. *English Historical Review* 2: 355–371.
Wroth, L. Kinvin, and Zobel, Hiller, eds. (1965). *The Legal Papers of John Adams.* Cambridge, MA. (Repr. New York, 1968.)
Wyly-Jones, Susan (2001). The 1835 Anti-Abolition Meetings in the South: A New Look at the Controversy over the Abolition Postal Campaign. *Civil War History* 47: 289–309.
Zagarri, Rosemarie (1995). *A Woman's Dilemma: Mercy Otis Warren and the American Revolution.* Wheeling, IL.
Zagarri, Rosemarie (2003). Review of Ryerson, *John Adams and the Founding of the Republic. Journal of Interdisciplinary History* 33(4): 658–659.

Zagarri, Rosemarie (2007). *Revolutionary Backlash: Women and Politics in the Early American Republic*. Philadelphia.
Zobel, Hiller B. (1970). *The Boston Massacre*. New York.
Zvesper, John (2003). *From Bullets to Ballots: The Election of 1800 and the First Peaceful Transfer of Political Power*. Claremont, CA.

Index

A Companion to John Adams and John Quincy Adams, First Edition.
Edited by David Waldstreicher.